Australia's Northern Shield?

Australia's Northern Shield?

Papua New Guinea and the Defence of Australia since 1880

Bruce Hunt

© Copyright 2017 Bruce Hunt

All rights reserved. Apart from any uses permitted by Australia's Copyright Act 1968, no part of this book may be reproduced by any process without prior written permission from the copyright owners. Inquiries should be directed to the publisher.

Monash University Publishing

Matheson Library and Information Services Building
40 Exhibition Walk
Monash University
Clayton, Victoria, 3800, Australia
www.publishing.monash.edu

Monash University Publishing brings to the world publications which advance the best traditions of humane and enlightened thought.

Monash University Publishing titles pass through a rigorous process of independent peer review.

www.publishing.monash.edu/books/ans-9781925495409.html

Series: Investigating Power

Series Editor: Clinton Fernandes

Design: Les Thomas

Cover image: courtesy of the National Archives of Australia. 'Personalities – Gough Whitlam – With Mr Somare at press conference (Chief Minister of Papua New Guinea), 1973'. NAA: A6180, 18/1/73/30.

National Library of Australia Cataloguing-in-Publication entry:

Creator:	Hunt, Bruce G., author.
Title:	Australia's northern shield? : Papua New Guinea and the defence of Australia since 1880 / Bruce Hunt.
ISBN:	9781925495409 (paperback)
Subjects:	National security--Australia--History.
	Papua New Guinea--Strategic aspects.
	Australia--Foreign relations--Papua New Guinea.
	Papua New Guinea--Foreign relations--Australia.

Printed in Australia by Griffin Press an Accredited ISO AS/NZS 14001:2004 Environmental Management System printer.

The paper this book is printed on is certified against the Forest Stewardship Council ® Standards. Griffin Press holds FSC chain of custody certification SGS-COC-005088.
FSC promotes environmentally responsible, socially beneficial and economically viable management of the world's forests.

CONTENTS

About the Author vii
Acknowledgements viii
Foreword x
Introduction xiii

PART I: THE SHIELD

Chapter 1
Securing the Shield 1880–1920 1

Chapter 2
The Shield is Raised 1920–1945 25

PART II: THE SPECTRE OF INDONESIA – PROTECTING PAPUA NEW GUINEA

Chapter 3
The West New Guinea Dispute 1949–1951 47

Chapter 4
The West New Guinea Dispute 1952–1956 74

Chapter 5
The West New Guinea Dispute 1956–1959 92

Chapter 6
The West New Guinea Dispute 1959–1962 122

Chapter 7
Indonesia, Confrontation and Protecting Papua New Guinea
1962–1963 152

Chapter 8
Indonesia, Confrontation and Protecting Papua New Guinea
1964–1966 180

Part III: Shifting Ground

Chapter 9
Shifting Ground: New Influences Emerge 1966–1972 202

Chapter 10
Redefining the Options 1972–1973 227

Part IV: The Settlement

Chapter 11
Towards a Common Understanding 1973–1975 253

Chapter 12
A Settlement is Reached 1976–1977 270

Chapter 13
The Defence Undertaking Revisited: The Joint Declaration of Principles
1987 and 2013 284

Notes 293
Bibliography 348
Index 364

ABOUT THE AUTHOR

Bruce Hunt is a Research Fellow in the School of History, College of Arts and Social Sciences, at the Australian National University. He was an officer in the Department of Foreign Affairs and Trade (DFAT) from 1974 until his retirement in mid-2011. He was posted to the Australian High Commission in Port Moresby from 1985 to 1987 and was Director of the PNG Section in DFAT from 1990 to 1994 and again from 2000 to 2003. In 1999 he was appointed Chief Negotiator in the Peace Monitoring Group on Bougainville. In 2000 he was an adviser to the Commonwealth Eminent Persons Group set up to examine the challenges faced by the Papua New Guinea Defence Force. His other postings have been to Bonn, Harare, Tel Aviv and as High Commissioner to the Kingdom of Tonga.

In 1996 he attended the Australian College of Defence and Strategic Studies (now known as the Australian Defence College). He is a Fellow of the College.

He was awarded a PhD from the University of New England in 2003.

ACKNOWLEDGEMENTS

This book had its origins in an essay I wrote while a participant at the Australian Centre for Defence and Strategic Studies in Canberra in 1996. I then turned to the question of the place of Papua New Guinea in Australia's strategic assessments in writing my PhD thesis in the late 1990s. It was during this period that I was fortunate enough to be supported and encouraged first by Chris Pugsley and then Frank Bongiorno of the University of New England. Chris's enthusiasm alone was essential during those early uncertain times, and Frank, now at the Australian National University has remained an invaluable mentor to the present day. Three other academic colleagues who have spent their careers studying Papua New Guinea have been a constant source of encouragement. They are David Hegarty, Anthony Regan and Dr Ron May from the Australian National University. I owe all three a great debt of gratitude.

I began writing this book in 2011 and since then the list of those whose support and encouragement should be acknowledged has grown immeasurably. I am bound to omit someone and for that I apologise. However, I do wish to acknowledge the guidance and encouragement of friends and colleagues notably Ric Wells who fully supported my proposal to turn the thesis into a book and Rob Flynn, Steve Waters, John Oliver, Ruth Pearce, Peter Hooton and Colin Milner for their continuing interest. Michael Wilson, who was my High Commissioner in Port Moresby in the mid-1980s, has been a great source of support, as was his late wife, Susan Stratigos. Dr Matt Jordan has been a font of advice and knowledge and has served as an invaluable sounding board for the exploration of ideas. Similarly, Dr Moreen Dee has been generous in providing comment and offering assistance. I have also appreciated the support of Dr Clinton Fernandes. I must acknowledge the great help given by Drs David Lee and Stephen Henningham and the guidance offered by Joan Beaumont, James Cotton, Garry Woodard and Neville Meaney, all distinguished historians of Australian foreign policy.

I have particularly benefitted by being able to draw on the first-hand knowledge of John Greenwell, Christine Goode and Alan Kerr, former officers of the Department of External Territories whose work in bringing Papua New Guinea to independence deserves much greater recognition than it has had to date. I am particularly indebted to Alan Kerr for his support and guidance.

Acknowledgements

I was fortunate to have been able to draw on the insights of Sir Peter Lawler and Peter Bailey, both senior officers in the Department of Prime Minister in the 1960s and 1970s and both note-takers in Cabinet meetings. Both were present at some of the critical meetings which decided the course of Australian foreign and defence polices in this period and were able to provide an intimate portrait of how the Cabinet functioned and the key personalities.

The writing of this book also reflects the influence and support of a number of people who have been instrumental in stimulating my interest in history. These begin with Professors Bruce Mansfield and Edwin Judge of Macquarie University who instilled in me the importance of always turning to the original source document when coming to an understanding of events and decisions. My great friends, Brian Croke, Fran Byrnes and Douglas Newton, all history students with me at Macquarie many years ago, have been an inspiration as we have discussed the many issues arising from our shared interest in both modern and ancient history. I owe a particular debt to Douglas Newton for his willingness to share documents and information, as well as advice, on the contents of the early chapters of this book.

I am indebted to Robert Webster whose knowledge of modern Indonesian history, politics and language has been invaluable. His comments on the early drafts of the book and his suggestions for revisions were an essential element in bringing this book to completion. Our mutual friend, Peter Michelson, who we first met in Port Moresby in 1986 and who served with the British Army in Malaysia during Confrontation and then with the Australian Army in Vietnam, has encouraged me over the years and has also been a source of inspiration and support.

A book such as this that has taken a long time to research and write owes a particular debt to the staff of the National Archives in Canberra, notably but not exclusively, Andrew Cairns, Michael Wenke, Leslie Wetherall, Kerri Ward, Megan Vasey, Ritchie George and Paul Croke who have responded to each request for assistance with great professionalism and dedication. I am also indebted to Beja van den Bosch in the Netherlands for tracking down and translating a number of documents from the Dutch Archives. I have also appreciated the support and guidance given to me by the great team at Monash University Publishing and by Gary Grey in proofreading the text.

Finally, I owe a great debt to my family. They have remained engaged and interested in the book as it has progressed from an idea to a manuscript.

Above all, I would not have completed this project without the support of my wife. I owe her the greatest debt.

FOREWORD

The island of New Guinea, and specifically that part which became the state of Papua New Guinea, has long featured prominently in Australia's perceptions of its national security. As early as 1867 the colonial government of New South Wales urged the British government, unsuccessfully, to take possession of New Guinea. Sixteen years later the Queensland government, concerned about the prospect of German imperialist expansion in the Pacific, 'took possession' of New Guinea and adjacent islands east of the border with Dutch New Guinea. This action was repudiated by the British Government, but after Germany established a protectorate over northeastern New Guinea and the Bismarck Archipelago the following year, Britain responded by claiming the southeast portion of the island, which was subsequently transferred to Australia, becoming the Protectorate of Papua. In 1914 an Australian expeditionary force took over German New Guinea, which in the post-war settlement became a mandated territory under Australian administration. But while the potential threat of German imperialism was removed, Japan, which in 1902 had become an ally of Great Britain and had gained Germany's Pacific territories north of the Equator, was now seen as a potential threat to Australia's security.

The Japanese invasion of New Guinea during the Second World War confirmed the common view in Australia that securing at least the eastern half of New Guinea was essential for the defence of Australia, providing a shield against aggression from the north. The shared wartime experience of Australians and Papua New Guineans also created continuing bonds between the two countries which persist, notably in the symbolism of the Kokoda Track.

In the period following the Second World War Australian threat perceptions shifted more firmly to Asia, particularly against the background of Britain's military withdrawal from 'East of Suez', Indonesian Konfrontasi in Malaysia and the dispute over West Papua. Defence of the Territory of Papua and New Guinea was seen as an essential element of Australia's defence strategy. During the early 1960s concerns about possible Indonesian expansionism towards Papua New Guinea prompted a surge of activity on Australia's part to increase, and localise, the military in Papua New Guinea (which on the eve of independence was still part of Australia's Northern Command) and strengthen security infrastructure along the Indonesia–Papua New Guinea border.

Foreword

In the years leading up to Papua New Guinea's independence in 1975, questions relating to future defence relations between Australia and Papua New Guinea came under increasing scrutiny. Australia was particularly reluctant to engage in a formal defence treaty with an independent Papua New Guinea, fearing it might be drawn into a conflict if the new state acted 'irresponsibly', for example in response to a border incursion by Indonesia. With apparent secessionist movements in Bougainville and Papua emerging on the eve of independence, Australia was also concerned about the future internal stability of the new state. Ironically, perhaps, Papua New Guinea was also keen to avoid formal treaty relationships, having adopted a foreign policy of 'Universalism' – friends to all and enemies to none – and not wanting to 'participate in the great powers' quarrels'. The final outcome of negotiations between the two countries was an amicable Joint Statement, released in 1977, which affirmed the two countries' agreement to sustain their close cooperation in defence matters and to consult at the request of either about matters affecting their common security. This position was reaffirmed, in terms which were generally seen to be slightly stronger, in a Joint Declaration of Principles, initiated by Papua New Guinea, in 1987 and again in a reworded Declaration in 2013 (which omits specific reference to defence but 'builds on' the 1987 agreement). The two countries have maintained a close relationship in defence matters and Australia has continued to support the Papua New Guinea Defence Force through its Defence Cooperation Program. But given Australia's defence commitments to unwinnable conflicts far from its shores, Papua New Guinea may have chosen wisely to avoid 'great powers' quarrels'.

The bare bones of this story have been documented elsewhere, but Bruce Hunt's study presents in rich detail both the elements of continuity in the story and the shifts that have taken place in strategic thinking over time in response to external events and changing actors. The book began as a meticulously researched PhD thesis for the University of New England. Subsequently Hunt gained access to Australian Cabinet Notebooks, which have provided new insights into the processes of policy formulation on the Australian side, particularly under the Menzies government and through notably John McEwen. It highlights the dramatic changes that occurred in Australia's thinking in the late 1960s and early 1970s as internal security issues in Papua New Guinea began to dominate Canberra's perceptions of the long-term defence relationship with Port Moresby. The study thus gives us not only a comprehensive account of the evolution of relations between Australia and Papua New Guinea in the field of geopolitical defence strategy but also a more general insight into the way in which policies are formulated. It also explores the relationship between Australia, Papua New Guinea, Indonesia and Southeast Asia more broadly.

As scholars and practitioners of my generation who have a continuous association with Papua New Guinea since before the country's independence move on, firsthand knowledge of the history of Australia's relations with Papua New Guinea is fading. At a time when many are calling for greater engagement with and understanding of Papua New Guinea, Australians need to know more about the history and context of relations between our two countries. Bruce Hunt's book is a major contribution to our understanding of Australian attitudes towards Papua New Guinea and its role in the evolution of Australia's defence policy and strategic assessments.

Dr Ron May
Emeritus Fellow
Australian National University
Canberra

INTRODUCTION

'The establishment of a foreign power in the
neighbourhood of Australia would be injurious to …
Australia's interests'.

T. J. McIlwraith,
Premier of Queensland, 1883

'Australia cannot be secure if our immediate
neighbourhood, including PNG, became the source of
threat to Australia'.

2016 Defence White Paper

A feature of the analysis and discussion of Australia's strategic environment over the past one hundred years has been the remarkable degree of continuity in the language used to describe and the prominence given to the place of Papua New Guinea (PNG) in Australia's defence outlook. In 1956 the holding of Papua New Guinea was described as 'vital to the defence of Australia'. It was seen as the 'most suitable area from which to launch air and sea attacks on the vital east coast of Australia' and as providing 'the best area for mounting an invasion of eastern Australia'. PNG gave Australia and her allies 'potential forward bases from which operations could be mounted against attacks from the northwest', i.e. Indonesia. It was 'essential in our last outer ring of defence, i.e. Cocos Islands–Darwin–New Guinea–Manus'.[1] More recently, for example in 1976, immediately after independence from Australia, Papua New Guinea's importance to Australia was described as 'resid(ing) in its geographic position and proximity; in the potential for trouble in PNG's relations with Indonesia; and in the security of extensive Australian interests in PNG'. In addition, 'military lodgement in PNG by a power unfriendly to Australia would facilitate attack against Australia and lines of communication to Australia's north. ... denial of (such) opportunity ... should remain an enduring objective of Australian national policy'. The objective of Australia's policy was to ensure that PNG saw Australia 'as its primary strategic partner'.[2] The 1987 White Paper, 'The Defence of Australia', drawing on the groundbreaking Dibb Report of the previous year, noted that 'our historic ties give Australia a strong interest in the security of Papua New Guinea, and this is reinforced by Papua New Guinea's geographic location which makes its security a major factor in our own strategic outlook'.[3] It added, 'because of the potential strategic implications, Australia would be understandably concerned should a hostile power gain lodgement or control in Papua New Guinea'.[4]

The seventh Australian Defence White Paper, published in February 2016, gave a similar prominence to Papua New Guinea in Australia's strategic environment. An early reference asserts that 'our nearest region, which encompasses Australia's borders and offshore territories, Papua New Guinea, Timor-Leste and the Pacific Island Countries and maritime South East Asia, is of the most immediate importance for Australia's security'. Elsewhere, it argues that 'Australia cannot be secure if our immediate neighbourhood, including Papua New Guinea ... becomes a source of threat to Australia. This includes a threat of a foreign military power seeking influence in ways that could challenge the security of our maritime approaches or transnational crime targeting Australian interests'. Furthermore, 'geography, shared history, business and interpersonal links tie Australia's interests closely to stability and prosperity in our immediate neighbourhood spanning Papua New Guinea'.[5]

How has Papua New Guinea come to occupy, over an extended period of time, such a prominent place in Australia's security outlook? Specifically, this book examines, from a historical perspective, the place of Papua New Guinea in Australia's strategic and defence environment in order to understand the forces that have consistently shaped Australia's approach to determining Papua New Guinea's role in that environment.

For over a century Australia has viewed the defence relationship with its closest neighbour to the near north, Papua New Guinea, in the context of the intrusion of foreign powers or an anxiety about the stability and dependability of the country itself. It has been the focus of Australian concerns about the ambitions of Imperial Germany, Japanese aggression and Indonesian threats of infiltration and subversion. More recently, as it approached independence in 1975, Papua New Guinea was seen by Australian

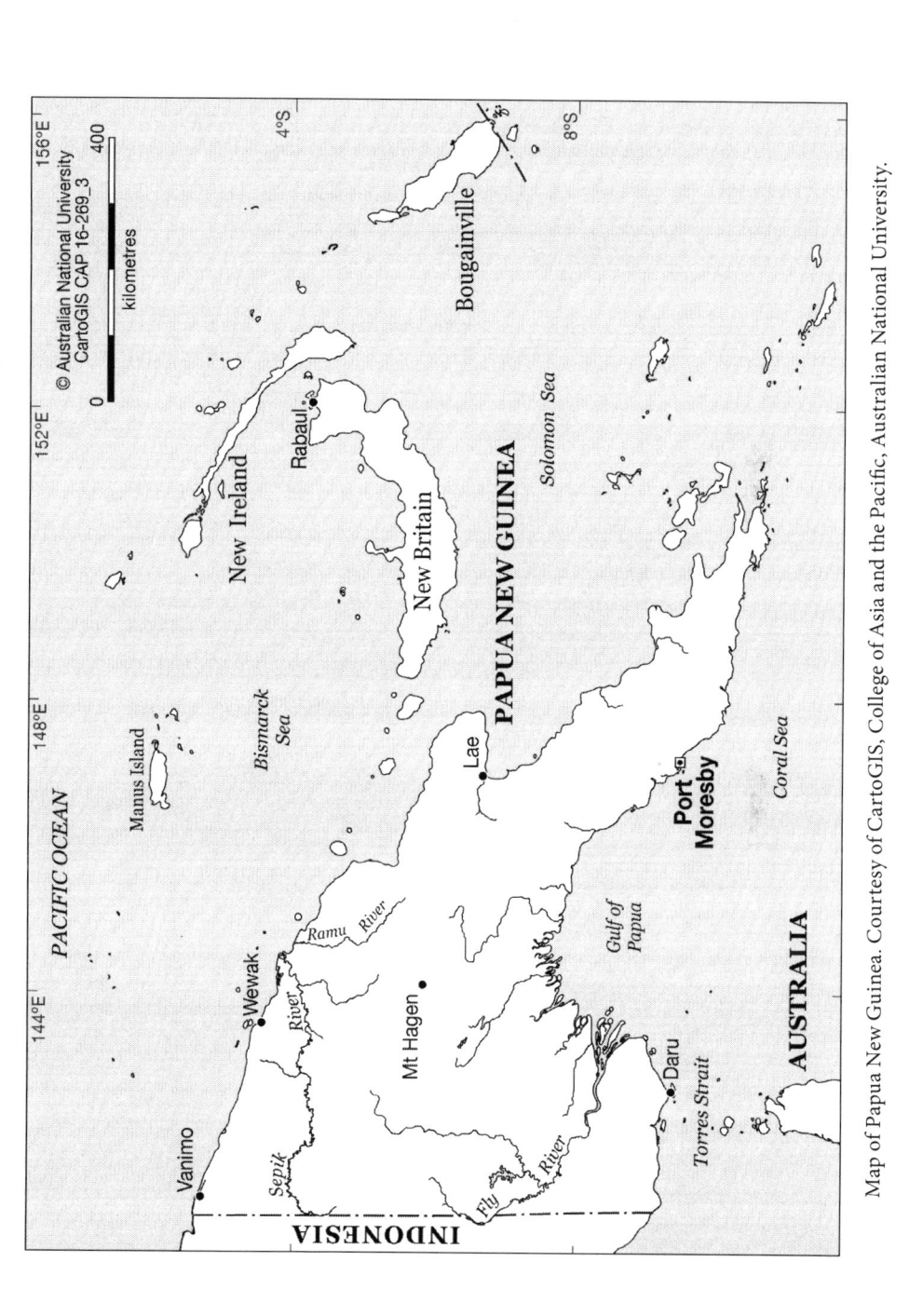

Map of Papua New Guinea. Courtesy of CartoGIS, College of Asia and the Pacific, Australian National University.

decision-makers as chronically unstable and liable to fall victim to internal instability and separatist divisions. It was feared that Australia would be forced to intervene to restore stability and unity. On occasion, Australia has also regarded Papua New Guinea as a liability whose immaturity in managing its relationship with Indonesia had the potential, in extremis, to embarrass the Australian Government.

From as early as the mid-1880s Australian political leaders had spoken of a special relationship between Australia and the eastern half of the island, as the western half had already been secured by the Netherlands. In 1884, at Australia's insistence, Britain acquired Papua, the southeast quarter of the island. In the final decades of the nineteenth and at the beginning of the twentieth century, leaders of the new Commonwealth of Australia, egged on by influential newspaper editors and the general public, asserted a claim to acquire Papua and New Guinea as an integral part of the new nation's manifest destiny and as a bastion to protect it from invaders.[6] Australia's Prime Minister during the First World War, William Morris Hughes, sought to assert an exclusive role for Australia in the region and advocated an Australian version of the United States's Monroe Doctrine covering South America to apply across the South Pacific, including Papua New Guinea. German New Guinea, the northeast quarter of the main island, and the Bismarck Archipelago, were occupied by Australian forces in the early days of the First World War. As part of the peace settlement at the end of the war, Australia secured all the former German possessions south of the Equator and administered New Guinea as a mandated territory under the League of Nations.

During the Second World War Papua New Guinea was the scene of some of the most brutal and crucial battles of the war involving Australian forces – battles whose ferocity and death toll quickly became etched into the psyche of a generation of Australians. The official estimate is that 114,000 Australians served in Papua New Guinea during the Second World War, although Hank Nelson, the noted academic on Papua New Guinea from the Australian National University, has also calculated that over 300,000 Australians served in Papua New Guinea – or one in twenty of the Australian population.[7] More Australians – 2165 – died in the broader Papuan campaign than in any other theatre in the war.[8] Nine of the twenty Victoria Crosses awarded to Australians during the Second World War were won in fighting in Papua New Guinea.[9] As Nelson has observed: 'in its influence on Australian attitudes to Papua New Guinea, three and [a] half years of World War II may have been more important and more

Introduction

enduring than nearly one hundred years of administrative history ... [A]s a result of the war New Guinea ... entered Australian nationalism'.[10] The psychological pull on decision-makers of the memories of the war was to last for a generation or more.

More recently, in the period 2001 to 2015, 44,475 Australians have walked the 96 kilometres of the Kokoda Track across the rugged Owen Stanley Ranges in Papua New Guinea, one of the most gruelling mountain jungle tracks in the world.[11] These trekkers were attempting to replicate and honour the experience of thousands of Australian soldiers who in 1942 repelled the Japanese threat to Port Moresby in the Battle of Kokoda. In his 1992 visit to the Kokoda war memorial, Prime Minister Paul Keating knelt and kissed the ground in front of the memorial, describing the location as a 'solemn place, a national shrine' for all Australians.

The nature of the relationship between Australia and Papua New Guinea is without parallel in Australia's history. It is a shared history. Papua New Guinea, with a population at Independence in September 1975 of close to three million, was the largest overseas community Australia had governed. Prior to Independence, Papuans were acknowledged as Australian citizens and British subjects while New Guineans were Australian protected persons. Both travelled on Australian passports however neither had an automatic right of residence in Australia. Australia governed the Territory through an Administrator who was appointed by the Governor-General and was responsible to the Australian Minister for Territories. Australia had introduced and sponsored a system of government, finance, public service, education, law and justice which were mirrors of its own. Australian currency was the sole legal tender in the Territory. Even the sports played in Papua New Guinea were transplanted from Australia. Between 1949 and 1974 approximately 2000 Australians had served as Kiaps or District Officers representing the Australian Administration in some of the most inaccessible parts of the country. Thirty thousand Australians were still resident there in 1975, with 2500 serving in the public service. At the time of independence, ten Commonwealth Government departments and nine agencies or instrumentalities were working in Papua New Guinea. Over 270 Acts of the Australian Parliament formed part of the Territory's internal laws. Australia had established, nurtured and trained the Territory's police and defence forces and had provided the commanders and senior officers of both forces. The defence force, with over 400 Australian service personnel still serving in it at Independence, was an integral part of the Australian Defence Force.

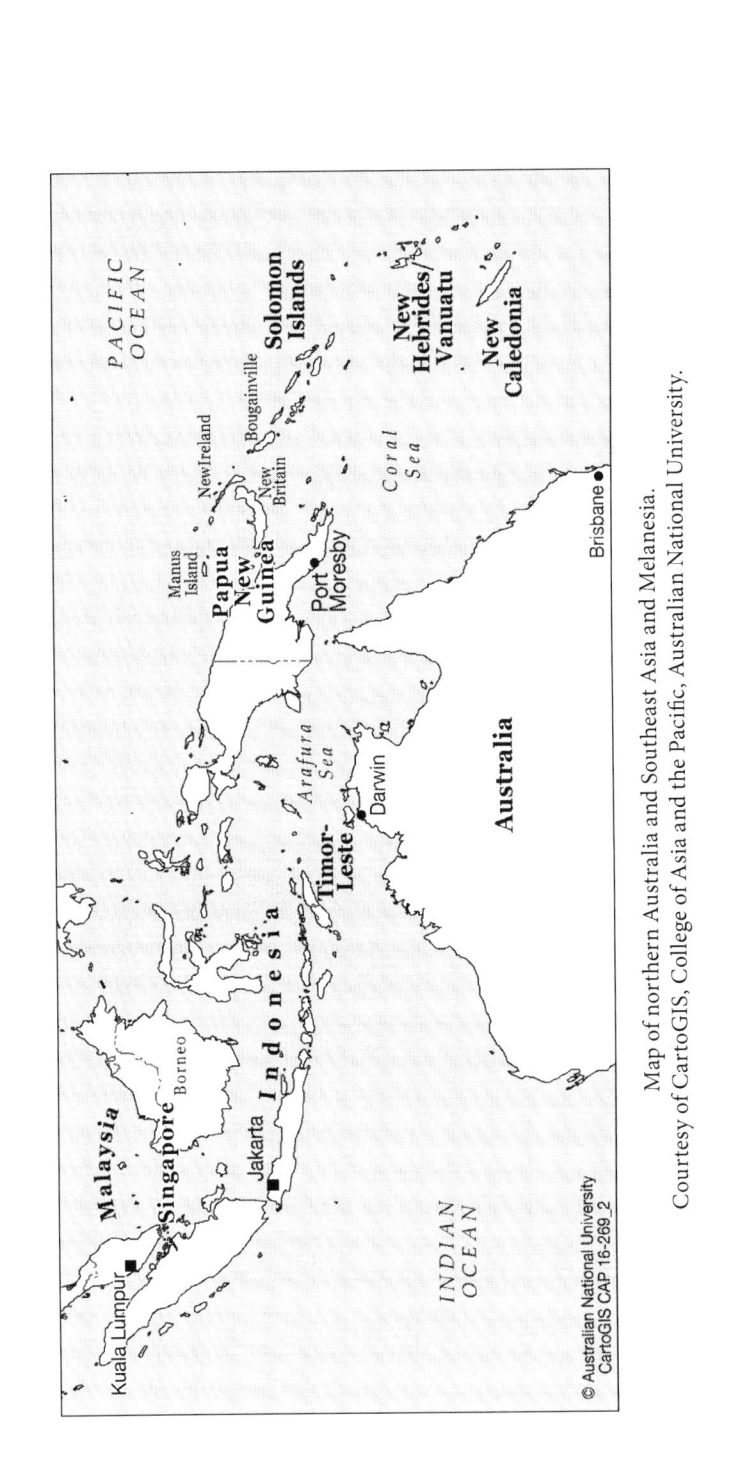

Map of northern Australia and Southeast Asia and Melanesia.
Courtesy of CartoGIS, College of Asia and the Pacific, Australian National University.

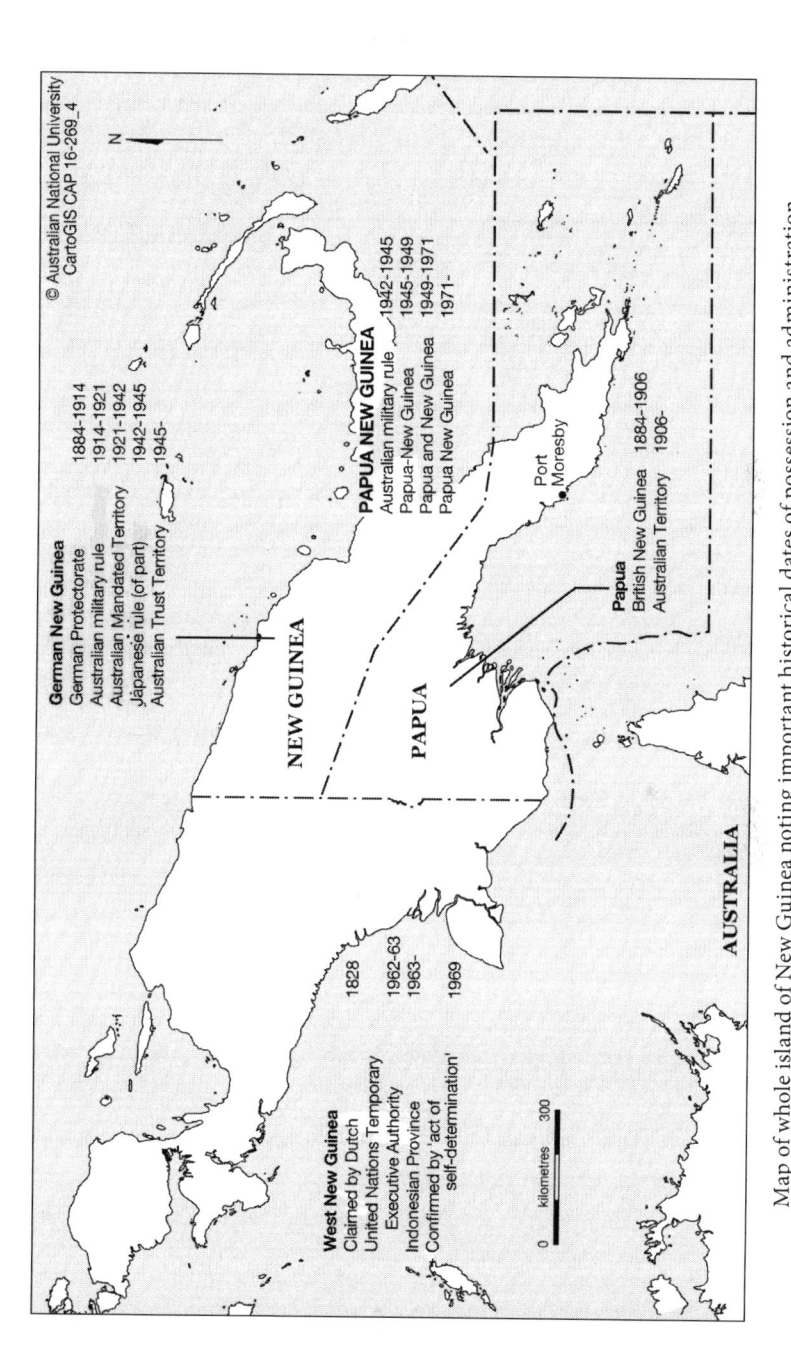

Map of whole island of New Guinea noting important historical dates of possession and administration. Courtesy of CartoGIS, College of Asia and the Pacific, Australian National University.

On the economic front, Australian investments dominated the local economy with an Australian-incorporated company operating the rich Panguna copper mine on Bougainville Island and another soon to open the equally rich Ok Tedi gold and copper mine near the border with Indonesia. Half of all public expenditure in Papua New Guinea was funded by Australia, while the incoming indigenous government relied on Australia for approximately half of total government receipts.[12] Australia was Papua New Guinea's largest trading partner. It was Papua New Guinea's largest export market and Papua New Guinea was Australia's fifth largest market. Papua New Guinea was the recipient at Independence of the largest economic development package in Australia's history and a Prime Ministerial–level commitment that it would have first call on Australia's overseas aid program. In the period 1945 to 1975 Australia was by far the dominant influence on the country's development. Such was the role of Australia that Prime Minister Robert Menzies in 1963 told a local audience in Port Moresby that Australia would in time be able to say that 'we have built a new Jerusalem of our own in this country'.[13]

The Strategic Assessment Papers, developed by Australian military planners and approved by Cabinet and which served as the fundamental guidance for the planning of Australia's defence preparedness, had, since the mid-1950s, identified Papua New Guinea as of central importance to Australia's defence. Papua New Guinea sat astride Australia's military and trade lines of communication to Southeast Asia and North Asia and to United States military bases in the Western Pacific. In 1970, for example, nineteen per cent in value and twenty one per cent in volume of Australia's trade with Japan, Hong Kong and Taiwan passed through the territorial waters surrounding Papua New Guinea. Traditionally it had been seen as a potential base for the conduct of enemy operations inimical to Australia's security. In more recent times its common border with Indonesia had ensured that it was of 'abiding' strategic interest to Australia. Until Independence Australia was responsible for Papua New Guinea's defence. In 1970, as the Australian Cabinet began to contemplate a self-governing Papua New Guinea, ministers were told:

> No matter what the constitutional position maybe, Australia will always have a close interest in whatever happens in Papua New Guinea. No matter how reluctant an Australian Government of the future may be to contemplate intervening to maintain order or to promote Australian interests, the possibility cannot be ruled out of its being requested to do

so or of circumstances in which it would feel compelled to do so even if the Territory had attained full independence.[14]

Paul Dibb, the author of a number of Strategic Basis Papers in the 1980s and now prominent among Australia's defence analysts, has noted Papua New Guinea has never been far from the centre of Australian strategic assessments and is still regarded as a primary area of Australia's defence interests.[15]

A further question behind this study is why, given this long historical association and the primary role of Papua New Guinea in Australia's defence assessments, did Australia not formalise its defence relationship with and its strategic interest in Papua New Guinea with a binding agreement at Independence to guarantee the country's security against external attack.

Several significant historical episodes have been chosen as a means of exploring this question and the changing importance of Papua New Guinea in Australia's strategic outlook. These episodes have been selected because they establish the proposition that, until shortly before the critical phase of preparing for independence, Australia made judgements about the importance of Papua New Guinea using external reference points as the focus of its assessments.

This book will detail the argument that defence and security interests and a fear of Australia's Asian neighbours dominated Australia's consideration of the value of Papua New Guinea. They propelled politicians in the last decades of the nineteenth century and the first two decades of the twentieth century to secure the territory for the new Commonwealth of Australia. In the first instance, the role of Imperial Germany and its naval fleet in the Pacific is relevant to the examination of why Australia sought to gain possession of Papua and later New Guinea. However, it was the assessment of Japan's ambitions in the Pacific before, during and following the First World War which dominated contemporary Australian political and defence analyses. These placed Japan at the centre of Australia's concerns about peace in the region. The threat from Japan became the major influence on Australia's view of the island as a buffer against invasion from the north. This led Prime Minister William Morris Hughes to go to extraordinary lengths at meetings of the Imperial War Cabinet in London and then at the Peace Conference in Paris to argue the case for Australia to secure the former German possessions in the Pacific south of the Equator. He preferred that Australia annex the islands but had to settle for the newly created concept of a League of Nations mandate over German New Guinea. Australia would be allowed to administer the mandated territory as if it were an integral part of Australia but was prohibited from taking defence measures to protect the territory.

By the end of the Second World War, following the desperate fighting of the New Guinea campaign, Papua New Guinea had been firmly established in the minds of all Australians as a shield protecting the country. In the opinion of Dr H. V. Evatt, the wartime Minister for External Affairs, one of Australia's principal postwar strategic imperatives was to secure 'complete and exclusive power'[16] over Papua New Guinea, a land he described as 'consecrated by the sacrifices of Australians in two world wars'.[17]

The third external reference point was Indonesia. It is inevitable in a study of the place of Papua New Guinea in Australia's strategic environment that Indonesia should figure significantly. Indeed much of the consideration and analysis of the place of Papua New Guinea by successive post–Second World War Australian governments was, at the same time, a commentary on the potential threat from Indonesia. The two critical episodes examined here, the West New Guinea dispute and Indonesia's declared intention to crush the newly formed Federation of Malaysia (Confrontation or *Konfrontasi*), were considered by the Menzies and Holt Cabinets on over sixty occasions in specific detail or in the context of analysing Australia's strategic environment. On nearly each occasion ministers linked Indonesia's actions to possible threats to Papua New Guinea. Such was the level of concern generated by Indonesia's threats that Prime Minister Menzies, at the height of Confrontation, repeatedly declared that Australia would defend Papua New Guinea against any infiltration or aggression by Indonesia – and that the United States, courtesy of the ANZUS Treaty, would be by Australia's side. The historian Gregory Pemberton has described a possible Indonesian threat to Papua New Guinea as the *casus belli* in Australia's response to Indonesia's attempts to crush Malaysia.[18] Both episodes studied are as much an examination of the place of Indonesia in Australia's security assessments over the period 1949–1966 as they are of Papua New Guinea's place in that environment.

However, it should be borne in mind that this book is not a detailed study of either episode. There is now a strong and exemplary body of published work on both. The official histories of Australia's involvement in Southeast Asian conflicts between 1948–1975, such as those by Peter Edwards, Gregory Pemberton, Peter Dennis and Jeffrey Grey, provide a comprehensive account of the decision-making behind Australia's involvement in all the major crises of the period and are an essential reference for this study.¹⁹ Rather, this book uses these two critical episodes to illustrate the place of Papua New Guinea in Australia's security environment and the debate within the Australian Government over the need to provide for the defence of Papua New Guinea. The case studies provide an essential background to understanding the strength and depth of Australia's belief that Papua New Guinea was a pivotal component in the defence of Australia.

A study of these two major disputes is best and uniquely seen through extensive references to the Australian Cabinet discussions recorded in the highly classified Cabinet Notebooks. Knowing that their views would not be made public for fifty years and often with no officials other than the Cabinet Secretary present, ministers spoke candidly and frankly of their suspicions and fears of how Australia should respond to developments in Asia, particularly Indonesia, as well as their doubts and anxieties about Australia's capacity to defend its interests. The Notebooks were not shown to ministers to be corrected or edited which adds to their value. Often punctuation marks were not included. In 1972 Prime Minister William McMahon told his Cabinet colleagues that the Notebooks should be destroyed. Fortunately for historians this suggestion was not implemented.²⁰ They are a rich treasure trove of information and insights and change many of the established assessments of the way Australian governments viewed and responded to the changes in Australia's security environment.

For the first time these minutes will be drawn on extensively to expand on the work of Edwards, Pemberton, Garry Woodard, John Subritzky, David Lee, Stuart Doran, David Lowe, David Goldsworthy, Moreen Dee and other historians who have examined this period, to illustrate the argument that the Cabinet was more deeply worried by the changing security environment in Southeast Asia than previously realised. At the same time the Notebooks reveal that ministers in the Menzies and Holt Governments were acutely aware of the implications of the actions they took for Australia's relations with the rest of Asia. Ministers were reflecting on these connections much earlier and in a much broader context than historians to date have been able to acknowledge. Similarly, the Notebooks reveal Australian ministers were less confident of the actions and reliability of Australia's major allies, notably the United States, in coming to their aid than research to date has shown. The views of Prime Minister Menzies and John McEwen, Deputy Prime Minister from 1958 and Leader of the Country Party, were particularly influential and will be followed in detail.²¹ McEwen's leading role in guiding the development of Australia's foreign policy towards Southeast Asia will, for the first time, be described. No decision on Australia's foreign and security policies from mid-1950 to 1970 was taken without his involvement and agreement.

The dramatic internal political developments in Indonesia in 1965 and the abandonment of the policy of *Konfrontasi* by the Suharto Government forced a reappraisal by Australia of its immediate security environment. Indonesia retained a critical place in strategic assessments into the 1980s but the focus was now on managing the international border between Papua New Guinea and Indonesia, the problem of border-crossers and the activities of pro-independence movements based in Irian Jaya. The rise to power of General Suharto was a positive development for Australia in one respect as it removed the need to focus on external military threats to Papua New Guinea. Indeed, the long history of Australia viewing the vulnerability of Papua New Guinea through external reference points all but ended at this point. In its place came concerns over the internal political stability and cohesion of Papua New Guinea. These concerns were to dominate the thinking of decision-makers from the late 1960s through to the post-independence period.

In the critical period (1970–1975) leading to Papua New Guinea's independence on 16 September 1975 Australia's assessment of its own interests shifted dramatically. Australian decision-makers became increasingly preoccupied by the uncertain and unstable internal security situation taking hold of the country. The disturbances associated with the riots in the Gazelle Peninsula in 1970, the political demands from the Papua Besena separatist movement, the long-standing secessionist claims of the leaders of the island of Bougainville and the continuing problem of tribal fighting in the Highlands, as well as more generalised fears about the internal law and order issues facing the country, contributed to an overwhelming determination by senior Australian officials and ministers not to be held hostage to a potentially unstable Papua New Guinea. Australian governments were deeply concerned that an unqualified commitment to defend Papua New Guinea would become a factor in PNG's own calculations and could lead it to pursue immoderate or risky policies, confident of Australian support.

This book will examine in detail the negotiations over the terms of the future defence relationship between Australia and Papua New Guinea. Particular attention will be given to the groundbreaking report 'Australia's Defence Relations with Papua New Guinea' examined by the Defence Committee in November 1973. The radical shifts in opinion set out in the Committee's assessment and later endorsed by the then Minister for Defence, Lance Barnard, questioned and qualified nearly a century of assumptions about the importance of Papua New Guinea to Australia's strategic environment. Australia sought to promote its defence interests in Papua New Guinea by ensuring that it became and remained that country's primary defence partner through a defence cooperation program rather than a treaty-based commitment.

The uncertainty generated by the speed of the process of preparing Papua New Guinea for independence in 1975; the realisation by the Whitlam Government that, given its sensitivity, the terms of a long-term defence relationship could only be negotiated with the government of a post-independent Papua New Guinea; and then the dramatic political events in Australia of November 1975 meant that responsibility for the final negotiations was passed to the Fraser Government. Fraser had little difficulty in accepting the limited nature of the defence arrangements proposed while, at the same time, confirming the objective of establishing Australia as Papua New Guinea's primary defence partner.

A postscript will examine the Hawke Government's early views on the strategic importance of Papua New Guinea and its subsequent decision to accept Papua New Guinea's initiative to sign a Joint Declaration of Principles aimed at setting out the fundamentals of the post-independence relationship, including the terms of a revised long-term defence understanding. The recent revision of the Joint Declaration signed in 2013 will also be discussed. Both documents are statements of political intent. The defence commitment from Australia has been left as a matter of trust rather than of obligation.

Finally, the author hopes that this book responds to the challenge posed by the noted journalist and observer of Papua New Guinea, Sean Dorney, in his recent book, *The Embarrassed Colonialist*, for Australians to return to the study of the relationship between Australia and Papua New Guinea and to demonstrate a renewed interest in trying to understand our shared history.[22]

* * *

History of the name 'Papua New Guinea'

In 1971 the House of Assembly in Port Moresby determined that the country would be called Papua New Guinea. Prior to this decision and from 1949 the country had been called the Territory of Papua and New Guinea and administered as such. This term reflected the separate histories of the two former territories. In 1884 Imperial Germany had taken control of the northeast quadrant of the island and the adjoining islands in the Bismarck Archipelago, including West and East New Britain, New Ireland and Bougainville. In 1884 Britain had formally annexed the southeast quadrant known as Papua. In September 1906 Australia assumed responsibility for British New Guinea and renamed it the Territory of Papua. In 1920, as part of the peace settlement following the First World War, Australia was granted a mandate from the League of Nations over the former German New Guinea.[23] The mandated territory of New Guinea was administered by Australia from 9 May 1921. In 1942, following the outbreak of war, Papua and New Guinea were placed under Australian military administration. At the end of the war civil administration of the territories was progressively restored under the Papua New Guinea Provisional Administration Act (1945–1946). In December 1946 the United Nations General Assembly approved the terms of a trusteeship agreement for the territory of New Guinea. In 1949 under the terms of the Papua and New Guinea Act (1949) the two halves, Papua and New Guinea, were placed under joint administration from Port Moresby under the title 'Territory of Papua and New Guinea', although New Guinea remained a trusteeship of the United Nations. The Territory became an independent country on 16 September 1975.

At times 'Australian New Guinea' or 'Eastern New Guinea' were used in public discussion as an easy reference to Papua New Guinea. To add to the confusion Australian ministers and officials, including Prime Minister Whitlam, also had the habit of informally referring to Papua New Guinea as 'New Guinea'.

Chapter 1

SECURING THE SHIELD 1880–1920

'We must take it [Papua]'.

William Morris Hughes, MP
19 November 1901

Australia's early interest in the South Pacific, and in the island of New Guinea, reflected a variety of influences, ranging from an anxiety about the threat generated by the presence (real or potential) of foreign powers both European and Asian in the region, to a concern not to be denied the chance to secure territory in the Pacific for itself. There were trade and economic ambitions represented by shipping, plantation and trading companies such as Burns Philp, and other imperatives such as missionary zeal, scientific curiosity and the need to secure, by 'blackbirding' or kidnapping, island labourers for use in the Queensland sugarcane fields. There was also a sense of 'Imperial duty' felt by Australians and New Zealanders to extend British rule over the islands of the South Pacific. However, above and beyond all these, as Brian Primrose has described, was an overwhelming and persistent sense that possession would allow Australia to turn the island of New Guinea into a shield which would guarantee the safety of Australia against invasion.[1]

Within a few decades of the establishment of British settlement on the east coast of Australia in 1788, colonial politicians, followed by colonial news editors, began calling for the expansion of the British presence in the Pacific to include possession of the islands to the immediate north and east of the continent. Colonial Australia saw the islands of the South Pacific as providing their 'geo-political setting … their buffer against possible aggressors'. The chief objective 'was simply defensive, to exclude all other foreign powers from the region'.[2]

In the first instance, it was New Zealand's Governor, Sir George Grey, who in 1848 called for the annexation of Tonga and Fiji.³ Britain declined to take up Grey's suggestion. Five years later in 1853 Grey pointed out to London that with the French now in possession of New Caledonia 'a position for attack against Australia and New Zealand had thus passed into foreign hands'.⁴ The Australian colonies had also shown an early interest in promoting the idea of annexing the islands. In 1867 the New South Wales Government submitted a minute to the Governor, Sir John Young, arguing that 'the increasing traffic between Australia and the Indian isles by way of the Torres Strait makes the possession of New Guinea by the British Empire a matter of the highest importance to Australian colonists'. The British Government declined to act.

In 1873 Captain John Moresby attempted to claim three islands at the eastern end of New Guinea on behalf of Britain. He was motivated, in part, by a sense that 'the occupation of this island [Hayter Island] by a foreign maritime power … would be a standing menace to Queensland'.⁵ However, his actions were not endorsed by the British Government. Two years later, in May 1875, the New South Wales Government asked the Governor, Sir Hercules Robinson, to forward to London its 'opinion' that it would be desirable 'in the highest interests of civilisation' for Britain to take possession of the island of New Guinea as well as the islands lying to the north and east of New Guinea, including New Britain, New Ireland, Bougainville, Solomon Islands, New Hebrides and the Marshall, Gilbert and Ellice Islands 'to all of which the traffic from the port of Sydney extends'.⁶ It added that the acquisition would 'extend dominion over these waters on the part of the British Empire … but would conduce much to the tranquillity and peace of these Australian colonies'.⁷ It further argued that 'the occupation by foreign Governments of large islands in the immediate neighbourhood of our coasts, and on the very tracks of our ocean communications with the mother country, might, and probably would, be in time of war fatal to our free navigation of the sea which adjoins our territory'.⁸ The New South Wales Cabinet also claimed that the colonies could not finance such acquisitions and that Britain alone would have to bear the costs.

The British Secretary of State for the Colonies in Disraeli's Conservative Government, the Earl of Carnarvon, rejected the proposals. Carnarvon told the New South Wales Governor that he would be unable to persuade the British Parliament that while the Australia colonies might have an interest in New Guinea it should be left to Britain to bear the financial costs for the administration of the area. He added that 'there is no present indication of any intention of a foreign state to annex islands in the Pacific'.⁹ The issue of who would underwrite the financial costs of any colonial administration in New Guinea frustrated these early attempts to secure London's support for annexation.

The Australian colonial governments were not content with Britain's reassurances. They were particularly anxious at reports that Imperial Germany was intent on expanding its new colonial empire into the region. Such was the level of concern that in 1883 'Queensland could no longer contain its frustration' and unilaterally attempted to take possession of the eastern half of New Guinea.¹⁰ On 20 March 1883, alarmed by news of the departure from Sydney of a German Corvette, SMS *Carola*, the Queensland Premier, T. J. McIlwraith, instructed the resident magistrate on Thursday Island in the Torres Strait, Henry Chester, to take possession of New Guinea east of the Dutch border and adjacent islands in the name of the Crown. The magistrate did so on 4 April 1883. The Governor of Queensland, Sir Arthur Kennedy, endorsed Chester's action telling the Earl of Derby, the Secretary of State for Colonies in William Gladstone's Government, that 'I have never heard any well-informed person doubt the great disaster which the occupation of New Guinea by a European Power would prove to Australia'.¹¹ On 11 July, Lord Derby replied that the Queensland Colonial Government had no authority to act beyond the geographic borders of its colony. Moreover, the 'apprehension entertained in Australia that some foreign power was about to establish itself on the shores of New Guinea appears to have been altogether indefinite and unfounded'.¹² He nevertheless told the House of Lords that 'England would regard it as an unfriendly action should any foreigners settle in New Guinea'.¹³

Margaret George and Brian Primrose have argued that a mix of reasons motivated the Queensland Premier in 1883 to instruct the magistrate to take possession of the eastern half of New Guinea. Both have acknowledged the pull of commercial ambitions but have concluded that anxiety over security dominated the thinking of the Queensland Government. Primrose, in particular, has drawn attention to the terms of an earlier request by the Premier of Queensland to the Governor of Queensland (Sir Arthur Kennedy) that Britain be asked to annex New Guinea. McIlwraith had argued that:

> Possession of New Guinea and the adjacent islands would be of value to the Empire and conduce specially to the peace and safety of Australia, the development of Australian trade and the prevention and punishment of crime throughout the Pacific.

> That the establishment of a Foreign Power in the neighbourhood of Australia would be injurious to British and more particularly to Australian interests.[14]

Roger Joyce has concluded that the actions by Queensland confirmed an impression at the time that Papua New Guinea would serve as a 'defensive shield' across Australia's north.[15]

The Australian colonies, and New Zealand, meeting at the Australasian Convention in Sydney in December 1883, resolved unanimously that 'further acquisition of dominion in the Pacific, south of the Equator, by any foreign power would be highly detrimental to the safety and well-being of the British possessions in Australasia, and injurious to the interests of the Empire'. This statement was interpreted as attempting to impose a Monroe Doctrine for the Western Pacific similar to the United States statement in 1823 warning against foreign interference in Central and South America.[16] In this case British (and colonial) maritime security interests were to be given primacy in the South Pacific and other powers warned off involving themselves in the region. The Convention also resolved that 'having regard to the geographical position of New Guinea ... such steps should be immediately taken as will most conveniently and effectively secure the incorporation with the British Empire of so much of New Guinea and the small islands adjacent thereto as is not claimed by the Government of the Netherlands'.[17] The added significance of the resolution was that the colonies offered to finance the Australian presence in New Guinea. Alfred Deakin, a leading Victorian politician and later Prime Minister of Australia (1903–1904, 1905–1908 and 1909–1910) noted at the time that a driving force behind the calling together of the Convention and the passage of the resolution was the 'dread of German aggression in New Guinea and of a French annexation of the New Hebrides coupled with the alarm occasioned by the arrival of escaped criminals from the [French] penal settlement in New Caledonia'.[18]

The concerns of the Australian colonial politicians as to Australia's 'strategic vulnerability' were dramatically realised when it was revealed on 19 August 1884 that Imperial Germany had ordered a German protectorate be established over north-eastern New Guinea and the New Britain archipelago.[19] The Victorian Premier, James Service, exclaimed 'at last the end has come ... The exasperation here is boundless'.[20] On Australia Day 1885, the *Sydney Morning Herald* commented that the action:

Signifies ... the possible establishment of a German colony within too convenient distance of Australian coasts, and thereby the loss of strength of isolation which had been, and should continue to be, more to us than any possible conditions of preparedness for war or defence. The probability of a speedy appearance of an armed man at the door of the Australian house has done more for Federation than any formal resolution. The sense of danger has been felt in every colony.[21]

The Gladstone Government, which had begun in August 1884 to consider the establishment of a protectorate over all of East New Guinea, responded on 23 October 1884 by ordering the British flag be hoisted at Port Moresby and the area claimed for Britain. On 6 November 1884 Commodore J. E. Erskine arrived in Port Moresby and proclaimed a British protectorate over southeastern New Guinea. By April 1885 Britain and Germany had reached substantial agreement on the boundaries between their respective jurisdictions and on 10 April 1886 an Anglo-German Declaration described and delineated the boundaries.[22] On 4 September 1888 Lord Salisbury's Conservative Government formally annexed the southeastern portion of the main island of New Guinea to the east of Dutch New Guinea and south of German New Guinea. The British portion was described as 'British New Guinea'.

The new Commonwealth takes control of Papua

The Commonwealth's Constitution of 1901 gave the Federal Government not only responsibility for external affairs but also for the 'relations of the Commonwealth with the islands of the Pacific'.[23] Neville Meaney has convincingly argued that this specific reference was a 'direct expression of Australia's anxiety for security in its own geographic sphere'.[24] Marilyn Lake has developed this argument further and has drawn attention to the views of Australia's first Prime Minister, Edmund Barton, as representative of the opinion of many of the new leaders of the Commonwealth towards the South Pacific.[25] Barton, Lake notes, told the Colonial Office in London that the Australian nation had been founded in dreams of Empire, an 'Island Empire' of the Pacific, and that the new Constitution had endorsed Australia's statutory right to exercise the 'power and influence of the Commonwealth in connection with the islands of the South Seas'.[26] Lake adds that control over the islands of the Pacific had been identified as a 'key federal power' in the creation of the Commonwealth and has drawn attention to Australia's early 'imperial' interest in acquiring the Cook Islands, Solomon Islands, Tonga, New Hebrides as well as British New Guinea.[27] In colourful and effusive language that soon characterised the debate over control of the islands of the South Pacific, Sir Malcolm McEachern, the member of the House of Representatives for Melbourne and a shipping magnate, told the Parliament that Australia's imperial ambitions would not end 'until the whole of the islands are under our control'.[28] Peter Overlack has pointed out that 'no Australasian political party was opposed to the imperialist program (of acquisition)'.[29]

In November 1901 Prime Minister Edmund Barton introduced a resolution in the Parliament that the Commonwealth Government should accept British New Guinea as a Territory of the Commonwealth, if Britain were willing to place it under Australian control and that an annual budget be allocated to fund the administration of the territory. The subsequent debate focused more on the question of providing an adequate budget for the territory but it also included a number of comments from parliamentarians which illustrated their approach to defining the place of New Guinea in Australia's strategic environment.

Barton saw New Guinea in a broader context of Australia, in time, assuming responsibility for other islands in the Pacific, notably the Solomon Islands and possibly the New Hebrides. He held out the image of Australia's 'destiny' to be fulfilled in the South Pacific with 'the hopes and aspirations of those who look forward to the creation of a federation in these seas'.[30] Andrew Fisher of the Labor Party welcomed the concept of Australia taking responsibility for British New Guinea and told the Parliament that 'it would be better … if we could secure the whole of New Guinea'.[31] William Morris Hughes (Labor Party) told his parliamentary colleagues:

> It is essential that we assume control of this territory as soon as we can. How any man can conceive it possible that British New Guinea, lying adjacent to these shores – within a stone's throw, so to speak – being to all intents and purposes part of Australia, can be permitted, as it were, to lie, a pearl in the Pacific Ocean, waiting for some marauder to pick it up, I cannot understand. We must take it.[32]

The views of Barton, Fisher and Hughes, along with those of Alfred Deakin, were to be of continuing importance in the years ahead.[33] Each served as Prime Minister of Australia and all four were involved in developing Australia's defence preparedness, with Cook and Deakin responsible for establishing a Royal Australian Navy. All played a critical role in defining Australia's defence interests and strategic environment. All, as Meaney has argued, had seen in 'the Pacific a primary threat to Australian security ... and [had sought] to build up a formidable local defence force'.[34] Deakin had been at the forefront when he had declared that 'foreign interests and risks surround us on every side. A Pacific policy we must have'.[35]

The resolution introduced by Barton was adopted by the Parliament in 1902 but it was not until November 1905 that the Papua Bill was passed. The Papua Act was proclaimed on 1 September 1906 and Australia accepted responsibility for its first external territory which was henceforth known as Papua.[36] As W. J. Hudson has argued in explaining the reasons for Australia's acquisition of British New Guinea, 'it was clear from the beginning that the defence interest was paramount ... possession was sufficient'.[37] This assessment would be shared by Atlee Hunt, the first Secretary of the Department of External Affairs, who in 1904 wrote that 'possession of British New Guinea by the Commonwealth may be regarded as an important defensive measure in as much as while it remains under British control its harbours cannot be availed of as store-houses and places of equipment for vessels of foreign powers'.[38]

Defining Australia's strategic environment

Successive governments in the first decade of the Commonwealth had created the framework of Australia's defence policy with the passage of the first Defence Act in 1903 and the presentation in February 1910 by Field Marshal Lord Kitchener of his 'Memorandum on the Defence of the Australian Continent' at the conclusion of his visit to Australia. Australia had also begun to acquire the military hardware to defend itself and to contribute to the defence of the Empire, notably beginning in 1907–08 with elements of its own navy.[39]

As political and military leaders set about the task of building an Australian defence force and identifying its role, the strategic environment, including the place of New Guinea in that environment, changed dramatically. Japan's comprehensive defeat of the Russian Navy in May 1905 at the Battle of Tsushima had the most profound significance, accompanied by the later decision in 1911 by Britain to withdraw its capital ships from the Pacific to bolster its home defence against Germany. Japan's victory over the Russian fleet forced Prime Minister Deakin and military planners to elevate Japan to the role of a direct military threat. Australia's leaders refused to be consoled by the fact that Japan was a formal ally of Britain following the signing of the Anglo-Japanese Alliance of 1902.[40] It was viewed as a challenger to Australia's presence in the South Pacific, as well as a nation which could take issue with the country's 'White Australia policy'. Japan was perceived as a threat to Australia's interests and, as Meaney has argued, 'for the first time, Australians came to entertain seriously the fear of invasion'.[41] Japan was to maintain that place in Australian military planning for the next forty years.

In the years immediately before the outbreak of the First World War, defence planners began to examine more rigorously the question of Australia's immediate strategic environment and to debate whether Australia had to be prepared to defend its interests in the South Pacific. In October 1911 Australian military strategists had drawn up a plan to capture Rabaul, the capital of German New Guinea,[42] while in 1912 at a three-day conference at Victoria Barracks in Melbourne chaired by the Minister for Defence, Senator George Pearce, senior Australian and New Zealand military officers debated a 'Scheme of Defence – Mobile Forces of Australia – Strategical Considerations'. The scheme noted the presence of a 'foreign territory' in the French possessions of New Caledonia and the German and Dutch possessions in the Bismarck Archipelago, New Guinea, and the Java and Flores Seas. It called for 'war preparations [that] must include plans for the occupation, if necessary, of probable hostile bases in these localities'.[43] This objective, and the listing of the ports in these locations, were incorporated into the 1913 General Scheme of Defence. Despite the alliance relationship between Britain and Japan, the General Scheme identified an 'Eastern Power', a euphemism for Japan, as being able to bring pressure to bear on Australia through raids rather than invasion. It suggested that an enemy pursuing such a policy would benefit from taking possession of Wilhelmshaven in German New Guinea (present day Madang) and Noumea in New Caledonia. It advocated a policy of 'active offence' to meet the challenge posed by raids from the 'Eastern Power' and reiterated the proposal to occupy the bases identified in the 1912 Scheme of Defence plan. It recommended the 'despatch of small expeditionary forces against foreign possessions which might be used as a base for operations against the Commonwealth in the East Indian Archipelago and the Pacific'.[44]

At the same time as defence planners were identifying areas in Australia's immediate environment to be occupied at the outbreak of hostilities, consideration was also being given to identifying the limits of Australia's strategic environment. In May 1913 Commander W. H. C. S. (Hugh)

Thring, Royal Australian Navy and a recently appointed assistant to the First Naval Member (Rear Admiral William Creswell) of the pre-eminent advisory body, the Naval Board, reported on the naval defence of Australia following a visit to Papua, Thursday Island and the Northern Territory. He had been accompanied by Captain C. Hughes-Onslow, Second Naval Member of the Board.[45] In his separate report Thring argued that Australia faced attack from the north rather than by raids against populated centres in the southeast. He identified Japan as a future threat to Australia. Thring asked his colleagues 'to imagine Australia in the hands of Japan and it is not difficult to forsee [sic] the greater part of Asia under Japanese control. It would entail the downfall not alone of British power in the East but that of every other European nation'.[46] He suggested that Japan would not try to take the whole of Australia but instead would occupy part of the country and 'stop all coastwise and sea trade'. In assessing the targets for Japan to occupy, Thring concluded that 'everything points to the Northern Territory, Papua, the Solomon Islands, Torres Strait and some harbours inside the Barrier Reef as the theatre of operations of the Fleet in war and our attention must be concentrated there'.[47] He then proposed that the defence of Australia and New Zealand should be guided by identifying and fortifying a 'naval frontier' which would run from Singapore, Java, Timor, Papua, Solomon Islands, Fiji and 'on this line we should attack the enemy'.[48] David Stevens has described this 'naval frontier' as a 'flexible tripwire' which, with the deployment of an intelligence system, wireless communications and coastwatchers, could alert Australia's defence forces to take action.[49] Finally, Thring suggested that two naval bases should be established with one at Bynoe Harbour southwest of Darwin and the other at the southeast end of Papua or in the Solomon Islands.

Thring's report was not well received by the senior member of the Naval Board, Rear Admiral William Creswell, and it ran into considerable bureaucratic difficulties.[50] Nevertheless, it is an interesting and illuminating insight into how defence planners were developing their thoughts on the detail and scope of Australia's strategic environment. Thring's description of a 'naval frontier' was, as will be seen in later chapters, remarkably close to that identified after the Second World War by Australia's defence planners as the preferred outer perimeter for Australia's defence. It also showed that the island of New Guinea was emerging as an important feature in Australia's defence planning as crises erupted in Europe and the world stumbled into a major global conflict. As Stevens has concluded, 'many of [the] features of the [Thring Plan] echo those enunciated in recent strategic policy guidance.

The combination of deterrence and decisive response continues to underpin Australian security planning'.⁵¹

Seizing German New Guinea

Australia 'jumped the gun' in offering to contribute troops to defend the Empire before London had formally declared war on Imperial Germany in 1914.⁵² It showed similar alacrity in responding to Britain's invitation that it launch a raid on the German New Guinea capital of Rabaul and seize German New Guinea and other German possessions in the South Pacific. On 6 August 1914, in the same telegram in which the British Government had accepted the offer by Australia to send 20,000 men to join the campaign against Germany, the Secretary of State for the Colonies, Lewis Harcourt, advised the Governor-General, Sir Ronald Munro Ferguson, and the Australian Government that:

> If your Ministers at the same time desire and feel themselves able to seize German wireless stations at Ytrop (Yap) in Marshall Islands, Nauru or Pleasant Islands and New Guinea we should feel this was a great and urgent Imperial Service. You will, however, realise that any territory now occupied must at the conclusion of war be at the disposal of the Imperial Government for purposes of an ultimate settlement. Other Dominions are acting in similar way on the same understanding in regard to Samoa.⁵³

On 10 August 1914 the Minister for Defence (E. D. Millen) asked the Naval Board to examine the feasibility of despatching a contingent of 1500 soldiers 'for the purposes of securing certain German possessions referred to in the recent Admiralty cablegram'.⁵⁴ On 19 August Harcourt cabled Australia and suggested 'that Rabaul be occupied as [a] base and thereafter subsidiary expeditions to Nauru, Yap and Angaur. Later, operations should be taken to occupy mainland of German New Guinea and as many as possible of the more valuable outlying islands, such as Feys'.⁵⁵ In late August the Naval Board ordered Australian 'submarines and tenders to leave Sydney for Palm Island and then to Rabaul in furtherance of the purpose of the expedition and the occupation of German possessions and destruction of wireless stations'.⁵⁶

On 11 September 1914, within six weeks of the outbreak of war and after some resistance from the local German forces, the Australian Naval and Military Expeditionary Force seized Rabaul and took control of German

New Guinea.⁵⁷ Six members of the landing party were killed and four wounded. Under the terms of the surrender dated 17 September all German possessions in the Pacific 'lately administered from Rabaul' were placed under the control of the Australian expeditionary force.⁵⁸ The Australian force then went on to capture Nauru on 6 November. The intention to seize and occupy the German islands north of the Equator (Yap, Carolines and Marshall Islands) was, however, frustrated when HMAS *Australia*, which was escorting the Australian expeditionary force, was diverted to protect the New Zealand naval attack on German Samoa. In the period during which HMAS *Australia* was absent, momentum was lost, Australia's military endeavour faltered and, contrary to expectations held in London, Japan, which had declared war on Germany on 23 August, took possession of the German-held islands north of the Equator.⁵⁹

The proposal that Australia should secure German New Guinea had strong and immediate popular support. On 19 August 1914, *The Age* had commented:

> In view of the intervention of Japan in Chinese waters, the duty of the Australian Commonwealth to plant the British flag on Germany's Pacific Ocean colonies has acquired a new and sharp significance … That they will be wrested from Germany is certain. But under what flag will they pass? To the captors belong the prize. Australia should be first well and good, but we cannot afford to take chances in a matter so closely affecting our national interests and the future of the Commonwealth.⁶⁰

The editorial had also identified an issue which was to confound Australia's Pacific policy until the peace settlement. The issue was the role of Japan in the Pacific following its own declaration of war against Germany. The initial assessment from London had been that Japan would concentrate on securing German-held Tsingtao in China. On 11 August Harcourt advised the Australian Government through the Governor-General that the 'action of Japan will not extend to the Pacific Ocean'. He followed this message up on 25 August 1914 with advice that Britain had 'received private assurances from the Japanese Government that they have no intention to seize territory outside China Seas such as German islands in Pacific'.⁶¹

Events, however, moved quickly and on 10 September the Colonial Secretary asked the Governor-General to 'inform your Ministers very confidentially that Japanese ships and destroyers may very likely cruise in the Pacific round Marianne and Caroline Islands in order to hunt down

German squadron which is believed to be in these ports'.[62] In October, a Japanese naval force temporarily occupied the island of Yap and took control of the German wireless station. Japan agreed to a British request that the island be occupied by Australia and an Australian military force was prepared under the command of Commander Samuel Petherbridge. On 23 November Harcourt advised of a change of plan. He directed that the Australian force should not proceed to Yap nor should it proceed north of the Equator. He confirmed that the islands north of the Equator were under military occupation by Japan. On 24 November he asked that Australia confine itself to the German islands south of the Equator, leaving the question of the future disposition of all the German island possessions to be settled after the war. On 3 December Harcourt repeated his request that 'should be glad if Australian expedition would confine itself to occupation of German Islands south of Equator'.[63] On 5 December the Governor-General advised Harcourt that the 'wishes of the Imperial Government will be complied with'.[64]

In a 'private, personal and very secret' letter, Harcourt later explained to Munro Ferguson that the change in Britain's instructions to Australia had been brought about by the need not to antagonise Japan while it was performing an essential role in augmenting the Allied naval effort in the Pacific and Indian Oceans, particularly as the German warships *Sharnhorst*, *Gneisenau*, *Emden* and *Dresden* were still active in the Pacific. He advised that the Japanese had called at Yap at Britain's request and had destroyed the German wireless stations which were still operating and had also called at Jaluit in the Marshall Islands to destroy the German coal reserves. He commented that 'all this has changed the character of the Japanese participation and no doubt of their eventual claims to compensation'. He added 'from information which reaches me I have very little doubt that it is the intention of the Japanese at the end of the war to claim for themselves all the German islands north of the Equator'. (In fact Japan had told Britain on 1 December that it intended to retain permanently all the German islands north of the Equator. Britain had not objected to the Japanese statement.)

Harcourt told Munro Ferguson that Britain was not prepared to risk a quarrel with Japan in order to oust its forces from the islands, particularly as it had been invited to occupy them 'more or less' by Britain. Harcourt also argued that such were the demands on the British Fleet that it was possible that Japan would be asked to serve in the European theatre of war. He then asked the Governor-General:

... in the most gradual and diplomatic way to begin to prepare the mind of your ministers for the possibility that at the end of the war Japan may be left in possession of the Northern islands and we with everything south of the Equator.

I know they won't like this, but after all the thing of most importance are [sic] those territories most contiguous to Australia and it will be of great gain to add German New Guinea to Papua and to have the whole of the Solomon Island group under the British flag.[65]

The critical question had emerged of how Australia's strategic environment was to be defined and whether Australia's interests were best defined by limiting that environment to the island of New Guinea and the area south of the Equator.

Over the next few months the Governor-General carried out the task set for him. In January 1915 he advised Harcourt that he was 'suggesting to trustworthy interlocutors the Equator as a likely line between British and Japanese sphere of influence in the Pacific'.[66] He reported Prime Minister Fisher as 'convinced that the islands south of the Line administered from Rabaul would leave Australia with enough on her hands'.[67] Other senior parliamentarians, such as Defence Minister Senator George Pearce, agreed with Fisher, although Pearce preferred Australia to 'keep a grip on the New Hebrides so that an Australian outer line of defence should run thence by the Solomons to New Guinea'.[68] A military point of view was provided by Colonel Gordon Legge, Chief of the General Staff, who was reported by the Governor-General as saying that he was not sure (as a military man) whether he would not rather be without them, describing the islands north of the Equator as 'expensive to hold, that the Japanese would seize them on the outbreak of war ... whilst if Japan held them they would still be a thousand miles away from our outlying possessions'.[69]

In May 1915 Fisher informally canvassed the views of his Cabinet and reported to the Governor-General that he anticipated 'no effective objection to continued occupation by Japanese of islands north of Line when question raised at end of war'. Moreover, he thought an 'Australian administrative area including New Guinea, Bismarck Archipelago and possibly Solomons would be favourably regarded' and the 'continued condominium [of the] New Hebrides considered better than our (i.e. British) withdrawal as a defensive measure'.[70] Fisher also assured the Cabinet that nothing would be conceded until the terms of the peace settlement had been reached. The Cabinet accepted this assurance.

The Colonial Office, and Harcourt in particular, were pleased with the assessment of Australia's attitude. Harcourt told Munro Ferguson that he had 'done splendidly with Fisher and Legge over the question of the late German islands' and that he was 'greatly relieved to hear that they will be satisfied with those (islands) south of the Equator'. He added that he would be prepared to 'hand over Bougainville and the British Solomons to the Commonwealth on certain conditions', although that might force Britain to surrender its share of the New Hebrides to the French as a way of soothing any criticisms they might express and 'greatly ease the future peace negotiations with France'.[71] Harcourt told his successor as Colonial Secretary, Andrew Bonar Law, in July 1915, that the ground had been 'prepared' in Australia on the question of the disposition of the Japanese-held islands north of the Equator and the possible transfer of the British share of the New Hebrides to France.[72]

Hughes takes charge

The London-born William Morris Hughes was elected by his Labor Party colleagues to the post of Prime Minister on 27 October 1915 following the resignation of Andrew Fisher. Fisher had followed Deakin in articulating a role for Australia in the South Pacific, had supported the Australian takeover of German New Guinea and had expressed a keenness to acquire the French interests in the New Hebrides and New Caledonia as a way of projecting Australia's presence in the region and in securing the outer perimeter of Australia's defensive line. He had also been interested in securing the British protectorate of Solomon Islands. Hughes, who had already demonstrated an interest in the Pacific, proved to be a far more outspoken and bellicose advocate of the same principles and objectives. But, as time would show, he was a poor judge of the broader changes emerging in the international environment as the war continued and as a new alignment of forces and a new set of international principles began to emerge to determine the post-war international environment.[73]

Munro Ferguson welcomed Hughes's appointment. He described Hughes to the British Prime Minister, Herbert Asquith, as 'a remarkable personality', a 'natural leader of men', as 'bold in adversity' and as 'clear in his views'.[74] He also told the Colonial Secretary, Bonar Law, that Hughes was 'highly strung and at times violent … He stands out above his whole party in intellect, courage and skill'.[75] Hughes was described as having a 'grasp of the difficulties which must attend the administration of [the] Pacific Islands by

Australia'[76] and as having an appreciation of 'the importance of the Pacific Question as it affects India, Japan, USA and Australia'.[77] The Governor-General also warned London that Hughes was a 'born politician and I am afraid that it is unlikely that his real opinions will remain unchanged in the face of Party prejudice or passions'.[78]

Hughes was the first of a long list of political leaders who were to prosecute Australia's argument that East New Guinea had to be in Australian hands if the country were to be free from the fear of invasion or subversion. He was to be joined later by Australia's leaders during the Second World War, notably Dr H. V. Evatt, Minister for External Affairs in the Curtin and Chifley Governments, and then by Prime Minister Menzies and External Affairs Ministers Spender, Casey and Barwick. A continuous, unbroken line of argument had formed and was shared by the major political parties in Australia and by the Australian press and community. Hughes held a number of senior ministerial posts in subsequent conservative governments and remained a member of parliament until his death in 1952. He thus had the opportunity to sustain his argument on the importance of New Guinea in the defence of Australia for over half a century.

Shortly after taking office, and in preparation for his first visit to London as Prime Minister, Hughes received an assessment from his Minister for Defence, Senator George Pearce, on the strategic value to Australia of the former German possessions in the Pacific. In contrast to the private remarks made by ministers and others in the Fisher Government and conveyed to London by the Governor-General, Pearce's statement, written following a conversation with Hughes on the Pacific islands, can be described as one of the first formal, endorsed assessments of Australia's immediate security environment and the place of New Guinea in that environment. Pearce dismissed the islands north of the Equator as:

> not of very great value to Australia. Their commercial value is small; they have essentially a tropical climate and their distance from Australia renders them of little value to us from a strategical point of view. In fact they might be a source of weakness whereas, in the hands of another power they cannot be of much danger to us because of their distance from us and the intervention of other islands.[79]

Turning to the islands south of the Equator, Pearce made clear his view that they were of 'incalculable value to Australia'. He added that:

> Their commercial value is already considerable and will be largely increased. ... the latest reports indicate that that portion of New Guinea, possessed by Germany, to be the richest portion and capable of great development. The climate is not by any means bad even for white people. Their strategic value is exceedingly great to Australia forming a shield to the northern portions of our continent. They possess many good harbours. In addition, New Guinea may be capable of carrying a considerable white population; the New Guinea native is capable of training for industrial pursuits and as a soldier and because of this, the holding of these islands with naval assistance is rendered fairly easy and the holding of these islands and outlying posts will ward off any invasion of Australia by a hostile power.[80]

Pearce also referred in detail to the New Hebrides which he described as forming a 'portion of a shield' and containing 'many excellent harbours, making ideal naval bases'. He acknowledged that while it remained with the French and British it posed no danger to Australia but said it would be a different matter if it were to be transferred to another power which in turn were to become hostile. Pearce concluded his letter by noting that 'my remarks regarding New Guinea apply equally to the Solomons and the islands of other groups south of the Equator'.[81]

Pearce's assessment had captured many of the ideas put forward in reports written for the Naval Board before the outbreak of the war. He had identified New Guinea as a shield lying across the northern portion of the Australian continent which would help to 'ward off any invasion of Australia by a hostile power'. Such terminology was to appear frequently over the next fifty years.

There is no record of Hughes's response to Pearce's assessment but the themes and arguments were consistent with his own thinking. Hughes was reported in the *Sydney Morning Herald* in the same month as Pearce's letter was drafted as having said that Australia was 'in deadly peril. ... Take a look at the map. Look where Australia is. We are five million people and we have challenged the whole Pacific to interfere with us'.[82]

Preparing for the Peace Conference

As Hughes turned his attention to the possible terms of a post-war settlement he had before him a number of additional assessments which set out the possible military dangers facing Australia. The documents reinforced

Hughes's own strongly held views on the need to protect Australia in the Pacific. In June 1916 the Naval Secretary, George Macandie, forwarded to the Prime Minister a report on the threat from Japan in the Pacific.[83] The assessment made clear the defence establishment's view that Japan 'wants a good deal that she has not got and has shown more than once that she will fight to get what she wants … they will not shrink from war as a means of getting it'.[84]

The Macandie assessment argued that by virtue of its occupation of the former German-held islands north of the Equator, Japan posed a real threat to Australia. A Japanese force 'could be assembled in full readiness for an attack not five days' steaming from the Australian coast'. It added that the 'permanent ownership of these groups is a matter of great importance to Australia'. It suggested that if it were not too late the islands should be handed over to Britain and then Australia but accepted that this might no longer be possible. As a consequence the 'retention of the groups in the hands of Japan (which seems now almost inevitable) or their restoration to Germany … confronts us with the probability that they will become bases for the quiet accumulation of stores, ships and troops from which an attack can be made quickly and without giving any clear intention of its real objective'. It speculated that a raid on the Australian coast could be launched in less than a week from the Japanese-held islands.[85]

A second paper on the 'Importance to Australia of German New Guinea and the Islands (lately German) North of the Equator' was forwarded to Hughes in July 1918 and was drafted by John Latham who was later to serve as an adviser to Hughes during the peace negotiations.[86] The report described in detail the value of the harbours and wireless stations in the islands north of the Equator to an enemy and to Australia. It concluded that 'the possession of these islands by an enemy [identified as Japan] would make it necessary to double the strength of the Australian naval and military forces; and the number of days necessary for mobilisation would probably be halved. The annual increase in cost to Australia would amount to many millions of pounds. … The possession of these islands by Japan might even make it impossible to defend all parts of Australia'.[87]

Latham went on to argue that:

> in enemy hands German New Guinea would form a perpetual and very serious menace to Australia. In Australian hands this territory would afford observation posts, advance bases and positions from which aeroplanes could watch the Straits thereby reducing the number

of cruisers required. It covered the most direct route by which an attacking force from the north could approach the eastern coast of Australia and formed a link in the sea frontier between Papua and the Solomons.[88]

Hughes was sympathetic to the assessments put forward by his military and civilian advisers. Indeed, they reinforced his own firmly held views. He believed that Australia's future depended 'upon the control of the Pacific being in the hands of the Empire and its Allies'.[89] At the same time, he appeared to accept that Australia could not secure the German-held islands north of the Equator. In response to advice from the British Government in February 1917 that Japan wished to secure British support for its claims to the islands, Hughes replied that Australia would not object to the 'occupancy' of the islands north of the Equator 'except for one or two small islands near the border line of which Nauru and Ocean Islands are typical'.[90] He later clarified the meaning of 'occupancy' by noting that he had 'no objection' to Japan's annexation of the North Pacific possessions in return for a Japanese promise to support the British Empire's claims to the South Pacific islands.[91] Later in the year Hughes told the British Government that Australian ministers' desire to emphasise that the islands in question south of the Equator should not be returned to the Government of Germany nor handed over to any foreign power'.[92] Hughes's attitude had the full support of the Australian Parliament which passed a number of resolutions in 1917 and 1918 expressing its opposition to any possible return to Germany of the islands and arguing that the defence of Australia now depended on the islands south of the Equator being held by Australia.[93]

Hughes left Australia in mid-1918 for Washington and London determined to ensure that Australia's strategic interests in the Pacific were secured in the peace settlement. He used the occasion of his visit to the United States to put his case for a peace settlement which took account of Australia's particular interests. He called on President Woodrow Wilson on 2 June and, in the only contemporary record of the meeting, prepared by the British Ambassador who accompanied Hughes, he:

> impressed on the President that it was vital to secure to Australia that Germany should never be allowed to hold any part of New Guinea or the islands of the Pacific. Mr Hughes made plain that Australia was not seeking all these islands for herself, that she had sufficient territory, but that her life would be menaced if Germany with her predatory designs held any of these islands, and he emphasized the

necessity of these belonging only to the British Empire and friendly powers.[94]

Wilson is recorded as saying he was 'sympathetic' and that he would refer the issue to a team of officials ('The Inquiry') he had assembled to study such issues. Hughes may have interpreted Wilson's near silence on the issue as indicating support but if he had done so he had badly misunderstood Wilson's philosophical approach to a post-war peace settlement which he would announce six months later in his Fourteen Points. Joan Beaumont has described Hughes's call on the President as 'probably a failure'.[95]

Hughes also used the occasion of his visit to the United States to deliver two speeches in which he put forward the concept of a Monroe Doctrine for the Pacific, an idea that had been previously aired by a number of colonial politicians, as well as Prime Minister Deakin. Hughes told a gathering in New York that:

> If Australia is to continue to be a Commonwealth of free people we must have guarantees against enemy aggression in the future. This involves the Australasian Monroe Doctrine in the Southern Pacific. … it is essential to [Australia's] territorial integrity that it should either control these islands itself or that they should be in the hands of friendly and civilised nations. For they stand in the same relation to Australia as, say Mount Kemmel does to Ypres, Amiens to Paris or as Calais and the Channel Ports do to England. To allow another nation to control them would be to allow it to control Australia. Hands off the Australian Pacific is the doctrine to which by inexorable circumstances we are committed.[96]

In his second speech Hughes presented a description of the pressures he felt Australia was under when he argued that 'the possession of islands within striking distance of us in unfriendly hands means that our country must always sleep with the sword half drawn'.[97] The speeches were widely reported in the Japanese press.

Negotiating the terms of a peace settlement

Hughes proceeded to London and for the next six months, in meetings of the Imperial War Cabinet and then later at the peace negotiations in Paris, argued Australia's case against the inclusion of a racial equality clause in the final peace treaty as sought by Japan and for Germany to accept full indemnity and pay reparations for the costs of the war.[98] He also made clear that 'as regards the Pacific Islands his attitude was that if anyone wanted to shift Australia from them they would have to come and get it'.[99] Contrary to the advice given to the Governor-General by Prime Minister Fisher, Hughes told the War Cabinet that Australia did not regard itself as responsible for the fact that Japan now occupied the former German-held islands north of the Equator and argued that 'it would be most unfortunate if such a claim were admitted'.[100] Leo Amery, Under Secretary of State for Colonies, described Hughes as 'quarrelsome and vain' while historians have judged his persistent and belligerent manner as a 'liability'.[101] Leaders such as Britain's Prime Minister David Lloyd George soon grew tired of him and sought ways to minimise his influence. Hughes had quickly worn out his welcome.

On 4 November 1918, following press reports of the views of Japan's Prime Minister, Marquis Okuma, on Japan's claim to the islands north of the Equator, Hughes wrote to Lloyd George and, in a seven page letter, set out his case for Australia to retain possession of the islands north and south of the Equator. He reminded Lloyd George of 'Australia's deeply rooted mistrust of Japan' and his wish to 'enter an emphatic protest on behalf of the Commonwealth against Japan's right or even claim to the islands mentioned by Marquis Okuma, viz, the Marshalls, Caroline and Ladrones'. Hughes added 'Japan has neither the right nor just claim to these islands and … menace to the trade and national safety of Australia and the Empire is involved' in its claim. He noted that the islands were 'most important to Australia from the point of view of defence and of possible offence'. He cited the value of the harbours in the islands and their use as locations for wireless stations and as advance bases for aeroplane and seaplane patrol. Hughes argued that if Australia were to retain the island of Yap, north of the Equator, it would serve as a monitoring station and provide early information and warning of possible enemy advance. He added:

> if, on the other hand, these islands were in foreign hands, Australia would lose all the advantages I have mentioned. The islands would serve as possible enemy bases and as points for the secret concentration of large naval and military forces, and all the consequential advantages would accrue to the armed forces using them. … Australia so profoundly distrusts Japan that its national welfare and its trade alike are seriously menaced by Japan.[102]

Hughes's argument fell on deaf ears. His relentless and quarrelsome style of representations had irritated Lloyd George to the point that, as shown in his reply to Hughes of 11 November 1918, the British Prime Minister was no longer prepared to tolerate his arguments and protestations.[103] In addition, Britain was not prepared to antagonise Japan by abandoning the secret agreement reached between the Foreign Secretary, Arthur Balfour, and Japan's Foreign Minister, Motono Ichirō, in February 1917 that Britain would 'support' Japan's claim in the peace settlement to the islands north of the Equator. Britain had traded this assurance for an undertaking by Japan to increase its naval assistance in the Mediterranean and around the Cape of Good Hope and Japan's acceptance of Britain's right to dispose of the islands south of the Equator in a post-war settlement.[104] While a statement of 'support' was weaker than a guarantee, it nevertheless represented a strong political undertaking from which it would be difficult to withdraw.

Hughes continued his campaign at the Council of Ten Meeting in Paris in January 1919 when he addressed the Allied leaders: President Wilson, Prime Minister Lloyd George, Prime Minister Georges Clemenceau of France, Prime Minister Vittorio Orlando of Italy and Baron Makino of Japan.[105] Hughes appeared before the Council on 24 January 1919 and, with the aid of a large map, set out Australia's case for its retention of New Guinea and other islands in the Pacific. To present his case, he used all the same rhetorical devices and flourishes he had employed on earlier occasions and focused almost exclusively on the strategic importance of New Guinea to Australia. He told the leaders that 'strategically the Pacific Islands encompassed Australia like a fortress' and that 'south east' of New Guinea was a 'string of islands suitable for coaling and submarine bases from which Australia could be attacked'. The islands 'were as necessary to Australia as water to a city. If they were in the hands of a superior power there would be no peace for Australia. ... Any strong power controlling New Guinea controlled Australia'. Hughes objected to the idea of a mandatory power acting under the authority of the League of Nations being placed in charge of a quarter of the island. He claimed this would 'overshadow' Australian authority. Perhaps with an eye directed at the Japanese representative, he noted that 'history showed that friends in one war were not always friends in the next' and that a mandatory power could develop into a potential enemy. He concluded by noting that 'Australia ... had a right to claim freedom from the menace of any enemy such as had weighed upon her before this war'.[106]

Hughes's presentation was not his best. He had spent a good deal of his allotted time retracing the history of Australia's interest in acquiring New Guinea and the various failed attempts in the 1880s. He had mentioned only in passing the issue of the 'rights of the natives' – a question of particular interest to President Wilson. In contrast, the presentations by General Louis Smuts (South Africa) in arguing for South Africa to secure South West Africa and William Massey (Prime Minister of New Zealand) to secure Samoa were more measured and more convincing. The presentation by Baron Makino of Japan's claims to retain possession of the former German islands focused solely on Japan's role in responding to the presence of German naval forces in the Pacific Ocean and its activities undertaken in the Pacific and Indian Oceans in cooperation with the British Navy. He argued that continued Japanese possession of the islands would allow Japan to 'continue to protect the inhabitants and to endeavour to better their conditions'.[107]

As the Council continued its deliberations the question which emerged to preoccupy the leaders was the form in which the German colonies were to be administered. The options were either annexation by a metropolitan power or the hastily developed concept of a system of mandates functioning under the overall responsibility of the League of Nations. Wilson, who had little sympathy for Hughes and his arguments as to the strategic significance of German New Guinea, opposed the concept of annexation and favoured a system of mandates aimed at promoting the development of the native population. Hughes challenged Wilson to identify 'what advantage was to be gained by the appointment of a mandatory for New Guinea in preference to handing it over to Australia'. He also challenged Wilson's view that Australia's security would be strengthened under a mandatory system. He again turned to a rhetorical flourish when he told the Allied leaders that 'were this mandatory principle applied to Great Britain, to America, to France, it would not work. As Ireland is to the United Kingdom, as Mexico is to the United States, as Alsace-Lorraine is to France, so was New Guinea to Australia'. He went on to argue that 'Australia had governed New Guinea; New Guinea was essential to the safety of Australia'. He added 'New Guinea was the outward and visible sign of the World's recognition that they (Australians) were worthy to be entrusted with the government of that country'.[108]

After three days of often intense and acrimonious debate and disagreement with Hughes, ever the nuisance at the centre of the argument, the Council of Ten reached a provisional agreement on the creation of a new, three-tiered system of mandates under the authority of the League of Nations.[109] Australia accepted a 'Class C' mandate over the former German New Guinea. It agreed to administer the mandate as an integral part of its own territory and as part of its legal and economic system. It also accepted the reference to the 'prevention of the establishment of fortifications or military and naval bases and of the military training of the natives for other than police purposes and the defence of the territory'. In a remark designed no doubt to save face, Hughes said it 'gives us all the power we want and all the safety too'.[110] Britain, Australia and New Zealand also accepted a mandate over Nauru with Australia as the administering authority on the island.

On his return to Melbourne Hughes, who tabled the Treaty signed at Versailles on 28 June 1919, reminded the House of Representatives that 'in order for Australia to be safe, it is necessary that the great rampart of islands stretching around the north-east of Australia should be held by us or by some Power in whom we have absolute confidence. ... It was difficult to make the Council of Ten realize how utterly the safety of Australia depended upon the possession of these islands. ... Those who hold it [sic] hold us'.[111]

Conclusion

Australia would have preferred to have annexed German New Guinea and to have had full and unfettered control over that quadrant of the island. The government was nevertheless satisfied that Australia's strategic interests had been strengthened and that its security had been improved. The decision in Paris had brought to an end a debate which had begun before the formation of the Commonwealth. Australia's security could best be guaranteed by the eviction of aggressive foreign powers from its immediate neighbourhood and the securing of the island of New Guinea by Australia or forces sympathetic to Australia, i.e. Britain and the Netherlands. Since the formation of the Commonwealth all Australian Prime Ministers had argued that Australia's security depended on it controlling the eastern half of New Guinea. In the first instance the threat to Australia's interests was seen as coming from Imperial Germany. However, from 1905 onwards the fear of Japan had gradually come to dominate the thinking of Australian military and political leaders and subsequently their attitude towards the terms of a peace settlement. Hughes was without peer in articulating these views. He repeatedly turned to arguments based on geography, security and an implied fear of Japan to emphasise his case for Australia to occupy and then secure German New Guinea. He saw Australia's defence and the role of the island of New Guinea in terms of forward lines of battlements and ramparts designed to keep an enemy at a distance. And that enemy was now Japan.[112] The arguments and vocabulary employed by Hughes would be drawn on by Australian political leaders over the next fifty years.

Chapter 2

THE SHIELD IS RAISED 1920–1945

'Australia could be saved in Papua and only in Papua'.

General Douglas MacArthur,
Supreme Commander,
Allied Forces,
Southwest Pacific Area, 1942

The twenty-one years between the close of the First World War and the start of the Second World War were firstly a period of hope and ambition to advance the cause of peace followed by a period of steady decline into global war. The establishment of the League of Nations was followed by a succession of treaties and agreements designed to promote peace. In 1928, under the terms of the Kellogg-Briand Pact, countries including Australia, renounced war as an instrument of national policy. Earlier, under the terms of the agreement reached at the conference on naval disarmament held in Washington from November 1921 to January 1922, the five major naval powers, Britain, the United States, France, Italy and Japan, agreed to reduce and then fix the tonnage of their naval capital ships by a formula based on proportionality. At the same conference four major Pacific powers (the United States, Britain, Japan and France) agreed to respect the existing territorial boundaries in the Pacific and to limit fortifications and naval bases in their possessions. The Washington Naval Treaty was seen at the time as making a significant contribution to promoting peace in the Pacific.[1] By a curious twist of history Australia's contribution to the reduction in Britain's fleet was the scuttling of HMAS *Australia*, the battlecruiser which had escorted the Australian military expedition to Rabaul in 1914.

Australia made its own contribution to the search for peace when, at the 1937 Imperial Conference in London, Prime Minister Joseph Lyons, without forewarning the British Government, launched one of Australia's few initiatives in inter-war diplomacy. He proposed the negotiation of a non-aggression pact in the Pacific to include Britain, Japan, and possibly the United States. Under the terms of the proposed agreement the signatories would renounce war as a means of achieving policy, accept the doctrine of non-aggression and put in place a process of 'political collaboration' to minimise the risk of countries turning to war.[2] The idea gathered little support in London and Washington and lapsed when Japan invaded China. The search for permanent peace in Europe and elsewhere proved elusive and, as the 1930s progressed, hopes of disarmament and a peaceful resolution of disputes were replaced by a slow descent into war.

Over the course of the inter-war period Australia, although crippled economically by the Great Depression, also sought to identify its national defence interests and to provide for the security of the country. In doing so it placed Japan squarely at the centre of its fears and concerns. At the same time it also sought to articulate the place of Papua New Guinea in its national interests and strategic outlook.

The first post-war strategic assessments

On 9 September 1920, six years after the Australian Naval and Military Expeditionary Force had occupied German New Guinea, and only a few months after having secured the territory as a mandate in the peace settlement, Prime Minister Hughes addressed the Parliament on Australia's post-war defence policy and expenditure. Neville Meaney has described the speech as 'masterly … perhaps the most comprehensive of all his speeches on defence and foreign policy in his eight years as Prime Minister'.[3] Hughes did not speak of any direct threat to Australia, although he referred to the hostility felt by some towards the White Australia policy and the need for Australia to be prepared to defend that principle. Most significantly he told the Parliament that 'as a result of the war the centre of gravity has again shifted. Between 1906 and 1920 the Pacific has assumed a new importance'. He reminded the Parliament that Australia not only had an obligation to defend 12,000 miles of coastline but that 'we have taken over the control of huge islands in the Pacific involving new obligations and responsibilities'. Hughes then returned to the ideas put forward by Commander Thring and articulated by senior parliamentarians such as

Sir George Reid in 1902 (later Prime Minister from August 1904 to July 1905) and Minister for Defence Senator George Pearce in 1910, to suggest a 'forward defence' policy for Australia. Hughes argued that 'if they come here we shall do our best; but it is better that they should not come here at all ... our lines of defence must be on the sea and in the air'. He outlined the structure of the post-war defence forces and concluded his speech by telling the Parliament that no matter the size of the effort and resources provided by the government, Australia's defence relied on the protection of the Royal Navy and, as a consequence, Australia had to contribute to the naval defence of the Empire.[4]

Hughes delivered a follow-up speech on 7 April 1921 on the government's approach to the Imperial Conference scheduled for June that year in London and the question on the agenda of the renewal of the Anglo-Japanese Treaty which, since 1902, had articulated the defence relations between Britain and Japan. In this speech he was less discreet in his comments about the perceived threat from Japan. He told the Parliament that Australia was 'securely sheltered under the broad wing of the mighty British Navy' and that Australia was a 'nation only by the grace of God and the power of the British Empire'.[5] However, Australia was faced with a direct threat from Asia. Australia stood:

> within a few weeks' sail of the great mass of the population of the world. We have boldly announced that we intend to retain this continent for ourselves and we have set up the banner of a White Australia. ... How long would that banner fly unless behind it there were massed the legions of the Empire, or unless ringed about it there was the protection of the British Navy.[6]

Hughes repeated his earlier comment that 'when we [Australia] speak of war and foreign policy we speak of foreign policy in relation to Pacific problems and of war as it may come out of the East'. Hughes concluded by noting that 'we desire above all things to live in peace and friendship with Japan. It is utterly wrong for the Japanese people to think that because we have passed certain laws we regard them as our inferiors'. However, 'we do not always invite our friends into our house'.[7]

The two speeches by Hughes, as well as his earlier comment in the House of Representatives when introducing the New Guinea Bill that a 'great empire ... has fallen to us' when referring to the former German territory, reflected Hughes's passionate belief that Australia's national defence interest was strengthened by its possession of Papua and New Guinea and that its future security was bound up in developments in the Pacific and the potential threat posed by Japan.[8] Hughes never wavered in his fear of Japan's ambitions. In July 1920 he forwarded a letter through the Governor-General to the Secretary of State for the Colonies, Viscount Milner, calling for consultations with Australia 'before any commercial treaties giving rights to aliens in British possessions in the Pacific are entered into'. In Hughes's terminology 'aliens' were either Japanese in particular or Asians in general. He argued that:

> many British possessions in the Pacific are in positions having a strategic importance for the defence of the Commonwealth, as for instance the British Solomon Islands, which are as important in regard to the defence of the Commonwealth as the former German possessions to the north and west of them. Foreign powers ... might seek to make use of the islands in times of peace in preparing their plans against the Commonwealth.[9]

Milner's successor as Secretary of State, Winston Churchill, replied to Hughes nearly twelve months later and reassured him that Britain was not proposing to enter into any commercial treaties in the Pacific.[10]

Hughes's letter to Milner and his earlier speeches in parliament were typical of his suspicions and phobias. He maintained these concerns throughout the inter-war period and became the first of a number of Australian politicians over the next fifty years to speak openly and forthrightly on the importance of Papua New Guinea to Australia. Much of the language used by his post-war successors, Dr Evatt, Percy Spender and Robert Menzies, can be traced back to Hughes.

The government's assessments of Australia's changed post-war security environment reflected the views of its senior advisers. Its senior civilian adviser, E. L. Piesse, Director of Military Intelligence from 1916 to 1919 and Head of the Pacific Branch in the Prime Minister's Department from 1919 to 1923, produced a number of assessments of Australia's strategic environment including the first, albeit crude, map identifying Australia's immediate sphere of interest. The map was very similar to one given to Hughes while in New York in 1918 by a group of American scholars and clearly identified New Guinea as in Australia's sphere of interest. Piesse placed importance on Australia maintaining a strong position in the Pacific. In a minute to the Secretary of the Prime Minister's Department in December 1920 he recommended that if Britain decided to divest itself of its possessions in the Pacific, Australia's interests would be furthered by its taking control of the British Protectorate of the Solomon Islands, the Gilbert and Ellice Islands (now known as Kiribati and Tuvalu) and the British half of the condominium covering the New Hebrides (now Vanuatu). He also believed that Australia should secure control of the French-governed New Caledonia. He argued that the principal objective of Australian policy should be to ensure that these islands should not pass into the 'hands of any power which might have aggressive designs against Australia'. He also argued that should the Dutch leave the Netherlands East Indies it was imperative that 'they shall not pass into the hands of a power stronger than Holland'.[11] Piesse fell out of favour with Hughes over the assessment of Japan's intentions towards Australia but Hughes did not disagree with Piesse's views of the importance of maintaining Australia's role in the South Pacific.[12]

In January 1920 the six most senior members of the Australian defence establishment gathered in Melbourne to examine and report to the government on the defence of Australia. The six, under the chairmanship of Lt General Sir Harry G. Chauvel and including Lt General Sir John Monash, drafted a comprehensive strategic assessment of the world Australia now faced.[13] They drew attention to the weakened state of a 'majority of nations' but did not hesitate to state that 'the Empire of Japan remains ... in the immediate future as the only potential and probable enemy' of Australia. Australia's 'great natural resources', sparsely settled population, extended coastline and the location of its industries and population on the coast made it 'peculiarly vulnerable to attack', while the maintenance of the White Australia policy was a potential *casus belli*. The report described Japan as 'one of the nations whose resources and offensive capacity are both relatively and absolutely greater than in 1914'. It warned that Japan could attack without warning and take advantage of the delay in the Royal Navy deploying to the Pacific to secure its objectives. Australia had no choice but to assume that 'any aggression against Australia will involve the whole of the British Empire'. The senior defence advisers concluded that the 'ultimate fate of Australia [was] dependent upon the security of the Empire's sea communications'.[14]

The strategic assessment acknowledged Australia's newly acquired responsibility for New Guinea and noted that 'should war come through some nations flouting the League, those territories will have to be defended and the Mandatory who has undertaken to administer will surely be the Power called upon to defend'. However, despite this reference, the newly acquired former German possessions did not otherwise feature in the assessment.

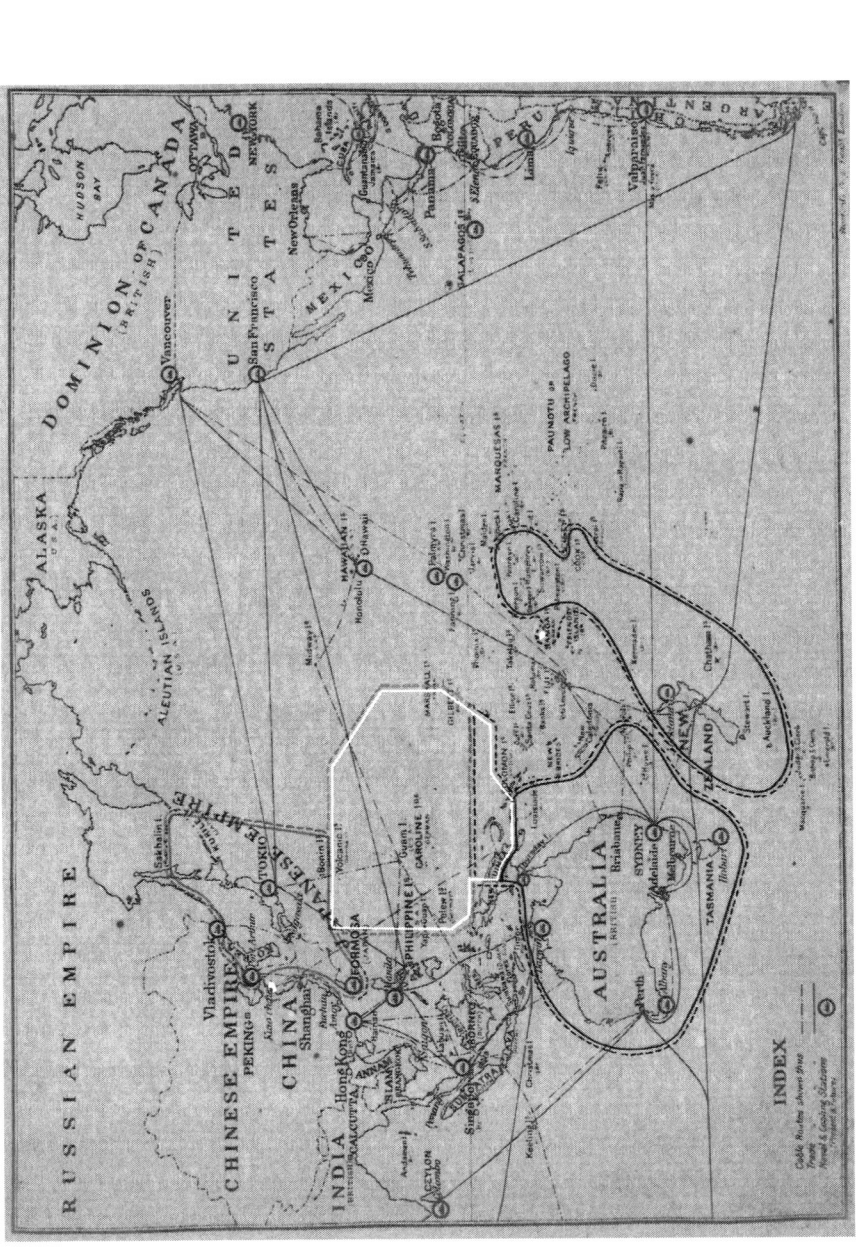

Map identifying Australia's area of strategic interest presented to Prime Minister W. M. Hughes, 5 June 1918, in New York by a group of prominent American scholars headed by James Shotwell, later an adviser to President Wilson at the Paris Peace Conference. Papers of William Morris Hughes, National Library of Australia, MS 1538, series 2 item 983.

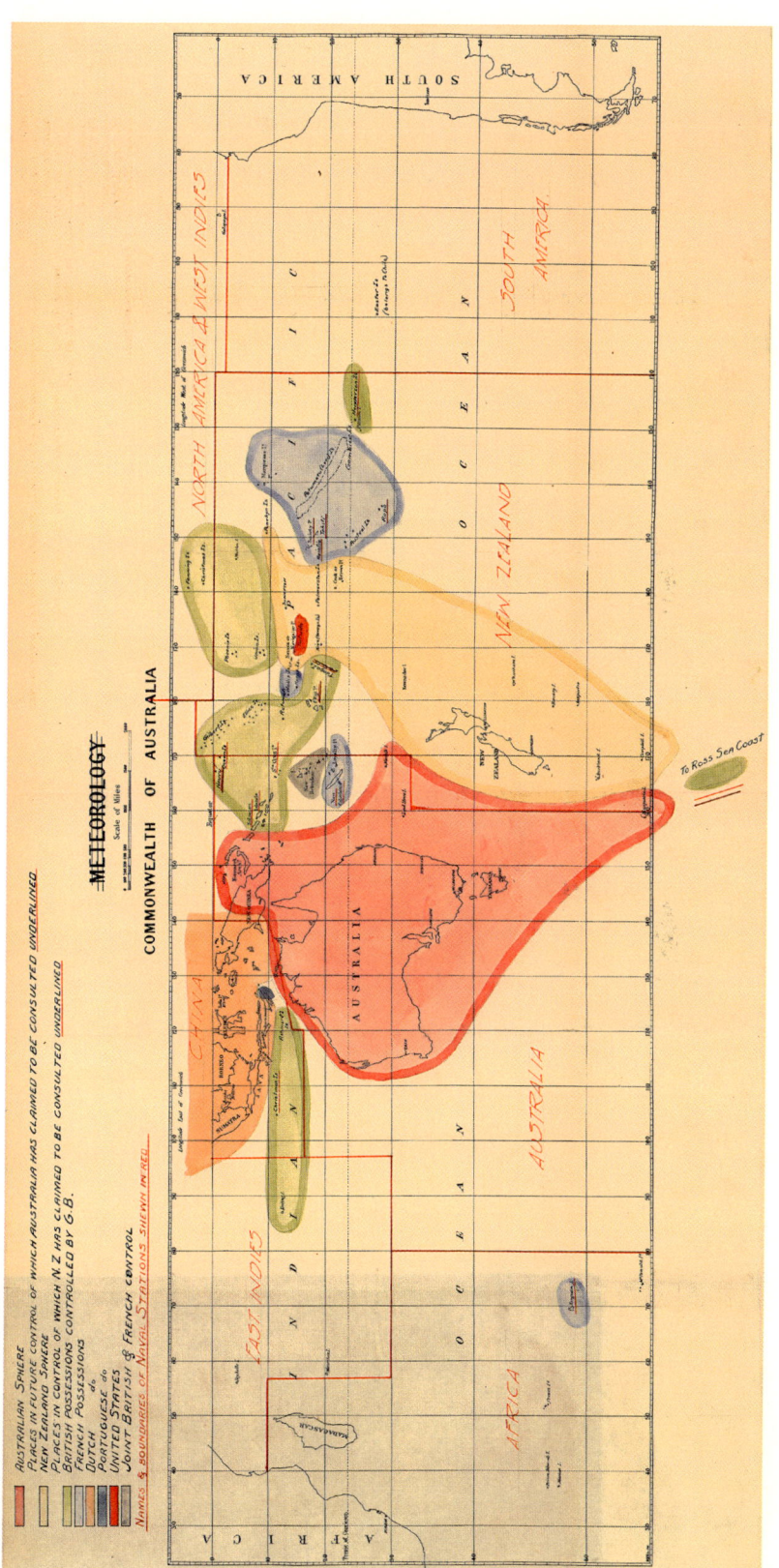

E. L. Piesse, *The Spheres of Influence of Australia and New Zealand*, 6 November 1920. Courtesy National Archives of Australia. NAA: MP1049/1, 1920/0465.

Instead, as Meaney has commented, 'in every respect the imperative driving the report and its recommendations was fear of Japan'.[15] Emphasis was placed on the need to secure the Pacific Ocean and to protect the ability of Britain to deploy the Royal Navy. New Guinea figured only marginally in this plan.

A similar report from the highly influential Naval Board to the Minister for Defence in 1920 was equally blunt in its assessment of Japan's ambitions.[16] The Board identified Japan's demand to be accorded a status equal to the Western powers, and in particular its objections to the White Australia policy, as driving it to adopt an aggressive military strategy similar to that pursued by Germany in 1914. The report asked 'why does she (Japan) place a Rear Admiral as the Governor of her newly acquired groups of islands in the Pacific, why does she place Commanders and other Naval Officers as administrators of these Islands, and why does she discourage shipping of other countries from trading with these islands?'[17] The Board recommended the maintenance of a strong naval force but also highlighted the critical role of the Royal Navy in defending Australia. It warned that 'with the command of the sea lost, the end is near'. The report reinforced the assessments emerging in the defence community of the threats to Australia and the critical importance now given to the Pacific in those assessments.

The place of Papua New Guinea in post-war assessments

It was not until 1924 that the first post-war assessment to focus on Papua and New Guinea and the island chain across the northeast of Australia was presented to the government's Council of Defence. It was a curious mix of views. In a paper entitled 'Strategical Aspect', the assessment identified the island chain stretching from New Guinea to New Caledonia and comprising the Bismarck Archipelago, Bougainville, Buka, the British Solomons, New Hebrides, New Caledonia and the Loyalty Islands as a 'broken chain' whose harbours represented their 'most important strategic aspect'.[18] The harbours were seen as 'potential bases for operations against Australia'. At the same time the harbours of the Japanese mandate-controlled Caroline Islands, north of the Equator, formed a 'natural stepping stone for operations to the South'.[19] The military adviser who contributed to the report noted that 'the seizure by the enemy of a safe harbour among the islands is an essential preliminary step … and it is likely that he will occupy suitable islands early in the war'. The wireless transmission station at Bita Paka near Rabaul in New Guinea was identified as the 'key position which the enemy will endeavour to destroy at the outset'. The military adviser argued that Australia's 'objective must be defensive – to deny these harbours to the enemy as long as we can, and, therefore, to hinder him in their use, by guerrilla warfare from the hinterland'.[20] The paper recommended the development of a mobile wireless transmission system and the formation of an intelligence gathering network to enable Australia to monitor enemy activity in the islands.

The strategic assessment was forwarded to the Council of Defence. A covering report, also by a military member of the Council's sub-committee, argued that Australia's approach to defensive measures in the islands should be guided by the following principles, in order of importance:

a. the defence of any essential naval interests of our own which exist therein;

b. the prevention of the seizure by the enemy of points which are likely to be of use to him in the prosecution of naval and/or military operations against Australia; and

c. the general defence of the Islands considered as an object in itself.[21]

However, the military adviser then argued that 'there [were] no essential naval interests of our own in the Islands' and that the security of the wireless installations 'though desirable' was 'not so essential as to justify the dispersion of force entailed at a time when the security of Australia itself [was] threatened'. Instead, any defence measure must be by local units. Moreover, the 'enemy [had] such a wide choice of apparently suitable harbours that it would be quite impossible to attempt to defend them all. If one or two were defended then the enemy would select other harbours to occupy'.[22] The military adviser agreed to the suggestion of establishing an intelligence or information-gathering service in the islands and supported additional local security around the Bita Paka wireless station, as well as the use of mobile wireless stations. The organisation of a volunteer force from among the European population in New Guinea was also endorsed, as was the military training of the native police force.

In 1926 officials incorporated sections of the 1924 report into the Commonwealth War Book. The War Book was a collection of contingency plans to meet an attack on Australia, as well as a list of responses to be taken by the government and the defence force following the outbreak of war. By including Papua and New Guinea in the contingency plans, officials were recognising its role in the defence of Australia and the need to establish its defence requirements. However, as an indication of the lack of urgency attached to Australia's defence preparations in the 1920s, a copy of the War Book was not forwarded to Port Moresby and Rabaul for comment until 1930.

Australia's pre-war and immediate post-war views on the need to secure German New Guinea and the island chain south of the Equator and the energy with which Hughes had pursued this issue in London and Paris might have suggested a pre-eminent role for both New Guinea and Papua, as well as the island chain, in Australian defence assessments. Hughes certainly believed so. However, the difficult economic position Australia faced in the post-war environment, the continuous reduction of the defence budget, the limitations on local defences inherent in the conditions of the mandate and the sheer scale of the preparations needed to defend the continent may explain its absence from the report prepared by Chauvel's Committee and the less than clear assessment contained in the subsequent report to the Council of Defence. In addition, the faith placed in international attempts to promote disarmament seen in agreements such as that reached at the Washington naval conference may have contributed to an attitude of complacency and benign neglect towards defence preparedness.

Mark Turner has argued that Australia exhibited very little interest in Papua New Guinea in the inter-war years and, when an interest was shown, it was limited to Papua New Guinea's role as an 'inert shield' to protect Australia from invasion.[23] Hank Nelson has described Australia in this period as having 'no immediate knowledge of, or emotional investment in, Eastern New Guinea … while Papua functioned on a pittance'.[24] This was certainly the case but it may also reflect the emergence of a characteristic in Australia's approach to Papua New Guinea: that Australia's political leaders often attached more importance to the island in Australia's defence than the military advisers. This was to become more evident in the post–Second World War period but it may help to explain the preoccupation of individuals such as Hughes and the passive approach of the government's military advisers.

A period of drift

Australia's defence preparations in Papua and New Guinea maintained a desultory pace as the 1930s progressed. The long-serving Lieutenant Governor of Papua based in Port Moresby, Sir Hubert Murray, responded to the contents of the War Book in April 1930 and advised that it was not possible to carry out many of the suggestions it contained.[25] Murray drew attention to the fact that there were only two wireless transmission stations in Papua from which to transmit intelligence information, and once these had been overrun there was no electronic means available to communicate with Australia. He noted there was no artillery in Papua, hence it would be impossible to prevent an enemy landing, although it might be possible to harass and hamper any enemy after landing.[26]

For his part, Evan Wisdom, the Administrator of New Guinea based in Rabaul, suggested that the objectives of local defence measures should be the 'maintenance of intelligence, compelling the diversion of as large a force of the enemy as possible thus ... helping other theatres and inflicting as much damage on the enemy as possible with the minimum damage to our own small forces'.[27] Wisdom also recommended an increase in the number of native police and that 'special bush training' be introduced.

In January 1933, in a letter to Prime Minister Joseph Lyons, Wisdom forwarded under a covering letter a draft defence scheme for the Territory prepared by the Superintendent of Police, Lt Col Walstab. Walstab proposed that the defence of New Guinea and Papua should be considered as a whole with the town of Wau in Morobe District as its headquarters.[28] He added that Port Moresby and Daru on the coast in the Torres Strait were not suitable as a headquarters as they were 'possibly the most useful jumping off places for [an] attack on Australia'. In his covering letter Wisdom stressed the importance of developing the Air Force with a capacity to defend Australia and New Guinea. He told the Prime Minister that if the air defence of Australia were to be taken seriously, 'we surely cannot afford to give away to an enemy such a valuable base as New Guinea. The defence of New Guinea becomes therefore a question of importance to the defence of Australia'. [29] Wisdom concluded his letter by supporting the assessment that 'there must be one scheme for the defence of the whole of our New Guinea possessions under one command, not for the Mandated Territory alone'.[30]

The delay in despatching the original report to Port Moresby and Rabaul was matched by the slowness in attending to the replies from Murray in 1930 and Wisdom in 1933. Officials noted Murray's comments but took no initiative until 1934 to review the papers in detail. The tardiness reflected the preoccupation of the Scullin and Lyons Governments with responding to the impact of the Great Depression and the collapse in government revenue.

The descent into war

In the decade following the departure of Hughes as Prime Minister in 1923, politicians were strangely silent on the question of Papua and New Guinea and its place in Australia's strategic environment. There was no one with Hughes's rhetorical flair, sense of drama (or melodrama) and colourful arguments and there were few who demonstrated the same passionate commitment to hold Papua and New Guinea.

It was not until the mid-1930s that Hughes had the opportunity again to express his views. In 1936 the Lyons Government was faced with the need to respond to Germany's reoccupation of the Rhineland and calls from the German Führer, Adolf Hitler, and from others within Germany, for its former colonial possessions to be returned as a means of correcting the harshness of the provisions of the Versailles Treaty.[31] David Bird has argued that Prime Minister Lyons was slow to reject the German suggestions and was possibly open-minded about their merit. The initiative in setting the government's position therefore fell to Senator George Pearce, now Minister for External Affairs.[32] On 13 March 1936 Pearce delivered what Bird has described as a 'savage, comprehensive denunciation' of Germany's suggestion that New Guinea and Nauru be returned.[33] He described Germany's claims as having reached a state of 'definite and openly-expressed demands ... officially and unofficially'. Pearce rejected the arguments put forward by Germany and made clear that:

> New Guinea, by virtue of its geographical position in relation to Australia, its natural harbours, its facilities for naval and military aircraft, is of considerable strategic value to Australia from a defence aspect, so long as the existing form of control and administration obtains. This value is emphasised by the fact that the territory is contiguous to ... Papua ... enabling [the] co-ordination of measures to be obtained in defence interests.[34]

Pearce concluded his statement by declaring 'it is unthinkable that Australia should even consider the handing over of any territory'. Moreover, 'every country is entitled to examine any international issue in the light of its own security and national interests and the inviolability and integrity of our Australian territories is as much one of the cardinal aims of our people as is the White Australia policy'.[35] Officials reflected the views of Pearce when they warned the Lyons Government in briefings prepared for the 1937 Imperial Conference in London that 'the return of New Guinea [to

Germany] would bring Australia face to face with the conditions prior to 1914 but in an accentuated form owing to the development of the air arm'.[36] German military bases in New Guinea 'or by an allied Pacific power[,] would lead to a feeling of constant disquiet and insecurity'.[37] Lyons and Richard Casey (Treasurer) told the Imperial Conference that the statement by Senator Pearce in 1936 remained government policy and that Australia would not agree to the return of the former German colonies in New Guinea and Nauru to Berlin's control.[38]

Hughes shared Pearce's strong objections. In response to a speech by Hitler at Bückeberg in October 1937 in which he demanded the return of Germany's former colonies, Hughes (then Minister for External Affairs in the Lyons Government and visiting Rabaul) announced in June 1938 that 'on this rock we have got our mandate ... what we have we shall hold'. Later in an interview with the *Sydney Morning Herald* he referred to the mandate as a 'sacred trust' and said that any return would be 'cowardly and unjust'.[39] Lyons finally made clear his view in November 1938 when he declared that 'The Australian Government has no intention of handing New Guinea to Germany or anybody else'.[40]

Hughes continued to deploy colourful descriptions of New Guinea's place in Australia's security in speeches during 1939. He described the eastern half of the island as 'like a mantel' over Australia and that for 'all practical purposes they were an integral part of Australia'.[41] He responded to an article in the German Nazi newspaper *Voelkischer Beobachter* in April 1939, which claimed that Australia intended to exploit New Guinea, by arguing that 'occupation of New Guinea by a potentially hostile power would be a dagger aimed at the heart of Australia'.[42] Elsewhere he told the New Guinea Mining Association that 'New Guinea is Australia's frontier and it is fundamental to the defence of Australia that New Guinea should be held by the men and women of our race'.[43]

Apart from the colourful references by Hughes, Papua New Guinea did not figure prominently in the public statements by other ministers until the clear approach of war in 1939. In twenty-six speeches delivered on defence in the period 1933 to early 1939 by either Prime Minister Lyons or Defence Minister Sir Archdale Parkhill or his successor Brigadier Geoffrey Street there were very few references to the island of New Guinea and no mention of its role in Australia's general strategic outlook. In one of the few exceptions, in a speech in December 1938, Street told the Parliament of both the government's decision to increase the defence budget from £44,500,000 to £63,000,000 and its intention to establish a base at Port

Moresby for mobile naval and air forces. He argued that the base, along with a similar base in Darwin and the British naval base in Singapore, could form an 'archway' across the north of Australia. This statement may represent one of the first references to the defence of Australia using the concept of a strategic arc across the north of the continent.[44]

The announcement by Street represented the tentative beginning of a reappraisal of Australia's defence preparedness and assessment of its strategic environment. In contrast to the view of the Chief of the Naval Staff, Admiral Sir George Hyde, in 1937 that the 'strategical importance of the Pacific Islands was not high' and that 'from the point of view of warlike operations, none of the islands are [sic] of very much value to us', by December 1938 defence officials were beginning to adopt a different approach. Planners noted that 'the time has come for greater security to be offered to Northern Australia and the Island Territories, thereby increasing the security of Australia as a whole'.[45] They identified the need for a base with an anchorage capable of accommodating cruisers and supply ships, a suitable aerodrome and harbour which could be easily defended and an existing town and infrastructure to draw on. The officials nominated Port Moresby as the ideal location.

As an indication of the changing attitudes, twelve months later Lt General Ernest Squires, Chief of the General Staff, reminded the Defence Council that 'Moresby [was] the most suitable place for any enemy base south of the Marshall and Caroline Islands. The importance of the harbour and port in enemy hands as a base for further operations would be considerable'.[46] However, on this occasion the Council noted that the improvements suggested by General Squires were not necessary 'at this juncture' and that other harbours were considered of higher priority.[47]

With the outbreak of war in Europe in September 1939 and as the prospects loomed of a war in the Pacific, Australian defence planners dramatically sharpened their assessment of the place of Papua and New Guinea in Australia's security environment. In February 1941 the Chiefs of Staff told Cabinet that:

> The desirability of preventing the Japanese gaining a foothold across this line, i.e. New Guinea–New Hebrides–New Caledonia–Fiji, and thus making the passage of American reinforcements most hazardous, is a strong argument for the need for adequate naval and air forces in the area and the advisability of strengthening the defences of our existing ports and bases there.[48]

The focus on New Guinea and the surrounding islands was shared by knowledgeable civilian observers. Sir John Latham had served as an adviser to Hughes at the Paris Peace Conference, was Minister for External Affairs from 1932 to 1934 and had taken up Australia's first diplomatic appointment to Tokyo in 1940. In August 1941 he warned Robert Menzies who had succeeded Earle Page as Prime Minister on 26 April 1939, to prepare for a 'blitz invasion' based on air power. He advised

> our policy should ... be to prevent either Japan or Germany ... from becoming established in any of the islands near Australia. Australia can have only one policy towards any hostile power seeking to establish itself in the neighbouring islands. That policy is 'keep out'. This must be absolute and not conditional. ... any other policy will almost certainly be fatal to Australia in time.[49]

As the prospects of war in the Pacific increased, the Menzies Government faced pressure from the European settler community in New Guinea to annex the former German territory unilaterally. It rejected the calls. At the same time the government rejected calls from two members of the Victorian Legislative Assembly, who had visited Port Moresby, to annex New Guinea and the Solomon Islands in order to strengthen Australia's defence preparedness.[50] The government did take some measures to bolster the defences in New Guinea with Australia welcoming the decision in October 1941 by the then neutral United States to use Rabaul as a base for naval operations, despite recent severe volcanic activity. Australia also agreed to increase the defence fortifications in Rabaul and Port Moresby.

However, there remained at times a strangely detached and aloof air to the Menzies Government's approach to the defence of Papua and New Guinea. In October 1939, shortly after the outbreak of war with Germany, the War Cabinet decided to 'despatch a telegram to the Administrator of New Guinea requesting his views on the adequacy or otherwise of the present defence of New Guinea, on the basis of the existing war with Germany, and the Japanese remaining neutral'.[51] On the one hand the government could be considered proactive in asking for guidance but on the other it was extremely late in the day to be posing such a fundamental question. (Five days later the War Cabinet also decided to explore the possibility of acquiring training aircraft from the Japanese!)[52]

War in the Pacific: The shield is raised

At the outbreak of war Australia had, as David Day has described, 'a defence force in name only'.[53] Peter Stanley, the former Principal Historian at the Australian War Memorial and now the Head of the Centre for Historical Research at the National Museum of Australia, has dismissed such assessments, arguing instead that 'there is an exaggerated perception ... that Australia's defences were "weak"'.[54] Stanley has listed the strength of the Australian forces in detail and concluded that they were 'more than enough to meet anything the Japanese could muster, especially in the vital and more vulnerable south-east'.[55] As Stanley notes, the Lyons Government had increased the defence budget to £43 million in 1938 (a 40 per cent increase over the previous year) and had begun to acquire much-needed defence equipment. Neville Meaney is more perceptive in his assessment, acknowledging only that Lyons 'spoke a new language' and that the 'emphasis was changing'.[56]

The Lyons Government had adopted its predecessor's policy that Australia's security was predicated on the assumption that the British naval base in Singapore would remain impregnable and that Britain would quickly deploy units of the Royal Navy to Singapore. As late as June 1939 Prime Minister Robert Menzies sought an assurance that Britain would deploy a fleet to Singapore 'within the appropriate time capable of containing the Japanese fleet to a degree sufficient to prevent an act of aggression against Australia'.[57] Prime Minister Neville Chamberlain confirmed that Britain remained committed to the deployment, although he cautioned that the size of the fleet would depend on the circumstances at the time. He reassured Menzies that Britain's intention was to prevent a 'major operation against Australia, New Zealand or India ... keep open our sea communications ... to prevent the fall of Singapore'.[58]

The assumptions underlying Australia's defence preparedness were shattered in the wake of Japan's attack on Pearl Harbour in December 1941. Japan's subsequent march through Southeast Asia, including the Dutch East Indies, the sinking on 10 December 1941 of the battleship *Prince of Wales* and the battlecruiser *Repulse* sent by Britain to Singapore, the extensive bombing of Darwin and Japan's assault on New Guinea and islands in the South Pacific, exposed Australia to attack and raised the prospect of possible invasion. The 'Singapore Strategy ... failed even before it was tested'.[59] Australia's wartime leaders grappled with the challenge of a collapsing military front to their north and the desperate need to recall

Australian troops from the Middle East. It was in this period that the place of Papua New Guinea in Australia's strategic planning assumed unprecedented importance.

In late February 1942, following the fall of Rabaul, the Chiefs of Staff warned that with the prospect of an attack on Australia, 'Port Moresby is most important to us as a strong position on the flank of enemy movements from either the Mandates or the Netherlands East Indies'.[60] However, defences were inadequate and the alternatives were either to provide Port Moresby with an increased garrison or to accept that it was to be 'regarded as indefensible and the present garrison withdrawn'. The second option was rejected. In a public broadcast in September 1942, John Curtin who had succeeded Arthur Fadden as Prime Minister on 7 October 1941, told the nation that Darwin and Port Moresby were the 'Singapores of Australia' and that if they fell Australia would be faced 'with a bloody struggle on our own soil, a struggle in which we would be forced to fight grimly, city by city, village by village, until our fair land might become a blackened ruin'.[61] Curtin repeated the warning in numerous broadcasts over the next few months.[62] At the same time, General Sir Thomas Blamey, Commander of the Australian Military Force and Commander Allied Land Forces, told the War Cabinet that 'it was imperative to hold Port Moresby' as while it was held 'it was improbable that an attack could be made on Australia'.[63] General Douglas MacArthur, Supreme Commander, Allied Forces in the Southwest Pacific, told a group of journalists that 'Australia could be saved in Papua and only in Papua'.[64]

Historians such as Peter Stanley have argued persuasively that Japan did not intend or plan an invasion of Australia. Instead, it sought to isolate Australia by seizing Fiji, New Caledonia and the Solomons, as well as Papua New Guinea and the islands of the Bismarck Archipelago. The aim was to neutralise Australia as a potential base for a United States-led counter-offensive.[65] Stanley is emphatic in his dismissal of the claims made by Australian civilian and military leaders that Australia was soon to be invaded. He has described Curtin's response as a 'great overreaction' and has presented a detailed, archives-based argument that there is no evidence that Japan planned to invade Australia or that the Papuan campaign was the beginning of a drive to invade Australia.[66] He has noted that by April 1942, a select group of Australian political leaders, including Curtin and Blamey, knew through the interception of Japanese intelligence messages that an invasion was no longer under consideration. The invasion 'crisis' had ended with the Battle of the Coral Sea and the Battle of Midway.

The evidence Stanley has presented is compelling and he has also qualified his argument by accepting, but not overstating, that there was 'an atmosphere of apprehension that permeated Australia in 1942'.[67] Joan Beaumont, however, argues more convincingly that in 1942 in Australia there was 'alarm, verging on near panic at the possibility of invasion'.[68] Stanley concedes that the fear of invasion was a 'reality of the mind rather than fact' but dismisses at every turn the idea that Japan intended to invade Australia. He has no hesitation in conceding that the battles fought in Papua and New Guinea were brutal and deadly. He has noted that more Australians died in the broader Papuan campaign than in any other operation in the war.[69] Beaumont is, however, more persuasive and Stanley may underestimate the fears held by the general population in Australia of the threat posed by Japan. He would nevertheless no doubt agree with Hank Nelson that 'as a result of the war, New Guinea ... entered Australian nationalism'.[70]

The bloody battle along the Kokoda Track and the defence of Port Moresby lasted until November 1942. By 1943, following the battles of the Coral Sea and Milne Bay, organised Japanese resistance in Papua had collapsed and the war had shifted to Lae, the north coast of the island and to Bougainville. In this period, as Mark Turner has described, 'the inert shield [of Papua New Guinea in Australia's defence] had sprung to life'.[71] The scale and intensity of the fighting with 2165 Australians killed during the battle for Kokoda, the sheer proximity of the battlefields to mainland Australia, the threat posed by defeat and the relief at eventual success all combined to create a sense of oneness between Australia and Papua New Guinea. Papua New Guinea was now 'known, significant and evoked national and personal sentiment' in the minds of those who had served, and the public and politicians who had supported them from home.[72]

This new bond had a particularly strong influence on Australia's wartime political leaders who now fully accepted that the arc of islands to Australia's north represented the most effective shield against invasion. Curtin and his Minister for External Affairs, Dr H. V. Evatt, firmly believed that Papua New Guinea was pivotal to Australia's defence. In March 1943, in response to some early thinking in his department on post-war policy towards the region, Evatt noted that 'the control or supervision of control over neighbouring territories will be vital to the future security of Australia as well as to other Pacific countries and we must have a full say in the determination of these questions'.[73] Evatt told an audience in New York in April 1943 that 'Australia will naturally regard as of crucial importance to its own security the arc of islands lying to the north and north-east of our continent ... Australia will be vitally concerned as to who shall live in, develop and control these areas so vital to her security from aggression'.[74]

In January 1944 Curtin and Evatt attempted to confirm, in one of the first international agreements negotiated and entered into by Australia without British involvement, the description of Australia's strategic environment. The Canberra or ANZAC Pact with New Zealand identified the two countries' areas of security interests as a 'zone of defence comprising the South-west and South Pacific areas ... stretching through the arc of islands north and north-east of Australia to Western Samoa and the Cook Islands'.[75] Curtin explained that:

> The fundamental concept of the Australian Government is that the best defence of Australia and New Zealand is to be secured by a system of defence based on an island screen to the north of these Dominions. The purpose of such a system of defence is to preserve the strategic isolation of Australia and New Zealand, whose security is linked with that of the adjacent islands. In the hands of ourselves or a friendly power and adequately defended they are a bulwark to the defence of Australia and New Zealand and points of offensive action against an enemy. In possession of an enemy they are spring-boards for offensive action against our mainlands.[76]

The two countries agreed to 'continuing consultation in all defence matters of mutual interest' and increased planning and exchanges on defence issues in the Pacific.[77] The ANZAC Pact had also called for an international conference of powers involved in the Southwest Pacific to discuss the problems of security, post-war development and native welfare in the islands. This was considered premature by Washington. London too was unimpressed by Canberra's initiative. Once the proposed conference failed to materialise the Pact could not gather momentum and ceased to have an enduring significance. The ideas behind the Pact did, in time, however lead to the formation of the South Pacific Commission.

Curtin's and Evatt's views on the post-war security environment were shared by General Blamey, who endorsed and forwarded to Curtin an assessment prepared by the Army's secret policy planning and assessment unit known as the Directorate of Research and Civil Affairs under Col. Alf Conlon's leadership.[78] The unit had been charged by Blamey to examine policy options for the development of Papua and New Guinea across a wide spectrum of subjects, including defence. In a covering letter sent on 5 February 1944, Blamey told Curtin that:

> Militarily, the operations in the Timor-Solomons arc have revealed, as though a screen had suddenly been removed, the world importance of these areas strategically. The chain of islands from Timor to the Solomons and New Caledonia is the forward base-area from which an Asiatic enemy can organise his forces to isolate or attack the Australian mainland, and the forward base-area from which Australian and Allied forces can attack his supply lines. ... The battle for Australia can possibly be won by either side in the island-chain. ... Australia would have learnt nothing from the sacrifices of the war if the world strategic importance of the whole New Guinea theatre had not become overwhelmingly obvious to the nation.[79]

Blamey's description of Australia's strategic environment suggested that the assessments that had first emerged in the works of Commander Hugh Thring before the First World War and later repeated by other military and civilian leaders had now become the orthodox view. A shield or arc across Australia's north beginning in Malaya and extending to Solomon Islands was the accepted description of Australia's immediate security environment.

Blamey's views were shared by his political leaders. J. B. (Ben) Chifley, who had been sworn in as Prime Minister on 13 July 1945 following the death of John Curtin on 5 July, made clear to the Australian Parliament that the 'Territory of New Guinea, in which so many of our men died in battle against the Japanese, is of such importance to the safety of this country that no agreement would be considered by us which restricted in any way our right to provide for the defence of New Guinea and consequently for the safety of Australia. We are permitted to plan and carry out measures directly relevant to the security of Australia itself'.[80] In the early negotiations over the establishment of the United Nations, Evatt secured for Australia a United Nations trusteeship over New Guinea. The terms of the trusteeship allowed for the administering authority to be responsible for the 'peace, order, good government and defence of the Territory'. It could also 'take all measures in the Territory which it considers desirable to provide for the defence of the Territory and for the maintenance of international peace and security'.[81] The new arrangements removed the constraints imposed by the League of Nations and presented Australia with an obligation under international law to defend the Territory of New Guinea. The eastern half of the island of New Guinea, which Evatt described as a land 'consecrated by the sacrifice of Australians in two World Wars', was now Australia's responsibility.[82] In 1949 the United Nations agreed that both Papua and New Guinea could be administered jointly as one unit from an administrative headquarters in Port Moresby.

In the first comprehensive strategic assessment prepared following the end of the war by the Chiefs of Staff, an Australian 'zone of strategic responsibility' was identified with Singapore, North Borneo and Manus Island north of the New Guinea coastline clearly identified as its key points.[83] The report also incorporated a line of bases from Singapore to Manus Island, New Ireland, Rabaul and eventually Fiji and referred to the need for an air base at Nadzab, near Lae. It accepted that Malaya was pivotal to the defence of Australia but acknowledged that New Guinea was of 'particular importance' to Australia's strategic position. The Council of Defence endorsed the assessment in April 1948 but noted that the 'vital question' was whether 'Australia has the resources to accept the responsibilities' to maintain a defence presence in the area.[84]

This question quickly emerged as critical to defence planning when Australia examined the sustainability of Manus Island as a naval base. In March 1944 Manus Island had been occupied by the United States Air Force and had been used as a base in the final phase of the war against the Japanese. After the war the question arose as to whether the base should continue to be used by the United States. Evatt sought joint control and use by Australia and the United States but Washington would not agree. The United States Air Force withdrew in 1947–48. In 1948 the Australian defence force assessed it as 'one of the essentials in the general strategy for the protection of the northern approaches to Australia'. In 1951 it was still seen as a 'bastion' in Australia's defence.[85] It was to remain as a useful asset and in 1962 the Menzies Government rejected calls by the Navy and its Minister, Senator John Gorton, for it to be closed.

Conclusion

The period 1919 to 1945 had witnessed the slow evolution of Papua New Guinea in Australia's defence planning and assessments from an overlooked and neglected territory to one seen as pivotal. It was an uncomfortable journey. The rhetoric used at the Paris Peace Conference had suggested that the island would have an important place in Australia's post-war strategic assessments. However, this did not immediately materialise. Australia's defence planners were focused on the broader threat from Japan and allowed military preparations to be subsumed within Britain's strategic plans. They placed a near total reliance on the building of a naval base at Singapore by

Britain and the deployment of units of the British Navy in the event of war. Some basic contingency plans covering Papua and New Guinea had been developed in the inter-war years but these had a desultory air to them and were always secondary to the wider strategic objectives of maritime defence and the promise of support from the Royal Navy.

The events of 1941 to 1945 changed this outlook. Malaya, Singapore and the Netherlands East Indies had fallen, contrary to all hopes and expectations. The 'shield' was now deployed and the islands of New Guinea were seen as the final barrier to the Japanese advance into the South Pacific and invasion of Australia. The proximity and brutality of the fighting, captured on news reports shown in cinemas, alarmed Australians. Significantly, the battles in Papua and New Guinea had entered the psyche of Australia from the ordinary citizen to the defence planners and, most importantly, to members of the government and opposition. The fear generated by the Japanese attacks across New Guinea, the islands of the Bismarck Archipelago, Solomon Islands and the Coral Sea, scarred a generation of Australian leaders and ensured that New Guinea would retain a significant place in Australia's strategic environment.

A fear of Japan had pervaded Australia's approach to New Guinea and the Pacific from the turn of the century. It had reached a crescendo in 1942. It had been extinguished in war but vestiges remained throughout the immediate post-war period. However, as Australia turned its attention to the challenges of post-war nation-building, a new country would emerge to unsettle Australia's leaders.

Chapter 3

THE WEST NEW GUINEA DISPUTE 1949–1951

> 'Australia's vital strategic interests in Dutch New Guinea, ... are, in fact, no less than Australia's vital strategic interests in Australian New Guinea and Papua'.
>
> Percy Spender,
> Minister for External Affairs, 1950

> 'Australians could not trust the Indonesians as neighbours in New Guinea in the event of a conflict between the free world and the communists'.
>
> Prime Minister Robert Menzies,
> 1950

On 19 December 1949 Robert Menzies was sworn in as Prime Minister of Australia for a second time. A week later, following years of bitter conflict and the transfer of sovereignty from the Netherlands, Achmad Sukarno, seven years younger than Menzies, was sworn in as President of Indonesia, a title he had held since his audacious declaration of independence in August 1945. In a curious twist of history both would govern and dominate the politics of their respective countries for the next sixteen years. Both would lead their governments through the challenges and threats which emerged over that period.

These two men, Menzies and Sukarno, were a study in contrasts. Menzies had been moulded in the principles of law and Westminster parliamentary democracy, having first been elected to the Victorian State Parliament in 1928 and then to the Commonwealth Parliament in 1934. He had served as Attorney General from 1934 to 1939 and as Prime Minister from 26 April 1939 to 29 August 1941. He had seen the Japanese invasion of Southeast Asia as the greatest threat his country had ever faced. For many Australians, Menzies included, it had demonstrated, once and for all, the country's vulnerability to attack from the north.

Sukarno's political career had been forged in the furnace of an anti-colonial struggle against Dutch rule over the Netherlands East Indies. He had carried the aspirations of his people as they sought a new identity in an independent nation emerging from colonial rule. For Sukarno, the Second World War and the Japanese invasion of the Netherlands East Indies had become the catalyst for a much longed-for drive for decolonisation and independence. He had led this struggle through the post-war period and had finally succeeded in negotiating independence for his homeland – a homeland which he firmly believed included all of the former Dutch East Indies and stretched from Sabang in Aceh to Merauke in West New Guinea. Sukarno had emerged as the symbol of Indonesia's new nationalism.

Menzies was conservative, orthodox, disciplined and cautious. He saw Australia's involvement in international issues as a means to secure the support of Australia's principal allies, Britain and the United States. He campaigned strongly at home and abroad against the threat of communism. He preferred the atmosphere and surety of the old world of Imperial Britain and, as Peter Edwards has described,

> like many Australians of his time, Menzies assumed that Australia's security was based in large measure on European dominance of most of Southeast Asia. The rapid post-1945 decolonisation of the European empires in Asia and Africa, especially in Southeast Asia, discomfited him.[1]

In contrast, Sukarno was emotional, undisciplined, reckless and a near-demagogue. He governed in an atmosphere of crises and diversions and enjoyed indulging in acts of brinkmanship. He saw the world through the prism of anti-colonialism and non-alignment and identified himself closely with leaders such as Nehru of India, Nasser of Egypt and Zhou Enlai of communist China. He regarded himself as a natural leader of the emerging Afro-Asian bloc. As President, Sukarno ignored questions of economic management, allowing his country instead to crumble into near bankruptcy and chronic instability. He flirted with the largest communist party outside of Russia and China, the PKI (Partai Komunis Indonesia), in order to retain power. Under Sukarno's leadership Indonesia became the second largest non-communist recipient of aid from the communist bloc after Nasser's Egypt.

From vastly different backgrounds and pursuing markedly different policies and objectives these two leaders dominated their respective countries' domestic and foreign policies for more than sixteen years. Both could be described as the product of their background and times. Menzies put his country on the path to prosperity but yearned for an older world and was disturbed by changes to institutions, such as the Commonwealth. Sukarno was the product of his own tumultuous upbringing and marked by his long campaign for Indonesian independence. His ill-disciplined behaviour and nationalist rhetoric reflected the frustration of leading a diverse country struggling to develop and prosper.

The two leaders met only once, when Menzies visited Indonesia in December 1959. There is no evidence that they corresponded with one another, despite Menzies being a prolific writer to world leaders and a regular international traveller (in his first eight years in office he was absent overseas for a cumulative period of close to two years).[2] Indeed, one of the surprising facts is that despite being engaged in two significant regional disputes in the 1950s and 1960s, Australia's and Indonesia's senior leaders only occasionally met one another – for example, there were only four meetings between President, Prime Minister and Ministers for Foreign Affairs in the eight years between 1955 and 1963.[3] Nevertheless, the assessment by Menzies and his fellow ministers of Sukarno and his government had a profound influence on the development of Australia's foreign and defence policies in the period between 1950 and 1966. It contributed to one of the most rapid build-ups in Australia's military preparedness beginning in the early 1960s. It also had a significant influence on the way defence planners approached the assessment of Australia's strategic environment and, as a consequence, ensured that Papua New Guinea remained a constant focus in Australia's defence planning.

It is hard to know what Sukarno thought of Australia. He would have had an intimate knowledge of Australia's sympathy for Indonesia's push for independence in the post-war period under the Chifley Labor Government and he kept the door open to Australian diplomats such as Tom Critchley who had been instrumental in securing Indonesia's independence.[4]

He may also have been impressed by the senior level of the Australian diplomat sent to Jakarta as Ambassador: John Hood (1950–1953), Walter Crocker (1955–1957), Lawrence (Jim) McIntyre (1957–1960), Patrick Shaw (1960–1962) and K.C.O. (Mick) Shann (1962–1966). But beyond that little is known. He never publicly criticised Australia, even during the height of Confrontation in the mid-1960s, and at times went out of his way to reassure Australia of his wish for a positive relationship. His personal opinion of Menzies is not known. In contrast, Menzies and his fellow Cabinet ministers distrusted Sukarno from a very early date and remained deeply suspicious of Indonesia's intentions. This feeling was pervasive and influenced Australia's decision-making throughout the 1950s and 1960s. By 1963 Menzies had lost all confidence in and respect for Sukarno and let drop an invitation for him to visit Australia.[5] At the same time, as an indication of the complex nature of the relationship, he and his colleagues acknowledged, albeit at times reluctantly, that Australia had to live with its northern neighbour and had to establish some type of a workable bilateral relationship.

If the two leaders did have a characteristic in common it was their skill as formidable and popular orators. Both were masters of the public arena with Sukarno in particular employing his charismatic personality to manipulate and win the support of the crowd and thereby secure his continued supremacy in the chaotic world of Indonesian politics. Sukarno was described by one Australian Ambassador to Jakarta as having a 'mesmeric hold over the urban and (to a lesser degree) the rural masses' secured through a 'mixture of astuteness and charm' and the 'guile to play off his potential challengers against one another'.[6] Menzies was forceful, authoritative and, at his wilful best, merciless in the prosecution of his argument as best demonstrated in his brutal demolition of the leader of the Labor Party, Dr Evatt, in October 1955 following the tabling in Parliament of the final report of the Petrov Royal Commission.[7]

Menzies and his Cabinet were tested for over a decade by the management of the relationship with Indonesia. The West New Guinea dispute was discussed in Cabinet on at least thirty-six occasions between 1950 and 1962 either in great detail or in the wider context of Australia's overall strategic outlook. Confrontation and the question of military assistance to Malaysia were discussed on over twenty occasions between 1963 and 1966. Both issues dominated the Cabinet room discussion more so than the Korean War, the Suez Crisis or Australia's entry into the war in Vietnam. The West New Guinea dispute and Confrontation were also the subject of regular correspondence and discussion between Menzies and his British and American counterparts for close to sixteen years and the subject of repeated assessments by senior officials. As the various crises unfolded in Indonesia in the 1950s and 1960s a recurring feature of the debates in Cabinet and elsewhere was the need to factor in the defence of Papua New Guinea in any calculation of how Australia could or should respond. Menzies and his ministers held uppermost in their minds the place of geography in determining Australia's strategic priorities, the importance of Papua New Guinea to Australia and the need to provide for its defence.

Early Australian interest

In December 1949 Australia enjoyed a positive and sympathetic standing with the incoming government of an independent Indonesia. On 9 July 1947, in response to the first Dutch 'police action' against the Indonesian nationalists, the Minister for External Affairs, Dr Evatt, had announced Australia's recognition of the *de facto* status of the Indonesian Republic while still appearing to accept the Netherlands *de jure* authority. In September 1947 following extensive negotiations at the United Nations, Australia accepted the invitation by the Republic to become its nominee on the United Nations Good Offices Committee (GOC).[8] Over the next four months, culminating in the signing of the Renville Agreement in January 1948, 'Australia found itself increasingly cast in the role of champion of the Republic'.[9] The Renville Agreement was at best an interim or temporary solution to the problem of Dutch–Indonesian relations and a new round of negotiations would be inevitable, particularly following the resumption of 'police action' by the Dutch in December 1948.

In July 1949, in the days preceding the beginning of the Round Table Conference intended to settle the terms of the transfer of Dutch sovereignty over Indonesia, the Netherlands surprised the international community when it made clear that it intended to retain sovereignty over Dutch New Guinea. The republican and federalist Indonesian delegations claimed that as the successor state to the Netherlands for the whole of the Dutch East Indies, Indonesia had the right to control West New Guinea. It was eventually recognised by all delegations at the Round Table Conference that postponement of negotiations over the status of West New Guinea was the only acceptable approach if the conference and the founding of Indonesia were not to be delayed. Under the terms of the Round Table Conference agreement it was acknowledged that the views of the parties remained 'in dispute'. It was agreed that negotiations on the 'question of the political status of New Guinea' would commence within a year of the date of the transfer of sovereignty, i.e. late 1950.[10]

Margaret George has argued that Australia's support for the continuation of Dutch sovereignty over West New Guinea 'contradicted its approach to the resolution of the Dutch-Indonesia dispute' based as it was on support for the moderate forces within the nationalist movement. George has concluded that 'whereas the Australian government had come to regard the Dutch as contributing to instability in Indonesia, their continuing control of West New Guinea was welcomed as a guarantee to stability within New Guinea and as a bulwark to Australia's external security'.[11] Australia's security interests were best promoted by obstructing 'any changeover to indigenous administration in West New Guinea' as this 'might enable revolutionary nationalism and or Asian Communism to penetrate New Guinea'.[12] Australia had supported the emergence of an independent Indonesia but felt best protected if the 'barrier' to the north were maintained by a reliable but distant European power. Garry Woodard, a senior Australian diplomat and later historian, has described Australia's objective in the West New Guinea dispute as 'keeping this undeveloped territory out of the hands of Indonesia while trying to control the damage to the bilateral relations'. He has also argued that this was 'Australia's most consistent foreign policy challenge in the decade up to [Sir Garfield] Barwick becoming Foreign Minister [1961]'.[13]

The second outcome from the early debate over the future of West New Guinea was that, in the mind of Australians, little distinction was drawn between the two halves of the island. When assessing the future of Dutch New Guinea, Australian decision-makers were also thinking of Australian New Guinea. The island was seen as one strategic entity despite the political division between the two halves. As a consequence, little distinction was made in assessing the military importance of either half to Australia. This attitude was to be carried forward by the incoming Menzies Government when it assumed office in December 1949.

New government: old ideas

A recent study of Menzies by Anne Henderson makes few references to his views on foreign affairs in the post-war period except for his rigid support for the British Commonwealth and a wish to see a stronger relationship between Britain and the United States.[14] This overlooks Menzies's view on issues such as continued Dutch rule of West New Guinea. Menzies was alarmed by the combination of rising nationalism in Asia and the calls for decolonisation. As early as 1945 he had told a Liberal Party convention that 'the very arguments used for throwing the Dutch out of the East Indies are the arguments which will be used to throw the British out of Malaya, to throw the British out of Burma, India, for throwing the Australians out of New Guinea'.[15] Menzies returned to this theme in February 1949 when he told the Australian Parliament that 'we cannot sensibly expect to maintain our own territorial integrity and our own national, racial and economic policies – which we are perfectly entitled to have and which we do have and hold strongly – if we take sides against European nations as though they were, of necessity, interlopers in countries where they have long been colonists, administrators and educators'. He went on to argue that, as a consequence of what he described as the Chifley Government's anti-Dutch stance, 'we have been assisting to put the Dutch out of the East Indies. If we continue to do that the same process will no doubt in due course, eject the British from Malaya and the Australians from Papua and New Guinea'.[16]

Menzies also showed his lukewarm attitude towards the newly-formed United Nations which was to characterise his time in government. He attacked the Chifley Government's support for the United Nations in facilitating the negotiations, describing it as interference in the sovereign affairs of a state and as a possible harbinger of future interventions in issues of domestic jurisdiction such as the White Australia policy. He also criticised the Labor Government for a policy which served 'to placate neutrals or former collaborators with the Japanese, (rather) than … play the game by our former allies'.[17] This was a reference to the links between Sukarno and his senior supporters and the Japanese occupying forces during the war. In a speech in Sydney in January 1949 Menzies had described members of Indonesia's independence movement as 'active Japanese collaborators'.[18] It was a description repeated by other members of the Liberal Party.

In the debate in parliament in February 1949, Menzies's senior colleague, Percy Spender, who had served as Minister for the Army from 1940 to 1941, a member of the War Cabinet in 1939 and would assume the portfolio of Minister for External Affairs and Minister for External Territories (i.e. responsible for Papua and New Guinea) in the Menzies Government, argued that by supporting the Indonesian independence movement the Chifley Government had 'allied itself to a policy which will ultimately destroy White Australia'.[19] Spender echoed Menzies's argument when he said that the consequence of the government's policy would be that 'the French should get out of New Caledonia, the Dutch out of Indonesia, the

English out of Malaya and the Portuguese out of Portuguese Timor. Then certainly we should be alone, and to whom should we turn to in time of trouble?'[20] Spender added that should Indonesia secure Dutch New Guinea and 'if the natives have a right to govern themselves in Dutch New Guinea why have they not a similar right to govern themselves in the mandated territory administered by Australia? If so, we ought to get out of there, if we are to be logical'.[21]

The arguments used by Menzies and Spender, drawing on the threat to Australia's immediate security in the region should Indonesia secure West New Guinea, had bipartisan support in the Australian Parliament. The Labor Party, although a supporter of Indonesia's drive for independence, firmly believed that Australia's security would be endangered if Indonesia secured West New Guinea. The former Minister for Immigration in the Chifley Government and later leader of the party, Arthur Calwell, told the House of Representatives in February 1950 that

> we can no more let the Indonesians into Dutch New Guinea than we can let them into Darwin. ... and we can no more trust an Indonesia that we have recognized under Soekarno than we could trust an Indonesia that was led by the same Soekarno when he was a Japanese puppet premier. If we allow the Indonesians into Dutch New Guinea there will be no hope of our holding the northern portion of Australia and the fate of this country would then be sealed and certain.[22]

Labor did not change its views throughout the period of the dispute.

Similarly, the Australian press, drawing on language first used by Prime Minister Hughes, echoed many of Spender's arguments with a recurring degree of alarm. In an editorial on 2 January 1950 the Melbourne *Sun* argued that an Indonesian takeover was a 'matter ... of vital interest to the Commonwealth. ... we would be entitled to view with some uneasiness a transfer which placed in the hands of relatively inexperienced administrators an area which would be an obvious springboard for any future aggressor'.[23] Earlier it had described a possible Indonesian takeover as 'a dagger pointed at Australia's heart'.[24]

The influential *Sydney Morning Herald* commented that 'it is an imperative requirement of Australia's security that no dangerously premature nationalism should be injected into New Guinea' and preferred the Dutch to remain to steer 'more safely and wisely' the area to self-government.[25] The *Sydney Sun* described the Indonesian Government's claim as 'the most serious threat to Australia's security since the Japanese advance on Rabaul' and that Australia would have 'a common front with an Asian nation of 75,000,000 in which is a strong communist element'. It would see the 'loss of a strategic buffer against possible aggression from Communist-dominated Far Eastern counties' and the 'disappearance of the last European neighbour and complete isolation from white communities'.[26]

The Australian press had captured the arguments which would form the basis of Australia's objections to an Indonesian takeover of West New Guinea: that Indonesia was an untested and potentially unreliable neighbour; that the Dutch were a more reliable and steady administrator; there were no cultural or community links between Indonesia and West New Guinea which would sustain the argument that it should be granted control of Dutch New Guinea; and that an Indonesian presence in the western half of the island was too close to Australia's interest in the eastern half of the island and to Australia in general. The Australian media remained unchanged in its opinions throughout the 1950s. As Woodard has concluded, 'after the experience of World War II, Australians of all political persuasions ... saw Australia's security interests as served by New Guinea being in reliable hands, certainly in the hands of a country which would keep out hostile powers'. He has also added to this argument by noting that Australia's security concerns 'were bound up inextricably with racial prejudice against Indonesia, which reflected public opinion'.[27]

Spender takes the initiative

Within three weeks of coming to office Spender began to put in place a plan largely developed on his own initiative to establish a security screen across Australia's northern coastline.[28] His intention was to create a barrier of friendly states which would serve to defend Australia. Crucial to this objective was that sovereignty over West New Guinea not pass to Indonesia. As part of this plan he also sought to secure control over the archipelago stretching across Australia's northeastern coast.

In January 1950, en route to a Commonwealth Foreign Ministers Conference in Colombo, Spender launched the first part of his strategy. On 14 January he wrote to the British Secretary of State for Commonwealth Relations, Philip Noel-Baker, and proposed that Britain's interest in the Anglo-French Condominium of the New Hebrides be passed to Australia. Spender cited Australia's 'close interest in the New Hebrides from a strategic point of view', as well as its interest in developing over 40,000 acres of land held by the Australian Government.[29] Spender also asked that

FUZZY PERCY: THIS ALL BELONG WHITE AUSTRALIA!
A reflection on Percy Spender's role in the West New Guinea dispute.
Charles Hallett, *Smith's Weekly*, October 1950.

Australia be involved in any talks with the French on the future of the New Hebrides. Britain responded positively to Spender's initiative with Prime Minister Attlee describing it to his Cabinet colleagues as a 'very good bargain for us'.[30] Shortly after, Spender was told that the French were, in principle, sympathetic to the proposal. Spender recommended to Menzies that the issue be put to the Australian Cabinet. He hoped ministers would endorse a 'proposal so obviously in the vital interests of Australia'. He added that it was a 'matter of supreme importance ... that for the effective protection of our eastern coastline we should step into the shoes of the United Kingdom. ... The New Hebrides are an important area, forming as they do with New Britain, New Ireland and Bougainville, a vital strategic screen for Australia'.[31] Spender's ambitions, and the language he used, were similar to those used by Hughes in 1919 and 1920.

The issue evolved slowly over the next few months. The government's Defence Committee advised Cabinet in July 1951 of its 'lukewarm' assessment of the strategic value of the New Hebrides to Australia's defence.[32] The Committee noted that 'all islands of the central and south Pacific may be regarded as having approximately equal strategic value to the defence of Australia'. The New Hebrides occupied a 'strategic position in the inner screen' of islands off the coast of Australia' but 'the group is only of limited importance in any foreseeable strategic situation'.[33] Over subsequent months Canberra's enthusiasm for the idea waned until it allowed it to pass. Finally, in June 1952 Australia advised the British Government that it would defer for at least two years any further consideration of the proposal 'due to difficulties in providing necessary administrative personnel' to support an Australian presence.[34] Canberra, as Goldworthy has noted, was content not to assume responsibility for Britain's half of the island as long as Britain remained *in situ* and protected any potential Australian interest.[35] It is a curious anomaly that in this period Spender made no formal demarche to the British Government to seek the transfer of the British Solomon Islands Protectorate to Australia. Its claim to a crucial role in Australia's defence perimeter due to its close proximity to both the north eastern coast of Australia and to Papua New Guinea was just as strong as those of the New Hebrides. It was not until 1956 and again in 1959 that ministers turned to the suggestion of acquiring the Solomon Islands but by then the Cabinet had lost interest. John McEwen, Leader of the Country Party and Deputy Prime Minister from 1958 to 1971, told his colleagues that Australia had too many other responsibilities and obligations to take control of the Solomon Islands. He later added that 'takeovers don't fit in today's world'.[36]

The second element in Spender's strategic plan was to ensure that the Dutch retained sovereignty and responsibility over West New Guinea. In January 1950 he visited Jakarta en route to the Commonwealth Foreign Ministers' meeting in Colombo. In his report to Menzies on his discussions with President Sukarno, Spender told the Prime Minister that there was 'evidence of sustainable good will towards Australia' and that the new government 'will obviously appreciate all the advice and assistance that can be given them by Australia'. For his part, he had 'confined [himself] to general expressions of our desire to give them whatever help we can and in particular to increase trade with Indonesia'. He noted the 'general air of confidence' and judged that 'if the present government can be sustained through full cooperation from the Dutch and help from the United States, Australia and others, there is good cause for optimism'. He was also confident that the bilateral relationship could be developed.[37]

On the subject of Dutch New Guinea, Spender was more cautious. He described the issue as 'an exceedingly delicate one' and that 'the Indonesians at present apparently feel very strongly on the matter' – a surprisingly naïve remark given the events of the previous twelve months. He commented that an article in the Australian press by Wilfred Kent-Hughes MP ridiculing Indonesia's claims to Dutch New Guinea 'had caused some excitement here' but added that to 'what extent this is a real question with the Indonesians as distinct from the politics behind it, is not possible at this stage to gauge'. He urged that 'public comment and speculation be discouraged at the present time'.[38]

In his memoirs Spender described his meeting with Sukarno in which the President had raised the issue of West New Guinea. Spender said he had cut Sukarno off, saying the President knew the views of the Australian Government on the issue and that 'in the light of them did he think that any discussion between us would be likely to be very productive'. Spender added that he didn't want the convivial nature of the meeting to be disturbed by 'any difference between us'.[39] In view of the seriousness of the issue and the Menzies Government's strong stance it is surprising he did not take this early opportunity to try to discourage Sukarno from pursuing Indonesia's claim. It would be another two years before an Australian Minister for External Affairs again had the chance to speak directly to Sukarno.

Spender used the occasion of his visit to deliver a speech over the Macquarie Radio Network to an audience in Australia. Speaking from Jakarta he described the emergence of Indonesia as a 'great experiment' that 'can have tremendous importance for the future of Southeast Asia and indeed for the whole world'. He drew attention to the fact that:

> Indonesia is, after all, our nearest neighbour, and [that] our future welfare, and especially our future security, might be vitally affected by what happens here ... This is a plain fact of geography; we simply cannot afford to be indifferent to events that take place next door to us.
>
> It is especially important that Indonesia should ... pursue a course of conduct which creates no clash of interests between us. Anything we can do to these ends will be a measure of insurance for our own future.[40]

Australia had begun a delicate balancing act which was to last for over a decade between developing a bilateral relationship with Jakarta and maintaining a position on the status of West New Guinea. Richard Casey, who would succeed Spender as Minister for External Affairs, described this policy as similar to trying to ride two horses at once.

On his return to Canberra Spender made clear Australia's full support for continued Dutch control over West New Guinea. In a letter to the Dutch Ambassador on 8 February 1950, he drew attention to the fact that negotiations between Indonesia and the Netherlands were to be held later in the year to settle the status of West New Guinea. He asserted that 'the Netherlands authorities will fully appreciate Australia's vital strategic interests in Dutch New Guinea, which are, in fact, no less than Australia's vital interests in Australian New Guinea and Papua'. As a result the Australian Government regarded itself 'as directly concerned in the determination of the future administration of Dutch New Guinea' – a point it intended to make separately to the Indonesian authorities. He then proceeded to articulate Australia's policy position:

> The Australian Government does not regard Dutch New Guinea as forming part of Indonesia. We believe that the peoples of Dutch New Guinea have little or nothing in common, except a past common administration, with the peoples of Indonesia. Their developmental problems are separate and the level of political development necessitates placing them in a category quite different from the States of the United States of Indonesia. In fact, we regard Dutch New Guinea as having much in common from both an ethnic, administrative and developmental point of view with our own territories of New Guinea and Papua.
>
> In our view, political and economic stability in the newly-created United States of Indonesia is vital, not merely to our own security interests, but also to those of all western peoples having interests in South-East Asia. The inclusion of Dutch New Guinea, however, with the United States of Indonesia would not, in our view, add to this stability, and may in fact result in Dutch New Guinea being undeveloped, undefended and a major weakness in South-East Asian strategic planning. Indeed, we would view with profound misgivings any transfer of sovereignty to the United States of Indonesia.[41]

Spender concluded his letter with a proposal that both governments exchange views on the future administration of their respective halves of New Guinea. He also held out the possibility that the 'Australian Government would be prepared to consider even more fundamental proposals on the future control of the territory'.[42] Spender had in mind a possible joint trusteeship arrangement over Dutch New Guinea.

Spender's letter to the Dutch Government encapsulated the principles the Menzies Government would articulate over the coming decade with an ever-increasing emphasis on security and defence. Indonesian control over such a large area was too close for comfort for a government still haunted by the experiences of the Second World War. In addition, the letter had suggested that an Indonesia which was already struggling with the demands of independence would be made more susceptible to internal instability by having to provide for the development needs of West New Guinea. It also hinted at the possibility that Indonesia could not be trusted to restrict its claims to just Dutch New Guinea and that it had ambitions to incorporate the whole island. The ethnic and anthropological arguments were particularly important because by describing the Papuans of Dutch New Guinea as having more in common with the indigenous population of Australian New Guinea, Spender was also drawing a picture of a potentially unified island. In terms of strategic planning it meant that the island was being seen by Australian authorities as one entity rather than Australia's interests being solely focused on Australian New Guinea.

The second point to note is that Australia had embarked on a policy without first seeking the support of either London or Washington. As Richard Chauvel has commented, Spender's policy approach was an 'attempt to conduct an indigenous and independent policy'.[43] Stuart Doran has developed this point further with an argument that Spender viewed Australia 'as the preeminent power in the area roughly south of Singapore and as the effective colonial power of the Southwest Pacific'. As a consequence it 'aggressively and relatively independently assert[ed] its predominance in the wider area through defence of its immediate Pacific sphere of influence east of the West New Guinea–Papua and New Guinea border and maintenance of its strategic buffer zone in West New Guinea'.[44] As we shall see, the behaviour of Spender in pursuing his objective gives support to Doran's thesis but the argument is weakened by the realisation that Australia had few diplomatic assets and no military wherewithal to back up any claims to assert superiority over Indonesia or to stake out a sphere of influence in Southeast Asia. Even Spender's 'stubbornness' and 'maverick trait' that characterised his dealings with his allies eventually undermined his standing and his support.[45] The 'highly volatile, almost manic' approach of Dr Evatt in the 1940s was replaced by the 'strong, self-assured personality' of Spender, leading Patrick Gordon Walker, the British Secretary of State for Commonwealth Affairs, to comment that, when assessing Australia's policy approach to the West New Guinea dispute, 'scratch a Spender and you'll find an Evatt'.[46] He could have added 'and a Hughes'.

At this time the Australian Government and the press were especially sensitive to any suggestion that Indonesia held expansionist ambitions and, in this regard, comments made on 30 January 1950 by Mohammed Yamin, a middle-ranking adviser to the Republican delegation at the Round Table Conference, caused considerable alarm. In an interview with the news wire service ANETA, Yamin was reported to have said that after Dutch New Guinea had been incorporated into Indonesia, talks should also be held about Australian New Guinea 'as this territory which is at present under Australian trusteeship is Indonesian, too'. He also identified Portuguese Timor and British North Borneo as areas to be included in Indonesia if colonialism were to be 'wiped out absolutely and unconditionally'.[47] The Australian press and the government reacted angrily to Yamin's comments. The *Sydney Morning Herald* described them as demonstrating 'Indonesian imperialist pretension' and that 'Djakarta's territorial appetite is visibly growing'. It again called for continued Dutch administration of West New Guinea or, if necessary, that it should be placed under a trusteeship. As for Eastern New Guinea, it 'is our charge, and we shall firmly hold it'.[48]

Spender similarly rejected Yamin's statement, adding 'the United States of Indonesia has not the slightest shadow of a claim to Australian New Guinea on any ground, ethnic (racial) or otherwise. Any such claim would not admit a moment's consideration. It would be immediately rejected'.[49] The Indonesian Government, through its Ambassador to the United Nations (L. N. Palar), formally advised the Australian Government on 6 February that the statement (by Yamin) was 'totally without foundation and my government denies it emphatically'.[50] Later, on 11 April, President Sukarno asked the Australian Ambassador 'to convey to his Minister his strongest assurance that Indonesians have no aspirations whatever regarding Australian administration of territories in New Guinea'.[51]

In late April 1950, Australia again approached the Dutch Government and expressed its alarm at any possibility of a compromise settlement being reached which would see Indonesia secure control of West New Guinea. Australia's diplomatic note made clear that 'we would regard our security interests adversely affected if Republican influence were confined to Dutch New Guinea. ... Inevitably Republican influence would step by step be increased and ultimately argument put forward in spite of present denials that our own territories should be similarly incorporated either wholly or in part'.[52] Australia suggested as an alternative to a possible Indonesian takeover that responsibility for West New Guinea be transferred to Australia or that a trusteeship be established with Australia a trusted power or a joint Netherlands–Australian trusteeship be created. Australia made clear that 'we could not contemplate trusteeship in which Indonesia was either alone or in conjunction with other power a trusteeship authority'.[53]

Menzies and Spender state Australia's case

After three months of international travel and active diplomatic campaigning, Spender turned his attention to the Australian Parliament where he delivered two major speeches setting out the government's foreign policy priorities. On 9 March 1950 he told the Parliament that Australia had a duty to ensure that 'nothing takes place [in the islands to the north] that can in any way offer a threat to Australian security. These islands are, as experience has shown, our last ring of defence against aggression'. He drew attention to New Guinea as a whole and described it as 'an absolutely essential link in the chain of Australian defence'. He added, with an oblique reference to Dutch New Guinea, 'it is not to be assumed by any one [sic] that should fundamental changes take place in any of these areas, Australia would adopt a purely passive role'.[54] Spender did not elaborate on what he meant by this last remark. It could be assessed as suggesting an aggressive diplomatic campaign to thwart any Indonesian initiative or, *in extremis*, a preparedness to use military force. Spender did not inform the Parliament of his discussions with the British Government over the New Hebrides but referred to Australia's interest in 'any developments in Timor, the New Hebrides and New Caledonia that might have unwelcome consequences for Australia' and Australia's preparedness to join in 'arrangements of mutual economic and security benefit'. He referred to Australian New Guinea in the context of the promotion of the local population and its development 'to serve Australia's security interests'.[55]

On 8 June 1950 Spender delivered the second of his speeches on Australia's immediate security environment and dealt at length with New Guinea. He reiterated many of the points he had earlier made in correspondence with Australia's allies as to the significance of the island to Australia. He again sought to create the image that the island's two halves should 'naturally' be considered as one and that 'strategically (they were) vital to our defence. ... We cannot alter our geography which for all time makes the mainland of New Guinea of vital significance to our security'.[56]

Spender had taken an early role in setting out Australia's objections to Indonesia securing control of West New Guinea. He and Menzies now took advantage of a program of visits over the next six months to London, The Hague and Washington to lobby allies to support their arguments. In July 1950 Menzies used his first visit to London since being elected Prime Minister to tell Kenneth Younger, Minister of State in the UK Foreign Office and acting Foreign Secretary, of Australia's concerns and suspicions about the newly independent Indonesia.[57] He reminded Younger that 'New Guinea had proved to be of vital strategic importance to Australia in the last war and would be equally important in any coming conflict'. Menzies, using language similar to his speech in Parliament in 1949 as well as to that used by the senior Labor parliamentarian, Arthur Calwell, in February 1950, went on to say:

> to be frank, the Australians could not trust the Indonesians as neighbours in New Guinea in the event of a conflict between the free world and the Communists. At a time when Australian blood was being shed in New Guinea the present Indonesian leaders had been making obeisance to the Emperor of Japan. Furthermore, Indonesia had no valid claim to Dutch New Guinea on ethnic, historical or other grounds. In fact their claim was purely colonial – on the basis that what had been a Dutch colony should be an Indonesian colony.[58]

He added that such was the strength of feeling in Australia that 'any proposal that the Indonesians should take over Dutch New Guinea would have to be resisted by Australia, even to the extent of a rupture with Indonesia. … What the Australians were not prepared to have was a long, indefensible, purely technical frontier with an Indonesian New Guinea over which they could not stop Chinese Communist or other infiltration'.[59] It is not clear what Menzies intended by his reference to Australia resisting an Indonesian takeover but it was similar to Spender's earlier reference to Australia not adopting a 'purely passive role' in its approach to the issue.

Younger expressed his sympathy for Australia's point-of-view but added his concern if 'the matter were allowed to vitiate Indonesian–Australian relations and become a major issue of East–West conflict, with the Asians supporting the Indonesian stand'.[60] Britain saw the dispute in the broader context of the global Cold War rather than regional security. It was preoccupied with the tense relationship with the USSR over Berlin and East Germany, the impact of the fall of China to the communist party, the threat to Formosa (Taiwan) and the Korean war which had begun just weeks earlier. It did not wish to add a quarrel over the sovereignty of half an island in Southeast Asia to global tensions. Both leaders agreed it would be best if the issue were kept out of the United Nations, with Menzies expressing his support for the question to be held in abeyance for a number of years. This latter idea had emerged as the preferred option for the management of the dispute, with a number of countries suggesting that the issue be placed in 'cold storage' until a solution could be found.

While Menzies returned to Australia Spender continued his aggressive campaign to thwart any possible Indonesian takeover of West New Guinea. On 28 August 1950 he visited The Hague for discussions with the government of Dr Drees. Spender and his Cabinet colleagues had been concerned either that the Dutch Government could weaken in its resolve to hold on to West New Guinea, or that the coalition government could collapse and be replaced by one that was prepared to negotiate a settlement. This concern was to remain present in Australian ministerial thinking for the remainder of the decade and was watched carefully by Australian diplomats in The Hague and by ministers in Canberra. After the talks he cabled Menzies that he was satisfied that the Dutch Government was opposed to any form of compromise and understood that the 'Australian Government's view was wholly opposed to any entry direct or indirect by Indonesia into Dutch New Guinea'. Spender told Menzies:

> The course which I have advanced is that of no compromise. I think this is the safest one to pursue at the moment. If we show any disposition to compromise we only worsen our position later on although it may be that Dutch trusteeship will be accepted in which Australian vital interests will be protected.[61]

He added that 'it was obvious that they welcomed our unequivocal stand and that this has produced over the past six months a stiffening of their attitude'.[62] Spender did acknowledge to Menzies that the Dutch attitude could change in the years ahead as Dutch commercial interests operating in Indonesia could try to pressure the government to reach a compromise. Nevertheless, he was confident that Drees would resist such pressures. (In a later report to Cabinet Spender noted that 'the matter still has its dangers because of the pressure from Dutch commercial interests'.[63]) Spender also advised Menzies that he had raised with the Dutch the question of 'collaboration in defence security and administrative problems in New Guinea' and his suggestion for an 'informal machinery for consultation on common defence security and similar problems in New Guinea'.[64] The Dutch authorities had taken note and had left it for 'future discussion'. (The Dutch record of the meeting with Spender noted that he had also drawn attention to the Australian naval base on Manus Island and by implication had raised the possibility of the Dutch using it.)[65] Spender concluded his message by noting that he had 'stressed to the Dutch that emphasis should be placed in their arguments on the welfare of the indigenous people of New Guinea' while in his approach to the United States and Britain he would 'place special emphasis on the security and defence aspects'.⁶⁶ Spender's comment reflected a decision by him on the tactics to be pursued in this debate. It is open to question whether this was a cynical ploy to hide Australia's overall objection to the newly independent Asian state coming closer to Australian interests in Papua and New Guinea or represented a genuine concern for Australia's security.

According to a later record of the meeting, the Dutch Prime Minister had also asked Spender not to make 'too strong [public] statements' on West New Guinea, perhaps reflecting a concern that Spender's uncompromising approach and blunt remarks in public could only serve to alienate Indonesian opinion.⁶⁷ Spender appeared to take little notice of the Dutch request when he issued a press statement in The Hague on 29 August in which he repeated all the arguments that now constituted Australia's case against any concession to the Indonesian claim. A clear emphasis was again placed on the need to secure Australia's defence interests against an ambitious Indonesia. He argued that:

> if the claim of Indonesia ... were conceded to any degree at all it would be but a matter of time, no matter how genuine may be assurances to the contrary, when the claim will be pushed further so as to include the Trust Territory of Australian New Guinea and its people. Experience has shown to Australians how strategically vital to Australian defence is the mainland of New Guinea.

At the same time as dismissing the Indonesian claim, Spender noted Australia's 'friendly attitude towards the Indonesian people' and Australia's 'not unimportant part in bringing nationhood to the Indonesian people'.⁶⁸ This was a convenient line of argument and one which sought to bring a degree of balance into the presentation of Australia's policy objectives but it was a hollow gesture given Spender's overall hostility towards Sukarno's Indonesia.

Spender next travelled to London. He called on British Prime Minister Clement Attlee and took up the issue of West New Guinea. Attlee agreed with Spender's argument that 'there was no real reason why New Guinea should be under the Indonesians' and he also 'recognized the strong strategic interests of Australia'. He told his colleagues that he 'thought we [i.e. the UK Government] should endeavour to keep the status quo at present'.⁶⁹ Spender was more direct and somewhat agitated in his conversation with the Foreign Secretary, Ernest Bevin, on 1 September 1950. He told Bevin that 'too many attempts were being made to find a solution' to the issue and that 'any solution which did not maintain Dutch control would mean a concession and no concession of any kind should be made to Indonesia'. He also told Bevin that 'if there were any Indonesian infiltration Australian troops would have to go in at once'. Moreover, any decision by the Security Council for participation by Indonesia in the administration of Dutch New Guinea would mean 'a break between Australia and the United Nations'. Spender had no authority from Cabinet to make such a statement and any initiative to include Indonesia along these lines could have been vetoed by one of Australia's allies on the Council. It indicated Spender's single-minded if somewhat emotional approach to the issue and his heightened distrust of Indonesia. Bevin tried to calm Spender by expressing a preference for the issue to be placed in 'cold storage' for a few years.[70]

The British Government described Spender as 'violent' in the presentation of his argument. His uncompromising approach disturbed the Foreign Office which at one point characterised his response to possible joint consultations on the issue with Britain as 'uncommunicative and unwilling'.[71] Reflecting on its own policy approach which sought not to antagonise Indonesia for fear that it would become hostile to the West and hence undermine the West's position in Southeast Asia, the Foreign Office assessed that:

> It is one thing to state a preference for Dutch control over West Irian but entirely another to go bald-headed for that objective. This is what the Australians are doing, and I do not see where it will lead them except to some strain on their relations with Indonesia.
>
> If Holland and Indonesia reached a mutually satisfactory arrangement, I really do not see what justification anyone else would have for trying to upset it: nor would such action be supported by other powers. If it were Australia who tried to upset it, then we would I am sure try to use our influence discreetly to help Australia, but it would be for the sake of friendship for Australia and not out of conviction that we were acting in the best interests of ourselves or indeed of Australia, and I doubt whether we would go as far as Australia would want us to go.[72]

British Ministers also questioned whether Spender's style and presentations had the full endorsement and knowledge of the Australian Cabinet. The Foreign Office summed up Spender as difficult to manage.[73] In contrast, it assessed Menzies as 'considerably more reasonable and long-sighted over this than Spender'.[74] It understood that Menzies had accepted the idea of maintaining the status quo for two or three years 'while passions all round had cooled' but described Australia in general, and Spender in particular, as 'simply not in the mood to accept a compromise' which would associate the Indonesians with the administration of West New Guinea. It also understood from the British High Commission in Canberra that Spender had threatened to resign if the Dutch and the Indonesians were to compromise over New Guinea.[75] Privately, the Foreign Office described Spender's threat as 'very unreasonable'.[76]

For his part Spender thought he had done well in his conversations in London. He cabled Menzies that British ministers:

> fully realize now the vital significance of the issue to Australia and the force of public opinion behind the Government. I think that they will support the Dutch trusteeship. At the very least they will play to prevent any decision being arrived at for some two or three years in the hope that by that time the heat will be off the issue.[77]

A military perspective

The views expressed by Menzies and Spender in London and The Hague were supported by their military advisers. In three reports, all prepared in the wake of the outbreak of war in the Korean Peninsula, culminating in a letter from the newly appointed Minister for Defence (Philip McBride) to Menzies dated 24 October 1950, the senior military advisers concluded that it was 'strategically important to Australia that, in a major war, Dutch New Guinea should be denied to a potential enemy. There [was] no internal or external threat at present but it is possible that Indonesia may become Communist dominated or unfriendly and attempt to gain control by force'. The military advisers recommended that 'Australia should support the Dutch, if necessary with military assistance, in their stand to retain control of Dutch New Guinea'.[78] In an earlier report, the Chiefs of Staff had commented that 'from a defence point of view, the Republic of Indonesia should not be regarded as a friendly power and, in the event of a hot war, it could become Communist dominated or unfriendly'. If it gained control of Dutch New Guinea 'it is likely that Communist influence would become established there. This may lead to the spread of Communism throughout New Guinea and have a consequential effect on the defence of Australia'.[79] The introduction into Australian strategic assessments and ministerial discussions of viewing Indonesia from the perspective of being communist or non-communist was to remain a feature of assessments made from this date until the fall of President Sukarno in late 1965.

Separately, the Chiefs of Staff described the strategic importance of Dutch New Guinea as providing depth to the defence and security of Australia and as a site for potential air and naval bases for use by allied forces. The occupation of Dutch New Guinea airfields by a potential enemy would constitute a threat to Australia and her territories, including Manus Island. The sea approaches to Australia could be threatened and the Australian territories of Papua and New Guinea would be threatened with attack, which, if successful, would put the enemy in possession of areas suitable for mounting an invasion of Australia. The internal threat to those territories would be considerably increased. Indonesia lacked 'both the means and the experience for firm control and effective administration and cannot be regarded as a stable and friendly regime at present'. For these reasons the Chiefs of Staff argued it was important to the defence of Australia that Dutch New Guinea remain under the control of an allied power, preferably the Netherlands.[80]

More diplomatic pressure

Australian ministers remained uncertain and concerned as to the future course of events. The Minister for Defence (Philip McBride) told his Cabinet colleagues that he thought the Dutch would 'sell out on us' while Spender also doubted the Dutch and asked 'Can we ensure that the Dutch will stand fast?' Spender also expressed some sympathy for the idea of a trusteeship over West New Guinea, but only if it were given to the Dutch to administer. He also told his colleagues that the American and British Ambassadors in Jakarta were placing pressure on their home governments to encourage a settlement of the dispute.[81] Spender renewed his representations to the Dutch and British Governments but such was the forcefulness of the Australian representations that the British Government intervened directly with Menzies and asked that he tell Spender to refrain from 'provocative' statements.[82]

Menzies returned to London in January 1951 and again raised the West New Guinea issue with Foreign Secretary Bevin. In his response Bevin acknowledged Australia's anxiety that West New Guinea remain under 'solid, reliable' Dutch control but argued that 'in the long run Australian interests will be best served by a policy designed to retain Indonesian goodwill … even if this sooner or later involves the Australian acceptance of Indonesia as the sovereign power in Western New Guinea'. Alan Watt, Secretary of the Department of External Affairs, who was accompanying

Menzies in London, described Bevin's argument as 'completely unsatisfactory'.[83] Menzies and his colleagues similarly dismissed Bevin's suggestion.

Menzies then turned to the United States in an effort to counter the pro-settlement arguments which it was thought were being promoted by Merle Cochran, the US Ambassador in Jakarta. Menzies wrote to Secretary of State Dean Acheson on 18 January 1951. He made a brief reference to the absence of ethnic and cultural links between West New Guinea and Indonesia, pointing out that a transfer of sovereignty to Indonesia would be 'no more than the conversion of one form of colonialism into another'. He then shifted the focus to his central argument that 'New Guinea is vital to Australia' and that he had 'sometimes pondered whether we should not declare some form of Monroe Doctrine in relation to it'. In making this suggestion he was in fact repeating the idea articulated by Australian colonial leaders during the nineteenth century, by Prime Minister Deakin and by Hughes during his visit to New York in 1918 en route to the Paris Peace Conference. Menzies went on to note that 'our experience in the recent war gave us a jolt and you may take it from me that Australian public opinion is on this matter both sensitive and strong'. He acknowledged the possibility 'in the long run' of some form of joint trusteeship emerging as a solution but said it would need to be one in which the Dutch and/or Australia had a hand. He sought Acheson's assistance 'as an act of singular friendship' in delaying any decision which might see the Dutch leave and thereby 'giving us an uncomfortable neighbour in the near north'. He concluded by reminding Acheson that 'who controls Dutch New Guinea can at will infiltrate into Australian New Guinea'.[84]

Acheson replied on 7 February 1951 to Menzies's 'friendly and frank' message but gave him little real comfort. He acknowledged that the issue of Dutch New Guinea 'has been and is a source of serious concern' to Australia but said that US policy was to remain impartial and to urge a resolution through negotiations. Acheson pointed out that the primary interest of the United States was to avoid a rupture in the relationship between the Netherlands and Indonesia as this would not only be detrimental to the interests of the two countries but 'could endanger the maintenance of that stability which is essential to the security of South East Asia'. He reiterated that such a development would have consequences not only for the Netherlands and Indonesia but also 'for Australia, the United States and in fact for all those nations interested in the peace and security of the area'.[85] Acheson's letter established two points: that in American eyes the handling of the West New Guinea dispute had to be considered in the context of a broader Cold War strategy and that the United States would remain neutral and detached for as long as it could. It was a policy position shared with Britain's Labour Government. Acheson's letter did nothing to reassure Menzies and his colleagues. Menzies told a worried Cabinet on 15 February that 'the Dutch won't stand firm – the commercial interests will give way'. Moreover, he did not expect the UK Foreign Secretary to be of 'any real assistance … because he is so ill'.[86]

Menzies's exchange with the US Secretary of State and his conversations with the British Government revealed a significant factor in Australia's approach to the West New Guinea dispute. It had embarked on its policy objectives without prior consultation or agreement with its major allies. The Menzies Government had not sought their endorsement of its tactics or objectives before presenting its views so forcefully to the Dutch. Over the next ten years Menzies and his colleagues sought to persuade Washington and London of the merits of Australia's case but found both capitals lukewarm at best. London and Washington were in the difficult position of juggling a response to Australia's policy with larger strategic problems associated with the Cold War, a 'dilemma' which, according to Richard Chauvel, 'seemed little understood by Australia'.[87] Chauvel has also concluded that the West New Guinea dispute 'was one of the few policies pursued by the Menzies Government which was not initiated or supported with any enthusiasm or much interest in Washington or London'.[88] As the dispute progressed over the decade there were frequent comments by Australian Cabinet ministers in private that American support could not be taken for granted. A sense of doubt and uncertainty as to the reliability of Australia's allies contributed to a sense of unease and insecurity in the Cabinet room.

In the deteriorating security environment following the outbreak of the war in Korea the Menzies Government introduced military conscription for home service and increased the defence budget. The government took one of its few post-war decisions to improve the military preparedness of Papua and New Guinea by re-establishing the Pacific Islands Regiment (PIR) as a single battalion of the Australian Army. It had been disbanded in 1946. At the same time it re-established the European-only New Guinea Volunteer Rifles as a reserve force. Although largely a symbolic gesture given the small size of the force and its lack of real resources, these measures and the decision in 1952 to open a patrol base at Vanimo on the northern border with Dutch New Guinea and on Manus Island in 1954 reflected the attitude of a nervous Cabinet. They nevertheless sit oddly with the decision by the Australian Army in the late 1940s and the early part of the 1950s to give back to the Administration in Port Moresby most of the land it had occupied or used as bases during the war.[89]

Spender departs

Australia's anxieties continued for the remainder of 1951 and beyond. However, the style and presentation of Australia's policy changed considerably with Spender's resignation on 26 April 1951 on the grounds of ill health. He was appointed Ambassador to Washington and was replaced by R. G. Casey. Nevertheless, while in Washington for the next eight years and as a member of the Australian delegation to the annual United Nations (UN) General Assembly in this period, he continued to advocate Australia's interest in West New Guinea. In doing so he was unrelenting. In 1954 Spender told the General Assembly's First Committee that 'Australia felt its destiny and defence (was) closely bound up with West New Guinea'.[90] David Lowe has described Spender as engaging in 'diplomatic high-handedness' and using 'militant language' in his pursuit of objectives such as the ANZUS Treaty and the Colombo Plan. At the same time Lowe sees him as 'one of the most independent and innovative thinkers in Menzies's first Cabinet'.[91] Lowe has also described Spender as 'aggressive', a 'fierce advocate' and 'not easily deterred' in his advocacy of the Colombo Plan and the ANZUS Treaty.[92] It is true that Spender was tenacious but he was also overly persistent and dogged in his advocacy of Australia's position and in laying the foundations for Australia's policy towards the West New Guinea dispute. He worried both the British and Dutch Governments with his robust and 'tactless' style and was at times insensitive to their own particular interests.[93]

In a language similar to that of Hughes in 1919, Spender had launched an initiative for Australia to take Britain's place in the New Hebrides, claiming that control over the islands of the archipelago lying across Australia's north would strengthen Australia's strategic environment.[94] He had forcefully articulated a case for continued Dutch possession of West New Guinea by pointing out the security implications for Australia, and for Australia's half of New Guinea, of the newly independent but politically volatile and immature Indonesia moving closer to Australian interests. The idea of a security shield across Australia's north would, in his opinion, be greatly weakened by Indonesia assuming control of West New Guinea.

Conclusion

In his comprehensive and consummate archives-based account of the West New Guinea dispute and the international diplomacy that accompanied it, Stuart Doran has also argued that the Menzies Government's response, and particularly that of Spender, was driven by a strong belief that Australia was 'the preeminent power in the area roughly south of Singapore and as the effective colonial power of the South West Pacific. It consequently behaved in a manner it saw befitting such degrees of 'imperial' authority – aggressively and relatively independently'.[95] Doran later described the government's approach as a 'crusade' and that 'Australia approached its relations with Indonesia confident of its supremacy' while its 'self-perceived superiority' allowed it to remain independent of the United States and Britain.[96] He has developed this view further by characterising Australia as a 'middle power' that 'ruthlessly and expediently looked to use the Dutch as a political and military proxy'. Doran saw Australia's policy and Spender as 'machiavellian' – perhaps the greatest compliment able to be given to a minister and his policy objectives.[97] In his view, Australia's determination to assert a status in Southeast Asia 'south of Singapore' continued until about 1957 and then folded as both London and Washington intervened to find a solution to the dispute.

Doran's analysis of the shifts within the West New Guinea dispute is exemplary but his secondary thesis is open to criticism as being wide of the mark, especially as it applies to the islands of the South Pacific held by other powers. He has taken Richard Chauvel's description of Australia's independence from the United States and Britain and developed an interpretation which does not reflect the comments and debate subsequently able to be seen in the Cabinet Notebooks of the period nor the strategic assessments. There is little indication in these discussions that Australia was seeking such a role for itself in the region. The government allowed the idea of securing Britain's half of the New Hebrides to lapse and made no claim to the Solomon Islands. Moreover, ministers realised that Australia did not have the military capability to assert a role in Southeast Asia and were worried that the Dutch could concede their claim to West New Guinea. Spender may have sought to construct a shield across Australia's north but it had very little substance. The sense of the debates in Cabinet in this early period was of a tentative, uncertain Cabinet assessing issues from a defensive point of view and not one intent on asserting a claim to be an 'imperial' or even 'middle ranking' power in the region. Sir Garfield Barwick, Minister for External Affairs from 1961 to 1964, described Australia's policies during the 1950s as 'essentially passive in nature in the sense that we had concentrated on seeking that no one interfere with us'.[98] He added that 'when the present [Menzies] government came to office there had been also some deliberate turning away from the practice of intruding into other people's business'. A 'passive' policy was 'understandable for a country which had no territorial aims'. Nicholas Tarling, in his comprehensive account of the West New Guinea dispute, drawing extensively on British archives, makes no claim that Australia sought the role of preeminent power 'south of Singapore'. In Tarling's account, British officials did not interpret Australia's policy in such terms.[99]

The threat of communism in Asia was the major concern of the government throughout the 1950s but, in terms of its immediate security environment, Australia had replaced the pre-war focus on Japan with Indonesia, particularly a possible communist-leaning Indonesia. As Woodard has concluded, Australia's approach to Indonesia and the West New Guinea dispute was driven by 'fear ... first of New Guinea offering a route for invasion from the north and then fear of Indonesia or perhaps one day a communist Indonesia constituting a threat through sharing a common border with Australian territory or through becoming a competitor for influence in Malaysia'.[100]

Spender could not have stopped the creation of an independent Indonesia – although he may have preferred this outcome – but he was determined to frustrate its attempts to secure control over West New Guinea. He believed that New Guinea was an integral part of Australia's defence system and a barrier to an invasion of Australia. Of equal importance he had succeeded in promoting the concept that, from the perspective of Australia's security and strategic outlook, the island of New Guinea should be seen as one entity despite the fact that sovereignty over the island was divided between two powers. Spender had promoted Australia's security through the negotiation of the ANZUS Treaty signed after his resignation in September 1951 and had launched the Colombo Plan in 1950 as a means of advancing Australia's presence in Asia. His policy towards Indonesia over West New Guinea, however, showed the limits to which he was prepared to go to identify himself and Australia with the new Asia that had emerged after the Second World War. On the question of West New Guinea, Australia's fears for its security, as well as its anxiety at the idea of an Asian state becoming a neighbour in New Guinea, triumphed over its desire to promote a positive relationship with Indonesia.

Chapter 4

THE WEST NEW GUINEA DISPUTE 1952–1956

> 'The holding of Australian New Guinea is …
> vital to the defence of Australia. The aim of national
> defence policy in relation to New Guinea must therefore
> be directed to the maintenance of Australia's control of
> Australian New Guinea'.
>
> Defence Committee Report, 1956

The newly appointed Minister for External Affairs, Richard Casey, brought to the position a wealth of experience as a parliamentarian and diplomat. Born in 1890 he had served at Gallipoli and on the Western Front in the First World War. Following the war he had been sent to London as Australia's diplomatic liaison officer. Casey had first entered the Australian Parliament in 1931 and had served as Treasurer in the Lyons Government from 1935 until 1939. He held ambitions to succeed Lyons as Prime Minister but he failed to win the leadership of the United Australia Party in a contest with Robert Menzies. He had resigned from Parliament shortly after the outbreak of the Second World War to accept Menzies's offer to serve as Australia's first resident minister in Washington – in effect Australia's diplomatic representative in Washington. In 1942 he accepted Winston Churchill's invitation to serve as Britain's Minister Resident in Cairo and then, in 1944, as Governor of Bengal. In 1949, at the age of 59, Casey re-entered Parliament and was appointed Minister for Supply and Development, later renamed National Development, in the first Menzies ministry. His early years as a diplomat in London and Washington had demonstrated his remarkable ability to win and retain friendships and confidences with the widest range of counterparts. He was to exploit this capacity further as Minister for External Affairs. Casey's weakness was an inability to carry an argument in the robust world of Australian Cabinet politics and decision-making. Paul Hasluck, his ministerial colleague for ten years, described him as 'ineffective' in Cabinet.[1] Casey retired from Parliament in February 1960. He was appointed Governor-General of Australia from 1965 to 1969.

At the time of Casey's appointment as Minister for External Affairs Australia's immediate security environment was deeply troubling. Australia had 5000 troops overseas in Korea, Japan and Malaya. The war in Korea and the involvement of China represented a major threat to world peace. The Emergency in Malaya was in its third year and the communist guerilla insurgency showed little sign of easing. Australian forces were still in Korea as part of a sixteen-nation United Nations sponsored coalition, while units of the Royal Australian Air Force had been deployed to Malaya to assist the British to put down the insurgency.[2] China posed a direct challenge to the Nationalist Government on Formosa. The French faced defeat in Vietnam. In Europe, Cold War tensions remained high. On a positive note, on 1 September 1951, Australia, New Zealand and the United States signed the ANZUS Treaty with its undertaking that if an armed attack occurred in the 'Pacific area on any of the parties' each party would 'act to meet the common danger in accordance with its constitutional processes'.[3] In October 1953, at a meeting in Melbourne, allied defence planners developed further the original concepts underlying ANZAM (Australia, New Zealand and Malaya). With its focus on Malaya, ANZAM had been created to expedite planning for the deployment of British, Australian and New Zealand forces in Malaya. ANZAM cemented further the idea of a forward defence strategy as the principle underpinning Australia's military planning.[4] It also confirmed the gradual change in Australia's defence planning that had been occurring in discussions beginning in 1950 from acceptance of a role in the Middle East to involvement in a more narrowly defined region of Southeast Asia.[5] Hence events and developments north and south of Malaya, including Indonesia, became of increasing importance in Australia's strategic outlook. In 1954 Australia accepted a further commitment to assist in the defence of Southeast Asia when it signed the South East Asia Collective Defence Treaty (SEATO). SEATO brought a wider range of states interested in the security of Asia, including Britain and France, into a closer defence relationship with Australia, but proved to be a weak reed when placed under pressure.[6]

Maintaining the diplomatic campaign

Casey did not deviate from the policy on West New Guinea established by Spender. One of his first overseas visits was to Jakarta in August 1951. He did not see President Sukarno and the West New Guinea issue was not raised by any Indonesian minister. For his part Casey 'refrained from raising the issue' partly at the wish of the Dutch Government.[7] Later in the year Casey told the Indonesian Ambassador in Canberra, Dr Oetoyo, that he had to date 'observed almost superhuman discretion' with regard to Dutch New Guinea. He reminded the Ambassador that it 'was a subject on which the Australian public was likely to be explosive – and I only hoped that it would be dropped as a subject of public discussion'. Casey told the Ambassador that Australia wanted to be friends with Indonesia but that 'nothing was more likely to disturb and muddy our relations as the possibility of Dutch New Guinea becoming a gambit'.[8] He made a similar point to the Indonesian Foreign Minister, Subardjo, at a meeting in Paris in November 1951. At that meeting he had told his Indonesian counterpart that it was 'essential to the future welfare of his country and mine to avoid trouble over New Guinea, a subject on which Australians were apt to see red'.[9]

In a visit to The Hague in November 1951 Casey told the Dutch Government that 'the Australian view was unchanged. This was a subject on which Australian public opinion had the strongest views. The Australian Government was completely behind the Netherlands Government in its determination to maintain New Guinea under Dutch control'.[10] The Dutch Prime Minister, Dr Drees, told Casey that in his view the United States and the United Kingdom were at best preoccupied with other major cold-war related issues (the war in Korea was at its height) or at worse ambivalent in their commitment to the Dutch position. He encouraged Casey to lobby the Americans and to 'stress to Acheson [Secretary of State] that Australia would take it very badly if there were a change in the status quo in New Guinea'. Casey followed Menzies's example and wrote to Acheson in December 1951. On 19 January 1952, again encouraged by the Dutch who were uncertain as to the strength of Britain's commitment, he wrote to his British counterpart and good friend, the Foreign Secretary, Anthony Eden. He ignored the advice given by Bevin to Menzies in January 1951 that Australia should attach the highest priority to developing relations with Indonesia and told Eden that:

> It would be unfortunate if the Indonesians were to become our immediate and close neighbours in New Guinea. The Indonesian Government

is weak politically and militarily. Their lack of political stability is such that they might swing rather wildly to the left at any time – and might be induced to agree to immigration arrangements in respect of Dutch New Guinea that would allow Japanese and even doubtful Chinese to enter Dutch New Guinea in numbers. Moreover the terrain is such that infiltration – by Indonesians and others – into our part of New Guinea would be difficult to stop. This could well create difficult problems in respect of Australian New Guinea. All these things are well in the minds of our people here and generate a good deal of anxiety.[11]

Casey's references to Japanese migrants 'and even doubtful Chinese' was strongly reminiscent of the arguments pursued by Australian politicians over previous decades as they defended the 'White Australia' policy. The reference to infiltration by 'Indonesians and others' also reflected claims by Australians in Papua and New Guinea at the time, picked up by the Australian press and reported in alarming tones, that 'infiltrators' had been spotted crossing the border and 'spying out the land'.[12] Casey also carried forward the concept that the island of New Guinea must be assessed as one political and strategic unit rather than two political jurisdictions. What affected West New Guinea was, in Australia's mind, of direct relevance to Papua New Guinea. Casey's objective was also to keep the issue of the future of Dutch New Guinea in 'cold storage' for as long as possible. In this he repeatedly turned to the United Kingdom to lobby the United States on Australia's behalf.

Casey had his first opportunity to put Australia's case directly to President Sukarno when he visited Jakarta on 5 April 1952. Unlike Spender, Casey did not baulk at the chance. According to his diary entry Casey drew Sukarno's attention to the lessons for Australia of the Second World War. He argued that there was 'an attitude of mind in Australia that New Guinea as a whole is important to us and that we have to ensure that even West New Guinea has to be in hands that will be secure'. He sought from Sukarno a 'most confident and close relationship' but said that 'nothing was likely to disturb this relationship so quickly or so gravely as Indonesia getting sovereignty over West New Guinea. Any change in sovereignty … would set the whole Australian people aflame'. When Casey raised a concern about the likelihood that should Indonesia gain sovereignty over West New Guinea it was likely to claim the east as well, Sukarno, according to Casey's account, offered him not only his hand that it would never happen 'but my whole arm – my arm will be the forfeit that that will never happen'.[13] According to a later departmental briefing note – which made no reference to Sukarno's assurances – Casey had also told the President that 'the New Guinea issue should not be allowed to develop and cut across the close and confidential relationship necessary to stand against the threat from the north. Soekarno however remained unconvinced. … The Minister made it quite clear that Australia supported the retention of Dutch sovereignty over the area'.[14]

Despite Sukarno's personal assurance and a subsequent similar statement to the press a few months later that Indonesia 'had no aspirations towards East New Guinea – no aspirations at all' and 'There is no threat to East New Guinea and that area will not be in danger when West Irian is in Indonesian hands', Australia remained highly sceptical and mistrustful.[15] Casey again wrote to Eden informing him of his discussions with Sukarno. He again expressed his concerns 'about the possibility of infiltration into Eastern New Guinea and the particular use which might be made of Western New Guinea'. Casey added that should a 'leftist' government come to power 'all these difficulties would be amplified many times' and said that 'such a situation would create in Australia a degree of anxiety which could be explosive'.[16]

Casey did not see Indonesia in a totally negative light. Like Spender, he realised that a relationship had to be established regardless of the West New Guinea dispute. In a press statement released on 6 February 1952, in the midst of Australia's lobbying to ensure the dispute remained in 'cold storage', he said that Australia had 'every desire to work closely, harmoniously and constructively [with Indonesia] … [and] desires close and friendly relationships with Indonesia and will do its best to secure them'. He cited Australia's wish to have Indonesia join the Colombo Plan and to provide technical assistance to Indonesia as a sign of Australia's intent. He placed the relationship in the context of the joint need to deal effectively with the 'risk of an attempted southwards drive by Communism in Asia'.[17] But developing the relationship would come second to the management of the dispute over West New Guinea and on that point he reiterated firmly Australia's opposition to a change in sovereignty.

More diplomatic pressure

Menzies travelled to London in late May 1952, where he held six meetings with Prime Minister Winston Churchill and his senior ministers on international security issues, defence policy and defence procurement. Menzies briefed Churchill and Eden on the recently signed ANZUS Treaty. He described it as means for Australia to gain a closer knowledge of US strategic and military planning, particularly in Southeast Asia. He told Churchill that he was not prepared to reopen the question of the membership of ANZUS to include Britain as this could see the revival of an earlier US suggestion that the Treaty include Japan, the Philippines and Indonesia. He made clear to Churchill that 'the Australian public opinion would not tolerate the inclusion of Indonesia or Japan' in the pact.[18] Menzies was correct in his assessment of Australian public opinion.

Menzies discussed the question of West New Guinea with Eden on 3 June. He made clear his concern that the Dutch would weaken and cede the territory if Indonesia would guarantee the security of Dutch commercial interests in the country. As to the political outlook for Indonesia and the impact of absorbing West New Guinea, Menzies was explicit in his view that:

> it was very doubtful if the Indonesian Government were firmly enough established to take on a new commitment of this kind. Above all, the presence of a weak and unreliable Government on the very frontiers of Australia would make it extremely difficult for any Australian Government in the future to accept overseas commitments in war. It was most important that the Dutch Government should be encouraged to stand firm.[19]

Eden undertook to continue to do 'everything in his power' to hold the Dutch to their position and to encourage the United States to remain supportive. In a letter from Eden to Casey dated 24 June 1952, Eden told Casey that he had raised the issue with Secretary of State Acheson, reminding him that Casey had 'written stressing the strength of Australian public opinion against any change of sovereignty in Netherlands New Guinea'. Acheson had 'entirely agreed' that the issue should be left in 'cold storage' and that 'there had been no change in the American point of view on the subject'. Eden told Casey that he could see no 'reason why you, we and the Americans should not continue to maintain a united front on this issue'.[20]

The reference in Menzies's meeting with Eden to the difficulty Australia would face in accepting any future overseas commitment in war reflected discussions which had been underway in Canberra for a number of months about whether Australia could maintain its post-war commitment to deploy forces to the Middle East given the deteriorating military outlook in Asia.[21] Menzies had made clear to Churchill in their meeting on 27 May that:

> If ... before a world war started the whole of South-East Asia had been lost to Communism and Chinese Communist influence had spread into Indonesia and New Guinea, it would be very difficult for any Australian Government to support a policy for sending Divisions and Air Forces to the Middle East in war.[22]

He was more explicit in his second meeting with Churchill on 29 May when he said that 'if communism had spread through South-East Asia and Indonesia, it would be difficult for any Australian Government to send forces overseas'.[23]

The six meetings had enabled Menzies to alert his British counterparts to Australia's decision to refocus its strategic outlook and priorities. David Lowe has suggested that Menzies had yet to be fully convinced of the need to redirect Australia's war effort away from a contribution to allied efforts in the Middle East and to Southeast Asia.[24] The strength of his argument in London would indicate that by mid-1952 he had made that adjustment and, as Peter Edwards has argued in his study of the development of the concept of 'forward defence' in Australia's security outlook, the government was now focused on the need to meet the challenges emerging in Asia.[25] The discussions in London had also allowed Menzies to press the point that the Australian public would object if Australian forces were to be deployed to distant areas such as the Middle East should Southeast Asia came under threat. He did, however, temper the negative nature of this message by advising the British Government of his government's decision to strengthen Australia's defence preparedness with the Navy to be increased to 17,000 men with 10,000 in reserve, the Army to be increased from 26,000 to 33,000 regular troops plus a citizen force of 97,000 including 67,500 National Service trainees, and the Air Force to be strengthened to 17 squadrons and 17,000 men.[26] Menzies did not comment on whether Australia could sustain this level of preparedness but he appeared to be a little more confident of Australia's defence readiness than in 1950 when he had told his Cabinet colleagues that 'we have an extensive building programme but we don't build anything which we want'.[27]

Despite the reassurances from Eden, the Menzies Cabinet continued to fear that a change of government or a new coalition of ministers in The Hague might lead to a change in policy. In part these concerns were allayed by the visit to Canberra in July 1953 of the Dutch Minister for Foreign

Affairs, Joseph Luns. Luns, whom Casey described as a 'great big pleasant intelligent extrovert', had been, and continued throughout the decade to be, the most determined and immovable advocate of Dutch policy towards retaining sovereignty.[28] His visit coincided with the presentation in Canberra of a Dutch aide memoire which stated that sovereignty over Dutch New Guinea continued to be vested in the Netherlands; the Netherlands would be prepared to give a guarantee that West New Guinea would not be used as a basis for action against Indonesia; the Netherlands was resolved to resist Indonesian actions directed against Dutch New Guinea; and the Netherlands was willing to cooperate with countries interested in the South Pacific.[29] Luns told Casey that he had been 'loudly applauded' by the New South Wales (Labor) Government at a luncheon when he had said the Netherlands intended to retain New Guinea 'for all eternity'.[30]

Luns's conversations with Casey concentrated on areas for cooperation between the two territories and he appears to have raised the issue of defence and military cooperation only in a private meeting with Alan Watt, Secretary of the Department of External Affairs, and then only in the broader context of defence arrangements in the Pacific. Luns had told Watt that 'the Dutch would, if necessary, defend New Guinea and were quite capable of doing so'.[31] It appears that Luns may have been more serious in his wish for a defence agreement with Australia than the report of his meeting with Watt suggests. In 1955 Alfred Stirling, who had been Ambassador in The Hague in 1953, recalled in a letter to Casey that 'Luns was anxious to bind the Dutch Government by a defence agreement with us for N. G. [New Guinea]'.[32] There is no other evidence available to elaborate on what Luns had in mind or how the issue was managed.

The fact that Luns had not raised the question of possible defence cooperation with Australia covering West New Guinea did not stop a suspicious Indonesian Government from speculating that both countries had entered into such an arrangement. Indonesia eventually sought an assurance from Luns that no 'treaty' had been entered into and that Australia's cooperation with the Netherlands extended only to administrative arrangements.[33]

Australian ministers nevertheless remained anxious that the Dutch could change their policy approach and seek a settlement with Indonesia. Alfred Stirling provided Casey with a number of reports on the strength of views of members of the Dutch Parliament. In an assessment of the visit by Luns to Canberra, Stirling told Casey of Luns's positive reaction to his meetings in Australia but, at the same time, warned that 'Luns (had) put Dutch parliamentary feeling about the retention of New Guinea a good deal too high. ... He is too optimistic'.[34] Stirling later advised Casey that 'Dutch opinion for the retention of New Guinea can never be taken for granted without our constant attention. ... (a change in attitude) could happen quickly'.[35] The question of whether the Dutch could pull out or be forced to compromise weighed heavily on the minds of ministers and featured in a number of discussions in the Cabinet room throughout the decade.

A revised strategic assessment

The views expressed by Menzies in London formed the foundation of the Strategic Basis Paper on Australian Defence Policy endorsed by the Defence Committee on 8 January 1953.[36] The paper confirmed the shift in focus from the Middle East to Southeast Asia. It emphasised the importance of holding Indochina for the defence of Southeast Asia and for providing 'defence in depth' to Australia and New Zealand.[37] It attached critical importance to defending Malaya. If Malaya fell in a global war a 'steady infiltration of communists throughout the islands of Indonesia could follow' and Australia would be 'confronted in due course by hostile land and air forces within 500 miles of the Northern Territory and have a common frontier with the communists in New Guinea'.[38] Even in a Cold War scenario it argued that if Malaya were lost and the communists 'successfully infiltrate throughout Indonesia, the threat to sea communications would be increased and a direct air threat to the mainland of Australia would exist'.[39] Australia would have to respond with 'ground forces for the occupation of the Island Chain (Admiralty Islands [Manus Island], New Guinea, the coastal waters of North and North-West Australia and the Cocos Islands)' as well as forces for the defence of sea communications.[40] The paper endorsed the concept of defending Australia through a system of frontiers or perimeters beginning in northeast Asia and descending first to Malaya, then the island of New Guinea and finally the northern coastline of Australia.[41] Malaya was the key barrier in the perimeter. The concepts were captured in the subsequent planning undertaken under the aegis of ANZAM. They had become central to Australia's thinking about its outer defence perimeter.

Cabinet again anxious

In August 1954 Cabinet again examined Australia's approach to the West New Guinea issue following reports that Indonesia intended to take its claim to the United Nations.[42] Ministers were suspicious. Casey told them of comments he had heard that Indonesia had 'thoughts of Australian New Guinea, Timor and British North Borneo'.[43] He did not provide any evidence as to the source of these comments but they were sufficient to cause alarm. Casey argued that if Indonesia were successful it would set a precedent for India to 'pinch off' Portuguese Goa to which Menzies added that 'Goa [would be] a precedent for Hong Kong, then New Guinea, then Malaya'.[44] John McEwen (Minister for Commerce and Agriculture) was equally suspicious and commented that the United States 'probably think we're right but will ditch us [Australia] to maintain *persona grata* with Indonesia to combat communism'.[45] Ministers were equally alarmed at the prospect of Indonesia succeeding in securing sufficient votes in the UN General Assembly to force negotiations. Menzies told his colleagues that 'if UN votes West New Guinea to Indonesia – then ours', i.e. Papua New Guinea, would become the subject of debate in the United Nations with some countries arguing for independence. McEwen added a strange twist to the scenario by noting that 'West New Guinea under Indonesia will endeavor to bring in Japs'. McEwen's comments reflected the concern contained in Casey's letter to Eden in January 1952 and the deep-seated Australian fear of Asian states and populations coming into ever closer proximity to Australia and Australian interests. Menzies concluded the discussion by noting that Australia should again speak to the United States and Britain at the forthcoming SEATO meeting on the 'implications of New Guinea on Australia's capacity to take [a] hand in SEATO, for with Indonesia in possession of New Guinea Australia must go entirely on the defensive and be last to making a contribution to South East Asia'.[46]

In the discussions in Cabinet Menzies had also raised in an incidental way the question of purchasing Dutch New Guinea. McEwen and Senator William Spooner (Minister for National Development and a powerful figure within the New South Wales Branch of the Liberal Party) supported the idea ('Aye, Aye') but Casey pointed out that it would 'land us with a bone of contention with Indonesia'.[47] The formal minute prepared to capture the outcome of the debate noted that Cabinet had discussed the question of possibly buying West New Guinea but had agreed that while 'there was a lot to be said' for this option 'if that were possible', it would put Australia into the dispute with Indonesia in place of the Dutch'.[48]

Throughout the remainder of the decade Australian diplomacy was focused on efforts to block attempts by Jakarta to have the United Nations call on Indonesia and the Netherlands to negotiate a settlement of the issue.

Australia sought and gained the support of Britain with the Foreign Office instructing its diplomatic missions to lobby on behalf of the Australian objectives. In November 1954 Casey also wrote directly to the newly appointed US Under Secretary of State, Herbert Hoover Jnr, seeking US support in the United Nations. The letter was a continuation of the effort begun by Menzies in 1951 to secure United States support for Australia's stance. Casey again set out in detail all the arguments which had characterised Australia's representations to date: the whole of the island was a 'vital part of the island chain in the Western Pacific'; if it passed 'into the hands of a government of doubtful stability and sympathies the strength of the island chain would be endangered'; Australia's situation if New Guinea passed to Indonesia would be 'serious'; Indonesia's attitude to opposing communism did not 'inspire ... great confidence'; Dutch control 'ensures the preservation of the eventual freedom of choice of the inhabitants'; the Netherlands Government 'is in a far better position from a financial, scientific and administrative point of view to benefit the indigenous population'; Indonesia had no claim on 'ethnic grounds'; public opinion in Australia was 'understandably strong as a result of the events of the war against Japan – and before that, of our military problems with the Germans in the first war'; and Australia 'cannot and will not countenance' the transfer of sovereignty to Indonesia. Casey concluded by noting 'I cannot stress too strongly the vital interest which the Australian Government has in this matter'.[49] Casey's arguments reflected Australia's deepening suspicions towards Indonesia and a continued preference for the status quo.

The Australian approach placed the United States in an awkward position. The Truman and Eisenhower Administrations had followed a policy of non-involvement. The United States did not wish to offend either of the principals (the Netherlands or Indonesia) while at the same time it understood the attitude of countries such as Australia. Its first priority, as Secretary of State Dulles explained to Menzies in March 1955, was in 'keeping Indonesia with its 80 million people from falling into Communist hands'. However, 'if it came to a real showdown about New Guinea, then the United States would back Australia 'right or wrong'.[50]

Casey continued to be sensitive to the problems created by Australia's firm stance on the West New Guinea dispute for the development of a bilateral relationship with Indonesia. In June 1955 he told his Cabinet colleagues:

> So long as the West New Guinea issue is outstanding between us – for at any rate the foreseeable future – we must take it as a fact that

this may prejudice friendly relations between Australia and Indonesia, that it impedes cooperation, that it will be a focus of discontent in Indonesia not only against Australia but to some extent against the West generally, and that it will be a theme on which Communist propaganda can play and on which Communist and anti-Western feeling can centre.[51]

Casey argued, and his colleagues accepted, that Australia would be facing a difficult battle at successive meetings of the UN General Assembly to deny Indonesia the two-thirds majority it needed to secure acceptance of its resolution calling for negotiations between it and the Dutch. In a wide-ranging discussion of policy options, ministers rejected the idea that the dispute might be referred to the International Court of Justice for adjudication. Menzies told his colleagues such a move would be a 'complete gamble' and that he had 'no faith' in an approach to the Court. Paul Hasluck (Minister for Territories) agreed with Menzies and added that an approach to the Court would 'admit doubts as to sovereignty', while McEwen thought such a step by Australia would 'allow an outside body to hand Dutch New Guinea to potential communists'.[52] (Ministers abandoned their concerns in 1959 when, in discussion with the visiting Indonesian Foreign Minister, Menzies and others suggested Indonesia take the issue to the Court. See Chapter 5.)

As the discussion in Cabinet continued Menzies reiterated the argument that 'it is vital that there be no Communist Government adjacent to Australian territory and that is possible. ... Australian public opinion will be revolted if they get access'. The Minister for Defence (McBride) agreed with his colleagues that the issue was 'vital' for Australia but argued that Australia had to 'do more than talk'. He suggested a program of cooperation with the Dutch on subjects such as trade and communications. He called for 'physical help not eloquent speeches'. Hasluck agreed that Australia should discuss with the Dutch enhanced cooperation between the two halves of the island and posed the question of whether we 'are prepared to envisage linking East and West New Guinea [and] say jointly with Dutch we are working to objective – in far future – to unification'. He accepted that such a proposal 'involves [a] trick of placing [the] fate of our territory in same basket as Dutch New Guinea'. Menzies endorsed McBride and Hasluck's idea of discussions with the Dutch.[53]

Casey continued to grapple with the two seemingly incompatible goals of strengthening the bilateral relationship with Indonesia and maintaining the government's policy on West New Guinea. He again visited Indonesia from 29 October to 2 November 1955. Prior to the visit the Indonesian Government had sent out feelers through India and the United States suggesting that it was prepared to enter into a Treaty of Friendship with Australia.[54] Casey and his department elected to respond to the suggestion by noting that it was 'something Australia did not do'.[55] In Canberra's eyes it was something third world or communist countries sought as a means of furthering a diplomatic relationship. Instead, it agreed to an Indonesian initiative that the two Foreign Ministers issue a Joint Statement on the bilateral relationship. The four paragraph statement issued during Casey's visit noted that the two countries were 'close neighbours and having a wide range of interests in common should make joint efforts to develop the greatest possible degree of cooperation'. The two ministers also declared that the two countries would 'respect each other's independence and territorial integrity and abstain from intervention or interference in each other's affairs'. Finally, on the critical issue of West New Guinea, the two ministers agreed that 'whilst maintaining their respective views … the matter should be dealt with by peaceful discussion and with the firm desire to uphold peace and stability in the South East Asian area'.[56]

In guidance sent to Australian diplomatic missions Casey said the reference to 'peaceful discussion' did not represent a change in Australia's policy. Australia continued to recognise Dutch sovereignty over West New Guinea and preferred to leave the issue in 'cold storage' and to 'concentrate on developing positive measures of cooperation'.[57] The Dutch, nevertheless, objected strongly to the reference to 'discussions'. Luns called in the Australian Ambassador to object. He saw the expression as implying doubt over Dutch sovereignty and was adamant that there 'could not and would not be any discussion whatsoever on the question of the sovereignty of West New Guinea'.[58] This would not be the last time that an effort by Casey to put on paper the Australian Government's views on the terms of a settlement would cause him diplomatic and political difficulties. He was to experience a similar controversy in 1959 when the Indonesian Foreign Minister, Dr Subandrio, visited Australia.

A mid-decade review

For six years Australia had been pursuing a twin policy of developing the bilateral relationship with Indonesia while maintaining support for the continuation of Dutch sovereignty over Dutch New Guinea. Government officials, particularly those in the Department of External Affairs, were acutely aware that the attempt to build the relationship was being frustrated by Australia's rejection of Indonesia's claims. K. C. O. (Mick) Shann, a senior officer in the Department of External Affairs, who had represented Australia as an observer at the Asian-African Conference of newly independent states at Bandung, Indonesia, in May 1955, had told Canberra that 'there does not seem to be much doubt that our good relations with Indonesia rest on a solution to the problem of West New Guinea'. Moreover, it was time for Australia to 'make an assessment as to whether the continued presence of the Dutch in Western New Guinea is more important to our security than friendly relations with Indonesia'.[59] He urged Canberra to take the initiative and suggest to the Dutch that they discuss the issue with Indonesia. Even Spender, writing from Washington, had suggested to the newly appointed Secretary of the Department of External Affairs, Arthur Tange, that, although still fully supportive of continued Dutch control over West New Guinea, he believed a 'thorough re-examination of the problem was necessary'.[60]

While not responding directly to Shann's and Spender's suggestions, Tange was receptive to the idea of a fundamental reassessment of the principles and assumptions underlying Australia's strategic assessment of Dutch New Guinea. He wrote to the Secretary of the Department of Defence (Sir Frederick Shedden) on 13 March 1956 suggesting that the Defence Committee prepare a new appreciation of the strategic importance of the island of New Guinea.[61]

In his letter, Tange, who possessed one of the finest analytical minds in the Australian public service, at first deconstructed the arguments which had characterised all post-war assessments. He noted that Australia's support for the retention of Dutch or 'friendly' control over West New Guinea was 'the foundation of a most important area of Australia's external political policy'. At the same time, the issue of sovereignty over West New Guinea was the 'major obstacle in the way of good relations between Australia and Indonesia' and that it would continue to be so as the issue was now one of 'national aspiration' for all Indonesian political parties, even the moderate parties. He argued that should a 'left-wing extremist Government under the dominance of Sukarno be formed we could expect the claim to be taken up and made a serious issue with Australia'. Tange was worried that a left-leaning, if not communist, government could emerge in Indonesia which would be 'more neutralist and relatively unfriendly'. As to the Dutch, Tange questioned whether it should be regarded that 'any future Netherlands Government will necessarily pursue as firm a policy as the present Drees Government'. Moreover, 'consideration of Australian wishes is unlikely to affect Netherlands decisions, if only because Australia is regarded in part responsible for the loss of Indonesia from Netherlands' colonial control'.

Tange argued for a new appreciation based on the 'balance of advantages and disadvantages' of the strategic significance of West New Guinea 'in the defence of Australia and in relation to the SEATO area'. He suggested the appreciation needed to consider the 'whole island, the inter-relationship of the two parts and their individual relationship to the whole island'. He specifically asked the review to examine 'the tenability of Eastern New Guinea if West New Guinea were occupied by hostile forces'.[62]

The Defence Committee issued its report in May 1956. It set out the most comprehensive description of Papua New Guinea's strategic importance to Australia. In doing so it often returned to language similar to that used before and during the First World War. It argued that:

> Australian New Guinea provides a most suitable area from which to launch air and sea attacks on the vital east coast of Australia and the communications to it, and would also provide the best area for mounting an invasion of eastern Australia. It also provides Australia and her Allies with potential forward bases from which operations could be mounted against attacks from the northwest. Conversely, while it remains in our hands, it provides additional depth for the defence of Australia and is essential in our last outer ring of defence, i.e. Cocos Island–Darwin–New Guinea–Manus. Moreover, Australian New Guinea is a vital link between Australia and the chain of islands through the Philippines to Japan, all of which are closely associated with the United States system of defence in the Western Pacific. The holding of Australian New Guinea is therefore vital to the defence of Australia. The aim of national defence policy in relation to New Guinea must therefore be directed to the maintenance of Australia's control of Australian New Guinea.[63]

In examining the relationship between the two halves of the island the report argued that 'the security of Australian New Guinea depends largely on Dutch New Guinea being occupied by a power which is neither hostile nor potentially hostile to Australia'. In friendly hands Dutch New Guinea provided greater depth for the defence of Australia and Australian New Guinea, bases which could be used by Australian and allied forces, and an assurance that sea and air bases in West New Guinea would be denied to a potential enemy. In contrast, in hostile, or potentially hostile, hands it could be possible for 'subversive and/or hostile elements to be infiltrated into Australian New Guinea which could, in time, create a serious threat to internal security'. Moreover, Dutch New Guinea could be used as a base, in time of war, from which sea, land and air operations could be mounted against Australian New Guinea. It was therefore 'most important for the defence of Australian New Guinea and the Island Chain that Dutch New Guinea should not be controlled by or available to a hostile or potentially hostile power'.[64]

The report then focused on the question of a communist or non-communist Indonesia and made clear that 'only if it were certain that in the long term Indonesia would remain non-communist could her control of Dutch New Guinea be strategically acceptable'. It was 'essential that a communist Indonesia should not obtain control of territory of strategic importance for the close defence of Australia'. Such a possibility was 'strategically unacceptable'.[65]

In one of its most significant recommendations, the members of the Defence Committee made clear their view that Australia should 'afford military support to the Dutch or other friendly government' should a hostile or potentially hostile government attempt to assume control of Dutch New Guinea 'by force'. They also recommended that if the threat of an attack became apparent or a communist government gained power in Indonesia, then Australia should seek defence talks with the Netherlands and other friendly governments 'with a view to ensuring the successful defence of Dutch New Guinea'.[66] The question of whether Australia should assist the Dutch militarily would become a critical issue over the next few years and generate a degree of confusion amongst Australia's allies.

Reiterating a point made by Menzies to Eden in 1952, the Committee set out in greater detail than previously the argument that Australia might have to choose between its commitments to its allies under SEATO and its obligation to defend Papua New Guinea, or at least divide its resources between the two. A threat to Papua New Guinea, for example through infiltration by Indonesia or the use of bases to stage 'nuisance raids … would have the effect of tying down Australian forces and thus weakening Australia's capacity to contribute to regional arrangements for collective defence in South East Asia'.

The 1956 report was the most comprehensive assessment to date of the place of Papua New Guinea in Australia's strategic outlook and the importance of the relationship between the two halves of the island. Committee members had reasserted the judgement that the island was 'vital' to the defence of Australia. They had also sustained the argument that New Guinea had a role both as a shield preventing an attack and as a staging area to help Australia deploy to Southeast Asia. There were also further indications of an awareness of the serious strain on Australia's limited defence capabilities should it be required to commit forces to regional security arrangements, while at the same time provide for the defence of Papua New Guinea. However, building on these conclusions, the report had emphasised the pivotal role of Indonesia in the strategic assessment of New Guinea and the deep concerns felt by defence planners about the consequences for Australia's strategic environment should Indonesia fall under the control of communists. Casey made clear his views when he told his Canadian counterpart, Lester Pearson, that a change in the status of West New Guinea 'would profoundly affect Australia's position in our own adjoining dependent territories and affect our ability to commit defence forces outside Australia. Australia will take no risks with a land frontier with a neighbour who could go communist'.[67]

Conclusion

The first six years of Menzies's prime ministership had seen the establishment of the principles guiding Australia's regional security policy. Menzies had come to accept that Australia's defence planning and commitments were no longer to be as a participant in an allied defence response in the Middle East but instead the focus was Southeast Asia and, in particular, Malaya. In 1953 the concept of ANZAM had been given greater clarification with the outer perimeter of Australia's defence and strategic area of concern now centred on Malaya. As Peter Edwards has noted, 'from 1953 Australia insisted that its military commitments would only be in what Menzies had much earlier called the "near north"'.[68] Australia's views as to the place of the island of New Guinea in its security environment had also been reasserted. Australia had continued its active diplomatic campaign with visits by Menzies and Casey to London, The Hague and Washington while Casey had set out in detail Australia's views directly to Sukarno in April 1952 – the first formal presentation by an Australian minister to the Indonesian President. A mid-decade strategic review had confirmed that Australian New Guinea was 'vital' to Australia's defence and that its security in turn was largely dependent on West New Guinea being occupied by a friendly power.

The attitudes of the members of the Menzies Cabinet had been largely formed from their experiences in the Second World War. In Menzies's first post-war Cabinet ten of his seventeen ministerial colleagues had held ministerial posts during his wartime government from 1939 to 1941. In the election of 1949, thirty-four of the fifty new Liberal/Country Party members had served in the war.[69] The memories of the invasion of Malaya, Netherlands East Indies and New Guinea influenced the government's decision-making throughout the 1950s.

Menzies, Spender and then Casey had promoted Australia's rejection of Indonesia's claim to hold sovereignty over West New Guinea using arguments based almost solely on security but reinforced by references to race, ethnicity and international law. The Australian Government told its allies that its strategic environment and its responsibility for the defence of Papua New Guinea would be severely compromised should Indonesia assume control of West Guinea. Reflecting a psychology developed during the Second World War, Australian ministers believed that the continued presence of a stable, reliable and friendly Netherlands in West New Guinea was of critical importance to Australia. An unreliable and possibly pro-communist Indonesia was not an acceptable alternative. Indeed, it was a dangerous option that had to be frustrated.

Chapter 5

THE WEST NEW GUINEA DISPUTE 1956–1959

'Let the Dutch out and the Indonesians in – how long would it be before we are fighting for Australian New Guinea[?]'.

Robert Menzies, 1958

'East New Guinea is ours and what we own we fight for'.

John McEwen, August 1958

The disagreement over the status of West New Guinea continued without any apparent prospect of resolution. Meanwhile Indonesia's leadership confronted serious internal dissent while Australia faced a changing world in Asia. The French had withdrawn from Indochina and the threat of communist expansion in the region had intensified. Australia's defence planning remained focused on Malaya as the pivotal element of the ANZAM barrier but the attention of Australian politicians rarely shifted from Indonesia.

At the end of May 1956 Menzies left Australia to attend a Commonwealth Prime Ministers Conference in London and to visit Washington and Ottawa. He had also accepted an invitation to visit Jakarta (and other Asian capitals) and preparations were well in hand for a visit to the Indonesian capital in August. The crisis over the nationalisation of the Suez Canal by President Nasser erupted while Menzies was in the United States and he returned to London where he was invited to chair a ministerial committee representing canal users and travel to Cairo to present the terms of a possible settlement to the dispute. Menzies's efforts were rebuffed by Nasser. His involvement in the Suez Crisis lasted until mid-September. As a result he was forced to abandon his proposed visit to Indonesia. An opportunity was thus lost for the first visit by an Australian Prime Minister to Indonesia and the possibility of building a firmer foundation for the bilateral relationship.[1] A further three years would pass before Menzies was able to visit Jakarta. He did, however, undertake the first visit by an Australian Prime Minister to the Territory of Papua and New Guinea from 24 to 28 April 1957 visiting Port Moresby, Rabaul and Lae.

Menzies' later description of his dealings with President Nasser are noteworthy because they anticipate the comments he was subsequently to make about President Sukarno. Menzies told his Cabinet colleagues on his return to Canberra that Nasser 'is full of himself. He has pulled noses over the Canal and is looking for fresh worlds to conquer. ... They [the UK] know that unless Nasser is cut back to size you will have a new Empire in the Middle East. My view is that we have to remember that you must not underestimate Nasser. He's had a victory over great powers'.[2] Menzies was to employ similar language about President Sukarno as the West New Guinea dispute escalated and was then followed by Indonesia's policy of Confrontation towards the newly created Malaysia.

Sukarno was equally active on the international scene. In the year following the Bandung Conference he visited the Soviet Union, China, Yugoslavia, Czechoslovakia and the United States where he met President Eisenhower. However, Sukarno's main preoccupation in the period 1956 to 1959 was with the chronic internal political problems facing Indonesia as the country moved from one coalition government to another and faced serious and destabilising revolts from dissident groups within the army in Sumatra, Sulawesi and other outer islands of Indonesia. Sukarno eventually emerged from these tumultuous events with greater, near autocratic power. In doing so he removed many of the democratic features of the Indonesian constitution and replaced them with his concept of 'Guided Democracy'.

In this period Sukarno also embarked on an increasingly dramatic campaign to harass and undermine Dutch economic activity in Indonesia. In 1954 he dissolved the Dutch-Indonesia Union and nationalised two major Dutch-owned utility companies. In 1956 he abrogated the Round Table Conference Agreements, repudiated all remaining government debts to the Netherlands and imposed a tax of over 50 per cent on Dutch businesses and increased to 60 per cent the charges on transferring funds to the Netherlands. He also acquired the shares the Dutch airline company KLM had held in the local airline, Garuda. In December 1957 the government seized Dutch companies operating in Indonesia and expropriated Dutch plantations. In 1960 Indonesia broke off diplomatic relations with the Netherlands and launched a more aggressive and threatening campaign to secure West New Guinea.

Sukarno also initiated a number of significant arms purchases, turning to the Soviet Union and its satellites, although some of the purchases were matched by deliveries from Britain and the United States. The possibility that the communist party could secure an influential role in the government and its leaders be brought into the Cabinet became a constant theme in discussions in Canberra and in military assessments of the future of the country.

A new strategic outlook: a sharper focus

Menzies arrived in Australia on 16 September 1956 and immediately faced a number of critical decisions regarding Australia's defence and strategic policies. On 10 October 1956, a month after his return, Cabinet examined the newly drafted 'Strategic Basis of Australian Defence Policy'.[3] As an indication of the pace of change in Australia's strategic environment this was the third to be presented to the Menzies Cabinet since it had taken office six years earlier. The assessment gave greater emphasis than previously to the threat posed by communist advances in Asia. It made clear that 'the first line of Australia's defence lies in South East Asia and no major threat to her security can develop … whilst Malaya is held'.[4] It argued that should Malaya be lost, Australian forces would be required to undertake operations 'to prevent key areas, particularly in New Guinea, coming under Communist control or the control of Indonesia either by means short of war or through a limited war'.[5] Similarly, Australia's forward defence would have to be 'based on north western Australia and areas in Dutch New Guinea including the Vogelkop Peninsula … whilst the Admiralty Islands [Manus Islands] and Australian New Guinea contain significant supporting bases which must be secured'.[6] It also noted that the dispute over West New Guinea 'remains a serious source of friction in our relations with Indonesia'.[7]

Ministers discussed the Strategic Basis Paper on 22 February 1957. The Minister for Defence (Philip McBride) told his colleagues that 'the fact that communism has been stopped in Europe increases the danger in Asia'. McBride argued that Australia's defence focus had shifted to Asia and suggested that in this environment 'the whole object of the exercise is to play our part in helping countries in Southeast Asia to build themselves up and to have confidence'.[8] Ministers were united in their view that Australia's security environment was now firmly set in Asia. Hasluck, now a senior member of the Cabinet, expressed some scepticism as to the reliability of the United States in defending the Pacific. He told his colleagues that 'we can rely on the US to rely on self interest but if it does not coincide with ours we can't rely on it in that respect'.[9] Senator William Spooner (Minister for National Development) shared Hasluck's doubts while Menzies was confident that the United States would 'fight for us and with us' and believed that it was becoming a 'little more understanding on Dutch New Guinea ... all we can do is to keep nudging them on Indonesia'.[10]

While all present accepted the broad terms of the strategic assessment, ministers showed a great reluctance to provide the defence force with an increase in its budget. Instead, they looked for savings and began to identify the cessation of the National Service training program as a cost-saving measure. Only Casey registered a note of concern when he drew attention to the defence force's budget of just less than £200 million for each of the past few years. He told his Cabinet colleagues that Australia 'could not send more than a battalion or so overseas and the Air Force could not fight a serious war for very long.'[11] At an earlier Cabinet meeting Casey had put it to the Defence Minister (McBride): 'Isn't it true that we couldn't send a single infantry brigade overseas without equipment?' to which McBride had replied: 'Yep – true'.[12]

The reluctance to increase the defence budget reflected a deeper argument within Cabinet over the priority to be given to the economic and social development of Australia versus the funding of defence preparedness. Hasluck best captured the sentiment when he told his colleagues 'what the US thinks, is no reason for a defence vote out of line with our economy. A stable economy is as useful as another battalion'.[13] McEwen, in particular, repeatedly voiced his opposition to a redirection of the budget away from national economic development to fund increased defence preparedness. However, by the early 1960s, he was to become the most consistent advocate in Cabinet for the deployment of forces overseas if and when asked to contribute to an allied defence effort. As Peter Edwards has argued, the limits placed on the defence budget and the priority attached to national development 'required the government to place an even greater emphasis on Australia's alliances to ensure its security. ... Australia could not defend itself'.[14]

A strain in the relationship

The issue of pursuing the two seemingly incompatible goals of developing a bilateral relationship with Indonesia and denying Indonesia's claim to West New Guinea continued to pose problems for Australia. The always unpredictable and erratic Indonesian Foreign Minister, Dr Subandrio, had told the newly arrived Australian Ambassador, Lawrence (Jim) McIntyre, that the issue was one on which 'the Indonesian Government was prepared for the present to agree to differ with Australia and not let it interfere with our good relations in other directions'.[15] McIntyre reassured Subandrio that this was also Australia's position. McIntyre was not, however, confident that the issue could be separated from the development of the bilateral relationship. Sukarno, after all, had told McIntyre in October that the issue of West New Guinea had created a 'great gulf' between Indonesia and Australia.[16] In November, McIntyre wrote to Casey and commented that 'we (Australia) can never cut any ice here as long as we are identified with Dutch obstinacy'. He added that Australia's past record of having supported Indonesia's push for independence was 'likely to be a wasting asset' and that 'our absolute and reiterated inflexibility is bound to tell more and more against us'. McIntyre concluded by advising Casey that 'without wanting to sound too alarmist I feel bound to suggest that the possibility of a steady and perhaps even accelerated deterioration in Australian–Indonesian relations will have to be weighed against the virtues of our present course'.[17]

Menzies and his colleagues understood McIntyre's assessment but were not prepared to change course. Instead Australia continued to look for international support for its policy towards Indonesia and the West New Guinea dispute. At the ANZUS Council meeting in Washington in October 1957 ministers listened to a pessimistic assessment from senior US officials, including the head of the Central Intelligence Agency, Allen Dulles, of the political situation in Indonesia and the growing influence of the Soviet Union on Sukarno. Dulles accepted that Sukarno was not a communist but thought that Sukarno believed he could use the communists to his advantage. Such was the delicate state of Indonesian politics that the United States did not wish to intervene overtly for fear of tipping it in the wrong direction, although it was prepared to sponsor clandestine activities in the outer islands. Similarly, despite arguments offered by both Casey and

Australia's Ambassador to Washington, Spender, the United States declined to change its voting record in the General Assembly from abstaining on the annual Indonesian resolution on West New Guinea for fear of sending the wrong signal to Jakarta. Secretary of State John Foster Dulles did accept that it 'would be contrary to the security interests of the United States for West New Guinea to come under Indonesian rule, especially if the threat of communist control was present. It would bring Indonesia closer to Australia and be a breach in the offshore island chain'.[18] The United States continued to assess Indonesia and the West New Guinea dispute in the context of the Cold War and the threat of further communist advancement in Asia. It was preoccupied with the communist threat in Laos and the aftermath of the defeat of the French in Vietnam. It was not prepared to change its now established policy of non-involvement nor change its vote in the General Assembly.

Indonesia's actions against Dutch interests, including the confiscation of property and the threatened expulsion of Dutch citizens, accelerated in the wake of a further defeat of the Indonesian resolution at the General Assembly. At this time Sukarno also launched a major reform of the Indonesian constitution under the guise of 'Guided Democracy' which, in effect, gave him near-undisputed political power but also raised the possibility that he could invite the communist party into his government. In this climate of uncertainty and confusion the Australian Cabinet met on 11 December 1957 to examine how it should respond to the Indonesian actions against the Dutch. The meeting, however, soon turned into a debate over the role of the United States and its policy towards both the dispute and to the internal political situation in Indonesia. In doing so it highlighted a shift in the thinking of some senior ministers towards Asia and Australia's relations with Asia in general and with Indonesia in particular.

Menzies described Indonesia's actions against the Dutch as a 'serious situation of outstanding importance'. He queried America's insistence on remaining neutral. Perhaps still smarting from American actions during the Suez Crisis, he commented that the Americans had 'taken neutrality … to great lengths – for all we know they are preparing for the obsequies now'.[19] Harold Holt (Minister for Labour and National Service) agreed that the internal political situation in Indonesia looked 'unstable and dangerous well into the future'.

Ministers took particular offence at a newspaper report that suggested the United States had offered to mediate between the Dutch and the Indonesians. Casey and others were unable to confirm the report which led McEwen to express his alarm at being denied this advice by the United States. He warned that 'this [was] the first time Australia has been precipitated into a world crisis in a direct fashion. ... We are in the front row – world must watch our attitude – we mustn't fumble'.[20] He then went on to set out the two principles which guided his thinking on the issue: 'the military need to hold West New Guinea as Dutch territory; and the need not to get into state of bad relations and enmity with Indonesia and therefore Asians generally'. He commented that it was possible that the second principle was more important than the first.

McEwen also revealed his sensitivity towards America's limited options if it were to involve itself in settling the dispute and commented that the 'Americans mustn't make themselves into enemies of Indonesia'. He set out a theme which was to characterise many of his thoughts on international diplomacy over the next few years: 'nations have to remember that their support or their alliances [are] vital – they can't afford to let allies down'. He suggested that Australia 'tell Americans that the prospects of a Communist state between us and Asia is unthinkable for us or them – plug that with Americans'. However, he also noted that 'an approach to US is no substitute for an Australian policy ... I want to see us fix on a policy here now'.[21]

McEwen was soon to take over the leadership of the Country Party and the newly-named portfolio of Minister for Trade.[22] He would act as Prime Minister on twenty-four occasions totalling 550 days from 1958 until his retirement in February 1971. He visited Papua New Guinea once in June 1964.[23] McEwen is usually thought of in terms of his role in developing and protecting Australia's trade and tariff policies but, as will be seen in this and subsequent chapters, this underestimates his considerable influence in Cabinet debates on regional and international security polices and the consistency of his views on Australia's relations with Southeast Asia and with its principal ally, the United States.

There was a general acceptance within the Cabinet of McEwen's assessment of developments and his advice on the correct policy approach. Casey added that 'a communist Indonesia would break the island chain and therefore break into basic policy – don't think Americans will let this drift'.[24] Hasluck agreed and thought that Australia should 'persuade them [the US] to assume their leadership role in this part of the world'. For the first time in a Cabinet discussion Senator Spooner presented the argument that 'the Dutch must by degrees and perhaps quickly get out of West New Guinea and then almost certainly out of Indonesia – that means probably a Communist Indonesia – this is a problem for America as well as us'. Menzies acknowledged that this was a 'critical point in history'. Against the background of the difficulties Australia faced of pursuing its policy towards the dispute while trying to build a relationship with Indonesia or at least not to alienate it, he commented that 'too much (has) gone into developing [a] friendship with Indonesia to do other than approach this with tact and caution'.[25]

In keeping with the practice he had begun early in his time as Prime Minister, Menzies followed up the discussions in Cabinet by writing on 12 December to Secretary of State Dulles.[26] He set out in detail Australia's concerns at recent developments in Indonesia and argued that no nation could be 'indifferent or inactive' to Indonesia's attempts to liquidate Dutch interests and 'the weakening of decent elements in Indonesian life'. Amongst other ideas he suggested that countries such as the United States could look at using their aid programs as leverage to encourage Sukarno towards a more reasonable attitude. He concluded by arguing that Australia was 'particularly concerned because we are close neighbours of Indonesia and a somewhat exposed member of the Western democracies. We would view with great apprehension the passing of Indonesia into lawless Communist control, the risk or substantial intervention by Russia or Communist China, or a persistent violation by Indonesia of the civilized rules of personal freedom and property'. He encouraged the United States to initiate direct talks with Indonesia so as to 'avert unpleasant possibilities'.[27] For his part Casey issued a similarly worded press statement on 12 December.[28]

Dulles replied on 31 December.[29] He agreed with Menzies that 'the situation is most serious' but disagreed with the suggestion that the US use its aid program as leverage to encourage Sukarno towards a more reasonable attitude. Dulles believed that the situation in Indonesia was so sensitive that any overt intervention by America could have the wrong effect and consequences. Similarly, he argued that any change in the American attitude of neutrality in the West New Guinea dispute would not be welcomed, as even those forces in open revolt against Sukarno supported Indonesia's claim. Dulles did reaffirm 'our common resolve to keep Indonesia out of Communist control. It is in the interests of the entire Free World that we should not fail in this effort'.[30] However, he was not prepared to alter America's policy towards Indonesia or the West New Guinea dispute.

The next six months saw further fundamental changes in the political and internal situation in Indonesia. Menzies described the outlook for Indonesia to newly appointed British Prime Minister, Harold Macmillan, as:

there is now a danger that a Communist-dominated Government might achieve power. The situation also contains the possibility of civil war, economic disruption and national disintegration. While these developments are by no means inevitable, the present weak and inept national leadership appears to be able to do little to avert them.[31]

By mid-1958 Canberra's assessment was that Indonesia remained in a 'critical' state with the prospect of a further 'slide towards chaos and increased dependence on the Sino-Soviet bloc'.[32] From his perspective in Jakarta, McIntyre described the Sukarno Government as 'whistling in the dark with alternate bravado and anxiety'.[33]

It was in this environment that the Australian Cabinet undertook a further comprehensive review of Australia's policy towards Indonesia and the West New Guinea dispute. Casey was soon to leave for The Hague and then to Washington for the annual ANZUS Council meeting and wanted to be confident that he had a full understanding of the Cabinet's attitude. On 29 July 1958, immediately prior to the Cabinet meeting, Casey wrote to Menzies setting out his thoughts on the question of possible Australian military support for the Dutch. He described the idea of openly aiding the Dutch as 'possibly one of the most fundamental decisions that we are called upon to make – with long range implications for our own relationships with the Asian peoples'. However, he felt that he needed guidance from Cabinet as to whether Australia would provide military assistance as the US Government would 'inevitably ask what we propose to do about it – and if I have nothing to say … I would be likely to be thrown out of the door, politely and metaphorically at least'.[34]

It is one of the remarkable features of the West New Guinea dispute that it returned again and again to Cabinet for assessment and guidance. Ministers examined it from the point of view of political developments in Indonesia, the state of the bilateral relationship, the deteriorating relationship between the Netherlands and Indonesia, the attitude of Australia's principal allies, notably the United States, and most consistently from the perspective of Australia's security outlook and the impact on Papua New Guinea. Frequent Cabinet discussion of the West New Guinea dispute exposed Australia's concerns and uncertainties about its regional neighbourhood but at the same time reflected Australia's recognition of the need to build a positive relationship with Indonesia.

A joint submission from Casey and McBride examined the dispute from the perspective of both Australia's defence and foreign policy interests.[35]

The two ministers made clear that the review was necessary as the risk had increased that Indonesia would resort to the use of force to make good its claim. Sukarno had successfully suppressed the rebellions by various armed groups across the archipelago. By doing so the Indonesian Government was now thought to have the military capacity to launch an attack on West New Guinea. At the same time Indonesia was acquiring substantial quantities of military equipment from the Soviet Union. For its part, the Dutch Government had suggested staff or military-related talks between Australia and the Netherlands to examine possible areas for defence cooperation over West New Guinea. The Dutch had also sought an assurance from Australia that if Indonesia should attack West New Guinea they would not be left to respond to the attack alone but that Australia would assist.[36]

At the outset of the submission, the two ministers asked for direction from Cabinet as to 'how much importance do we attach to the Dutch remaining in Western New Guinea? What are the offsetting disadvantages of their remaining? Is there any desirable or acceptable alternative?'[37] Ministers had before them extracts from two recently prepared reports from the Defence Committee on 'The Strategic Importance of New Guinea' and 'The Importance of Indonesia to Australia and Regional Defence'.[38] Both reports and assessments were sharper, more focused and definitive in tone than those prepared in 1956 and more sensitive to the threat posed by Indonesia to Australia's defence interests in Papua and New Guinea.

Unlike the 1956 assessment the revised report made clear that 'as part of Australian territory, Australian New Guinea should be defended'.[39] This was the first time such a statement had been made in such bald terms. It then reverted to familiar language by noting that Australian New Guinea could provide an enemy with a suitable area from which to launch air, sea and land attacks on the east coast of Australia. Conversely, it provided Australia and her allies with potential forward bases to defend the northwest and provided defence in depth for the Australian mainland.[40] It asserted that the 'holding of Australian New Guinea should ... be a primary objective of Australian defence policy'.[41] In turn, 'the security of Australian New Guinea depend[ed] among other things upon Netherlands New Guinea being in the hands of a power possessing a relatively stable government ... which is unlikely to pursue policies inimical to Australian interests. The Netherlands satisfies these conditions; Indonesia at present does not'.[42] The defence of Australian New Guinea would be 'seriously prejudiced' and Australia would be faced with a 'grave potential strategic threat' should a communist-controlled Indonesia secure control of West New

Guinea.⁴³ The preferred outcome would be a West New Guinea which remained under the 'control of a friendly power or, failing that, under neutral control'.⁴⁴ The latter was a reference to the possibility of the territory being placed under a UN-sponsored trusteeship arrangement. The assumption behind such a trusteeship arrangement was that Indonesia would not be a partner in its administration.

The Cabinet submission set out the pros and cons of the continuation of Australian policy towards West New Guinea from the dual perspectives of Australia's defence and external affairs interests. It argued that the administration and development of Australia's half of the island would proceed more 'safely and smoothly if administration in the western half is friendly and along similar lines. … Indonesian administration or trusteeship in which an Asian element was strong, could very well create difficulties and dangers for us'. Independence or self-government in the western half of the island could lead to calls for a similar outcome in Australian New Guinea while 'propaganda and other appeals could be made to detach eastern New Guinea from Australian influence'.⁴⁵ On balance, the submission recommended continued support for the Netherlands. At the same time it argued against Australia entering into military commitments with the Dutch unless the United States was also prepared to enter into such an undertaking. Staff or military planning talks with the Dutch should not be held until after consultations with the United States.

The Cabinet discussion took place over two days. The main speakers were Menzies, Hasluck, Casey, McBride and Senator Spooner, with McEwen also playing a leading role. The length of time given by Cabinet to discussing the Dutch New Guinea dispute was considerably greater than that to any other foreign and defence policy issue until the debate over the Vietnam War in the 1960s. Ministers quickly dismissed the idea of a study of alternative arrangements, such as a trusteeship, and described the suggestion of staff talks with the Dutch as premature. Instead ministers focused on the question of the possible use of force by Indonesia to secure its claims, the likely Australian response and whether Australia was prepared to assist the Dutch militarily. Casey also briefed the Cabinet on his assessment of whether the Dutch Government of Dr Drees would stay the course or succumb to calls from the Dutch Labour Party and others to abandon the issue in order to protect Dutch investments in Indonesia. Casey was confident that Drees would hold firm but 'we can't be sure of this lasting'.⁴⁶ McBride and Casey also alerted ministers to the revised assessment of capabilities of the Indonesian Army following its success in defeating the various rebellions in the outer islands. McBride frankly admitted 'all the appreciations that I was given during the revolt were wrong. The Indonesians were better than we believed'.[47] He added that Indonesia could land a battalion in West New Guinea 'with little warning and they could do this in spite of the Dutch and of us'.[48] The critical question, however, was whether Australia should respond to a threat by Indonesia and what effect the response would have on Australia's relations with the rest of Asia.

The discussion revealed a Cabinet wavering in its views and unsure as to how Australia should respond to the new pressures being applied by Indonesia. In addition, it was acutely aware that the gradual running down of the Australian defence force had limited its capacity to respond quickly or effectively to any possible Indonesian military activity. Australia had only vague assurances of support from its major allies and no firm guarantees. Spender's decision in 1950 to pursue Australia's policy without first securing allied support was now beginning to haunt the Cabinet. The self-confidence and single-mindedness that had characterised the government's approach to the issue a few years earlier was faltering. Menzies summed up the mood when he said 'this is not a problem we can stall. As the menace increases so our boldness has oozed away'.[49] At times ministers returned to the fundamentals of the issue, following Senator Spooner's lead in the previous Cabinet room discussion to question whether the Dutch would remain in West New Guinea, whether the territory was vital to Australia's defence and if the United States would provide military support if Indonesia used force to impose its claim. The Menzies Government was having difficulty in identifying a policy which would adequately address a complex situation and also provide guidance in the event of rapidly-changing circumstances. The choice was to carry on as before with representations to allies seeking support for the status quo, to find a new approach or to do nothing.

McEwen opened the debate by asking 'What is Indonesia's attitude to East New Guinea?'[50] It was a curious opening question but it reflected the linkages he and other ministers drew between Indonesia's attitude to West New Guinea and the potential for difficulty in Papua New Guinea. Casey replied that 'they have never made a claim to it and they have always disclaimed it'.[51] This did not settle the issue and ministers returned to the question later in the discussion. Casey also told his colleagues that the 'Dutch have a few suspicions of us. They say Dutch New Guinea is more important to you than us'.[52] This opened up the question of the strategic value of West New Guinea and whether Australia would support the Dutch militarily. McBride noted that 'Defence has always regarded West

New Guinea as very important. It is firmer of course about Australian New Guinea. With a friendly Indonesian hold of New Guinea it would not matter'. On the question of whether Australia could help militarily, the Minister for Defence added 'we can't do a great deal to help the Dutch'. Menzies reacted angrily to McBride and to Casey's comment that Defence, and the Chief of the Air Staff, Frederick Scherger, would 'look with horror' on the 'idea of a war with Indonesia' with the reply that 'I suppose that he would equally look with horror on fighting for Australian New Guinea. Let the Dutch get out and the Indonesians in, how long would it be before we are fighting for Australian New Guinea? This is an expansionist movement which has nothing to do with race'.[53] This was the first time Menzies had described Indonesia as 'expansionist'. He was to use the phrase frequently in the 1960s.

The initial questioning by ministers of the threat to West New Guinea turned to a debate over the broader strategic environment. McEwen identified a danger posed by Indonesia and told his colleagues 'it is hard to get excited about the Indonesians in West New Guinea compared with their threat to us in Indonesia itself'. He added that 'a fracas over this is a fracas with Asia', although he accepted that 'an Indonesia infested with Russian submarines, Chinese volunteers etc is a very dangerous Indonesia'. The change in the mood of some ministers in Cabinet was summed up by McEwen's comment:

> some years ago I would have fought for Dutch New Guinea. But a hostile Indonesia would impose such a strain on us as would stultify our development. We would have to step up our defence preparations. Our own parties would demand more preparations in the face of a hostile Indonesia.[54]

He warned that Australia:

> had more at stake [in this dispute] than anyone else. ... It is not vitally important either to the Dutch or the Indonesians. If Australia is thrown into a different relationship with all Asian countries that could ultimately affect the fate of Australia. ... So this decision could be more decisive as to Australia's fate than the world wars. ... If we say that we will fight with the Dutch we may begin a chain of consequences.[55]

McEwen was showing a breadth of understanding of the complexities of the issue that elevated him above most of his colleagues in the Cabinet. He had recently led the negotiations in 1957 on a groundbreaking commercial agreement with Japan. This may have given him the authority and confidence to speak in broader, more strategic terms, although his reference to 'all Asian countries' is odd as he had a very good understanding of Japan's approach to the region following his negotiations of a new trade agreement.

Ministers, including Hasluck, initially questioned whether Indonesia would 'go for East New Guinea if they get into West New Guinea'. Hasluck also made clear his firm belief that the principle of supporting an ally against aggression should be maintained and that 'we can't allow Australian New Guinea to be threatened'.[56] Menzies asked his colleagues: 'If we are not prepared to fight for West New Guinea are we prepared to fight for East New Guinea?' McEwen replied: 'East New Guinea is ours and what we own we fight for'.[57] Menzies agreed and summed up part of the discussion by noting:

> I begin by assuming that Australian New Guinea is vital to Australia's defence. So, if this is so, West New Guinea is of great importance to Australian defence.[58]

Menzies also expressed his sympathy for the Dutch and their treatment at the hands of the Indonesians but thought Australia should avoid responding if questioned about support for the Dutch in the event of an Indonesian attack on West New Guinea. The discussion then turned to the question of whether the United States or others would provide military support to the Dutch. Menzies and McEwen expressed their doubts with Menzies commenting that 'the US would drop us in this matter'. McEwen assessed it as 'probable' that the US would abandon Australia and the Netherlands. McEwen reflected on the Suez crisis and said 'this is exactly what the US did in the Suez Crisis. And they did it to avoid turning the Arab world against them. Will they not treat the Dutch and us in the same way to avoid turning the Asian world against them?'[59]

At the end of the second day of discussions the Chairman of the Chiefs of Staff Committee, Lt General Sir Henry Wells, was invited to brief ministers on the military importance of Australian New Guinea and the significance of Indonesia securing control of West New Guinea. He described the two halves of the island as providing both defence in depth and bases for the defence of Australia: 'Australian New Guinea would be more important if West New Guinea [were] lost'.[60] In answer to a specific question as to the implication of the loss of New Guinea to Australia, Wells responded that 'we would have only Northern Australia for depth'.[61]

The Cabinet discussions had revealed ministers to be deeply anxious and more prepared than previously to weigh up the pros and cons of continued support for the Dutch. They neither wanted to encourage the Dutch to believe that Australia was ready to back them militarily nor to leave them with a sense of abandonment. Ministers were now more sensitive to the impact on the rest of Asia if Australia were to respond militarily to any Indonesian use of force and more prepared than in the past to look at the issue from a broader perspective of how Asian states would react to developments. However, there is no sense emerging from this discussion of a broader policy towards Indonesia or Asia in general. The Menzies Cabinet remained on the back foot, waiting on developments and uncertain as to how to push the government's policy objectives. Ministers hoped the Dutch would not weaken in their resolve but had no policy position yet on how best to protect Australia's interests, only a determination to protect Australia's position in the Territory of Papua and New Guinea.

On 9 September 1958 Casey met Secretary of State Dulles and senior departmental officials in Washington. Casey gave prominence to the Cabinet's concern at the possible use of force by Indonesia to secure control of West New Guinea. He made clear that the Dutch were 'most anxious on this score' and had asked Australia to give an 'undertaking to support them by force of arms if such an attack were to be made'.[62] Australia had declined 'at present' and was 'most anxious' to 'head off' any possibility of the use of force. He added that 'such a development would place the Australian Government in a grave dilemma … the first shot fired by an Australian in West New Guinea would destroy the whole basis of the friendly relations with Asian countries which Australia had patiently built up since the last war'.[63] He acknowledged, however, that public opinion in Australia 'might well oblige any government to go to the aid of the Dutch'. Casey asked Dulles to consider adopting a change in United States policy to make it a condition of the supply of any future civil and military aid to Indonesia that it refrain from using force in West New Guinea. Dulles agreed that the principle should be maintained that force should not be sanctioned to settle disputes but would not go further. He also acknowledged that it would be a 'disaster' if Indonesia attacked West New Guinea. In such an event the United States would 'throw its full support behind any defence of West New Guinea'. However, the details and type of support were not discussed except that economic sanctions could be deployed. Casey pulled back from encouraging the possibility of the use of US military force and told Dulles that 'he did not wish to suggest at this stage that the United States should undertake to use force'. Other 'deterrents' should instead be considered.[64] Dulles ended the conversation by noting that Australia had not given the Dutch a commitment to assist in the defence of West New Guinea; however, the United States 'would not mind if we did'.[65] The discussion in Cabinet and the conversation in Washington had brought the question of a response to the possible use of force by Indonesia to the forefront of assessments and debate. The question was to remain the principal focus as the issue continued to evolve over the next few months.

Indonesia's Foreign Minister visits

Throughout 1958 Indonesia's Foreign Minister, Dr Subandrio, had made it known that he saw value in developing a closer relationship with Australia and that he would be prepared to visit. It had been seven years since the last visit by an Indonesian Foreign Minister to Canberra and three years since Casey's last meeting in Jakarta. Subandrio had also tried on several occasions to appease known Australian concerns about the possible use of force by Indonesia to secure its claim to West New Guinea. In August 1958 the Indonesian Ambassador had, on instructions, called on the Acting Minister for External Affairs, Philip McBride, to assure him that Indonesia had 'no intention to use force over West New Guinea because this would not be in conformity with the neighbourly relations between Indonesia and Australia'.[66] Prime Minister Djuanda had given Ambassador McIntyre a similar assurance in November 1958, although Djuanda had added that as for Sukarno, Irian Barat [West New Guinea] was after all 'his hobby' and 'he could not be controlled'.[67] Despite these assurances Australia remained sceptical, particularly in view of a new round of weapons purchases by Indonesia from the United States and the United Kingdom which had evoked strong protests from Menzies to Macmillan and Dulles. McIntyre told the Head of Indonesia's Foreign Ministry, Sowito, that a 'completely unequivocal public statement renouncing the use of force' was needed to assuage Australia's suspicions.[68] Subandrio had also floated the idea of a mutual defence or security arrangement but Australia had not responded.[69]

In preparation for the visit Cabinet re-examined its policy in December 1958 and in January 1959 and again sought to develop an appropriate response. The key issues remained the question of the possible use of force by Indonesia and the response to any Dutch request for military assistance. McEwen was direct in his interventions. He told his colleagues that Australia had to 're-plan' its policy approach and that perhaps Cabinet had not thought the policy through sufficiently when it took its fundamental decisions in 1950 and 1951.[70] He warned his colleagues 'can we really expect the Americans to come in with us against Indonesia solo – they won't go to war against Asia – don't let us pull our own legs'. McEwen added that 'we shouldn't say or sufficiently imply that we will fight with Dutch if necessary. We are in deep enough now but don't get in deeper'.[71] Holt agreed with McEwen's line of argument and told his colleagues that he had 'real doubt about the matter of whether Australia and Dutch should engage in a war against Indonesia – could divide the country and very likely the Government. ... Our job is to keep US in position where intervention not impossible – Indonesia could not assume that US will not'.[72]

At the commencement of the Cabinet's full-day major review of the dispute on 5 January 1959 Casey described Sukarno as a 'fanatic' and said that a 'momentum [had] built up [in Indonesia] and [a] lust for New Guinea'.[73] Menzies followed McEwen's earlier example and said that 'we must take a good look at our policies to date and admit mistakes if they exist'. He added that the focus to date had been on the Dutch rather than on Indonesia. Menzies was surer in his assessment than in the discussions six months earlier and warned his colleagues that:

> if Indonesia does launch an attack in whatever form it will be from that moment a communist satellite – Communists will be the providers and backers and technical experts and the West will cut off supplies – therefore they are de facto communists. If we fight with the Dutch we are at war with Indonesia – not a skirmish in New Guinea but a war with bases being attacked.[74]

He added that if Australia gave a commitment to the Dutch to use force 'we are potential enemies of Indonesia and all for a wasting and disappearing asset'. Moreover, 'Indonesia will, if an enemy of ours, present a much more direct threat to our security than their possession of New Guinea does – a map proves this'. Menzies concluded his assessment by noting that Australia could not string the Dutch along nor should it give a commitment to the Dutch. He made clear that 'we can't go into [a] commitment except with US and UK – cards on table. Indonesia [is] much more important to us than New Guinea to [the] Dutch'.[75] In Menzies's mind the key to Australia's position was clear support from its principal allies. Without it Australia could not act.

McEwen agreed with Menzies's assessment, again noting that this was 'a matter of enormous importance to us because geography is with us and we cannot declare war on Asia'.[76] In keeping with his overall philosophy of supporting the actions of the United States, he added that 'if by some unexpected chance the US say here we put in a peg, we also join in. But this is unlikely'.[77] He was not keen on the idea of an Australian trusteeship over West New Guinea ('we would only attract Indonesian hostility to ourselves on top of the huge cost') nor of giving the Dutch any further encouragement to stay.[78] Ministers agreed that Australia could not give the Dutch a guarantee of support but were still deeply concerned about the future. Spooner noted that 'if we hand over to Indonesia we get Communists right across our top, including Papua'. Hasluck described the situation as 'communist bully tactics'. In his first recorded intervention on the issue in Cabinet, the newly appointed Attorney-General, Sir Garfield Barwick, commented 'we couldn't honestly, physically promise support to the Dutch. Further, we shouldn't do so – shouldn't support Dutch colonialism – we can't afford to do so'.[79] Barwick brought a new voice to the Cabinet discussions and was clearly on the side of keeping Australia out of any possible conflict over West New Guinea. In some respects the Cabinet sensed that the tide was turning in the West New Guinea dispute. After a long period in which the issue had been kept in 'cold storage' it was soon to emerge and be the subject of new debate and new pressures. A more complicated environment was on the horizon. McEwen was now leading the debate in Cabinet over West New Guinea and reminding his colleagues of the broader consequences for Australia of alienating Asian opinion. Ministers may have shared McEwen's views but he captured the strategic arguments more succinctly than others. He was also more aware of the consequences for Australia's relationship with Asia than his colleagues, although the Cabinet was not anti-Asian in sentiment. Nevertheless, at all times, the place of Papua New Guinea was still very much central to any discussions.

Dr Subandrio visited Australia from 10 to 15 February 1959. The government decided at the outset to accord the visit the utmost importance and seriousness. In the now close-to-ten years of the Menzies Government the visit was the most critical event to date in the development of Australia's relationship with Indonesia. It would see Menzies and the Australian Cabinet in direct conversation with one of the most influential members of the Sukarno Government. The government set as its objective to treat Subandrio in a way 'that will have the effect of lessening or appearing to lessen the tension between Indonesia and Australia which results from our support of the Dutch in New Guinea'. At the same time the government did not want to allow Subandrio to 'drive a wedge between ourselves and the Dutch'. It acknowledged that this 'would not be any easy task'. Ministers would look for 'any opportunity to help take the heat out of the situation provided it does not compromise our position'.[80] For his part, it would appear that Subandrio's aim was to test the strength of Australia's commitment to the Dutch remaining in West New Guinea, including its military commitment, and to assess the conditions under which Australia would accept a settlement.

Subandrio was invited by Menzies to join him in a meeting with the Cabinet in Canberra, held a private meeting with Menzies and Casey at the Hotel Windsor in Melbourne and had a conversation with Casey on the flight between Canberra and Melbourne. In the opening phase of his meeting with Subandrio Menzies did not deviate from stated government policy. He reminded Subandrio that 'New Guinea has great significance in the Australian mind' while Indonesia had an 'even greater significance'.[81] He referred to the sentiment born out of the experience of the Second World War when he said that for Australians 'various events, including events in the war, have put New Guinea into the Australian mind and there is an instinctive point of view that New Guinea does not easily divide into two parts and that Australia must be concerned in the future of New Guinea'.[82] At times Menzies appeared to revert to his experience as a barrister in the style and tone of his presentation and the questions he posed. He asserted that Australia's acceptance of Dutch sovereignty over West New Guinea was founded in international law. He made clear that 'it was Australia's policy to respect those [Dutch] rights and, as a corollary, to resist any challenge to them which was based on force or aggression in any form'.[83] For the first time in the now decade-long dispute Menzies also put to Subandrio that Australia was not a party principal in the matter. Australia had no claim of its own. In contrast to the position adopted by Spender in 1950, he described Australia as a 'by-stander. But a very interested by-stander because we are interested in the future of New Guinea'.[84] For his part Casey, reflecting the views of senior officers in his department chose to remind Subandrio of the importance of recognising the concept of self-determination in assessing the attitudes of the indigenous population of West New Guinea. Casey also hoped that the dispute might, once again, be placed in some form of 'cold storage'.[85]

At their second meeting in Melbourne Menzies felt obliged to restate his position as he was not confident that Subandrio had understood the strength of Australia's commitment to support Dutch sovereignty. For Menzies it was both a legal and a moral commitment. He reiterated that 'we are neutral on whether negotiations are held but we are not neutral on the question of sovereignty'. He did add that:

> just as we respect sovereignty and just as we respect the present sovereignty so we would respect any altered sovereignty if reached ... by some appropriate process of law – which means to say by adjudication or by agreement freely and fairly arrived at. In these circumstances we would accept any new position fully and without ill will and I am definite that we would not stand in the way of any negotiations.[86]

Menzies told Subandrio he was prepared to have his views reflected in a communiqué. Menzies's remark that his government would recognise a settlement arrived at freely and fairly through adjudication represented a significant departure from the policy developed by Percy Spender. In the early 1950s Australia had gone to great pains to shore up Dutch resolve not to settle the dispute. It is difficult to understand why Menzies made this statement to Subandrio. It had not been part of Australian policy beforehand nor had it been discussed in Cabinet before Subandrio's arrival. It reflected the advice given to Spender and Menzies by the UK Foreign Secretary, Bevin, in 1950 and 1951 but which, at the time, had been ignored. As a highly trained lawyer Menzies would have recognised the logic of Bevin's earlier advice but this fact offers no insight into why he volunteered the remark to Subandrio in 1959. Alternatively, he may have known that the Dutch were unlikely to agree to any transfer of sovereignty and hence it represented no real concession.

In his remarks to the Cabinet, and privately to Menzies and Casey, Subandrio did not deviate from known Indonesian policy towards West New Guinea. He did tell the Cabinet that in his government's view 'no territorial dispute can nowadays be settled by the use of force'. If Indonesia were to use force 'it would mean facing not only the Dutch, or the Dutch and Australia, but also the United States and the United Kingdom'. China and Russia could then be dragged in and 'West New Guinea would be further from Indonesia's reach than ever and Indonesia itself would be open to fragmentation and disintegration'.[87]

As to the possible relationship between an Indonesian-controlled West New Guinea and Australian New Guinea, Subandrio acknowledged that Australia 'may be fearful of Indonesia as a neighbour ... but there were no grounds for this'. Importantly for his Australian audience he commented that Indonesia had 'no territorial ambitions beyond West New Guinea'. He cited Indonesia's history of living on friendly terms with Borneo and Portuguese Timor as proof of its intentions. He also argued that Indonesian control of West New Guinea could work to Australia's advantage. Indonesia could not remain neutral in any conflict involving East New Guinea while its possession of West New Guinea would be likely to deter China from any aggression in New Guinea as China would not attack another Asian country. Casey accepted Subandrio's statement that Indonesia rejected the use of force and suggested that he take an opportunity while in Australia to make these views known publicly.[88] Ministers did not respond to the other elements of Subandrio's argument.

The Joint Announcement released by Casey and Subandrio at the conclusion of the visit emphasised the importance of building the bilateral relationship and co-operating as 'good neighbours sympathetically concerned in each other's material progress'.[89] On the issue of the West New Guinea dispute, the ministers noted that the two countries held different views and that Australia recognised the Netherlands' sovereignty over the area and the principle of self-determination. In keeping with Menzies's commitment to Subandrio, the announcement stated that 'if any agreement were reached between the Netherlands and Indonesia as parties principal, arrived at by peaceful processes and in accordance with internationally accepted principles, Australia would not oppose such an agreement'.[90] For his part Subandrio acknowledged that force should not be used to settle territorial disputes.

The Joint Announcement met with a wave of criticism. It was seen as potentially conceding West New Guinea to Indonesian control and thereby exposing Australia to a threat from Indonesia. The Returned and Services League (RSL) reacted with a claim that 'once they [Indonesia] get into West New Guinea there is nothing to stop them from claiming East New Guinea'.[91] A number of newspapers vigorously pursued a similar line with the Sydney *Sun* capturing a popular sentiment when it asked 'of what value will his [Dr Subandrio's] assurances be if Indonesia falls into the hands of a communist government … New Guinea is Australia's last bastion against a southward march of international communism'.[92] The *Daily Mirror* joined in the protest by noting that the 'Menzies Government sees no danger in handing over a territory which is of crucial strategical importance to a country which could at any moment go communist'.[93]

The strength of the reaction caught the government off guard and it was forced to defend its decisions in a heated debate in Parliament. The leader of the Australian Labor Party, Dr Evatt, attacked the government arguing that the Second World War had demonstrated that the whole of New Guinea was 'absolutely vital to the security and defence' of Australia. Evatt argued that sovereignty unquestionably rested with the Netherlands but, in keeping with his long-held advocacy of the use of regional and international arrangements to help build relationships, suggested that a tripartite mutual regional security and welfare pact between Australia, the Netherlands and Indonesia be negotiated to oversee the development of the island.[94] Evatt also placed considerable importance on the concepts of governing for the welfare and interests of the indigenous population, a concept he felt had been down-played by the government.

The government was forced to bring in Menzies, Casey and McEwen to defend the terms of the Joint Announcement. Menzies set out in detail the government's policy, emphasising Australia's belief that sovereignty rested with the Netherlands. He argued that the discussions with Subandrio had not changed that policy. Menzies was also at pains to point out his government's 'genuine interest in the welfare of the young and growing nation of Indonesia ... whose goodwill is so important for our own future'.[95] Casey argued that the statement of Australia's attitude towards a possible settlement represented a description of a 'hypothetical' situation and was 'no new departure in our policy'. Nor could it be 'represented as advice to the Netherlands or to Indonesia on the question of negotiations upon the matter'.[96] As the academic Jamie Mackie has commented, 'whatever the Government's intention may have been at the time the joint announcement was signed, after the press and public uproar it hastened to erase any impression that it had intended a concession to Indonesia'.[97] The government survived the debate and controversy but it had been reminded of the sensitivities within the Australian community towards New Guinea and Indonesia and of the continuing lack of trust by the Australian public in the words of Indonesian leaders when speaking of Australia's security interests.

The broader security environment – implications for defence

The Menzies Cabinet faced another awkward debate over the contents of the 1959 Strategic Basis Paper produced by the Defence Committee.[98] On this occasion the debate was conducted within the bureaucracy in Canberra. The paper, a revision of the Committee's 1956 paper, elevated the place of Indonesia in Australia's strategic outlook. The assessment noted that Indonesia's military strength had been 'considerably increased by foreign aid' and that it now had the capacity to 'pose a significant threat to Netherlands New Guinea and a small threat to Northern Australia and the Australian islands territories of Cocos and Christmas'.[99] Indonesia did not pose a threat to the Australian mainland but it could provide bases from which external communist forces could operate against Australia.

The strategic importance of Australian New Guinea was assessed in terms very similar to those in the 1956 report. The paper noted that as part of Australian territory 'it should be defended' and that 'it provided the final defence in depth of the Australian mainland and it must be the primary objective of our defence strategy to hold it'. Its security depended in part on Netherlands New Guinea being in the hands of a 'relatively stable government which is unlikely to pursue policies inimical to Australian interests'. A 'grave potential strategic threat would ensue if a Communist-influenced Indonesian government held possession of Netherlands New Guinea'.[100]

Ministers accepted the broad strategic analysis contained in the paper but reacted strongly against the proposition contained in the section on the 'Shape of the Australian Defence Force' that the organisation of the defence force should take into account a possible future situation where Australia 'may be called upon to defend New Guinea or the north-western approaches by our independent efforts'. The section also proposed that the defence force should, over time, 'be designed primarily to act independently of Allies'.[101] In a rare departure from his practice of letting the relevant minister open the debate in Cabinet, Menzies began the discussion by making clear that he was totally opposed to that proposition and was 'against the idea of breaking with existing policy of operating with allies'. He added that the paper contained 'revolutionary ideas about (the) Army' and that it was 'politically and financially impossible'.[102] Menzies was not prepared to shift Australia's defence preparedness to one based on self-reliance.

McEwen, who also had a habit in Cabinet discussions of biding his time and waiting until most ministers had spoken before intervening, joined Menzies in strongly attacking the paper. He commented that he could not see where Australia would deploy independently of allies: 'if it's Malaya, I assume we have allies, if not, I don't think they'll be going overseas'.[103] He added that 'my approach is that in peacetime the Australian Army has not been and cannot be a fighting force ready on an instant, but only a cadre – this on the basis that we have allies who are larger and take the first shock and we tune in later. If we are fighting independently [we] will be fighting at home'.[104] Later in the debate McEwen commented that 'we are too small to run a complete expeditionary force and maintain an acceptable home defence – it is unmanageable or too expensive or both'. As to Indonesia, McEwen told his colleagues: 'I put my faith in diplomats and politicians – if they can't avoid us getting into a tangle with Indonesia that's that. The soldiers can't then win for us. Even to fight is to lose'.[105] In an earlier discussion of the Strategic Basis Paper and its suggestions for a possible reshaping of the defence force he rejected out of hand the idea tentatively raised by some ministers that Australia should strengthen its defence capability by acquiring nuclear weapons. He bluntly told his colleagues 'if we were to drop one on Djakarta [we] would never live in Asia again'.[106] He argued that Australia had to 'develop our associations and economic relations with Indonesia – get to know them better. Take initiatives ourselves so that the chance that they will jump the gun against us [is] reduce[d]. We have gained ground over past twelve months in this. Also the Dutch have less expectation that we would go in with them'.[107] McEwen was again thinking in the broadest terms of the ramifications in Asia of Australia's foreign and defence polices. Although he supported military action in concert with Australia's allies, he continued to demonstrate a keen awareness of the long-term consequences for Australia.

Menzies was momentarily, and uncharacteristically, less confident that Australia's allies, notably the United States, would support it immediately in a conflict over New Guinea. It had 'adopted [an] equivocal position re New Guinea – they have certain words of assurance but they have other policies and views which could deter them. So it is conceivable that we should be fighting on our own or with the Dutch against Indonesia. A hell of a situation but not an impossible one'.[108]

The Cabinet discussion continued to show the strain emerging in the thinking of ministers towards Indonesia and the resolution of the West New Guinea dispute. The pressure on ministers was increasing and they were leaning more towards avoiding military action to defend Dutch sovereignty over West New Guinea. A frustrated Menzies had ended the discussion by noting that 'we've got a navy and an air force which can fight now. But the Army can't. We haven't got a fighting force and we can't let it go at that'.[109] Nevertheless, at a later Cabinet meeting ministers agreed to the abolition of the National Service training program as a cost-saving measure.[110] The Australian defence budget in 1958–59 stood at £189 million and was projected to rise to £193 million in 1959–60.

Menzies visits Indonesia

Menzies arrived in Jakarta on 1 December 1959 on the first official visit by an Australian Prime Minister to Indonesia ten years to the month after becoming Prime Minister. He was at the height of his powers. He was unchallenged in Cabinet and in Parliament. He, rather than Casey, determined Australian foreign policy. He had the strong support of the media and the population in general. Menzies had the status of an elder statesman, being one of the longest-serving political leaders on the world stage. Sukarno had emerged triumphant from the threat posed by army rebels in the islands and was in total command. He too was unchallenged. He too was a world statesman as a leader of the newly formed Non-Aligned Movement representing developing countries.

In all his public speeches in Jakarta Menzies adopted a positive and encouraging tone and emphasised the willingness of Australia to help in Indonesia's development. He told his audience that 'this great republic of Indonesia lying there on the north west of Australia is our greatest and most powerful neighbour and we are interested in what goes on'.[111] Later, he added 'we [Australia] believe in our hearts that you can become great, not aggressively powerful, but great and strong and free and happy. And in that task, whenever you feel that you need a friend you have only to turn in our direction'.[112] Menzies adopted a similarly co-operative tone in his meetings with First Minister Djuanda, Foreign Minister Subandrio and Minister for National Security and Chief of the General Staff, General Nasution.[113] (Shortly after Menzies' departure Australia and Indonesia signed a trade agreement. Australia's exports to Indonesia at the time totalled £3,221,000 while imports, mainly of oil and petroleum, totalled £29,438,000.[114] Between 1950-1951 and 1963-1964, 943 Indonesian students studied in Australia under the Colombo Plan. This was close to twenty per cent of the total intake of students under the scheme.[115])

Menzies met President Sukarno at Bogor Palace on 6 December for their official conversation.[116] It was perhaps the most important meeting between an Australian and an Asian leader since the end of the Second World War and one of the most important in Australia's post-war history. It could be argued that various meetings with the leaders of Japan and their outcomes had established the basis for Australia's economic and commercial growth but these meetings were non-controversial compared to the issues confronting Australia and Indonesia. It was a meeting which combined ceremony and substance and went to the core of the relationship between

Australia and Indonesia and the issue which bedevilled it. Djuanda, Subandrio and Tamzil, Chief of the President's Cabinet, were present with Sukarno. Menzies was accompanied by Ambassador McIntyre, Maurice Timbs from his own department and Peter Heydon from External Affairs in Canberra.

The conversation focused entirely on the West New Guinea dispute. Sukarno described the issue 'as the one question standing against the development of close and friendly relations between Indonesia and its near neighbour'. At Menzies's invitation he explained the history of the dispute and Indonesia's frustration at the Netherlands' refusal to honour a 'gentleman's agreement' to transfer sovereignty as expected in 1949. The President described the issue as 'paramount in the minds of Indonesians since it represented the principal element of incompleteness to their independence'. He asked why Australia always appeared to side with the Dutch and described the Dutch as being 'largely influenced by Australia'. Menzies replied that Australia was not a party principal in the matter and, in a further departure from established policy and, contrary to the views Cabinet had expressed in the mid-1950s, suggested that the dispute could be settled in the International Court of Justice. He added that Australia would 'unhesitatingly accept' the Court's decision. Sukarno did not respond to this suggestion. Menzies also referred to the assurance that Dr Subandrio had given in February that Indonesia would not use force to pursue its claim. Sukarno 'repeated that there was no question of any use of force'. He also told Menzies that he could be quoted on this and that he would 'underline Subandrio's declaration three times'. Menzies referred to his discussions with Subandrio in Australia and, despite the earlier public criticism of the terms of the Casey–Subandrio Joint Announcement, he repeated his undertaking that 'if the Netherlands and Indonesia reached an agreement over the future disposition of the territory, freely negotiated under no threat of force, Australia would respect it'.

Menzies took the opportunity to set out the reasons for Australia's interest in New Guinea 'as a whole'. He noted that in two world wars 'New Guinea in hostile hands had offered a threat to Australia and Australians had fought there'. He added that he 'well understood and respected the profound emotional significance of West New Guinea to Indonesians. But it must be understood that Australians also entertained deep feelings about New Guinea'. Sukarno appeared to dismiss this argument, noting that 'the days of colonialism in Asia were over; nationalism was the new driving force'. Germany and Japan were distant countries and 'Indonesia now stood between Australia and the rest of Asia'. This drew Menzies to raise the spectre of 'aggressive communist imperialism the threat of which extended southward from China through North Vietnam'. Menzies acknowledged the efforts by the Sukarno Government to curb the influence of the Chinese community but added that 'Australia contemplated with apprehension the risk that Communism might somehow come to power in Indonesia. ... The greatest danger might be that of subversion and covert infiltration'. Sukarno 'gave his personal guarantee that this would not happen as long as he was the leader of Indonesia'.

Menzies spoke of the importance Australia attached to the principle of self-determination in Papua New Guinea. He also outlined his government's programs 'to bring the inhabitants to the stage where they could decide for themselves about their own future'. This was his only specific reference to Papua New Guinea and he made no attempt to refer to it in the context of Australia's security interests. He next raised the issue of the 'racial differences' between the people of Indonesia and the 'Melanesians of West New Guinea'. Sukarno and Subandrio rejected the observation, with Subandrio arguing that 'race is no longer the valid criterion of nationality; economic, political and geographical ties and interests were more cogent'. Menzies was more direct when he remarked that some Australians 'saw no reason why the Melanesians of West New Guinea should exchange Dutch colonialism for Indonesian colonialism'. Again, both Sukarno and Subandrio 'amicably but emphatically' denied that the transfer could be regarded in this light.

Menzies drew the discussion to a close by referring to the points of common interest between the two countries and 'expressed the view that whatever differences might remain – and it was only natural and proper that there should be some differences of view – genuine friendship and understanding could be fostered'. Sukarno was unimpressed and, according to the Australian record of the meeting, 'sounded sceptical ... he came back again to the point that there could be no real improvement in relations until the West New Guinea issue was settled and out of the way'. Both leaders agreed that in their comments to the press they would report Sukarno's declaration that Indonesia had 'no intention of resorting to force' to acquire West New Guinea. Menzies closed the discussion by extending an invitation to Sukarno to visit Australia.

Menzies left Jakarta for Kuala Lumpur and the cooler climate of the Cameron Highlands, satisfied with the outcome of his discussions. He had obtained what he wanted which was a reaffirmation from President

Sukarno of Subandrio's earlier commitment that force would not be used by Indonesia to secure its objectives in West New Guinea.[117] Menzies attached great importance to a leader's word or commitment and he would now hold Sukarno to his undertaking. It was fundamental to the question of trust and Menzies now had something very concrete by which to judge Sukarno. This would prove vital in Australia's handling of the dispute over the next two years and would influence Menzies's attitude towards Sukarno and his ministers as events unfolded over West New Guinea and then during *Konfrontasi*.

For his part, Sukarno may have been pleased that he had explained fully Indonesia's position to Menzies and had rebutted or rejected a good number of the assumptions or claims put forward by the Australian leader. Sukarno offered no hint of a possible compromise, such as a trusteeship arrangement, but on 'several occasions hinted that Australia could help persuade the Dutch to come to terms with the Indonesians ... without asking'. Whether deliberately or not, he had inserted the word 'intention' in his comments about the use of force to settle the dispute, perhaps providing him with a loophole as the word could be interpreted to mean that he had no plans at that moment. Sukarno had remained firm in his belief that Indonesia was entitled to and would eventually acquire West New Guinea from the Dutch.

On his return to Canberra Menzies briefed the Cabinet on his talks. He drew a stark contrast between Sukarno, Indonesia, Prime Minister Tunku Abdul Rahman and Malaya. He described 'the Tunku' as being 'very friendly towards Australia', as having 'no objections to [the] white Australia policy', and as having made 'no suggestion of objections to Australian troops'. Malaya was 'very friendly towards Australia' and the Tunku was a man of 'great charm and trust'.[118] In contrast, Menzies described Sukarno as being 'quiet', while the President's 'guided democracy' was not a 'cover for democracy but for a dictatorship'. He added that Sukarno 'behaves and lives as a dictator'. Indonesia was living from 'one crisis to another [with] everything coming away in your hands'.[119] Sukarno was not interested in economic and administrative problems and the country was heading 'back to [a] rural peasant economy'. Menzies did remind his colleagues that the President had 'affirmed no use of force on West New Guinea' and had done so publicly. In response to a question from Holt as to the strength of Indonesia's commitment to West New Guinea, Menzies noted that 'none of the ministers raised it' and that it was an interest of 'Sukarno only'.[120] He also reminded the Cabinet that he had invited the President to visit Australia.

Conclusion

The three years dating from Casey's meeting with Sukarno in 1956 had been difficult ones for Menzies and his government in their dealings with Indonesia over West New Guinea. They had struggled with assessing the implications of the dispute for Australia and had produced few new ideas. Indeed, the government had reversed some of the principles which had previously guided it. The confidence which had characterised the government's handling of the dispute in the first half of the decade began to slip away as it faced the question of whether it would support the Dutch if Indonesia used force to pursue its claim. A new sense of anxiety and frustration had begun to emerge as ministers contemplated the repercussions of military involvement. The Cabinet was aware of the weakened state of Australia's defence preparedness. It was also showing a greater awareness of the implications for Australia's relations with Asia should it intervene militarily. All ministers were increasingly sensitive to this aspect of the problem but Deputy Prime Minister John McEwen expressed it most frequently and clearly. The pressure that ministers felt they were under also caused them to express increasing degrees of scepticism as to the reliability of the United States in providing support, including military support, should Australia (and the Dutch) face Indonesian aggression.

Australia had taken comfort from the comments by Subandrio and Sukarno that force would not be used to resolve the issue but had also conceded, for the first time, that if Indonesia and the Netherlands reached an amicable agreement which settled the issue then Australia would not object. Menzies had also suggested that the International Court of Justice could be used to settle the outstanding issue. He had conceded significant elements of Australia's policy – that Australia was an interested party to the dispute and believed it had a voice in how the dispute should be resolved. Perhaps Menzies knew that the Netherlands would not reach such an agreement and hence it was a hollow gesture but it was an important point to concede publicly.

Menzies's meetings with first Subandrio and then, most importantly, Sukarno were historic. Both were long overdue and both could have been of significance in setting the tone for the future relationship between the two countries. At face value Menzies and Sukarno achieved their objectives of explaining their respective points of view over West New Guinea. The meeting did go some way towards establishing a degree of mutual understanding between the leaders of each country. Menzies was to place considerable store on this point in the years ahead as he sought to hold Sukarno to account for his promise not to threaten to use nor indeed to use force to secure West New Guinea. But Menzies had not been won over by Sukarno. His comments to the Cabinet suggest that he saw Sukarno as a dictator of a country steadily falling into economic ruin. Menzies saw little reason to trust Sukarno and did not seek to contact him again during the remaining six years of his Prime Ministership.

Both leaders, but particularly Menzies, were soon to discover that they were not the only parties actively interested in the outcome of the West New Guinea dispute. A change in Administration in Washington was to bring about a fundamental change in approach leading to a negotiated settlement. Australia was caught off guard by the new policy ideas emerging from the Kennedy White House and was forced to adjust quickly. The anxieties which had been revealed in the Cabinet discussions in 1958 and 1959 were to be heightened further.

Chapter 6

THE WEST NEW GUINEA DISPUTE 1959–1962

'East New Guinea is Australian territory – for us to take an attitude that we would not defend it would be unthinkable – we must defend it and we would – nothing else would satisfy either our obligations or our conscience – so an attack on East New Guinea is an attack on us'.

Robert Menzies, 11 January 1962.[1]

By the end of 1959 Menzies was riding a wave of success. He had secured a stunning victory at the elections in November 1958, winning a thirty-seat majority over the now divided and broken Labor Party. Lord Peter Carrington, the British High Commissioner in Canberra, described Australia in 1959 as a country with a 'greater sense of maturity and self-confidence'. Economic performance had been 'outstanding' while 'abroad there is also a surer touch'. He added that there was now 'a conscious realization that Australia is a South East Asian power'. It appeared certain that 'as time goes on Australia will concern herself more and more with her Asian neighbours on whose goodwill and markets her security and prosperity will increasingly depend'. The change in emphasis from Europe and the Middle East to Southeast Asia had been 'swift and marked', although Australia retained a very close attachment to both the United States in defence relations and with Britain in defence and economic relations. Australia remained emotionally and sentimentally closer to Britain than any other country. Carrington acknowledged the hard work of Casey and External Affairs in refocusing Australia towards Asia but attributed the overall success of Australia to Menzies whom he described as the 'outstanding figure in the political scene ... he dominates public life as much as he dominates the Cabinet. His authority and success are acknowledged even by his political opponents'.[2]

In Indonesia Sukarno had by 1959 acquired near absolute power. In his comprehensive biography of Sukarno, John Legge described him as the 'dominating figure, the source of authority and of ideological leadership and the centre of a glittering court'.[3] Politics in Indonesia in 1960 was, according to Legge, 'in great measure the history of a shifting balance' between 'the President, the army and the P.K.I. (Communist party)'.[4] Guided Democracy was now established as the political philosophy for Indonesia but Indonesia's future would also be determined by its vulnerability as the economy crumbled in the face of declining exports and accelerating inflation.[5] In his valedictory despatch in February 1960 McIntyre described the 'picture' in Indonesia as 'opaque if not indeed black ... the political, economic and security situations are all bad and they are inseparable, each one contributes to the worsening of the others. Over everything hangs an atmosphere compounded of a queer mixture of emotion, envy, sincerity, opportunism, cynicism, timidity and intrigue ... the nation is being fed on slogans passed down from on high'.[6] Sukarno relied increasingly on bravado, bluster, brinkmanship and adventurism to hold power. The West New Guinea dispute continued to serve his purposes.

An inconclusive debate in Cabinet

In the months before Menzies's visit to Jakarta the Department of External Affairs, at Tange's direction, and with Casey's full support, had been drafting a new Cabinet submission dealing with West New Guinea. The submission was one of three to be presented which sought to re-examine Australia's relationships with its northern neighbours. The first was to address the 'The Future of Netherlands New Guinea'. It was to be accompanied by a separate submission from the Minister for Defence (Athol Townley) on 'The Military Importance of Netherlands New Guinea' and the third, from the Minister for Territories (Paul Hasluck), on 'The Unity of New Guinea'.[7] This last submission dealt with the questions of whether Australia should seek the transfer from Britain of the Solomon Islands Protectorate and a possible political union of the Solomon Islands with Papua and New Guinea.[8] The three submissions were to form the first instalment of six submissions, as well as discussions without submissions, in

Cabinet in 1960 on West New Guinea, followed by a further four debates in 1961. It was a period described by the Acting Secretary of External Affairs (Peter Heydon) as one in which the relationships with both Indonesia and the Dutch were 'going to be in a more or less constant state of crisis'.[9] It saw ideas and options proposed and examined then rejected; assumptions questioned and upheld or dismissed. It ended with Australia's security environment irreversibly changed.

Casey retired from the Cabinet and Parliament on 4 February 1960 and Menzies assumed his responsibilities as Minister for External Affairs, holding the portfolio until December 1961 when it was passed to Sir Garfield Barwick. Menzies accepted responsibility for the submission on the 'Future of Netherlands New Guinea' prepared under Casey's direction. The External Affairs paper sought endorsement for the continuation of a policy to encourage and support continued Dutch administration of West New Guinea, or, as it stated, the 'primary objective of [Australian] policy should be by means short of force to prevent Indonesia from occupying or controlling any part of West New Guinea'.[10] This was an imperative. At the same time it said that while pursuing this policy objective 'we should do all we can to reduce the damage to our relations with Indonesia'.[11] The submission acknowledged the fact that at some stage in the future the Dutch would leave West New Guinea and argued that if they were to leave before self-government, Australia should 'seek, in the extremely difficult situation that would follow, at least a form of international control which would limit Indonesian opportunities for interference to a minimum, give Australia a maximum voice in the administration of the territory and keep open the possibility of ultimate unification of New Guinea'.[12] It acknowledged the possibility of a UN-negotiated trusteeship agreement which would place the territory under Australian administration, although it readily acknowledged this would be difficult to obtain and arouse intense opposition from Indonesia. It also accepted as a possible outcome a UN-only trusteeship arrangement.

The submission also canvassed the consequences of Indonesia securing control of West New Guinea. It recognised that such a development would remove the one major irritant in the relationship, as well as strengthen the West's position in Indonesia by removing a rallying call used by the communists. However, on balance, it suggested that any short-term gain would be compromised by the long-term consequences as Australia and Indonesia would be 'bound to be competing for influence in New Guinea for decades'.[13] The paper judged Indonesian competition with Australia in

East New Guinea as a possibility and noted that Indonesia's capacity to do so would be 'considerably greater if they had control of West New Guinea'. Indonesia's strong sense of 'anti-colonialism' could encourage it to call for change in Australian New Guinea. If Indonesia were to be controlled by communists then West New Guinea 'would inevitably be used by Indonesia for the systematic subversion of East New Guinea and the territories beyond in Melanesia'. Even a non-communist Indonesia could spread its influence into Melanesia.[14]

The separate submission from the Minister for Defence repeated many of the judgements from earlier strategic assessments. It argued that 'in friendly hands Netherlands New Guinea (NNG) ensures the security of Eastern New Guinea (ENG) and reduces the requirement of Australian forces for its protection'; 'occupation of bases in NNG would represent a breach in the island chain and greatly increase Indonesian capability to attack ENG'; 'Indonesia could not obtain ENG by force' as long as substantial help were available to Australia under ANZUS; 'the loss of ENG would be the loss of Australian territory and the maintenance of our territorial integrity is a cardinal aim of defence policy'; Indonesian 'possession of ENG would result in a further breach in the Pacific island chain'; and, the 'retention of NNG in friendly hands is the best guarantee of the security of ENG'. In terms of strategic guidance the submission nevertheless reminded ministers that in January 1959 Cabinet had agreed that 'the strategic importance of Indonesia is of greater importance to the United States and to Australia than Netherlands New Guinea'.[15]

The Defence Committee's more detailed assessment of the military importance of Netherlands New Guinea to Australia, which was attached as an annex, drew on the earlier references by Menzies in his conversations in the United States and the United Kingdom that a hostile Indonesia would cause Australia to 'reconsider our contributions to our regional arrangements under SEATO and ANZUS [and] might require Australia to be prepared to devote a large part of its defence effort to the protection of East New Guinea'.[16] Over the next decade this argument was to feature more prominently in Australia's assessment of how to respond to regional conflicts.

In the consultations held between departments before the Cabinet meeting it had become apparent that Hasluck held strong objections to the External Affairs draft. In an unusual step he put his views direct to Menzies before the Cabinet meeting.[17] Hasluck described the submission on the Future of Netherlands New Guinea as showing 'an imperfect knowledge' and being based on incorrect assumptions. In keeping with the views he had expressed in earlier Cabinet room discussions, he argued for Australian diplomacy to focus on keeping the Dutch in West New Guinea 'for another twenty years'. He added that 'every ounce of diplomatic skill we have and our thinking on policy should be directed to keeping the Dutch there'.[18] He told Menzies that Australian policy should try to secure greater recognition from the United States and Britain of the importance of West New Guinea.

Cabinet discussed the three submissions on 2 March 1960.[19] Ministers concentrated their attention on the External Affairs submission and left the other two virtually untouched. There was no interest amongst ministers or in the bureaucracy for Hasluck's proposal to acquire the Solomon Islands and to link it to Papua New Guinea. Christopher Waters has written of Hasluck's 'dreams for the Southwest Pacific'. If Hasluck held such dreams then they evaporated in the disinclination of ministers to share them.[20] Instead ministers focused on the question of policy towards West New Guinea. The discussions in 1959 leading to Menzies's visit to Jakarta had shown a small but an increasing number of ministers who felt the policy of support and collaboration with the Dutch had exposed Australia unnecessarily and that it was time to distance Australia from the Dutch. At issue now was whether a consensus had formed in Cabinet in favour of change. As expected Hasluck led the argument, describing the assumptions contained in the submission as inaccurate or 'wrong'.[21] He dismissed the inference in the paper that the Dutch would leave or that self-government would be granted in fifteen years. Hasluck said the Dutch had assured him otherwise and described the consequences of a Dutch withdrawal as 'chaos'. In keeping with the views he had strongly put in earlier discussions in the Cabinet room, he argued that, once having committed itself to the Dutch claim of sovereignty, Australia could not now resile in the face of Indonesian intimidation. He made clear his view that 'our policy surely must be to do our utmost to keep [the] Dutch in'.[22] Menzies deployed a different argument and reminded Cabinet that existing policy was based on a solid judicial view of the Dutch claim to sovereignty. He had told President Sukarno that Australia was not a party principal in the dispute and that Australia would not cut across a freely determined settlement of the dispute. He also reminded his colleagues that Cabinet had decided that the strategic importance of Indonesia was of more consequence than Netherlands New Guinea. Menzies's preference was to keep Australia out of any written commitment with the Dutch and 'not egg on either party'. He added:

the strategic importance of New Guinea can be very easily over-rated. ... We must face up to the fact that we are not going to invest troops in [the] defence of New Guinea. The Australian people will not be prepared to go to war with a country of 80 million people with backstopping of Russia and [the] Chinese. So we must not take ourselves to the point where we can't recoil with honour.[23]

McEwen supported Menzies and warned that if the Dutch had begun to consider possible options for an act of self-determination in fifteen years time or later, they 'were mentally out of New Guinea' and, as a consequence, 'we are not to be entangled by [the] Dutch into embarrassing commitments'. He cautioned that 'we have no long history of close friendship with [the] Dutch and the plain fact is that they are trying to use us and we them'. McEwen was not prepared to change existing policy but he showed his increasingly pragmatic nature by adding 'geography will endure and Indonesia will always be where it is. We have to hope to ride the problem out'.[24] Sir Garfield Barwick (Attorney-General) agreed with his colleagues and added 'my view has solidified along line that [the] strategic importance of New Guinea [is] overstated and also that we should not be fearful of Indonesia coming into New Guinea'.[25] Senator Spooner maintained his earlier argument in favour of Australia distancing itself from the issue. He noted that 'my first reactions on this ... were that we should oppose even by force any Indonesian move ... [but] we can't wisely resist'. He told his colleagues that the government had to begin to prepare the public for a change in policy.

Australia preferred the status quo but this was under increasing pressure. Whichever way ministers looked at the West New Guinea dispute it had implications for Australia's security and regional relationships and innovative solutions were not obvious. Moreover, the issue was becoming increasingly entangled with the question of the future political development of the Australian half of New Guinea and, more generally, Australia's relations with Asia. The government had committed itself to supporting a distant but like-minded Netherlands holding on to the last remnants of its pre-war empire while recognising that a change of government in The Hague could bring about a change of policy towards West New Guinea. At the same time Australia wanted to develop a sound relationship with Indonesia. The twin objectives were in conflict with one another and could not easily be sustained. Australia was also dependent on the sympathetic attitude of its major allies, Britain and the United States, to support its policy towards the dispute. The discussions in Cabinet, recorded in the Cabinet Notebooks, revealed ministers who were aware of the implications of Australia's current policy but could not bring themselves to change course formally and to trust Indonesia to become a near neighbour in New Guinea.

In one of the few positive developments in this period, the Menzies Government received a letter from the Indonesian Foreign Minister, Dr Subandrio, in which he tried again to reassure Australia that Indonesia had no ambitions towards East New Guinea, or Australia. Subandrio told Menzies that:

> We certainly have no irredentist intention towards Australian territory. Certainly we are fully prepared, after recognition of our sovereignty over West Irian, to discuss ways and means of how to develop the territories under our respective jurisdiction and how to safeguard the frontier between Indonesia and Australia. I am adding this thought, because especially lately the rumours have been spread around, as if after the solution of the West Irian problem in our favour, we will embark upon an adventurous policy of expansion upon other territories, including East Irian [East New Guinea].[26]

Menzies acknowledged the letter and 'welcome[d] your friendly sentiments towards Australia and the Australian Territory of Papua and New Guinea'. However, in private, he told Patrick Shaw, the newly appointed Ambassador in Jakarta, during a meeting in January 1961 in Canberra that 'on the dangers of Indonesian control [of West New Guinea] … even if there were no immediate threat, it would cause constant irritation in East New Guinea, stimulation of agitation in, or actual independence movements, and so on'.[27] Menzies remained unconvinced of Indonesia's *bona fides*.

The United States begins to change tack

At the same time as the Menzies Government was examining the implications of the unresolved problem of West New Guinea for the security of the region and for bilateral relations, officials in London and Washington, in separate initiatives, were beginning to turn their attention to possible solutions. The re-examination in both capitals would see the abandonment by Washington of its decade-long policy of non-engagement with Australia being caught off-guard by the swiftness and completeness of the new policy approaches towards Southeast Asia being developed by the incoming Kennedy Administration.[28] Sir Garfield Barwick (appointed Minister for External Affairs in December 1961) was later to comment in Cabinet that 'we didn't act soon enough in getting into rapport with US [on West New Guinea] – we didn't have a meeting of minds'. Menzies acknowledged Barwick's assessment with the comment 'Barwick's historical point about events in West New Guinea is powerful'.[29]

The State Department had had the issue of West New Guinea under review from mid-1960 and, on 30 November 1960, a few weeks after John F. Kennedy had been elected President but before he took office, Graham Parsons, Assistant Secretary, Far East, in the State Department, called in the Australian Ambassador with the intention of briefing Australia on the results of the State Department's review.[30] Howard Beale, who had succeeded Sir Percy Spender as Ambassador to Washington in March 1958, had served in the Menzies Cabinet from 1949 to 1958. Parsons made clear to Beale that in Washington's mind 'free world interests had been damaged by the continuance of the quarrel between the Netherlands and Indonesia ... and that this damage would continue. ... The Communist bloc has benefitted from the situation. The Communists had exploited it both externally and internally'.[31] He added that the current US policy 'was not considered good enough'. In fact, the US position was now 'lamentable'. Parsons went on to argue that, while all solutions presented difficulties, the State Department was inclined to favour a United Nations trusteeship with the UN itself as trustee, an idea which had earlier been floated by Malaya's Prime Minister Tunku Abdul Rahman. Such a structure 'would take the issue out of the present atmosphere of crisis and diminish the risk of hostility' while 'Indonesia was much less likely to cause trouble in Netherlands New Guinea if the United Nations were there'. The collateral objective was 'preventing Indonesia from going Communist'. Parsons acknowledged that 'in his view Australia was the country most interested' in the type of settlement which could emerge. Australia's reactions, he said, 'would influence the State Department on whether it would continue on its present train of thought or cast about for alternatives'.[32]

Beale, who was scheduled to return to Canberra for consultations, responded to Parsons by noting that Australia 'had never set our face completely against the possibility of a trusteeship. We were most anxious to get the problem out of the area of conflict and controversy'.[33] He nevertheless questioned whether a trusteeship administered by the United Nations would 'achieve our objectives both politically and for the welfare of the natives of the territory'.[34] Beale undertook to consult Canberra but it soon became evident that he had not appreciated the full significance of the conversation with Parsons. Woodard has described Beale as having 'completely misjudged US policy on Indonesia and New Guinea'.[35]

Beale was invited to attend a Cabinet meeting on his return to Australia. His presentation did not ring any alarm bells. He told his former colleagues that the United States was 'very worried' about the West New Guinea dispute and 'impatient' with the Dutch. He added that in his view the 'strong attitude' of the United States was 'that they did not want Indonesia sovereignty' and that they had 'put up this idea of UN sovereignty without knowing just how it would operate'.[36] Beale had failed to alert ministers to the beginning of a major shift in US policy which gathered momentum once the Kennedy Administration had taken office in January 1961.[37]

The re-examination of policy options in Washington was matched in London where the Macmillan Government examined closely the concept of promoting a Federation of Melanesia embracing the Solomon Islands, Australian New Guinea and Netherlands New Guinea. The Federation was seen as a long-term option intended in part to provide a more solid structure in which the weaker West New Guinea could develop.[38] Australia would be obliged to include its half of New Guinea in the Federation but would not have a role in its administration. A similar idea had been current in some non-governmental quarters in Australia. The British idea, which was always rather vague, faded as a preference emerged for Washington's suggestion of a UN trusteeship arrangement over West New Guinea. As both Washington and London began to consider new options for a settlement, Australia soon found itself tested as to whether its diplomacy could keep pace with the rapidly changing turn of events as the West New Guinea dispute entered a phase of negotiation.

Australia challenged as events gather pace

The Australian Cabinet twice examined the US overture. At its first meeting on 6 February 1961, Menzies, also serving as Minister for External Affairs, advised his colleagues that his preferred approach was to 'show objective interest … temporize and point to the problems'. The second meeting, held immediately before Menzies was due to call on President Kennedy, took a harder line and noted that 'this proposal bristled with difficulties and that its publication might encourage the Indonesians to take precipitate action in the area'. Ministers agreed that Australia ought not to resist the principle of the idea of a trusteeship but the administering power should be the Netherlands. It again recommended the adoption of 'politically delaying tactics'.[39]

Menzies arrived in Washington four weeks after Kennedy's inauguration. He was the first in a series of leaders Kennedy met over the next three months from those countries with a direct interest in the dispute or who had a capacity to influence the parties principal. The President's meetings with Macmillan, Sukarno, Dutch Foreign Minister Luns, and Australian Ambassador Beale were used by him to gain a full understanding of the problem and to search for a possible solution. In this he was assisted by Secretary of State Dean Rusk and senior officers in the State Department who worked quickly to take advantage of what the President's Deputy Special Assistant for National Security Affairs, Walt Rostow, described as a 'unique but transient opportunity for action which might solve the problem'.[40]

In the papers prepared for Kennedy, officials advised that Australia's interest in the West New Guinea dispute derived from its territorial interests in the eastern half of the island and a 'defence interest based on their memories of the threat posed by the Japanese on New Guinea during World War II'.[41] The briefing warned that, 'apprehensive of Indonesia's turbulent political scene and strong Communist party, Australia fears that Indonesian control of West New Guinea might cause unrest in East New Guinea, pose a threat to the security of Australia itself, and prejudice Australian objectives with respect to East New Guinea'. It concluded that Australia considered potential Indonesian influence in East New Guinea to be a greater danger than an 'Indonesian nation drifting in the direction of more dependence on the Communists and greater hostility towards the West because of frustration over the non-attainment of its objective' (in West New Guinea).[42] Officials advised the President to 'assure him [Menzies] in this context that we regard very seriously our responsibilities under our Mutual Defence Treaty'.[43]

In a style which was to characterise his approach to most conversations on the subject, Kennedy first invited Menzies to set out Australia's position on the problem. In response, according to the White House record of the meeting, Menzies:

> reviewed the historic involvement of New Guinea in both world wars, mentioned its proximity to Australia and its importance from the standpoint of Australia's national security. He said all Australians feel emotionally and strongly about the West New Guinea issue and

react immediately to any danger that it might fall into the hands of a Communist-dominated Indonesia. He described the Indonesian position and the political, rather than legal, basis on which the Indonesians advance their claim. He questioned in this connection whether one could have assurance that control of West New Guinea would be the limit of Indonesian ambitions once control had been secured. He summarized the Indonesian position as a substitution of brown colonialism for white colonialism, and mentioned Australian sympathy for The Netherlands, whose property in Indonesia had been 'stolen' from them.[44]

Menzies added that he thought the ideal solution would be continued Dutch administration under a trusteeship but acknowledged that this was not politically feasible. He was dismissive of the other options that had been mooted, including Tunku Abdul Rahman's 'fantastic' proposal that a trusteeship might be created for a brief interval for the purpose of turning the territory over to the Indonesians. Both Kennedy and Menzies dismissed the British idea of a Federation of Melanesia. Menzies 'showed scepticism in regard to Indonesian attitudes and motives'.[45] The record acknowledged that Menzies had left the impression of 'genuine and continuing concern from the Australian national viewpoint over what, to Australia, was a potentially most serious problem'.[46]

Menzies's presentation of Australia's concerns had changed little over the decade since he had spoken in the Australian Parliament in 1949 or had argued his case to Kenneth Younger, Minister of State in the Foreign Office, in London in July 1950. They were the same concerns derived in the first instance from Australia's experience in the Second World War and sustained by its fear of the consequences of an Asian country coming in close proximity to Australian-controlled interests. While the discussions in the Cabinet room in Canberra had shown hints of flexibility and pragmatism, Menzies and his colleagues could not bring themselves to convey to Australia's allies a view other than one of not trusting President Sukarno and Indonesia. Menzies was still trapped in a mind set formed in the late 1940s.

Menzies was very pleased with the discussions in Washington. He had been greatly impressed by Kennedy's 'lively' mind and cabled McEwen and Holt to tell them that the President had given him 'over a couple of hours an opportunity to tell him about the New Guinea problem in its proper historic and national setting. I am sure that no American administration has been so completely put in the picture on this matter'.[47] Menzies referred to 'notions' from the 'official level in the State Department about a trusteeship for West New Guinea which would exclude the Netherlands'. He assured McEwen and Holt that this idea 'has not been adopted by either Kennedy or Rusk, and that after our discussions there may be a healthy disposition to preserve the status quo in West New Guinea'.[48]

As events were to prove over the next twelve months Menzies was incorrect in his assessment of the new administration's approach. Woodard has described Menzies as making 'a rare misjudgement about an American President' and as not being 'in tune with the White House's New Frontiersmen'.[49] Just as Prime Minister Hughes had misread President Wilson's mind on the terms of the peace settlement when they had met in 1918, Menzies had misread the new President's thinking. He had failed to appreciate Kennedy's deeper concerns about events in Asia, notably Laos and Vietnam, and the need to neutralise issues which could be used by communist elements in the region to strengthen their popular standing. Kennedy would pursue a strategy which, in quick time, would see him reverse the decade-long policy of non-involvement in the West New Guinea dispute preferred by the Eisenhower Administration. Australia's policy could not withstand the forceful pragmatism of Kennedy's approach to the issue.

The initiative in seeking a possible solution to the West New Guinea dispute was seized by the Kennedy Administration. Kennedy discussed the problem with Britain's Prime Minister Macmillan and Foreign Secretary Lord Home in Washington on 5 April 1961.[50] He drew attention to the fact that Sukarno would be visiting Washington on 24 April. Kennedy specifically asked Macmillan and Home what the Australian attitude would be to a trusteeship arrangement and whether Australia would be concerned if 'there were no response from their major allies in the event of an Indonesian attack on West New Guinea'. Home advised Kennedy that he thought Menzies would accept a trusteeship solution 'though he was not enthusiastic about it' and that 'the Australians would certainly be concerned at the prospect of West New Guinea in the hands of an Indonesia which itself might come under Communist rule'.[51] Macmillan privately told Beale that his assessment of the conversation with the President was that 'Kennedy would warn Sukarno off',[52] although the acting Permanent Secretary of the Foreign Office (Sir Roger Stevens) told the High Commission in London that the talks in Washington had revealed that the warning would not be made 'with much heart'. The Foreign Office added that 'the President regards the problem as a dangerous one and the Dutch as "wrong"'.[53]

President Kennedy was still searching for options when he held a private meeting with Beale on 6 April. Kennedy asked Beale: 'Tell me, how seriously does Australia really view the idea of Indonesia getting Dutch New Guinea?'[54] Beale relied on arguments similar to those presented by Menzies. He said 'the whole Australian nation would view it very gravely indeed'. He gave as the reasons 'the threat to the rest of New Guinea if a Communist Indonesia became our land neighbour; also the threat of an expansionist Indonesian dictatorship having a land border to our territory from which it could infiltrate and subvert the native population, leading probably to a claim to other parts of the island'. Beale reiterated Australia's support for the principle of self-determination and added that 'to permit more than one third of them [i.e. the indigenous population of West New Guinea] to be taken over by Indonesia was to perpetuate colonialism'. As to a trusteeship, Beale commented that 'a genuine trusteeship was a mirage because Indonesia simply would not accept [it], nor indeed would most of the Asians'. In response to the President's question 'What is the solution?' Beale said the 'sheet anchor to which I felt we should all cling was the principle of self-determination' to which Kennedy agreed but asked: 'What steps could be taken consistent with this principle to head-off the Indonesians?' Beale concluded by commenting that Kennedy 'made no specific proposal' but appeared to be looking for options. He added that he could not judge what effect 'his reputed anti-colonial sentiments and those of some of his advisers, may have' on policy development.[55] Beale had failed to appreciate the fundamental changes which were occurring in America's foreign policy under the new President and their impact on issues such as the US approach to the West New Guinea dispute and Indonesia.

The fourth meeting held by Kennedy was with the Dutch Foreign Minister, Luns, on 10 April. Luns warned the President that his country would not turn West New Guinea 'over to the Indonesians ... if they did so, this crisis might disappear but new crises would follow as the Indonesians moved against the Australian portion of New Guinea or against the Portuguese island of Timor'.[56] The President pressed Luns on why the Dutch were determined to remain in a 'faraway island which was really a great burden for them'. Luns had difficulty in articulating a case and offered Kennedy no suggestions for a solution to the dispute.[57] In a separate conversation with Secretary of State Rusk, Luns stressed the importance of the new US Administration sending an early and clear signal to Sukarno that it would not accept an act of aggression by Indonesia to secure West New Guinea.[58]

The final meeting in this series occurred on 24 April when President Sukarno, accompanied by Foreign Minister Subandrio and Deputy First Minister Leimena, called on President Kennedy.[59] Again, Kennedy used the meeting to pose questions and seek explanations. He pointedly asked Sukarno: 'Why do you want West Irian?' Sukarno replied just as directly that 'it is part of our country; it should be free'. Kennedy also raised the subject of Australia's attitude to the dispute and asked 'What about the eastern part of New Guinea?', to which Sukarno replied: 'This was never part of Indonesia, we have no claim to it, but West Irian is different. Long before the Dutch came, West Irian was Indonesian territory'. Later in the conversation Kennedy returned to the West New Guinea issue and said the 'problem was a very great concern to us [United States] and that Australia was disturbed. ... We want to see this matter come to an amicable conclusion'. Subandrio replied on Sukarno's behalf that 'several years ago these [relations between Australia and Indonesia] approached hostility. Australia wanted no relations with Asia. This has changed recently, however. Prime Minister Menzies was moving forward, demonstrating greater interest in establishing good relations with his Asian neighbours'. Kennedy added that 'Mr Menzies feels that if communism is successful in Indonesia it would constitute a greater threat to Australia if West Irian were in the possession of Indonesia. He pointed out that the US too was concerned about international communism in the area'.[60]

Unlike Luns, Sukarno and Sudandrio suggested a solution. Subandrio told the President that Indonesia would be 'willing to consider a trusteeship for a period of one or two years to make the transition to Indonesia's possession easier'. There could be no alternative to Indonesia taking possession of the area. Sukarno had earlier poured cold water on the idea of a plebiscite to allow the local population to determine whether they wanted to join Indonesia. Kennedy brought the meeting to a close by expressing his strong hope that Indonesia would not resort to force to secure its claim. Subandrio gave Kennedy the same assurance that Sukarno had given Menzies in 1959 that Indonesia had 'no intention of taking military action against West Irian'.[61]

The conversation between President Kennedy and his Indonesian counterpart at least confirmed that the new Administration had listened to the arguments put by Menzies and Beale as to Australia's interests in the dispute and its views on the implications of a settlement which would result in Indonesian control. Unfortunately for Australia, it also confirmed that the new Administration was actively searching for a solution to the dispute and was beginning to move away from a position of neutrality.

A further conversation with Indonesia

Australia had a further, and perhaps last, opportunity to present its views and to influence events when General Nasution, Indonesia's Minister for National Security, Chief of Staff of the Army and Chairman of the Government's National Front for the Liberation of West Irian, visited Australia in late April 1961. It was the first meeting between a senior Indonesian minister and senior Australian ministers in nearly eighteen months.

Nasution was accorded an almost identical welcome to that given to Subandrio in 1959. He was seen by Canberra as the Indonesian leader most capable of resisting the influence of communism in Indonesia and the most likely successor to Sukarno should the latter be removed from the scene. He met the Cabinet in Canberra and held two private meetings with Menzies and the Minister for Defence, Athol Townley, in Canberra and Sydney. If the Australian Government had hoped that Nasution might present a more moderate assessment of Indonesia's claims to West New Guinea it was disappointed. He did not deviate from the arguments presented by Sukarno and Subandrio in their meetings with Menzies in 1959 or with Kennedy in April 1961. He offered no hint that Indonesia was prepared to compromise its position or agree to a settlement based on a trusteeship arrangement. Nasution did however address directly what he described as Australian fears of Indonesian 'intentions', specifically that Indonesia would also want to claim East New Guinea. He 'assured ministers that this would not occur'.[62] He dismissed 'another fear that Indonesia would turn communist and become a tool of major communist powers to be used against the security of Australia'.[63]

At the private meeting in Sydney with only Menzies, Townley, General Nasution and Tange from External Affairs present, Menzies sought to assure Nasution that Australia had no secret military agreement or arrangements with the Netherlands. He did, however, add that Australia could not be 'indifferent if force were used' against West New Guinea but he was confident following the assurances given by President Sukarno, Subandrio and now Nasution that Indonesia contemplated no such thing. Nasution agreed that the government could make public his reiteration of that assurance. Menzies used the remainder of the conversation to speak of Australia's support for the principle of self-determination. He described Australia's attitude as 'it could be said that we do not support the Dutch but rather we support self-determination', a policy approach that was strongly supported by officers in the Department of External Affairs.[64]

Menzies was not fully won over by Nasution's statements and told New Zealand's Prime Minister Keith Holyoake that 'any breach of those undertakings [i.e. respect for the principle of self-determination and not to resort to the use of force] would create an entirely new situation in which Australia would have to reconsider the whole position'.[65] For his part, Nasution went away from the meeting pleased to hear from Menzies that Australia had no military arrangements or understanding with the Dutch.[66] Australia stayed in touch with Nasution over the next few years through a series of personal letters from Townley (cleared with External Affairs) which often referred to outstanding defence issues.

The ground moves from under Australia

The Australian Government's confidence that the West New Guinea issue was unfolding at a pace and in a direction consistent with its objectives was disturbed on 1 August when the Dutch Government presented an Aide Memoire which advised that it had been in discussion with the United States on an initiative in the United Nations to bring the issue to some form of resolution based on an act of self-determination and the creation of a UN trusteeship, assuming that Indonesia would be excluded as a trustee.[67]

The Dutch initiative was matched by a US proposal for a 'solution to the problem' which called for the appointment of a group of countries to report to the UN General Assembly 'with suggestions for a solution' while acknowledging that 'no form of trusteeship solution appeared practicable'.[68] At the same time the UK let it be known that it had been thinking of an alternative trusteeship arrangement. The presentation of all three ideas sparked a period of intense consultation in Canberra leading to a Cabinet meeting on 16 August.

The discussion in Cabinet again highlighted the complexity of the issue and the critical point reached in ministers' thinking. As the record in the Cabinet Notebook illustrates, their approach to the policy implications of developments often evolved during the course of the Cabinet room discussion.[69] McEwen began the meeting by noting 'first there is still a defence significance. Next we must contain Indonesia – it is expansionist and dangerous to us. We should keep it out of New Guinea. ... not use force but play for time'. As the meeting progressed and the debate turned to the question of whether the Dutch were seeking to extricate themselves from West New Guinea, McEwen told his colleagues:

> My interest in international affairs is my own national interest – that's the only reason why I'm interested in international affairs – and one thing in international affairs doesn't change – geography. We began with Billy Hughes declaring certain attachments to New Guinea – since then we have changed but [the] first change was still that we would fight to defend New Guinea – we were unanimous about that – but now, are we so certain – if we fight, win, lose or draw, we lose in terms of Asia. I feel we are hanging on too long to our Dutch attachment. We are the last to be attached. US and UK don't really mean it – we should disengage. … We can talk about self-determination – that's empty – what is it – Congo has it – I'd rather see the Indonesians get it (as I believe they will) – preserve what chance of stability there may be – the Indonesians have been driven into the arms of the Communists by its failures in [the] UN – it has gone to a military build up as an alternative – Dutch have contributed to this – so have we – we're in a new situation and should recognize it.[70]

McEwen concluded his remarks by recommending that while Australia should continue publicly to defend the concept of sovereignty, he would prefer a position of 'letting it fade away as a plank'.[71] McEwen's aim was to ensure that Australia was not left isolated and committed to fighting a rearguard action with the Dutch.

The Defence Minister, Athol Townley, had also changed his view to one of accepting the inevitability of an Indonesian takeover. He argued that:

> Indonesia now has such weapons and equipment that New Guinea [was] irrelevant to their ability to tackle Australia – of course [we would] rather have friendly Europeans there but if the alternative is to have a possibly friendly Indonesia there or certainly hostile Indonesia (if we adopt certain attitudes) better to seek the former – we're going to have to live alongside Indonesia and need to trade. Therefore I'm for being very careful about attitudes of anti-Indonesian kind.[72]

The thought of an unfettered Indonesian takeover appalled Senator William Spooner (Minister for National Development and Leader of the Government in the Senate). He told his colleagues 'I can't take any comfort in Indonesia getting New Guinea – I regard Indonesia as Communist or on the way to it – so I would feel we should look to a trustee arrangement'. Spooner, who had argued against continued support for the Dutch in earlier Cabinet meetings, added that he felt 'the situation is deteriorating against us – the Dutch patently fed up – UK have no stomach for it – US doubtful – Indonesia appetite increasing – must face fact' and support a trusteeship over West New Guinea.[73] Of the other ministers who took part in the debate, Hasluck remained resolute in his view that Australia should continue to support the principles of self-determination and Dutch sovereignty. He saw no reason to shift from established policy.

All ministers agreed that the use of force by Australia to support the Dutch position was not an option. Menzies summarised this point by noting 'we must not be thought by the Dutch or the world as being the backers of the Dutch because if that's so, when fighting occurs, we won't be there'.[74] This comment was made in the context of Australia having to deploy forces without the backing of the United States or Britain. In the past, the Australian Government, and particularly ministers such as McEwen, had strongly advocated the need for Australia to deploy forces if asked by the United States or the United Kingdom. A fortnight after Cabinet had discussed and rejected the idea of using force unilaterally to stop the Indonesians in West New Guinea, Menzies told ministers that Australia had to assist the United States in any emerging conflict in Laos in order to avoid a domino effect throughout Asia: 'as we need US [so] we must be willing to assist them'.[75]

The debate in Cabinet revealed the deep sense of unease about where Australia's support for Dutch retention of West New Guinea had left the country. Those ministers, such as McEwen, Holt, Hasluck and Menzies, who had debated the issue for at least ten years, applying arguments ranging from geography, history, race, anthropology, international law but primarily security, were now faced with the realisation that time was up. The involvement of a new American administration, keen to keep Indonesia from falling under communist influence, was having a profound effect. Menzies was dismissive of the early attempts by the Kennedy Administration to find a solution to the issue, describing Washington as 'playing around vaguely with an international solution – but nothing that will run'.[76] By October 1961 he had changed his assessment and warned his colleagues that 'one thing [that] becomes clearer in relation to West New Guinea and may apply to our New Guinea, is that our large friends are becoming wibbly wobbly'.[77]

Kennedy and Macmillan change the game

Over the next three months Australia was actively involved in discussions with Washington, London and The Hague as the Dutch, against Australia's advice, put a proposal to the UN General Assembly for the terms of a settlement. At the same time the possibility that Indonesia could turn to the use of force became an issue of immediate concern as Indonesia threatened to initiate a military offensive to secure West New Guinea. With this development came the vital question of whether Western leaders were prepared to act to deter Indonesia. In early October Indonesia's Foreign Minister, Dr Subandrio, warned Australia's Ambassador in Jakarta, Patrick Shaw, of a 'break' between the two countries and even the possibility of 'hostilities' following Australia's advocacy of self-determination during the UN debate on West New Guinea.[78] Newspaper articles in Jakarta and speeches by Sukarno and other leaders advocated direct confrontation as the only way to resolve the dispute. Following an alarming report from the US Ambassador in Jakarta of an imminent Indonesian attack, President Kennedy on 9 December sent a personal message to Sukarno urging restraint and also hinting at the possibility of further US involvement in finding a settlement to the dispute.[79] Britain reinforced the US message and also discussed with Subandrio possibilities for the commencement of a round of negotiations leading to a settlement.[80] Sukarno agreed to respect Kennedy's request. Nevertheless, on 19 December, in his Heroes Day speech he issued a rhetorical 'command' for a general mobilisation to retake West Irian in the near future and for the Indonesian flag to be raised over the territory.

Sukarno's 'command' coincided with a scheduled meeting in Bermuda of President Kennedy and Harold Macmillan on 22 December 1961. The subject of West New Guinea had not been included on the meeting's original agenda and the UK delegation hurriedly had to ask London for briefing on Australia's policy position. The discussion was to prove a turning point in London's and Washington's attitudes towards the dispute and in the search for a settlement. It would also be a turning point for Australia.

At Bermuda, where the other issues discussed included the Berlin Crisis, the war in the Congo, the Indian takeover of Goa and the resumption of nuclear testing in the atmosphere, both leaders placed the West New Guinea dispute in the context of East–West relations and the Cold War.[81] They were not prepared to create a new area of crisis in Southeast Asia nor to offend Indonesia and thereby possibly force Sukarno into the arms of the communists. While alert to and possibly sympathetic to Australia's security concerns, they were not willing to allow those concerns to dominate the course of events if the consequence were to be the emergence of the third largest communist state after the Soviet Union and China. After ten or more years of continuous diplomacy and representations, Australia's declared interests were to be abandoned, as London and Washington were not prepared to oppose Indonesia directly and militarily. Kennedy is reported to have confided to Macmillan prior to India's annexation of Goa in December 1961 and before the conference in Bermuda, 'let's face it, if at the end of the day Goa becomes Indian and West Irian becomes Indonesian, neither you in Britain or we in America are going to suffer any irrevocable damage. We must keep a sense of perspective about this'.[82]

According to the more detailed British record, the meeting was told that the US assessment, following recent talks with the Dutch Ambassador in Washington, was that the Dutch would be 'glad to extricate themselves ... if they could do so without national humiliation' and that they 'were prepared for a negotiated settlement which would leave the Papuans with a right of self-determination'.[83] The Dutch were reluctant to discuss these questions with the Indonesians alone and had said they would prefer to engage the 'good offices' of one or more representatives of another country. In response, Kennedy said that if the Dutch were now only concerned with finding an honourable way out then 'it would be a mistake for the Western Powers to involve themselves in supporting the Dutch in military operations'. He added that his administration had accepted 'no commitment to help the Dutch even by logistic support to resist such an attack and they would not wish to become involved in any new commitment of this kind'.[84] Macmillan noted Britain's obligation to provide logistic support but that he 'would be sorry to have to do this as it would have the effect of increasing tension between Indonesia [and] ... Malaysia and Singapore'. Kennedy added that 'the most likely result of military operations would be to strengthen the Communist position in Indonesia – which would be contrary to the interests of the West as a whole'.[85] Both leaders agreed that the position the Dutch had taken had 'largely' been due to the 'personal influence of ... Luns's and it was possible that other members of the Dutch Government would be prepared to look for ways to extricate the Netherlands from the territory. They suggested a direct approach be made to the Dutch Prime Minister, Jan de Quay, and the Minister of Finance, Jelle Zijlstra, thereby circumventing Luns. They also agreed that Dutch commercial representatives could be used as a lobbying mechanism to 'supplement' the approaches.

Both leaders were uncertain as to whether Australia would initiate any unilateral counter-measures against an Indonesian attack and agreed that they 'should each impress on the Australian Government the desirability of avoiding military operations in West Irian and ... it would be preferable that the Western Powers should refrain from offering to support the Dutch in resisting an Indonesian attack'. They also noted that the Australian Government 'could be reminded ... that active Western help to the Dutch ... was likely to provoke the Indonesians to take retaliatory action against Western interests in Indonesia which would be even more damaging to Australia than Indonesian occupation of West Irian'.[86]

In keeping with his undertaking to the President, Macmillan wrote to Menzies on 27 December with an account of the meeting. He told Menzies that if the West helped the Dutch in military operations 'we must assume that retaliatory action would be taken against Western interests in Indonesia. ... The President and I were inclined to think that the preservation of those interests and the discouragement of Communist influence in Indonesia are more important to the West than the maintenance of the Dutch position in Dutch New Guinea'.[87] As a result the Dutch should be persuaded to find a 'tolerable means' to 'extricate themselves' from the present position. Macmillan added 'we realize of course that Indonesian ambitions in New Guinea present special problems for you and the recent developments must be causing you a good deal of anxiety. I fear that we are faced here with a choice of evils'.[88]

A choice of evils

Tange told the US Chargé d'Affaires that 'Australia [had] bowed to what appeared to be inevitable' following news that the United States, Britain and the Netherlands all favoured negotiations. He added that Australia's attitude had not been arrived at 'without considerable misgivings'.[89] The misgivings were that 'the negotiations were likely to lead to Indonesian control of West New Guinea and that in this event Australia was faced with a real prospect of continuing friction with Indonesia in New Guinea'. Tange went on to say that 'what was on his mind was that in the long term given present Indonesian leadership, the ideologies being cultivated in Indonesia, the immensity of domestic Indonesia problems which would be a continuing temptation to resort, as a means of distraction, to external issues – we were bound to expect difficulties with Indonesia'.[90] Tange, possibly reflecting a degree of bitterness, directly asked for the United States to make clear whether it would respond with military action should Indonesia resort to force to secure West New Guinea. He added 'it was one thing to keep Indonesia uncertain and another to leave Australia so'.[91]

On 12 January 1962 Cabinet began a two-day meeting to consider its response to developments. It was the third time in twelve months that ministers had discussed the dispute in detail as well as its impact on Australia's security environment. In preparation for the meetings the ever-realistic John Bunting, Secretary of the Department of Prime Minister and Secretary to Cabinet, advised Menzies that 'we have to begin to break down in the public mind the idea that the retention of West New Guinea in friendly hands is essential to our defence'. He noted that Australia 'remain[ed] opposed to the use of force and we expect both undertakings – as to the avoidance of force and as to no claims on East New Guinea – to be honoured'. He reflected on the outcome of the discussions in Bermuda and noted 'we march with the US and the UK on all matters. It is not in our interest to act alone'.[92]

Cabinet had before it a long and detailed submission from the newly-appointed Minister for External Affairs, Sir Garfield Barwick.[93] Barwick, a brilliant Sydney barrister, had been elected to Parliament in 1958 and had immediately been appointed Attorney-General. He had acted as Minister for External Affairs during Menzies's absences overseas and had been appointed Minister for External Affairs on 22 December 1961. Historians such as Peter Edwards and Garry Woodard have argued that 'Barwick gambled his political career in unhesitatingly making [the West New Guinea dispute] the first matter on which he set out to change policy and Australia's regional image'.[94] Moreover, 'he 'turned his government around' on the issue and that 'no one else could have done it'.[95] Stuart Doran has pursued a different line of argument to that of Edwards and Woodard. He has argued, without the benefit of the Cabinet Notebooks, that the decisions by Kennedy and Macmillan in Bermuda had isolated Australia and that it was forced to 'surrender' its position on West New Guinea to the decisions taken by Kennedy and Macmillan. In Doran's opinion, 'the notion that Barwick's personal influence was decisive in changing Australian policy is incorrect. ... At most he added his voice to the general agreement that Australia was alone'.[96] Like Doran, Edwards and Woodard did not have access to the Cabinet Notebooks when drawing their conclusions. If they had they would have been alert to the changes in ministers' attitudes which had been occurring over the previous two to three years. A pragmatism had emerged in the approach of influential ministers, such as McEwen. In short, Barwick was facing a sympathetic audience.

Barwick took ministers back to basics and argued against the continuation of a decade-long policy approach. He acknowledged the 'two policy targets' which had guided Australia throughout the 1950s, notably that the Dutch remain in West New Guinea and Australia's wish to build a positive bilateral relationship with Indonesia. These 'targets were in truth from the beginning antithetical' and they were 'now fast moving to the point where they are mutually exclusive, if indeed that time has not already passed'.[97] His assessment was that 'the point has now arrived ... when the Dutch inevitably must go. ... The choice either now or in the near future is whether the Dutch go before or after a military attack or go in pursuance of a negotiated settlement'.[98]

The argument then turned to the question of Australia's interests and Barwick argued that 'Australia's real interest lies above all with a friendly and cooperative, and if at all possible, a non-Communist, Indonesia'. This was the 'paramount policy to be pursued'. In part, he argued that a friendly Indonesia would be a 'greater bulwark against the southward march of Communism than a Papuan State of New Guinea created and existing without Indonesian goodwill could ever prove'.[99] He also told Cabinet that his 'fundamental conclusion [was] that whatever else we must avoid a white-coloured war over New Guinea especially as the Asian's view is that the logic is with Indonesia'.[100] The hard-line Hasluck questioned Barwick's last statement, arguing that 'we should not act by our estimation of the Asian mind ... we must adhere to principles of international conduct – if we don't we throw civilization overboard'.[101]

The immediate objective according to Barwick was to resolve the dispute between the Netherlands and Indonesia. It could no longer drift or wait for a start of hostilities. He suggested that Australia break with its long-standing practice of remaining on the sidelines as an interested observer and instead take the initiative and join Britain and the United States in searching for the terms of a negotiated settlement. He acknowledged that the public held very strong views as to the importance of the island for Australia's security, describing it as 'a frontier beyond the frontier'. The public had been warned that an Indonesian takeover of part of the island would have consequences for East New Guinea and that Indonesia also held ambitions to secure the whole of the island. Barwick offered no suggestions as to how to manage this aspect of the issue except to argue that Australia would contribute to any United Nations force formed to suppress aggression and to maintain peace in the area.

The Cabinet agreed with the assessment that West New Guinea would sooner or later pass to Indonesia and, with the exception of Hasluck, most agreed that it was no longer 'vital' to Australia's security outlook. Ministers also agreed with Menzies's assessment that 'we must not get into a position where we have military obligations to fight the Indonesians on behalf of the Dutch in West New Guinea – we would be on our own and there is no need for us to get into that position'. For the first time Menzies suggested that 'if there is any remaining doubt in Dutch mind we should tell them plainly that we won't be aiding unilaterally if there is fighting – we can't ourselves promote what would be a Dutch surrender'. He added that a war with Indonesia 'won't be an affair of outposts and West New Guinea [would] therefore not [be] vital'.[102] Ministers also endorsed Menzies's view that the United States should be told that Australia firmly believed that the use of force [by Indonesia] should be prevented. Menzies even proposed to the Cabinet that 'we ought to stop using [the expression] "self-determination" but if we do we'll be in trouble with having abandoned the ark of the covenant – problem therefore [is] to get less ambiguous expression'. Senior officials in the Department of External Affairs had been the strongest advocates of promoting the principle of self-determination. At this critical point in the development of policy towards the West New Guinea dispute they had lost their influence and their views were replaced by others in the Department.[103] While ministers acknowledged this change of sentiment, Menzies took the opportunity to reaffirm the assessment that:

> East New Guinea is Australian territory – for us to take an attitude that we would not defend it would be unthinkable – we must defend it and we would – nothing else would satisfy either our obligations or our conscience – so an attack on East New Guinea is an attack on us – we would have allies if ANZUS and SEATO mean anything – but even if not we would defend.[104]

As he had done when responding to Casey's submission in early 1960, Hasluck held firmly to the established Cabinet line and showed little inclination to modify it. He argued that 'neat capitulation is not a method of getting success in negotiations … we have a considerable rearguard action to perform … I would look for some check to Soekarno', possibly through the UN. He expressed his disquiet that Barwick proposed to 'run away from our obligations to the Dutch', even though he (Hasluck) accepted that the Dutch would not be present in West New Guinea forever. He argued that 'if Dutch colonization is not acceptable why should we facilitate Indonesian colonialism?' He objected to rewarding 'Soekarno's antics and threats of war' by offering a solution to the dispute and suggested instead that the issue be referred to the United Nations.[105]

As had been evident in the earlier Cabinet room discussions, McEwen showed greater flexibility in his thinking than his colleagues. He argued that 'as between the two alternatives of yielding to the threat of force in order to save fighting or to uphold the principle of not yielding at the risk of war, I would take the first. It means … international safety and also political sense'.[106] He acknowledged that 'possession of West New Guinea in Dutch hands may not be critical in same degree that it is critical to have friendly power in Indonesia. If we continue to frustrate Indonesian ambition to have West New Guinea we will be in state of unfriendliness'. Defence Minister Townley agreed with McEwen while Hasluck maintained his hard-line attitude and told his colleagues that 'the defence significance is not that we don't have West New Guinea but that some unfriendly power does'. He acknowledged the intelligence assessment before them that East New Guinea interests would be damaged if Indonesia secured control of West New Guinea. He asked 'what happens to East New Guinea if Indonesia gets West New Guinea?' to which McEwen replied 'frankly I leave that to history'.[107] Hasluck continued to argue against the idea of placing Indonesia as a first priority. He told his colleagues that 'we shouldn't assume that we can buy Indonesia's friendship by some assisting action now – if their self-interest or ambitions inclined them to some other course in future they will follow that'.[108] McEwen accepted Hasluck's logic but added 'while you can't win friendship necessarily you can win animosity if you frustrate'.

A policy of 'doing nothing'

Ministers did not, however, support Barwick's proposal for Australia to look for ways to promote a formula to solve the dispute. McEwen convinced his colleagues that 'we ought not to think that having no policy and having a policy of doing nothing are synonymous. … my policy is [to] know what I want (which I do) but to do as close to nothing as possible, except in the direction of developing public opinion'.[109] Ministers agreed that an initiative such as that proposed by Barwick was 'unnecessary and inappropriate' but also wanted the US and UK to be advised of 'the enduring importance to the Western world of the principle of strength in the face of threats of aggression for territorial purposes and to the possible embarrassment to Australia of the continuance of threats of the use of force.[110] Menzies released a public statement on 12 January which summarised the Cabinet's views and reminded Indonesia of its 'explicit assurances' that it would not use arms to enforce its claim to West New Guinea and that it 'did not and would not make any claim to that portion of Papua and New Guinea for which Australia had direct responsibility'. He added that Australia 'recognizes and will discharge its prime responsibility for the security of Australia, its territories and its people'.[111] Hasluck made a similar statement in Port Moresby in February 1962 and Barwick told the House of Representatives that 'we have territorial rights which we will defend to the utmost'.[112]

Australia's continuing alarm at the possible use of force by Indonesia was made known to the US State Department when Beale called on Rusk on 16 January 1962. Barwick had cabled instructions to Beale for his use in the meeting. His tone was forthright and robust, perhaps more so than the more nuanced conversation in the Cabinet room. Barwick nevertheless drew on those discussions and referred to Australia's anxiety at the absence of a response from the international community to Indonesia's threat to use force. He described Indonesia's own response when assurances not to use force were sought as 'evasive and almost contemptuous'.[113] Australia was worried that Indonesia's 'demagogic and irresponsible leader' would be unable to resist the temptation to use force. Australian public opinion felt a 'profound uneasiness at the implications for the world in the 1960's if this kind of sword-waving passes without rebuke, much less warning of consequences if force is used'. This would lead the Australian community to ask 'why President Sukarno should be believed when he says there is no Indonesian interest in Australian New Guinea, and what other expansionist pretensions we may expect in the air and sea spaces and territories adjacent to Indonesia'.[114] Barwick urged Beale to tell the United States to use its influence to turn Indonesia away from the threat to use force and towards negotiations, otherwise 'it may be difficult for us to maintain our policy' of recognising a settlement arrived at without duress.[115]

Rusk responded to Beale's representations and the expressions of concern at possible future Indonesian 'aspirations' by asking whether Australia had sent reinforcements to Australian New Guinea and whether we had suffered any inconvenience in the use of sea or air communications.[116] Beale advised that the government had not sent reinforcements although he did not 'discount the possibility of this happening'. Rusk asked Beale whether 'there was any nervousness in Australia about whether the United States would assist in protecting Australian territory' to which Beale had replied that 'many Australians' held some doubts. Beale later told Rusk that there was a feeling in Australia that the United States, in respect of the New Guinea problem, was 'ignoring vital Australian interests'. Rusk took offence at the suggestion and, according to Beale, 'cut back quickly and curtly with a rhetorical question as to whether Australia itself had mobilized' and that if it had done so 'it would be more persuasive'.[117] Rusk concluded by telling Beale that the United States preferred not to deliver ultimatums to Jakarta but would instead focus on creating the atmosphere to promote negotiations. He told Beale 'why should the United States fight and give up any hope of good relations with 100 million Indonesians for the sake of a few people in West New Guinea'. Beale concluded his report of the conversation by noting that 'Rusk [had] added that the United States was not ignoring our part of the world – the despatch of 3000 American troops to Vietnam was evidence of this'.[118]

The difficulty with Australia's argument was that it did not have the military means available to initiate or sustain a military response, even if it were so inclined. Menzies and others may have referred to the government's determination to defend Australia's interests but they had few options available to them to do so.[119] The choices amounted to declarations without real substance, particularly military substance, to support them. The government had embarked on a build-up of the navy but this would take a number of years. In contrast to that decision, in one of the few defence-related initiatives at this time specifically related to Papua and New Guinea, Cabinet rejected a proposal from Senator John Gorton (Minister for the Navy) to close the naval base at Manus Island on the grounds that it had not been adequately maintained. Most ministers opposed the idea. Holt described the base as a 'political asset' and said that 'to abandon it would be a mistake'. Townley agreed, while Menzies summed up his views by noting 'the overwhelming political view is that we should not be giving any impression of withdrawal from Manus'.[120]

As events unfolded throughout 1962 leading to the initiative to appoint the American diplomat Ellsworth Bunker to act as a mediator in the negotiation of a settlement to the dispute, Australia continued to highlight the threat to use force. This was discussed at the ANZUS Council meeting in Canberra in May, with Barwick warning of the consequences but also reminding the US of Australia's concern that, as an outcome of a settlement, 'instead of a friendly power to our north we had the prospect of an Indonesian West New Guinea and an Indonesia under communist domination'.[121] The communiqué issued following the Council meeting drew attention to the application of the ANZUS Treaty to the 'island territories under the jurisdiction of any of the three governments'.[122] Barwick drew specific attention to this reference in his press conference following the meeting.

Barwick paid his first visit to Jakarta in July 1962 as part of a tour through Southeast Asia. The visit was intended to try to pave the way for a more balanced and productive relationship between the two countries but the tensions which were accompanying the negotiations over a settlement to the Dutch New Guinea dispute overshadowed the visit. In his conversation with Sukarno, Barwick made clear Australia's opposition to the use of force, arguing that such actions 'bred suspicion of Indonesian motives and doubt of its good faith ... [it] endangered the friendship of the Australian people'.[123] In response to Barwick's question, President Sukarno confirmed that Indonesia had claims only to the former Dutch East Indies, while Subandrio, who was present at the meeting, added that Indonesia had no claim to North Borneo or to East New Guinea.[124] Subandrio repeated this statement during his separate meeting with Barwick, adding that a claim to East New Guinea would be inconsistent with the principles underlying Indonesia's claim to West New Guinea.[125] On his return to Australia Barwick provided the press with an outline of his conversations in Jakarta, including 'an assurance (from Subandrio) that Indonesia had no claim nor design upon any Australian territory and in particular East New Guinea'.[126]

While senior officials, such as Tange, were sceptical of Indonesia's intentions, Indonesia's repeated assurances must have gained some acceptance in Canberra as Menzies had told his British counterpart in June that he did not think Indonesia would assert any claim to East New Guinea and that communist opinion would be satisfied by the acquisition of West New Guinea. Menzies added that 'if the Indonesians had further territorial ambitions they were more likely to look to the north. They might be tempted to attack Timor or even the Borneo Territories. This was one of the reasons why he favoured the creation of a Greater Malaysia'.[127]

After a round of difficult negotiations marked by Indonesian intransigence and requiring the intervention of President Kennedy with the Indonesian Foreign Minister, agreement on the terms of a settlement was reached on 31 July and formally signed on 15 August. West New Guinea would be placed under a UN Temporary Authority on 1 October 1962 and transferred to Indonesian control on 1 May 1963. An exercise in self-determination would be held before the end of 1969. Barwick briefed his Cabinet colleagues on the terms of the settlement on 6 August with Holt asking the only question on the financial arrangements governing the cost of the UN administration.[128] On 17 August Barwick wrote to Subandrio welcoming the settlement and promising a 'spirit of continuing cooperation' between the administrations of both halves of the island.[129]

Conclusion

The settlement of the West New Guinea dispute ended a difficult twelve-year-long period in Australia's relations with Indonesia. In Woodard's assessment, 'the New Guinea dispute [had] carried enormous baggage arising out of Australia's deep-seated fear of threats from Asia and from Sukarno's Indonesia in particular; the doubtful dependability of great and powerful friends and the invidious responsibilities of orderly decolonisation at the height of international anti-colonialism'.[130] Edwards has added a further dimension by arguing that 'the divergent policies of the US and Australia towards West New Guinea established a major concern, seldom expressed publicly, for the Australian Government ... [as] the Americans were taking a different stance on an area of extreme strategic sensitivity to the Australians'.[131] Pemberton agrees with this analysis and has noted that 'the US alliance was of little value as an instrument of Australian policy because of the conflict in Australian–US interests'. He has also argued that Indonesia's responses during the US-sponsored negotiations were a 'further humiliation' for the Menzies Government and 'cruelly expos[ed] its impotence'.[132]

The fourth historian who has examined the dispute in detail, Stuart Doran, as noted in Chapter 3, has argued that in the early phases of the dispute Australia sought to project itself as a 'preeminent power' in Southeast Asia and that it behaved with a sense of 'imperial authority'. He has concluded that by 1962 'Australia's view of itself as the power south of Singapore was utterly destroyed'.[133] Moreover, the 'country was now completely dependent in the area – both militarily and politically – on its two main allies. ... Australia was no longer allowed to determine its own path in offshore SEA [Southeast Asia] and, for the first time, it shared a land border with a threatening Asian power'.[134] Doran's thesis that Australia claimed the status of a preeminent power in Southeast Asia is, as argued earlier, wide of the mark and not substantiated by the debates in Cabinet. It is true, however, that as a result of the West New Guinea dispute Australia was now increasingly dependent on the policy directions to be pursued in Asia by its two allies. This was to become evident in the months immediately ahead.

Australian leaders, scarred by the events of the Second World War but also protective of the fundamentals of the White Australia policy, elected to treat Sukarno's Indonesia as a threat. A distrust of Indonesia was fundamental to Australia's strategic outlook in this period. Alan Renouf, former Secretary of the Department of Foreign Affairs, has described the Australia of this period as 'The Frightened Country'.[135] This is an apt description of Australia's approach throughout the 1950s towards Indonesia and towards a settlement of the West New Guinea dispute. The British Labour Government in 1950 had told Spender and Menzies that Australia's long-term interests were best served by building a relationship with Indonesia. Menzies and his colleagues, supported by the Labor Opposition and the Australian press, preferred to keep Indonesia at a distance, and certainly as far removed from Australian territory as possible, despite occasionally admitting to themselves the need to build a positive relationship with Australia's northern neighbour.

Australia's need to defend Papua New Guinea had played a significant part in the response to Indonesia's campaign to secure West New Guinea. It was a constant in assessments beginning in 1950 through to the end of the decade, a fact highlighted by Edwards in particular. It rose to sharper prominence as the decade progressed and the prospect of Indonesia securing West New Guinea appeared closer. It formed part of the political argument employed by Menzies, Spender, Casey and Barwick in conversations with Australia's allies, as well as part of the assessments prepared by the country's military advisers. It featured repeatedly in discussions in the Cabinet room with ministers unanimous in their view that Australia was not only obliged to defend Papua New Guinea against Indonesia but that this was a fundamental element of Australia's national identity and interests. Pemberton has drawn on the views of General John Wilton, Chief of the General Staff, to conclude that for Australia, 'if Indonesia's takeover of West New Guinea had been its "Munich", then an Indonesian threat to Papua New Guinea would be its "Poland": a *casus belli*'.[136]

Australia had faced a complex set of international and regional security problems in the 1950s. It was soon to find that the regional and international environment was to become even more dangerous. Militarily, Australia had been unprepared for the challenges of the 1950s and was soon to find itself even more exposed as a new episode of confrontation with Indonesia erupted and it faced new defence obligations in Vietnam.

Chapter 7

INDONESIA, CONFRONTATION AND PROTECTING PAPUA NEW GUINEA 1962–1963

'We will defend these territories [Papua and New Guinea] as if they were part of our mainland; there must be no mistaken ideas about that'.

Robert Menzies 1963

The early years of the 1960s were unexpectedly difficult times for Menzies and the Liberal–Country Party Government. The coalition had suffered a near fatal setback at the 1961 general elections due to its economic policies and had retained government with only a two seat majority – or one seat after it had provided a Speaker for the House of Representatives. Menzies was unsure of the longevity of his government. He told his British counterpart, Harold Macmillan, that his 'nominal majority includes one or two people who would be quite happy to make mischief in my absence (overseas)'.[1]

Menzies survived this uncertain period to emerge victorious in the 1963 election for the House of Representatives and to remain in government until his retirement in January 1966. His Cabinet throughout this period was a mixture of experience and ambition. In 1961 the British High Commissioner in Canberra, Lord Peter Carrington, provided London with a portrait of its leading members.[2] Menzies was once again described as the dominant personality both in parliament and in the country and 'head and shoulders above the average Australian'. He was also portrayed as 'an arrogant man' who was not good at delegating. After Menzies, Deputy

Prime Minister McEwen was described as the only Cabinet member 'of any real stature' with a 'keen and intelligent interest over a wide field of economic affairs'. (Carrington made no reference to McEwen's growing influence over Australia's foreign policy and its relations with Asia.) Harold Holt (Treasurer) was seen as a disappointment. He was well informed but had 'not so far showed the necessary qualities of leadership and statesmanship or lived up to the promise he earlier showed'. The newly appointed Defence Minister, Athol Townley, 'has yet to show any outstanding qualities as a statesman or politician'. William McMahon (Minister for Labour and National Service) had 'little ability or force of character', although there was more to him 'than he looks or sounds'. He was, however, seen as 'intensely ambitious'. Senator John Gorton (Minister for the Navy) was also called 'intensely ambitious', although 'he tends to give the appearance of a lightweight'. Paul Hasluck (Minister for Territories) was clearly difficult to assess. His hard work in a sensitive portfolio was admired but he was acknowledged as a 'difficult minister' who stood 'aloof because of his intellectual qualities'. Finally, Sir Garfield Barwick (Minister for External Affairs and Attorney-General) was seen in 1961 as lacking in parliamentary experience and political 'nous' but with his 'obvious ability' was 'progressively establishing himself as a possible successor to Mr Menzies'. These men were to lead Australia through the next crisis with Indonesia.[3]

There was an air of expectation that the Labor Party could win the next election due in 1963 given the dramatic fall in the government's popularity. Arthur Calwell had succeeded Dr Evatt as leader of the Labor Party on 7 March 1960 with E. Gough Whitlam as his deputy. Calwell was to lead the party in its opposition to the re-introduction of conscription and Australia's involvement in the Vietnam War. Such was the possibility that Calwell could become Prime Minister that he was invited to call on President Kennedy on 23 July 1963 during his first overseas visit since the late 1940s. Despite his precarious position in the Parliament Menzies slowly reasserted control as the Opposition fumbled key security and foreign policy issues. Australian politics was to remain unchanged for the next decade.

In contrast, Indonesia under Sukarno continued its steady economic decline. James Ingram, Deputy Head of Mission in Jakarta whose reporting style was a perfect counterbalance to the sharply-focused but nevertheless quicksilver, uninhibited, almost stream-of-consciousness style of K. C. O. (Mick) Shann, who had taken up duty as Ambassador to Indonesia in November 1962, sent Canberra a portrait of Sukarno and Indonesia in 1964.[4] Ingram described Sukarno as a 'potentate who rules through a court, playing favourites, compartmentalizing his aides while exploiting their weaknesses whether it be pride, cupidity, avarice or sexual appetite'. His power was 'paramount' and 'becoming increasingly absolute' and he had achieved this status as a 'function of his charisma, his shrewdness and the appeal of his ideology'. His 'system of rule puts a premium on amorality and lack of character as the dominant quality of his subordinates'. Sukarno's 'main assistants were opportunists and sycophants', while Foreign Minister Subandrio was 'the epitome of the clever, ingratiating lackey who, however, lacks any real guts'. As to where Sukarno was leading Indonesia, Ingram described him as 'obsessed with Indonesia's destiny as the dominant power in the region'. As a consequence 'if there were a settlement on Malaysia, Sukarno would have to turn to another external adventure'. Indonesia's future was seen as possibly a 'national communist' state which could be expansionist in outlook.[5]

As noted in the earlier chapters on the West New Guinea dispute, a strong body of writing also exists on Confrontation and Australia's response and it is not the intention of this book to repeat those assessments of the crisis. Instead the aim is to assess the place of Papua New Guinea in determining how Australia responded to developments and the importance Australian decision-makers attached to Papua New Guinea when making decisions about Confrontation.[6]

Malaysia formed – trouble erupts

Indonesia's policy of Confrontation towards the newly formed Malaysia was a more complex international and regional issue than the West New Guinea dispute. It was conducted, as John Subritzky has argued, in a period of heightened Cold War tension involving challenges from the Soviet Union and Communist China to Britain and the United States in both Europe and Southeast Asia.[7] The Vietnam War was beginning to escalate, while Laos remained under serious threat from insurgents. The United States was under pressure to finalise a policy position on the extent to which it wished to be engaged militarily in Southeast Asia. In addition, Confrontation involved a number of significant Southeast Asian regional states, principally Indonesia, Malaysia, Singapore and the Philippines.

In November 1961 in principle agreement had been reached on the establishment of the Federation of Malaysia incorporating Malaya and Singapore. Agreements reached in subsequent months saw the British North Borneo Territories of Sabah and Sarawak included in the Federation.

The November agreement, negotiated by Britain, Malaya and Singapore, was that the Federation would come into being on 31 August 1963 and that Britain would retain unrestricted access to the defence facilities in Singapore.[8] Initially, as Subritzky has noted, Subandrio, privately and later publicly at the United Nations, expressed his country's support for the concept of the Federation.[9] However, the steady and favourable early path towards the formation of Malaysia was blocked as Indonesia came to believe that the proposed Federation would in fact lead to Britain remaining in Southeast Asia to meet its obligation to defend Malaysia. Indonesia perceived the proposed Federation as a 'neo-colonial construct of an imperialist power'.[10] Sukarno's hostility crystallised following the suppression by British troops in December 1962 of a revolt in Brunei led by Sheik Azahari. On 20 January 1963 Subandrio announced that Indonesia would pursue a policy of 'confrontation' against the proposed Federation. In April 1963 'volunteers', widely assumed to be supported by Indonesia, crossed the Sarawak border and clashed with British troops.

In late May and early June 1963 attempts were made to promote a dialogue between Malaysia, the Philippines and Indonesia and a solution to the crisis appeared possible. Hopes were dashed, however, when Indonesia reacted negatively to the announcement on 9 July 1963 that Britain, Singapore and Malaya had reached agreement (the London Agreement) on the establishment of Malaysia, with provision for the maintenance of British bases. Further attempts to reach a negotiated settlement were made at the Manila Summit of July–August 1963 between the leaders of Indonesia, Malaysia and the Philippines but these too failed. By late July 1963 Sukarno had accelerated his campaign against the proposal, declaring on 15 September 1963, the day before 'Malaysia Day', that Malaysia was illegal and would not be recognised by Indonesia. This was followed by the attacks on the British Embassy and the Malaysian chancery in Jakarta. Indonesia launched a publicly declared policy of 'Crush Malaysia'.

On 25 September 1963 Menzies told the Parliament that Australia would contribute to Britain's efforts to defend Malaysia's territorial integrity and independence. On 13 October 1963 Sukarno formally announced: 'Now I declare officially that Indonesia opposes Malaysia'. Further violent clashes, subversive activities in Singapore and Indonesian guerrilla attacks on British Borneo contributed to a rapid deterioration in relations. A summit meeting between Sukarno and Malaysia's Tunku Abdul Rahman in Tokyo in June 1964 failed to achieve a resolution of the dispute, leading to heightened fears of an escalation of fighting. Indonesian military attacks broadened to major military operations, including seaborne landings by Indonesian troops on the Malayan peninsula.

In response, Britain and its allies, including Australia, deployed significant military assets to defend Malaysia. At the height of Confrontation, Britain had 68,000 servicemen in Southeast Asia and a fleet of 80 naval vessels, including two aircraft carriers.[11] Australia had accepted an undertaking in 1959 to assist in the defence of Malaysia through its participation in the Commonwealth Strategic Reserve, its earlier commitment through ANZAM to defence coordination and planning with Britain, New Zealand and Malaysia and, more generally, through SEATO. Nevertheless, the key links, as Moreen Dee has noted, were through ANZAM and SEATO.[12] As discussed earlier, Australia also had a long-established belief that its security began with the preservation of a defensive line stretching from Malaya to the South Pacific. However, the government adopted a cautious and highly graduated approach to the timing and scope of the actual deployment of its troops to Malaysia. In October 1964 the first clash occurred between Australian and Indonesian troops in West Malaysia. In December 1964 Malaysia appealed to the United Nations for assistance should Indonesia continue with its acts of aggression. Indonesia responded to this appeal, and to Malaysia taking a seat on the Security Council, by withdrawing from the United Nations and its agencies in January 1965.

Throughout 1965 Britain was focused on the need to build its military resources to meet the threat from Indonesia. While attention was directed to this issue, internal pressures within the Federation caused Singapore to secede on 9 August 1965, although Malaysia and Singapore remained resolved to defend themselves against Indonesian confrontation. It was not until the attempted coup on 30 September 1965 which saw a dramatic realignment of political forces in Jakarta that tensions between Indonesia and its neighbours lessened. Eventually Confrontation was officially abandoned on 11 August 1966, although few if any clashes had occurred between the major parties in the six months beforehand.

The same dilemma which had confronted the Menzies Cabinet throughout the West New Guinea dispute had returned during the period of Confrontation: how to maintain the elements of a sound bilateral relationship with Indonesia while protecting its national and regional defence and security interests. It was also a test of Australia's capacity to judge the extent to which its interests in maintaining an open relationship with Indonesia could be weighed against its need to protect its interests in Papua New Guinea.

Australia's wartime leaders in London, 1918. In civilian dress from left to right: Sir Joseph Cook (Minister for the Navy), William Morris Hughes (Prime Minister), Andrew Fisher (former Prime Minister and serving as High Commissioner in London) and Senator George Pearce (Minister for Defence).
Source: National Archives of Australia; M4063, 1.

Australian Minister for External Affairs, Percy Spender with President Sukarno and Fatmawati Sukarno at the Istana Merdeka, Jakarta, January 1950.
Source: Department of Foreign Affairs and Trade.

Prime Minister Menzies on arrival in Port Moresby on 24 April 1957 for his first visit to the Territory of Papua and New Guinea. He is seen accompanied by the Police Commissioner C. Normoyle. *Pacific Islands Monthly*, Vol. XXVII No 10 May 1957, page 19; reproduced courtesy *Fiji Times*, Suva.

Indonesia's Minister for Foreign Affairs, Dr Subandrio being met on arrival in Australia by R. G. Casey, Minister for External Affairs and John McEwen, Deputy Prime Minister and Minister for Trade, February 1959. Source: National Archives of Australia; A8281, 13, IFM 1/1.

President Sukarno welcomes Prime Minister Menzies, Istana Negara (State) Palace, Jakarta, December 1959. Source: National Archives of Australia; A1775, RGM2.

Prime Minister Robert Menzies with President Sukarno at Istana Negara, Jakarta, December 1959. Source: National Archives of Australia; A1775 RGM 1.

John McEwen, Deputy Prime Minister and Minister for Trade with President John F. Kennedy, The White House, 1963.
Source: National Archives of Australia; M60, 100.

Menzies Cabinet in November 1963. Prime Minister Menzies is seated at the centre of the table with John McEwen, Deputy Prime Minister and Minister for Trade on his right, and Harold Holt, Treasurer on his left. Paul Hasluck, Minister for Territories is on the far right at the table. William McMahon, Minister for Labour and National Service is seated at the far left.
Source: National Archives of Australia; A1200, L45498.

Paul Hasluck, Minister for External Affairs, with President Sukarno, Presidential Palace, Jakarta, June 1964. Standing in the background are Keith Waller, First Assistant Secretary, Division 1, Department of External Affairs, and K. C. O. Shann, Australian Ambassador to Indonesia.
Source: Department of Foreign Affairs and Trade and National Archives of Indonesia.

Prime Minister Gough Whitlam, PNG Chief Minister Michael Somare and Minister for External Territories, Bill Morrison, January 1973.
Source: National Archives of Australia; A6180, 18/1/73/30.

Minister for Defence, Lance Barnard and PNG Chief Minister, Michael Somare, Port Moresby, January 1973.
Source: *Post Courier*, page 3, 26 January 1973.

Arrival in Port Moresby of Prime Minister Gough Whitlam, September 1975. Met by Chief Minister Michael Somare and T. K. Critchley, High Commissioner of Papua New Guinea.
Source: National Archives of Australia; A6180, 22/9/75/28.

Minister for Defence, James Killen and PNG Minister for Defence, Foreign Affairs and Trade, Sir Albert Maori Kiki, Parliament House, Canberra, 1976.
Source National Archives of Australia: A6180, 6/7/76/11.

Confrontation – implications for Australia, fears for Papua New Guinea

The period from late 1962 witnessed a rush of assessments and opinions on the likely course of events in Indonesia with an emphasis on its possible ambitions to assert a role in the region. As early as February 1961, Australia's Ambassador in Washington, Howard Beale, had reported the views of Allen Dulles, Director of the Central Intelligence Agency, that he (Dulles) had no doubt that 'if they [Indonesia] got West New Guinea they would then lay claim to other territories in the area ... mentioning Sarawak, Borneo and the rest of New Guinea as possible future objectives'.[13] Later, in June 1962 in talks with H. D. (David) Anderson, visiting from the Department of External Affairs, the United States Embassy in Jakarta canvassed a number of scenarios as to Indonesia's possible intentions and suggested that the most likely target was East New Guinea or Borneo.[14]

The Department of External Affairs continued to demonstrate the pessimism about Indonesia's attitude to Papua New Guinea which had characterised its assessments during the West New Guinea dispute. In briefing notes prepared in September 1962 for a meeting between Australia's Minister for External Affairs, Sir Garfield Barwick, and US Secretary of State Dean Rusk, the Department encouraged Barwick to remind Rusk that:

> Australia will face a new and tricky situation, with major implications not only for the future of East New Guinea but possibly for the wider area of the Pacific islands and Australia itself. By the take over of West New Guinea Indonesia is projected a great deal further eastwards; what eventuates in Indonesia – a subject on which it is hard to be optimistic – will henceforth be reflected in West New Guinea and will in turn have an effect on two million people in our territory.[15]

For his part Menzies remained sensitive to the possibility of difficulty between Australia and Indonesia if the latter chose to destabilise its neighbours, including Papua New Guinea. However, in the brief pause between the end of the West New Guinea dispute and the launch of Confrontation, he continued to reflect the views expressed in the Cabinet room during the West New Guinea dispute that a relationship had to be maintained with Indonesia, but not if Indonesia posed a threat of any sort to Papua New Guinea. In a record of his meeting on 31 October 1962, Shann, Ambassador-designate to Indonesia, noted that the Prime Minister:

Did not think that the Indonesians intended to absorb East New Guinea, and was confident that it was going to be possible to live sensibly with what in due course would be a rich and powerful neighbour. Neither did he imagine that the Indonesians would cause trouble in Borneo, although their distaste for the concept of Malaysia was clear ... While it was clear that in due course Indonesia must have the whole of Timor our reaction at any rate for the time being to any sign of her trying to extend her territory beyond the confines of the old Netherlands East Indies should be sharp and immediate. ... In the development of New Guinea ... we must adopt an attitude friendly to Indonesia and that his own personal view was that there should be no diminution in cooperation and contact between the two sides of New Guinea following the replacement of the Dutch by the Indonesians. He realised that in a few years' time a very tricky situation might develop between the two sides as they come towards the time for making decisions about their future. Each side might tend to attract the other at some stage or other.[16]

The pause in Menzies's suspicion of Sukarno and Indonesia did not last long, while his assessment of Indonesia's attitude towards Borneo soon proved wide of the mark.

Barwick shared his Prime Minister's sensitivities over possible difficulties with Indonesia. Shann recorded Barwick as telling Tange and himself that 'our [Australian] reaction to any monkey business in Portuguese Timor, Borneo or particularly East New Guinea should be sharp and quick'.[17] On 9 January 1963 he wrote to Shann advising him that Australia's tolerance of Indonesia's behaviour towards its neighbours had been 'strained' by recent events and that 'a time is approaching when it will be necessary to warn the Indonesians that whatever they may get away with in Borneo or Timor, Australia is prepared to defend its own frontier and that of Papua/New Guinea against subversion or direct attack'.[18] Barwick argued that while Australia had come to accept Indonesia's claims regarding West New Guinea, 'we do not accept Indonesia's right to interfere in any other territory whether in Borneo or East New Guinea'.[19] He concluded by reminding Shann that 'any activity (whether crudely labelled as aid by 'volunteers' or not) which is hostile to Australia's position in New Guinea would have an immediate and profound effect not only on Australian public opinion but on the Government's whole attitude to Indonesia'.[20]

Shann replied to Barwick's letter of 9 January and, in doing so, questioned whether the judgement could be made conclusively that Indonesia was expansionist in outlook.[21] In his first despatch to Canberra, Shann told his minister that he believed that 'the Indonesians [were] for the moment quite sincere in their claim that they have no ambitions whatsoever towards East New Guinea, and this claim is strengthened by their distress as to what they have found in West New Guinea'.[22] [Shann was referring to the economic and social conditions in West New Guinea.] He was wary of Indonesia's intentions but, at this stage in the evolution of Confrontation, he took a more pragmatic approach and was not convinced that Indonesia would threaten Papua New Guinea militarily, nor subvert Australian interests there.

Other members of the Cabinet drew on the suspicions of Indonesia they had first developed during the West New Guinea dispute. Hasluck, who had held out longest in the Cabinet room in defence of the Dutch claim to West New Guinea and had argued for a stronger line against Indonesia, told a largely Australian audience in Port Moresby in September 1962 that:

> in matters of defence the Australian Government regards Papua and New Guinea in the same way as it regards the Australian mainland. It will defend both. ... Furthermore, the territory of Papua and New Guinea is regarded as the same as any other Australian territory for the purposes of the ANZUS Treaty which ensures that in any act of aggression against Australian territory we will have powerful Allies.[23]

Hasluck's assurance that Australia would defend Papua New Guinea was one of the first of a number of such public statements over the next three years by Australian political leaders.

Canberra's patience towards Indonesia was strained when on 20 January 1963 Subandrio publicly announced a policy of Confrontation (*Konfrontasi*) against Malaysia. As he had flagged in his letter to Shann on 9 January, Barwick called in the Indonesian Ambassador on 21 January and warned him of the 'risk to relations between Australia and Indonesia of suspicion and antagonism aroused by rash steps by Indonesia'. In this context 'Australians would stand no nonsense where East New Guinea was concerned. Australians expected solemn obligations to be performed. It was basic to our relations that Indonesia understood these things fully'.[24] Barwick's meeting with the Indonesian Ambassador was immediately followed up by a letter from External Affairs to Shann. The letter advised Shann that 'Australia could not accept Indonesian involvement in Papua-New Guinea'. Moreover, 'the Secretary [Tange] feels that without in any way threatening or striking attitudes, we bring home to responsible Indonesian officials our determination to defend our territory and to honour our international agreements'.[25] Shann was encouraged to speak to the Indonesian Minister for Defence informally and 'get the message across both about Australian New Guinea and our close relations with Malaya ... and the extreme seriousness with which Australia would regard expansionist activity by Indonesia ... [which] would meet resolute opposition'.[26]

Australian ministers were becoming noticeably more convinced that Indonesia's actions against Malaysia could lead to possible Indonesian hostility towards Papua New Guinea. They were also increasingly sceptical of Sukarno's broader intentions. At this time Menzies let it be known that officials should go cold on following up with Jakarta his invitation to Sukarno to visit Australia. John Bunting (Secretary, Prime Minister's Department) told Tange that 'no energy (was to be) devoted towards firm arrangements for a visit or towards hastening one ... he (Menzies) does not feel that the Australian public would receive a visit happily'.[27]

Britain raises the stakes

On 15 January 1963 Britain proposed that talks be held with Australia and the United States in the wake of Indonesia's involvement in the rebellion in Brunei and its assessment that Sukarno's ambitions 'do not seem to be satisfied by the acquisition of West Irian. ... He is looking for new adventures'.[28] As to New Guinea, the British assessment passed to Canberra argued that:

> with half of New Guinea in their hands, the Indonesians are eventually going to want the other half. ... A time will surely come when the Indonesians will push the Papuans under their own control to demand union with their brothers 'under Colonialist oppression'. The Indonesians would hope to extend their control over the whole of Melanesia and thus become a major Pacific Power.[29]

The assessment noted that Indonesia's ambitions 'put itself in the grip of either the Russians or the Chinese in the course of extending its conquests. ... From many points of view it is already identified with the Communist Bloc'.[30] The UK paper asked whether Australia shared this analysis of Indonesia's ambitions and sought 'their own views about the dangers ahead of us'.

Woodard has described Britain as having 'weakened their case by overstating it' and certainly Canberra's initial response was to question the urgency of the British initiative and to doubt the conclusions drawn by

London.³¹ Contrary to the strong views External Affairs had been expressing to Barwick and to Shann about Indonesian threats to Australian interests in Papua New Guinea, Tange told the UK Deputy High Commissioner that 'there was a good deal more "heat" in the analysis than we ourselves felt at present'. He agreed that some of the activity by Indonesia described in the assessment could occur but 'we did not expect any activity against Australian territory for some time ahead'. He admitted that Australia expected some 'eventual meddling' by Indonesia in Australian New Guinea and was 'taking steps in anticipation of this'.³²

Barwick decided to seek Cabinet endorsement for the position which Tange, who was representing Australia along with the Ambassador to Washington, Sir Howard Beale, would take at the talks scheduled for February in Washington. In a note circulated to Cabinet he told his colleagues that Australia should accept Malaysia as the best available solution to the internal problems facing the territories concerned and that Australia should encourage Indonesia and the Philippines to support its formation. Australia should also make clear its disapproval of Indonesia's campaign of subversion and infiltration into the territories. Barwick saw a link between Indonesia's actions against Malaysia and possible ambitions towards Papua New Guinea and argued that Australia was to make clear its:

> determination to defend Papua-New Guinea and must be prepared to resist Indonesian attempts to interfere in the transition of the territory to self-government. Australia would expect the understanding, approval and assistance of its friends in this.³³

At the same time, reflecting the point reached by Cabinet during the West New Guinea dispute, Barwick argued that 'we must be prepared to understand and accommodate some Indonesian interest in what is in fact a neighbouring territory ... and we [Australia] must seek to improve relations with Indonesia in all fields'.³⁴

In briefing his minister for the Cabinet meeting Tange warned him that Australia 'cannot ignore the possibility that an Indonesian Government of any political complexion will interest itself in internal political developments in Papua New Guinea'.³⁵ Moreover:

> an Indonesian Government not concerned with maintaining good relations with Australia is likely to turn its attention at some time in the future towards Papua New Guinea whether Australian administered or not. I conclude that it is essential to leave Indonesia in no doubt

as to our determination to bring Papua New Guinea to the stage of self-determination without interference from outside. This can be done without giving the impression of fear or hostility. We should make it clear, however, that Indonesia's respect of the 141st meridian will be in our view a major test of our future relations.[36]

Tange's comments to Barwick reflected the now well-established attitude held by Australia that the defence of Australia's interests and its presence in Papua and New Guinea was qualitatively different from its approach to other regional issues. While the government spoke of seeking a positive relationship with Indonesia in particular and Southeast Asia in general, ministers and officials such as Tange placed Papua and New Guinea in a different category. They were not prepared to compromise Australia's position.

Although the issue had moved on from West New Guinea to the creation of Malaysia, the interventions by ministers in Cabinet were similar in tone and sentiment to those which had characterised discussions in the 1950s. At the Cabinet meeting on 5 February 1963 held to discuss Barwick's note, ministers accepted the need to strike a balance between building a friendly relationship with Indonesia while opposing it if it embarked on expansionist activities that threatened Australia's interests. Barwick told his colleagues that 'the worst of all worlds is to create standing ill-will with Indonesia but we must nevertheless support the Tunku' (i.e. Malaysia).[37] He said Australia must make clear 'our opposition to Indonesian expansion and meddling in the affairs of others'.[38] He was adamant that 'we should be quite emphatic that we won't stand for Indonesian expansion'. Barwick's comments were directed more at Indonesia's perceived ambitions towards Borneo and Timor but Menzies believed they spread further. Using language similar to that he had first used to describe President Nasser during the Suez Crisis (see Chapter 5), he told his colleagues that:

> Sukarno's expansion aims are not concluded. [The] British and US [are] waking up to this a little late in the day. His ideas appear to run to Borneo, to Timor and conceivably to East New Guinea. As to East New Guinea, we propose to oppose by arms – and we would hope to have friends to assist.[39]

Menzies argued that Australia had to be prepared to assist Britain in the defence of Malaysia as '[Australia] can't take an attitude that we're interested only when it comes to East New Guinea'.[40] Menzies described Greater Malaysia as a '*cordon sanitaire* against Soekarno's northern ambitions', while

Barwick added that it was 'our best guarantee against an eventual monolithic structure from Indonesia northwards'.[41] Only McEwen sounded a note of caution when he bluntly warned 'if we get to the point of conflict we go along with our friends. ... but don't let us brook a situation in which we become number one enemy of Indonesia'. He linked Australia's attitude to military action against Indonesia and the government's wider plans for national development and added 'we can't mobilize and develop'.[42]

Ministers agreed that Australia should support the concept of Malaysia and should participate in the talks in Washington. The preferred policy position was to avoid 'policy initiatives which might lead to the point where Australia came to be seen by Indonesia or other countries as a standing adversary. The objective ... must be to achieve the greatest available degree of mutual understanding'.[43] Nevertheless, they were wary, in light of the experience of how the West New Guinea issue had been settled, of whether the major powers (Britain and the United States) would show 'firmness against Indonesian expansion'.[44]

The quadripartite talks in Washington, held on 11 and 12 February 1963, met Australia's objectives. Britain made clear that it accepted primary responsibility for the defence of Malaysia, a sentiment readily accepted by both the United States and Australia with Averell Harriman (Assistant Secretary of State for Far East Affairs) making plain the US view that 'Britain was in the lead, with both Australia and New Zealand a stride behind and the United States a few strides further behind them'.[45] Officials were in general agreement that Indonesia's future actions were uncertain, with Britain expressing the most pessimistic view of Sukarno's expansionist ambitions. Beale told the meeting that Australia was aware of the need for caution in its policy towards Indonesia and of the danger that Sukarno might be pushed into Russian hands but it could not accept an Indonesia that could 'lay hands on other people's territory'. In this respect, 'as far as Australian Papua/New Guinea was concerned, Australia had made clear its determination to defend the territory, a matter in which United States defence commitments under ANZUS were involved'. Harriman 'confirmed the application of ANZUS to Papua/New Guinea', adding that the United States was 'willing to make the understanding even plainer'. Beale resisted the offer and told the meeting that a further assurance was not required.[46]

Defence shortcomings exposed

At the same time as ministers were debating their approach to the defence of Malaysia they were also acutely aware of the pressure being brought to bear to increase Australia's defence capabilities and its military engagement in Southeast Asia. The United States had first made this point at the 1962 ANZUS talks in Canberra early in the term of the Kennedy Administration. In February 1963 Beale told Canberra that he believed the Administration was expecting its allies to assume a greater share of the defence burden and that this attitude was stiffening.[47] Beale argued that 'our ability to influence their policies and actions in our favour may, in the future, depend upon how much we are willing to put into an area which, in their mind, is even more vital to us than it is to them'.[48]

While in Washington for the quadripartite talks Tange experienced at first hand such pressure from the Administration when he called on Secretary of State Rusk. Rusk was 'serious and emphatic' and 'was not seeking information but conveying an opinion' when he asked whether 'Australian defences are in adequate shape to assume the burdens arising in this area' and 'whether we had "reserves of trained men" to call upon to meet any situation'.[49] Rusk told Tange that the United States supported the formation of Malaysia but it was a British Commonwealth responsibility to look after it. He added 'if anyone had any idea that the United States would repeat anywhere else the situation in Vietnam where they had 12,000 men suffering casualties, they were mistaken. The United States would not be the gendarmes of the world'.[50] Tange explained the government's preference for 'smaller forces fully trained and available to be used in South East Asia within two or three weeks of the call'.[51] In private comments to his colleagues he revealed his own frustrations and concerns at the 'manifest insufficiency of the Australian defence forces to meet the variety of diplomatic challenges with which Australia might be confronted'.[52] Rusk later reassured Beale that the US was 'unequivocally bound under ANZUS to come to Australia's defence in the event of an attack on Australia or her territories in the Pacific area' and that if Australian forces were involved in fighting Indonesia to protect Malaysia and 'Australian forces were in trouble', the US 'would regard itself as just as bound to assist Australia as she would in a case involving ANZUS'.[53]

As ministers grappled with the implications of Indonesia's hostility to the formation of Malaysia they also had before them at least half a dozen complex submissions dealing with Australia's regional security environment and defence preparedness.[54] Although Menzies brought his customary outward calm and ordered approach to decision-making, there can be detected in the recording of the Cabinet's discussions and subsequent decisions a deepening concern, if not alarm, as ministers raced to make up for a decade of inactivity in relation to Australia's defences. Holt described the proposed increases before Cabinet as the biggest build-up in the defence budget since the government had taken office in 1949.[55]

The first submission on the broader question of 'Australia's Strategic Position' had been prepared by the Defence Committee in February 1963 and had identified two threats to Australia: Indonesia and the advance of communism in Indochina and Southeast Asia. Communist expansionist aims promoted by China and backed by military power were seen as the 'underlying threat to Australia's national security', while Indonesia was considered a more immediate danger.[56] The report assessed the Indonesian Government's attitude to Australia as 'one of reserve' while it was 'too early to estimate Indonesia's long term attitude and intentions in respect of eastern New Guinea'. However, reflecting the thoughts of Tange, it warned that 'an Indonesian Government not concerned with maintaining good relations with Australia is likely to turn its attention at some time in the future towards eastern New Guinea – whether Australian administered or not'. Indonesia would be deterred from open warfare while the ANZUS Treaty applied to the Territory but it could pursue techniques short of war to force a 'political settlement in her favour'.[57] The report highlighted the US Administration's call for allies to contribute more to the defence of the region and noted that 'in some cases, such as might develop over eastern New Guinea, the degree of obligation which America feels to Australia under ANZUS could be influenced by the contributions which Australia makes to the common defence'.[58]

Ministers accepted the Defence Committee's arguments, including its description of Indonesia's growth as a military power, opposition to Malaysia, hostility to colonial regimes and use of power in respect of diplomatic aims.[59] It agreed that 'there should be an increase in the present scale of defence programming ... not only to ensure the security of the Australian mainland and East New Guinea but also to enable us to make an effective and sustained contribution in South East Asia and to present a deterrent to possible activities by Indonesia inimical to our strategic interests'.[60]

The second submission on the narrower subject of 'The Strategic Importance to Australia of New Guinea' was the first prepared on the island since the settlement of the West New Guinea dispute. It began by noting that 'for the first time Australia will through the territories of Papua and New Guinea share a common land frontier with a country whose long term friendship cannot be assumed'. It anticipated a likely 'conflict of interest' between Australia and Indonesia given their different 'outlook and aspirations' and warned of the possibility of 'external pressures, including communist pressures ... being directed towards ... Eastern New Guinea aimed at creating disaffection'.[61] It also acknowledged that problems could arise due to the 'incomplete and inadequate definition of the border'. This, in turn, could lead to infiltration 'directed at creating disaffection with our administration [in the Territory]'.[62] It concluded that 'the strategic importance of West New Guinea under Indonesian control [Indonesia was scheduled to assume administrative control on 3 August 1963] will lie mainly in its potentiality as a base for the conduct of activities, particularly of a subversive nature, prejudicial to our interests in Eastern New Guinea'.[63]

Turning to Eastern New Guinea itself, the submission argued that it would 'continue to remain of great strategic importance to Australia for the foreseeable future' and, as long as it remained Australian territory, Australia had a responsibility to defend it. The report placed considerable emphasis on Papua and New Guinea's role in protecting Australia's lines of communications to its forward defence positions in Southeast Asia. The denial of Eastern New Guinea to an enemy would 'play a most important part in maintaining the security of our sea and air communications with North America ... and United States bases in the Pacific'. It was envisaged that 'Manus and possibly Rabaul and Port Moresby would be used for convoy support forces and air staging'.

The Defence Committee's review received strong support within the bureaucracy. In particular, the Department of the Prime Minister showed itself to be increasingly alarmed at the state of Australia's defence preparedness in the face of what it saw as a deteriorating security environment in Southeast Asia. One of its senior advisers on foreign and defence issues, Alan Griffith, who was close to McEwen and later Prime Minister Malcolm Fraser, believed that Australia had to adopt a tougher approach to Indonesia and warned against what he saw as a soft approach from External Affairs. Griffith, described by Woodard as one of many officials close to Menzies who had 'strongly held anti-communist views', saw a clear link between the situation in Southeast Asia and Australia's security interests in Papua New Guinea.[64] He identified Papua New Guinea's role as providing 'staging facilities for a line of communication into Southeast Asia, whenever it becomes necessary to circumvent Indonesia'.[65] In addition, Griffith held strongly to the view that unprecedented pressure was now placed on Papua New Guinea through Indonesia's assumption of control over West New Guinea. He warned that 'subversion [was] a probability and we must be prepared for incidents particularly on questions of border demarcation and refugees'.[66] Over the next few months Griffith continued to put before Menzies and other senior ministers his deep concerns about an Indonesian threat to Papua New Guinea. In doing so he 'drew on the decades of fear of Indonesia constituting a threat through control over West New Guinea'.[67]

Strengthening Papua New Guinea's defences

In conjunction with its examination of the strategic importance of New Guinea, Cabinet also examined a further submission proposing 'immediate' measures to improve both the defence of Papua and New Guinea and Australia's ability to defend its broader strategic interests using Papua and New Guinea as a forward base.[68] The submission recommended the creation of an intelligence organisation to provide 'warning of infiltration or subversion' in Eastern New Guinea; the 'orderly' expansion of the Pacific Island Regiment over a three year period through the recruitment of more indigenous soldiers and the placement of indigenous officers in command and control positions; and increased coastal security with the creation of a marine branch. The submission examined the possibility of developing military bases for the conduct of defensive operations but judged they were not necessary as an overt military attack in the near future was considered unlikely.

The submission and the subsequent discussion in Cabinet provide a further insight into the increasing anxiety that ministers were experiencing. Such was the sense of frustration at Australia's inability to respond effectively to this changing environment that the government's most senior adviser, John Bunting, raised directly with Menzies his criticisms of the proposals. He described them as 'a small idea or two about more intelligence and a bit more on the Papuan Infantry Regiment. ... It seems to me that Cabinet should note the Defence papers, but then get down to the tin tacks of discussing the policy of doing something extra or not, and if yes, in what fields.'[69] Bunting's criticisms played into Menzies's broader concerns about the state of Australia's defence preparations in Papua New Guinea.

A reading of the Cabinet Notebook for the meeting suggests that Barwick was not present on 2 May when ministers discussed the submission and Townley may have been absent due to ill health. Instead Hasluck, who had served as Minister for Territories since 1951, led the discussion.

He emphasised the need to 'reassure' the Australian public in the wake of Indonesia's success over West New Guinea and now its attitude of confrontation with Malaysia. He argued that a 'large proportion of the Australian people [was] very concerned with the security of East New Guinea and doubts [were] popularly held about Soekarno's intentions'. As a result, there was a 'need to reassure [the] Australian public by indicating that East New Guinea will be held and we are not being taken for suckers'.[70] Moreover, 'we must give visible evidence that we are serious about [the] defence of New Guinea' to reassure both the 'native and non-native' communities. He made clear to his colleagues his 'central thesis [was] that we must, as [an] essential element in our defence, build confidence in New Guinea and in Australia'. In keeping with this argument, Hasluck called for a significant increase in the size of the Pacific Islands Regiment (PIR), and at a much faster rate than that proposed, and a military base, wharf and 'first class' all-weather air field should be built at Wewak in East Sepik province, close to the border with Indonesia, to serve as a military 'centre'. The formation of a locally-based intelligence organisation was also supported 'to provide warning of infiltration or subversion'.[71] Hasluck's presentation was consistent with many of the points he had made during the latter stages of the West New Guinea dispute. He remained both suspicious of Indonesia and an advocate of a strong, sustained military response to protect Australia's interests in the region.

Hasluck found widespread support in Cabinet. Menzies readily agreed, adding that the government had a responsibility not only to reassure both the Australian and territory populations but to 'make clear an intention to defend'. He emphasised the need to 'have substantial forces in being and visible – trained and equipped and disciplined – otherwise border incidents [will go unchecked]'. He commented that, if practical, we 'proceed on the sound principle of reassurance of our New Guinea people'. Menzies noted the need to 'expand [the] PIR effectively – this is the operative word'.[72] Menzies held a subsequent meeting with the Secretary of Defence (Sir Edwin Hicks) and the Chair of the Chief of Staff Committee (Sir Frederick Scherger) and reached agreement that the PIR would be increased more rapidly than first proposed, with an emphasis on an 'effective' expansion.[73]

In subsequent months the size of the PIR was increased from 72 Australian Army personnel and 660 local troops to 185 Australian Army personnel and 1188 local troops. Menzies directed that the increase be undertaken 'at full effective speed' and, if possible, completed sooner than planned. The Cabinet decision noted that the build-up in local defence capability was considered especially important 'in the context of a need to provide the people of Papua and New Guinea (and also the people of Australia) with visible evidence of capacity and intention to act in the defence of the Territory'.[74] Cabinet later endorsed the proposal for the development of an airfield at Boram (Wewak, East Sepik Province).[75] The Defence Department had argued that the airstrip would allow for the patrolling of the Indonesia–Papua New Guinea border and the transit of aircraft from Australia to Southeast Asia.[76] Cabinet also approved the rehabilitation and extension of the Nadzab airstrip (near Lae) for use as a transit airfield for flights to Southeast Asia.[77]

These decisions drew Papua New Guinea more closely into a broader strategic concept which linked it to developments in Southeast Asia and to questions of Australia's overall defence preparedness. They marked the beginning of a shift in Australia's thinking as to the role of Papua New Guinea in Australia's defence environment. Historically, Papua New Guinea had been seen as a shield lying across Australia's north, well-placed to defend Australia against invasion. That view was now being modified. Papua New Guinea was still seen as a barrier against invasion but it was also now a platform or staging post to assist Australia in its deployments into Southeast Asia and Indo China.

Menzies captured the mood of the Cabinet in a statement to Parliament on 22 May 1963. He referred to the 'uncertainties' in Laos, the 'acute problems' in South Vietnam, the 'conflicts' which existed over the creation of the Federation of Malaysia and the 'events in and concerning' West New Guinea. He made no specific reference to Indonesia, although early in his statement, reflecting the discussion in Cabinet over the need to reassure the Australian and local communities in Eastern New Guinea, he made clear that 'we will defend these territories as if they were part of our mainland; there must be no mistaken ideas about that'.[78] Menzies was to repeat this pledge on at least four further occasions over the next six months as confrontation escalated and as he sought to portray himself as a staunch defender of Australia's security interests.[79] He made the same commitment when he visited Port Moresby in September 1963.[80]

Menzies went on to advise the Parliament of the major increases in the capability and preparedness of each element of the defence force. The total budget (excluding the cost of a new strike-reconnaissance aircraft) would be increased from an earlier figure of £1313.4 million to £1519.2 million or rising from £212.2 million in 1962–63 to £269.5 million in 1967–68. This was the beginning of a series of revised and increased defence budgets over the next few years as confrontation with Indonesia continued and engagement in the Vietnam War deepened. Tange told his departmental colleagues that the Prime Minister's statement was a clear message to Indonesia that 'Australia is preparing itself more to defend its vital security interests, including the territory neighbouring Indonesia against attack or threat from any quarter'. Cabinet's urgency in approving increased defence spending was 'not only to ensure the security of the Australian mainland and East New Guinea, but also to enable us to make an effective and sustained contribution in Southeast Asia and to present a deterrent to possible activities by Indonesia inimical to our strategic interests'.[81] Over the next twelve to eighteen months the suspicion and distrust which had formed in Menzies's mind and that of his colleagues during the West New Guinea dispute towards Indonesia, and President Sukarno in particular, deepened.

Crisis over Malaysia

Australia continued to be concerned at the possibility of Indonesia becoming more openly aggressive as the date for the inauguration of the Federation of Malaysia drew closer.[82] Barwick told the UK Parliamentary Under Secretary of State for Foreign Affairs, Peter Thomas, in April 1963 that he 'remained highly sceptical about Indonesia and thought that the ultimate sanction was that the United States should let it be plainly understood that they would not stand for any nonsense'.[83] However, America's attitude was less accommodating than Australia wished. At a meeting with the Menzies Cabinet on 7 June 1963, Averell Harriman, now Under Secretary of State for Political Affairs, told ministers that 'Soekarno [was] a problem but has qualities we can't ignore ... a strong nationalist ... our feeling is that it is best to work in with Soekarno and Indonesia rather than hit them over the head'. He repeated earlier assurances from senior US State Department officials when he said '[I] have noted [the Prime Minister] has said that Australia will fight for its part of New Guinea. I have said and now repeat that ANZUS applies to New Guinea'.[84] Harriman continued to argue that responsibility for Malaysia was first a UK problem and then a Commonwealth responsibility, i.e. an Australian and New Zealand responsibility. He drew on the sentiments expressed by Rusk to Tange in February 1963 when Rusk had said that the United States could 'not take on a new country at this time for political reasons'. Harriman then created a degree of confusion over whether the ANZUS Treaty would apply if Australian troops in Malaysia were attacked. Firstly, he said that it would, adding 'we haven't stood aside yet when our friends [were] in need', but later, under questioning from McEwen, he left open the question of whether it would be invoked in 'grey areas' involving conflict with Indonesian-sponsored 'volunteers'.[85]

The importance of Harriman's reaffirmation that the ANZUS Treaty applied to both Papua and New Guinea and that it could also apply in certain (undefined) circumstances to Malaysia was that it gave Menzies and others the confidence to think in terms of deploying Australian troops to Papua New Guinea in the knowledge that they would ultimately be supported by the United States. The UK High Commission in Canberra reported to London that the 'Australians have been much comforted by the strong line taken in public by Mr Harriman when he re-affirmed that the Americans would regard an attack on Papua and New Guinea as coming under the ANZUS Treaty'.[86]

Menzies travelled to London and Washington in June and July 1963 where the principal topic of conversation was the establishment of Malaysia and the danger posed by Indonesian threats to destabilise it. At the same time, the possible Indonesian threat to Papua New Guinea remained very much on his mind. He told Macmillan that 'Australia was becoming increasingly worried about East New Guinea and this was one reason why they had recently increased the size of the Pacific Islands Regiment'.[87] Menzies noted that 'the Chiefs of Staff no longer believed that East New Guinea was as important as they had at one time thought; this was partly because Indonesians would no doubt take Timor fairly soon and that was as near as New Guinea to Australia'.[88] This was a curious comment given his remarks to his own Cabinet and his increasingly negative view of Sukarno and Indonesia's intentions but should be seen in the context of Indonesia possibly securing control over East Timor.[89] Menzies had earlier told Peter Thorneycroft (Defence Secretary) that 'any estimated threat from Indonesia ... might ultimately be directed in part against Australian New Guinea [although he thought this was unlikely to develop in the near future]. This would involve a direct threat to our own interests and place priority demand on our resources, but it would also bring the ANZUS Treaty into operation'.[90]

In Washington, Menzies talked up Australia's strengthened military preparations. He told Rusk of the 'substantial increase in the Australian defence programme ... with additional expenditure of £50 million per annum'. A further £100 million would be committed if a new strike bomber were to be acquired. He added 'this is quite a breakthrough' and said that 'Australia is now stiffening up her defence potential in East New Guinea'.[91] In response, Rusk referred specifically to 'possible Indonesian attempts at infiltration or other action to undermine Australian authority in Papua and East New Guinea'.[92] The record of the meeting noted that 'he put it to Sir Robert that Australia should be sensitive over the first Indonesian motion. The Indonesians should find out straight away that Australia is resolved to take firm action to keep Indonesian influence out of the territories'. Rusk added that if 'you get into trouble on this, we will be with you'. It would appear that the Kennedy Administration, through Rusk, while rejecting the role of a global policeman, was prepared to extend its military support to cover Australian action in Papua New Guinea. The record concluded by noting that Menzies had drawn Rusk's attention to his recent Defence Statement and that he had added 'we regard East New Guinea as part of our territory and we will resist promptly any interference'.[93] In a press conference on 14 July 1963 on his return to Australia, Menzies told the Australian public that he had also reiterated to the President that the 'defence of Australian New Guinea and Papua was regarded by us in exactly the same way as the defence of our mainland and that any overt attack on it would be resisted in the same way… it is well understood and agreed that should such an event occur, ANZUS would operate and we would have the assistance of the United States of America'.[94]

As the date for the creation of Malaysia drew closer Indonesia's aggressive and uncooperative behaviour continued to arouse concerns in Canberra. In May 1963 Barwick publicly described Indonesia as a 'militant power … [with] a disposition to expand'.[95] In August 1963, following the outcome of the Malaysian–Philippine–Indonesian leaders' talks, a frustrated and disillusioned Menzies wrote to Barwick that 'once more Sukarno has succeeded in his policy of threats … I think we are in great danger in taking and encouraging too soft a line with Sukarno. Like all the dictators he will get what he can by threat and bluff. Each concession made to him increases his appetite'.[96]

In Cabinet, ministers showed a further hardening in their attitude towards Indonesia. Barwick had suggested in a Cabinet meeting on 6 August 1963 that there may be some advantage in consulting Indonesia as an interested party on regional political issues. Hasluck immediately disagreed and instead described Indonesia as not wanting 'consultations except that which brings the concessions it wants – we can't escape the fact that we must thwart Indonesia – not consult and humour it'.[97] Later in the meeting he said he 'regard[ed] Indonesia as imperialist and expansionist. Indonesia is seeking [to] develop as the continuing dominant power in South East Asia – don't think that suits us at all – our job, without getting into conditions of enmity with Indonesia is not to knit Indonesia-Philippines-Malaysia but to keep them apart. ... We must continue our military aid to Malaysia and by diplomacy weaken the bonds of Malphilindo'.[98] Menzies also saw a problem with Barwick's suggestion of consulting Indonesia. He commented that if taken to its logical conclusion Indonesia would have a 'legitimate interest in PNG'.[99] Menzies, who since 1950 had engaged in countless discussions in Cabinet on Indonesia, had lost patience with Sukarno and was much less inclined to adopt a conciliatory line.[100] Barwick floated the idea of a non-aggression pact between Indonesia and Malaysia which 'would assist our presentation of our stationing of forces in Malaysia'. Cabinet rejected the suggestion with McEwen arguing that it 'would give a nudge to neutralism and [the] closing down [of] our bases. Out go our forces – would suit the Indonesians'.[101]

The six months from July to December 1963 were one of the most challenging and difficult periods in the history of Australia's response to developments in Southeast Asia. The government's in-principle support for the concept of Malaysia did not falter nor did its preparedness to associate Australia with the defence of Malaysia in some way. The government was under increasing strain and ministers felt the need to clarify whether and under what circumstances the ANZUS Treaty would apply to Australian military activity in Malaysia.[102] In this environment Barwick embarked on a round of consultations beginning in Jakarta in September and ending in Washington, first for a series of bilateral meetings with the Kennedy Administration and then a quadripartite meeting with senior representatives from the UK, US and New Zealand on a policy response to Confrontation. Harold Holt also visited Washington and described Indonesia to the President as 'behaving like a juvenile delinquent'.[103] Eventually Barwick negotiated a form of words to cover the question of the application of the ANZUS Treaty to include overt attacks by Indonesia on Australian forces in Malaysia. In the middle of this hectic period of diplomacy Menzies, on 14 October, called an election for the House of Representatives confident that he could use differences with the Labor Party over foreign and defence policies to his advantage.[104]

Australia to defend Malaysia and Papua New Guinea

Shortly before Barwick left to attend the ceremonies marking the formation of Malaysia, Cabinet took the decision to 'associate' itself with the revised UK–Malaysia defence arrangements to come into effect on Malaysia Day, i.e. the day Malaysia was to be officially created. Rather than opting to become a full party to the Anglo-Malaysian Defence Agreement or negotiating its own agreement with Malaysia, Australia instead decided to 'associate' itself with the revised Anglo-Malaysia Agreement. In doing so the government made clear that the 'primary responsibility for the security and defence of Malaysia clearly remains a UK responsibility' although it also argued that 'the extended geographical area and the enhancement of the threat from Indonesia does, in fact, mean that Australia under the new arrangement would be accepting a greater commitment than hitherto'.[105] Menzies formally advised the House of Representatives on 25 September 1963 of the government's decision. He told the House that if Malaysia were subject to 'armed invasion or subversive activity – supported or directed or inspired from outside Malaysia – we shall to the best of our powers ... add our military assistance to the efforts of Malaysia and the United Kingdom in the defence of Malaysia's territorial integrity and political independence'.[106] Holt later told President Kennedy that this was 'the strongest guarantee that Australia had ever issued'.[107] Menzies's statement had been made in the wake of Indonesian mobs attacking the British and Malaysian diplomatic missions in Jakarta.

As Barwick prepared to visit Jakarta Menzies paid his second visit to Papua and New Guinea as Prime Minister. He delivered a radio broadcast in Port Moresby on 6 September 1963 in which he spoke of the government's commitment to continue to assist the development of the territories and pointed to a 25 per cent increase in the territories' budget in 1963 over the previous year. He referred to the 'bitter and devastating experience' of invasion and repeated the words of his statement in Canberra that 'we will defend these territories as if they were part of our mainland'. Menzies again referred to the 'staunch backing of our ANZUS partner the United States's in the defence of Papua and New Guinea'.[108]

In contrast to the welcoming audience for Menzies in Papua and New Guinea, Barwick met an 'obdurate' Sukarno in a 'determinedly irrational mood'.[109] Barwick could not budge Sukarno from his implacable opposition to the formation of Malaysia.[110] He cautioned Sukarno that Australia and other countries 'were beginning to doubt the *bona fides* of Indonesia' as it raised repeated objections to the Michelmore-led UN sponsored survey of opinion in Sarawak and North Borneo. He warned that 'a sharp deterioration in relations between Indonesia and Australia would be tragic' but 'the ordinary Australians would react against current Indonesian behaviour'. Barwick continued to press the argument that Indonesia's obduracy risked long-term consequences for the good will and relationship between the two countries and called for a period of quiet. Sukarno told Barwick that he wanted a close relationship with Australia but this would not divert him from his present course of opposing Malaysia. There was no mention of East New Guinea in this meeting. It was raised in the meeting with Subandrio but only in the context of a discussion of the placement of border markers on the Irian Jaya/East New Guinea border. Barwick also gave Subandrio an undertaking that Australia would not allow dissident groups to use Papua and New Guinea as a base for radio broadcasts into Irian Jaya – a claim made earlier in the year by Indonesia.

Barwick's meetings in New York and Washington with senior officials from the Kennedy Administration, culminating in a meeting on 17 October with the President, focused on Indonesia, Malaysia and clarifying the terms under which Australia's possible involvement in a conflict in Malaysia would invoke the ANZUS Treaty. He also used the meetings to set out the case in the clearest terms that Australia now viewed Indonesia as driven by 'extreme nationalism' and 'the need for foreign adventures' which had become 'a dynamic which was no longer under full control'. Barwick described Indonesia as suffering from a 'form of national paranoia' which allowed it to think there was a plot to deny it the 'greatness entitled to them'.[111] He identified Portuguese Timor and possibly East New Guinea as the likely targets of Indonesian interest, after Malaysia.[112] Barwick told Walt Rostow (Chair of the State Department's Policy Planning Council) and George Ball (Under Secretary of State) that 'in due time' Indonesia's anti-colonialism would lead it to 'turn on East New Guinea' and that Indonesia had said it would support any dissident movements should they appear in the territory.[113] He told Rusk of Indonesia's reluctance to cooperate on the photographing of the Irian Jaya/East New Guinea border and other recent complaints to which Rusk replied that 'he hoped that we would react "like a fire cracker" at the first sign of Indonesian tinkering in East New Guinea'.[114] Barwick also felt obliged to make the point in these conversations, albeit reluctantly, that despite the differences over Malaysia, Australia wanted to build a positive, long-term relationship with Indonesia.

In his conversation with the President on 17 October Barwick repeated his earlier remarks that he had 'tried to avoid antipathy with Indonesia although this had caused him to be called an appeaser'. He told Kennedy that 'Sukarno had told him quite frankly that he would support a dissident movement in East New Guinea. He did not feel that Indonesia had a plan for East New Guinea but that they were generally ambitious'. Barwick added that 'they would have a dissident movement in East New Guinea, however, and that Sukarno would try to support it'.[115] Kennedy is not recorded as directly responding to Barwick's remarks. He instead pointed out that US policy was more nuanced or 'ambivalent' than Australia's policy approach. Its aim had been 'not to face Sukarno with a white trio and to avoid a polemic between Sukarno and the United States'.[116] However, he could foresee a time when the United States might have to change its policy towards Indonesia.

The final meeting in Barwick's round of consultations in Washington was the Four Power Talks held with the United States, Great Britain and New Zealand to discuss a policy approach to Confrontation. In preparing for the talks the British had recognised the sensitivity and importance of Papua New Guinea to Australia and Australia's concern that 'Sukarno's ambitions extend further than Malaysia (this would include their New Guinea territories)'. The British decided to use these concerns to their advantage and briefed their delegation to ensure that 'we must make absolutely certain it [East New Guinea] is not overlooked. … The Americans have given clear undertakings to defend it and they should be warned that if by misjudgement they let Malaysia slip away they will soon be called upon to honour their pledge in New Guinea'.[117]

Barwick was forceful in his arguments. He again described Indonesia as 'expansionist' and driven either by 'paranoia or territorial greed'. He went further than in his earlier conversation when he said that 'Indonesia had adopted a suicidal attitude of open and implacable hostility to Malaysia'. He asked:

> what more could now be done by way of 'carrot and stick' without creating perils for Australia as well as other countries in the region? Timor would be an embarrassment but we've got East New Guinea and so [to Harriman] have you! The Indonesians have said they would support a dissident movement in East New Guinea and not withstanding our great efforts for the territory, the Indonesians could undoubtedly rake up some malcontents. Could the West then bear

Sukarno up any longer. ... The day a stronger Indonesia decided to confront Australia it would be too late for 'carrots and sticks'.[118]

Barwick did not confine his argument to an American audience. He told Lord Home, the British Foreign Secretary, in a meeting in New York that Australia faced a difficulty with Indonesia given its ability to interfere with flights between Australia and the Philippines and Australia and Singapore. He also alerted Home to 'Indonesia's capacity to make trouble in Australian New Guinea where it was not likely Australia would be able to do enough or move fast enough to prevent malcontents actual or spurious arising'.[119]

Barwick would have been justified in assessing his talks with the Kennedy Administration and with Britain and New Zealand at the quadripartite talks as a success. He had negotiated a more precise description of the geographic range and application of the ANZUS Treaty to include Malaysia, under certain circumstances.[120] He had secured from the United States a written understanding that the ANZUS Treaty would be invoked in the event of an overt attack by Indonesian armed forces on Australian defence forces in Malaysia. (Holt had earlier told Kennedy that Australia had made its public commitment on 25 September to assist in the defence of Malaysia on the assumption that Australia's actions were covered by ANZUS.)[121] The question of the exact nature of US assistance was left vague while the US made clear that ANZUS would not be invoked if clashes arose from subversion or guerrilla warfare. The United States had made clear that ANZUS would apply to Papua and New Guinea (as long as they remained Australian territories).[122] The UK High Commission in Canberra commented to London that 'the change in Australia's policy seems quite genuinely to date from the time of Sir Garfield Barwick's visit to Indonesia in September which clearly convinced him about Indonesia's long term ambitions (of which Sir Robert Menzies himself had never been in doubt)'.[123]

Barwick (and Holt) had acknowledged in their conversations in Washington the importance of maintaining a functional, long-term relationship with Indonesia. This remained a key government objective in the months ahead but the balance was moving towards an assessment that Sukarno's Indonesia was a threat to Australia's interests in the region and that, if left unchecked, this threat could, possibly, extend to East New Guinea. The question was how to respond.

Conclusion

The period of calm which had characterised the months between the end of the West New Guinea dispute and the beginning of Confrontation was a brief interlude that allowed for some more mellow judgements about Indonesia and President Sukarno. It did not last long. Instead, as Confrontation began to escalate, concern deepened in Canberra as to Sukarno's ambitions and whether Australia was able militarily to respond to them to defend its interests. A sense of panic began to take hold as ministers looked for immediate measures to improve the defence preparedness of Papua New Guinea and Australia's own defence preparations. Australia embarked on one of the most rapid increases in its defence budget in its peacetime history. Menzies made clear for the first of a number of times that Australia would defend Papua New Guinea if it were the subject of Indonesian subversion or infiltration. Australia sought and gained a clarification of the application of the ANZUS Treaty which reassured ministers but they nevertheless remained alarmed and nervous about Sukarno's ambitions. Again, the place of Papua New Guinea in Australia's security environment emerged as a major consideration in ministers' thinking.

Woodard, in his book *Asian Alternatives*, provides a masterful insider's account of Barwick's management of the early phase of Confrontation. His thesis is that Barwick was more pragmatic and independent in his approach to foreign policy and as such would have pursued a policy which sought to build a relationship with Indonesia rather than antagonise it. Similarly, Barwick's focus on Indonesia meant that he would have resisted attempts to lead Australia into a commitment to the war in Vietnam. According to Woodard, 'Barwick regarded going to war against a regional country, especially Indonesia, which was so important to the region and to Australia, as an enormous step with incalculable consequences in the long-term'.[124] Woodard holds Barwick in the highest esteem, describing him as 'the most powerful independent voice in Cabinet until his departure'.[125] Peter Edwards shares Woodard's assessment of Barwick and has praised his skill and statecraft in convincing the Cabinet 'to adopt a nuanced and subtle approach' towards Confrontation and Indonesia.[126]

At the time of its publication in 2004 Woodard's account of the Menzies's Government's foreign policy did not have access to the Cabinet Notebooks. Edwards's article, published in 2015, may also not have had access to all of the discussions in Cabinet over Confrontation. As argued elsewhere, the debates in Cabinet were more subtle and arguments about

Indonesia more discerning than historians have to date described. With the exception of Hasluck who, in this period, held the most conservative and dogmatic views about how Australia should relate to Indonesia, ministers, notably McEwen, were sensitive to the impact of Australia's actions in Southeast Asia. Woodard and Edwards present Barwick as almost a lone voice in Cabinet arguing for maintaining a relationship with Indonesia. This underestimates the role of some of his colleagues who were just as influential in guiding policy.

Chapter 8

INDONESIA, CONFRONTATION AND PROTECTING PAPUA NEW GUINEA 1964–1966

'If we get into [a] conflict in Borneo in less than war I would be astounded if Indonesia didn't retaliate [in] New Guinea. Cost them nothing'.

John McEwen, May 1964

Throughout the campaign leading to the House of Representatives election on 30 November 1963 Menzies spoke repeatedly on defence and foreign policy issues. He argued in favour of close cooperation with Australia's allies, commenting that 'we must have their help in times of difficulty and they must have ours. To prepare to defend Australia purely on Australian territory would assume that our allies had been defeated'.[1] He laid out the case in favour of the proposed United States–operated North West Cape Naval Communications Station at Exmouth in Western Australia. In doing so he taunted the Labor Party that it was controlled by thirty-six 'faceless men' following the release of a photograph of the ALP leaders Arthur Calwell and Gough Whitlam waiting to receive policy directions from the ALP Special National Conference meeting in Canberra. He questioned Labor's commitment to a forward defence policy and its preparedness to defend Malaysia. He played up the decision to acquire the F111 aircraft and to boost the strength of the navy and army. He described their need to be mobile 'in order to cooperate with our allies to keep war out of Australia'.[2]

In his policy speech on 12 November Menzies said: 'we have made clear that we will defend Papua and New Guinea against attack as if it were part of the Australian mainland. That promise of ours is as a result of ANZUS, completely backed by the United States'.[3] He did not mention Indonesia in his speeches while Barwick later remarked that the Prime Minister had been at pains to resist drawing it into the campaign. Menzies led the Liberal–Country Party coalition to a resounding victory, possibly aided by the shock felt in the community at the assassination of President Kennedy on 22 November.

In December Menzies reshuffled his ministry moving Hasluck to Defence. He appointed the Country Party member, Charles Barnes, as Minister for Territories. Menzies moved Hasluck to External Affairs in April 1964 following the nomination of Barwick to be Chief Justice of the High Court.[4] Senator Shane Paltridge was appointed Minister for Defence.

The selection of Barnes as Minister for Territories was to prove crucial as he was to hold the portfolio until January 1972.[5] Barnes was deeply conservative by nature and saw little need to encourage political or constitutional change in Papua and New Guinea. His poor communication skills and blunt, disdainful manner alienated Papua New Guineans and those wishing to see progress. He was ill-at-ease with the emerging leaders of the Territory and preferred the company of the more conservatively-minded expatriate and indigenous communities in the Highlands. Yet despite his reputation and the criticisms emerging in the media, he retained the strong support of his Cabinet colleagues. None disagreed with policy nor his management of the portfolio.

The new Defence Minister, Shane Paltridge, was to prove a stronger performer in Cabinet than Townley, who had been ill for most of the last year of his appointment. Debates on defence and strategy in the 1950s and early 1960s had been characterised by a lack of involvement and leadership from the Defence Minister who had deferred to his military advisers and left wider strategic issues and assessments to Menzies, McEwen or the Minister for External Affairs. Even the service ministers such as John Gorton (Minister for the Navy from 1958 to 1963) rarely intervened and almost never spoke of wider strategic interests or objectives. Paltridge was to broaden the interventions beyond comments on acquisitions and supplies to include strategic concepts and priorities. Allan Martin has described Paltridge as one of the 'triumvirate' with Menzies and Hasluck who were to be of 'crucial importance in the final shaping of foreign relations'.[6] In all, Menzies, McEwen, Hasluck, Paltridge and Holt determined Australia's response to the worsening regional security situation with McEwen again showing a close involvement in the Cabinet room discussions.

The period was also marked by the retirement of Harold Macmillan on 18 October 1963 as Prime Minister of Great Britain and his replacement by Sir Alec Douglas-Home, an equally close friend of Menzies. In the week before his death on 22 November, President Kennedy had again reviewed US policy towards Indonesia and had reconfirmed the administration's priority to minimise the influence of the communist party in the politics of the government in Jakarta and not to antagonise Sukarno to the extent that he would shift closer to the communist bloc. The President had tentatively agreed to the suggestion of a state visit to Indonesia in 1964 but his officials had cautioned that this could only go ahead if Confrontation had ceased. The administration had also given some thought to including Australia and other countries in the region in that itinerary.[7]

Shann and Barwick try to assess Indonesia's intentions

At this time Shann and Barwick exchanged views on the likely future direction of Indonesia and the options for Australia's policy response. Shann had been in Jakarta for twelve months and used the anniversary to place before the minister his considered reflections on Indonesia and Sukarno. The exchange reflected the difficulties in finding an appropriate policy response to the increasingly febrile, chaotic and dangerous political and economic environment in Indonesia. As brilliant an analyst as Shann was – and during his time in Jakarta Shann was at his sharpest – he had yet to come to a point where he was completely sure he understood Sukarno and Indonesia.[8]

Shann described Indonesia under Sukarno as 'a difficult neighbour' suffering from 'delusions of grandeur' with a population in need of 'excitement and circuses' or 'gimmicks and slogans' to distract it from internal troubles. Indonesia was pursuing an 'aggressive anti-colonial nationalism' and was 'dangerous, expansionist and uncontrollable either from outside or from within'. He criticised US policy as 'vacillating and soft' when firmness was most needed. He anticipated a 'protracted period of extreme difficulty in our relations with this country' and was 'absolutely convinced that if Malaysia fails … we are in for real trouble, and it will not be many years before Australia and Indonesia are snarling at each other across the border between East and West New Guinea'. He did not discount the possibility of Indonesia being prepared to go to war against Australia but warned that if Australia were to initiate a war 'it would take 50 years to put the pieces together again'. He foresaw relations with Indonesia as 'difficult, exhausting and extremely worrying' and requiring a policy response of 'patience, forbearance and much careful thought', as well as firmness.[9]

Barwick did not disagree with Shann's analysis. He accepted that Australia's support for Malaysia had meant that it was seen by Indonesia as hostile but this was a price he was prepared to pay. He described a possible defeat and crushing of Malaysia as a 'disaster of the first magnitude and one which could have terrible effects on the security of the region'.[10] He acknowledged the 'threat to Papua/New Guinea which an expanding Indonesia could represent' and thought it could develop regardless of Confrontation: 'the tendency to interfere in Papua/New Guinea will develop in any case and ... we must be alert to anticipate it'.[11] Later, he noted that 'acute difficulties are bound to arise in New Guinea and they could even lead to hostilities ... we must make clear our intentions to defend Malaysia and Papua/New Guinea, no matter how little Indonesia likes this'.[12] However, elsewhere in his reply to Shann, Barwick rejected the assessment that Indonesia posed a direct military threat to Australia. While Barwick agreed on the need for firmness he placed importance on maintaining some elements of a bilateral relationship with Indonesia, including a small aid program, 'to convince them that we are not merely a British outpost but independent and sensitive to our neighbours'.[13] As Moreen Dee has argued, Barwick saw continued value in a policy of persuasive but quiet dialogue with Indonesia in order to avoid the possibility of pushing Indonesia further down a more a dangerous path.[14]

The exchange between Shann and Barwick continued into the New Year with Shann becoming increasingly alarmed at the direction Indonesia was taking and concerned at its capacity to undermine or threaten Australia's position in East New Guinea.[15] Writing on 17 January 1964 Shann agreed with Barwick's conclusion that Indonesia was not a direct military threat to Australia principally because Indonesia's economic and industrial base was too weak to sustain a military campaign of such magnitude to threaten Australia. He assured Barwick that 'there is no need for panic'. However, if Indonesia succeeded in causing the collapse of Malaysia he anticipated a number of countries in Southeast Asia – the Philippines, Thailand and perhaps Burma and Cambodia – would seek an accommodation with Indonesia and, as a result, 'Indonesian hegemony of the Southeast Asian region would be established'.[16] In such circumstances 'Australia's capacity to maintain its power in East New Guinea, either directly or through an independent Government closely aligned to us, might be seriously impaired'.[17] Shann argued that if one accepted the thesis that Indonesia was 'seeking to carve out as big a sphere of influence as possible' then East New Guinea was in its sights and Australia was not only 'a threat to its ambitions' but the 'only country of the South East Asian/South Pacific region which has the military potential to thwart or at least make very difficult, the attainment by Indonesia of its objectives'.[18]

In his public remarks Barwick referred to the need to maintain a balance in the relationship with Indonesia. In the Roy Milne Lecture on 25 January 1964 he used more diplomatic language when he described the need to balance a 'policy of friendship pursued with patience and understanding' with a recognition that 'wherever the vital interests of ourselves or our allies and friends are concerned we should be firm and unequivocal'. He added that Australia would not tolerate 'unacceptable international conduct' and that 'there must be no interference in the affairs of others and no expansionism'. More specifically, he commented that 'our own territorial integrity and that of our territories, Papua and New Guinea and our other territories, must be clearly indicated as inviolable'. He did not anticipate war with Indonesia but he made clear to his audience that if it did eventuate then Australia would face it with 'calmness and resolution'.[19]

The exchanges between Shann and Barwick, as well as the latter's public remarks, illustrated the sensitive game Barwick was trying to play in managing Australia's relations with Indonesia. However, in spite of the inducements he was prepared to offer Indonesia, Barwick (and his colleagues) were determined to respond swiftly and firmly to any Indonesian threat against Papua New Guinea.

How to defend Malaysia

In September 1963, following the official declaration of the establishment of Malaysia and the subsequent attack on the British and Malaysian Embassies in Jakarta, Macmillan sounded out Menzies as to a possible Australian contribution to counter-insurgency operations in the defence of Malaysia. He suggested this could be done by drawing on units from the Australian forces serving in the Commonwealth Strategic Reserve. Macmillan made clear his view that Malaysia was the subject of an external attack.[20] Barwick forwarded an interim reply to Duncan Sandys, the Secretary of State for Commonwealth Relations and for the Colonies, noting that Australia wished to examine 'carefully the international political implications and the timing of any military response'.[21] He also told Sandys that Australia had 'examined the retaliation Indonesia can bring to play such as interference with our civil and military air and shipping connections and meddling in New Guinea, and we are developing plans to meet these contingencies'.[22]

The newly-established Foreign Affairs and Defence Committee of Cabinet (FADC) considered its response to the British request on 19 December 1963 when it reviewed an assessment prepared by the Defence Committee. The latter had concluded that there was 'no pressing military need at present for Australian military assistance in eastern Malaysia' and if the government were to make a military contribution it would be to the detriment of Australia's ability to make a contribution to any regional SEATO commitment. The Defence Committee drew ministers' attention to the possibility that 'Indonesia might engineer diversionary incidents against the Papua/New Guinea border and take obstructive action against our sea and air communications'. The 'diversionary incidents' could include 'attacks by 'volunteers' against soft targets near the [New Guinea] border'; infiltration for the purpose of subversion; and subversion by indirect means such as infiltrating local communities. The consequences would be 'that these would force Australia to disperse her efforts by sending troops to eastern New Guinea'.[23]

Ministers were faced with the predicament of trying to respond to the British request with limited resources and a number of potential commitments. This dilemma was to preoccupy the Cabinet for the next two years with ministers repeatedly drawing attention to the adverse impact on Australia's ability to defend Papua New Guinea if it committed troops to Southeast Asia and Indo China. During the period of the West New Guinea dispute Australia had been faced with the sole prospect of deployment to the war in Korea. Following the ceasefire there in 1953 Australia had only relatively minor external military commitments. The government had therefore been able to concentrate the focus of its defence efforts on the possibility of Indonesian aggression in West New Guinea and even East New Guinea. During the period of Confrontation Australia faced a complex set of potential commitments ranging from Indonesian aggression in Malaysia, Indonesian pressure on the border with East New Guinea and the escalating war in Vietnam. Papua New Guinea was one element in a larger, more demanding strategic environment and was ever-present in the minds of decision makers.

In the Cabinet discussions in December 1963, McEwen warned his colleagues that 'we've got political commitments beyond our capacity ... we may get [a] diversionary attack on our territory. ... What I see is difficulty, all difficulty'.[24] Barwick agreed and noted that Britain was looking for partners in Malaysia while Australia 'on the other hand [didn't] want to be implicated beyond what [was] necessary'.[25] Menzies was more inclined to look for ways to assist Britain and chided the Defence Committee representatives present, saying that they 'looked for what we can't do rather than what might be possible'.[26] Nevertheless, Menzies accepted the argument in favour of caution and wrote to Douglas-Home on 24 December 1963.[27] He told his newly-appointed British counterpart that 'for lack of clear military justification ... (a) further military contribution by us ought not to come at this stage'. He also admitted to Douglas-Home that 'we are not so flush with forces that we can allot any of them prematurely'.[28]

The content of Menzies's message to Douglas-Home anticipated the type of response his government would give to most requests from Britain over the next few months. It was a strategy of balancing the need to stand firm in the face of Indonesia's provocative acts against Malaysia while, at the same time, maintaining the semblance of a relationship with Indonesia based on a broader, but still very limited bilateral agenda. In managing this strategy ministers showed a keen sensitivity towards the need to defend Papua and New Guinea and the implications which any deployments to either Malaysia or Indo China would have on that requirement. At times ministers were more sensitive to this issue than officials, although some, for example in External Affairs, highlighted Australia's exposed position. External Affairs argued that:

> Indonesia would be tempted by our weakness in New Guinea. The Indonesians could calculate that some interference in border regions would create considerable public unrest in Australia and cause a diversion of troop disposition. The Indonesians are well placed geographically to intrude; several former Dutch administrative towns are near the border and the Indonesian presence is well established in and around them; by contrast Australian border regions are more deserted and our administrative centres further away. Minor forms of Indonesian meddling would be difficult to prevent and difficult to bring effectively to international notice.[29]

In the first six months of 1964, in an atmosphere of increasingly hostile Indonesian behaviour towards Malaysia, ministers returned frequently to the question of how to respond. Cabinet met on five occasions between December 1963 and April 1964 to discuss its response to Confrontation before announcing on 17 March 1964 and on 16 April its decisions to provide additional military aid to Malaysia.³⁰ In one of the early debates in Cabinet leading up to those announcements Hasluck (Minister for Defence), who, during the West New Guinea dispute had shown a preference for a strong military response against Indonesia, continued to make clear his view that Indonesia had a 'very ugly and very determined ambition and what will stop them is the certainty that they will not succeed – we must make it clear beyond doubt that we intend to see Malaysia stand'.³¹ On 28 January when Cabinet considered a program of defence aid for Malaysia, McEwen was more cautious and reluctant to see Australia respond disproportionately to what, at this stage, he considered to be minor incursions by Indonesia. He warned his colleagues that Australia should 'not get into a military situation with Indonesia in which we're not sure that the US will back us – keep ourselves under ANZUS umbrella'.³² He urged caution, telling his colleagues that in deciding on the aid package 'we want to play it in accordance with Australian interests and not with British interests'. He added that Australia should provide the defence aid but 'give it quietly – don't flaunt what you do'.³³ (He nevertheless held a dim view of Sukarno whom he described to UK Prime Minister Home during a trip to London at this time as a 'crazy dictator' whose actions were unpredictable.)³⁴ McEwen continued to urge restraint as Britain placed further pressure on Australia to contribute forces to Malaysia. By May 1964 he warned his colleagues that:

> Our area is Malaysia and if something happens there, we'll be in it. But not anxious to put our toe in unnecessarily – we still have to live with Indonesia and we could, if we act prematurely, get ourselves on world stage as invading Indonesia – may provoke retaliation across Papuan border'.³⁵

McEwen and his colleagues were not appeasers of Indonesia. They were realistic about the low level of Australia's defence preparedness and, in McEwen's case, sensitive to the broader implications of Australia acting against Indonesia, either alone or with its allies. McEwen was prepared to act but only if the circumstances fully merited it and the consequences had been thoroughly considered. It was at this time, in June 1964, that McEwen paid his only visit to Port Moresby when he accompanied the Governor-General to the opening of the House of Assembly.

In their discussions in early 1964 ministers juggled with the need to find resources to send to Malaysia while meeting commitments in Papua New Guinea. In the Cabinet discussions immediately before the second announcement on 16 April 1964 ministers had before them a report on 'the implications for Australian preparedness to meet overt aggression, or the more likely eventuality of covert Indonesian retaliatory and diversionary attacks along the Papua/New Guinea border if Australian forces were committed to anti-insurgency operations in Borneo'.[36] The Defence Committee's report repeatedly drew attention to the fact that Australia would be caught short in responding to any threat to Papua and New Guinea if it provided military assistance to Malaysia. In particular, it noted that the provision of two coastal minesweepers and four Iroquois helicopters to Malaysia would have an impact on the current defence deployments to Papua and New Guinea, on Australia's ability to monitor the Indonesia/Papua and New Guinea border and to respond to overt Indonesian naval activity around Papua and New Guinea.[37] McEwen, in particular, strongly endorsed the Committee's assessment and advised Menzies, who was in London attending a Commonwealth leaders' meeting, that the despatch of the Australian battalion to Eastern Malaysia, as requested by Britain, might lead to Indonesian retaliatory action on the New Guinea border, with the Australian public in turn demanding the deployment of Australian troops to defend the border.[38]

As a further reflection of Canberra's increasing sensitivity towards Indonesia, defence officials in April 1964 developed 'Plan Pygmalion' designed to meet possible covert Indonesian action along the border and the promotion of insurgency inside Papua New Guinea. The plan reflected the argument that 'Indonesia may attempt to divert our attention and our forces [deployed to Sabah and Sarawak] by covert action against East New Guinea'.[39] The plan was periodically updated over the next few years and formed one of a number of contingency plans developed to meet possible Indonesian military activity in Southeast Asia, including Papua New Guinea.

Hasluck broadens the policy debate

Hasluck had taken over as Minister for External Affairs on 24 April 1964 and soon after left for meetings in Jakarta, London and Washington. In his talks in Jakarta Hasluck referred to Papua New Guinea only in passing. With Subandrio he discussed the need to push ahead with the demarcation of the boundary between Irian Jaya and Papua and New Guinea and other practical administrative issues concerning management of the border. He did raise with General Nasution whether Indonesia would 'arrogate to itself a right to support any dissident movement which might grow up against

Australian Administration in East New Guinea' to which Nasution replied 'no, not there'.[40]

Hasluck's visit to Washington was to attend a meeting of the ANZUS Council with the New Zealand Prime Minister Keith Holyoake and the US Secretary of State Dean Rusk. The war in Vietnam dominated discussion. In his bilateral conversations before the Council meeting Hasluck did not pursue the forceful line of argument that Barwick had set out six months earlier over possible Indonesian threats towards Papua and New Guinea. He made no mention of Papua and New Guinea during his meeting with President Johnson.[41] He told Robert McNamara (Secretary of Defence) that Australia had 'no wish to be an aggressor and had no designs whatsoever upon Indonesian territory'.[42] For his part, McNamara told Hasluck that the United States did not think Australia's defence budget and forces were adequate for the international situation facing the country.[43]

At the ANZUS Council meeting Hasluck did not mention Papua New Guinea or possible Indonesian threats. He described the military situation in Malaysia as 'manageable' and that 'patience would be required over a long period while Sukarno continued to irritate'.[44] Perhaps showing the influence of McEwen on his thinking, he added that 'Australia faced the long-term question of living in perpetuity with Indonesia. Australia would strive to survive the current crisis without doing lasting damage to relations with Indonesia'.[45] As Gregory Pemberton has observed, events were moving quickly and Washington's attention was now dominated by Vietnam. Hasluck followed suit and increasingly moved Australia's focus towards Indochina and the war in Vietnam.[46] By the time of the next ANZUS Council Meeting in June 1965 the debate over the future course of the war in Vietnam was almost the sole focus of discussion and only minimum mention was made of Confrontation.

The Australian Government was faced with increasing pressure from Britain for a greater defence effort in Malaysia. It also anticipated US overtures for an increased contribution to the war in Vietnam. The government's response was to continue to draw attention to the pressures it perceived in Australia's own strategic environment. In Menzies's absence in London, Cabinet considered a further request from Britain for the deployment of, firstly, the Australian battalion in the Commonwealth Brigade and later the whole Brigade to Borneo. McEwen, who was acting Prime Minister, made clear to his colleagues that Australia did not have the resources to conduct a war in Borneo and meet its SEATO commitments. He also made clear his concern that 'if we get into [a] conflict in Borneo in less than war I would be astounded if Indonesia didn't retaliate [in] New Guinea. Cost them nothing. Retaliation to hot pursuit'. An an earlier Cabinet meeting McEwan had said that 'we still have to live with Indonesia and we could, if we … prematurely get ourselves on [the] world stage as "invading" Indonesia [over Malaysia] Indonesia may provoke retaliation across Papuan border'.[47] McEwen conveyed his views to Menzies while noting that 'Indonesia could organize retaliatory incidents even with nationalistic West Irians, cross border raids and general harassment in the New Guinea border regions. While these would not constitute a real military threat they might give rise to an immediate and irresistible clamour in Australia for the posting of Australian troops to meet what the public would regard as an imminent threat of invasion'.[48]

As an indication of the concern within Cabinet to defend Papua and New Guinea, ministers in August quickly approved a submission from the Minister for Air (Peter Howson) to rehabilitate the airfield at Nadzab near Lae to enable it to serve as a transit or ferry airfield to allow flights from Australia to Southeast Asia by Mirage aircraft and thereby bypass Indonesian airspace.[49] Separately, the Defence Minister sought approval for the proposed airfield at Boram near Wewak, which was to be used in both covert and overt operations against Indonesia in Irian Jaya if these were required, to be completed earlier than planned but to a less sophisticated standard. He advised his colleagues of an intention to seek ministerial approval to develop a chain of airfields near the border area to allow for enhanced mobility and flexibility in the deployment of troops to meet both covert and overt threats.[50] Both submissions were approved with the minimum of discussion.

Juggling commitments

The sense that Australia was facing too many security challenges and was being asked to contribute forces simultaneously in a number of areas increasingly preoccupied the Menzies Cabinet. As Woodard and Edwards have argued, there was 'certainly a sense of apprehension (in Cabinet) that Australia was faced with more threats than it had the capability to meet'.[51] On 3 September 1964 ministers examined the issue of a possible commitment to the war in Vietnam. In doing so they also discussed the range of commitments facing Australia. Paltridge told his colleagues that Australia 'did not have the military resources to become seriously involved with combat forces in all three areas', i.e. South Vietnam, Malaysia and in Papua/New Guinea. He added that 'any substantial contribution to mainland South East Asia even in an insurgency situation would be at some expense to our present contribution to the defence of Malaysia and could affect our ability to provide forces for Papua/New Guinea'.[52] In the discussion in Cabinet McEwen questioned how Australia would respond 'if we get into a SEATO plan and are faced with activity in New Guinea as well – we will have extra forces north of Malaya and will need extra forces for New Guinea'. Menzies also acknowledged the dilemma and suggested ministers 'decide which is our priority commitment'. He identified South Vietnam as the 'most urgent situation'. McEwen agreed on the need to identify a priority and added 'we could be in for great torment. We must not be in a position where in a crisis we fail US, UK or ourselves'. He said that he did 'not think Borneo [was] first priority – Malaysia could well be – Vietnam could be'.[53] The Cabinet decision noted that ministers had agreed that Australia's formal commitments 'would in total be beyond our capacity to satisfy'.[54] The Cabinet discussions also canvassed the possibility of introducing some form of military conscription, including for overseas service, to overcome the shortfall in manpower in the army.

The debate about concurrent and conflicting commitments continued in the Cabinet's discussion of the 1964 Strategic Basis Paper.[55] The paper concluded that Australia's strategic environment had undergone a 'further substantial deterioration'. It reviewed security developments throughout Indochina and Southeast Asia and, in particular, warned that 'Indonesia will aim to achieve regional hegemony and to eliminate from the area the British or any other influences inimical to her'. Indonesia posed the only direct threat to Australia and its territories. It anticipated that Indonesia would continue a policy of confrontation against Malaysia and argued that Sukarno was moving 'steadily into a closer association with the communist powers'. It warned that Indonesia was 'likely to interfere increasingly in Papua/New Guinea' and argued that Indonesia could place pressure on Australia if 'anti-Administration movements' were to develop. Once Papua and New Guinea was independent it could 'exploit emerging political parties opposed to Australia's aims for the area'. The paper suggested that, if the United States were heavily committed elsewhere, Indonesia might be tempted to step up her activity to a type of military confrontation in Papua New Guinea similar to that now being conducted in Borneo. It noted that 'in Papua/New Guinea it is conceivable that an insurgency situation stimulated and assisted by Indonesia could also require the commitment of Australian forces'. The paper ascribed a level of vulnerability to Papua New Guinea which had not been present since the Second World War.

The concerns expressed in the Strategic Basis Paper regarding Indonesia were matched by continuing expressions of alarm from within the bureaucracy. In briefing the Prime Minister on the 1964 Paper, officials from his department emphasised their deep concern at the competing demands of dealing with Malaysia, Indonesia and Papua New Guinea and the management of the tensions and pressures within a tri-polar security environment. They argued that 'the real commitment we have entered into in terms of current demand is in respect of Malaysia which in turn involves us with Indonesia which in turn places a priority on New Guinea defence'.[56] They drew attention to the critical assessment in the paper that 'for the first time a direct threat' to Australia had clearly been identified – Indonesia. The officials asserted that the 'defence of New Guinea ... is emerging as the real claimant for priority attention in the present defence review'. They argued that:

> Australia now has a long frontier in New Guinea with Asia. The extent to which Australian defence is divisible from New Guinea defence is the only adjustment which we can make to the concept that Australia has a common land frontier with Asia. From this kind of consideration, it emerges that we must accompany a forward defence policy with a policy of territorial defence based on the defence of New Guinea.[57]

The briefing note also argued that the Chiefs of Staff had not allocated sufficient resources to the defence of Papua New Guinea and, indeed, that the Australian Army was understaffed to meet the needs of the strategic environment. The Department advised the Prime Minister that an army of 55,000 was needed, not 33,000, 'if we are to take our obligation to New Guinea seriously'.[58]

From his perspective in Jakarta, Shann contributed a pessimistic assessment of Sukarno and Indonesia.[59] He described Sukarno following his 'hysterical, chauvinistic harangue' speech on 17 August 1964 in which he had launched his 'Year of Living Dangerously', as in an 'egotistical mood' with 'delusions of importance'. He added that 'Indonesians like turmoil and excitement. ... If they do not have West Irian, then it seems they must have a Malaysia. If they do not have a Malaysia, I think they will have to have an Eastern New Guinea, or something like that'. He assessed Indonesia to be a 'thoroughly unpleasant neighbour'. He concluded that it would be a 'tragedy for Australia's position in this part of the world to become involved in hostilities with Indonesia ... but I conclude with some regret that we have to prepare against such an eventuality ... and that such a war may, as things turn out, be quite hard to avoid'.[60]

Ministers were in broad agreement with the analysis in the Strategic Basis Paper. Menzies described the situation as 'deteriorating to serious proportions'.⁶¹ McEwen said the overall situation had 'dramatically changed'. Holt reminded his colleagues of the increased defence budgets approved over the previous two years, although Paltridge responded by telling his colleagues that 'our picnic is over' and more resources had to be found.⁶² There was a general acceptance of this argument although it served to lead once again to the question of whether compulsory military service was needed to boost the Army.

In terms of specific issues, Menzies, reflecting the brief from his department, asked 'have we paid enough attention to the possibility that Indonesia may stir the pot in our New Guinea?'.⁶³ McEwen shared Menzies's concern and told his colleagues that:

> in a situation of escalation in New Guinea we haven't the equipment there to handle a guerrilla war – Australian public would however insist that we fight it – the US won't come into it – What I [look] ... for is a separable, detachable unit which would cope with a New Guinea situation. We ought not to rush into bombing Indonesian bases without endorsement of US but we must have provision to fight a guerrilla action in New Guinea – public opinion will demand it – this New Guinea aspect is the new strategic factor – perhaps political factor more than military. We must provide for that.⁶⁴

Menzies agreed fully with McEwen's comment and posed the question to General Sir John Wilton, Chief of the General Staff, who was present during the discussions, whether 'we could put into New Guinea a force of any substance'. Wilton replied that a battalion and support units could be deployed to assist the Pacific Islands Regiment (PIR). He described the PIR as best at 'reconnaissance, screening and activity operations and was not sure as to their capacity as assault troops or defending troops. But with Australian regulars behind them would be effective'. In response to McEwen's question, Wilton said the PIR could respond to 'probing incidents' by Indonesia into New Guinea.⁶⁵ Ministers endorsed the Strategic Basis Paper but, in keeping with the remarks by Menzies and McEwen, flagged in their decision the question of whether 'the possibility of Australian forces being required to act without the assistance of the United States armed forces against Indonesian activities in Papua New Guinea is sufficiently recognized and sufficiently provided for in military planning'.⁶⁶

Compromised by obligations

The government responded to the question of whether the resources allocated to the defence forces were sufficient when it introduced the 1964 Defence Review into Parliament on 10 November 1964. Menzies spoke at length about the deteriorating regional security environment, the tension between Indonesia and Malaysia and the risk of war. He announced a further 50 per cent increase in the defence budget and the introduction of selective military service which might involve deployment overseas. The Prime Minister reflected the conversations in the Cabinet room and assessment in the Strategic Basis Paper when he rated the defence of Papua New Guinea as one of the three principal obligations of Australian defence planning in 1964, along with Malaysia and South Vietnam. He specifically linked the actions of Indonesia in the region to the need to defend Papua New Guinea and warned that 'we must prepare for all eventualities including the control and, if necessary, defence of the frontier between West New Guinea and the territory of Papua New Guinea'.[67] Subritzky has argued that the announcements made on 10 November were both a reflection of Menzies's influence and powers of persuasion in Cabinet and an acknowledgement of the 'genuine fears' of both himself and his 'contemporaries concerning recent political developments in their region of the world'.[68] In listing the 'contemporaries' it is important to acknowledge the role of McEwen, a hitherto hidden voice in guiding the development of Australia's foreign and security policies.

In the course of the campaign for the half-Senate election held on 5 December 1964, Menzies showed a new willingness to criticise Indonesia publicly. He had by now lost all respect for Sukarno and had earlier described him as the 'ineffable Dr Soekarno'.[69] In his opening address in the campaign Menzies referred to 'the truculence with which Soekarno and those with him speak to us and to the world'. He told the electorate that 'a nation which will not hesitate in breach of all the rules of international conduct to invade, even in a small way, a peaceful neighbour, won't have too many doubts about making some infiltration into our side of New Guinea if they think it is profitable'. He added 'and therefore in our programme we have had to step up, quite materially, what we are doing to defend New Guinea and Papua'.[70] In the course of the campaign Menzies repeated his earlier statement that 'we have declared that we will defend the frontiers of New Guinea and Papua just as we would the frontiers of our own country. … any attack on our territories in the Pacific invokes the operations of the great ANZUS pact to which the United States is a party'.[71] He also used the need to defend Papua and New Guinea to justify the introduction of selective military conscription, stating 'we need this higher figure because we have obligations to perform to our own country, to Papua and New Guinea, to Malaysia ... to Vietnam'.[72] Menzies also began to articulate more forcefully the view that Australia had a number of defence obligations which needed to be met, including 'developing our strength in Papua and New Guinea'.[73]

The election result was mixed for the Liberal/Country parties, with Labor campaigning heavily against the introduction of conscription. Menzies failed to gain the resounding victory he had achieved in 1963. Instead the two parties were tied in numbers in the Senate with the government now dependent on the support of the anti-communist and pro-defence spending Democratic Labor Party. Nevertheless, when addressing regional security issues, Menzies and his colleagues continued to employ the argument they had used during the election campaign that Australia faced a range of commitments which strained its ability to respond to regional developments.

On 15 January 1965, the newly elected Prime Minister of Britain, Harold Wilson, wrote to Menzies suggesting that a more robust response to Indonesia's threats against Malaysia was now necessary. Australian ministers were again cautious in their response. Hasluck commented that Australia was being asked for resources 'in two areas' – battalions for Borneo and South Vietnam. He added that 'we alone in Australia [are] in this position'.[74] McEwen told his colleagues that Sukarno would 'suck us dry by present tactics' and suggested that instead of Malaysia, 'our vital interest is that they [USA] remain there [in Vietnam] fighting'.[75] In his reply, McEwen, as Acting Prime Minister, told Wilson that Australia's obligations in Southeast Asia were 'tending to run in two directions'. He noted that 'in addition to our commitment to assist you in the discharge of your defence obligations to Malaysia we feel a deep concern over the situation developing in Vietnam and a strong desire to help our American allies in that theatre within the limits of our resources'. He also drew Wilson's attention to the fact that Australia 'must also bear in mind the possibilities of events on our frontier in New Guinea should relationships further deteriorate'.[76]

While McEwen's message could be seen as prevaricating he had no such hesitation when it came to assessing requests for military assistance in Vietnam from the United States. In response to the escalation of fighting and anticipating a likely request from the United States (and South Vietnam) for a commitment of forces, McEwen's views were clear: 'if the US become engaged with formations and they ask us to be in. This is the acid test. The only barrier between us and China. Either we go in or crawl out. I would go in almost asking no questions'. His only caveats were the need for South Vietnam to ask for Australian involvement and the desirability of broadening the list of countries providing troops. He bluntly told his colleagues that it was desirable to 'get some brown skins in if you can: Thais, Philippines'.[77] The caution Australia had shown in responding to Britain's requests for assistance during Confrontation was not evident when the United States broached the question of a contribution to Vietnam.

In his meetings in London in February 1965, while attending the funeral of Sir Winston Churchill, Menzies continued to highlight the competing commitments now facing Australia and its defence force. In a discussion on 1 February with Wilson, senior UK ministers and New Zealand Prime Minister Holyoake, Menzies noted, according to the British record of the meeting, that Australia had a number of 'obligations'. The first was the 'almost instinctive obligation, unwritten but nonetheless, to do all … to help Britain'. Second, 'there were the contractual obligations under ANZUS'. Third, 'there were the Treaty obligations of SEATO'. Fourth, 'there was the commitment to Malaysia itself'. Fifth, there were Australia's 'obligations to defend Papua and New Guinea', and finally there was the 'question of the territorial defence of Australia itself'. He told his British colleagues that 'he found it very difficult to get clear in his own mind what the priorities were' and suggested that in such an environment 'it was all the more important that there should be a closer possible political consultation … to get quite clear an agreed order of priorities'. Menzies also drew attention to the 50 per cent increase in the Australian defence budget and the introduction of compulsory military service overseas. Later in the conversation, after agreeing to consider the possible deployment of sixty SAS troops to Malaysia, Menzies said, according to the UK record, that 'as far as Australia was concerned the last thing [it] wanted was a war with Indonesia. It was not merely because Indonesia had 100 million people but because, for Australia, a war with Asia was a bad prospect. He, for his part, felt that the right way to avoid such a war was to demonstrate that we were not frightened of one. He described Mr Subandrio as an eel soaked in oil and President Soekarno as a nut'.[78]

Hasluck employed a near-identical argument when he told the United States *Chargé d'Affaires* in Canberra in February 1965 that:

> Australia was being required to consider requests for help or to maintain its commitments in respect of Malaysia, South Vietnam, SEATO planning, the defence of the New Guinea border and the defence of

Northern Australia. There was a consequent risk of a dissipation of our limited resources without advantage either to our allies or to ourselves.[79]

By making these connections he sustained the view that the need to defend Papua New Guinea had to be acknowledged when making judgements about commitments to the more violent confrontations happening in Southeast Asia. However, Hasluck's broader philosophical approach to foreign policy and security issues was revealed in his first major address on foreign policy to the House of Representatives on 23 March 1965. In that speech Hasluck established a theme that was to dominate his time as minister: the war in Vietnam and the threat posed by China to the region. These issues steadily took the place of Indonesia and Confrontation.[80]

Critical decisions

1965 was a critical year in the development of Australia's foreign and defence policies. Confrontation escalated and Australia responded by agreeing to the deployment of an SAS squadron to Malaysia and for the Australian battalion (3 RAR) serving with the Strategic Reserve to be made available for active deployment in Malaysia. The Australian Cabinet took the decision to despatch a battalion to Vietnam. Singapore and Malaysia separated after a difficult period as a Federation. Lastly, the attempted coup in Jakarta on 30 September/1 October 1965 by pro-communist party sympathisers saw the end of Sukarno's period of undisputed leadership and his replacement within a few months by General Suharto. It also signaled the eventual end of Confrontation as Suharto began to reverse many of the elements of Sukarno's foreign and defence policies and to repair relations with Malaysia.

On 7, 20 and 21 April 1965 the Cabinet considered the question of nominating a battalion to serve in Vietnam.[81] In a briefing note to Menzies, the Secretary of his Department, Sir John Bunting, assured the Prime Minister that an increased commitment to Vietnam had 'no unacceptable implications' for Australia's responsibilities towards Malaysia and Papua New Guinea.[82] In the meeting on 7 April Hasluck, who at the time was developing the concept that Southeast Asia should be looked at as one single security-related area and not different theatres of operation, questioned whether the deployment of the battalion to Vietnam would 'involve a dissipation of our forces'.[83] Both McEwen and Menzies, who fully supported the despatch of the battalion, took the view that any dispersal of Australia's forces 'should be against an assurance of our allies that they will take the place of our battalions or release them in time of need'.⁸⁴ Menzies was firmer in his view that 'we should mention East New Guinea – our problem there must be understood and assistance assured'.⁸⁵ Ministers rejected a proposal from Hasluck to develop a 'paper' setting out Australia's responsibilities and seeking assurances of assistance in other theatres if Australia were pressed. McEwen argued that Australia's ability to respond to problems in New Guinea and Oceania would be delayed but not 'removed' by having a battalion in Vietnam. He added 'if Indonesia becomes active we need assistance – US more certain to provide it if we have supplied a battalion to Vietnam than if we haven't'.⁸⁶ The question of the US and UK providing some form of assurance that they would provide military support if Australia faced problems in East New Guinea was included in the decision reached by Cabinet and conveyed to both governments.⁸⁷ The British Government declined to give an assurance, citing the need to be prepared to deploy troops to Borneo and the Persian Gulf. The US Government was more sympathetic.⁸⁸

In his public comments following the decision to despatch a battalion to Vietnam Menzies continued to refer to the difficult relationship with Indonesia. In May 1965 he told an audience in Melbourne that Australia 'continued to do everything in our power to maintain some friendly contacts with Indonesia. ... Nothing could be more terrifying for us than to think we might by erroneous judgements or foolish actions find ourselves in conflict with the whole of the people of Asia'. He went on to say that nevertheless 'our objective is to defend our own security and that of our territories'.⁸⁹ Later in the year Menzies returned to the theme and spoke of Australia's 'obligations', including 'the defence of New Guinea and Papua which we have accepted as part of the defence of Australia'.⁹⁰

While ministers focused on military developments in the region, they were taken by surprise at the announcement that Singapore had left the Federation with Malaysia. Hasluck told his Cabinet colleagues that the break 'involves very real risks – that Singapore will go Communist ... that confrontation will be dodged, that Singapore and Malaysia become at loggerheads. These are risks over five years'.⁹¹ He recommended that Australia put the best possible face on the news and adopt an air of confidence when answering questions about the future of the two countries. McEwen said the 'only crisis out of this is if Singapore goes Communist – vital to us. UK and USA to see that Singapore remains as is'.⁹² Menzies agreed. McEwen, reflecting the sudden and unexpected nature of the break, added that the lesson learned was that 'it is impossible to be close to Asians. We believed we were on closest terms. But we were ignored and dumped'.

Menzies again agreed and added that 'part of this lesson is that we need to be more wary still and recognize that we don't necessarily understand Asians even when we think we do'. McEwen concluded the conversation by suggesting that 'we go on co-operating but within the limits of our self interest, not in a "do-good" context'.[93] Menzies and his senior colleagues had believed that they were developing an understanding and a relationship with a good number of countries in Asia, notably Japan, Malaysia and Singapore. The shock of Singapore's departure showed how sensitive they were to events in the region and not quite at ease with the politics of many of the new and developing nations in Southeast Asia.

If Australian ministers were distressed at the news of the break-up of the Federation, they were equally concerned at developments in Indonesia. Robert (Bob) Furlonger, a senior officer in External Affairs and later Ambassador to Jakarta, looked back on the period and described the prospect of Indonesia moving in one of three different directions: 'becoming a thoroughgoing communist state in close alliance with Peking and Hanoi'; short of that outlook, 'to become a kind of Cuba on the early Castro pattern ... intent on driving Western influence out of South East Asia and on fomenting revolution throughout the region'; or 'if neither of these happened, to drift towards internal chaos, probably civil war, and perhaps disintegration. ... in any of these eventualities, Indonesia would have been a major problem for Australia'.[94] Australia faced a set of dangerous challenges.

The concerns of the Australian Cabinet were in time allayed. The developments in Indonesia following the abortive coup of 30 September 1965, including the eventual replacement of Sukarno by General Suharto and the repression of communists or communist sympathisers throughout Indonesia, were, as Edwards has described, 'a major turning-point in the politics of Indonesia and all of Southeast Asia'.[95] Edwards is perhaps a little too quick off the mark with his further conclusion that 'as far as the Australian public ... were concerned, the preoccupation with Indonesia was over'.[96] The possibility of Indonesia applying pressure on Papua New Guinea continued to be a feature of assessments, as evident in a further review conducted in February 1966 by the Defence Committee and in March of that year by the Cabinet.[97] In the still uncertain outlook for Indonesia, defence planners persisted with the argument that Papua New Guinea was a potential target for Indonesian 'hegemony' and that Indonesia could have a potential interest in subverting the emerging indigenous political leadership of the country and in undermining Australia's interests there.

However, Australia's regional security focus was in the process of shifting quickly to the war in Vietnam and, in this new environment, concerns about Indonesian interest in or threat to Papua New Guinea began to be redirected to the question of the management of the Indonesia-Papua New Guinea border rather than threats of overt incursions. Australia's immediate security concerns were soon reduced to an overwhelming preoccupation with the war in Vietnam and the impact of Britain's decision to withdraw its military forces 'East of Suez'.

Conclusion and the fading spectre of Indonesia

The gradual fall from power of President Sukarno following the attempted coup of 30 September 1965 and the retirement of Menzies on 26 January 1966 brought to an end a sixteen-year period of parallel, though contrasting, careers. In the sixteen years of tension between Australia and Indonesia, first over the issue of West New Guinea and then Confrontation, Menzies had not changed his mind about Australia's northern neighbour. He knew, and said publicly, that Australia had to develop and sustain a relationship with Indonesia. In this he recognised the inevitability of geography. But he did little personally to promote a positive relationship. He travelled out of Australia on a regular, almost annual basis throughout his term as Prime Minister but only once visited Indonesia. His comments and attitudes towards Sukarno and Indonesia in general, as revealed in the discussions in the Cabinet room, instead suggest that Menzies remained suspicious and wary of Indonesia under Sukarno throughout his term as Prime Minister. In 1950 Menzies had regarded Sukarno as a wartime collaborator with the Japanese who could not be trusted. By 1959 the Australian leader was at least prepared, albeit reluctantly given his aversion to travelling in the tropics, to journey to Jakarta to meet him. The visit represented a temporary pause in Menzies's attitude and by the early 1960s he was again openly critical of Indonesia and the threat it posed to the region. He saw Sukarno as a quasi-dictator and demagogue who was ambitious, expansionist and intent on building an 'Indonesian Empire'. He saw him in much the same light as he had President Nasser of Egypt during the Suez Crisis. Menzies and his senior ministers, notably Paul Hasluck, rarely moved beyond this deeply-held feeling of mistrust. McEwen on the other hand showed more pragmatism and flexibility.

In this unstable environment Menzies and his colleagues were consistently mindful of the place of Papua New Guinea in Australia's security environment and the need to defend it. In part, Menzies reflected the attitude of the generation of Australians who had endured the campaigns of the Second World War in New Guinea. He felt obliged to say publicly on at least five occasions that Australia would defend Papua New Guinea against Indonesian infiltration or aggression. He was also acutely aware of the strain that such an obligation placed on Australia's other commitments in the region, although it could be said that he used this card to his advantage in arguing against a sizeable deployment of Australian troops to Malaysia, as sought by Britain. Papua New Guinea and, more broadly, New Guinea, also had a place in Menzies's view of Australian defence planning. It was, as Greg Pemberton has described, a *casus belli* should Indonesia threaten it. The mood in Cabinet throughout the 1950s and 1960s was such that it was unlikely that ministers would have hesitated to defend Papua New Guinea if Indonesia had threatened it militarily. By the mid-1960s it was both an island to be defended but also a platform from which Australia could shift defence assets to Southeast Asia and Indo China.

Historians such as John Subritzky and Greg Pemberton and others have rightly examined Australia's response to developments in the region in the mid-1960s through the perspective of Australia's immediate response to events in Malaysia and then Vietnam. It is clear that these were the dominant foci for Australian decision-makers. However, it is also true that Australian ministers, as revealed in the conversations in Cabinet, were highly sensitive to the place of Papua New Guinea in this picture and rarely concluded an analysis of developments and their repercussions without drawing attention to it and the need to provide for its defence.

The assumption of power by General Suharto began a slow but, in time, fundamental change in Australia's assessment of the place of Indonesia and, by extension, Papua New Guinea, in Australia's strategic environment. Indonesia remained the close object of Australia's concerns and suspicions but now on a gradually decreasing scale. The emphasis shifted, as will be seen in subsequent chapters, from concerns about an ambitious, expansionary Indonesia to one focused on the internal problems of Papua New Guinea as it moved to self-government and independence. By 1983 the Strategic Basis Paper setting out Australian Defence Policy asserted that 'at best a strong, stable and friendly Indonesia could be a defensive shield between Australia and hostile developments further north. At worst, a belligerent, or weak and divided, Indonesia could seriously threaten our security'.[98] The replacement of Papua New Guinea with Indonesia as the 'defensive shield' represented a transformation in Australia's defence thinking.

Chapter 9

SHIFTING GROUND: NEW INFLUENCES EMERGE 1966–1972

> 'Papua/New Guinea is of abiding strategic interest to Australia'.
>
> Defence Committee, September 1970

On 26 January 1966 Harold Holt was sworn in as Prime Minister. He succeeded Sir Robert Menzies who had announced his retirement a few days earlier. Holt was to serve just short of two years before he drowned in December 1967. Holt's death signalled the beginning of a five-year period of political uncertainty and division in Australia with three Prime Ministers (including a brief interim appointment of John McEwen as Prime Minister immediately after Holt's death), five Ministers for External or Foreign Affairs, four Defence Ministers and three Treasurers holding office. The stability of the Menzies era had disappeared. A lack of cohesion and direction permeated the Cabinet as it struggled with a complex, demanding and rapidly changing regional security environment. As Peter Edwards has described: 'the Australian government was in a state of policy paralysis'.[1]

The post-Menzies Liberal–Country Party governments were faced with three continuing defence-related problems: the dramatically changing and uncertain political environment in Indonesia after the removal of President Sukarno; the announcement by Britain that it would withdraw its forces 'East of Suez', leading to the negotiation of new defence arrangements with Malaysia; and the escalating war in Vietnam. Looming above these was the question of the constitutional future of Papua and New Guinea.

A change of direction in Indonesia

The Cabinet debates in the first twelve months of the Holt Government were conducted against the backdrop of an uncertain outlook in Indonesia. Sukarno's power was increasingly on the wane. The Australian Embassy in Jakarta warned that he was still 'capable of destroying any new initiative' to end Confrontation through a strong personal attack on Malaysia and its leaders but thought that possibility was diminishing.[2] General Suharto gradually strengthened his hold over the country by crushing communist party supporters and appointing pro-Suharto loyalists to government positions. Paul Hasluck (Minister for External Affairs) had told Prime Minister Harold Wilson in April 1966 that he thought Confrontation would 'wither away rather than end in a formal sense'.[3] In response, Wilson, reflecting the views of Bevin in 1950 and 1951, told Hasluck that in his view 'Indonesia should in the long term not be in a posture of hostility to Australia but should form part of a defensive island chain to protect the Australians'.[4] An alliance might be too much to hope for but 'good relations should surely be attainable if only the Indonesians could be brought to accept the existence of Malaysia'.[5] Hasluck agreed and Australia encouraged Indonesia and Malaysia as they progressed towards a negotiated settlement. An end to Confrontation was announced on 11 August 1966 and the Holt Government expressed its 'delight' at the outcome.

Hasluck visited Indonesia in August 1966 for talks with the new leadership and to discuss a broadening of the aid program. In the conversation with Dr Adam Malik, who had replaced Dr Subandrio in March 1966, Hasluck only briefly mentioned Papua New Guinea and only in the context of noting its eventual independence. He did mention the impending vote of ascertainment or free choice in West New Guinea and was assured by Dr Malik that the vote would go ahead.[6] Privately, Hasluck, reflecting the attitudes he had formed as Minister for Territories, was cautious in his approach to possible cooperation between Australia and Indonesia over West New Guinea. He told Gordon Jockel, a senior officer in External Affairs and soon to emerge as a major influence on policy, that he did not want the impression to develop that any close cooperation was likely. Instead he thought the two territories would go their 'separate ways'.[7]

In a report he allowed to be passed to the British Government on his visit, Hasluck noted that he was optimistic that the end of Confrontation 'may well be the prelude to Malaysian and Indonesian friendship, perhaps even an emotional closeness'. However, he cautioned against assuming that all would settle quietly, and, again reflecting many of the points he had made in Cabinet in recent years, argued instead that 'Indonesia will still be seeking to cut a figure on the international scene. ... We should not imagine ... that Indonesia has become less nationalistic or more pro-Western. In foreign policy its interpretation of non-alignment will probably be to establish itself as a leader in new groupings of Asian nations'. He assessed 'as genuine' their 'friendliness and respect towards Australia' and with 'Confrontation ended they see no matters of dispute with us and Malik would go further and see a large measure of common interest'.[8] In his brief remarks to Cabinet on his return to Canberra, Hasluck noted that Indonesia was still 'intensely nationalistic – not western in outlook'.[9]

In 1968 Cabinet approved an increase in Australia's aid program to Indonesia from $6.1 million to $12.7 million. As an indication of the change in mood in Canberra since the end of Confrontation, Cabinet accepted Hasluck's argument of the 'supreme importance to Australia of stability in Indonesia ... to our very great national disadvantage if we fail to act'. McEwen supported the increase in the aid program and told his colleagues it was 'enormously important to us that it (Indonesia) should be stable and that we should be well regarded ... Support for trade reasons but not press. But do press for national foreign policy reasons'.[10] The hostility towards Indonesia previously expressed by Cabinet ministers such as McEwen and Hasluck who had been members of the Cabinet throughout the West New Guinea dispute and then Confrontation, was changing. McEwen was even prepared to acknowledge the early work by Dr Evatt in laying the foundations for a positive relationship. He nevertheless still saw Indonesia as the 'only great power in the world which could still threaten us'.[11]

John Gorton, who had succeeded McEwen as Prime Minister in January 1968, visited Indonesia in June and spoke in positive, friendly terms about the future of the relationship.[12] In 1969 ministers again examined the aid program to Indonesia and approved a further increase in its budget. In the short discussion before deciding on the new level of funding ministers made no reference to security concerns nor to anxieties about the direction Indonesia could take.[13] In 1970 the aid program was further increased to $53.8 million over three years with Cabinet accepting the argument that 'Australia does not have an option of disengagement from Indonesia and its problems'.[14] In March 1971 Cabinet agreed to lift all controls first imposed in 1965 and modified in October 1966 on the export of goods for use by the Indonesian Armed Forces.[15] Australia's relationship with

Indonesia was further enhanced with the visit by President Suharto to Australia in February 1972, the first visit by an Indonesian Head of State. The communiqué issued at the end of the visit made only passing reference to the Papua New Guinea–Indonesia border and no reference to a future relationship between the two countries. Prime Minister McMahon who had succeeded Gorton in March 1971 paid a return visit to Jakarta in June 1972. The only reference to Papua New Guinea was an expression by Indonesia that 'understanding and cordial relations' should be developed between the two countries as Papua New Guinea moved to independence.[16]

In the period following the end of Confrontation the question which preoccupied Australian defence analysts was how Indonesia would manage the border between it and Papua New Guinea. Officials and ministers maintained a constant watch on cross-border movements and were alert to possible cross-border raids by Indonesian troops to pursue dissident movements opposed to the incorporation of Irian Jaya. These questions influenced later decisions on the role and size of the defence force in an independent Papua New Guinea and the debate within Australia on the nature of its long-term defence support to an independent Papua New Guinea.

An ally departs – how to juggle new demands

While the issue of developing a positive relationship with Indonesia was of importance to Canberra it was the announcement by Britain that it would withdraw its military forces from 'East of Suez' that shook the Australian Government and forced a fundamental reappraisal of its attitude toward long term or unconditional written military commitments in the region.

During his visit to Australia in February 1961, Lord Mountbatten, Chief of the Defence Staff, had hinted that Britain could not sustain its defence presence in Asia given its global commitments and increasingly difficult financial position.[17] In fact, as early as May 1960, as David Goldsworthy has pointed out, Mountbatten had set alarm bells ringing in Canberra with some injudicious comments on the future of the naval base in Singapore.[18]

By the mid-1960s Britain's economic and financial position was under serious threat and the Labour Government of Harold Wilson was forced into a major reconsideration of Britain's military priorities. Throughout 1965 Menzies and Wilson exchanged messages on the question of the future presence of British forces in Southeast Asia, with London seeking a greater financial and defence cooperation or burden-sharing from Australia and Canberra sidestepping any such commitments.

In January 1966 it was announced that the UK Secretary for Defence, Dennis Healey, would visit Canberra to brief the government on the thinking behind the UK Government's review of Britain's defence priorities. Cabinet met on 5 and 10 January to prepare for the Healey visit. It was wary of Britain's intentions but uncertain as to how to react. Hasluck argued that Australia should encourage Britain to remain in Singapore and 'not abandon bases in Asia'.[19] He added that Australia should reject any suggestion that Britain transfer its military resources to a possible base in Western Australia. McEwen suggested that Australia propose a treaty arrangement to keep Britain in the region. Perhaps reflecting the 'sentimental' attachment of politicians of the Menzies era to Britain described by Goldsworthy, he told his colleagues 'we should be trying for as firm a treaty as possible to pin her there'. He added 'I want to survive. If Britain goes home from [the Far East] our survival would be a chancy matter. I'd pay a hell of a lot for [a] treaty which kept Britain and America there. I wouldn't come down on the side of taking a chance'.[20] In a subsequent meeting McEwen agreed that Australia would not formally raise the idea of a treaty but instead work towards that objective with a 'softly, softly approach'.[21] He subsequently told his colleagues there was 'no denying that British reasons for being in Singapore belong to the past. Ours and US belong to the future'.[22]

The discussions with Healey took place over two days in early February 1966.[23] He assured the Foreign Affairs and Defence Committee of Cabinet that Britain had not come to any firm decision on the future of its engagement in Asia. He 'viewed a continued British presence in the Far East as a pre-condition to a continuation of an American presence' and still saw Britain as having a role in the region countering Communist China at least until Confrontation and the war in Vietnam had ended.[24] Healey nevertheless made clear that Britain could not sustain actions such as those against Indonesia for many more years. (Confrontation had all but ceased to be an active military issue following the rise to power of General Suharto but a formal settlement between Indonesia and Malaysia had yet to be agreed.) He described Confrontation as a 'wasteful distraction' and that Indonesia 'would be far better acting as a counterpoise to China in Asia'.[25] Healy noted that current British plans were based on Confrontation having ended by 1970 and raised the possibility of Britain withdrawing from its naval base in Singapore as part of a deal necessary to achieve a settlement with Indonesia. He also flagged the possibility that Britain could leave Singapore regardless due to local pressures and non-cooperation. In this context he mentioned the idea of building a new naval base in Australia.

In reply Holt argued that Australia already had a range of extensive military commitments in the region which limited its capacity to take on new responsibilities. Holt, who had served as Treasurer from 1958 until January 1966, may still have been thinking from the perspective of that portfolio, made only one reference to Papua and New Guinea when he drew attention to the need to budget for its development. He made no reference to the need to provide for its defence.[26] Holt instead drew attention to Healey's assessment of Indonesia and the prospects for a settlement to Confrontation. He questioned whether 'an end of Confrontation [would] really mean [a] quiet and constructive Indonesia. ... After Confrontation – what? Something almost certainly. Timor. NG [New Guinea]. We see no sense of security from end of Confrontation. Fortunately Indonesians have [a] sense of friendliness for Australia but opposition is equivocal at present'.[27] McEwen pressed Healey on the strength of Britain's willingness to remain in Malaysia, while Hasluck joined Holt in raising questions about Britain's approach to an end of Confrontation. Hasluck described Britain's possible approach to ending Confrontation as 'ceding to Indonesia all asked for' at a time when 'we feel we cannot rely on Indonesian promises. If Confrontation ends in circumstances which give them what they want, they will try something more. ... We rather hope it will fade away but not try to save Indonesia's face'.[28] Healey returned to his earlier theme by noting that Britain could hardly face retaining 50,000 men permanently in the area and could not refuse negotiations. He did, however, hope that Confrontation would 'fade away'. The talks ended with an agreed minute which noted that Britain proposed to continue its global defence role and maintain its military presence in the Far East. It also foreshadowed further talks, including with the United States. Privately, ministers felt uneasy and unsure as to the future direction of Britain's policy.[29] They were not impressed and McEwen told his colleagues 'I do not believe Britain would end Confrontation by force. So will walk out'.[30] Hasluck later told the New Zealand Prime Minister (Holyoake) that the 'essential point was that the British stay East of Suez, that there should be no diminution of their influence, that they stay on the Asian mainland'.[31]

Two weeks after Healey's visit US Vice President Hubert Humphrey arrived in Canberra on 19 February 1966 as part of a regional tour.

Humphrey confined his discussions to the political developments in Asia, the threat to Southeast Asia posed by communism and the state of the war in Vietnam.[32] He made no specific request for an increase in Australia's contribution to the war. In his one-on-one conversation with Humphrey and in the meeting with the Cabinet, Holt returned to one of the themes he had pursued in his meeting with Healey. He told the Vice President that Australia had embarked on a program to strengthen the defence force and that 'it must continue to grow'. However, 'at the same time we have other tasks of development in various directions, including in New Guinea, which we must not only not neglect, but, in fact, prosecute with vigour'.[33] At the Vice President's meeting with the Foreign Affairs and Defence Committee, Holt, again perhaps reflecting his perspective as the former Treasurer, returned to this point when he said 'Australia also had immediate tasks in bringing stone-age New Guinea into the modern world in the quickest possible time'.[34] Holt was referring to the effect on the budget of providing Papua New Guinea with economic and developmental support rather than commenting on its place in Australia's strategic outlook. His argument represented a change in emphasis as Australia struggled to assess the impact of regional developments on its security commitments. In his letter to President Johnson after the meeting, Holt again referred to the need to develop Papua New Guinea but placed it in the context of the competing demands and costs on Australia to contribute forces to Malaysia and Vietnam.[35]

On 15 February Cabinet examined the question of an increase in the Australian contribution to the war in Vietnam. There was a general sentiment in favour of an increase although Holt preferred not to rush to an immediate decision and noted that 'a further question is how we stand in relation to our New Guinea defence'. McMahon and McEwen agreed, while McMahon asked 'whether we can do this without running ourselves short in relation to New Guinea and further Confrontation'.[36]

Cabinet resumed its discussion on 2 March and agreed to the despatch of a task force to Vietnam. Ministers noted that Australia would retain the capacity 'after the commitment of the task force to contribute to a situation suddenly arising in New Guinea'.[37] Holt addressed the Parliament on 24 March 1966 and informed members of the government's decision to increase Australia's contribution to South Vietnam. In doing so he noted that the increased deployment was 'fully consistent with our obligations and requirements to retain adequate forces for the defence of Australia and its territories, including Papua and New Guinea'.[38]

Holt continued to receive strong support in Cabinet for the decision to increase Australia's commitment to the war in Vietnam.[39] McEwen and Hasluck believed it was in Australia's interest to be seen by the United States to be prepared to contribute. McEwen, in particular, argued strongly in favour of a further commitment of troops to Vietnam in 1967, telling the Cabinet on a number of occasions that, in his view, the 'only real thing to ensure our survival is US willingness to be with us in South East Asia. ... US involvement in Vietnam is enormously to our interest'.[40] Later he told his colleagues 'the primary aim is to keep the US there [in Asia]. What we want from the Americans (i.e. staying on the mainland) requires us to stay ourselves'.[41] He added 'you stand by your allies in adversity, not less. Two dramatic incidents of history are UK withdrawal from Asia and PM's close relationship with the President of the US. Can think of nothing more important that this be strengthened, cemented and welded by every possible means. ... The posture of an ally of US is so important as not to be tinkered with'.[42] As to Britain, McEwen was equally disturbed by its proposed withdrawal and argued that Australia should try to convince Britain to 'keep any force there – even a company – or even a sloop'.[43] In these discussions there was no longer, as there had been in the early 1960s, any mention of the need to hold troops in reserve to defend Papua New Guinea. The five commitments or obligations that Menzies and others had articulated up until 1965 were no longer uppermost in ministers' minds. Instead their focus had narrowed to the immediate issues of Vietnam and the British withdrawal.

A new Prime Minister and a new approach to regional engagement

Holt drowned on 19 December 1967 and Deputy Prime Minister McEwen held the Prime Ministership on an interim basis until Senator John Gorton was elected leader of the Liberal Party and sworn in as Prime Minister on 10 January 1968. US Secretary of State Dean Rusk described Gorton as 'helpful, friendly and staunch' with a 'reputation as a lone wolf in political circles and apparently inclined to reach snap judgements and personal conclusions before he has considered the full advice of his more experienced colleagues and his departments. He will take a bit of handling but sees the general situation in the Pacific and Australian national interests pretty much as did Holt'.[44] The British High Commissioner in Canberra, Charles Johnson, preferred to characterise Gorton as a 'rogue-elephant' rather than a 'lone wolf'.[45] Johnson described him to London as having a 'curious, almost schoolboyish streak of immaturity in him. ... He would come out with something designed to shock but would not persist with it once I had done what I could to answer it'. Johnson was worried by what he perceived as Gorton's view that 'nothing could stop our two countries [Australia and Britain] drifting further apart' and Gorton's questioning of the relevance of the Commonwealth.

From the time of his appointment to Cabinet as Minister for Navy in 1958, Gorton had only occasionally intervened in discussions on defence and security issues, leaving the debate to the more experienced ministers such as Menzies, McEwen, Holt and Hasluck. He had been more involved during Holt's term as Prime Minister but there were few indications of his overall approach to security matters or that he held views contrary to established policy. Gorton's approach to discussions and deliberations in Cabinet, as revealed in the Notebooks, soon became apparent. In contrast to the practice adopted by Menzies, Gorton preferred to speak early in the discussion, to pose questions and to challenge the concepts underpinning existing policy. He would often open up an issue for discussion without the benefit of a ministerial submission or departmental paper. At times he did this because he had a genuine interest in re-examining a policy, while at other times, for example on the question of the timing of a withdrawal of troops from Vietnam or a continued defence-based commitment to Malaysia and Singapore, he appeared uncertain and unsure of his own position.[46] Hasluck has described Gorton as having 'so many likes and dislikes and so many fixed ideas that the search for wise guidance from him had to run the hazard of surviving his prejudices before one could reach the point for decision'.[47] Some ministers, for example, Malcolm Fraser, found Gorton's style difficult to accept and preferred the established procedures of relying on expert opinion and a well-argued and agreed submission. By mid-1970 Gorton had alienated a number of his colleagues.[48]

George Thomson, Secretary of State for Commonwealth Relations, arrived in Canberra on 11 January 1968, one day after Gorton had been sworn in as Prime Minister. The purpose of his visit was to brief the Cabinet on the soon-to-be settled decision by the Wilson Government to accelerate Britain's departure from Southeast Asia. In response to Thomson's presentation Gorton commented that Britain's decision 'fills me with anxiety and some dismay' while the 'creation of a partial military vacuum in part of the Far East which US not covered leaves a dangerous hole in area. ... I would not like to be reported that we accept this new step. Could not accept and would have to protest'.[49] McEwen told Thomson that he was 'tremendously fearful of state of affairs when Britain withdraws ... a serious step ... intolerable ... this frightens me'. Gorton concluded the discussion by saying that the Cabinet was 'dismayed' at the decision and that he had 'no confidence' that any new arrangement could be settled.[50]

Goldsworthy has described Gorton and Australia as adjusting 'quickly' to Britain's decision and as taking the initiative in the 'construction of alternative arrangements'.[51] This does not reflect the difficult discussions which preoccupied the Cabinet over the next few years as ministers debated whether to be part of a defence arrangement covering Malaysia or Malaya and the extent of that commitment. Gorton in particular held strong views on limiting Australia's role in Southeast Asia. In May 1969, following the Chinese/Malay race riots in Kuala Lumpur and the request by the Malaysian Government for additional military assistance, Gorton argued against a positive response from Australia, telling his colleagues that he feared for the future stability of Malaysia and that he could 'see overtones of [a] beginning of a new Vietnam'.[52] He was wary of any commitment to Malaysia. On this occasion, McEwen responded that if the security of the Malaysian Government was threatened 'our first job is to contribute ... to sustain it'.[53] In more immediate terms, Australia's representations to Britain did have the effect of postponing the withdrawal of British forces from Malaysia and Singapore by nine months until 31 December 1971. It was not until the Conservative Party under Edward Heath came to power that the British decision was modified further.

Britain's decision to withdraw from Southeast Asia was significant for two reasons. It represented the departure of one of Australia's principal allies from the region. Britain retained some residual defence forces but its role and importance to the defence of the region and to Australia's defence was now greatly diminished. The second impact was more psychological. Britain's announcement and the sense that Australia had been let down created great uncertainty and unease in the minds of defence planners. Ministers were dismayed and an air of floundering in an uncertain environment became apparent. At this time the idea began to take root in the minds of ministers and senior officials that Australia should avoid, at all cost, replacing Britain as one of the principal guarantors of security in Southeast Asia.[54] Similarly, ministers and officials, notably Gorton and McEwen, adopted the view that Australia should avoid entering into long-term, unqualified commitments to defend countries in the region. David Goldsworthy has described in detail the impact on Australia of the decision by Britain to withdraw from Southeast Asia. He has quoted John Subritzky as describing the decision as fundamentally transforming Australia's view of the region.[55] Australia was now faced with relying on a sole ally, the United States, and on re-defining Australia's role in the region.

The importance of this period of re-examination became clearer as Australia articulated its response to a proposed new security arrangement with Malaysia and Singapore. Thomson had advised the Cabinet of Britain's intention to terminate the Anglo Malaysia Defence Agreement (AMDA) with effect from 1 January 1972 and with it Britain's unconditional and unlimited commitment to defend Malaysia. In December 1969 it had proposed the negotiation of a new protocol. Negotiations proceeded over the next twelve months, eventually leading to the signing of a Five Power Defence Arrangement involving Britain, Australia, New Zealand, Malaysia and Singapore in 1971. The new security undertakings did not include an unconditional commitment to defend Malaysia or Singapore from external attack or externally-sponsored subversion. Instead, a non-treaty-based document, issued in the form of a communiqué, declared that:

> in the event of any form of armed attack externally organised or supported or the threat of such attack against Malaysia or Singapore, their Governments would immediately consult together for the purpose of deciding what measures should be taken jointly or separately in relation to such attack or threat.[56]

These words, or a closely similar sentiment, with the emphasis on consultation are significant as similar language would eventually be used in the text of the long-term defence undertaking agreed between Australia and Papua New Guinea in 1977. Australia had recast its defence relationship with the region to give it a greater degree of flexibility in how it responded to developments and to remove a sense of automatic commitment. This was the lesson Australia had learned from the end of Confrontation and the withdrawal of Britain from the region and, in time, it was to bring this appreciation to the negotiation of a long-term defence relationship with Papua New Guinea.

As a further indication of Australia's response to the changes occurring in the region and in its revised assessment of threats to Papua and New Guinea, Cabinet decided in September 1968 to call a halt to the build-up of the Pacific Islands Regiment (PIR). In 1963, at the height of concerns about the ambitions of Indonesia, a decision had been taken to increase the size of the PIR to three battalions. Cabinet now acknowledged that the change in direction in Indonesia meant that an increase was no longer necessary.[57] As a similar example of the same trend, in July 1969, during the debate in Cabinet on the preparation of the government's budget, Gorton queried the need for the funding of repairs and maintenance of the oil storage facilities at the Manus Island naval base and questioned its role. Gorton called for a review of the future need for the base.[58]

What to do about Papua New Guinea – first thoughts

The Holt Government faced the third major issue of its early period in government in March 1966 when it turned to a submission from the Minister for Territories, Charles Barnes, on the question of the long-term constitutional status of Papua New Guinea. The Cabinet was asked to adopt a policy approach to talks scheduled to take place with the Papua and New Guinea Select Committee on Constitutional Development, chaired by the Papuan leader Dr John Guise.[59] It was expected that the Select Committee would seek an indication of the government's thinking on the future status of the territory and its long-term relationship with Australia. The options were seen as self-government, independence or some form of association with Australia, including possibly statehood.[60]

The submission also examined Papua New Guinea's strategic significance and placed it squarely in the context of a 'forward defence strategy to hold South East Asia'.[61] It moved away from seeing Papua New Guinea solely in terms of being threatened by Indonesia and set it in a broader context. It argued that:

> in terms of this policy the retention of facilities in Papua and New Guinea is of great importance in ensuring the passage of our forces between Australia and South East Asia and the maintenance of communications between Australia and United States bases in the Pacific. We also need to retain these facilities for the defence of the Territory itself particularly against Indonesia, and in some circumstances, to reduce the risk to our Eastern seaboard. Should Papua and New Guinea come under the control of an administration unfriendly to Australia and the West in general, this would, in addition to the direct military consequences, facilitate the further penetration of the Pacific by hostile influences.

> In the interest of Australian defence as well as the defence of the area it is important that access to the Territory of Papua and New Guinea and its base facilities be maintained.[62]

The paper suggested that future defence arrangements should settle three related issues: the retention of present and planned base and transit facilities in the Territory; the right to maintain forces as required in Papua and New Guinea; and, dependent on the first two, a commitment to defend the Territory against overt and covert aggression. In one of the earliest references in a Cabinet submission to the implications for the ANZUS Treaty of an independent Papua New Guinea, it noted that the Treaty would no longer apply to Papua and New Guinea once it became independent and 'there could be great difficulties in obtaining the United States agreement to any modification'. An overt attack on Australian forces in Papua and New Guinea would nevertheless be covered.

The submission stressed that 'the importance of Papua and New Guinea in Australian defence and security is such that total Australian policies towards Papua and New Guinea should be directed to achieving the securest possible tenure for Australian defence positions and interests in the Territory'. It concluded that this could best be achieved by securing the goodwill of the people and government of the day in Papua and New Guinea rather than relying on constitutional forms, although a form of association would be a preferred option rather than a policy directed towards disengagement.[63]

In the discussion in Cabinet, ministers agreed fully with the views expressed by McEwen that the government should maintain 'flexibility' in the talks with the Select Committee and 'avoid precision'. He acknowledged that the Territory's leadership held the prerogative to 'terminate their status … and be independent'. Nevertheless, he thought it would not do this until the Territory had obtained a greater degree of economic viability. He argued that 'as a matter of mutual self-interest we would think that there would be, under independence or otherwise, a defence relationship and a trade relationship'.[64] The formal Cabinet decision closely reflected McEwen's argument although it noted that 'the defence relationship would derive from the Territory's need of Australian aid in defence and from Australia's interest, from a defence point of view, in New Guinea'.[65]

This was not the first time that ministers had examined the strategic importance of Papua and New Guinea. However, it was one of the first occasions in which they had examined it in the context of the long-term political and constitutional relationship which Australia and the Territory's leaders envisaged for the two countries. The strategic value of Papua and New Guinea was assessed as important but not sufficient to push Australian ministers to embrace the idea of including the Territory as a state in the Commonwealth. That idea was unacceptable to Cabinet. Australia's interests had been identified as securing bases in the Territory and maintaining sea links through the region to the north and east. Cabinet's views were shared by Sir Henry Bland, Secretary of the Department of Defence (1968–1970), who, following a visit to Port Moresby, told his colleagues that 'in all our thinking about the Territory, we must see it not as part of Australia nor anything resembling an extension of Australia. For our purposes the Territory is a country of South East Asia'.[65a]

Internal problems in Papua New Guinea erupt

The concerns which had begun to preoccupy the minds of ministers in 1966 over internal stability, the inadequacies of the police force and the possible use of the army to assist in quelling local security problems, resurfaced dramatically in 1969. In 1969 civil unrest erupted in the Gazelle Peninsula over land issues and the establishment of a multi-racial local council. The campaign by the Mataungan Association and local political parties from 1968 until 1972, culminating in demonstrations, calls for secession, acts of political brinkmanship, arrests and the killing of a District Commissioner, deeply disturbed the administration in Port Moresby and the Gorton Government. At the same time there were the first signs of a serious political crisis emerging on Bougainville Island as Conzinc Rio Tinto (CRA) began the development of the Panguna mine in the centre of the island. These concerns deepened in August 1969 when the population of Rorovana Village at Loloho rioted and were removed by the police to make way for a new wharf to service the mine.

In this period the Papuan separatist movement, Papua Besena, under the leadership of Josephine Abaijah, also emerged to argue the case for Papua to remain a separate entity from New Guinea. It attracted support from the Papuan community with Abaijah elected to the House of Assembly in 1972. Papuan separatism and Josephine Abaijah were to be a thorn in the side of the administration in Port Moresby and the government in Canberra until independence in 1975. Smaller groups also emerged such as a Papuan Black Power Group and the Highlands Liberation Front which, while very few in numbers and of marginal influence, nevertheless created a sense of anxiety in Canberra about the future of a unified Papua New Guinea. The outbreak of serious fighting between New Guineans and Papuans in Port Moresby in July 1973 following an inter-regional football game marked a nadir in law and order and in Canberra's confidence about the prospects for a peaceful, united Papua New Guinea.

In May 1969 Barnes sought Cabinet's views on how the government should respond to present and future secessionist movements 'and generally towards national unity in the Territory'.[66] Barnes's submission focused on Bougainville and the threat to the development of the mining project should violence increase. As to the question of preserving the unity of the Territory, Barnes told his colleagues that 'it should be made clear that the Government's attitude is that secession of any part of the Territory cannot be accepted at this stage of the Territory's development'. He also sought Cabinet's agreement to the Minister for Defence, in concert with other senior ministers, being given the authority to recommend to the Governor-General that the Pacific Islands Regiment (PIR) be called out to aid the civil powers to guard important points or, as a last resort, reinforce the police.

Ministers supported the idea of sustaining the Territory as a united entity but were alert to the possibility that the House of Assembly in Port Moresby could take a different approach and endorse the secession of part of the Territory. Gorton questioned whether Australia would use force against the recommendations of the Assembly. He described the prospects of such a development as creating an 'international situation' and referred to 'Biafra'[67] then in the process of breaking away from Nigeria resulting in a bloody civil war. Malcolm Fraser (Minister for Education and Science and a former Minister for the Army) argued that if the Assembly approved an act of secession 'we couldn't use force'. Allen Fairhall (Minister for Defence) agreed, noting that the PIR was not trained for internal security roles and that 'public disorder should be handled by civil means'. He also saw the possibility of the PIR splintering along race lines with 'many tribes and white officers' with a result that it 'could escalate into white versus black'. McEwen was adamant. He told his colleagues that 'CRA [was] not an Australian company' and that he didn't want 'to see us getting in with white troops or black troops to support CRA. This troubles me immensely. ... Preserve law and order but don't get involved at behest of foreign companies'. He did support the concept of national unity if promoted by the House of Assembly but added 'if the House of Assembly says Bougainville should secede we'd have to agree'. However, he accepted the idea of calling out the PIR if the police were unable to maintain law and order.[68]

Ministers agreed that Barnes could be authorised to 'express the Government's belief that the interests of the people of Papua–New Guinea are best served by national unity and to say that the Government endorses the House of Assembly declaration in this regard'. Ministers did not come to a view on the question of the deployment of the PIR, noting that this had 'wider implications of great significance' and calling for a further study of the issue.[69] There was no appetite within the Australian defence and foreign affairs community to support the deployment of the PIR, with its large attachment of Australian soldiers, to manage the country's internal security problems. Tange, who had been appointed Secretary of Defence, and now chaired the Defence Committee, was adamant that the PIR should not be deployed and argued that 'the moment we make a move we are on the road to involvement in situations of civil order. This could develop to the point where we would have to commit Australian troops to retrieve the situation'.[70]

The problems on the Gazelle Peninsula continued to defy resolution. At its height over 25 per cent of Papua New Guinea's police force was deployed to the Peninsula. Similarly, Bougainville continued to fester as a political problem while the administration in Port Moresby was also dealing with outbreaks of tribal fighting in the Highlands.[71] In response to a directive from Cabinet in June 1970 an inter-departmental committee of officials studied the internal security problems facing the Territory. The study endorsed the assessment of the National Intelligence Committee that the state of law and order was 'deteriorating' with the 'growing possibility of significant disorder' which the police alone would be unable to contain. The study also acknowledged that the 'main threat to the integrity of Papua New Guinea is likely to be internal ... while the outlook for internal security ... will impose severe strains on the whole internal security apparatus'.[72] In a separate report in 1970, the National Intelligence Committee thought the prospects for Papua New Guinea were finely balanced between 'weak New Guinea [which] could degenerate into another Congo but one which would be on Australia's northern borders. A stable New Guinea will have a beneficial influence amongst neighbouring islands and the Pacific peoples'.[73]

The slow road to self-government and PNG's strategic significance adjusted

It was against this background of uncertainty over the future stability and unity of Papua New Guinea that Gorton undertook an extensive visit to the Territory from 5 to 11 July 1970, the first by an Australian Prime Minister since 1963. (Gorton had served in the New Guinea theatre as a pilot during the Second World War.) A month earlier he had paid his first visit to Indonesia. The visit to Port Moresby and major regional centres was intended to be the occasion for a major announcement by Gorton of the further transfer of responsibility and decision-making to elected members of the House of Assembly. This was seen by the Gorton Government as a significant step on the road to internal self-government. However, Gorton's visit was overshadowed by the continuing trouble on the Gazelle Peninsula and the threat of violence. Gorton used his visits to Bougainville, Lae and elsewhere to argue the importance of national unity. In his farewell broadcast from Port Moresby he acknowledged that 'the Territory is on the road which leads to self-government. There can be no turning back from that road. It must be travelled to the end. But it is not for the Australian Government to dictate the speed at which the ultimate goal is reached'. He also expressed a 'hope' that the Territory would 'remain un-fragmented and that the different parts of it will not secede. ... [as] each separate part will be economically and politically less strong than the whole'.[74] His government would wait for Papua New Guineans to come to their own decisions about the timing of the next stage in their political development.

The troubles on the Peninsula and the threats from the Mataungan Association, combined with the emerging problems in Bougainville, the threat from the Papua Besena Movement, as well as the continuing breakdown in law and order across the Territory, served to shift the focus of Canberra's attention away from external threats to concentrate almost exclusively on internal law and order problems. Opinion in Canberra was united on the seriousness of the problems facing Papua New Guinea and how Australia should respond. Sir Keith Waller, Secretary of External Affairs, warned his senior departmental colleagues that 'the longer we delay independence the harder it may become to grant it because of separatist tendencies within PNG'.[75] Waller feared not only for the future of the Territory but also for Australia's ability to exercise freely its policy options.

Although the Gorton Government was not prepared to accelerate the transfer of powers to Papua New Guinea nor to think in terms of possible independence for the Territory, work in Canberra began to turn slowly in the direction of self-government. In September 1970 the Defence Committee concluded its three-year-long review of the defence forces in Papua New Guinea in preparation for decisions on its eventual size and function.[76] In examining these questions the Committee inevitably revisited the issue of the strategic significance of Papua New Guinea to Australia. It judged that:

> Papua/New Guinea is of abiding strategic interest to Australia because of its geographical position astride our military and trade lines of communication from our eastern seaboard to South-East Asia, Japan and the United States bases in the Western Pacific; because of its common border with Indonesia; and because of its potential as a base for the conduct of operations inimical to Australian security interests.[77]

At this time nineteen per cent in value and twenty one per cent in volume of Australia's trade with Japan, Hong Kong and Taiwan passed through the strait between New Ireland province and Buka Island, north of Bougainville, the Vitiaz Strait between New Britain and the Huon Peninsula near Lae or through the Torres Strait.[78]

In addition, the assessment noted the 'continuing requirement for unrestricted passage of our military shipping through New Guinea waters in support of our regional security arrangements'. As a consequence, this required the maintenance of a refuelling facility for naval escorts in the area, i.e. the HMAS *Tarangau* naval base at Manus Island. The land frontier with West Irian 'could provide Indonesia with opportunities to threaten the security of Papua/New Guinea and thereby embarrass Australia'. The report also examined the 'very long term' prospect that:

> should Papua/New Guinea be taken over, or come under the influence of a power unfriendly or hostile to Australia this would open the way to further penetration of the south-west Pacific, facilitate military operations down the eastern Australian coast and expose our important trade routes with Asia to interruption.[79]

The Defence Committee went on to record that:

> It is in Australia's interest that an independent Territory of Papua New Guinea (TPNG) should remain well disposed towards Australia. It would serve our defence interests if TPNG should seek an understanding or an arrangement on defence matters. Although Australia

has no legal obligation to give to Papua/New Guinea a defence capability, there is a general expectation that we should.[80]

The assessment endorsed by the Committee contained familiar language and themes. It also contained interesting new phraseology noting that Papua New Guinea was of 'abiding strategic interest'. The reference to an 'understanding or an arrangement' had been mentioned previously but departed from the report prepared by the lower-ranked Joint Planning Committee which had left this issue undefined. Nevertheless, the reference was still open to interpretation and fell short of any suggestion of a long-term, unconditional commitment. Of equal importance, the Committee acknowledged that it could no longer determine these questions in isolation from local (Papua New Guinean) opinion.

A changing of the guard

The personal animosities and divisions which had plagued the Gorton Cabinet came to a head in March 1971 with the resignation of Malcolm Fraser as Minister for Defence. In explaining his actions Fraser cited Gorton's style of decision-making, noting in particular his handling in July 1970 of the decision to approve the call-out of the PIR during the crisis in the Gazelle Peninsula.[81] A subsequent challenge to Gorton's position as Prime Minister was won by his deputy, William McMahon.

McMahon succeeded Gorton as Prime Minister on 10 March 1971 and Gorton assumed the office of Minister for Defence. McMahon had served as a minister in the Menzies Cabinet from July 1951 and had risen to the posts of Treasurer (1966–1969) and Foreign Minister (1969–1971) in the Holt and Gorton Cabinets. He had visited Papua New Guinea once in 1954. A reading of the Cabinet Notebooks for the period 1950 to 1969 reveals a person of limited initiative and confidence in foreign and security matters. He lacked Barwick and Hasluck's intellectual capacity to articulate a clear set of principles to guide the development of Australia's foreign policy. His preference was for the maintenance of the status quo even when debating the inevitability of changing policy. His approach to Papua New Guinea was to let his energetic and open-minded minister, Andrew Peacock, take the lead. He did not discourage Peacock from moving more purposefully towards self-government for the Territory but expressed no opinion of the possibility of eventual independence. He cancelled at the last minute a planned trip to Port Moresby scheduled for early August 1972.

Shifting Ground: New Influences Emerge 1966–1972

In addition to the change in Prime Ministers, the late 1960s and early 1970s were marked by the departure of Paul Hasluck from the post of Minister for External Affairs in February 1969 following his appointment to the position of Governor-General, the retirement of Allen Fairhall as Minister for Defence in November 1969 and, most significantly, the retirement of John McEwen in February 1971. Charles Barnes also retired as Minister for External Territories in January 1972 giving way to Peacock.

Hasluck had provided the intellectual framework for the Holt and Gorton governments' policies towards Asia and the war in Vietnam and had redefined Australia's concept of 'forward defence' to a more subtle concept of 'engagement in regional security'. He had also shifted the emphasis in the presentation of Australia's regional defence outlook away from a focus on Papua New Guinea and did not pursue its importance with the same vigour as Barwick had done in his meetings with members of the Kennedy and Johnson administrations. He had been the last minister to accept the need to change Australia's policy towards the West New Guinea dispute and had shown a similar conservatism and stubbornness towards Indonesia throughout the period of Confrontation.

However, it was McEwen's retirement which was perhaps the most significant. He had been elected to the Federal Parliament in 1934 and had been Minister for External Affairs in 1940 in Menzies's wartime government. He had served with Menzies since 1949 and his position from 1958 as Deputy Prime Minister and Leader of the Country Party had given him a status in Cabinet equal only to that of Menzies. McEwen had adopted Menzies's approach of letting other ministers set out the policy options before intervening with a statement of principles which often brought the meeting back to its essential purpose and gave it direction.

McEwen is more widely known for his work as Minister for Trade and his role in protecting the development of the Australian economy; however, he was an active participant in all Cabinet debates on foreign and defence issues and no decision was taken on Australia's security policies in the 1950s and 1960s without his full support. He believed that Australia's interests were best served by being an absolutely reliable and dependable ally of the superpowers. He told his ministerial colleagues in 1967 at the height of the war in Vietnam 'you stand by your allies in adversity not less'.[82] At the beginning of the crisis over the Suez Canal in September 1956 he told the Cabinet that, while he did not think the issue would see the use of force, 'if the United Kingdom is in – we're in. That's my view'.[83] Later he warned the Cabinet, as it assessed the deteriorating security environment in Asia, 'we are not any longer in 1914 or 1939 – we can't be in a position of letting the US know "in a few days" – we're either in or out – we must take the basic decision that we are with the US. ... we must be in'.[84] He did not hesitate to argue the case for Australia's participation alongside first Britain and then the United States in military engagements in Asia – from the Dutch New Guinea dispute, to Confrontation and finally the war in Vietnam. Even in those conflicts which had not developed into full scale military campaigns, such as the tensions over Formosa in the mid-1950s and the crisis in Laos in 1962, McEwen had fully supported the principle of Australian participation if requested by the United States. Woodard is therefore slightly wide of the mark in his conclusion that McEwen may have supported Barwick if the latter had argued in Cabinet against a deployment to Vietnam.[85]

McEwen believed that Australia's interests were best served by keeping the United States in Asia, even if the price were Australian participation in a military campaign. However, he also recognised that Australia could not engage in any military campaign in Asia by itself – except in the defence of Papua New Guinea. He had had no hesitation in declaring that Australia's interests in Papua New Guinea should be defended as a first priority against any threat from Indonesia. At the same time he could see the broader danger of military conflict with Indonesia and warned during the West New Guinea dispute that 'a fracas over this is a fracas with Asia'. He accepted that Australia's future was in Asia and that Australia could not afford to offend Asia through ill-thought-out military involvement, such as a strike against Indonesia during the critical months of Confrontation. He had shared Menzies's distrust of Sukarno and was fearful of Indonesia's potential to disrupt Australia's position in Papua New Guinea. In his last years in office he had steered the government away from any suggestion that Australia take the place of Britain in the defence of Malaysia, although Gorton shared this view. He, rather than Gorton, had been the initial advocate in Cabinet of the view that Australia should only commit itself to defend the peninsula of Malaya, not Malaysia. In the 1950s and early 1960s he had argued that Australia's need for economic development should be placed ahead of financing the nation's defence. By the mid 1960s and the escalation of the Vietnam War he had accepted that this objective could no longer be sustained.

The 1971 Strategic Basis Paper

As Minister for Defence Gorton presented his first and only Strategic Basis Paper to the McMahon Cabinet in May 1971.[86] Regarding Papua

New Guinea, the paper examined the Territory from the perspective of both its pre- and post-independence status. It drew on earlier language to describe Papua New Guinea as of 'abiding strategic interest to Australia' because of its 'geographic position aside our military and trade lines of communication ... because of its common border with Indonesia; because in hostile hands it could provide facilities for the conduct of operations inimical to Australian security'.[87]

Turning to the post-independence period, the paper revealed a heightened sense of concern and alarm. It assessed the 'principal threat to the integrity of the Territory after Independence is foreseen as the general decline in law and order or the activity of secessionist movements which could lead to conflict beyond the limits of capability of the security forces'.[88] A further 'danger' was the 'possibility of hot headed reactions or provocations ... [that] could lead to armed clashes with Indonesian forces in the border area. Any of these sources of conflict could conceivably lead to calls for Australian combat assistance'.[89] The paper also canvassed Australia's response to a possible act of secession and noted that Australia 'should not exclude the possibility of furnishing the New Guinea Government with organizational, training and logistic support and in the last resort, physical assistance'. It added that such support 'should not be assumed to be automatic'.[90] It also drew attention to Australia's potential responsibilities when it noted that 'whether there be a formal Australian New Guinea defence agreement or not, Australian interests will lie in affording the New Guinea Government reasonable assurance of combat support against the emergence of any substantial, unprovoked and persisting Indonesian aggressive actions'.[91]

The paper also highlighted two further elements in Australia's defence relationship with Papua New Guinea. It repeated the need for a naval refuelling installation off the north coast of New Guinea and noted the need to develop air facilities also on the north coast for strategic transport, maritime patrol and combat air support operations. However, it warned that 'we should proceed with caution on the establishment of any new facilities in [the Territory of Papua New Guinea] required only by Australian forces'.[92] Overall, the 1971 paper was an important development in the evolution of Australia's assessment of the strategic importance of Papua New Guinea. Indonesia was still seen as a potential threat but not to the same extent as in the papers of the 1960s. It was now 'unlikely' to pose a threat to Australia. West New Guinea was no longer described as a potential staging ground for an attack on Australia or for incursions into Papua New Guinea. There was a degree of optimism about the future direction of Indonesia under President Suharto.

Australia, however, was now preoccupied by the prospects for Papua New Guinea's unity and stability. In June 1970 the Cabinet ordered a 'special study of the situation in relation to internal security' in Papua New Guinea.[93] Over the next three years senior officials and ministers repeatedly returned to the issue and the associated question of the possible circumstances in which the PIR could be called out to assist the police to put down civil unrest. All decision-makers in Canberra were appalled at the idea of such a possibility. In May 1971 the Administrator, Les Johnson, was authorised by McMahon and Barnes to release a statement making clear the Australian Government's policy was to 'advance Papua and New Guinea to internal self-government and independence as a unified country'.[94] Sir Keith Waller again reflected the 'unease' of senior officials in his department, notably his Deputy, Mick Shann, about the future of the Territory when, on 14 December 1971, he wrote to David Hay, Secretary of the Department of External Territories. He now made clear the views he had only expressed 'in-house' that 'it would be wrong to conclude … that it would be in the best interests of both Australia and the Territory to slow down the move towards self-government'. He argued that 'the longer we delay independence the harder it may become to grant it, not least because of the separatist tendencies already apparent within the Territory'. Waller told Hay 'the longer we stay in PNG the more we will become disliked and the more difficult it will be for us to control a law and order situation which has already shown signs of strain'. He concluded his letter by emphasising the need to encourage the local population to assume greater responsibility as 'it is the people of the Territory who will decide the pace of progress towards self-government'.[95] Hay acknowledged Waller's letter and did not take issue with his arguments. The implications of the serious and deteriorating internal security situation and its potential to impact on the country's unity had emerged as the critical element in Australia's strategic assessment of Papua New Guinea.

In March 1972, the Minister for Defence, David Fairbairn, tabled the *Australian Defence Review* in Parliament. It noted that the extent of Australia's obligations and 'accompanying rights in the defence of that country [Papua New Guinea] will depend on the wishes of the Government of the new nation and the terms of a negotiation with Australia. This is for the future'.[96] In his speech accompanying the presentation of the *Review* Fairbairn argued that Australia 'must, however, recognise the contingency that in some way or in some measure the future security of the country [Papua New Guinea] may be threatened. Fairbairn told the Parliament that it was 'the Government's view that this and future governments must be provided with the means to act militarily in support of the Papua New Guinea Government if the need should arise, if our help is sought and if we should wish to respond'.[97] The new caveat could be seen as the first public indication of a more cautious approach to the terms of the future defence relationship. It placed an emphasis on local opinion and interests and less of an emphasis on Australia pursuing its national interests, regardless of local opinion.

In June 1972 Fairbairn visited Port Moresby – his first visit since 1944. He told the Administrator's Executive Council that he placed importance on close consultation on defence matters with the leaders of Papua New Guinea. He also suggested the appointment of an indigenous defence spokesman in the House of Assembly who would have responsibilities for answering questions and making statements on defence matters, consulting the Administrator and leading discussion in the Administrator's Executive Council on the development of the defence force'.[98] In August 1972 the Chief Minister of Papua New Guinea, Michael Somare, was appointed the Defence spokesman. He held that post until August 1973 when he was succeeded by Albert Maori Kiki. Kiki was one of the strongest advocates of a 'special relationship' with Australia and was pro-Australian principally due to his extensive contacts with the Australian union movement.[99] Kiki was to continue in the position after independence.

In a press conference at the conclusion of his visit Fairbairn commented on the question of the post-independence long-term defence relationship and the circumstances in which Australia might assist Papua New Guinea, particularly in internal security matters. He said that 'there would be a need for agreements and possible pacts, defence pacts between the two countries and this is a matter which would come for consideration between Australian and Papua New Guinea Governments at that time'.[100] This was his only specific reference to a possible post-independence defence relationship. In response to a further question from an ABC reporter as to the importance of PNG to Australia's defence, Fairbairn commented that:

> I think it is important to say that just from the point of view of a base for Australia or denying a base to the enemy that PNG has lost its importance. On the other hand, it is extremely important to us that PNG ... should be friendly and should not be taken over by an enemy.[101]

Fairbairn's remark reflected the changes which were emerging in Australia's approach to the strategic importance of PNG and of its place in Australia's defence planning. The unequivocal stance of the early 1950s and 1960s, especially the views held by Menzies, McEwen and Hasluck, was in the process of being reassessed. New language was being developed to describe PNG's importance and a more circumspect attitude emerging. The last year of the Liberal Country Party Government was witnessing the emergence of new thinking which was to gain greater prominence with the election of a Labor Government in December 1972.

Conclusion

The Holt, Gorton and McMahon governments had all struggled with some of the most difficult and complex issues in the evolution of Australia's regional security policy. They had been shocked by Britain's decision to withdraw 'East of Suez'. They had refused to assume Britain's responsibilities in Malaysia and the region and had been wary of entering into any undertaking which committed Australia to come unconditionally to Malaysia's defence. At the same time as adjusting to the new realities in Malaysia, successive governments were faced with managing Australia's involvement in and then withdrawal from the Vietnam War.

The Australian Government had begun this period with an open commitment to defend Papua New Guinea against attack, infiltration or subversion from its neighbours. It remained deeply concerned by the incidents of cross-border infiltration from Indonesia but as the period progressed it redefined its interests to focus on the internal security situation emerging in the country and less on external threats. The shift of attention to the seemingly intractable internal security problems facing Papua New Guinea and the rise of separatist movements fundamentally changed Australia's perception of its responsibilities towards Papua New Guinea and how it should manage those responsibilities. This unsettled environment was bequeathed to the incoming Whitlam Government which had a clear idea of how it wished to be seen by the world and by Papua New Guinea.

Chapter 10

REDEFINING THE OPTIONS
1972–1973

'We must take all steps to minimise the possibility of Australia becoming involved, or looking as if it is involved in a military sense after Independence'.

Lance Barnard, Minister for
Defence, January 1973

On 5 December 1972 the Australian Labor Party, led by Gough Whitlam, assumed government in Canberra.[1] Under Whitlam's leadership the Labor Party had displayed a close interest in political, economic and social developments in Papua New Guinea.[2] Whitlam had visited Papua New Guinea (PNG) six times as an opposition MP from 1953 to 1972 and nearly all senior members of the parliamentary party, notably Kim Beazley, had developed close personal relationships with the country's emerging leaders.[3] As early as 1963, encouraged by Whitlam, the party had declared that Australia's policy towards PNG should be 'to develop the Territories to independence at the earliest possible time, and that it must then withdraw'.[4] By January 1970, in an address to over 11,000 protesters in Rabaul, Whitlam had declared that a Labor Government would 'let New Guineans govern themselves'.[5] At the end of his visit Whitlam released Labor's 'Plan for New Guinea'.[6] It declared that 'New Guinea will have home rule as soon as a Labor Government can make the necessary arrangements'.[7] It added that none of the problems facing PNG 'require colonial rule for their solution'.[8] Whitlam's tour of Papua New Guinea was described by *The Australian* as having a 'catalytic value' in accelerating the pace and changing the direction of the debate in Canberra over the future constitutional status of the Territory.⁹ The Liberal Country Party Government was forced to embrace the idea of an accelerated shift in powers and authority from Canberra to Port Moresby and an earlier date for self-government.

Whitlam fervently believed that Australia should not continue in the role of colonial power. He had made clear to officials that he did not wish there to be 'any appearance of "imperial power" in Australia's participation in New Guinea's development'. Nor would Australia make any 'special claims on Papua New Guinea'.¹⁰ In Whitlam's view such a role detracted from his government's efforts to promote Australia in the Asia-Pacific region as a sympathetic and equal partner in development.¹¹ In his speech at the beginning of the campaign for the 1972 election Whitlam reiterated the point that his government would 'cooperate whole-heartedly with the [Papua] New Guinea House of Assembly in reaching successfully its timetable for self-government and independence'.¹² He added that it was 'wrong and unnatural that a nation like Australia should continue to run a colony'. He also declared that Australia would have 'four commitments commensurate to our power and resources'. After nominating 'our own national security', he listed as second 'a secure, united and friendly Papua New Guinea'. A closer relationship with Indonesia was the third priority while the 'promotion of peace and prosperity of our neighbourhood' was the fourth.¹³

Whitlam's active interest in PNG was shared by his deputy and Shadow Minister for Defence, Lance Barnard who had accompanied Whitlam on a visit to Papua New Guinea in 1960.¹⁴ Barnard took full responsibility for determining the principles behind Australia's long-term defence relationships and in his quiet, understated manner he steered Australia towards a new assessment of the defence relationship with PNG. In this he was joined by Bill Morrison who, as Minister for External Territories and later Minister assisting the Minister for Foreign Affairs on matters relating to Papua New Guinea, was determined to bring PNG to independence as soon as practicable. Of all the ministers in the Labor Government involved in PNG Morrison had had the least exposure to the country, having visited it for the first time with Whitlam in January 1971.¹⁵

Morrison's introduction to Papua New Guinea coincided with the deepening concern in Canberra at the future stability and unity of the country. He believed that the Territory's ability to respond to the internal security challenges it faced was best ensured by a dramatic overhaul of the country's poorly funded, badly resourced and inadequately trained police force. Andrew Peacock had recognised the same shortcomings of the police force but had had little time as minister to address the issue. Morrison argued for a significant increase in funding for the police force and suggested that such funding be drawn from the Australian-provided budget for the PNG Defence Force. He had support in Canberra for his views, particularly from within the Department of Foreign Affairs. He also had some support from Sir Arthur Tange, Secretary of the Department of Defence, who railed against plans presented to him by the Australian military that anticipated the PNG Defence Force being created as an image of the Australian Defence Force. As time would tell Morrison was to be frustrated in this goal.[16] He was, however, determined to ensure that Australia did not enter into an open-ended commitment to defend an independent PNG

The Whitlam Government's counterparts in Port Moresby were a group of young, inexperienced but determined men on whose shoulders was placed the responsibility of leading their country to independence. Michael Somare was thirty-six years old and had first been elected to the House of Assembly in 1968. He had received some early education from the Japanese during the occupation of the East Sepik region in the Second World War and had been a primary school teacher and then radio broadcaster before entering politics. He was an early advocate of self-government and in 1967 had helped form and then lead the PANGU Party. Following the 1972 election he became Chief Minister in the House of Assembly. He had little experience in governing or in administration. The ANU scholar Hank Nelson provided a contemporary description of Somare in 1972, writing that he was:

> not a reader, a visionary nor is he committed to a particular ideology; he has a great capacity to gather men and ideas, exercise power without displaying an arrogance of office, win and retain the trust of close staff members or crowds at political gatherings and work long hours; and he is committed to an improvement in the life of all the people of Papua New Guinea. No group thinks he will deceive them.[17]

Somare's great gift was to seek a compromise as a means of solving a problem. He was a master of the 'Melanesian Way' – a style of finding a solution through discussion, consultation and compromise. At the same time he had a clear vision for his country and was determined to see it become self-governing and independent as soon as practicable. He, as much as Whitlam and Morrison, pushed the country towards these objectives. He did not baulk at seeking the transfer of powers and authorities from Canberra nor in acting as the decision-maker in the Port Moresby Government.

As such he was called upon on a daily basis to make decisions of fundamental importance on all aspects of government. He did this while holding together a coalition of parties and individuals in government, fending off threats of secession from various quarters, negotiating with the outgoing Australian administration and presenting to the region an image of himself and his country and its views on international issues. Donald Denoon has described Somare as the 'focus of huge and contrary pressures' from a wide variety of sources.[18] The monumental task of preparing the country for independence would have overwhelmed a lesser person. In January 1975, with the road to independence clearly marked, *The Sydney Morning Herald* described Somare as 'having pursued a policy of moderate nationalism with dogged pressure, compromise and the lively touch of a successful gambler'.[19]

Somare's key ally in the PANGU Party and in government was Albert Maori Kiki. Kiki had been born in 1931 in Gulf Province in Papua and hence was slightly older than Somare. He too had undertaken a teacher training course and had taught for two years in the early 1950s before studying at the Suva Medical School in Fiji and then working as a laboratory technician at the Port Moresby Hospital. Kiki had drifted into political activity in the early 1960s before joining PANGU. He became its National Secretary in 1967 and was elected to the House of Assembly in 1972. He also had had an active career in PNG's trade union movement and had served in senior positions in a number of unions in the late 1960s and early 1970s. In 1972 he was appointed Minister for Lands and Environment and then, in 1973, Minister for Foreign Relations and Defence. He was to prove to be very competent in both portfolios. Kiki initially held some anti-Indonesian views and was cautious in his approach to building a relationship with Jakarta but these concerns eroded over time and he worked hard to build a relationship with his counterpart, Adam Malik. Kiki was one of the strongest advocates of early self-government and independence.

Somare, Kiki and the other emerging leaders of PNG – Julius Chan and Father John Momis, and a team of young and untested public servants such as Tony Siaguru in Foreign Relations, Noel Levi in Defence, Mekere Morauta in Finance and Charles Lepani in National Planning – faced enormous challenges in deciding on the nature and style of government they believed was appropriate for Papua New Guinea.

On 3 December 1972 following Whitlam's election, Somare issued a statement in which he said he knew 'that our two governments will be able to work together in the same spirit that has been established with Mr Peacock and the Liberals during the last nine months'. He added that 'Mr Whitlam can justifiably claim some of the credit for the recent changes of Australian policy towards Papua New Guinea after his visits to our country in 1969 and 1971'. He concluded by noting that as a consequence of these visits 'there is already a great deal of understanding established between us'.[20]

A new approach

The Labor Government was determined to move to self-government and then independence in its first term in parliament. It established early timelines to achieve these objectives and galvanised the Australian public service through a program entitled 'Gearing Up' led by a small group of senior officers in the Department of External Territories under the direction of its Secretary, David Hay, and including John Greenwell, Pat Galvin and Alan Kerr. The group's purpose was to accelerate the transfer of responsibilities and authority to ministers in the House of Assembly. It worked closely with local politicians in Port Moresby and had the unwavering support of leaders such as Somare and Kiki.

Barnard had taken some interest in the question of the establishment of a local defence force in Papua New Guinea and of Australia's role in an independent country but he admitted that his thoughts had not yet fully matured. In an address to the Australian Army Staff College in May 1972 he had acknowledged the Labor Party's close interest in the political and social development of PNG but conceded that the 'future of Australian defence relations with Papua New Guinea has not received any concentrated attention in the policy writing of the Labor Party'.[21] He drew attention to the reference in the Party Platform to the proposal for a defence treaty and to the creation of a Pacific Islands Division in the Department of Foreign Affairs but noted that Labor's thoughts did not go beyond these two proposals. Barnard argued that:

> Australian military policy has fashioned military units in Papua New Guinea which are closely integrated into Australia's armed forces. To a very large extent the New Guinea forces are facsimiles of Australian units. It is likely that this pervasive Australian influence will persist for many years to come. There is every reason why the forces of Papua New Guinea should be modelled on the Australian pattern. But policy should be directed towards weaning these indigenous forces away from Australia so when the final wrench comes it is not a traumatic experience for either country. Obviously Papua New Guinea will be

a heavy charge on our defence resources for years to come. This will put a burden on Australian facilities for training and logistics support. It is a responsibility that must be accepted, but it reinforces Labor's belief that Australia's major effort should be swung away from South East Asia to Papua New Guinea.[22]

Barnard went on to identify the areas for 'rapid policy implementation' if Papua New Guinea were to have a self-sustaining defence force. He called for the establishment of a third battalion of the Pacific Islands Regiment, the rapid expansion of naval units to facilitate coastal surveillance, the development of an air capability to allow for the monitoring of the border and, finally, the building of an infrastructure for the administration of defence policy and the armed services. Barnard conceded that these initiatives could not be easily realised in the short term and that they involved considerable costs.[23]

Barnard had also acknowledged early in his remarks to the Staff College that Labor Party policy was to negotiate a defence treaty with PNG but he did not elaborate on this proposal. His comments had instead focused on the need to develop the PNG defence force's practical capabilities rather than suggesting that Australia should extend its commitment to defend Papua New Guinea. In this respect Barnard may have been influenced by another section of the Labor Party Platform in which the party expressed its opposition to the commitment of forces overseas unless under the aegis of the United Nations. At the same time he could have been preparing to re-position the Party's policy away from a formal defence treaty towards an emphasis on a significant level of practical cooperation. This assessment would accord with his subsequent actions and private comments shortly after becoming minister.

As Minister for Defence for two and a half years, Barnard was instrumental in shaping Australian defence policy towards PNG. However, while forthright in his views, on practical matters Barnard pursued much the same path that Fairbairn had begun to map out during the McMahon Government. Barnard's significant contribution was that he quickened the pace of the decision-making. Fairbairn can be credited with identifying the basic policy parameters, while Barnard should be acknowledged as the minister who further developed them and nearly brought them to fruition.

Morrison had visited PNG from 4 to 8 January and had called on Somare in Wewak to introduce himself and to pass on to Somare a sense of the new government's priorities. In turn, Somare announced that he would visit Canberra to discuss the timing of self-government and, amongst other issues, the transfer of responsibility for defence. Somare was expected to arrive in Canberra on 17 January 1973. At the same time Barnard agreed to accept an outstanding invitation to visit Port Moresby over the Australia Day (26 January) long weekend to attend the redesignation ceremony of the Papua New Guinea Defence Force (PNGDF). Whitlam had also accepted an invitation to visit Port Moresby in mid-February before proceeding to Indonesia. After being in power for only four weeks the new government had created a number of opportunities through scheduled bilateral visits to establish a framework for a defence policy towards Papua New Guinea.

In preparation for the visit to Canberra by Somare, the Labor Government had before it a number of assessments by the intelligence and defence communities on the short and long-term prospects for PNG. The reports focused almost exclusively on the internal political and security situation in the country. Their general tone was one of caution, if not pessimism. An assessment prepared in January 1973 by the Joint Intelligence Organisation concluded that the:

> prospects for the future stability and even unity of Papua New Guinea are uncertain. The most likely threat to the viability of Papua New Guinea would be a general decline in law and order leading to large-scale civil disturbances and dissent, possibly going as far as attempted secession from central government rule by parts of Papua New Guinea. ... It is almost inevitable that the central government of Papua New Guinea will, through the period of self-government and independence, face substantial problems in holding Papua New Guinea together.[24]

It is noticeable that the interest in possible Indonesian threats to PNG had diminished greatly. Similarly, other external threats were now given little attention. Instead, the assessments concentrated on the same issues which had featured in papers prepared for the previous Gorton and McMahon Governments: the possible secession of Bougainville, political disturbances in the Gazelle Peninsula and in Papua, and the difficult law and order situation in the Highlands.[25]

Shortly before Somare arrived in Canberra, Barnard met Morrison, Senator Reg Bishop, the Minister Assisting the Minister for Defence, Admiral Sir Victor Smith, Chairman of the Chiefs of Staff Committee and Les Johnson, the Administrator of PNG. The purpose of the meeting was to come to an initial understanding as to how to resolve the question of the need to assist Papua New Guinea to meet its internal security problems, plan for the handover of a defence capability to a localised defence force and identify any Australian defence requirements in a post-independent PNG.[26]

Morrison was keenly aware of the need to strengthen the local authorities' capacity to meet the challenges posed by the country's internal security problems.[27] He expressed his concern at the demands being placed on the police force and commented that its shortcomings could lead to the possible use of the military to assist in restoring order. If this were to occur there would be clear implications for Australia due to the presence of Australian personnel in the PNG Defence Force. Morrison persisted in his advocacy of the view that the limited financial resources of PNG, including the funds held under the defence cooperation scheme, should be directed away from the military and towards the police force. He also argued for the creation of a single security force combining the police and defence force. When this point was lost he suggested that a police field force along the lines of the Malaysian model he had seen while serving in the Australian High Commission in Kuala Lumpur should be established with a battalion from the PNGDF being converted to serve as a field force. Its role would be to engage in the policing of law and order in rural areas, riot control and border liaison and supervision.[28] Later, in four letters over the period January to May 1973, Morrison doggedly pushed his argument in favour of a stronger local police force at the expense of the Defence Force.

In response to Morrison's presentation Barnard made clear to his colleagues that:

> We must take all steps to minimise the possibility of Australia becoming involved, or looking as if it is involved in a military sense after Independence. It was quite clear Papua New Guinea would not be able to maintain the Pacific Islands Regiment (PIR) at its present level without financial assistance from Australia ... It was also clear that before independence we must decide what facilities we might require in Papua New Guinea after Independence and which might be offset against any defence assistance granted by Australia.[29]

The meeting recorded that Barnard went on to note 'while he did not favour a formal treaty he foresaw some form of understanding being negotiated about the time of Independence which clearly covered these matters'.[30]

At this early point in the life of the Whitlam Government, Barnard and Morrison had redefined some of the government's key policy principles.

Barnard may have been responding to Morrison's assessment of the internal security challenges facing the country when he said that Australia 'must take all steps to minimise the possibility of becoming involved' but his comments could be seen as applying equally to an external threat. Both had recognised the challenges faced in responding to the weakening internal security environment in the country and both had ruled out the possibility of Australia, or more specifically the Australian Defence Force, intervening to restore order once PNG had ceased to be an Australian responsibility. Barnard had acknowledged that 'while it was agreed that there was no external threat at present, we must take account of what might arise in the future. There must be and ought to be a defence force and Australia should be prepared to assist in the maintenance of such a force'.[31] But he did not want the defence force involved in quelling outbreaks of civil disorder, thereby raising the possibility of PNG calling on Australian military personnel for support. At a later meeting with Morrison in April 1973 Barnard made his views clearer on the need for PNG to have a military capability when he noted that 'it was necessary to have a viable defence force in Papua New Guinea otherwise Australia would have to accept the burden of defending Papua New Guinea'.[32] Barnard was intent on Australia maintaining all possible options as his government began to address the question of the defence relationship with a post-independent PNG.

Barnard had also identified a further key issue: the question of continued access to defence facilities in an independent PNG. It is possible that the reference in Barnard's remarks to an 'understanding' could have applied to the question of the use of or access to facilities by the Australian Defence Force in PNG given that Barnard, in summing up the meeting, agreed that 'in the final negotiations Australia must seek to retain access to facilities it might require in Papua New Guinea [e.g. Manus]'.[33] He had also made clear his view that it was not necessary to enter into a 'formal treaty' to secure Australia's interests in an independent PNG. He was clearly moving away from his party's platform declaration to 'seek a defence treaty with Papua New Guinea' but had yet to express a view on the scope of any long-term defence commitment or relationship.

While one assessment of this first meeting of relevant ministers and senior officials in the Whitlam Government could be that it set a clear agenda for the government's approach to establishing the defence relationship, Donald Denoon has offered an alternate view. He has argued that, faced with Morrison's calls for a field force and a revised set of functions for the PNG Defence Force, senior Australian defence officials in both

Canberra and Port Moresby decided to ignore the government's wishes and to continue to create a defence force which suited Australia's objectives and one which could work closely with the Australian defence force. This battle of ideas was to continue for the next three years.[34]

Somare seeks to build a relationship with Indonesia

At the same time as the Whitlam Government was settling into office Somare was giving consideration to Papua New Guinea's relationship with Indonesia. In late 1972 he had decided to visit Jakarta and, in preparation for the visit Bob Furlonger, Australia's Ambassador in Jakarta, visited Port Moresby from Canberra on 5 December to brief Somare on President Suharto and the policy priorities of Suharto's Government.[35] Somare told Furlonger that he 'expected Papua New Guinea's relations with Indonesia would be harmonious'. He did not want 'the Indonesians to feel that Papua New Guinea was anti-Indonesian and hoped that the 'West Papuan people' who crossed into Papua New Guinea would not be a cause of friction between the two countries. Somare added that he also did not wish to 'harbour people who had made trouble on the Indonesian side [of the border]'. Furlonger told Somare that in his view Indonesia 'wanted to be good neighbours and the type of relationship they had built up with their ASEAN partners would also be extended to Papua New Guinea'. He added that Indonesia was 'primarily concerned to achieve stability in South East Asia so that they could be left to get on with the job of economic development'. Somare agreed and added his assessment that 'the Indonesians now had no expansionist ambitions and that there was every prospect for good relationships between the two countries, based on many common interests'.[36]

Furlonger had an opportunity to discuss PNG when he called on Suharto on 11 December, shortly after his visit to Port Moresby. He told Canberra that the President had expressed a 'desire that Indonesia should be a good neighbour there [Papua New Guinea] as elsewhere'.[37] He 'recognised that there were … residual fears of Indonesian expansionism and there were tribal problems in both parts of the island'. The President 'developed the recurrent Indonesian theme of the possibility of instability flowing from the uneven economic development of the two parts of the islands'. He expressed 'the hope that the remaining boundary and border problems with Papua and New Guinea could be solved in the near future'. Suharto also told Furlonger that 'Australia and Indonesia would continue to share an interest in the stability of Papua and New Guinea even after Independence and everything possible needed to be done to avoid Papua and New Guinea becoming a problem in relations between Indonesia and Australia'.[38] Suharto added that he believed increased political and cultural contacts between Indonesia and PNG would strengthen the understanding and links between the two countries.

Somare visited Jakarta from 9 to 14 February 1973 and called on the President on 12 February, accompanied by Furlonger.[39] Suharto assured Somare that 'Indonesia would never dominate other peoples. It was, on the contrary, anxious to develop close cooperation with its neighbours, as exemplified by ASEAN'. For his part, Somare told Suharto that he agreed 'on the need for friendship and very close cooperation between the two countries'. He added that 'Indonesia and Papua New Guinea formed a bridge between the Indian and Pacific Oceans and he was anxious to see this bridge developed as much as possible'. Both leaders spoke of the value of increased awareness and knowledge on the part of their respective countries. There was only a brief reference by the President to West Irian, while Suharto told Somare that 'he appreciated the problem of national unity with which Papua New Guinea was confronted'.[40]

The exchange between Somare and Suharto had the effect of further removing from Australian assessments and forecasts the idea that PNG faced an external threat, notably from Indonesia. The possibility remained of misunderstandings along the border but the positive atmosphere generated by the talks meant that these could be managed and would not escalate into a stand-off between the two countries.

Australia and Papua New Guinea: a first round of talks – setting the parameters

Somare held an initial meeting with Whitlam on 17 January 1973. The question of the defence relationship was not discussed. Instead, Somare focused on a date for self-government and the transfer of further powers from Canberra to Port Moresby. He then met Barnard, Morrison and Senator Bishop on 18 January 1973. At this meeting Somare specifically sought the new Australian Government's views on the level of 'defence aid', including financial aid, it would continue to provide after independence. He also raised the issue of Australia's policy for the period between self-government and independence, and the post-independence defence relationship between the two countries.[41] Somare opened the discussions by making clear his preference for Papua New Guinea to continue to have a defence force. He did not wish it to be used to control riots but instead envisaged a small force which 'could be used to help in the development of the country and be seen by the people as their Army'. He described the reasons behind retaining an army as:

(a) any independent country needs some armed forces even when there is no visible threat;
(b) an Army could serve a useful role in nation building particularly in a developing country like Papua New Guinea – it should not simply be oriented towards war on the traditional British model; and
(c) individual skills developed in the Army were useful to the community when servicemen left the force.[42]

Somare also expressed his preference for the creation of a police field force to undertake internal security tasks, including riot control.

Barnard had no hesitation in supporting Somare's views on the role of a small defence force focused on nation building. As to the practical questions of assistance raised by Somare, Barnard agreed to the attachment of trainers to the police college to assist in training for the establishment of a possible police field force. Beyond this question Barnard did not express a view on the nature of the post-independence defence relationship nor the extent of any Australian commitment to PNG.[43] Somare's outline of the role of the army created few policy difficulties for Barnard and his fellow ministers. However, as Ron May, historian of PNG and a long-standing observer of the PNG defence force has argued, it was the beginning of an accelerated discussion between the two countries over the size, style, function and budget of a defence force for an independent PNG.[44] However, it should be noted that most if not all of the work done on these questions was first carried out in the Department of Defence in Canberra with PNG officials brought into the deliberations at the last moment.

Barnard took advantage of his visit to Port Moresby a week later for a dedication ceremony to mark the conversion of the Pacific Islands Regiment to the Papua New Guinea Defence Force (PNGDF) to reinforce some of the points he had made in his discussions in Canberra. In his meeting with the Administrator's Executive Council on 25 January, Barnard told the Council members that 'while there appears to be no external threat to Papua New Guinea at present we should not assume that this will always be the situation. For this reason alone therefore it is necessary to maintain in being a viable defence force ... with a capability to contribute in peacetime to important national development projects'.[45] In response to a question as to whether there would be a defence agreement committing Australia to PNG's defence in the event of external aggression, he replied that:

> it is not possible to give a precise answer but we have accepted certain responsibilities and this [sic] will continue. Personally, we believe it would be out of character if the Australian Government and people did not recognise that any problem Papua New Guinea had was also an Australian problem.[46]

In response to a similar question from another member of the Executive Council as to whether Australia would defend PNG, Barnard went even further and commented, 'I unhesitatingly say yes – it could not be otherwise. It is not only your security but ours too. There would of course be highest level consultation'.[47]

Barnard's remarks went beyond the policy positions his government appeared to be setting for itself. That said, his comments were less than clear and precise and could have been misinterpreted. At the same time, Barnard did not hold out the prospect of an open commitment to the defence of Papua New Guinea. Instead, he had emphasised the need for 'highest level consultation'. Barnard had earlier told the Council that Australia considered 'this area as strategically important and Papua New Guinea is our closest neighbour'.[48] At best, Barnard may have left the Council members with a slightly misleading impression. He had told Australian defence officials in several private conversations during the visit that 'he did not favour a formal treaty. He preferred an arrangement similar to our defence cooperation arrangements with Indonesia with the possible addition of an agreement to consult in the event of external threat and/or aggression to PNG'. This was interpreted by Australian defence officials to mean 'an agreement along the lines of the Five Power London Communiqué' covering Malaysia and Singapore.[49] Senior Defence Department officials also told their Foreign Affairs counterparts that their priority was increasingly directed to putting in place 'arrangements to cover status of forces and visiting forces agreements rather than an over-arching defence agreement embracing a long-term commitment'.[50] Defence officials were moving to ensure that Australia would be PNG's primary defence partner rather than a guarantor against external aggression.

Barnard's presentation had continued many of the themes first developed by Fairbairn during his visit to Port Moresby in June 1972. Indeed, Barnard also visited Manus Island and, as Fairbairn had done seven months earlier, expressed the interest of the Australian Navy in continued access to the oil refuelling facilities located at the naval base. In a later press interview he described Manus as 'desirable to Australian Defence for refuelling purposes'.[51] The visit also highlighted the continuing debate surrounding the role of the Defence Force in responding to breakdowns in internal security, with Barnard making clear to his officials that 'this ought to be the role of the police and only of interest to the army in the circumstance of ultimate crisis'.[52] There was, however, general recognition that the police force 'needed improvement of a qualitative rather than quantitative character'.[53]

This issue remained unresolved for a number of months with Morrison continuing to push for increased involvement by the better-resourced defence force. In May 1973 he pushed unsuccessfully for the transfer of part of the budget of the PNGDF to the police force following Somare's statement that his government felt that 'the greatest foreseeable threat to Papua New Guinea's security is that the Police Force will not be able to contain the internal security situation'.[54]

The attitude of the new Labor Government was slowly beginning to crystallise. It had a clear interest in seeing a viable but small and financially self-sustainable defence force established in Papua New Guinea. It was also willing to assist in practical ways in the development of such a force. Similarly, there was a wish to encourage Papua New Guinea to accept full responsibility for its own defence. At the same time the Whitlam Government was preoccupied with identifying what residual interest Australia had in securing access to bases and facilities and in securing the terms and conditions to underwrite the continuing presence of Australian defence personnel in the PNGDF. In addition Barnard, like his most recent predecessors in the defence portfolio, and perhaps reflecting the changes in thinking which had marked the negotiations over the Five Power Defence Arrangements with Malaysia and Singapore, had sought to avoid a public statement committing Australia to defend Papua New Guinea against external attack. Barnard's less than clear explanation of his government's policy may have carried this argument further than intended at this stage but he had not gone into any detail as to how Australia might commit itself to defend Papua New Guinea. The intention behind Barnard's presentation, as it had been with Fairbairn, was to encourage consultations on the practical questions of the development of Papua New Guinea's own capacity to defend itself and to initiate discussion on the practical aspects of inter-service defence cooperation and support.

The third opportunity to discuss the establishment of a local defence force and the post-independence defence relationship came during the visit to Port Moresby by Whitlam in February 1973. In his meeting with Somare, Whitlam made clear his view that responsibility for law and order should be in the hands of the police and not the army. He commented that the Defence Force had Australian officers and his government would be held responsible if the Australian Army were involved in the shooting of Papua New Guineans. He added that 'he did not want the Army involved as that involved Australia'.[55] In keeping with this theme, but also reflecting growing concern about the internal security situation in the country and the strength of the separatist movements in Papua and Bougainville, Whitlam in his public remarks emphasised the importance of maintaining national unity in the face of such elements. He said that he saw it as Australia's duty to 'hand over to the Central Government and the House of Assembly a united Papua New Guinea'.[56] Whitlam and his senior ministerial colleagues were forced to make repeated statements in the months leading up to independence in 1975 in support of national unity as the country continued to face threats of secession from Bougainville, the Gazelle Peninsula and Papua.

Whitlam left Port Moresby for his first official visit to Indonesia. In his public comments in Jakarta Whitlam told his audience that 'we seek no binding treaty or formal alliance [with Indonesia], merely an understanding based on mutual trust and friendship. We will be charting a new course in our foreign policy with less emphasis on the kind of military pact that is no longer relevant to the realities of the 70s'.[57]

Two further speeches served to draw this initial period to a close. The first was by Barnard in an address to the National Press Club in Canberra on 15 March 1973 in which he described the future defence relationship with Papua New Guinea as a 'matter of high priority [and] where it is welcomed, Australia will be prepared to contribute to the maintenance of a defence force in Papua New Guinea after independence'.[58] He made clear his view that the size and functions of the defence force were issues to be settled by Papua New Guinea, although this remark ignored the considerable work being done in Canberra on these questions. His reference to assistance 'where it is welcomed' was similar to Fairbairn's remark in 1972 that Australia would only act militarily to support Papua New Guinea 'if our help should be sought and if we should wish to respond'. Barnard showed the same caution that Fairbairn had demonstrated when discussing a long-term commitment to Papua New Guinea and, just as Fairbairn had done in 1972, chose to concentrate on the practical aspects of developing the defence force.

The second occasion was Whitlam's foreign policy address in the House of Representatives on 24 May 1973. In that speech he described the defence cooperation arrangements with Indonesia as the model which the government would follow and that it would have as its:

> guiding aim ... to promote self reliance and the capability to resist external threats. It does not favour the permanent stationing of Australian military forces abroad, but looks to ... cooperation in such areas as technical aid, training assistance, joint exercises and continuing consultations. The Government will seek cooperation of this kind with our regional neighbours on an informal basis without the need for fixed and formal military pacts.[59]

Turning to Papua New Guinea, Whitlam told the House that 'Papua New Guinea will occupy a special position in Australia's network of relationships, but we do not seek an exclusive relationship with Papua New Guinea which will want to find its own place in the international community'.[60] Somare wrote to Whitlam expressing his support for Whitlam's concept of defence cooperation as set out in the speech. Somare added that 'my government's views on the impracticality of signing formal defence treaties (either bilateral or multilateral) are one and the same with those of your government'.[61] He noted that no 'final decisions on the future size, shape or composition of the Defence Force had been taken' and that planning for a separate defence force would 'follow realistic standards of economy'.[62]

At this time the government also announced the commencement of a study of the future disposition of defence bases and facilities within Australia to ensure their suitability for the defence of Australia, and their support of Australia's external commitments. This study, and the decisions arising from it regarding the establishment of new facilities in northern Australia, were to have important consequences in determining the long-term significance to be attached to maintaining access to facilities in Papua New Guinea. In particular, the decision to establish an air force base in the Northern Territory made obsolete the arguments which had featured in assessments in the early 1960s that access to air bases in Papua New

Guinea, particularly Nadzab near Lae, was necessary if Australia wished to project forces into Southeast Asia. From this time on the RAAF took less interest in the issue of access to facilities in Papua New Guinea. The service department which sustained that interest was the Navy, which continued to raise the question of access to the oil storage facilities at Manus Island.

A revised strategic assessment

The first Strategic Basis Paper prepared for the Whitlam Government was endorsed by the Defence Committee chaired by Tange on 1 June 1973. It was the first of three significant documents to confirm a change in the assessment of the strategic importance of Papua New Guinea to Australia.[63] The paper dealt first with Indonesia which was described as of 'the greatest strategic significance to Australia because of its position. Australia's relations with Indonesia are of profound and permanent importance to Australia's security and national interest'. It assessed that 'Indonesia will see Australia as an ally rather than an enemy' and that the likelihood of Indonesia threatening Australia was 'remote'. Indonesia had a 'legitimate, abiding interest' in Papua New Guinea. It acknowledged that difficulties could continue over the management of the border and problems could emerge if dissidents from Irian Jaya sought haven in Papua New Guinea but it dismissed as 'highly improbable' and 'remote' the possibility of 'significant military intrusion' by Indonesia into Papua New Guinea. Although canvassing 'highly remote' and hypothetical scenarios, the paper argued for a policy of considerable tolerance and forbearance towards Indonesia over Australia's interests in its relationship with Papua New Guinea.

Turning to Papua New Guinea itself, the paper focused on the internal security pressures facing the Territory and argued that its major problems 'are likely to arise from pressure for increased regional autonomy' while 'swollen urban populations, traditional hostilities in the Highlands and elsewhere and a general deterioration in law and order could lead to dissidence of varying degrees of seriousness and violence'. It anticipated 'no threat of military attack ... by an external power'. In a separate section on 'Australian Interests', the paper acknowledged that the question of any involvement by Australia in Papua New Guinea's internal security problems, post-independence, represented a very difficult policy issue. Moreover, any intervention by Australia (particularly in response to actions by secessionists) would be 'earning the hostility of significant political forces in Papua New Guinea'.[64] The paper acknowledged that a 'weak, fragmented Papua New

Guinea may prejudice Australia's long-term strategic interest' but concluded 'if the Papua New Guinea government itself were unable to cope with the situation politically and by military pressure, it is difficult to see what would justify Australian military intervention'. The overall judgement was that 'there appear[s] to be strong arguments against Australian intervention in the internal security situation ... and a desirability of avoiding any commitment to intervene'.

The 1973 Strategic Basis Paper confirmed the trend which had been emerging since 1970. The possibility of an external attack on Papua New Guinea was seen as remote. Australia's need to transit Papua New Guinea waters and airspace en route to the war in Vietnam was lessening. The focus in assessments was now firmly on Papua New Guinea's internal security problems. This, in turn, was leading decision-makers in Canberra to recommend both a hands-off approach and an avoidance of a commitment to intervene. There was a general acceptance that the political and diplomatic costs to Australia of intervening in internal security matters would be too high. There was also a tentative acceptance that a fragmented Papua New Guinea would make only a marginal difference to Australia's security environment.

Papua New Guinea was now seen as neither the robust shield of the Second World War era nor the necessary staging ground for deployments by Australia into Southeast Asia. The country still had a role as part of the geographic barrier stretching over Australia's northern approaches but it also presented a complex set of problems and pressures which needed to be managed carefully due to the stresses and strains of internal division and instability.

A question of bases in Papua New Guinea

The Strategic Basis Paper was followed by a report by the Joint Planning Committee of the Department of Defence on the question of *Australian Access to Base Facilities in Papua New Guinea after Independence*.[65] The question of maintaining Australian-built military bases in Port Moresby, Lae, Wewak, the small patrol base at Vanimo and the naval base on Manus Island had been a fundamental element of Australia's defence thinking since the Second World War. They were seen as part of Australia's strategy of forward defence or, in the case of Manus, as staging and refuelling centres to assist in the deployment of troops to Southeast Asia or further north.

The review made the critical judgement that 'the circumstances in which Australia would require access to base facilities in Papua New Guinea after independence are so doubtful that it would not be justifiable to outlay major expenditure to maintain or to develop these facilities, nor to enter into a defence commitment in support of Papua New Guinea in return for access to facilities'.[66] However, if they were available the facilities would 'enhance the operational capability of our naval and air forces should circumstances ever arise which required an Australian presence or intervention in Papua New Guinea'. The report suggested that the value of the navy refuelling and communications facilities at Manus Island were such that Australia should seek 'an arrangement' to maintain the facilities in association with the PNG Defence Force should it not wish to do so itself.[67]

The conclusions were in keeping with the changes that had been occurring in Australian defence analysis in the early 1970s. In the 1960s Cabinet had examined on two separate occasions the question of whether the base and refuelling facility on Manus Island played a role in Australia's defence profile and had rejected suggestions that they should be closed. Defence planners now couched the need for bases and access to facilities in judgements which emphasised the remote possibility of military action by Indonesia. The official assessment may still have been that Australia had 'abiding' strategic interests in the country but these were now under serious re-examination as Australia approached the prospect of formally deciding on the terms of a defence relationship with an independent Papua New Guinea. The report also contained the important acknowledgment that Papua New Guinea might have its own views on issues and might not wish its position compromised by providing Australia access to its facilities.

The question of a commitment or not

On 1 November 1973, the Defence Committee continued the rapid transformation in Australia's re-appraisal of the strategic importance of Papua New Guinea when it examined a comprehensive report on *Australia's Defence Relationship with Papua New Guinea*.[68] The Committee comprised Sir Arthur Tange as Chairman and Secretary of the Department of Defence; the senior representatives of the armed services; K.C.O. ('Mick') Shann, the former Ambassador to Jakarta (1962–66) and, on this occasion, Acting Secretary of the Department of Foreign Affairs; Sir David Hay, former Administrator of Papua New Guinea and now Secretary of the Department of External Territories; and Gordon Jockel, Director of the

Joint Intelligence Organisation and former Ambassador to Jakarta (1969–1972). Jockel had undertaken wide-ranging visits to Papua New Guinea in 1966 and again in November 1972. The report had been written solely by Bill Pritchett, First Assistant Secretary, Defence Planning Division, Department of Defence and a former senior officer in External Affairs with minimum consultations with other departments.[69] (Pritchett had served as Commissioner in Singapore from 1965 to 1967. In 1979 he succeeded Tange as Secretary of the Department of Defence.)

All these senior officials had been closely involved in the development of Australia's foreign and defence policies towards Southeast Asia and Papua New Guinea over the previous decade. All had expressed, over the course of those years, strong views on Australia's responsibility to defend Papua New Guinea and all had accepted the concept that Australia had a strategic interest in the Territory. In recent years Shann, in particular, but aided by his Secretary, Sir Keith Waller, and Deputy Secretary L. H. Border who had day-to-day responsibility for overseeing the department's engagement in the process towards independence, had taken the lead in Foreign Affairs in raising questions as to the role Papua New Guinea could play in the region and how it would manage its relationship with Indonesia. Shann had encouraged his colleagues to look at Papua New Guinea as an independent country whose internal dynamics needed to be understood. He was not prepared to take the country for granted and wanted to know how it would act and respond on the international stage. In November/December 1972 he had visited Papua New Guinea to try to further his own knowledge of the country. He had previously visited in 1963. In his subsequent conversations within Foreign Affairs, Shann had also raised questions about the responsibilities and size of the proposed defence force for an independent Papua New Guinea and had argued against it being a duplicate of the Australian Army in structure and functions. Shann had also argued that Papua New Guinea could not afford to maintain a defence force which, by tradition, had next-to-no role in responding to breakdowns in internal security. Earlier, Border had put to Sir Keith Waller, Secretary of Foreign Affairs, the idea that Australia could offer an independent Papua New Guinea a security assurance to 'consult' on defence issues drawing on similar language to the Five Power Arrangement covering Malaysia.[70] Waller had suggested that the idea be held over until a later date.

The senior officers now serving on the Defence Committee came to judgements which crystallised many of the tentative conclusions which had begun to emerge in the last years of the Gorton and McMahon governments and in the early months of the Whitlam administration. The Committee's report was to serve as the basis of Australia's approach to a long-term defence commitment to Papua New Guinea for the next decade or more. It was the reference document used by ministers and officials during the negotiations of the long-term defence arrangement finalised in 1977. It was again used during the negotiation of the revised defence obligations contained in the 1987 Joint Declaration of Principles.

The report had three distinct parts: a paper setting out the nature of the defence relationship and the options for a post-independence defence commitment; a paper on the 'Strategic Importance of Papua New Guinea to Australia'; and a short note on the application of the ANZUS Treaty to an independent Papua New Guinea.

The key document before the Committee, and the only one considered in detail, was the paper prepared by Pritchett on Australia's defence relationship with Papua New Guinea. The paper acknowledged that PNG was of 'abiding strategic relevance for Australia' and that:

> Australia's defence interest relates to the lodgement in PNG of an unfriendly power able to offer us a significant threat, or such other developments there as would facilitate that threat or limit Australia's ability to counter it and the protection of Australian interests in regard to trade routes and sea and air passage through the area and its waterways.[71]

On the question of how critical PNG was to Australia it advanced the key judgement that:

> control of PNG by a hostile power would seriously disadvantage Australia's defence. However, loss of PNG to an unfriendly power would not necessarily mean that Australia could no longer be effectively defended. Our defence policy should not be based on the assumption that exclusion of an unfriendly power from PNG is ultimately critical to Australia's own defence. ... [nor] automatically require military resistance from Australia. ... on balance we may decide to accept the situation.

Pritchett's paper stated that Australia's policy objective 'will be ... if possible, to secure the exclusion from PNG of an unfriendly power' and this might require the commitment of military forces. However, 'short of this it will be desirable for Australia to secure and retain the ability to influence, and if possible prevent, the development of circumstances in which the questions of foreign intrusions and resistance to it might occur'. It argued that one way to ensure this outcome was to create in the mind of any foreign power contemplating an act against PNG the thought that it would also have to consider Australia's response to such an intrusion. Pritchett concluded that 'Australia's defence relationship with Papua New Guinea should therefore be the primary regional defence relationship of that state'.

The paper then addressed itself to the issue of how best to give expression to the desired relationship. In doing so Pritchett examined the question of the long-term defence commitment and relationship Australia could enter into with an independent Papua New Guinea. He initially identified three possibilities: an unqualified commitment; no commitment; and a commitment to consult.

Regarding the first option of an unqualified commitment, the paper argued that it 'appears undesirable at this time that this [the expression of Australia's defence relationship] be done by formal Australian commitment to the defence of PNG in all circumstances'. It was 'altogether inappropriate when PNG was moving to independence and Australia is relinquishing obligations and responsibilities'. Moreover, a defence commitment to PNG was 'unnecessary'. An external threat to PNG was 'unlikely' and Australia's 'own defence interest [was] not in the security of PNG as such but the exclusion from there of a foreign power inimical to Australian defence interests'. This contingency was 'unlikely within the foreseeable future'. The paper envisaged the need to 'prevent, contain and end any local conflict in which PNG might become involved' but 'we must be free … to decide for ourselves whether our own interests and the circumstances of the day favour our military intervention; we should not, in the present and likely circumstances, bind ourselves to intervene'. Pritchett added that an unqualified defence commitment could also encourage PNG to 'pursue immoderate or risky policies, involving Australia beyond our own interests in disputes with other governments'.

Turning to the second option of 'no commitment', the paper argued that acceptance of this option would accord with Australia's recognition of PNG's status as a fully sovereign and independent state. It would acknowledge the 'improbability of intrusion by an unfriendly external power' and be in accord with Australia's 'requirement not to be involved by PNG beyond our own interests in disputes with other governments'. If later developments changed this outlook then it would be possible to move to a firmer commitment. Pritchett argued that 'no commitment need not mean no influence' and drew attention to the very close relationship Australia would expect to maintain in all fields, including the defence relationship. He envisaged Australia as the 'primary source of defence support' for Papua New Guinea. He also argued that any sensitivities which might be felt by Papua New Guinea if Australia did not offer a defence commitment could be managed by presenting 'a suitably worded statement ... expressing in general terms [both countries'] common interest in regional security and their intention to work for these objectives'.

There was an acknowledgement that the option of 'no commitment' may, however, 'not be politic in terms of all our interests in PNG and the PNG government's wish for [a] defence assurance'. He therefore proposed the concept of a 'consultative relationship'. This could be of a formal character similar to the formulation in the Five Power Arrangements with Malaysia and Singapore or it could be a general reference in an agreed statement that the two governments would consult about their common defence interests and about developments affecting the security of the region.

Pritchett presented four options for Australia: a formal commitment to defend PNG in all circumstances; a mutual commitment to consult in the event of external threat to Australia or PNG; an informal and generalised intention to consult about common defence interests; and a general statement between the two governments expressing their common interest in stability and regional security and intention to work towards these objectives. Pritchett's recommendation to the Defence Committee was that no 'automatic commitment' be offered or accepted. If a consultative arrangement were preferred 'it should for the present be of the general and informal character' and reflect their common defence interests. He also recommended that there be consultations with PNG at ministerial level on this issue and that a decision be deferred until PNG reactions had been obtained.

The paper also examined the implications for Australia's defence interests of PNG's internal instability. Pritchett acknowledged that internal instability would affect various Australian interests 'but not necessarily the defence interest' as that was focused on a 'foreign intrusion inimical to Australia'. It followed from such an assessment that 'there can be considerable internal instability in PNG without the defence interest being directly affected. ... This relative lack of concern extends even to the possible break up of Papua New Guinea. The continued unity of the present state ... is in itself not essential to the Australian defence effort'. The paper immediately set this thinking to one side and acknowledged that 'the defence interest will share with other interests, political, economic, communications etc., the objective of a unified and stable PNG because instability and division would make it more difficult to exercise the influence our defence interest seeks'. It repeated the judgement that it was undesirable to intervene militarily in problems related to internal security. The paper did not rule out completely the possibility of responding to a request to intervene to restore order or to rescue Australian citizens but preferred not to establish any criteria for particular scenarios.

The Defence Committee gave a 'general as distinct from detailed' endorsement of the paper. It modified some of the language used by Pritchett but did not raise any fundamental objections. It amended the paper's wording to read 'Australia's defence interest is that Australia's defence relationship with PNG be the primary defence relationship of that State'. As to the form of a defence commitment, the committee agreed with the four options summarised in the paper but added that 'it would not be wise for the Australian Government to reach final decisions until PNG views had been obtained'. It also agreed that such was the 'high policy implications' of the issue that discussions with PNG should be at ministerial level.

The committee members also considered a section of Pritchett's paper on access to bases and facilities in Papua New Guinea. They concluded that 'the question was not one of maintaining Australian facilities' in Papua New Guinea but rather whether special measures should be adopted to ensure access to any particular facility. They agreed that 'it was in Australia's interest to seek to retain access to refuelling facilities at Manus should PNG decide to continue to base its maritime element there and to use influence to ensure that PNG retains a potential for the future development of Wewak airfield'.

The Defence Committee's 'general as distinct from detailed' endorsement of Pritchett's paper and its conclusions were approved by Barnard on 11 December 1973. He did not seek Cabinet endorsement of his decision, a fact which demonstrated a confidence in his own judgement and his hold over policy development. The committee's conclusions were referred to in later Cabinet submissions presented to the Fraser Government.

The thinking behind Pritchett's analysis of Australia's long-term defence interest in Papua New Guinea had not developed in isolation. It reflected a pragmatism evident in the writings of Australian academics interested in defence and security issues, such as Hedley Bull, Robert O'Neill, T. B. Millar, Jamie Mackie and J. D. B. Miller. In a series of articles and speeches beginning in the late 1960s all had identified the problems of internal security and instability as the greatest threat to Papua New Guinea and had warned against the Papua New Guinea Defence Force and the Australian Defence Force becoming directly involved. They had strongly cautioned against Australia entering into an open commitment to come to Papua New Guinea's assistance if attacked. Instead, they had advocated a very limited definition of Australia's security interests in the country, largely confined to protecting maritime and air routes. O'Neill had warned that 'Australia should be chary of more direct involvement ... putting Papua New Guinea back together again is likely to be beyond Australia's capacity'.[72] Bull had shared O'Neill's view on the significance of the problem of internal security when he argued in early 1973 that 'we should ... make it clear to the government of an independent Papua New Guinea that we will not underwrite the internal security or unity of that country'. Bull had taken a harder line on the scope of any future defence obligation when he had argued that 'our ultimate objective should be to have no closer strategic connection with Papua New Guinea than with any other neighbouring country'.[73] Later, at a meeting of the Australian Institute of International Affairs in May 1975, Bull had cautioned against a neo-colonial relationship emerging and had argued that 'Australia's long-term objective must be to disengage'.[74]

Jamie Mackie, one of Australia's keenest observers of developments in Indonesia and author of the authoritative book on Confrontation, had come to the same conclusion as his peers but had also viewed the issue from the perspective of regional security policy.[75] He had argued that 'it is of the highest importance for Australians to avoid creating any misleading impressions that we would or could underwrite the defence of Papua New Guinea in the event of conflict between her and Indonesia'. He had added that 'our national interests in not being dragged into hostilities with [Indonesia] is almost ... greater than our residual interests in Papua New Guinea'.[76]

The terms of a possible Australian defence commitment to Papua New Guinea continued to be discussed over the next few years, with writers such as F. A Mediansky largely accepting the argument advanced by O'Neill and Bull against a formal defence arrangement containing a guarantee of assistance. Mediansky described such an option as 'undesirable ... [as it was] still too uncertain for Canberra to underwrite Papua New Guinea's foreign policy from the outset'. Mediansky nevertheless suggested that an arrangement to 'consult' in the event of an armed attack might be a practical alternative to an open guarantee. He argued that to do less would be 'imprudent and ungenerous'.[77]

The only academic to question this accepted line of argument was Owen Harries from the University of New South Wales, who had described it as a 'rather brusque, tough dismissal' of Papua New Guinea.[78] Harries argued that Australia had a residual responsibility based on the special nature of Australia's historical role in and responsibility towards Papua New Guinea. Harries was subsequently to emerge as an influential adviser on foreign policy issues in the Fraser Government.

With the exception of Harries, the academic community showed an absence of sentimentality in their assessments of Papua New Guinea and any associated Australian obligations. The empathy which had formed during and after the Second World War and had influenced Australian policy decisions during the West New Guinea dispute in the 1950s had begun to fade by the late 1960s, at least in this community. The emerging possibility that Papua New Guinea would soon be independent and a free agent on the regional stage, while still plagued by internal security questions, was serving to focus the attention of the academic community as quickly as it was that of the government's policy makers.

Conclusion

The period following the election of the Whitlam Labor Government in December 1972 witnessed an accelerated consideration of the themes which were beginning to emerge in Australian assessments as to the place of Papua New Guinea in Australia's post–Vietnam War environment. Some elements of Labor's approach to the significance of Papua New Guinea were similar to those evident in the last months of the Liberal Government. However, Labor endorsed a fundamentally new approach when the Minister for Defence, Lance Barnard, approved the Defence Committee's recommendations on the future of the long-term defence relationship. Australia's interests were now less influenced by concerns about foreign infiltration or subversion or by the need to retain Papua New Guinea as a base for the projection of Australian forces into Southeast Asia. Rather, they now took into account concerns over the long-term stability and reliability of the country and how best Australia should respond to those concerns. The emphasis had shifted to the need to avoid a long-term, open-ended commitment and to a position in which Australia retained the flexibility to determine how it responded.

Chapter 11

TOWARDS A COMMON UNDERSTANDING 1973–1975

'Neither side [Australia or PNG] were in favour of a defence commitment of the ANZUS nature. [...] There can no longer be any thought of automatic involvement of Australian forces in Papua New Guinea'.

Lance Barnard, Minister for Defence, August 1974

'Neither Government wishes to enter into a formal defence commitment'.

Lance Barnard, Minister for Defence, October 1974

At the beginning of their second full year in government Barnard, Morrison and their officials focused on a number of interconnected defence-related issues as Papua New Guinea moved to self-government and then independence. The senior ministers and officials were closely involved in the process of establishing the structure, style, role and responsibilities of the soon to be re-designated Papua New Guinea Defence Force (PNGDF). They were also preoccupied with negotiating a Status of Forces Agreement on the role and responsibilities of the Australian Defence

Force personnel who would continue to serve in the PNGDF after independence. As well, officials looked for a mechanism to allow Australia to be consulted if its defence personnel serving with the PNGDF were to be deployed to what were described as 'politically sensitive situations', usually defined as breakdowns in internal security or possible clashes with Indonesian forces on the border. Finally, officials were involved in settling the terms of a supply support arrangement to ensure continued Australian matériel assistance to the PNGDF. The question of the long-term defence relationship with an independent Papua New Guinea stood apart and was managed separately as a whole-of-government issue.

A feature of the consultations and negotiations surrounding these issues, as Paul Mench has commented, was that they were increasingly carried out with indigenous Papua New Guineans serving in the PNGDF or in the government.[1] Somare and Kiki were in the forefront of the negotiations, with Noel Levi, Secretary of the Department of Defence, also closely involved. Admittedly, there remained a considerable number of Australians in the administration who briefed local officials and who participated in these discussions but the trend was increasingly for decisions to be taken by Somare and Kiki. This suited the Whitlam Government's approach to Papua New Guinea. Although the active participation of Papua New Guineans in negotiations had begun to occur in the last years of the Liberal–Country Party Government, Whitlam and his colleagues insisted that Papua New Guinea ministers and officials were to be treated as equal partners by their Australian counterparts.

A second feature was that the negotiations were conducted during a period when Australia was increasingly worried by the internal security problems plaguing the country and the threat of secession, in particular from Bougainville. As noted earlier, Australian ministers and senior officials were preoccupied by the threat that Papua New Guinea would break apart, as firstly the Papua Besena Movement initiated a unilateral declaration of independence for Papua and then, in mid-1975, Bougainville launched a much more serious attempt to secede from Port Moresby's impending administration. Whitlam, his senior ministers and the Administrator (supported by statements from the United Nations) repeatedly made clear, publicly and privately, that Australia supported a united Papua New Guinea and would only provide assistance to a government based in Port Moresby.

Reshaping the party platform and quarantining the ANZUS Treaty

The Whitlam Government took the first step in clarifying its approach to the issue of the long-term defence relationship and the terms of a commitment to defend Papua New Guinea when, at its July 1973 Federal Conference, the Labor Party dropped the reference in its 1971 Federal Party Platform to a commitment to negotiate a 'defence treaty' with Papua New Guinea. The initiative to remove the reference was taken by Morrison as the New South Wales delegate on the conference drafting committee.[2] His aim was to give the government the maximum flexibility in its approach to this issue. Other key delegates, including Barnard, agreed to Morrison's decision to remove the reference. Morrison's action received little attention and there was minimum debate on the issue at the conference.[3] Mench has suggested that the reference was removed 'because of fears that a rigid treaty arrangement might possibly lead to Australian military intervention in Papua New Guinea's internal affairs'.[4] Whitlam noted, in response to a submission from the Department of Foreign Affairs shortly after the conference, that the decision was designed to 'simplify the plank not to repudiate the idea'.[5] Regardless of Whitlam's justification, Morrison had made sure that it was no longer Labor policy to conclude a 'defence treaty' (of whatever description and scope) with Papua New Guinea. One of the important foundation stones of Labor's policy approach to Papua New Guinea, adopted in opposition, had been removed.

At the same time as the Labor Party was recasting its policy approach, Australian officials settled the question of whether the ANZUS Treaty would be extended to include an independent Papua New Guinea as a signatory state. The application of the Treaty was, on the surface, the most straightforward and powerful mechanism available to provide Papua New Guinea with a guarantee of its defence against an external aggressor.

In 1962, at the height of the West New Guinea dispute, the Minister for External Affairs, Garfield Barwick, had secured a strong reference in the ANZUS Council meeting in Canberra to the application of the Treaty to the Territory of Papua and New Guinea and had followed this up with a statement at a press conference that 'if our island territories come under attack we can rely upon the United States of America and New Zealand to be standing with us and giving us assistance'.[6] In 1963, Averell Harriman, the United States Under Secretary of State, had confirmed that the United States 'would fight' to defend Papua New Guinea. Shortly afterwards the United States senior State Department official, Lucius Battle, confirmed that the United States would support Australia against an aggressor in Papua New Guinea.[7] Dean Rusk, Secretary of State, had given similar assurances to Australian ministers and senior officials.

At regular intervals throughout the late 1960s and 1970s Australian officials had examined the question of whether coverage of the ANZUS Treaty would extend to an independent Papua New Guinea or include Australian troops operating in an independent Papua New Guinea. Officials were consistently of the view that the Treaty would cover Australian troops on active defence duty in Papua New Guinea. However, they concluded that, despite its former colonial status as an Australian territory, an independent Papua New Guinea would not automatically be covered by ANZUS. Papua New Guinea could only be included if the existing partners agreed to amend the Treaty. It was noted that such a decision would be subject to confirmation by the United States Senate.

As early as 1963 Tange had commented to the Defence Committee that 'no US Senate is likely to mortgage itself to an independent New Guinea Government which would involve it in a war with Indonesia'.[8] At the time of its consideration of the 1973 report on *Australia's Defence Relations with Papua New Guinea* discussed earlier, the Defence Committee had also examined a paper on the implications for the ANZUS Treaty of Papua New Guinea gaining independence. In preparation for this discussion the Department of Foreign Affairs had formally sought from the United States Embassy an opinion as to whether, from the perspective of the United States, the Treaty would extend to Papua New Guinea on independence. The report to the Defence Committee drew on the advice from the State Department that the Treaty would not apply to an independent Papua New Guinea, unless specific action were taken by the parties to include it.[9] The Defence Committee noted that the United States Senate was 'most unlikely' to 'accept a new security commitment in the Asian–Pacific areas'. Moreover, efforts to secure the acceptance of Papua New Guinea as a Treaty partner 'could not be expected to succeed' and, if the question were raised in the Senate, it 'could … stimulate some unwelcome criticism in the United States of the Treaty commitment to Australia'. In view of this assessment, Australian officials argued that 'an effort to secure Papua New Guinea's membership of the ANZUS Treaty is not warranted'.[10]

Strongly implicit in this judgement was the view that the ANZUS Treaty was too important to Australia's own security outlook to risk it being weakened through redrafting or rejection in a United States Senate debate over widening its geographic coverage to include Papua New Guinea.

Australia was not prepared to jeopardise the fundamental pillar of its own defence policy for the sake of extending the ANZUS security guarantee to Papua New Guinea. In coming to this assessment Australian policy makers also noted that to extend the Treaty to Papua New Guinea might arouse resentment elsewhere in the South Pacific at Papua New Guinea's 'preferred status' and 'could be taken in Indonesia as implying that Australia considered Papua New Guinea likely to be threatened by Indonesia, a view it is in our interest to avoid'.[11] It may also have been the case that the Whitlam Government was wary of putting the ANZUS Treaty before the Nixon Administration given the serious division which had emerged between the two governments in late 1972 and early 1973 over the bombing of North Vietnam. The intensity of the Nixon Administration's hostility to Whitlam, as revealed by James Curran in *Unholy Fury: Whitlam and Nixon at War*, would not have boded well for any reasoned discussion about re-negotiation of ANZUS to include Papua New Guinea.[12]

The question of the possible extension of the ANZUS Treaty was not raised in the discussions between Australia and Papua New Guinea over the options to express a long-term defence commitment. There is no evidence to indicate that Papua New Guinea considered becoming a signatory to the ANZUS Treaty. Its preference for a foreign policy of 'universalism' meant that it wished to avoid public commitments and alliances with the superpowers.

PNG's first thoughts on a post-independence arrangement

In early 1973 officials from both Australia and Papua New Guinea had begun to discuss the details of the future structure, responsibilities, budget and role of the PNGDF. On 5 February 1974 the talks extended to the scope of the post-independence defence relationship. At this meeting Papua New Guinea officials canvassed the possibility of an 'arrangement' which, in the broadest terms, would:

(a) give Papua New Guinea some form of assurance, in mutual terms, which would ensure that in the event of external aggression beyond Papua New Guinea's capability to handle, Australia would help;

(b) be flexible, in relation to the type of events and circumstances;

(c) provide machinery for consultation which would keep the two countries informed of each other's attitudes and intentions and enable them to discuss particular developments;

(d) could be supported and elaborated if desired by unilateral statements of policy from time to time;

(e) not appear to be directed towards any specific third country or countries; and

(f) find practical expression for example through joint Australian/Papua New Guinea exercises.[13]

The scope of the possible 'arrangement' was the most detailed outline yet put forward and surprisingly it came from the PNG side. It is difficult to assess the strength of indigenous input into this description. Kiki and Levi were clear in their thinking but they were surrounded by Australian defence officers serving in senior positions in the PNGDF, including its commanding officer. The 'arrangement' did not propose a formal defence treaty or commitment. Instead it spoke only of an 'assurance' which would be 'flexible' and a 'machinery for consultation'. It approximated some of the elements examined in the Defence Committee three months earlier as it did not seek a formal, unrestricted, unlimited commitment from Australia. The reference to joint exercises serving as a practical expression of the defence relationship was also in keeping with Australian thinking, along with supply support arrangements.

The concern that Papua New Guinea would press Australia for an unconditional or unlimited public commitment to come to its defence proved unfounded. On 4 April 1974, Kiki met Barnard, Morrison and Senator Don Willesee, who had taken over as Minister for Foreign Affairs from Whitlam in November 1973. In his opening remarks, Barnard made clear his view that it was 'important for both countries that Papua New Guinea be seen domestically and internationally to be a sovereign country and responsible for its own defence'.[14] Barnard knew that this approach would resonate with Kiki given the latter's clearly expressed sentiments in favour of an independent Papua New Guinea. Kiki nevertheless raised the issue of the nature of the long-term defence relationship and referred to the common interest of both countries in a close relationship. He commented that he 'foresaw a particularly close relationship in the shorter term while Australia provided financial and personnel assistance to the PNGDF'. Kiki added that Papua New Guinea would like there to be:

> a general expectation within the region that the close relationship between the two countries resting on historical and geographical considerations and the defence assistance provided by Australia would mean that an attack on one would be seen as an attack on the other.[15]

Importantly, he commented that Papua New Guinea did not believe that this close relationship needed to be the subject of a formal arrangement. Instead, Papua New Guinea would prefer an 'understanding' between the two countries and this 'understanding' would include a mutual acceptance that the two governments would 'consult' each other should a threat develop. Kiki added that he did not wish to formalise this 'understanding' in a major public presentation or a formal agreement as this 'could lead to pressures on Papua New Guinea for similar arrangements with other countries'.[16]

Barnard and Willesee both readily accepted Kiki's argument and proposal, with Barnard noting that Australia also did not want a formal agreement. Barnard added that it would be 'better to have an understanding that there would always be an opportunity to consult should there be an appearance of a threat, i.e. a mutual acceptance by both governments that the opportunity to consult is there if the need arises'. Senator Willesee added that an announcement to this effect could also refer to the 'historical and geographical relationship between the two countries'. Barnard also advised Kiki that Australia would not be seeking to maintain its own defence facilities in Papua New Guinea but would look for access to facilities, with the minimum of formality, for visits and exercises. Australia, in particular, wished to retain limited access to the refuelling facilities at Manus, for the short term. Kiki accepted Barnard's proposal and added that such cooperation in the use of facilities would be part of the defence relationship as 'understood' between the two countries.[17]

The meeting had served the purpose of allowing both sides to articulate their vision for the future defence relationship. As such it reflected the themes emerging in both countries' foreign and security policies. In Papua New Guinea's case this had meant a reaffirmation that it wished to be seen as independent, sovereign and not, in public at least, tied to an ally or major power. This was consistent with its wish to pursue a course of 'universalism' – friend to all and enemy to none – in its relations with other states. At the same time it demonstrated the lack of a clear alternative for Papua New Guinea in establishing a security policy. Papua New Guinea was inevitably linked, at least for the short term, to Australia. The approach by Papua New Guinea to the management of this possible contradiction was to disguise that relationship by referring to it in terms of an 'understanding' rather than a formal, public statement of commitment. This suited Papua New Guinea's philosophical approach to its foreign and security policies but the deliberate vagueness of an *understanding* had the potential to create uncertainty and misunderstanding, not least in the minds of those who were responsible for managing the policy.

From Australia's perspective, the Papua New Guinean approach fully suited its policy objectives. The proposals were well aligned with Australia's concept of the future defence relationship. The option of an 'understanding' was in keeping with Labor Party policy of avoiding new international military obligations which would have occurred if the post-independence defence relationship were to be formalised in an international treaty. It also met the objective identified by the Defence Committee of maximising Australia's options as to how it would respond to an external threat to Papua New Guinea, and in particular, of avoiding an open commitment. Kiki's positive response to the advice that Australia would seek only access to the naval base at Manus also accorded with the Defence Committee's recommendation. The similarity in the two countries' positions on these issues was, as Mench has argued, not unexpected.[18] Kiki was determined to ensure that Papua New Guinea asserted a strong degree of independence from Australia in its foreign and security policies and that this should be reflected in the post-independence security arrangements.

In his first sixteen months as Minister for Defence, Barnard had effectively steered the question of the long-term defence relationship away from any possibility that it would be represented by a treaty-level document which included the concept of an open commitment to come to Papua New Guinea's defence. He had made an early judgement that Australia should not involve itself in trying to restore order and stability in Papua New Guinea and he had also accepted the assessment that Papua New Guinea was not likely to be threatened by Indonesia. The two conclusions combined to reinforce his view that Australia's best approach was to keep a distance from the country once its formal obligations ended at independence. He agreed with the view that Australia needed to support Papua New Guinea and its defence force but considered that this would be through a defence cooperation program similar to those he advocated with other regional partners.

Kiki sets out PNG's defence policy

On 25 April 1974 Kiki addressed the House of Assembly on his government's defence and security policy. This was one of the first comprehensive statements by a Minister for Defence to the House of Assembly and, as such, carried great weight both internally and in Australia. The speech set out a number of decisions taken by the government on the functions, responsibilities and structure of the defence and police forces. Kiki also used the occasion to speak on Papua New Guinea's external environment. He commented:

> There is nothing which would lead us to believe that ... an attack is at all likely in the foreseeable future. If such attacks did occur, we would count on the fact that our more powerful neighbours could not avoid being concerned in the interests of their own security.[19]

Later, in answer to a parliamentary question, Kiki added:

> The Australian Government and the Australian people look towards this country as their close neighbour and in the event of attack and so on Australia will come and assist.[20]

Kiki's argument was consistent with the rather ambiguous statements he had made in previous months. He saw the new nation of Papua New Guinea as having few enemies in the world due to its comparative isolation and its desire to work cooperatively with its neighbours. He also wished to think in terms of Papua New Guinea being independent, particularly from its former colonial administrator, and able to manage its problems. Nevertheless, he maintained the view that there would be some ultimate form of assistance from Australia, if necessary. Australia's desire, which Kiki understood, was to keep open the option of how it would respond to any request for assistance. The Australian Government welcomed Kiki's statement although it made no reference to Kiki's remarks regarding a possible response to an external threat.

By mid-1974, after two years of discussion with PNG officials, Australia's position could be summarised as an acceptance of the idea that 'the principal instrument' in the defence relationship would be a Defence Cooperation Agreement, formally registered with the United Nations. As Pritchett pointed out to Barnard, this would meet an earlier concern held by the Labor Party that Australian forces serving overseas do so under an international agreement.[21] Subsidiary agreements would then follow such as a Loan Agreement specifying arrangements for the stationing of Australian personnel and units in Papua New Guinea and establishing safeguards for the use of Australian personnel serving in the PNGDF, particularly in areas of political sensitivity. A Status of Forces Agreement would establish the respective rights and obligations of the two governments in respect of visiting forces in each other's country. A Defence Aid Program would allow for defence aid to be directed to the PNGDF and finally a Financial

Understanding would allow for Australian subventions to the PNG defence budget.[22] The four agreements and programs would form a policy platform which would ensure another key Australian objective was realised, that is, that Australia would be Papua New Guinea's primary defence partner in the region. As to the long-term defence relationship and the issue of a long-term commitment, Pritchett advised Barnard that the discussions with PNG ministers and officials had established that:

> the defence commitment itself would not be a formal agreement. ... it is not in our interest or, we understand, PNG's wish, to have a formal agreement. We want to avoid any commitment that involves us automatically in PNG's external defence, or internal security. Our policy is to limit our mutual relationship in this respect to a statement of our common strategic interests, our intention to maintain contact and cooperation in the defence field and willingness to consult about circumstances affecting PNG's security from external threat or attack. ... this statement [would] not be embodied in any formal undertaking but declared in a communiqué.[23]

Somare and Kiki took the opportunity of the visit by the Chairman of the Chiefs of Staff, Sir Victor Smith, to Port Moresby in July 1974, to restate their reluctance to seek a treaty or formal agreement to serve as the text of a defence commitment.[24] Both expressed a strong preference for the more functional arrangements covering defence cooperation to be based on a mutual understanding rather than a formal agreement. Kiki once again expressed his concern that the proposed defence relationship should not be formulated in such a way as to arouse the curiosity and suspicion of neighbouring countries, particularly Indonesia. He acknowledged the Australian Government's policy preference for an international agreement to cover the stationing overseas of Australian troops but, such was his reluctance to accept the idea of international treaties on defence issues, that he argued an exception to this policy preference should be made based on a confidence drawn from the existing closeness of the two countries.

Barnard outlines the framework of the post-independence defence relationship

Barnard captured the essence of his approach to the defence relationship when he addressed the Chief of General Staff Exercise at Duntroon in August 1974. He made clear to the assembled members of the Defence Force that:

neither side [Australia or PNG] were in favour of a defence commitment of the ANZUS nature. [...] there can no longer be any thought of automatic involvement of Australian forces in Papua New Guinea. Nevertheless Ministers foresee continuing close relations in the defence field based in the long term on various strategic interests shared by the two countries and in the short term on Australia's willingness to continue to assist Papua New Guinea. ... Central to the defence relationship would be a mutual acceptance that the opportunity to consult is there, if the need arises.[25]

On 24 October 1974, Barnard advised the Australian Parliament of the outcome of the discussion between the two governments on the terms of a future defence relationship. Barnard reminded the Parliament that the government's approach to the question of the transfer of defence powers had been that 'decisions concerning Papua New Guinea's post-independence defence capability and the structure and roles of its force, belong with the Papua New Guinea Government'.[26] He then outlined the basic decisions announced by the Papua New Guinea Defence Minister in his speech in April 1974 regarding the size, functions, and structure of the PNGDF. He also advised that it was intended to transfer formal defence responsibility to Papua New Guinea at a date to be agreed by both countries. (Somare's request that the transfer take place on 1 December 1974 was subsequently amended to 4 March 1975.)[27] Barnard then set out the proposed principles to govern negotiations on the post-independence defence relations. He noted that these included:

> Neither Government wishes to enter a formal defence commitment.
>
> Both Governments wish to project a relationship which truly demonstrates the independent and sovereign status which Papua New Guinea will soon acquire.
>
> Both Governments foresee continuing close relations in the defence field, based in the long term on our common interests as immediate neighbours, and in the shorter term on Australia's willingness to continue to assist in the development and support of the Papua New Guinea Defence Force.
>
> Both Governments see as central to the defence relationship a mutual acceptance that the opportunity to consult is available if the need arises.[28]

Barnard also canvassed the issue of the possible involvement of Australian personnel in operational situations and noted that it was both governments' wish to avoid or minimise such a possibility. He referred to the continuing discussions on mechanisms to consult each other before possible deployment in what he described as 'quite exceptional circumstances'. These were taken to be occasions when the PNGDF could be called on to assist the police to restore law and order. Barnard concluded by noting that 'no external threat to Papua New Guinea is foreseen' and the Defence Force would only be used as a 'last resort' in restoring public order and internal security.[29] In Port Moresby, Kiki delivered an almost identical speech to the House of Assembly to describe the wish of both governments regarding the future defence relationship and long-term commitment.[30]

The two speeches drew together the ideas and suggestions that had been raised in the various conversations over the previous eighteen months concerning how best to express the long-term defence relationship. As such they represented the crystallisation of the ideas first examined by officials in February 1974 and later refined by Kiki and Barnard. At the same time the speeches also served to bring to a close this period in the negotiations and consultations. The major policy outlines had been established and accepted publicly by both governments with no disagreement on key principles. Barnard retired as Minister for Defence and from the Australian Parliament on 6 June 1975, one week before a scheduled visit to Port Moresby. He was succeeded by Bill Morrison. Morrison also held the portfolio of Minister Assisting the Minister for Foreign Affairs in matters relating to Papua New Guinea.

New obstacles block negotiations

By October 1974 the basic principles of the post-independence defence relationship had been agreed upon. A final document could have been concluded and the details of the post-independence defence relationship could have been made public at that time. However, a number of uncertainties and conflicting demands emerged to delay the drafting of the final text and the securing of ministerial agreement. The delays, in part, can be attributed to the sheer volume of administrative work now before both governments as they prepared for independence. Such was the demand that in June 1974 Somare moved the date for independence to 16 September 1975. Whitlam agreed to this new arrangement. He had also made clear to officials that 'we cannot expect to make enduring or acceptable arrangements with Papua

New Guinea [on a long-term defence arrangement] until she can negotiate as an equal independent state'.[31] This view was consistent with comments he had made the year before to officials in Foreign Affairs when he noted that 'defence and economic arrangements with a country before independence produce post-independence regrets and resentments'.[32]

Whitlam was also aware of the intense pressure on Somare from the leaders of the Bougainville secessionist movement to accede to their demands for independence and their intention to promote their cause internationally. He took the opportunity to state not only for Somare's benefit but also for that of other leaders in Papua New Guinea that the 'Australian Government's policy is that Papua New Guinea should come to independence on 16 September as one country, in accordance with the wishes of the overwhelming majority of Papua New Guinea's elected representatives. The Australian Government will give no sympathy, aid or support in any form to any groups in Papua New Guinea working to undermine their country's unity'.[33] With the pressure from the separatist movement in Bougainville undiminished as 16 September approached, Whitlam and other Australian ministers regularly repeated the Australian Government's wish that Papua New Guinea come to independence as a united country.

Finally, the uncertainty that gripped Australia in the second half of 1975, as a result of the constitutional crisis that ended in the dismissal of the Whitlam Government on 11 November, ensured that there would be no quick conclusion to the defence negotiations. In regional terms, the period also saw an increase in activity by the Irian Jaya separatist movement, Organisasi Papua Merdeka (OPM), and a loss of equilibrium in Indonesia's relations with both Australia and Papua New Guinea following Indonesia's invasion of East Timor at the close of 1975.[34]

A further issue emerged reflecting the increasing assertiveness of indigenous Papua New Guinean officials. In August 1975 Papua New Guinean defence officials advised that Australian servicemen serving with the PNGDF would be subject to the jurisdiction of the soon-to-be-established Village Courts. The Village Court system was intended to administer indigenous and customary law at the village level in both civil and criminal matters. The courts would have highly modified judicial procedures regarding the taking of evidence, the role of witnesses, the form of punishment and the absence of an avenue of appeal. Procedures and punishments would vary from court to court depending on local custom.

The Australian Chiefs of Staff objected strongly but Papua New Guinean ministers would not compromise. They quickly articulated the view that this was an important test of the new nation's ability to introduce its own system of justice, with its own forms of punishment and to determine who should appear before the courts. This single issue stymied any further progress on settling the terms of the future defence relationship. A further twelve months elapsed before a solution was found. The effect was to delay the completion of negotiations on post-independence defence arrangements until early 1977.

As the Australian delegation travelled to Port Moresby in mid-September 1975 to celebrate Papua New Guinea's passage to independence there was little attention given to the outstanding defence issues. The briefing prepared for Whitlam outlined the stage reached in the negotiations and the difficulties over the jurisdiction of the Village Courts. It did not encourage Whitlam to try to resolve this problem. In the speeches marking the celebration Whitlam did not refer to the long-term defence relationship. Instead, he spoke enthusiastically of the prospects for the broader relationship between the two countries.

With Papua New Guinea's now independent Australia's responsibilities for New Guinea under the United Nations Trusteeship Agreement lapsed. Australia also ceased to have an international obligation to defend the territory of New Guinea. It was no longer responsible for the administration of Papua. Australia passed to Papua New Guinea a Defence Force of about 3600, a small maritime capacity and a very small air capacity. It also passed on about $70 million in defence assets and undertook to introduce a defence cooperation program with a budget of about $15.7 million in its first year and a one-off defence financial assistance grant of $8 million. In addition, 650 Australian servicemen, of whom about 490 were integrated into the PNGDF as 'loan' personnel, remained in the country to serve as specialist, technical and support personnel. Only about six Australians were stationed in PNGDF combat battalions.[35]

On 9 October 1975, in one of the last acts of the Labor Government, Morrison, (Minister for Defence), tabled in the House of Representatives a set of documents relating to the interim defence understandings between Australia and the now independent Papua New Guinea. The first document represented an interim Status of Forces Arrangements. The second related to interim undertakings governing loan personnel attached to the PNGDF. The third set out the consultative mechanisms to ensure the Australian authorities were informed and approved of the deployment of Australian loan personnel to 'politically sensitive situations'.[36] The fourth document listed the Australian Defence Force units in Papua New Guinea.

The Joint Statement by Australian and PNG Defence Ministers accompanying the tabling of the documents 'confirmed that neither Government wished at this time to finalise arrangements which could bind the post-independence Government of Papua New Guinea. The ministers declared however that, as soon as practicable, the two governments would negotiate the long-term defence relationship along the lines of the interim arrangements'.[37] The letters exchanged between the two governments established the intention of both to continue with the existing program of defence cooperation.[38] The documents and the accompanying press statements made no reference to the earlier discussions on the nature of a possible long-term defence commitment between the two countries.

Conclusion

The Whitlam Government had agreed on the set of revised judgements about the strategic importance of Papua New Guinea to Australia. It had accepted that:

i) PNG was of abiding strategic relevance to Australia.
ii) Control of PNG by an unfriendly power would seriously disadvantage the defence of Australia.
iii) Australia's principal interest was that its defence relationship with PNG be the primary defence relationship of the State.
iv) The main elements of that relationship should be defence aid, continued access to the naval facilities at Manus Island and a public expression of the relationship – but preferably not in terms of a formal commitment to the defence of PNG in all circumstances.
v) A decision on the nature and presentation of the defence relationship should be deferred until PNG views were obtained.
vi) Australia should avoid close involvement and specifically military intervention in PNG's internal security affairs.[39]

It had also endorsed the recommendation set out in the 1973 Report by the Defence Committee regarding the type of defence commitment Australia should enter into with an independent Papua New Guinea. Papua New Guinea retained its place as one of the countries of prime strategic importance to Australia, but it was no longer considered 'vital' to the defence of Australia, nor was there an expectation that Australia would come to its defence in any and all circumstances. The Labor Government did not accept the argument that Papua New Guinea served as a shield for the defence of the Australian continent. Nor did it wish to use Papua New Guinea to project Australia's military capabilities further into Southeast Asia. Both these concepts were contrary to Labor's views on how it wished Australia to be seen by its neighbours.

The Whitlam Government, and particularly Barnard and Morrison, who set the policy directions on this issue, shared a preference for the pragmatic approach recommended by senior defence and foreign affairs advisers. Morrison, quietly but quickly, abandoned the Labor Party's commitment expressed in its platform to negotiate a defence treaty with an independent Papua New Guinea. He realised the dangers and complications for Australia of such an undertaking. He and Barnard also saw the danger of being held hostage to a new and internationally immature state whose own actions could potentially drag Australia into a dispute with its neighbours. He and Barnard had wanted to avoid this possibility. Australia feared that, in such an eventuality, it could be asked to intervene and rescue Papua New Guinea. In doing so, Australia's relations with Southeast Asia, and in particular Indonesia, could be placed at risk.

Whitlam and Barnard also shared their senior advisers' strong preference for not jeopardising Australia's own security assurance with the United States under the ANZUS Treaty by advocating the extension of the treaty to an independent Papua New Guinea. Such a solution was risky not only from the point of view of the treaty partners becoming involved in Papua New Guinea's own disputes, but also because the debate on the extension in the United States Senate carried with it the possibility of the Treaty being weakened and hence undermining one of the fundamental pillars of Australia's own defence policy. Australia was not willing to take this chance for the sake of securing a multilateral defence guarantee covering Papua New Guinea.

However, while concern about the actions of an independent Papua New Guinea in its relations with its neighbours was a major influence on Australia's approach to this issue, the overriding influence on Australian decision makers was a continuing fear of being drawn into Papua New Guinea's internal security problems. Australia wanted Papua New Guinea to come to independence as a united country. This had prompted Whitlam to make his statement in June 1975 confirming Australia's strong preference for a united Papua New Guinea. The government was prepared to be as helpful as possible to promote Papua New Guinea's independence, but it, and senior defence and foreign affairs officials, were equally determined to resist any prospect that Australia would have to intervene in resolving internal security disputes.

The Whitlam Government was fortunate that Papua New Guinea did not press for a formal and specific defence commitment. The wish by Somare, and more particularly Kiki, that Papua New Guinea be seen by the international community as free and independent of Australia, and prepared to establish its own relationships without the suggestion of Australia acting as guarantor, coincided with and suited Australia's interest. A close relationship with Australia was accepted as inevitable, so long as it did not undermine the perception of independence. A formal defence tie would be seen by Papua New Guinea as doing just that. Kiki's references to an 'understanding' were vague and, at times, they confused both Papua New Guineans and Australians, but the ambiguity was sufficient to satisfy his political requirements and not detract from the new nation's sense of independence.

Chapter 12

A SETTLEMENT IS REACHED
1976–1977

> 'Although neither country seeks formal undertakings it will be important that they maintain close consultations regarding any developments that could affect their security'.
>
> Australian Defence White Paper
> 1976

Malcolm Fraser was sworn in as Prime Minister on 22 December 1975 after securing an overwhelming victory at the general election following the dismissal of the Whitlam Government. Fraser had been familiar with the issues surrounding the defence relationship with the then Territory of Papua and New Guinea from his earlier appointments as Minister for the Army (1966–1968) and Minister for Defence (1969–1971). While serving as Minister for the Army he had undertaken his first visit to Papua New Guinea in May 1967.[1] As Minister for Defence he had been closely involved in July 1970 in the controversy over the proposal to allow for the call-out of the Pacific Islands Regiment (PIR) to assist the police in controlling rioters in Rabaul. Fraser had attended the independence celebrations in Port Moresby in September 1975.

Fraser appointed Andrew Peacock as Minister for Foreign Affairs. Peacock too was familiar with Papua New Guinea from his time as Minister for the Army (March 1971–February 1972) and Minister for External Territories (February–December 1972). He had visited Port Moresby as recently as August 1975. Peacock had earlier brought a new level of energy to the portfolio of External Territories after the 'dead-hand paternalism' of Barnes and had been quick to engage the emerging leaders of Papua New Guinea, both elected and non-elected, in discussion about the future constitutional arrangements for the Territory.[2] In May 1972 he had written to Somare on the need for accelerated movement towards self-government and in July 1972 he had chaired one of the early meetings between Australian and Papua New Guinean ministers and officials on the transfer of responsibility and decision-making to the Territory.[3] He had encouraged Papua New Guineans to 'not just sit back and wait for [self-government] to happen', although he did not speak of independence. He took the view that 'Papua New Guinea will be our closest foreign neighbour; while we will be her closest source of aid and expertise'.[4] However, while Papua New Guinea would 'occupy a very special position in Australia's policy' Australia would not seek or assert 'an exclusive relationship' with an independent Papua New Guinea.[5]

The third appointment of relevance was that of James Killen as Minister for Defence. Killen had served as Minister for the Navy (November 1969–March 1971) and in that capacity had visited Papua and New Guinea in early 1970 and had, on Gorton's instructions, met with the leaders of the Mataungan Association.[6]

The joint Liberal–National Party policy platform for the 1975 election had placed an emphasis on maintaining a close relationship with an independent Papua New Guinea. It made no specific reference to a defence relationship.

Two new governments – same issues

During the first weeks of the Whitlam Government, Whitlam and his ministers had visited Port Moresby and had come under pressure to make early decisions on the management of the bilateral relationship. In a striking historical parallel, the Fraser ministry came under early pressure to receive Somare. Papua New Guinea's new Prime Minister had asked to visit Canberra to discuss the terms of the aid relationship agreed with the Whitlam Government and the immediate problems faced by his government to maintain its foreign exchange reserves. He had written to Fraser on 30 January 1976 and warned that the decisions taken in 1975 by Australia on the composition of its aid commitment had 'left us in such a precarious financial position' that it could lead 'to major difficulties for our relationship. ... It would be all too easy for an Australian government to accidently destroy our future prospects' while there would be clear 'threats to regional stability ... if a nation fails to surmount [its difficulties]'.[7]

In preparation for Somare's visit the Foreign Affairs and Defence Committee of Cabinet (FADC) examined three submissions on the bilateral relationship with Papua New Guinea, the threatened secession of Bougainville and the future long-term defence relationship with Papua New Guinea. In responding to the first two submissions ministers made clear that 'Australia had an overriding national interest in the maintenance of a stable, viable and united Papua New Guinea'.[8] They also 'expressed concern that this interest might be prejudiced if adequate Australian support was not provided'.[9] Fraser told his ministers that 'it would be infinitely costly for Australia if Somare fails' and that Australia had to 'help him in the eyes of [his] own people'. He emphasised the 'overriding interest of Australia in a unified and stable PNG'.[10] Alan Renouf, who had succeeded Sir Keith Waller as Secretary of the Department of Foreign Affairs in February 1974 and had attended the meeting of the FADC, told his departmental colleagues that the Cabinet committee had emphasised the assessment that 'a united Papua New Guinea was very definitely in the interests of both Australia and Papua New Guinea'.[11] In coming to these views the Fraser Government had not deviated from the policy position adopted and articulated by the Whitlam Government.

On Bougainville specifically, the Cabinet agreed to assure Somare of Australia's 'support in his pursuit of a united Papua New Guinea'. In a departure from established policy ministers asked for a new paper which would examine the options open to Australia to assist Port Moresby in its dispute with the secessionist movement on Bougainville. In a letter from the Department of Defence to Foreign Affairs in September 1976, Defence advised that it was the 'firm recollection' of its Secretary, Sir Arthur Tange, who was present at the Cabinet meeting on 2 March 1976, that:

> Cabinet was not so concerned about possible involvement of Australian servicemen in support of PNG Government operations in Bougainville. Cabinet had already ruled on this aspect. Rather it wanted a paper which examined the implications of all options open to Australia to assist the PNG Government to maintain or reassert its authority in Bougainville – including the use of force from Australia. The Government did not exclude the possibility of military intervention from Australia in Bougainville. The decision would depend upon the circumstances pertaining at the time. What the Government wanted

was a clear indication of the consequences domestically, internationally and within PNG of Australian intervention or, conversely, a decision to stand aside.[12]

An indication of Fraser's thoughts on the issue of military intervention were revealed in an interview with Peter Hastings in May 1976 when, in response to a question as to whether there were any circumstances under which Australia would contemplate military intervention, Fraser responded:

> that's a very hypothetical question. I wouldn't want to rule out the possibility. But at the same time I would very much hope that the skill of the Papua New Guinea Government, the general support that Australia can provide in many other ways which I'm not going to define would make any such eventuality quite unnecessary.[13]

As events unfolded, the paper sought by the Cabinet did not eventuate. Meetings and negotiations continued between Somare and the leaders of Bougainville, concluding with the signing of the Bougainville Agreement on 7 August 1976 and the inauguration of a Provincial Government on 26 November 1976. As part of the agreement, Somare had accepted the introduction of a provincial government in Papua New Guinea.[14]

The third submission sought guidance on the question of the future long-term defence relationship.[15] On this issue Fraser and his colleagues did not deviate from established policy. The Minister for Defence (Killen) advised his colleagues of the situation that had been reached prior to independence and the dismissal of the Whitlam Government. He noted that neither government wished to enter into a formal commitment to the defence of the other; both governments were seeking to project a relationship which demonstrated Papua New Guinea's independent status; and both governments accepted that the concept of the opportunity to consult would be available if the need arose. Killen also put before his colleagues the recommendations made by the Defence Committee in November 1973 and its emphasis on ensuring that PNG's primary defence relationship should be with Australia. Killen noted that a further meeting of the Defence Committee in October 1975 had confirmed the views set out in November 1973.[16]

Killen warned his colleagues that a 'firm commitment' from Australia could also encourage 'some elements in the PNG government and the Defence Force Command … to think in terms of the early use of military force, e.g. regarding border incursions from the Indonesian side and the situation in Bougainville'. He added that a 'firm commitment from Australia could encourage this disposition and expose Australia to pressure for support. Even though a commitment related only to external defence, a PNG government under serious internal challenge may well not observe this distinction'.[17] While he had highlighted the need to be aware of Indonesia, he added that 'substantial Indonesian military penetration of PNG, beyond possible limited border forays, was assessed by the Defence Committee as improbable. ... [An] external threat from any other source [was] also assessed as improbable'.[18]

The assessment by the Defence Committee and the references in the Cabinet paper reflected the doubts that Australia continued to hold regarding the behaviour of an independent Papua New Guinea. Australia was not prepared to place its full trust in the actions of the newly independent state and was not prepared to open up the possibility that Australia would have to respond in some way to Papua New Guinea's actions against Indonesia, notably on the border.

Killen then went on to set out the elements of the long-term defence relationship which had been discussed under the previous government. He noted that it was proposed that a Joint Statement be issued by the two defence ministers. It would refer to the desire of both governments to continue close relations in the defence field based on the common strategic interests of PNG and Australia as immediate neighbours. The Statement would also record a 'request from PNG for continuing assistance in the development and support of the PNGDF and the willingness of Australia to continue to provide this support'. It:

> would specifically affirm that both governments stood ready, as part of this continuing close defence relationship, to consult together at any time, at the request of either, about any matter which might affect their strategic involvement or any aspect of their mutual defence relations.[19]

Killen sought Cabinet endorsement of the recommendation that there be no formal Australian defence commitment to defend Papua New Guinea and that instead there be practical, cooperative relations, including a Defence Cooperation Program, that would in part 'establish the primacy of PNG's defence relationship with Australia'. He sought approval to negotiate a Joint Statement along the lines he had set out.

The Cabinet decision simply states that the Foreign Affairs and Defence Committee 'took note of the paper'.[20] In subsequent correspondence with the Department of Defence it was recorded that 'there was very little discussion of this item'.²¹ In correspondence between the Secretary of Cabinet, John Menadue, and the Department of Defence, Menadue advised that the Prime Minister had directed that a fresh submission be prepared on the subject of the defence relationship. To add to the confusion he suggested that it also 'reflect some of the thinking on the importance that the Australian Government attaches to its support for a unified Papua New Guinea and ... canvass the implications and the political prospects associated with secessionist movements (particularly Bougainville)'.²²

Somare arrived in Canberra on 4 March 1976. Both he and the Australian Government were preoccupied with the question of how the Bougainville issue could be defused and how to resolve the very acrimonious debate that had developed over the level of development assistance Australia would provide to Papua New Guinea. These two issues dominated the discussions.

The communiqué issued following Somare's visit highlighted the close nature of the relationship between the two countries and their 'many abiding common interests'. It also stressed that the relationship would be based on the sovereign, independent status of each country and on a mutual appreciation of each country's independent national interest. The aid issue, as well as the outstanding question of the country's foreign reserves, were resolved with a new level of development assistance put in place and an increase approved in the standby arrangements to the Bank of PNG from the Reserve Bank of Australia. On Bougainville, the communiqué noted that Bougainville was an internal issue for Papua New Guinea and that Australia was no longer directly involved. The long-term defence relationship was mentioned only in passing, along with other outstanding issues in the bilateral relationship yet to be settled, with both governments agreeing to 'proceed steadily towards completion of appropriate agreements or understandings'.²³

Clarifying outstanding issues

Killen had been disappointed that the discussion in Cabinet in March had led only to his submission being 'noted'. He had hoped for a clear endorsement of the policy positions he had put forward and approval to enter into negotiations with his counterpart, Kiki. He was determined to have the issues re-examined in Cabinet and in July 1976 presented a new submission.²⁴

Killen sought Cabinet endorsement of the recommendations regarding a long-term defence relationship which he had made in his earlier submission. He put forward no new argument or information. On this occasion a briefing note to the Prime Minister from his department stated that officials had 'reservations' about the recommendation that 'there be no formal Australian commitment to defend Papua New Guinea'. It described the wording as 'ambiguous' and argued that 'we see the need to avoid a formal defence agreement with Papua New Guinea but we also think that Australia should have a defence policy of preparedness to defend PNG if required'.[25] In the discussion in the Foreign Affairs and Defence Committee Cabinet, Ian Sinclair (Minister for Primary Industry) argued that a defence agreement 'need not commit us positively' and, from the relevant entry in the Cabinet Notebook, appears to have suggested an ANZUS-type arrangement. He told his colleagues that he 'would be disappointed if it were only a statement. Australians feel there should be something'.[26] Fraser added that 'something more than a joint ministerial statement' was needed. He thought an exchange of letters could be a possible solution. Ministers agreed that the Minister for Defence, in consultation with the Minister for Foreign Affairs should:

> explore further with Papua New Guinea the modalities of a long-term arrangement including the possibilities for:
>
> i) a Government to Government Agreement; or
> ii) an Exchange of Letters; or
> iii) a Joint Statement by Prime Ministers or Defence Ministers.[27]

Two new governments – new strategic assessments

On 2 December 1976 Kiki tabled in the PNG Parliament the first detailed strategic assessment prepared since independence. The *1975–1976 Defence Report* identified the 'most immediate powers to be reckoned with are Indonesia and Australia'. It stated that 'in the foreseeable future the Government does not anticipate there will be a major conventional invasion of Papua New Guinea' but noted that the activities of anti-Indonesian dissidents in Irian Jaya could cause Indonesian security forces to spill over the border. The report identified the most 'relevant' threat to Papua New Guinea as that posed to the country's maritime resources, particularly through illegal fishing. The report reiterated the government's policy that 'we do not intend to enter into military pacts and alliances with the great powers. We wish to follow a path of universalism and will not participate in the great powers' quarrels'.[28] It did refer to the existing interim defence arrangements with Australia covering practical issues such as supply support mechanisms and noted that permanent understandings were to be negotiated. The *Defence Report* also made clear that the government regarded the major function of the PNGDF as meeting external threats and that any involvement in internal security issues would be as a last resort.

The first post-independence defence assessment marked a significant milestone in the creation of a separate identity for Papua New Guinea's defence policy. Papua New Guinea was still closely linked to Australia but was confident enough to set out its own guiding principles and identify its own priorities. From Australia's perspective, the statement had emphasised the importance of Australia's practical measures of support to the PNGDF while at the same time it had confirmed that Papua New Guinea would not seek a defence treaty.

At the same time as Papua New Guinea was preparing and then delivering its inaugural defence paper Australian officials were also preoccupied with drafting a new strategic outlook for the Fraser Government. A resulting document, *Australian Strategic Analysis and Defence Policy Objectives* (ASADPO) was endorsed by the Defence Committee in September 1976.[29] The ASADPO paper described Indonesia as possessing 'in relation to Australia attributes of both an ally and an adversary' and said there was 'no present likelihood of significant military threat to Australia from or through Indonesia'. It identified a 'possible but unlikely contingency of small-scale Indonesian military pressure against PNG'. It noted that 'Indonesia has legitimate interests in the stability of PNG and in its security'.[30]

Turning to Papua New Guinea, the paper identified the same themes which had appeared in strategic assessments since the late 1960s:

> Papua New Guinea's importance for the Australian defence interest resides in its geographic position and proximity; in the potential for trouble in PNG's relations with Indonesia; and in the security of extensive Australian interests in PNG, including some thirty thousand citizens. Past and present close association also gives Australia important obligations for the support of PNG, and these include defence support.[31]

The document also acknowledged the traditional argument that 'military lodgement in PNG by a power unfriendly to Australia would facilitate attack against Australia and lines of communication to Australia's north'. This contingency, however, was 'on today's outlook improbable and would be remote in time'.[32] The paper canvassed the issue of low-level incursions by Indonesian troops across the border and argued that as long as any incursion was limited and incidental there was no obvious Australian defence interest. If, however, Papua New Guinea attempted to use military force to prevent Indonesian forays it could in such circumstances ask for Australian assistance. The paper argued that 'it would not be in Australia's interests to allow PNG to involve Australia in a bilateral dispute with Indonesia brought to a crisis by PNG's own irresponsible conduct'.[33]

While the ASADPO paper had examined some of the contingencies surrounding an external threat to PNG, its authors devoted most of their attention to the issue of the country's internal instability. They argued that 'Australian strategic policy can tolerate a significant degree of internal disorder – while preferring, of course, more stable conditions'.[34] The possibility that PNG could seek Australian defence support in its internal security operations was assessed as 'unlikely beyond the present level of limited logistic, transport and communications support'.

The paper's reluctance to endorse the concept that Australian defence forces could become involved in responding to internal disorders was amplified dramatically when examining the question of the possible fragmentation of Papua New Guinea. It assessed fragmentation as having 'major disadvantages for Australia's strategic interests' and stated that 'the defence preference for a united PNG is clear'.[35] The paper examined in detail the pros and cons of Australian military involvement on Bougainville and concluded that any such decision 'would require very careful assessment' at the time.

On the question of the long-term defence relationship with Papua New Guinea the ASADPO paper made clear that:

> a basic requirement of Australian strategic policy is a defence relationship with PNG that sustains PNG's acceptance of, and confidence in, Australia as its primary strategic partner. The relationship should make Australia's major interest clear also to other powers, and to PNG's expatriate population, on whom the national working and development of PNG so heavily depends.[36]

In referring to the principles of a long-term defence relationship it noted that:

> This relationship involves a clear statement of the common strategic interests of the two countries and their intention to maintain defence cooperation; on-going consultations about strategic developments and

policy requirements; and a substantial practical working defence relationship embodied in arrangements for project aid, training, attachment of service officers, supply support, military exercising, and operational support as circumstances require and the Government approves.[37]

In November 1976 Killen tabled in the House of Representatives a sanitised version of the *Australian Strategic Analysis and Defence Policy Objectives Paper* entitled *Australian Defence*.[38]

Negotiating the long-term defence relationship

Killen presented his third Cabinet submission in twelve months on Australia's defence relationship with Papua New Guinea when in December 1976 he sought Cabinet approval for the terms of a Joint Statement on the long-term relationship. In addition, he sought Cabinet agreement to the terms of the Supply Support Arrangements, the Status of Forces Agreement and procedures covering the deployment of Australian personnel in the PNGDF to politically sensitive areas of operation.[39] He referred to the statement by Kiki in the 1975–1976 PNG Defence report reiterating PNG's wish that it not enter into a pact or alliance and recommended to Cabinet that Australia accept PNG's suggestion that the statement instead be issued by both Prime Ministers during Fraser's proposed visit to Port Moresby in February 1977. Killen noted that 'pressure for any more formal accord could be counter-productive and could be represented as a departure from our own public statement in the Defence White Paper that neither government seeks formal undertakings'.[40]

Killen advised his colleagues that the proposed Joint Statement would note:

> The two Prime Ministers affirmed that, on the basis of their historic links and their common strategic concerns, both their Governments:
> - attached high importance to maintaining close cooperation in defence matters;
> - recognised the importance of their defence relationship in the context of their common desire to strengthen peace and stability in their region; and therefore
> - stood ready to consult at any time, at the request of either, about any matter which might affect their security or any other aspects of their defence relationship.[41]

As it turned out, after nearly five years of debate in Canberra and negotiations with Port Moresby, the record in the Cabinet Notebook of the final consideration of the long-term defence relationship consists of two lines with Peacock asking Fraser whether he was 'happy' with the proposed joint statement and Fraser replying 'yes'.[42]

In January 1977 officials conducted their final round of negotiations in Canberra with the text based on the earlier themes and the outline presented to Cabinet by Killen. In a further historical echo Somare visited Jakarta prior to the arrival of Fraser just as he had visited Jakarta before Whitlam's visit to Port Moresby. Shortly before he left Jakarta Somare again confirmed that 'Papua New Guinea did not intend to establish any military pacts with other countries such as Australia or New Zealand'.[43]

Fraser, accompanied by Foreign Minister Andrew Peacock, travelled to Port Moresby and held a formal round of consultations with Somare and Kiki on 8 February.[44] The talks covered a wide range of bilateral as well as regional and international questions with the outstanding matters associated with the negotiation of the Torres Strait Treaty the most contentious bilateral issue. Discussion on the terms of the long-term defence relationship was relatively straightforward. Both sides repeated their opposition to a formal defence commitment. Kiki said that 'it was pointless for Papua New Guinea and Australia to have a formal defence agreement'. He argued that 'if one existed other countries such as the Soviet Union could also want to seek such an agreement with PNG'. Kiki added that he 'considered that no formal defence agreement was necessary. What happened to Australia and PNG was such that he considered no formal defence agreement was necessary'. Somare agreed with Kiki and added that 'there was a certain trust and confidence between the two countries which made a formal defence agreement unnecessary'. Moreover, 'Australia and PNG understood and trusted each other and should continue on the understanding between the two governments and peoples'. Fraser expressed his full agreement with these sentiments. He added that 'the two countries shared common interests which were born out of history and geography. Regardless of how tight defence agreements were the important thing that mattered was the relationship which existed between the two countries at any one time'.[45] The two Prime Ministers accepted the terms of the proposed Joint Statement drafted by officials.

The Joint Statement was released on 11 February 1977 in the form of a press statement shortly before Fraser left Port Moresby. The other elements of the 'defence package' including the terms of the Status of Forces Agreement and the Supply Support Arrangements, were also formalised and made public at this time. The Joint Statement read:

> The two Prime Ministers affirmed that both their Governments attached high importance to continuing the close cooperation between their two countries in defence matters. They acknowledged their Governments' desire to contribute to the strengthening of peace and stability in their common region. They declared that it was their Governments' intention to consult, at the request of either, about matters affecting their common security interests and about other aspects of their defence relationship.
>
> Mr Fraser confirmed Australia's willingness to continue, at the request of the Papua New Guinea Government, to assist in the development of the Papua New Guinea Defence Force, and in development projects carried out by Australian Service Units in Papua New Guinea ...[46]

The Joint Statement had a strong 'political' status or at least represented a political intent as it had been authorised by the two Prime Ministers. But it did not represent a binding commitment under international law. It avoided any specifics as to the likely type of event or circumstance which would trigger consultations and did not establish any mechanism for such consultations. Australia had drawn on the terms of the Five Power Defence Arrangements with Malaysia and Singapore rather than those of the ANZUS Treaty with its ANZUS Ministerial Council as the means to facilitate consultations. While visits were to be frequent, the first formal meeting between defence officials to discuss the defence cooperation program did not take place until 1979.

There was little media interest in the Joint Statement. Fraser responded to one general question at a press conference on departure from Port Moresby by describing the Statement as a 'communiqué and understanding that would carry us through in the future'.[47] He made no mention of the Joint Statement in his letter of appreciation sent to Somare after the visit.[48]

It was left to Killen when tabling the statement and accompanying documentation in the House of Representatives on 23 February 1977 to note that:

They demonstrate, in a practical way, the importance Australia and Papua New Guinea attach to a continuing and close relationship in the defence field.

The agreement between the Australian and Papua New Guinea Governments to sustain their close cooperation in defence matters and the joint affirmation of their intention to consult at the request of either about matters affecting their common security is not the less significant – for each and for others – because their friendship is already so firmly and so openly established. This Parliament may look with pleasure and with no little pride upon the fact that in this new era of Papua New Guinea's independence and national sovereignty it has joined with Australia to reaffirm a clear and mutual interest in close cooperation and consultation in defence matters.[49]

The Joint Statement ended five years of deliberation, debate and negotiation over the nature of the long-term defence relationship Australia wished to have in place with an independent Papua New Guinea. Australia's objective was to secure its role as Papua New Guinea's primary defence partner and ally but to retain flexibility over the level and type of commitment it was prepared to conclude to maintain that objective.

Conclusion

The Fraser Government shared the concerns of the Whitlam Government about the future stability and unity of Papua New Guinea. Ministers had been particularly worried by the continued threat from the leaders of Bougainville that the island would secede from Port Moresby's control. These concerns influenced the government's approach to the negotiation of the terms of the long-term defence relationship. The Fraser Government also adopted the Whitlam Government's policy position of wishing to maintain maximum flexibility in responding to possible internal and external security problems that could erupt in the country. In this the Fraser Government was fortunate that the Somare Government, greatly influenced by its Defence Minister Maori Kiki, also wished to avoid any visible sign of dependency on its former colonial administrator.

The Fraser Government had accepted the orthodox view that Papua New Guinea was of strategic importance to Australia but that Australia's interests were best protected by avoiding a treaty-level formal commitment to come to its defence under any circumstance or to become embroiled in its internal troubles. Australia had secured its objective of articulating a sense of commitment without entering into a legally binding, open-ended guarantee. Australia had also secured the equally important objective of ensuring that it remained, and was seen by others in the region, as Papua New Guinea's primary defence partner. This close but not exclusive relationship ensured that Papua New Guinea would continue to occupy a significant place in future assessments of Australia's regional security environment.

Chapter 13

THE DEFENCE UNDERTAKING REVISITED: THE JOINT DECLARATION OF PRINCIPLES 1987 AND 2013

In 1974, the then Minister for Foreign Affairs, Senator Don Willesee, had posed the question to the incoming High Commissioner to Papua New Guinea, Tom Critchley, 'Would a broad treaty of friendship be a useful umbrella for our general relationship, possibly incorporating arrangements in regard to some of these subjects (Torres Strait matters, aid, cultural relations, defence, fisheries and civil aviation)?'.[1] The idea was not pursued within the Australian Government and lapsed. A similar concept had been suggested by Kim Beazley in the early 1970s prior to the election of the Whitlam Government.[2]

In August 1986, in the wake of financial pressures affecting the Australian budget, the Hawke Labor Government, elected in 1983, advised Papua New Guinea that the five-year aid program set out in the 1985 Memorandum of Understanding would be amended and that the level of aid would be reduced by $10 million for the period 1986–1987.

The reduction in the aid program caused great consternation in Port Moresby, not so much due to the size of the cut but rather because it was seen as a breach of faith. This was the first such negative measure implemented by Australia since 1975 and had come with little warning. As a result, many in Papua New Guinea began to view Australia as a somewhat unpredictable partner. The government of the recently-elected Prime Minister, Paias Wingti, accepted Australia's decision but decided that the relationship with Australia needed to be redefined. Wingti believed that a new arrangement was required which drew a line under the post-colonial period and set the two countries on a new path in their relationship. In this line of thinking he was assisted by Bill Dihm, the Secretary of PNG's

Department of Foreign Affairs. Both Wingti and Dihm represented a new generation of PNG leaders who were less closely associated with those who had taken the country to independence in 1975 and were less sentimental in their approach to the relationship with Australia. Both placed more importance on securing formal written assurances than on relying on personal ties and shared history to guide the relationship.

In December 1986 the Wingti Government presented Australia with the draft of a proposed Joint Declaration of Principles (JDP) and an Integrated Development Package (IDP). The draft JDP was a comprehensive document the scope of which embraced nearly all aspects of the bilateral relationship, ranging from trade, investment, private sector cooperation, development assistance, legal cooperation, border administration and assistance in combating smuggling to terrorism and crime. It strongly emphasised the principle of mutual respect for each nation's independence, sovereignty and equality. Perhaps reflecting the sense of uncertainty which had entered Papua New Guinea's relationship with Australia, Wingti proposed that the JDP be a treaty-level document. As such, it would be more difficult to break or amend and would be enforceable under international law. The PNG proposal included the idea of a Ministerial Forum which would meet regularly to review issues in the bilateral relationship.

Although taken by surprise, Australia welcomed the Wingti Government's initiative and endorsed the fundamental principles underlying it. Officials met in Port Moresby in 1987 to discuss the terms of the proposed declaration and reached agreement on almost all the text proposed by Papua New Guinea. However, the draft JDP also contained a set of clauses which sought to revisit the terms of the defence commitment agreed by Prime Ministers Somare and Fraser in 1977. The proposed redefinition was to cause a particular concern for the Australian Government.

In August 1987 Bill Hayden, Minister for Foreign Affairs and Trade, sought Cabinet's endorsement for Australia's approach to the draft Joint Declaration and for the negotiation of the articles dealing with the revised terms of the defence relationship.[3] Hayden was generally sympathetic to the PNG initiative and acknowledged that the draft reflected the 'desire of the PNG Government ... to put relations with Australia on a more balanced footing and a PNG attempt to establish its identity with Australia'.[4] He drew attention to a 'problem mainly in the area of defence' and advised his colleagues that the PNG Minister for Foreign Affairs had said that a 'major consideration behind the JD (Joint Declaration) is PNG's desire to strengthen Australia's security commitment to it'. (In attachment C to the Cabinet Submission it is stated that PNG proposed a commitment as follows: 'the two Governments shall cooperate in meeting common threats to their security, including armed attacks against either country, in accordance with their respective constitutional processes'.)[5] Hayden made clear his strong objections to the PNG draft proposal. He described it as 'provid[ing] for cooperation in meeting unspecified common threats'. He warned that to go beyond the terms of the 1977 Prime Ministerial Joint Statement, which he strongly supported, would present 'real dangers … not the least being a very real potential for PNG to interpret any new wording as an explicit and concrete commitment in circumstances where, I am concluding, we would be prudent and sober enough not to want to act'. Knowingly or not, Hayden drew on similar arguments to those that had circulated in Canberra in the late 1960s and 1970s when he said that 'an explicit and concrete undertaking' could 'make us hostages to the impulsive and unwise behaviour of an unsteady and poorly led PNG Government'. He also questioned how Indonesia would comprehend the signing of such a commitment and concluded that 'our bilateral ties with PNG would, at the very least, be regarded by Indonesia with suspicion and even hostility'.

Hayden was mystified as to why Papua New Guinea had proposed such a strong defence commitment with Australia when it had only months earlier signed a Treaty of Mutual Respect, Friendship and Cooperation with Indonesia. He accepted that his strong objections to the PNG draft might not be endorsed by his ministerial colleagues and proposed, 'only most reluctantly', a fall-back position which would not 'explicitly or implicitly commit us unreservedly to the defence of PNG in all circumstances'; allow Australia 'ample flexibility of response'; reflect the historical and strategic relationship between Australia and Papua New Guinea; encourage Papua New Guinea to act responsibly with its neighbours; and oblige it to maintain a reasonable level of defence effort.[6]

In an attachment to his submission Hayden presented Cabinet with a comprehensive review of the question of the strategic importance of Papua New Guinea to Australia and examined the pros and cons of various alternate wordings intended to capture the terms of a revised defence relationship and commitment.

In explaining the strategic significance of Papua New Guinea to Australia the paper reflected many of the themes that had appeared in similar papers written in the 1960s and 1970s. It argued that:

PNG's importance for Australian defence interests rests on three basic considerations: its proximity to north-eastern Australia and to the sea lines of communication to our north; the presence in PNG of substantial numbers of Australian citizens; and the potential in PNG's relations with Indonesia for disturbance of Australia's relations with Indonesia. This combination of factors gives PNG unique strategic importance to Australia.[7]

Again, reflecting the arguments of earlier Strategic Basis Papers, the document described how the historical ties with PNG gave Australia 'a strong interest in the security of PNG'. It warned that Australia's security would be significantly disadvantaged if a hostile power were to gain lodgement in or control over PNG as this would allow such a power to project maritime force over Australia's east coast and sea lanes. It also warned that should Indonesia exercise a dominant influence over PNG, the 'range of issues over which differences could arise between Australia and PNG would ... be considerably extended and would give rise to increased uncertainty in our strategic prospects'. The paper drew ministers' attention to the fact that successive Australian governments had pursued a policy of 'ensuring that PNG's primary strategic relationship is with Australia and is seen by Indonesia to be so'. As long as Indonesia believed that Australia exercised 'effective and favourable influence' in Papua New Guinea it would not try to advance its own influence in the country.

The paper attached to Hayden's Cabinet submission drew ministers' attention to the conclusions of the Review of Australian Defence Capabilities (the Dibb report) which had been accepted by the Hawke Government as a document of fundamental significance in determining its defence policy. Paul Dibb had long been a leading advocate of the critical importance of geography in guiding a nation's assessment of its strategic priorities. He had developed and publicised the concept of an area of 'direct military interest' for Australia and had represented this zone as Australia's northern air and sea approaches and the island and archipelagic states to the north through which a threat could be mounted.[8] The Dibb report, as quoted in the Cabinet submission, had judged that Australia 'would be likely to have few options other than to support PNG's territorial integrity if it were to be threatened' but also judged that the 'contingency of [a] major Indonesian attack on PNG lacks credibility'.[9] The Dibb report, again as quoted in the Cabinet submission, had however, assessed that the 'strategic significance of Papua New Guinea for Australia's security was not of such a dimension as to require a comprehensive', unqualified security commitment and that Australia's 'interests were served by elements of ambiguity' in any undertaking to Papua New Guinea. At the same time, Australia 'would not want Papua New Guinea to assume that it could provoke Indonesia safe in the knowledge that Australian military support would be forthcoming in all circumstances'.[10]

Returning to the question of how to respond to the Papua New Guinea draft proposal, Hayden argued that acceptance would disadvantage Australia in that the wording in the draft text was stronger than either the ANZUS Treaty or the Five Power Defence Arrangement and would be interpreted by other countries, notably Indonesia, as marking a major shift in Australia's defence policy and posture 'to a more offensive orientation'.[11] He suggested the three most appropriate options were: to retain the wording of the 1977 Joint Statement; employ similar wording to that in the Five Power Defence Arrangements; or use a weaker form of wording than in the Five Power Defence Arrangements. The paper examined in detail the advantages and disadvantages of these three options.

Other departments objected to Hayden's recommendation that Australia not go beyond the terms of the 1977 Joint Statement in responding to the PNG draft. The Department of Prime Minister and Cabinet argued that such a response 'carries a high risk of affecting adversely PNG's perception of the value of defence relations with Australia and also of exacerbating PNG's suspicions that Australian interest in PNG's future prospects is declining'. Defence agreed that 'Australia's strategic and defence policy objectives can best be maintained by providing PNG with a stronger undertaking'.[11a]

The decision reached by Cabinet clearly indicates that Hayden's recommendation was rejected. The decision noted that Australia agreed in principle to the proposal for a Joint Declaration but rejected PNG's suggestion that it be a treaty-level document. As to the proposed defence commitment, ministers rejected Hayden's preferred option not to go beyond the words in the 1977 statement and agreed that the following text be proposed:

> the two Governments will consult, at the request of either, about matters affecting their common security interests. In the event of external armed attack threatening the national sovereignty of either country, such consultation would be conducted for the purpose of each Government deciding what measures should be taken, jointly or separately, in relation to that attack.[12]

The decision also recommended that 'it should be made clear to PNG that the ... formulation does not necessarily imply the measures taken would be military measures and that they could be diplomatic ones'.[13]

In the ensuing negotiations Papua New Guinea accepted the text proposed by Australia and the Joint Declaration of Principles was signed on 9 December 1987 by Prime Minister Wingti and Prime Minister Hawke during Wingti's visit to Canberra.[14] The final text recognised that 'each government had primary responsibility for its own security' and valued their 'historical links and shared strategic interests'. The two governments undertook to continue to engage in defence cooperation and reaffirmed the existing agreement and arrangements covering the status of service personnel, supply support arrangements and consultations on the deployment of Australian loan personnel to politically sensitive situations. The Joint Declaration then set out the terms of the defence commitment using the words approved by the Australian Cabinet. The JDP was not elevated to a treaty-level document as first sought by Papua New Guinea. However, by virtue of being signed by two Prime Ministers it had the status of a document of 'political intent', that is, that Australia and Papua New Guinea assumed a political obligation to respect the terms of the Declaration.

A new Joint Declaration of Principles was signed in May 2013 during the visit by Prime Minister Julia Gillard to Port Moresby.[15] The new text noted that its undertakings would 'build on' the 1987 Joint Declaration of Principles. The 1987 commitment remains current and subsumed within the 2013 Declaration. The new Declaration noted that both countries were 'committed to strengthening their enduring defence partnership', particularly their 'mutual security interests, including maritime and border security, regional peacekeeping and disaster relief'.[16] The emphasis was placed on the bilateral defence cooperation program rather than mechanisms for responding to threats to either country. Like its predecessor, the 2013 text is a declaration of political intent and is not of treaty-level status. However, again, the fact that the document carries the signature of two Prime Ministers means that there is a strong responsibility on the part of both countries to meet their obligations. Consistent with its undertakings in 1977 and in 1987, Australia has reserved the right to determine how to respond to possible external threats to Papua New Guinea.

Although the various statements of Australia's commitment to the defence of Papua New Guinea could be described as being of 'political intent' rather than legally binding, this fact should not be interpreted as an indication of a declining Australian interest in the strategic importance of PNG in the region. In 1983 the Minister for Defence in the Hawke Government, Gordon Scholes, described Papua New Guinea as a 'major factor in Australia's security. Its geographical location, the potential for difficulties in its border relations with Indonesia, historical ties and continuing Australian involvement there contribute to PNG's abiding strategic importance for Australia'.[17] The 1986 Dibb 'Review of Australia's Defence Capabilities' described Australia as having a 'special interest' in Papua New Guinea and concluded that PNG was in a 'sphere of primary strategic interest'.[18] In 1989, the Minister for Foreign Affairs, Senator Gareth Evans, described 'Indonesia and Papua New Guinea [as] of particular importance because of the inescapable geographical reality that any military threat to Australia – unlikely though that currently is – would almost certainly be posed from or through our north'.[19] As noted in the Introduction, the Australian Defence White Paper, published in February 2016, argued that 'Australia cannot be secure if our immediate neighbourhood, including Papua New Guinea … becomes a source of threat to Australia'.[20]

Australia has maintained high-level defence consultations as well as an active defence cooperation program aimed at providing technical and other military training and assistance to strengthen the capability of the PNGDF. It has pursued a policy of ensuring that it is PNG's primary defence partner and, as a consequence, the government spends more of its defence cooperation funding with PNG than with any other country.[21] In 2015–2016 the budget for the program was $40 million. This is in addition to a non-defence aid program of over $558 million in the same period. In its 2013 Defence White Paper, Papua New Guinea noted that 'due to our historical, geographic and personal ties, Defence Cooperation with Australia remains the most important and most enduring partnership'.[22] A bilateral defence ministers' meeting between the two countries was held in Canberra in December 2011 where agreement was reached to hold an annual PNG–Australia security dialogue involving senior defence and foreign affairs officials.[23]

***

The place of Papua New Guinea in Australia's security environment and thinking has evolved in parallel with the changing definition of Australia's national interests and developments in the broader international security situation. Papua New Guinea is no longer seen as a shield or bulwark to protect Australia from invasion. Each country now assesses the security environment on the basis of its own national interests and sees a close, cooperative defence relationship as being advantageous to both nations. The closeness of Australia and Papua New Guinea, based on geography, history and social interaction, ensures that the two countries remain of unavoidable strategic importance to each other.

In July 1972, Michael Somare reflected on the internal problems facing his country and the relationship with Australia. He wrote in *The Age*:

> Papua New Guinea has gained many advantages under Australian administration but it has also inherited many Australian made problems. It will not be enough for Australians to sit back when Papua New Guinea becomes independent and say – 'Well, considering all the problems, I don't think we did a bad job'. Australia will never be able to sit back contentedly while Papua New Guinea lies at its northern doorstep.[24]

NOTES

Introduction

1. Defence Committee 30 May 1956, Agendum No 54/1956 and Attachment No 129/1956, Strategic Importance of New Guinea, NAA A2031, 129/1956.
2. Australian Strategic Analysis and Defence Policy Objectives, September 1976, in Stephen Frühling (ed.), *A History of Australian Strategic Policy Since 1945*, Defence Publishing Services, Canberra, 2009, paras 224 and 227.
3. The Defence of Australia 1987, Australian Government Publishing Service, Canberra, 1987, para 1.40.
4. ibid., para 2.53.
5. 2016 Australian Defence White Paper, Department of Defence, Canberra, 2016, paras 2.2, 3.7 and 2.62.
6. See Joan Beaumont, The Evolution of Australian Foreign Policy, 1901–1945, Occasional Paper Number 1, Australian Institute of International Affairs, Dyason House, East Melbourne, 1989, p.4.
7. H. Nelson, 'The Enemy at the Door: Australia and New Guinea in World War II,' seminar paper delivered at Tsukuba University, Japan, 21 July 1998, p. 8. Nelson has based his larger figure of over 300,000 on the number of troops attached to Australian Divisions which served in Papua New Guinea. The exact number is not known. A Department of External Territories draft Cabinet submission dated 19 May 1970 referred to a figure of 114,500 Australian troops as having served in Papua New Guinea. This may account for Army personnel only. NAA A452, 1970/1327.
8. Peter Stanley, *Invading Australia: Japan and the Battle for Australia, 1942*, Viking Press, Camberwell, 2008, p. 188.
9. L. Wigmore (ed.), *They Dared Mightily*, Australian War Memorial, Canberra, 1963.
10. Nelson, 'The Enemy at the Door,' p. 13.
11. Kokoda Track Authority, wwwkokodatrackauthority.org, 6 December 2016.
12. E. Wolfers (ed.), *Australia's Northern Neighbours: Independent or Dependent?*, Nelson in association with the Australian Institute of International Affairs, Melbourne, 1976, p. 7.
13. Speech by Robert Menzies in Papua New Guinea, NLA Papers of Sir Robert Menzies, MS 4936, Series 6, Box 277 Folder 187.
14. Cabinet Submission 327, June 1970, Papua New Guinea: Implications for Early Self-Government. NAA A5873 Vol 2, p. 9, para 20.
15. Paul Dibb, in 'The Importance of the Inner Arc to Australian Defence Policy and Planning', *Security Challenges*, Vol 8, No 4 (Summer 2012), pp. 13-31. A collection of Strategic Basis Papers dating from 1946 to 1976 is contained in Stephen Frühling (ed.), *A History of Australian Strategic Policy Since 1945*, Defence Publishing Service, Canberra, 1987.
16. Cable 1005, Evatt to N. J. O. Makin, Leader of the Australian Delegation to the Second Part of the First Session of the UN General Assembly, 20 July

1946, in W. J. Hudson and W. Way (eds), *Documents on Australian Foreign Policy (DAFP)*, Vol X, Australian Government Publishing Service (AGPS), Canberra, 1993, p. 56.

17 Cable 393, Evatt to Keith Bailey, member of the Australian delegation to the second part of the First Session of the UN General Assembly, 22 November 1946, containing text of message from Evatt to John Foster Dulles, United States alternate representative at the second part of the First Session of the UN General Assembly, ibid., p. 398.

18 Gregory Pemberton, *All the Way: Australia's Road to Vietnam*, Allen & Unwin, North Sydney, 1987, p. 105.

19 Peter Edwards with Gregory Pemberton, *Crises and Commitments: The Politics and Diplomacy of Australia's Involvement in Southeast Asian Conflicts 1948–1965*, Allen & Unwin, North Sydney 1992, Peter Dennis and Jeffrey Grey, *Emergency and Confrontation: Australian Military Operations in Malaya and Borneo 1950-1966*, Allen & Unwin, St Leonards, 1996 and Peter Edwards, *A Nation at War: Australian Politics, Society and Diplomacy during the Vietnam War 1965–1975*, Allen & Unwin, St Leonards, 1997.

20 Cabinet Notebook 1/336 of 26 January 1972. NAA A11099 1/336. A duplicate record of the meeting can be found in Cabinet Notebook 1/121. The advice that ministers were not shown the notebooks was provided to author by Fred Chaney, Minister Administrative Services (1978), Aboriginal Affairs (1978–1980) and Social Security (1980–1983).

21 The discussions in Cabinet were recorded by the note-taker in an abbreviated or shorthand form and in the present tense (reflecting the speed of the exchanges in Cabinet). Almost no attention was paid to punctuation. They have been reproduced here in their original form often without full stops or commas to note the end of a comment. At times the handwriting is indecipherable or open to interpretation but a best effort has been made to be as accurate as possible. See Fact Sheet 128 from the National Archives of Australia for a history of the Notebooks.

22 Sean Dorney, *The Embarrassed Colonialist*, Lowy Institute, Penguin Books, Sydney, 2016.

23 The League of Nations mandate was conferred on His Britannic Majesty, King George V, to be exercised on his behalf by the Government of the Commonwealth of Australia. In 1946 the United Nations placed the territory of New Guinea under a Trusteeship to be administered by Australia. The text of the mandate and the Trusteeship Agreement are in T. B. Millar, *Australia in Peace and War*, Australian National University Press, Canberra, 1978, pp. 443-444 and 450-452 respectively.

Chapter 1

1 Brian Primose began his authoritative study of Australian political involvement in New Guinea with the statement that 'the underlying reason for the Australian colonies' involvement in New Guinea was the growing fear that their strategic and economic well-being was in danger. In danger because of the lawlessness in an area with which there was increasing colonial contact, and in danger because of the increasing expansion of European and American interests into the Pacific region'. B. N. Primrose, Australian Involvement in New Guinea 1883–1908, MA Thesis, School of History, University of New South Wales, 1968, p. 1.

Notes (Chapter 1)

2. N. Meaney, *The Search for Security in the Pacific 1901–1914, Vol 1*, Sydney University Press, Sydney, 1976, p. 9.
3. Statement and subsequent extracts compiled in a memorandum prepared by E. Piesse, 'The Spheres of Interest of Australia and New Zealand', 6 November 1920. Piesse held the position of Director of Pacific Branch, Prime Minister's Department. NAA MP1049, 1920/0465.
4. ibid.
5. J. Moresby, Discoveries and Surveys in New Guinea, London, 1876, quoted in J. Whittaker, N. Gash, J. Hookey and R. Lacey, *Documents and Readings in New Guinea History*, Jacaranda Press, Milton, 1975, p. 439.
6. Minute of the Cabinet of New South Wales sent by Premier John Robertson to the Governor, Lord Rosemead, 31 May 1875 for transmission to London. ibid
7. ibid.
8. ibid.
9. Reply from the Secretary of State for the Colonies to the Governor, 8 December 1875. ibid.
10. A. Kerr, *A Federation in These Seas*, Attorney General's Department, Barton, Canberra, 2009, p. 15. Kerr's thorough and masterly presentation of the legal and legislative background to the acquisition by Australia of its overseas territories is an essential reference book.
11. Despatch dated 26 April 1886 from Kennedy to Derby quoted in Whittaker et al, *Documents and Readings in New Guinea History*, ibid, p.446.
12. Despatch Derby to Kennedy 11 July 1883 quoted in Whittaker et al, ibid, pp. 447-449.
13. Alan Kerr, ibid., p. 16.
14. B. N. Primrose, Australian Involvement in New Guinea 1883–1908, MA Thesis, School of History, University of New South Wales, 1968, p. 38. See also M. George, 'The Annexation of New Guinea', *ANU Historical Journal*, 1966, Vol 1, No 3-8, pp. 17-23.
15. R. B. Joyce, 'Australian Interests in New Guinea before 1906', in W. J. Hudson (ed.), *Australia and Papua New Guinea*, Sydney University Press, Sydney, 1971, pp. 11-12.
16. See Piesse's compilation of statements on the Pacific. The resolution is titled 'The Inter-colonial Convention. The Monroe Doctrine for the Western Pacific South of the Equator', loc. cit. p. 7.
17. ibid.
18. Quoted in Whittaker et al, p. 454.
19. Stuart Ward, 'Security: Defending Australia's Empire', D. M. Schreuder and S. Ward (eds), *Australia's Empire*, Oxford University Press, Oxford, 2008, p. 237.
20. E. Piesse, loc cit., p. 19.
21. *Sydney Morning Herald*, 26 January 1885, p. 6.
22. Kerr, ibid. p. 19.
23. See Chapter 1, Part V, Clause 51 (xxx) of the Australian Constitution in P. H. Lane, *An Introduction to the Australian Constitution*, The Law Book Company Limited, Sydney, 1974, p. 246.
24. N. Meaney, *The Search for Security*, p. 33.

25 Marilyn Lake, 'The Australian Dream of an Island Empire: Race, Reputation and Resistance', *Australian Historical Studies*, Vol 46 No 3 September 2015, pp. 410-424.
26 ibid.
27 ibid, p. 411 and p. 415.
28 idib., p. 417.
29 P. Overlack, '"Bless the Queen and Curse the Colonial Office", Australasian Reaction to German Consolidation in the Pacific 1871-99', *The Journal of Pacific History*, Vol 32:2, September 1998, p. 150.
30 Australia, House of Representatives, 1901, *Debates*, Vol V1, 12 November 1901, p. 7079.
31 House of Representatives, *Debates*, Vol VI, 19 November 1901, p. 7415.
32 House of Representatives, *Debates*, Vol VI, 19 November 1901, p. 7446.
33 Neville Meaney has provided a more extensive list of early members of the Commonwealth Parliament who were influential in developing Australia's foreign and defence polices. See N. Meaney, *Search for Security*, ibid, p. 13.
34 ibid, p. 13.
35 Quoted in Stuart Ward, loc cit., p. 243.
36 See A. Kerr, ibid, Chapter 3 for a detailed analysis of the debate in Parliament.
37 W. J. Hudson, *Australia and the Colonial Question at the United Nations*, Sydney University Press, Sydney, 1970, p. 13.
38 Minute, Hunt to Minister for External Affairs, 1904, NAA A1108, Vol 61.
39 See Peter Overlack, '"A Vigorous Offensive": Core Aspects of Australian Maritime Defence Concerns before 1914', in David Stevens and John Reeves (eds), *Southern Trident: Strategy, History and the Rise of Australian Naval Power*, Allen & Unwin, Crows Nest, 2001, pp. 140-159 for an analysis of Australia's defence policy in the pre-war period.
40 See, for example, text of interview given by Deakin to the Melbourne *Herald* on 12 June 1905 and Deakin's statement in House of Representatives, in *Debates*, 1905 Session Vol 11, No 31. The Anglo–Japanese Alliance was renewed in July 1911. The Japanese battle cruiser HJIMS *Ibuki* escorted the Australian convoy which left Albany in November 1914 with Australian and New Zealand troops bound for the Middle East and Europe.
41 Meaney, *Search for Security*, ibid, p. 123.
42 Cited in Douglas Newton, *Hell-Bent: Australia's Leap into the Great War*, Scribe Publications, Melbourne, 2014, p. 48.
43 Scheme of Defence – Mobile Forces of Australia – Strategical Considerations, NAA B197, 1856/4/156.
44 General Scheme of Defence, Commonwealth of Australia 1913, p. 18, NAA MP826/1, 3(B).
45 See David Stevens, 'Defend the North: Commander Thring, Captain Hughes-Onslow and the beginnings of Australian Naval Strategic Thought' in David Stevens and John Reeve (eds), *Southern Trident: Strategy, History and the Rise of Australian Naval Power*, Allen & Unwin, Crows Nest, 2001, pp. 225-241.
46 'Report on the Naval Defence of Australasia' by Commander W. H. Thring, R.A.N., 5 July 1913, NAA MP1049, 1915/054.
47 ibid.
48 ibid.

Notes (Chapter 1)

49 David Stevens, 'Defend the North', ibid., p. 234.
50 ibid., pp. 237-240.
51 ibid., p. 240.
52 See Douglas Newton, *Hell-Bent: Australia's Leap into the Great War*, 2014 for a detailed account of Australia's decision to offer support to Britain.
53 Text of telegram in NAA MP1049/1, 1914/0307 and UK Archives ADM 137/5.
54 Memorandum by the Minister for Defence to the Naval Board, 10 August 1914, ibid.
55 Briefing Note, 'Pacific Islands – Pelew, Marianne, Caroline and Marshall Groups – Occupation by Japanese', NAA A981, MARS 2, part 3.
56 Handwritten minutes from the Naval Board, 27 August 1914, ibid.
57 See Joan Beaumont, *Broken Nation: Australians in the Great War*, Allen & Unwin, Crows Nest, 2014, pp. 28-31 for a description of the campaign to seize Rabaul.
58 A detailed history of the preparations and execution of the order to seize German New Guinea is contained in the 'Report by the Minister of State for Defence on the Military Occupation of the German New Guinea Possessions', 10 October 1921, NAA A5954, 1085/2.
59 See H. Frei, 'Japan in World Politics and Pacific Expansion, 1870–1919' in J. Moses and C. Pugsley (eds), *The German Empire and Britain's Pacific Dominions 1871–1919, Essays on the Role of Australia and New Zealand in World Politics in the Age of Imperialism*, Regina Books, Claremont, California, 2000, p. 187, for an analysis of Australia's campaign to secure the islands north of the Equator.
60 *The Age*, 19 August 1914.
61 Cablegrams of 11 August 1914 and 25 August 1914 from Secretary of State for Colonies to Governor-General for forwarding to the Prime Minister, NAA A981, MARS 2, part 3. Harcourt's message was in response to a cable of 24 August 1914 from the Prime Minister in which an assurance was sought that 'Japanese action will not extend to territory except on Continental Eastern Asia. This is important'. ibid.
62 Cablegram of 10 September 1914 from Secretary of State for Colonies to Governor-General for forwarding to the Prime Minister, ibid.
63 Briefing, 'Pacific Islands', ibid.
64 ibid.
65 Letter, Harcourt to Munro Ferguson, 6 December 1914, NLA MS 696/1306-07.
66 Personal Despatch from Munro Ferguson to Harcourt, 23 January 1915, NLA MS 696 Box 1, Roll 1, item 524-998.
67 Cable, Munro Ferguson to Harcourt, 18 February 1915, MS Harcourt Papers, 479, Bodleian Library, Oxford University.
68 Letter, Munro Ferguson to Harcourt, 13 May 1915, ibid.
69 ibid.
70 Telegram, Munro Ferguson to Secretary of State for Colonies, 19 May 1915. NLA MS 696, Box 9, items 6616-6720.
71 Letter, Harcourt to Munro Ferguson, 27 March 1915, Harcourt Papers Bodleian Library, ibid. In his letter of 24 March 1915 Harcourt also mentioned handing over not only Solomon Islands but also Bougainville, New Ireland and New Guinea to Australian authority.

72 Letter, Harcourt to Munro Ferguson, 13 July 1915, Harcourt Papers, Bodleian Library, ibid
73 For a comprehensive account of Hughes's approach to the New Guinea question and the negotiations at the peace conference, see P. Spartalis, *The Diplomatic Battles of Billy Hughes*, Hale and Ironmonger, Sydney, 1983 and more recently C. Bridge, *William Hughes' Australia*, Haus Publishing, London, 2011.
74 Letter, Munro Ferguson to British Prime Minister Asquith, 5 December 1915, NLA Munro Ferguson Papers, MS 696, Box 1, Items 654-812.
75 Letter, Munro Ferguson to Bonar Law, 8 November 1915, ibid.
76 Letter, Munro Ferguson to Asquith, 5 December 1915, ibid.
77 Letter, Munro Ferguson to Secretary of State for Colonies, 25 January 1915, NLA Munro Ferguson Papers MS 696, Box 9, items 6904-6994.
78 ibid.
79 Letter, G. F. Pearce, Minister for Defence, to Hughes, 14 January 1916. Pearce papers, Australian War Memorial, 3DRL, 2222/1/148. Also in P. Heydon, *Quiet Question: A Study of George Forster Pearce*, Melbourne University Press, Carlton, 1965, p. 231.
80 ibid.
81 ibid. Pearce repeated a similar argument to the Secretary of his Department in May 1917 and told him that the 'Commonwealth would strongly object to those islands and territories lying south of the Equator and formerly in German possession being either handed back to Germany or to any other foreign power'. Letter, Pearce to Secretary, Department of Defence, 30 May 1917. NAA B197, 1851/2/81.
82 *Sydney Morning Herald*, 14 and 18 January 1916.
83 'Report on the Japanese Danger' dated 24 June 1916 and prepared at the end of 1915 attached to letter of 3 February 1917 from the Naval Secretary to the Secretary of the Prime Minister's Department. NAA MP1049/1, 1915/054.
84 ibid.
85 ibid.
86 'The Importance to Australia of German New Guinea and the Islands (Lately German) North of the Equator, 11 July 1918. NAA MP 1049/1, 1915/054.
87 ibid.
88 ibid.
89 Hughes reported in *The Age*, 18 and 19 May 1917, quoted in N. Meaney, *Australia and World Crisis, 1914–1923*, Sydney University Press, 2009, p. 246.
90 Letter from Hughes dated 7 February 1917, ibid. p. 250.
91 Letter dated 8 February 1917, ibid.
92 Letter dated 13 August 1917, ibid.
93 For details of the resolutions passed by the Australian Parliament, see A. Kerr, *A Federation in These Seas*, ibid., pp. 71- 75.
94 Cable from Reading [British Ambassador, Washington] to A. J. Balfour [Foreign Secretary] and W. Long [Colonial Secretary], 2 June 1918, Balfour Papers, British Library, BL ADD 49741, Folio 200.
95 Joan Beaumont, *Broken Nation: Australians in the Great War*, Allen & Unwin, Crows Nest, 2014, p. 439.

96 Hughes speech of 31 May 1918 reprinted in the *New York Times*, 1 June 1918 p. 9. A slightly different ordering of the speech also appeared in the *Argus*, 1 June 1918, MP1049/1, 1920/0465. Hughes's speech was reported extensively in the press in Japan. See reports in NAA B197, 1877/5/155.
97 Hughes speech of 1 June 1918 reprinted in the *Argus* on 13 July 1918. ibid.
98 For a fresh history of Hughes's arguments before the Allied leaders, see Joan Beaumont, *Broken Nation*, pp. 442-450 and 530-551.
99 Imperial War Cabinet (IWC), Meeting No 31, 14 August 1918. NLA Minutes of Meetings of the War Cabinet and the Cabinet 1916–1939. Microfilm G15719-15777.
100 IWC Meeting No 36, 5 November 1918, ibid.
101 Joan Beaumont, *Broken Nation*, p. 531 and p. 505.
102 Letter, Hughes to Lloyd George, 4 November 1918, House of Lords, London, Lloyd George Papers, F/28/2/7. Also cited in L. F. Fitzhardinge, *The Little Digger 1914–1952: William Morris Hughes – A Political Biography*, Vol II, Angus and Robertson, Sydney, 1979, pp. 348-349.
103 See letter, Lloyd George to Hughes, 18 November 1918, Lloyd George Papers, ibid.
104 Ian Nish, *Alliance in Decline: A Study in Anglo-Japanese Relations 1908-1923*, The Athlone Press, London, 1972, pp. 196-211.
105 Joan Beaumont, *Broken Nation*, pp. 532-539.
106 Secretary's Notes of a Conversation held in M. Pinchon's Room at the Quai d'Orsay, Paris, 24 January 1919. *Papers relating to the Foreign Relations of the United States (FRUS) The Paris Peace Conference 1919*, Vol III, United States Government Printing Office, Washington, 1943, pp. 720-722.
107 Meeting on 27 January 1919, ibid., pp. 738-740.
108 Meeting on 27 January 1919, ibid., pp. 746-747.
109 See P. Spartalis, *The Diplomatic Battles of Billy Hughes* and N. Meaney, *Australia and World Crisis* for comprehensive accounts of Hughes at the Peace Conference.
110 Quoted in Fitzhardinge, *The Little Digger* Vol II, p. 397. The League of Nations approved the mandate on 17 December 1920.
111 Australia, House of Representatives, 1919, *Debates*, Vol LXXXIX, 10 September 1919, pp. 12173-74.
112 Andrews contends that Hughes's arguments at the Peace Conference were based on an antipathy towards Japan and that he pursued an objective to thwart Japanese interests. See E. Andrews, *The ANZAC Illusion: Anglo–Australian Relations during World War I*, Cambridge University Press, Cambridge, 1993, p. 208.

Chapter 2

1 For details of the terms of the Washington treaty and subsequent naval disarmament negotiations, see T. B. Millar, *Australia in Peace and War*, Australian National University Press, Canberra, 1978, pp. 96-98.
2 For a detailed account of the proposed Pacific Pact, see David Bird, *J. A. Lyons – the Tame Tasmanian: Appeasement and Rearmament in Australia 1932–39*. Australian Scholarly Publishing, North Melbourne, 2008, pp. 183-190.
3 Neville Meaney, *Australia and World Crisis 1914–1923*, 451.

4   Australia, House of Representatives, 1920, *Debates*, Vol XCIII, 9 September 1920, pp. 4386-4394.
5   Australia, House of Representatives, 1921, *Debates*, Vol XCIV, 7 April 1921, pp. 7262-7270.
6   ibid.
7   ibid.
8   Australia, House of Representatives, 1920, *Debates*, Vol XCIII, 14 September 1920, p. 4452-4457.
9   Letter, Hughes to the Governor-General and the Secretary of State for the Colonies, 7 July 1920, NAA A2219, External Relations, Vol 20.
10 Letter, Churchill to Hughes, 13 May 1921, ibid.
11 Note from Piesse, Director Pacific Branch to the Secretary, Prime Minister's Department, 8 December 1920, NAA A2219, External Relations, Vol 20.
12 See Neville Meaney, *Fears and Phobias: E. L. Piesse and the Problem of Japan 1909–39*, National Library of Australia, Canberra, 1966 for a detailed analysis of Piesse's views on the threat posed by Japan.
13 *Report on the Military Defence of Australia by a Conference of Senior Officers of the Australian Military Forces, 1920, Vols I and II.* AWM 1, 20/7.
14 ibid.
15 Neville Meaney, *Australia and World Crisis 1914–1923*, ibid. p. 438. See also P. Twomey, 'Small Power Security through Great Power Arms Control? – The Australian Perceptions of Disarmament, 1919–1923', *War and Society*, Vol 8, No 1, May 1990, pp. 71-99.
16 *An Appreciation of the Present Position of Australia with regard to Defence: The Potential Enemy*, 1 July 1920, NAA MP 1049, 1920/0215.
17 ibid.
18 Defence of Mandated Territory, Council of Defence Agenda No 13/1924, Council of Defence Sub-Committee Agenda 7/24 Mandated Territories – Defence Measures: Notes by Military Member of Sub-Committee. NAA B197, 1851/2/211.
19 ibid.
20 ibid.
21 ibid.
22 ibid.
23 M. Turner, *Papua New Guinea, The Challenge of Independence: A Nation in Turmoil*, Penguin Books Australia, Ringwood, 1990, p. 7.
24 H. Nelson, 'The Enemy at the Door: Australia and New Guinea in World War II', Seminar Paper, Tsukuba University, Japan, 1998, p. 8.
25 Letter, Lieutenant Governor, Sir Hubert Murray to Prime Minister James Scullin, 28 April 1930. NAA MP729/6. 16/401/187.
26 ibid.
27 Letter, Wisdom to Secretary, Prime Minister's Department, 17 May 1930. NAA MP729/6, 16/401/187.
28 Letter, Wisdom to Prime Minister Lyons, January 1933 quoted in letter, M. L. Shepherd, Secretary, Department of Defence to Secretary, Prime Minister's Department February 1935, ibid.
29 ibid.

30 ibid.
31 See article by Hjalmar Schacht, Minister for Economics (1934–1937) in the Nazi Government. H. Schacht, 'Germany's Colonial Demands', *Foreign Affairs*, Vol 15, No 2, January 1937, pp. 223-234.
32 David Bird, *J. A. Lyons – The 'Tame Tasmanian': Appeasement and Rearmament in Australia, 1932–1939*, Australian Scholarly Publishing, North Melbourne, 2008, pp. 144-145.
33 ibid., p.145.
34 Australia, Senate 1936, *Debates*, Vol 149, 13 March 1936 p. 121.
35 ibid., p. 123.
36 Document No 3, Germany – Question of Colonies: Memorandum prepared for Delegation to Imperial Conference, no date, *Documents on Australian Foreign Policy, 1937–1938*, Vol 1, Australian Government Publishing Service, Canberra, 1975, pp. 12-14.
37 ibid.
38 Document No 37, 2 June 1937 Minutes of Eleventh Meeting of Principal Delegates to Imperial Conference, ibid. p. 122.
39 Quoted in David Bird, *J. A. Lyons – 'The Tame Tasmanian'*, p. 273.
40 ibid., p. 274.
41 Hughes Address to the New Guinea Mining Association, reported in *The Argus*, 17 April 1939. See NAA 518, S118/2.
42 Hughes Address to the New Guinea Mining Association, *Sydney Sun*, 19 April 1939. ibid.
43 Hughes Address to the New Guinea Mining Association, *Sydney Morning Herald*, 17 April 1939, ibid.
44 Australia, House of Representatives, 1938, *Debates*, Vol 158, 6 December 1938, pp. 2754-2768.
45 Meeting of the Defence Committee, 2 December 1938, 'Establishment of an Advanced Base to the Northward as part of the extended Defence of Northern Australia' para 2, NAA A2031/4 Roll 2, 1/1934-88/1938.
46 Minute by General Squires to Secretary, Defence Committee, 'Defence of Port Moresby', 14 December 1939, NAA A816. 14/302/134.
47 Minutes of the Defence Committee, 'Defence of Port Moresby', 18 December 1939, ibid.
48 War Cabinet Agendum 64/1941, 'Combined Far Eastern Appreciation of Australian Chiefs of Staff, February 1941', NAA A2672, 64/1941.
49 Sir John Latham, 'Invasion of Australia', NAA A5799, 110/1941.
50 For the exchange with the settler community and Menzies's comments on the proposals by the two members of the Victorian Legislative Assembly, see NAA A518, S118/2.
51 Minutes of the War Cabinet Meeting, 20 October 1939, Item 56. 'Defence of New Guinea', NAA A5954, 803/1.
52 Minutes of the War Cabinet Meeting, 25 October 1939, Item 63, 'Possibility of Obtaining Training Aircraft from Japan', ibid.
53 David Day, *The Great Betrayal: Britain, Australia and the Onset of the Pacific War, 1939–1942*, Oxford University Press, Melbourne, 1988, p. 14.

54 Peter Stanley, *Invading Australia*, Viking, Penguin Books, Cambellwell, 2008, p. 133.
55 ibid., p.134.
56 Neville Meaney, *Fears and Phobias: E. L. Piesse and the Problem of Japan 1909–39*, National Library of Australia Occasional Papers Series, Canberra, 1996, p. 56.
57 Personal cable (no number) dated 24 June 1939 from Menzies to Chamberlain, NAA A1608, F15/1/1.
58 Cable dated 29 June 1939 from Chamberlain to Menzies and cable of 20 March 1939, ibid.
59 Peter Stanley, *Invading Australia*, p. 97.
60 Minutes of War Cabinet, Agendum 96/1942 'Defence of Australia', NAA A2670, 96/1942.
61 Quoted in D. Horner, *Inside the War Cabinet: Directing Australia's War Effort 1939–1945*, Allen & Unwin, St Leonards, 1996, p. 139.
62 See broadcast on 26 January 1943 NAA A5954/69, 579/2 Box O.
63 ibid.
64 B. Edgar, *Warrior of Kokoda: A Biography of Brigadier Arnold Potts*, Army Military History Series, Allen & Unwin, St Leonards, 1999, p. 126. The remark by MacArthur was recorded by the war correspondent George Johnston.
65 Peter Stanley, *Invading Australia*, p. 102.
66 ibid.
67 ibid., p. 150.
68 Joan Beaumont (ed.), *Australia's War 1939–45*, Allen & Unwin, St Leonards, 1966, p. 30.
69 ibid., p. 188.
70 H. Nelson, 'The Enemy at the Door: Australia and New Guinea in World War II'. A seminar paper delivered at Tsukuba University, Japan, 21 July 1998, p. 8.
71 Turner, *Papua New Guinea*, p. 11.
72 Nelson, 'The Enemy at the Door', p. 9.
73 Cable, Evatt to Sir Owen Dixon, Minister to the United States, 31 March 1943 in Hudson and Stokes (eds) *Documents on Australian Foreign Policy, Vol VI*, Canberra, p. 316.
74 Address on 'Post War Settlement in the Pacific' delivered by the Rt Hon Dr H. V. Evatt, Minister for External Affairs, at the Overseas Press Club, New York, 28 April 1943. Reprinted in *Current Notes on International Affairs, (CNIA)*, Department of External Affairs, Vol 14, No 5, 1943, pp. 146-147.
75 Text of ANZAC Pact in Millar, *Australia in Peace and War*, p. 444. An assessment of the ANZAC Pact is in D. Day, 'Pearl Harbor to Nagasaki' in Bridge (ed.) *Munich to Vietnam*, p. 62 and W. Reynolds, 'Imperial Defence after 1945', in Lowe (ed.), *Australia and the End of Empire*, pp. 60-61.
76 Statement by the Rt Hon John Curtin, 'The Defence of the South-West Pacific Region' to the Australia–New Zealand Ministerial Conference on the Future of the South-West Pacific Region, Canberra, 18 January 1944. NAA A816, 104/301/1 part 1.
77 See text of ANZAC Pact in Millar, *Australia in Peace and War*, p. 448.
78 For a description of the role of Conlon and the Directorate in post-war planning, see G. Sligo, *The Backroom Boys: Alfred Conlon and Army's Directorate of Research*

and Civil Affairs, 1942–46, Big Sky Publishing, Newport, 2013. See also G. Gray, 'The Next Focus of Power to Fall under the Spell of This Little Gang': Anthropology and Australia's Post-war Policy in Papua New Guinea', *War and Society*, Vol 14, No 2, October 1966, pp. 101-17; B. Jinks, 'Alf Conlon, Directorate of Research and New Guinea', *Journal of Australian Studies*, No 2, June 1983, pp. 221-33; B. Jinks, 'Australia's Post-war Policy for New Guinea and Papua', *Journal of Pacific History*, Vol 17, No 2, April 1982; and B. Jinks, Policy Planning and Administration in Papua New Guinea, 1942-1952 with Special Reference to the Role of Colonel J. K. Murray, PhD thesis, University of Sydney, 1975.

79 Letter, Blamey to Curtin, 5 February 1944. NAA CP637/1/1, 45.
80 Australia, House of Representatives, 1946, *Debates*, Vol 188, 7 August 1946, pp. 3853-55.
81 The text of the Trusteeship Agreement is in T. B. Millar, *Australia in Peace and War*, p. 450.
82 Cable 393, Evatt to Keith Bailey, 22 November 1946 with the text of a message from Evatt to John Foster Dulles, US Alternate Representative at the UN General Assembly, in Hudson and Way (eds), *Documents on Australian Foreign Policy*, Vol X, p. 398.
83 Council of Defence Agendum 'The Strategic Appreciation of Australia: Review by the Chiefs of Staff Committee', September 1947, NAA A816, 14/301/321.
84 Council of Defence Minute, 20 April 1948. NAA A5954, 1628/3.
85 Joint Planning Staff Report No 12/48. 'The Case for Manus as a Naval Base'. NAA A9707, 2 para 4 and Defence Committee Minute, 'The Strategic Importance of Manus', 29 October 1953. NAA A816, 7/301/64, para 2.

Chapter 3

1 Peter Edwards, 'Learning from History: Some Strategic Lessons from the "Forward Defence" Era', *Strategy*, May 2015, p. 8.
2 Menzies had been scheduled to visit Indonesia in 1956 but changed his travel plans once the Suez crisis erupted. In his memoirs, Arthur Fadden notes that he served as acting Prime Minister for 692 days from 1949 to his retirement in 1958, or six weeks short of two years. Arthur Fadden, *They Call Me Artie: The Memoirs of Sir Arthur Fadden*, The Jacaranda Press, 1969, p. 151. The figure is repeated in John Howard, *The Menzies Era: The Years that Shaped Australia*, Harper Collins Publishers, Sydney, 2014, p. 266.
3 Minister for External Affairs Casey visited Jakarta in 1955, Prime Minister Menzies in 1959 and External Affairs Minister Barwick in 1963. Indonesia's Foreign Minister Subandrio visited Australia in 1959.
4 On 27 February 1963 Critchley, accompanied by Ambassador K. C. O. Shann, held a secret meeting with President Sukarno to discuss Malaysia and Confrontation. Critchley (High Commissioner, Kuala Lumpur) had been asked by Canberra to go to Jakarta and to try to convince Sukarno to modify his policies towards Malaysia. Document 44, *Australia and the Formation of Malaysia 1961–1966: Documents on Australian Foreign Policy*, Department of Foreign Affairs and Trade, Canberra, 2005, p. 72.
5 Letter, Bunting to Tange, 17 January 1963. NAA A1838, 3034/10/1 part 12.

6   Despatch No 1 of 4 February 1960 from Laurence McIntyre, Ambassador, Jakarta. NAA A1838 TS696/2/2 part 10.
7   See John Murphy, *Evatt, A Life*, New South, Sydney, 2016, pp. 347-351 for a description of Menzies speech in the Parliament.
8   On 28 January 1949 the Good Offices Committee was renamed the United Nations Commission on Indonesia and given enlarged powers.
9   Margaret George, *Australia and the Indonesian Revolution*, Melbourne University Press, Carlton, 1980, p. 96.
10 See text of Round Table Agreement, NAA A10570, 1.
11 Margaret George, *Australia and the Indonesian Revolution*, ibid., p. 160.
12 ibid., p. 145.
13 Garry Woodard, *Asian Alternatives: Australia's Vietnam Decision and Lessons on Going to War*, Melbourne University Press, Carlton, 2004, p. 33. Woodard joined the Department of External Affairs (DEA) in 1952 and served as Ambassador to Burma (1973–1975), China (1976–1980) and High Commissioner to Malaysia (1980–1984). He was the first head of the Policy Planning Unit of DEA established by Tange. He retired to take up an academic post at Melbourne University.
14 Anne Henderson, *Menzies at War*, New South, Sydney, 2014. See page 207 for details of Menzies's speech to the American Australian Association in New York, October 1948.
15 David Goldsworthy, *Losing the Blanket: Australia and the End of Britain's Empire*, Melbourne University Press, Carlton South, 2002, p. 24. The quote is drawn from David Lowe, 'Making Sense of Decolonization', p. 438.
16 Australia, House of Representatives, 1949, *Debates*, Vol 201, 15 February 1949, p. 269.
17 ibid., p. 271.
18 Speech by R. G. Menzies, Sydney Town Hall, 20 January 1949. Menzies papers, NLA, MS4936/6/20 Box 254.
19 Australia, House of Representatives, 1949, *Debates*, Vol 206, 16 February 1949, p. 356.
20 ibid.
21 ibid.
22 Australia, House of Representatives, 1950, *Debates*, Vol 206, 23 February 1950, p. 75.
23 Melbourne *Sun*, 2 January 1950.
24 Melbourne *Sun*, 4 January 1950.
25 *Sydney Morning Herald*, 4 January 1950.
26 Sydney *Sun*, 29 January 1950.
27 Woodard, *Asian Alternatives*, pp. 34-35.
28 See David Goldsworthy, *Losing the Blanket: Australia and the End of Britain's Empire*, pp. 63-66 for a description of Spender's policy approach.
29 Letter, Spender to Noel-Baker, 14 January 1950, letter attached to Cabinet Memorandum C. P. (50) 136, 26 June 1950. UK Archives CAB 129/40/36. See also David Goldsworthy, *Losing the Blanket*, pp. 63-70 for a detailed analysis of Australia's interest in the New Hebrides and Solomon Islands.
30 UK Cabinet Notebook, 29 June 1950, UK Archives CAB 195/8/14.

31 Cable 12 of 12 September 1950 from London to Canberra from Spender to Menzies. NAA A461, B350/1/19 part 2. In the same cable Spender advised Menzies that the British had told him that the French were sympathetic to the proposal. I am grateful to Stephen Henningham for providing the text of the cable to me.
32 David Goldsworthy, *Losing the Blanket*, p. 64.
33 Telex D485, 17 July 1951 from Acting Secretary, Department of Defence to the Secretary, Department of External Affairs, NAA A1838, 935/9/12, part 1.
34 Cable 2121 of 15 June 1952 Canberra to London, NAA A1838, TS699/5, part 1.
35 David Goldsworthy, ibid, p. 66.
36 ibid., pp. 67-70. The Menzies Cabinet discussed the possible acquisition of the Solomon Islands in 1956 and 1959. In 1956 John McEwen, who had served as Minister for External Affairs in Menzies's wartime Cabinet and who had despatched troops to seize New Caledonia, told his colleagues that he had regarded Australia assuming control of the Solomon Islands as 'inevitable' but he also believed that Australia had too many responsibilities and obligations to take on the task. Other ministers (Menzies, Casey and Hasluck) shared his assessment. At the meeting in March 1959 McEwen told his colleagues that 'Takeovers don't fit in today's world – my mind would go more into gradually insinuating yourself in with British'. Cabinet Notebook 1/22 meeting on 15 May 1956 and Cabinet Notebook 1/41 meeting on 3 March 1959. NAA A11099 1/22 and 1/41.
37 Cable 16 of 7 January 1950 from Batavia to DEA, Canberra. NAA A4357, 353/3.
38 ibid.
39 Percy Spender, *Politics and the Man*, Collins, Sydney, 1972, p. 287.
40 Mr Spender's Visit to Indonesia – Speech broadcast over Macquarie Network, 10 January 1950, NAA A4357, 353/3.
41 Letter, Spender to H.E. Mr P. E. Teppema, Netherlands Ambassador, Canberra, 8 February 1950. NAA A1838, TS3034/6/1 part 1.
42 ibid.
43 R. Chauvel, 'Up the Creek without a Paddle: Australia, Western New Guinea and Great and Powerful Friends' in Frank Cain (ed.), *Menzies in War and Peace*, Allen & Unwin, St Leonards, 1997, p. 67.
44 Stuart Doran, Western Friends and Eastern Neighbours: West New Guinea and Australian Self-perception in Relation to the United States, Britain and Southeast Asia, 1950–1962, PhD Thesis, Australian National University, July 1999, p. 13.
45 ibid., p. 6.
46 Quoted in Neville Meaney, 'Look Back in Fear: Percy Spender, the Japanese Peace Treaty and the ANZUS Pact', Discussion paper No IS/01/426, The Suntory Centre, September 2001, p. 3.
47 See 'Some Statements on West New Guinea made by Indonesian Leaders since January 1950', NAA, A1838, TS3036/6/1 part 2.
48 *Sydney Morning Herald*, 1 February 1950, quoted in 'New Guinea – Miscellaneous – Suggested Annexation of Dutch New Guinea by Indonesia', NAA A518, CK836/1 part 1.
49 Spender's remarks quoted in *The Sun*, 1 February 1950. NAA A1838, 309/4/1.

50 Letter dated 6 February 1950 from L. N. Palar, Indonesian Ambassador to the United Nations to J. D. L. Hood, Minister in Charge, Australian Mission to the United Nations, New York. Letter forwarded to Canberra by memo No 178 dated 8 February 1950 and by cable 59 dated 8 February 1950 from New York to Canberra. NAA A1838, 309/4/1.
51 Cable K374 from Jakarta to Canberra of 11 April 1950. NAA 1838, 309/4/1. In an interview with AAP reported on 6 June 1950 Sukarno argued that Indonesia's control over West New Guinea would have a positive impact on Australia's security. See *The Age*, 6 June 1950. NAA A518, CK836/1 part 1.
52 Text of Australian Aide Memoire contained in Cable 265 of 26 April 1950 from UK High Commission Canberra to London, UK Archives FO 371/83703.
53 ibid.
54 Australia, House of Representatives, 1950, *Debates*, Vol 206, 9 March 1950, p. 633.
55 ibid.
56 Australia, House of Representatives, 1950, *Debates*, Vol 208, 8 June 1950, p. 3973.
57 Record of Conversation, Minister of State (Kenneth Younger) and Menzies, 20 July 1950, Foreign Office, London. UK Archives, PREM 8/1148. At the time Foreign Secretary Bevin was ill and Younger was acting as Foreign Secretary.
58 ibid.
59 ibid.
60 ibid.
61 Cable 4126 of 1 September 1950 from London to Canberra from Spender to Prime Minister. NAA A1838, TS3036/6/1 part 2.
62 ibid.
63 Cabinet Notebook 1/8 of 21 November 1950. NAA A11099, 1/8.
64 Cable 4126 of 1 September 1950 from London to Canberra. NAA A1838, TS3036/6/1 part 2.
65 Royal Netherlands Archives, Dutch–Netherlands Relations 1950–1963, NIB 50-63, No 3587. Record of meeting between Stikker and Spender.
66 ibid.
67 Despatch No 10/51 of 19 November 1951 from Casey to Menzies reporting on his meeting with Prime Minister Drees and Foreign Minister Stikker on 17 November 1951. NAA A4231, 1951/The Hague.
68 Statement to the press dated 29 August 1950 released in The Hague. NAA 1838, 559/1/44.
69 Note by UK Prime Minister Attlee, 4 September 1950. UK Archives PREM 8/1121.
70 Conversation between the Foreign Secretary and Mr Spender at the Foreign Office, 1 September 1950. UK Archives FO371/83706. The record suggests that Secretary of State Younger was also present at the meeting.
71 Letter 19 December 1950 from R. H. Scott (FO) to Sir Esler Dening, UK Roving Ambassador to the Far East, Office of the Commissioner-General, Singapore. UK Archives FO 371/83709.
72 ibid.
73 Brief dated 1 December 1950 for Bevin's talks with Gordon-Walker. UK Archives FO 371/83707.

Notes (Chapter 3)

74. Letter 19 December 1950 from R. H. Scott (FO) to Sir Esler Dening, ibid.
75. Letter 19 December 1950, Foreign Office to Sir Esler Dening, ibid. See also letter 8 December 1950, Nichols, UK Embassy The Hague to J. D. Murray, South East Asia Department, Foreign Office, FO371/83708.
76. Minute by Lloyd (FO) dated 14 December 1950. UK Archives FO371/83708.
77. Cable 4269 of 8 September 1950 from London to Canberra from Spender to Menzies. NAA A1838, TS851/1/1/6.
78. Letter, McBride to Menzies dated 24 October 1950, 'Australian Strategy in Relation to Communist Expansion in the Pacific, South-East Asia and the Far East During the Cold War Period'. NAA A816, 14/301/407.
79. Minute by Chiefs of Staff Committee at Meeting held on Thursday 14 September 1950, Agendum No 17/1950, No 28/1950, 'Australian Strategy in Relation to Communist Expansion in Pacific, South-East Asia and the Far East Areas during the Cold War Period'. NAA A816/25, 14/301/407.
80. Minute by the Defence Committee, 21 September 1950 Agendum No 100/1959 plus attachment, No 172/1950 Strategic Significance of Dutch New Guinea. NAA A5954/69, 1682/13.
81. Cabinet Notebook 1/10, 23 January 1951. NAA A11099, 1/10.
82. Message from UK Ministers (Bevin and Gordon Walker) contained in letter dated 28 December 1950 from UK High Commissioner, Karachi, to Menzies. Menzies sent Spender the message in Cable 332 dated 28 December 1950 from Karachi to Canberra. NAA A1838, TS3036/6/1, part 2. See cable 6067 of 6 December 1950 from Canberra to London for text of Spender's instructions to the High Commission. NAA A1838, TS3036/6/1 part 2.
83. Cable 18 of 13 January 1951 from London to Canberra. Cable contains the text of Bevin's letter to Menzies. NAA A1838, TS3036/6/1 part 3.
84. Text of letter contained in cable 303 dated 18 January 1951 from London to Canberra. NAA A1838, TS 3036/6/1 part 3.
85. Text of letter in cable 188 dated 7 February 1951 from Washington to Canberra. NAA A1838, TS3036/6/1 part 3.
86. Cabinet Notebook 1/11, 15 February 1951. NAA A11099, 1/11.
87. Richard Chauvel, 'Up the Creek without a Paddle: Australia, West New Guinea and "Great and Powerful Friends"', in Frank Cain (ed.), *Menzies in War and Peace*, Allen & Unwin, St Leonards, 1997, p. 67.
88. ibid., p. 55.
89. Correspondence on this issue over the period 1945 to the late 1940s contained on NAA A518, K815/1/2 part 1.
90. General Assembly, First Committee, Summary Notes 727th meeting, 24 November 1954 quoted in Stuart Doran, 'Western Friends and Eastern Neighbours: West New Guinea and Australian Self-Perception in Relation to the United States, Britain and Southeast Asia, 1950–1962', PhD Thesis, July 1999, Menzies Library, Australian National University, Canberra, pp. 46-47.
91. David Lowe, *Menzies and the 'Great World Struggle'*, UNSW Press, Sydney, 1999, p. 48 and p. 54. See also David Lowe, 'Percy Spender, Minister and Ambassador' in Joan Beaumont, Christopher Waters, David Lowe with Garry Woodard, *Ministers, Mandarins and Diplomats: Australian Foreign Policy Making, 1941–1969*, Melbourne University Press, Carlton, 2003, pp. 62-87.
92. David Lowe, *Percy Spender, Minister and Ambassador*, ibid., pp. 64-65.

93 See comments by UK Foreign Office officials B. C. Keeble, 24 April 1950 and G. D. Young, 29 April 1950 on Spender's proposal to write to the Indonesian Government setting out Australia's interest in West New Guinea. UK Archives FO 371/83703.
94 In June 1952 Casey advised the British Government that Australia wished to defer consideration of any proposal to assume control over UK responsibilities in the New Hebrides for at least two years. Casey noted the delay in discussions with the French on the terms of Australia's involvement and that the 'need for additional administrative services in our existing Australian territories has been growing and we are feeling that our resources in experienced administrative personnel cannot keep pace with our requirements'. Letter, Casey to Oliver Lyttelton, Secretary of State for the Colonies, 19 June 1952. UK Archives CAB 129/62/25.
95 Stuart Doran, 'Western Friends and Eastern Neighbours', PhD thesis, Australian National University, July 1999, p. 13.
96 ibid., p. 21.
97 ibid., pp. 30-31.
98 Record of Policy Review 30 and 31 January 1963. Officers present: the Minister (Barwick), the Secretary (Tange), Messers Waller, Shaw, Jockel, Rowland, Loveday, Loomes, and Peachey. NAA A1838, 551/13/12 part 1.
99 Nicholas Tarling, *Britain and the West New Guinea Dispute 1949–62*, The Edwin Mellon Press, Lewiston, New York, 2008, see pp. 1-67.
100 Garry Woodard, *Asian Alternatives*, p. 34.

Chapter 4

1 Paul Hasluck, *Foreign Affairs: Public Addresses and Articles (other than Speeches in Parliament and Official Statements)*, Vol 1, 1946-1964, Hasluck papers, NLA MS 5274, Box 37, p. 22. For an assessment of Casey as Minister for External Affairs, see Joan Beaumont, Christopher Waters, David Lowe, with Garry Woodard, *Ministers, Mandarins and Diplomats*, and Melissa Conley Tyler, John Robbins, and Adrian March (eds), *R. G. Casey: Minister for External Affairs 1951–60*, Australian Institute of International Affairs, Deakin, 2012.
2 For a comprehensive analysis of the defence issues facing Australia in the early 1950s see Peter Edwards with Gregory Pemberton, *Crises and Commitments: The Politics and Diplomacy of Australia's Involvement in Southeast Asia Conflicts 1948–1965*, Allen & Unwin, North Sydney, 1992, Peter Dennis and Jeffery Grey, *Emergency and Confrontation: Australian Military Operations in Malaya and Borneo 1950-1966*, Allen & Unwin, St Leonards. 1996, Gregory Pemberton, *All the Way: Australia's Road to Vietnam*, Allen & Unwin, North Sydney 1987 and T. B. Millar, *Australia in Peace and War*, Australian National University Press, Canberra, 1978.
3 For text of ANZUS Treaty, see T. B. Millar, *Australia in Peace and War*, pp. 452-454.
4 See Peter Edwards with Gregory Pemberton, *Crises and Commitments*, pp. 162-163 for a detailed description of the origins of ANZAM.
5 Peter Edwards, 'Learning from History: Some Strategic Lessons from the "Forward Defence" Era', *Strategy*, May 2015, pp. 5-25.

Notes (Chapter 4)

6. See T. B. Millar, *Australia in Peace and War*, pp. 454-458 for text of SEATO Treaty, ibid. The participating countries were Australia, France, New Zealand, Pakistan, Philippines, Thailand, Great Britain and the USA. The treaty did not specify that military planning amongst parties would occur but it did provide for consultations on the subject. It had no standing defence force and gradually lost relevance although the Menzies Government attached considerable importance to its existence, more so than the United States. Millar has described the treaty as a means to ensure that any threat from China or Indochina to the security of the region was contained on the Asian mainland. ibid. p.211.
7. See draft report to Cabinet dated 24 August 1951. NAA A1838, 3034/11/28 part 1.
8. Minute, Casey to Watt, Record of Conversation with the Indonesian Ambassador, 2 October 1951. NAA A1838, 3034/10/1 part 1.
9. Despatch 10/51 of 19 November 1951 from The Hague. NAA A4231, 1951/The Hague.
10. ibid.
11. Letter, Casey to Eden, 19 January 1952, NAA A1838, 3036/6/1 part 3B.
12. Editorial in the *Courier Mail*, 21 March 1951, 'Is New Guinea Guarded?'. NAA A518, M16/2/6.
13. R. G. Casey, *Australian Foreign Minister: The Diaries of R. G. Casey 1951–60*, Collins, London, 1972, pp. 80-81.
14. Briefing, 'Dutch New Guinea', no date, possibly May 1952. NAA A1838, TS 3036/6/1 part 3.
15. Comments from interview given by President Sukarno to United Press, 29 August 1952, Department of External Affairs paper 'Recent Statements by Indonesia on West New Guinea'. NAA A1838, TS 3630/6/1 part 4.
16. Letter, Casey to Eden, 7 May 1952, NAA A1838, 3036/6/1 part 3B.
17. Statement by the Rt Hon R. G. Casey, Minister for External Affairs, Dutch New Guinea, 7 February 1952. NAA A1838, 3034/10/1 part 1. Australia provided $15.8 million in economic development and technical assistance to Indonesia in the period 1952–53 to 1966–67.
18. Meeting, Menzies and Churchill, 27 May 1952, Prime Minister's Room, House of Commons, UK Archives DO 121/173.
19. Meeting, Menzies and Eden, 3 June 1952, Minutes of Meeting held in the Prime Minister's Map Room, Ministry of Defence. UK Archives DO 121/173.
20. Letter, Eden to Casey dated 24 June 1952, NAA A1838, TS 3036/6/1 part 4.
21. See David Lowe, *Menzies and the 'Great World Struggle': Australia's Cold War 1948–1954*, UNSW Press, Sydney, 1999, Chapter 6 in particular.
22. Meeting, Menzies and Churchill, 27 May 1952, Prime Minister's Room, House of Commons. UK Archives DO 121/173.
23. Meeting, Menzies and Churchill, 29 May 1952, ibid.
24. David Lowe, *Menzies and the 'Great World Struggle'*, ibid.
25. Peter Edwards, 'Learning from History: Some Strategic Lessons from the "Forward Defence" Era', *Strategy*, May 2015, pp. 5-25.
26. Meeting, Menzies and Churchill, 29 May 1952, 10 Downing Street, UK Archives DO 121/173.
27. Cabinet Notebook 1/8, 21 November 1950, NAA A11099, 1/8.

28 Letter, Casey to J. C. G. Kevin, Minister, Australian Embassy, Djakarta, 25 May 1953. NAA M1129, Kevin, J. C. G.
29 Aide Memoire contained in cable 163 of 1 July 1953 from Canberra to The Hague. NAA A1838, TS45/1/3/15/1/2.
30 Record of Conversation, Casey and Luns, 30 June 1953, ibid.
31 Minute dated 3 July 1953 by Watt reporting conversation with Luns, ibid.
32 Letter, Stirling to Casey, 19 May 1955, NAA M1129, Stirling/A.
33 Cable 424 of 9 November 1953 from The Hague to Canberra. NAA A1838, 3034/10/1 part 1.
34 Letter, Stirling to Casey, 4 August 1953, NAA M1129, Stirling/A.
35 Letter, Stirling to Casey, 18 August 1953, ibid.
36 A Strategic Basis of Australian Defence Policy, (1953), NAA A816, 14/301/576. Also contained in S. Frühling (ed.), *A History of Australian Strategic Policy Since 1945*, Defence Publishing Service, Canberra, 2009, pp. 167-197.
37 S. Frühling, *A History of Australian Strategic Policy Since 1945*, ibid., para 37.
38 ibid., para 48.
39 ibid., para 68.
40 ibid., para 69 c (i) and (ii).
41 See L. Strahan, 'The Dread Frontier in Australia's Defence Thinking' in G. Cheeseman and R. Bruce (eds), *Discourses of Dangers and Dread Frontiers: Australian Defence and Security Thinking After the Cold War*, Allen & Unwin, Canberra, 1996. p. 152.
42 See Nicholas Tarling, *Britain and the West New Guinea Dispute 1949–1962*, The Edwin Mellen Press, Lewiston, New York, 2008, Chapter 1 for a detailed account of Britain and Australia's attempts to frustrate Indonesia's initiatives to secure UN support for its claim.
43 Cabinet Notebook 1/129 meeting on 17 August 1954. NAA A11099, 1/129.
44 ibid.
45 ibid.
46 ibid.
47 ibid.
48 Cabinet Minute No 3, Without Memorandum – Dutch New Guinea, 17 August 1954. NAA A4940, C508 part 1.
49 Letter, Casey to Hoover, Under Secretary of State, 5 November 1954, NAA A1838, 3036/6/1 part 13.
50 Memorandum of Conversation, Menzies and Secretary of State John Foster Dulles, Washington, 14 March 1955, *Foreign Relations of the United States (FRUS)*, 1955–1957, Vol XXII, Southeast Asia, United States Government Printing Office, Washington, 1989, pp. 143-144.
51 Cabinet submission No 412, Dutch New Guinea, 27 June 1955, and Cabinet Decision No 482 of 28 June 1955. NAA A 4940/1, C508 part 1.
52 Cabinet Notebook 1/137 meeting on 28 June 1955 Submission 412 'Dutch New Guinea'. NAA A11099 1/137.
53 ibid.
54 See cable 322 of 29 September 1955 from New Delhi to Canberra and cable 1074 of 25 September 1955 from Washington to Canberra. NAA A1838, 3034/10/1 part 2.

Notes (Chapter 5)

55 See DEA minute of 30 November 1955 from R. Fernandez to J. Quinn. NAA A1838, 3034/10/1 part 2.
56 Text of Joint Statement attached to memorandum No 1231 of 3 November 1955 from Australian Embassy Djakarta to Canberra. NAA A1838, 3034/10/1 part 2.
57 Savingram 20 Canberra to All Posts dated 10 November 1955. NAA A1838, 3034/10/1 part 2.
58 Cable 291 of 4 November 1955 from The Hague to Canberra. NAA A1838, 3034/10/1 part 2.
59 K. C. O. Shann, Report of Asian–African Conference at Bandung, 9 May 1955, NAA A1838, 3034/10/1 part 6.
60 Letter, Spender to Tange, 17 January 1956, NAA A1838, 3036/6/1A.
61 Letter, Tange to Secretary, Department of Defence, 13 March 1956. NAA A1838, TS3036/6/1 part 4.
62 ibid.
63 Minute by Defence Committee, 30 May 1956, Agendum No 54/1956 and Attachment, No 129/1956 Strategic Importance of New Guinea. NAA A2031, 129/1956. Tange was present at the Defence Committee meeting along with the Secretary of the Department of Defence (Shedden), Chief of the Air Staff (McCauley), Chief of the General Staff (Wells) and Chief of the Naval Staff (Dowling).
64 ibid.
65 ibid.
66 ibid.
67 Letter, Casey to Lester Pearson, 10 January 1957, NAA A1838, 3036/6/1A.
68 Peter Edwards, 'Learning from History: Some Strategic Lessons from the "Forward Defence" Era', *Strategy*, May 2015, p. 8.
69 Figure quoted in the biography of R. G. Menzies by A. W. Martin, *Australian Dictionary of Biography*, Vol 15, Melbourne University Press, Carlton South, 2000.

Chapter 5

1 Menzies had visited Batavia, capital of the Netherlands East Indies, on 28 January 1941 en route to London. He held talks with the Dutch Governor General. A. W. Martin and P. Hardy (eds), *Dark and Hurrying Days: Menzies's 1941 Diary*, National Library of Australia, Canberra, 1993.
2 Cabinet Notebook 1/23, 30 November 1956. NAA A11099, 1/23.
3 The Strategic Basis of Australian Defence Policy (1956), pp. 199-245 in S. Frühling (ed.), *A History of Australian Strategic Policy Since 1945*, Defence Publishing Service, Canberra, 2009.
4 ibid., p. 206.
5 ibid., p. 209.
6 ibid., p. 232.
7 ibid., p. 244.
8 Cabinet Notebook 1/23, 22 February 1957. NAA A11099, 1/23.
9 ibid.
10 ibid.
11 ibid.

12   Cabinet Notebook 1/33, 8 August 1956. NAA A11099, 1/33. Notebook 1/33 also contains further details of the debate over the priority to be attached to the budget for the defence force.
13   Cabinet Notebook 1/25, 1 July 1958. NAA A11099, 1/25.
14   Peter Edwards, *Australia and the Vietnam War*, Newsouth, Sydney 2014, p. 40.
15   Record of Conversation, McIntyre and Dr Subandrio, 13 May 1957. NAA A1838, 3034/10/1 part 4.
16   Memo 1852 of 18 October 1957 from Djakarta to Canberra. NAA A1838, 3034/10/1 part 5.
17   Letter, McIntyre to Casey, 13 November 1957, NAA M1129, McIntyre.
18   United States Minutes of ANZUS Council Meeting, Washington, 4 October 1957. *FRUS* 1955–1957, Vol XXII, pp. 466-470.
19   Cabinet Notebook 1/36, 11 December 1957. NAA A11099, 1/36.
20   ibid.
21   ibid.
22   McEwen had served as Minister for Commerce and Agriculture from 1949 until 1956 when the portfolio was abolished and the Department of Trade created.
23   I am indebted to Paul O'Donnell, Charles Sturt University, Regional Archives for an informative biography of McEwen including the times he acted as Prime Minister.
24   ibid.
25   ibid.
26   Text of letter in cable 1298 of 12 December 1957 from Canberra to Washington. NAA A1838, 3034/10/1 part 6.
27   ibid.
28   Department of External Affairs Press Statement 116 of 12 December 1957 'Cabinet Discussion on Indonesia'. NAA A1838, TS696/2/2 part 5.
29   Text of letter in cable 1369 Canberra to Washington of 31 December 1957. NAA A6706, 34.
30   ibid.
31   Letter, Menzies to Macmillan dated 31 December 1957 contained in cable SC10 of 1 January 1958 from Canberra to Washington. NAA A6706, 34.
32   Cable 176 of 7 June 1958 Canberra to Ottawa. NAA A1838, 3034/10/1 part 8.
33   Letter, McIntyre to Casey dated 2 January 1958. NAA A1129, McIntyre/L.
34   Letter, Casey to Menzies, 29 July 1958, NAA A3401,37.
35   Cabinet Submission 1312 of August 1958 'Netherlands New Guinea and Indonesia'. NAA A4940, C508 part 1. Discussed in Cabinet on 12 August 1958.
36   ibid., para 1 of submission.
37   ibid., para 2.
38   Minute by Defence Committee on 19 June 1958, Agendum No 74/1958, Item No 86/1958, Strategic Importance of New Guinea, NAA A2031, 86/1958. Minute by Defence Committee on 28 July 1958, Agendum No 94/1958, Item No 103/1958, Importance of Indonesia to Australia and Regional Defence, NAA A2031, 103/1958.
39   Minute by Defence Committee on 19 June 1958, Agendum No 74/1958, Item No 86/1958, 'Strategic Importance of New Guinea', para 6. NAA A2031, 86/1958.

Notes (Chapter 5)

40. ibid.
41. ibid.
42. ibid., para 8.
43. ibid., para 15.
44. ibid., para 11.
45. ibid., para 3 c.
46. Cabinet Notebook 1/26, 12 August 1958, NAA A11099, 1/26.
47. ibid.
48. ibid.
49. ibid.
50. ibid.
51. ibid.
52. ibid.
53. ibid. Frederick Scherger was Chief of the Air Staff and later the Air Force. In 1961 he was appointed Chair of the Chiefs of Staff Committee, the most senior position in the Defence Force. He held that post until May 1966.
54. ibid.
55. ibid.
56. ibid.
57. Cabinet Notebook 1/26, 13 August 1958, ibid.
58. ibid.
59. ibid.
60. ibid.
61. ibid.
62. Cable 1773 of 9 September 1958 Washington to Canberra, NAA A1838, TS3036/6/1 part 6.
63. ibid.
64. ibid.
65. ibid.
66. Record of Conversation, Acting Minister McBride and H.E. Dr Helmi, Ambassador of Indonesia, 21 August 1958. NAA A1838, 3034/10/1 part 8.
67. Cable 724 of 21 November 1958 from Jakarta to Canberra. NAA A1838, 3034/10/1 part 9.
68. Cable 712 of 13 November 1958 from Jakarta to Canberra. NAA A1838, 3034/10/1 part 9. McIntyre made the same suggestion to Subandrio in October 1958 and reminded him of the strength of public feeling in Australia on the New Guinea question and its objections to the threatened use of force. Cable 685 of 24 October 1958 from Jakarta to Canberra. NAA A3092, 221/11/6 part 2A.
69. Cable 680 of 22 October 1958 from Jakarta to Canberra. NAA A1838, 3034/10/1 part 8.
70. Cabinet Notebook 1/40, 10 December 1958, NAA A11099 1/40.
71. ibid.
72. ibid.
73. Cabinet Notebook 1/40, 5 January 1959, NAA A11099, 1/40.
74. ibid.
75. ibid.

76   ibid.
77   ibid.
78   ibid.
79   ibid.
80   Cable 119 of 6 February 1959 from Canberra to Washington. NAA A3092, 221/11/6 part 3A.
81   Cabinet Notebook 1/40, 9 February 1959, ibid.
82   ibid.
83   Cabinet Minute, Decision No 36, 11 February 1959. NAA A4943, Vol 1.
84   Cabinet Notebook 1/40, 13 February 1959. NAA A11099, 1/40.
85   Discussions between Mr Casey and Dr Subandrio, 12 February 1959. The discussion took place during a flight between Canberra and Melbourne. NAA A1838, 3034/10/11/5 part 1.
86   Cabinet Notebook 1/40, 13 February 1959, ibid.
87   Cabinet Minute Decision No 36 of 11 February 1959. NAA A4943, Vol 1.
88   At his press conference in Canberra on 11 February 1959, Subandrio responded to a question regarding the possible use of force by drawing on the same language he had used in the Cabinet discussions. He said that 'If I say that we are not going to use force in the first place it is because I'm convinced – or we are convinced – that nowadays no force can be employed for territorial claims not even by big powers and certainly not by Indonesia. Nobody has ever been successful in using force for their territorial claims. Secondly if I use force I know I've not only to face the Netherlands – or perhaps Australia – but that I have also to face the power of the United States and Britain'. Transcript of Dr Subandrio's press conference, Parliament House, Canberra, 11 February 1959. NAA A4940, C2314.
89   The text of the Joint Announcement was tabled in the House of Representatives by Casey on 18 February 1959. Australia, House of Representatives *Debates* Vol 22, 18 February 1959, pp. 37-39.
90   ibid. pp. 38-39.
91   Sydney *Daily Mirror*, 16 February 1959. NAA A1838, 3036/6/1 part 35.
92   Sydney *Sun*, 16 February 1959, ibid.
93   Sydney *Daily Mirror*, 16 February 1959, ibid.
94   Australia, House of Representatives, 19 59, *Debates* Vol 22, 18 February 1959, p. 39.
95   ibid., 24 February 1959, p. 197.
96   ibid., pp. 214-216.
97   Mackie, *Australia and Indonesia 1945–1960*, p. 307.
98   Strategic Basis of Australian Defence Policy January 1959 in S. Frühling (ed.), *A History of Australian Strategic Policy Since 1945*, Defence Publishing Service, Canberra, 2009, p. 253
99   ibid., para 14, p. 255.
100 ibid., para 10, p. 269.
101 ibid., para 44, p. 261.
102 Cabinet Notebook 1/41, 23 March 1959. NAA A11099, 1/41.
103 ibid.
104 ibid.

Notes (Chapter 6)

105 Cabinet Notebook 1/45, 29 October 1959. NAA A11099, 1/45. (The debate on the Paper had been adjourned in March and resumed in October 1959.)
106 Cabinet Notebook 1/41, 23 March 1959, NAA A11099, 1/41. The question of whether Australia should acquire tactical nuclear weapons as a means of strengthening the defence force had been raised by Senator Spooner, Minister for National Development and Alexander Downer, Minister for Immigration.
107 Cabinet Notebook 1/45, 29 October 1959, ibid.
108 ibid. In his public remarks Menzies expressed no doubts or reservations about a US response to a possible attack on West New Guinea. In an address to the Washington Press Club on 25 May 1959 he said 'I scarcely see how the United States under all these circumstances in the East, or ourselves, or Great Britain, or whoever it may be, could be indifferent in that event, and I'm sure that they wouldn't be'. Washington Press Club Luncheon, Washington, 25 May 1959. NLA Papers of R. G. Menzies, MS4939/6/118 Series 6, Box 268 Folder 118.
109 ibid.
110 Cabinet Notebook 1/45, 9 November 1959 and 24 November 1959. NAA A11099, 1/45. At the Cabinet meeting on 9 November the Minister for Defence, Athol Townley, had described the Army as 'rundown'.
111 Speech at Dinner given by Indonesia's First Minister Djuanda, 2 December 1959, NLA Papers of R. G. Menzies, MS 4936/6/118, Series 6, Box 268, Folder 122.
112 Speech at Merdeka Barat, Jakarta, 5 December 1959, NLA Papers of R. G. Menzies, MS4936/6/118, Series 6, Box 268, Folder 122.
113 Cable 629 of 5 December 1959 from Jakarta to Canberra. NAA A1838, 3034/10/11/5 part 2.
114 Briefing note 'Australian Trade with Indonesia', NAA A1838, TS3036/6/1/6.
115 Jemma Purdey, 'Scholarships and Connections: Australia, Indonesia and Papua New Guinea', Working Paper Series Two, Alfred Deakin Research Institute, August, 2004, p.8.
116 Summary of Conversation at Bogor Palace 6 December 1959 between President Sukarno and the Right Honourable R. G. Menzies. NAA A1838, 3034/10/11/5 part 2. The extracts quoted below are from this record.
117 Cable 190 of 24 December 1959 from Canberra to London contained the record of the meeting and drew attention to the 'one new element', i.e. Sukarno's endorsement of Subandrio's undertaking not to use force. Menzies responded positively to a request from Allen Dulles, Director of the CIA, for a copy of the record. A copy was also passed to the State Department. See cable 37 of 8 January 1960 from Canberra to Washington. NAA A1209, 1959/1194.
118 Cabinet Notebook 1/158, 15 December 1959. NAA A11099 1/158.
119 ibid.
120 ibid.

Chapter 6

1 Cabinet Notebook 1/55, 11 January 1962, NAA A11099, 1/55.
2 Despatch from Lord Carrington, UK High Commissioner, Canberra to London, 1 October 1959. UK Archives DO 35/9011. Paul Hasluck has also provided a pen portrait of members of the Cabinet in the 1950s and 1960s in Paul Hasluck, *The Chance of Politics*, Text Publishing, Melbourne, 1997.

3   J. D. Legge, *Sukarno: A Political Biography*, Allen Lane The Penguin Press, London, 1972, p. 311.
4   ibid., p. 319
5   ibid., p. 329.
6   Despatch 1/1960, 4 February 1960, NAA A1838 TS696/2/2 part 10.
7   Submission No 550 The Future of Netherlands New Guinea; Submission No 551 The Military Importance of Netherlands New Guinea to Australia; and Submission No 554 The Unity of New Guinea. NAA A4940, C508 part 2.
8   See Christopher Waters, 'The Last of Australian Imperial Dreams for the South West Pacific: Paul Hasluck, the Department of Territories and a Greater Melanesia in 1960', *The Journal of Pacific History*, Vol 51, No 2, 2016, pp. 169-185.
9   Letter, Peter Heydon, Acting Secretary, DEA to Shaw, Ambassador, Jakarta, 16 May 1960. NAA A1838, TS3036/6/1 part 10.
10 Cabinet Submission 550 The Future of Netherlands New Guinea, NAA A4940, C508 part 2.
11 ibid.
12 ibid.
13 ibid.
14 ibid.
15 Cabinet submission 552 The Militiary Importance of Netherlands New Guinea to Australia, 19 February 1960. NAA A4940, C508 part 2.
16 Annex to report by the Defence Committee 'The Military Importance of Netherlands New Guinea to Australia', para. 27. NAA A4940, C508 part 2.
17 Letter, Hasluck to Menzies, 26 February 1960. NAA A4940, C508 part 2.
18 ibid.
19 In a memorandum of Tange to Sir Edwin McCarthy, Ambassador, The Hague, 28 March 1960, Tange advised McCarthy of the outcome of the Cabinet deliberations but added that 'none of this has come to public knowledge in any way in Australia. The Cabinet met at night and I do not believe that even the fact of the meeting was known to the press. At any rate the meeting does not appear to have been reported'. Unnumbered memo of 28 March 1960, signed by Tange. NAA A1838, TS3036/6/1 part 10.
20 See Christopher Waters, 'The Last of Australian Imperial Dreams for the South West Pacific: Paul Hasluck, the Department of Territories and a Greater Melanesia in 1960', *The Journal of Pacific History*, Vol 51, No 2, 2016, pp. 169-185.
21 Cabinet Notebook 1/46 of 2 March 1960. NAA A11099, 1/46.
22 ibid.
23 ibid.
24 ibid.
25 ibid.
26 Letter, Dr Subandrio to Menzies. The letter is undated and was carried to Canberra by Shaw at the end of January 1961. NAA A1838, 3036/6/1 part 44.
27 Record of Conversation, Menzies and Shaw, 30 January 1961. NAA A1838, 3036/6/1 part 44.
28 See Paul M. McGarr, *The Cold War in South Asia*, Cambridge University Press, Cambridge, 2013 for an analysis of the Kennedy Administration's approach to South Asia.

Notes (Chapter 6)

29. Cabinet Notebook 1/60, meeting on 30 April 1963. NAA A11099, 1/60.
30. I am indebted to Stuart Doran for providing me with an unpublished paper on 'United States Policy toward the West New Guinea Dispute, 1949–1962'.
31. Cable 3217 of 30 November 1960 from Washington to Canberra, 'Netherlands New Guinea'. NAA A4940, C508, part 2.
32. ibid.
33. ibid.
34. ibid.
35. Garry Woodard, *Asian Alternatives*, Melbourne University Press, Carlton, 2004, p. 127.
36. Cabinet Notebook 1/49, meeting on 12 December 1960. NAA A11099 1/49.
37. The newly appointed Secretary of State, Dean Rusk, had told Beale in January 1961 that his thoughts on a possible solution were along the lines of a 'trusteeship resting on self-determination'. Beale had taken the opportunity of the call on Rusk to set out Australia's objections to a possible takeover of West New Guinea by an 'expansionist or a Communist Indonesia', 'infiltration into our territory, propaganda and subversion of a primitive native people' and the 'laying of claims to other parts of New Guinea'. Cable 185 of 27 January 1961 from Washington to Canberra. NAA A1838, TS3036/6/1 part 11. For details of the new Kennedy Administration's views, see R. Hilsman, *To Move a Nation: The Politics of Foreign Policy in the Administration of John F. Kennedy*, Doubleday and Company, New York, 1967. A later assessment is in T. Maga, *John F. Kennedy and the New Pacific Community, 1961–1963*, Macmillan Press, London, 1990.
38. For details of the British option, see UK cable No 552 of 6 March 1960 from Washington, and minute from F. A. Warner FCO to R. Ledward, British Embassy Washington, of 7 March 1961. UK Archives FO371/160007. In Australia, the idea of a federation was promoted by the Sydney lawyer (and later Governor-General) John Kerr.
39. Cabinet Minute 21 February 1961, Decision No 1229, Submission No 696 United Nations Trusteeship for Netherlands New Guinea. NAA A4940, C508 part 2.
40. Memorandum from the President's Deputy Special Assistant for National Security Affairs (Rostow) to the Deputy Under Secretary of State for Political Affairs (Johnson). 12 May 1961. *FRUS*, 1961–1963, Vol XXIII, United States Government Printing Office, Washington, 1994, p. 391.
41. Memorandm for the President. Subject: Memorandum for Meeting with Prime Minister Menzies, 22-24 1961, Indonesia and West New Guinea, Kennedy Presidential Library, NSF, Australia 1/1/61-3/2/61, Box 8.
42. ibid.
43. ibid.
44. Summary record of meeting at White House, 24 February 1961. Participants: The President, Prime Minister Menzies, Australian Ambassador Beale, the Secretary of State and Assistant Secretary of State Parsons. ibid.
45. ibid.
46. ibid. The communiqué issued at the end of the meeting made no reference to West New Guinea or Indonesia. It did refer to the two leaders reiterating their strong faith in SEATO and ANZUS as bulwarks for the maintenance of peace in the Pacific. NAA A1209, 1969/375.

47 Cable 131 of 4 March 1961 from Geneva to Canberra for McEwen and Holt. NAA A1838 TS3036/6/1 part 12.
48 ibid. Menzies gave a brief report of his meeting with Kennedy to Cabinet on his return to Canberra but did not provide any details of the conversation regarding West New Guinea. See Cabinet Notebook 1/50, 10 April 1961. NAA A11099, 1/50.
49 Woodard, *Asian Alternatives*, p. 37 and p. 127.
50 Record of a meeting held at the White House, 5 April 1961. Present: Prime Minister Macmillan and Foreign Secretary, Lord Home and President Kennedy and Secretary of State Rusk plus others. UK Archives CAB 133/244.
51 ibid.
52 Cable 844 of 8 April 1961 from Washington to Canberra. From Beale to Menzies. NAA A 1209, 1961/590.
53 Cable 1703 of 11 April 1961 from London to Canberra, ibid.
54 Cable 825 of 6 April 1961 from Washington to Canberra for Prime Minister from Beale. NAA A1838, TS3036/6/1 part 12.
55 ibid.
56 Memorandum of Conversation, 10 April 1961, West New Guinea. Participants: The President, George Ball, Under Secretary for Economic Affairs and Foreign Minister Luns and the Ambassador of the Netherlands and others. *FRUS*, 1961–1963, Vol XXIII p. 347.
57 ibid.
58 Memorandum of Conversation, 10 April 1961 'West New Guinea', Participants: Secretary of State Rusk, Foreign Minister Luns and others. ibid, pp. 352- 356.
59 Memorandum of Conversation, 24 April 1961. Participants: President Kennedy and President Sukarno plus officials. *FRUS*, 1961–1963, Vol XXIII, pp. 382-390.
60 ibid.
61 ibid., p. 390.
62 Record of Meeting between Australian Ministers and General Nasution and Admiral Martadinata, Cabinet Room, Canberra, 18 April 1961. NAA A4940, C3306.
63 ibid.
64 Report of Meeting with General Nasution, Minister for National Security and Chief of Staff of the Army, Republic of Indonesia, Kirribilli House, Sydney, 26 April 1961. NAA A 4940, C3306. Menzies used a speech in Parliament on international issues to report on the conversations with General Nasution. He referred to the assurance he had given Nasution that Australia had no secret military arrangement with the Netherlands. He also referred to Nasution's renewed assurance that Indonesia would not use force to secure its claim. Menzies told the House that Nasution had rejected the need for an act of self-determination for West New Guinea as it was part of Indonesia and had rejected any form of trusteeship unless its purpose was to transfer West New Guinea to Indonesia after a brief intervening period. Text of Statement contained in NAA A4940, C508 part 3. Menzies spoke along similar lines at a Press Conference on 30 April. See NLA Papers of Sir Robert Menzies, MS4936, Series 40, Box 576, Folder 42. On the question of support for the concept of self-determination I am indebted to James Ingram, a senior Australian diplomat who served in the

Notes (Chapter 6)

South East Asia Branch of External Affairs from 1961 to 1962 and then in the Australian Embassy in Jakarta from 1962 to 1964, for his insights into the policy developments in External Affairs at his time. Interview with James Ingram, 23 and 30 May 2016, Canberra.

65   Cable 146 of 21 April 1961 from Canberra to Wellington. From Menzies to Holyoake. NAA A1838, TS3036/6/1/6.
66   Minute, Heydon, DEA to Minister (Menzies), 20 April 1961 and report by Blakeney on visit, ibid.
67   Content of Aide Memoire contained in Cabinet Submission No 1305 'Netherlands New Guinea', of 12 August 1961. NAA A4940, C508 part 2.
68   ibid.
69   See Cabinet Notebook 1/52, 16 August 1961. NAA A11099 1/52.
70   ibid.
71   ibid.
72   ibid.
73   ibid.
74   ibid.
75   Cabinet Notebook 1/50, 1 May 1961 'Laos and SEATO', ibid.
76   Cabinet Notebook 1/52, 16 August 1961. NAA A11099 1/52.
77   Cabinet Notebook 1/54, 24 October 1961. NAA A11099 1/54.
78   Despatch No 15 of 3 October 1961 from Jakarta. NAA A1838, 3034/10/1 part 11.
79   UK cable No 665 of 13 December 1961 from Washington. UK Archives FO 371/160009.
80   UK cable No 836 of 20 December 1961 from Jakarta, ibid.
81   See Nicholas Tarling, *Britain and the West New Guinea Dispute 1949–1962*, The Edwin Mellor Press, Lewiston, New York, 2008 for a detailed account of the meeting. See Stuart Doran, 'Toeing the Line: Australia's Abandonment of "Traditional" West New Guinea Policy', *The Journal of Pacific History*, Vol 36, No 1, 2001, pp. 5-18 for an assessment of Australia's response to the meeting.
82   Comment retold by Lord Harlech, British Ambassador in Washington, in oral history interview held at the John F. Kennedy Library and quoted in Paul. M. McGarr, *The Cold War in Asia, Britain, the United States and the Indian Subcontinent, 1945–1965*, Cambridge University Press, 2013, p. 138.
83   Record of a meeting at Government House, Bermuda, 22 December 1961. UK Archives CAB133/299. Those present included President Kennedy, Secretary of State Rusk, Prime Minister Macmillan and Foreign Secretary Lord Home. There was no reference to West New Guinea in the communiqué issued following the meeting.
84   ibid.
85   ibid.
86   ibid.
87   Letter, Macmillan to Menzies, 27 December 1961 UK Archives CAB 21/5557. An extract of the letter is contained on NAA A1838, TS3036/6/1 part 14.
88   ibid.
89   Record of Conversation, Tange and W. Belton, US Charge d'Affaires, 3 January 1962. NAA A1838 TS696/2/2 part 10.

90   ibid.
91   ibid.
92   Minute, Bunting to Prime Minister, 11 January 1962. NAA A4940, C508 part 4.
93   Cabinet Submission 10, 'West New Guinea', and supplementary memorandum, 11 January 1962. NAA A4940, C508 part 3.
94   Woodard, *Asian Alternatives*, p. 46.
95   ibid., p. 39.
96   S. Doran, 'Toeing the Line: Australia's Abandonment of 'Traditional' West New Guinea Policy', *The Journal of Pacific History*, Vol 36, No 1, 2001, pp. 14-15.
97   Cabinet Submission 10, 'West New Guinea', Supplementary memorandum, ibid.
98   ibid.
99   ibid.
100 Cabinet Notebook 1/55, 11 January 1962, 'West New Guinea'. NAA A11099, 1/55.
101 ibid.
102 ibid.
103 I am indebted to James Ingram for his comments on the role of Robert Hamilton Snr and Tange in advocating the policy of self-determination in the Department of External Affairs.
104 Cabinet Notebooks 1/55 ibid.
105 ibid.
106 ibid.
107 ibid.
108 ibid.
109 ibid.
110 Cabinet Minute 11 and 12 December 1962, Decision No 3. NAA A4940, C508 part 3.
111 Statement No 2/1962, 'West New Guinea' by the Prime Minister, the Rt Hon R. G. Menzies, 12 January 1962, ibid.
112 Press Statement, Hasluck, Port Moresby, 17 February 1962. NAA A1838, 3036/6/1 part 65. Barwick, House of Representatives, *Debates*, 1962 Vol 34, 25 March 1962, p. 897.
113 Cable 74 of 15 January 1962 from Barwick to Beale. NAA A1838, TS 3036/6/1 part 14.
114 ibid
115 ibid.
116 Cable 107 of 16 January 1962 from Washington to Canberra, ibid.
117 ibid.
118 ibid.
119 See Pemberton, *All the Way*, p. 105.
120 Cabinet Notebook 1/56, 15 March 1962. NAA A11099, 1/56.
121 Meeting of ANZUS Council, Canberra, 8th and 9th May 1962. NAA 1838, 3034/10/1 part 11. The Australian Cabinet met with Rusk and New Zealand Prime Minister Holyoake on 8 May prior to the Council meeting. West Berlin, nuclear testing, disarmament issues, Laos and Vietnam were discussed but not Indonesia or West New Guinea. Cabinet Notebook 1/56, 8 May 1962. NAA A11099, 1/56.

122 Communiqué 1962 ANZUS Council Meeting, *Current Notes on International Affairs (CNIA)* Vol 33, No 5, 1962 pp. 5-8.
123 Record of Conversation, Sir Garfield Barwick and President Sukarno and others, Bogor Palace, Jakarta, 2 July 1962. NAA A1838, 3034/10/11/7 part 1.
124 ibid.
125 Record of Conversation, Sir Garfield Barwick and Dr Subandrio, Jakarta, 3 July 1962, ibid.
126 Minister's Press Conference at Sydney Airport, 5 July 1962. NAA A3034/10/1 part 11.
127 Record of Meeting at Admiralty House, London, 4 June 1962. Present: Menzies, Prime Minister Macmillan and Foreign Secretary Lord Home. UK Archives DO 169/91.
128 Cabinet Notebook 1/57, 6 August 1962. NAA A11099, 1/57. See also Cabinet Minute 6 August 1962, Decision No 374. NAA A4904, C508 part 4.
129 Text of letter contained in cable 612 of 17 August 1962 from Canberra to Jakarta. NAA A1838, 3034/10/1 part 11.
130 Woodard, *Asian Alternatives*, p. 46.
131 Edwards, *Australia and the Vietnam War*, p. 66.
132 Pemberton, *All the Way*, p. 100 and p. 105.
133 Doran, 'Western Friends and Eastern Neighbours', p. 225.
134 ibid.
135 Alan Renouf, *The Frightened Country*, Macmillan Company, South Melbourne, 1979.
136 Pemberton, *All the Way*, p. 105.

Chapter 7

1 Letter, Menzies to Macmillan, 15 January 1962. UK Archives PREM 11/3644.
2 UK High Commission Canberra 'Notes on Australian Ministers', Biographical Sketches of Menzies Cabinet Members. UK Archives DO 164/67.
3 Australian crafted assessments of the ministers in Menzies's Cabinet can be found in Paul Hasluck *The Chance of Politics*, Paul Hasluck, *Foreign Affairs*, Vols I and II, NLA Hasluck Papers MS5274, Box 37, Joan Beaumont, Christopher Waters, David Lowe, with Garry Woodard, *Ministers, Mandarins and Diplomats: Australian Foreign Policy Making 1941–1969*, and Melissa Conley Tyler, John Robbins and Adrian March (eds), *Ministers for Foreign Affairs*, The Australian Institute of International Relations, Deakin, 2014.
4 I am indebted to Michael Wilson, a departmental colleague of Shann from the early 1950s, for his assessment of Shann's style and approach to work.
5 Report by James Ingram, 'Indonesian Politics – Final Reflections'. No date but likely to be written in June or July 1964. NAA A1838, 3034/2/1 part 42. Ingram had served in Jakarta from 26 July 1962 until 7 July 1964.
6 For a document-based study of the formation of Malaysia, see Moreen Dee (ed.), *Australia and the Formation of Malaysia 1961–1966*, Documents on Australian Foreign Policy, Australian Department of Foreign Affairs and Trade, 2005. Also Moreen Dee, *'Not a matter for negotiation': Australia's commitment to Malaysia 1961–1966*, Department of Foreign Affairs and Trade, 2005 and D. Lee and M. Dee, 'Southeast Asian Conflicts' in Goldsworthy (ed.), *Facing North, Vol 1,*

pp. 262-309. John Subritzky, *Confronting Sukarno: British, American, Australian and New Zealand Diplomacy in the Malaysian–Indonesian Confrontation, 1961–65*, Macmillan Press, London, 2000. Gregory Pemberton, *All the Way: Australia's Road to Vietnam*, Allen & Unwin, North Sydney, 1987 and Peter Edwards with Gregory Pemberton, *Crises and Commitments: The Politics and Diplomacy of Australia's Involvement in Southeast Asian Conflicts 1948–1965*, Allen & Unwin, North Sydney, 1992. The most thorough account of Confrontation remains J. A. C. Mackie. *Konfrontasi: The Indonesia–Malaysia Dispute 1963–1966*, Oxford University Press, London, 1974.

7   J. Subritzky, *Confronting Sukarno*, p. 18.
8   The date for the inauguration of the Federation was later amended to 16 September 1963 following a wish to await the outcome of a United Nations survey (the Michelmore Report) of the wishes of the population of the territories.
9   J. Subritzky, *Confronting Sukarno*, p. 33.
10 See Moreen Dee, 'Not a Matter for Negotiation': Australia's Commitment to Malaysia 1961–1966, p. 7 and Subritzky p. 39.
11 Dee, ibid., p. 7.
12 Moreen Dee, 'In Australia's own interests: Australian Foreign Policy during Confrontation 1963–1966', PhD thesis, University of New England, 2001, p. 54.
13 Cable 283 of 8 February 1961 from Washington to Canberra contains report of meeting between Beale and Dulles. NAA A1838 TS3036/6/1 part 11.
14 Letter, H. D. Anderson to A. J. Eastman (DEA Canberra), 3 June 1962, NAA A1838, 3036/6/1 part 74.
15 Department of External Affairs, Minister's North American Brief, 'West New Guinea: Implications of Indonesian Control', September 1962, NAA A1838, 3034/10/1 part 11.
16 Record of Conversation, Menzies and Shann, 31 October 1962, NAA A1838, 3034/10/1 part 12.
17 Record of Discussion, Barwick, Tange and Shann, 29 October 1962, ibid.
18 Letter, Barwick to Shann, 9 January 1963, ibid.
19 ibid.
20 ibid.
21 Letter, Shann to Barwick, 7 February 1963, NAA A1838, 3034/10/1 part 13.
22 Despatch No 1, 'Some First Impressions of Indonesia', Shann, 21 January 1963, NAA A4231, 1963 South East Asia.
23 Address by the Minister for Territories, the Hon Paul Hasluck, to the Annual Congress of the Public Service Association of Papua and New Guinea at Port Moresby, 1 September 1962, NAA A3092 221/13/4/part 3.
24 Record of Conversation, Barwick and General Suadi, Indonesian Ambassador, 21 January 1963, NAA A1838, 3034/10/1 part 12.
25 Letter, Waller to Shann, 24 January 1963, ibid.
26 ibid.
27 Letter, Bunting to Tange, 17 Janaury 1963, ibid. Tange annotated the letter that Barwick agreed with the Prime Minister's instruction.
28 Letter, Kimber (UK High Commission, Canberra) to Bunting, 15 January 1963 with attachment 'Instructions sent to the British Ambassador Washington'.

Notes (Chapter 7)

    NAA A4940, C3739. Also contained in cable 115 of 11 January 1963 from Washington to Canberra. NAA A1838, 696/3/3 part 2. The talks were later expanded at Australia's request to include New Zealand.

29 Attachment to letter, Kimber to Bunting, 15 January 1963. NAA A4940, C3739.
30 ibid.
31 See Record of Conversation, Tange and Kimber, UK Deputy High Commissioner, 17 January 1963. NAA A1838 3034/10/1 part 12. Garry Woodard, *Asian Alternatives*, p. 72.
32 Record of Conversation, Tange and Kimber, ibid.
33 Note for Cabinet, 'Indonesia', 5 February 1963, NAA A1838, 3034/10/1 part 12.
34 ibid.
35 Note, 'Indonesia – Quadripartite Talks in Washington', Tange to Barwick, 4 February 1963, NAA A1838, 3034/10/1 part 12.
36 ibid.
37 Cabinet Notebook 1/59, 5 February 1963, NAA A11099, 1/59.
38 ibid.
39 ibid.
40 ibid.
41 ibid.
42 ibid.
43 Cabinet Minute 5 February 1963, Decision No 632 'Indonesia – Quadripartite Talks'. NAA A1838, 3034/10/1 part 12. See also despatch from the UK High Commission, Canberra, 'Australian Attitude Towards Malaysia', 19 March 1963 which analysed the dilemma facing Australia as it sought to support Malaysia and at the same time not offend Indonesia. It described Indonesia as 'the most important external problem for the Australian Government' while 'a fundamental aim of Australian policy is the maintenance of good relations with Indonesia'. UK Archives, DEFE 7/1559.
44 ibid.
45 Record of Ambassadorial Discussion on Indonesia, Washington, 11 and 12 February, 1963. NAA A1945, 146/1/14 and A1945, 41/4/1. Australia was represented by Ambassador Howard Beale and Sir Arthur Tange, Secretary, Department of External Affairs.
46 ibid.
47 Cable 334 of 3 February 1963 from Washington to Canberra from Beale to Menzies and Barwick. NAA A6364, WH1963/01
48 ibid.
49 Cable 401 of 11 February 1963 from Washington (from Tange) to Canberra, 'Australian Defence Position'. NAA A1838, 3034/10/1 part 13.
50 ibid.
51 ibid.
52 Record of Conversation, Tange, Waller and Brennan, 4 January 1963. NAA A1838, 696/3/3 part 2. Waller and Brennan were senior officers of the Department of External Affairs.
53 Cable 587 of 5 March 1963 from Washington to Canberra. NAA A1838, 3034/10/1 part 13.

54 See Cabinet Submission No 552 of 6 February, 'Australia's Strategic Position', NAA A4940, C3640; Cabinet Submission No 560 of 15 February 1963, 'The Strategic Importance to Australia of New Guinea', NAA A4940, C3750; Cabinet Submissions No 603 and 651 of 29 April 1963, 2 May 1963 and 7 May 1963, 'Defence Review', NAA A4940, C3640; Cabinet Submission No 651 of 18 February 1963, 'Territory of Papua/New Guinea – Immediate Defence Moves', NAA A4940, C3750; Cabinet Submission No 551 of 8 February 1963, 'Retention of Australian Forces in Malaya', NAA A4940, C1473 part 1; and Cabinet Submission No 601, 'Australian Cooperation with Indonesia in New Guinea'.

55 Cabinet Notebook 1/60, 25 February 1963 and 25 March 1963. NAA A11099, 1/60. In January 1963 the government announced that it would purchase a third guided missile destroyer and acquire four Oberon class submarines.

56 Cabinet Submission No 552 of 6 February and attached Report by the Defence Committee on 'Australia's Strategic Position', NAA A4940, C3640.

57 ibid.

58 ibid.

59 Cabinet Minute of 5 March 1963 Decision No 675. NAA A4940, C3640.

60 ibid.

61 Cabinet Submission 560, Report by the Defence Committee 'The Strategic Importance to Australia of New Guinea', February 1963, NAA A4940, C3750.

62 ibid., para. 8 (d).

63 ibid., para. 27.

64 Woodard, ibid., p. 86.

65 Briefing note, Alan Griffith, Prime Minister's Department, on Cabinet Submissions Nos 560 and 561, undated, likely to be March 1963. NAA A4940, C3750. Sir Peter Lawler, Deputy Secretary, Prime Minister's Department throughout this period, advised the author in a personal interview of Griffith's close relationship with McEwen.

66 ibid.

67 Woodard, ibid., p. 274.

68 Cabinet Submission No 561, 'Territory of Papua New Guinea – Immediate Defence Moves', 7 February 1963, para. 6, NAA A4940, C3750. See also Edwards with Pemberton, *Crises and Commitments*, pp. 269-72 for details of the Defence review and Cabinet's decisions to increase Australia's defence preparedness. The major decisions arising from the 1963 Review were the enlargement of the Army to provide for a field force of three battle groups in addition to the battle group in Malaysia, the reconstitution of the Regular Army reserve, the enlargement of the Citizens' Military Force and the acquisition of 40 Mirage III fighters, 18 Caribou aircraft and 8 additional Iroquois helicopters. The Navy was increased with the acquisition of an escort maintenance ship. Cabinet also agreed to the despatch of a team of experts, led by the Chief of the Air Staff, to investigate the options for a medium range bomber with strike and reconnaissance capabilities. This would eventually lead to the purchase of the F-111 aircraft.

69 Minute on Defence and External Affairs Cabinet Papers, Bunting, 4 March 1963, NAA A4940, C3389. There is no addressee on this minute. It was most likely given to the Prime Minister for use in Cabinet.

NOTES (CHAPTER 7)

70 Cabinet Notebook 1/61, 2 May 1963. NAA A11099, 1/61.
71 In a minute dated 13 October 1969, J. L. Legge, Defence Liaison Officer, Department of Territories, commented that 'the mainspring of the proposal [to establish the Territory Intelligence Committee and increase intelligence surveillance] was the situation vis-a-vis Indonesia ... and [to service] the requirement for information on internal developments in Papua New Guinea as the Territory moved towards self-determination'. NAA A452, 1962/7075.
72 Cabinet Notebook 1/61, 2 May 1963. NAA A11099, 1/61.
73 ibid. Comments reflect note in the margin of Notebook recording a meeting on 9 May between Menzies, Paltridge, Sherger, Hicks and Bunting. See Cabinet Minute 8 May 1963 Decision No 791 for details of the decisions made by Cabinet. NAA A4940, C3750.
74 Cabinet Decision No 791, 8 May 1963, para. 2, NAA A4940, C3750. See also Cabinet Submission No 118, 'Papua New Guinea – Military Requirements', 7 April 1964, ibid. The submission from the Minister for the Army provided details on the program to improve local service facilities as a consequence of strengthening the defence role in Papua New Guinea.
75 ibid.
76 Cabinet Submission No 388, Report by the Chiefs of Staff Committee, 'Defence of Papua/New Guinea – Airfield Requirements', August 1964, para. 6(e), NAA A4940, C3750.
77 Cabinet Decision No 440, 3 September 1964, NAA A4940, C3750.
78 Australia, House of Representatives 1963, *Debates*, Vol 38, 22 May 1963, pp. 1668-72. Menzies later repeated his remarks in a radio broadcast during a visit to Port Moresby, 6 September 1963, *Current Notes on International Affairs (CNIA)*, Vol 34, No 9, 1963, pp. 53-56. In a minute dated 28 May 1963 Gordon Jockel, A/g First Assistant Secretary Division 1 to Secretary, said that the Defence Statement had been written by the Prime Minister 'in his own crystal-clear language and with Indonesia evidently very much in mind'. NAA A1838 3034/10/1 part 14.
79 See Press and Radio Conference by the Prime Minister, the Rt Hon Sir R. G. Menzies, 14 July 1963, NLA Papers of Sir Robert Menzies, MS 4936, Series 40, Box 576, Folder 43. Speech in House of Representatives, 25 September 1963 on Malaysia and Defence, NLA Papers of Sir Robert Menzies, MS 4936, Series 6, Box 277, Folder 187. 1963 General Election Policy Speech delivered on 12 November 1963 by Menzies ('we have made it clear that we will defend Papua and New Guinea against attack, as if it were part of the Australian mainland. That promise of ours is, as a result of ANZUS, completely backed by the United States') and Liberal Party pamphlet Policy Speech, 12 November 1963. NLA Papers of Sir Robert Menzies, MS4936, Series 6, Box 277, Folders 190 and 191.
80 Broadcast by Sir Robert Menzies, Port Moresby, 6 September 1963. *The Prime Minister in Papua New Guinea*, issued under the authority of the Hon Paul Hasluck, M.P., Minister of State for Territories, 1963. Also in *CNIA*, September 1963, Department of External Affairs, Canberra, 1963.
81 Minute, 'Defence Policy and Indonesia', on meeting between Tange and departmental officers, 28 May 1963, NAA A1838, 3034/10/1 part 14.
82 For details of the evolution of Confrontation and Australia's involvement in the conflict, see Peter Dennis and Jeffery Grey, *Emergency and Confrontation*, Part 2, pp. 167-325, Allen & Unwin, 1996; Peter Edwards with Gregory Pemberton,

Crises and Commitments: The Politics and Diplomacy of Australia's Involvement in Southeast Asian Conflicts 1948–1965, Allen & Unwin, 1992, Chapters 14 and 15; and Gregory Pemberton, *All The Way: Australia's Road to Vietnam*, Allen & Unwin, Chapters 6, 7 and 8.

83 Record of Conversation Barwick and Peter Thomas, UK Parliamentary Under Secretary of State for Foreign Affairs, 4 April 1963. UK Archives FO371/169690.
84 Cabinet Notebook 1/61 of 7 June 1963, 'Meeting with Averell Harriman'. NAA A11099, 1/61.
85 ibid.
86 Letter, Larmour (UK High Commission, Canberra) to Anthony Golds, Head Far East and Pacific Department, Commonwealth Relations Office, 7 June 1963. UK Archives DO 169/92.
87 Record of Conversation between the Rt Hon Harold Macmillan and the Rt Hon Sir Robert Menzies, Admiralty House, London, 24 June 1963, others present. NAA A1209, 1968/9231 and UK Archives DO169/92.
88 ibid.
89 The possibility of Portuguese Timor being absorbed into Indonesia had been identified in the British paper passed to Canberra in January 1963 and had been nominated as an example of Indonesia's ambitions in the region. It had also been discussed in Cabinet in Canberra and had been accepted as a near-inevitability by ministers. However, East Timor remained a Portuguese colony until the collapse of Portuguese colonial rule and its takeover by Indonesia in 1975.
90 Record of Conversation between Menzies and UK Secretary of Defence, the Hon Peter Thorneycroft, 19 June 1963, London. Record attached to memo No 1007 of 21 June 1963 from Australian High Commission London to Canberra. NAA A1209, 1968/9231.
91 Record of Meeting, Menzies and Rusk, 8 July 1963, NAA A1838, 3034/10/1 part 16.
92 ibid.
93 ibid.
94 Press Radio and Television Conference by the Prime Minister, the Rt Hon Sir R. G. Menzies, 14 July 1963. NLA Papers of Sir Robert Menzies, MS 4936, Series 40, Box 576, Folder 43.
95 Extract of Barwick's interview in Wellington on 27 May 1963 contained in cable 260 of 28 May 1963 from Wellington to Canberra. NAA A1838, 3034/10/1 part 14.
96 Letter, Menzies to Barwick, 8 August 1963. NAA A1838, 3006/4/7 part 10.
97 Cabinet Notebook 1/61, 6 August 1963. NAA A11099, 1/61.
98 Cabinet Notebook 1/61, Cabinet Committee of Foreign Affairs and Defence, 12 August 1963, ibid. Malphindo was a loose confederation of Malay states comprising Malaya, the Philippines and Indonesia established in June 1963 at the initiative of President Macapagal of the Philippines to help defuse tensions between Indonesia and Malaya.
99 Cabinet Notebook 1/61, 6 August 1963, ibid.
100 Larmour (UK High Commission, Canberra) advised London that 'He, himself [i.e. Menzies] seems certainly not at all disposed to trust Sukarno, either over Malaysia or in his wider ambitions for the future'. Letter, Larmour to Golds

NOTES (CHAPTER 7)

of 26 July 1963, UK Archives DO 169/92. Menzies told the visiting Japanese Prime Minister, Ikeda, on 1 October 1963 that 'Sukarno's performance over Malaysia was deplorable'. He said that Australia had exercised a 'great deal of patience with Sukarno and had made a great deal of allowances ... but to go on following this course would be retreating before his obduracy. His international behaviour was now so bad that pressure must be brought to bear upon him to come back to accepted international standards of behaviour'. Minute, Waller to Tange, 1 October 1963 recording briefing by Bunting on discussions between Menzies and Ikeda. NAA A1838, 3034/10/1 part 17.

101 Cabinet Notebook 1/61, 12 August 1963, ibid. The Cabinet's rejection of the idea of a non-aggression pact is contained in Cabinet Minute Foreign Affairs and Defence Committee, 12 August 1963, Decision No 976 (FAD). NAA A1838, TS383/6/1 part 7.

102 See Pemberton, *All the Way: Australia's Road to Vietnam*, pp. 166-191 for an examination of the debate over the application of the ANZUS treaty to Malaysia.

103 See Memorandum of Conversation, President Kennedy and Holt, 2 October 1963, *FRUS*, Vol XXIII, pp. 730-734. Kennedy made clear that, contrary to the Australian view, the United States did not accept that the ANZUS Treaty came into effect if Australian troops were attacked by Indonesian guerrilla units in North Borneo. He also disagreed with the Australian assessment that it needed to be made clear to Sukarno that Indonesia faced US power as well as UK and Australian power.

104 In his speech in the House of Representatives on 15 October 1963, advising the House that an election had been called, Menzies spoke almost entirely on foreign and defence policy issues. He identified three major policy differences: the government's support and Labor's objection to the establishment of a US-controlled Very Low Frequency (VLF) naval radio signaling station in Port Hedland, West Australia; the defence of Malaysia with Labor calling for a treaty to cover the deployment of troops to Malaysia; and Labor's support for a nuclear-free zone south of the Equator. Menzies speech contained in NAA A1838, 3034/10/1 part 17.

105 Content of decision contained in Cable 565 of 15 August 1963 from Canberra to Kuala Lumpur and cable 885 of 19 August 1963 Canberra to Jakarta. NAA A1838, 3034/10/1 part 16.

106 Australia, House of Representatives 1963, *Debates*, 25 September 1963, pp. 1338-1339. Tange advised the Defence Committee on 26 September 1963 that the final sentence of Menzies's statement 'should be regarded as a carefully defined statement of intent to provide Malaysia with military assistance if certain circumstances arise. It is to be clearly understood that Britain has full responsibility with Malaysia for the defence of Malaysia against external aggression and that any assistance given by Australia would be supplementary to that given by Britain. Such assistance should not be, or be seen to be, simply a part of British military effort. It is important that Australian forces do not become regarded by other countries as assisting so-called imperialist or neo-colonialist purposes'. Assistance had to be in response to a request from Malaysia. Minute by the Defence Committee, 26 September 1963, NAA A1838, 3034/10/1 part 18.

107 See Memorandum of Conversation, President Kennedy and Holt, 2 October 1963, ibid.

108 Broadcast by Sir Robert Menzies, Port Moresby, 6 September 1963, *The Prime Minister in Papua and New Guinea*, issued under the authority of the Hon Paul Hasluck, MP, Minister of State for Territories. In his speech at the opening of the Sirinumu Dam in New Guinea on 7 September Menzies told his audience that 'Jerusalem can be built in Papua and New Guinea'. NLA Papers of Sir Robert Menzies, MS4936, Series 6, Box 277, Folder 186.

109 Cable 825 of 14 September 1963 Jakarta to Canberra. NAA A1838, 3034/10/11/7 part 2.

110 At the time of Barwick's meeting with Sukarno the Michelmore Enquiry and Report sponsored by the UN Secretary General at the request of Malaya, Philippines and Indonesia to ascertain the views of the population of Sarawak and North Borneo on inclusion in Malaysia had just concluded. It had found the population of both territories in favour of inclusion into Malaysia.

111 Cable UN1250 of 28 September 1963. Conversation, Barwick, Rusk and US Ambassador to the UN, Adlai Stevenson. NAA A1838, 3034/10/1 part 17.

112 Record of Conversation, Barwick and George Ball (Under Secretary of State for Economic and Agricultural Affairs), 15 October 1963. Barwick told Ball 'the Australian public was now rather unhappy about Indonesia; their attitude was that Sukarno was looking about with greedy eyes, which might next fall on Timor – and then on East New Guinea'. NAA A1838, 250/9/10/2 part 1.

113 Record of Conversation, Barwick and Walt Rostow (Counsellor and Chair, Policy Planning Council, Department of State), 15 October 1963. NAA A1838, 3034/10/1 part 17.

114 Cable UN1308 of 5 October 1963 Meeting between Barwick and Rusk. NAA A1838, 270/1/1 part 1.

115 US Memorandum of Conversation, 17 October 1963, Kennedy and Barwick. *FRUS* 1961–1963 Vol XXIII and Kennedy Library, Australia, General, 10/18/63–11/16/63 Folder Box 8.

116 ibid. For an analysis of the Kennedy Administration's policy towards Indonesia, see R. Hilsman, *To Move A Nation: The Politics of Foreign Policy in the Administration of John F. Kennedy*, Doubleday and Company, New York, 1967 and Timothy P. Maga, *John F. Kennedy and the New Pacific Community 1961–63*, Macmillan, London, 1990.

117 UK Brief for Quadripartite Talks, October 1963. UK Archives FO371/169909.

118 Record of Four Power Talks, Washington, 16 October 1963. NAA A1838, 3034/10/1 part 17.

119 Cable SAV 85 of 5 October 1963 New York to Canberra, ibid.

120 The Record of Understanding covering ANZUS can be found on NAA A1838, 270/1/1 part 3.

121 See Memorandum of Conversation, President Kennedy and Holt, 2 October 1963, *FRUS*, Vol XXIII, pp. 730-734.

122 The question of the geographic application of the ANZUS Treaty and whether it continued to cover Malaysia after the end of confrontation was raised again by Australia in October 1967 during a visit to Washington by Hasluck, Minister for External Affairs. See cable 4241 of 9 October 1967 from Washington. NAA 4940, C1473 part 3.

123 Report, Lamour (UK High Commission, Canberra) to London, 22 October 1963, UK Archives FO 371/169909.

NOTES (CHAPTER 8)

124 Woodard, *Asian Alternatives*, p. 340
125 ibid., p. 106
126 Peter Edwards, 'Learning from History: Some Strategic lessons from the "Forward Defence" Era', *Strategy,* May 2015, p. 16.

Chapter 8

1   Broadcast No 6 on 26 November 1963 by the Prime Minister the Rt Hon Sir Robert Menzies, ABC National Stations. NLA Papers of Sir Robert Menzies, MS4936, Series 6, Box 278, Folder 195.
2   Final Broadcast 27 November 1963 by the Prime Minister the Rt Hon Sir Robert Menzies over National Television. NLA Papers of Sir Robert Menzies, MS4936, Series 6, Box 278, Folder 196.
3   1963 Policy Speech delivered by the Prime Minister, the Rt Hon Sir Robert Menzies, 12 November 1963. NLA Papers of Sir Robert Menzies, MS 4936, Series 6, Box 277, Folder 190. The statement was repeated in a pamphlet produced by the Liberal Party of the Policy Speech, 12 November 1963. NLA Papers of Sir Robert Menzies, MS4936, Series 6, Box 277, Folder 191.
4   There is some debate as to the circumstances of Barwick's elevation to the High Court with Edwards and Pemberton drawing attention to Barwick's loose references to the application of ANZUS during a press conference in Sydney on 17 April 1964 and subsequent debate in Parliament (see Edwards with Pemberton, *Crises and Commitments*, p. 281). Menzies has recorded in his papers that Barwick approached him on 25 March 1964 about the impending retirement of Sir Owen Dixon and his wish to succeed him on the court. The two met again on 20 April when Barwick confirmed his wish to succeed Dixon. Barwick also told Menzies that he did not intend to contest his seat at the next general election. NLA Papers of Sir Robert Menzies MS4936 Box 578, Folder 55.
5   The Department of Territories was renamed the Department of External Territories on 28 February 1968.
6   A. W. Martin, *Robert Menzies: A Life*, Vol 2 1944–1978, Melbourne University Press, Carlton, 1999. p. 487.
7   See R. Hilsman, *To Move A Nation: The Politics of Foreign Policy in the Administration of John F. Kennedy*, pp. 405-407.
8   In a comment to Canberra in May 1964 on the state of Indonesian politics Shann said 'I am fairly sure that the Indonesians have little idea where they are going at the moment, I am quite sure that I don't'. Cable 541 of 19 May 1964 from Shann from Djakarta to Canberra. NAA A1838 3034/10/1 part 20.
9   Despatch No 5/1963 of 29 November 1963. NAA 4231, 1963 South East Asia.
10 Letter, Barwick to Shann, 31 December 1963. NAA A1838, 3034/10/1 part 18.
11 ibid.
12 ibid.
13 ibid.
14 Dee, *In Australia's Own Interests*, p. 196.
15 Letter, Shann to Barwick, 17 January 1964. NAA A1838 3034/10/4 part 19.
16 ibid.
17 ibid.
18 ibid.

19 Extract of the Roy Milne Lecture of 25 January 1964 contained in cable 198 of 25 January 1964 from Canberra to Washington. NAA A1838 3034/10/1 part 19. Hasluck made similar comments in a speech on 6 January 1964 to the Summer School of the Council of Adult Education, Melbourne, when he said that 'if the Territory of the new state [of Papua New Guinea] is to be kept inviolable it will only be … because Australia and her allies are ready and able to fight any aggressor who threatens it … Up to the point of self government we have to defend Papua and New Guinea and protect it from invasion, subversion or pressure from any quarter'. Text of speech on NAA A1838 936/1/3.
20 Letter, Macmillan to Menzies 20 September 1963 NAA A6705 35.
21 Letter, Barwick to Duncan Sandys, Secretary of State for Commonwealth Relations, 16 December 1963. Text of letter in cable 5286 of 16 December 1963 from Canberra to London. NAA A1838 270/1/1 part 2.
22 ibid.
23 Submission No 1 'Military Implications for Australia of the Malaysian Situation', 19 December 1963. NAA A4940, C1473 part 1.
24 Cabinet Notebook 1/65 meeting on 19 December 1963. NAA A11099, 1/65.
25 ibid.
26 ibid.
27 Message, Menzies to Home, 24 December 1963 attached to letter, Bunting to UK High Commissioner Oliver, 24 December 1963. NAA A6706, 35.
28 ibid.
29 Department of External Affairs paper 'British/Malaysian Request for the Use of Australian Forces'. The paper is undated but would appear to have been written in December 1963. NAA A1838, 3034/10/1 part 18.
30 Text of Hasluck's statement to the House of Representatives contained in cable AP50 of 16 April 1964. NAA A1838, 3034/10/1 part 20. On 17 March 1964 the government announced the decision to assist Malaysia in the form of material training and the secondment of Australian officers to assist Malaysia in developing and expanding its own forces. On 16 April the government announced the decision to provide two RAN Coastal minesweepers with the provision of two further vessels to be considered in early June. An Army engineer squadron with plant and equipment would be provided to construct airfields, roads and bridges in Borneo and four Iroquois helicopters would be made available for operations on the Thai–Malaysia border. The movement of the personnel and equipment would be undertaken by HMAS *Sydney*. For additional comment, see Edwards with Pemberton, *Crises and Commitments*, p. 289 and Pemberton, *All The Way*, pp. 224-231.
31 Cabinet Notebook 1/65, meeting on 15 January 1964. NAA A11099, 1/65.
32 Cabinet Notebook 1/65, meeting on 28 January 1964, ibid.
33 ibid.
34 Record of Conversation, Home and McEwen, London, 16 March 1964. UK Archives PREM 13/800.
35 Cabinet Notebook 1/66 of 12 and 29 May 1964. NAA A11099 1/66.
36 Report by the Defence Committee 'Australian Forces for the Defence of Malaysia' attached to Cabinet Submission No 136 of 14 April 1964 'Australian Forces for the Defence of Malaysia'. NAA A4940, C1473 part 1.
37 ibid.

Notes (Chapter 8)

38 Edwards with Pemberton, *Crises and Commitments*, p. 291.
39 See NAA A452, 1964/5917 and NAA: A452, 1972/4342.
40 Record of Conversation, Hasluck and General Nasution, 5 June 1964. NAA A1838 3034/10/1 part 21.
41 Memorandum of Conversation, President Johnson and Hasluck 16 July 1964, *FRUS*, 1964–1968, Vol XXVII Document 2.
42 Records of Conversations Hasluck and Rusk, 16 July 1964 and Hasluck and McNamara 16 July 1964. NAA A4940 C1473 part 1.
43 Record of Conversation Hasluck and McNamara, 16 July 1964. NAA A4940, C1473 part 1.
44 ANZUS Council Meeting 17–18 July 1964, Washington, Summary Record of Discussion. NAA A1838 270/2/14.
45 ibid.
46 Pemberton, *All the Way*, p. 217.
47 Cabinet Notebook 235 of meeting on 1 July 1964. NAA A11099, 235. Cabinet Notebook 1/66 of meeting on 12 May 1964. NAA A11099 1/66.
48 Cable 3245 of 3 July 1964 from Canberra to London from McEwen to Menzies. NAA A1838 TS687/9/3 part 1.
49 Submission 368 of 5 August 1964. NAA A1945 24/2/21. Decision 440 of 3 September 1964 in NAA A4940 C3750.
50 Submission 388 of 27 August 1964. Decision 439 of 3 September 1964. NAA A4940 C3750.
51 Woodard, *Asian Alternatives*, p. 289.
52 Submission 399 of 28 August 1964 'Defence Implications of the Situation in Vietnam'. NAA A4940 C4643 part 1.
53 Cabinet Notebook 1/69 of 1 September 1964. NAA A11099 1/69.
54 Cabinet Minute, 3 September 1964, Decision No 451 (FAD) NAA A4940 C4643 part 1.
55 'Strategic Basis of Australian Defence Policy (1964)' in Stephen Frühling (ed.) *A History of Australian Strategic Policy Since 1945*, Defence Publishing Services, Canberra, 2009, pp. 309-336.
56 Notes on Cabinet Submission No 493 by A. Griffith, 2 November 1964, NAA A4940, C3640.
57 ibid.
58 ibid.
59 See Despatch 4/1964, 2 September 1964, "Indonesia – Abandonment of Non-Alignment', NAA A1838, 3034/2/1 part 42.
60 ibid.
61 Cabinet Notebook 1/70, 4 November 1964, NAA A11099 1/70.
62 ibid.
63 ibid.
64 ibid.
65 ibid, 5 November 1964.
66 Cabinet Minute 4 November 1964 Decision No 592. NAA A5828 Vol 2.
67 Australia, House of Representatives 1964, *Debates*, Vol 44, 10 November 1964, p. 2716. In his early, hand-written drafting of the Defence Statement, Menzies

had referred to Indonesia's hostility towards Malaysia as part of building 'an Indonesian Empire'. He had also written that 'in spite of all promises made in the past the Indonesian leaders may well be prepared to send people across the frontier of West New Guinea to stir up trouble in Papua and New Guinea'. Although these words were not used in the final text they reveal Menzies's continuing mistrust of Sukarno in particular and Indonesia in general. Handwritten drafts of the Defence Statement held in Menzies papers. NLA Papers of Sir Robert Menzies, MS 4936, Series 6, Box 281, Folders 214 and 215.

68 Subritzky, *Confronting Sukarno*, pp. 134-135.
69 Speech to the Liberal Party of Australia (NSW Division), 7 October 1964. NLA Papers of Sir Robert Menzies, MS 4936, Series 6, Box 281, Folder 211.
70 Report to the Nation 19 November 1964 delivered by the Prime Minister. NLA Papers of Sir Robert Menzies, MS4936, Series 6, Box 281, Folder 216. Also contained in cable 1230 of 20 November 1964 from Canberra to Jakarta. NAA A1838, 3034/10/1.
71 Television speech by Menzies, 25 November 1964. NLA Papers of Sir Robert Menzies, MS4936, Series 6, Box 281, Folder 217.
72 Television speech by Menzies, 30 November 1964. NLA Papers of Sir Robert Menzies, ibid.
73 Final broadcast in election campaign, 2 December 1964. NLA Papers of Sir Robert Menzies, ibid, Folder 218.
74 Cabinet Notebook 1/236 of meeting on 18 January 1965. NAA A11099, 1/236.
75 ibid.
76 Message, McEwen to Wilson, 19 January 1965. Cable 269 of 19 January 1965 from Canberra to London. NAA A1838, TS687/9/3 part 1.
77 Cabinet Notebook 1/235 of 17 December 1964. Meeting of the Foreign Affairs and Defence Committee, 17 December. NAA A11099, 1/235.
78 Record of Conversation between Menzies, Wilson and Holyoake on 1 February 1965. Also present were UK Foreign Secretary Stewart, Defence Secretary Healey, Commonwealth Secretary Bottomley, and the Chief of the Defence Staff, Lord Mountbatten. UK Archives FO371/18126.
79 Record of Conversation, Hasluck and Lydman, 11 February 1965 NAA A1838 3006/4/7 part 33.
80 Australia, House of Representatives 1965, *Debates*, Vol 45, 23 March 1965, pp. 230-238.
81 See Pemberton, *All The Way*, for an analysis of the decision to send a battalion to Vietnam, pp. 279-297, and Edwards with Pemberton, *Crises and Commitments*, pp. 351-375.
82 Minute, Bunting to Menzies 7 April 1965, NAA A4940 C4643 part 2.
83 Cabinet Notebook 1/72, meeting on 7 April 1965. NAA A11099 1/72. A more polished and final version of the Cabinet discussion of 7 April is attached to the Cabinet Minute and Decision No 859. NAA A4940, C4643 part 2.
84 Cabinet Notebook 1/72 meeting on 7 April 1965. NAA A11099 1/72.
85 ibid.
86 Meeting on 21 April 1965, ibid.
87 Cabinet (Foreign Affairs and Defence Committee) Minute, 7 April 1965 Decision No 859 and cable 883 of 9 April 1965 from Canberra to Washington. NAA A4940, C4643 part 2.

88 Cable 2980 of 14 April 1965 from London to Canberra and cable 1281 of 13 April 1965 from Washington to Canberra, ibid.
89 Speech by Sir Robert Menzies at Young Liberal Rally, Hawthorn Town Hall, Melbourne, 21 May 1965. NLA Papers of Sir Robert Menzies, MS4936, Series 6, Box 282, Folder 224.
90 Press, radio and television conference by Sir Robert Menzies at Parliament House, Canberra. NLA Papers of Sir Robert Menzies, MS4936, Series 40, Box 577, Folder 44.
91 Cabinet Notebook 1/75 meeting of 10 August 1965, Foreign Affairs and Defence Committee. NAA 11099 1/75.
92 ibid.
93 ibid.
94 Furlonger's assessment contained in Jakarta Despatch No 5 18 January 1973 'The Soeharto Regime: Australian–Indonesian Relations (Part 1)', NAA A1838 3034/10/6/9 part 1. Furlonger had served in the Joint Intelligence Organisation as well as in senior positions in External Affairs before his appointment as Ambassador to Jakarta in 1972. Furlonger was later appointed the first Director-General of the Office of National Assessments.
95 Peter Edwards, *Australia and the Vietnam War*, New South Publishing, Sydney, 2014, p. 132.
96 ibid., p. 139.
97 Defence Committee report No 5/1966 'Review of Defence Situation in Papua/New Guinea', 11 February 1966 attached to Cabinet Submission 71, 'Papua New Guinea – Ultimate Status', 10 March 1966 and Defence Committee Report No 9/1966 'Future of Papua/New Guinea – Defence Considerations', 17 February 1966, NAA A1946, 1968/838.
98 Strategic Basis of Australian Defence Policy 1983, Chapter 6 para 31. NAA A11116 CA805 part 1.

Chapter 9

1 Peter Edwards, *Australia and the Vietnam War*, p. 187.
2 Cable 415 of 15 April 1966 from Djakarta to Canberra. NAA A4359, 201/2/2.
3 Record of Conversation, Wilson and Hasluck, London, 19 April 1966. UK Archives PREM 13/890 and PREM 13/1945, C675175.
4 ibid.
5 ibid.
6 Summary record of meeting between Malik and Hasluck, 9 August 1966. NAA A1838, 3034/10/1 part 28.
7 Minute, Jockel to H. D. Anderson, 28 March 1967. NAA A1838, 3034/10/1/4 part 1.
8 Letter, Knott to Garner, Permanent Under-Secretary of State, Commonwealth Office, London, 11 August 1966. The letter included a report by Hasluck on his visit to Indonesia which he had asked to be passed to the UK Government. UK Archives FO 371/186041.
9 Cabinet Notebook 1/81, 16 August 1966. NAA A11099, 1/81.
10 Cabinet Notebook 1/91 meeting of 28 February 1968. NAA A11099, 1/91. Cabinet Notebook 1/258 contains a record of the same meeting prepared by

Peter Lawler. There are some differences between the two records but not such as to change the sense of Cabinet's views.
11   Cabinet Notebook 1/258, NAA A11099, 1/258.
12   See Speech by Prime Minister Gorton at banquet given by President Suharto, Jakarta, 13 June 1968. NAA A1209, 1968/8679.
13   Cabinet Notebook 1/272 meeting of 27 March 1969 Submission No 515 'Australian Aid Programme for Indonesia 1969/70'. NAA A11099 1/272.
14   Cabinet Submission 182, March 1970 'Australian Aid to Indonesia' and Decision No 257 of 25 March 1970. NAA A5869, Vol 9.
15   Cabinet Submission 684 of 15 February 1971 'Review of Strategic Controls Over Exports to Indonesia' and Decision No 10 of 12 March 1971. NAA A5869, Vol 3.
16   See NAA A1838, 3034/10/7/1 part 2 for text of communiqué issued on 7 February 1972 following President Suharto's visit to Canberra and NAA A1838, 3034/10/4/5 part 4 for text of communiqué issued on 8 June 1972 following Prime Minister McMahon's visit to Jakarta.
17   See UK Archives CRO DEF 89/77/2 and DO 164/67 for the records of Mountbatten's discussions in Canberra.
18   David Goldsworthy, *Losing the Blanket: Australia and the End of Britain's Empire*, Melbourne University Press, Carlton South, 2002, p. 158.
19   Cabinet Notebook 1/238, FAD Committee meeting on 10 January 1966. NAA A11099, 1/238.
20   ibid.
21   Cabinet Notebook 1/77, meeting on 19 January 1966. NAA A11099, 1/77.
22   Cabinet Notebook 1/78, meeting on 26 January 1966. NAA A11099, 1/78.
23   In addition to the Australian and British ministers, the New Zealand Minister for Defence, Dean Eyre, also participated. See Cabinet Decision No 22 (FAD) of 2 February 1966 for a full, edited record of the discussions, NAA A5839, Vol 1. Cabinet Notebook 1/324 contains the unedited record of the meeting. NAA A11099, 1/324.
24   Cabinet Decision No 22 (FAD) of 2 February 1966. NAA A5839, Vol 1.
25   ibid.
26   Cabinet Notebook 1/324 of 1 February 1966. This reference is not included in the record of the meeting contained in Decision No 22 of 2 February 1966, ibid.
27   Cabinet Notebook 1/324 of 1 February 1966. NAA A11099 1/324.
28   ibid, meeting on 2 February 1966.
29   Curiously, such was the Cabinet's uneasiness at the prospect that Britain could decide to leave the region that it rejected a submission later in the year from the Attorney-General, Snedden, that Australia should abolish the right of legal appeals to be heard by the Privy Council in London. The initiative was too sensitive given 'the importance for Australia of encouraging the maintenance of a British presence East of Suez'. Decision No 339 of 13 July 1966 and Submission No 254 'Appeals to the Privy Council'. NAA A5841, Vol 9.
30   ibid, meeting on 2 February 1966 of Holt, McEwen, Hasluck, McMahon and Gorton prior to resumed meeting with Healey.
31   Record of meeting between Paul Hasluck and Keith Holyoake, Wellington, 7 May 1966. NAA A1838 370/8/5/2.

Notes (Chapter 9)

32 Note on Discussion in Prime Minister's Office between Holt and Vice President Humphrey, 19 February 1966. NAA A1209, 1966/7066.
33 ibid.
34 Cabinet Minute, Foreign Affairs and Defence Committee, 19 February 1966 Decision No 25 (FAD). NAA A5839 Vol 1.
35 Holt referred to 'our special responsibilities in New Guinea' when he wrote to President Johnson after the visit of Vice President Humphrey. Letter forwarded to the White House by the Australian Ambassador on 25 February 1966. Lyndon Baines Johnson Library and Museum, Austin, Texas, Head of State Correspondence File (Box1).
36 Cabinet Notebook 1/78 meeting on 15 February 1966. NAA A11099, 1/78. In the formal Cabinet Minute of the meeting the ministers' comments have been recorded as asking whether 'there would be sufficient capacity and flexibility left in the force at home to respond effectively to any increase or spread of hostile Indonesian activity'. Cabinet Minute, 15 February 1966 Decision No 32. NAA A5839, Vol 1.
37 Cabinet Minute of 2 March 1966, Decision No 60. NAA A5839, Vol 1.
38 Australia, House of Representatives, 1966, *Debates*, Vol 50, 24 March 1966, p. 618.
39 For details of Australia's commitment to the Vietnam War in 1967, see P. Edwards, *A Nation at War: Australian Politics, Society and Diplomacy during the Vietnam War 1965–1975*, pp. 139-156, Allen & Unwin, St Leonards, 1997.
40 Cabinet Notebook 1/319 meeting of 28 July 1967. NAA A11099, 1/319.
41 Cabinet Notebook 1/87 meeting of 28 September 1967. NAA A11099, 1/87.
42 Cabinet Notebook 1/87 meeting of 6 September 1967, ibid.
43 Cabinet Notebook 1/85 meeting of 18 July 1967, ibid.
44 Rusk's comments contained in cable 44 from Rusk to the Department of State and the President, Canberra, 6 April 1968, *FRUS* 1964–1968 Vol XXVII, Mainland Southeast Asia: Regional Affairs, Document 36.
45 Letter, Charles Johnson to Sir John Johnson, Commonwealth Office, London, 1 August 1968. UK Archives PREM 13/1945, C675175.
46 See, for example, the discussion of Submission No 81 'Military presence in Malaysia and Singapore', 15 May 1968. Cabinet Notebook 1/326. NAA A11099, 1/326. The uncertainty generated by the Cabinet's indecision over a continued forward defence commitment to Malaysia resulted in Secretary of State Rusk calling in Ambassador Waller to clarify whether Australia was 'withdrawing' from Malaysia. Hasluck warned that we 'must try to breakdown appearance of crisis, uncertainty etc' to which Gorton replied 'But we are in a period of crisis'. Cabinet Notebook 1/326,. ibid.
47 Paul Hasluck, *Foreign Affairs, Public Addresses and Articles (Other than Speeches in Parliament and Formal Official Statements)*, Vol II 1964–1968, NLA Hasluck Papers, MS5274, Box 37, p. 7.
48 See, for example, Cabinet Notebook 1/110 of meeting on 22 April 1970 to discuss a response to President Nixon's announcement of a withdrawal of troops from Vietnam and the testy exchange between Gorton and Fraser. At one point Gorton cut off his Defence Minister in mid-sentence. NAA A11099 1/110.
49 Cabinet Notebook 1/256 meeting of 12 January 1968. NAA A11099, 1/256.
50 ibid.

51 David Goldsworthy, *Losing the Blanket*, p.170.
52 Cabinet Notebook 1/101, meeting on 29 May 1969. NAA A11099, 1/103.
53 ibid.
54 See discussion recorded in Cabinet Notebook 1/320 of meeting on 25 January 1968.
55 David Goldsworthy, *Losing the Blanket*, p. 176.
56 Relevant section of Five Power Arrangements quoted in T. B. Millar, *Australia in Peace and War*, p. 246, Australian National University Press, 1978. See also Andrea Benvenuti, *Anglo–Australian Relations and the 'Turn to Europe'*, The Royal Historical Society, The Boydell Press, 2008, pp.153-162.
57 Cabinet Decision of 18 September 1968 and Cabinet Submission No 274 'Papua New Guinea: Strength of the PIR'. NAA A1838, TS698/2 part 4.
58 Cabinet Notebook 1/102, meeting on 22 July 1969, NAA A11099 1/102.
59 An earlier round of talks had taken place in January 1966 in Port Moresby between Barnes and the Select Committee. Barnes had briefed the Cabinet on these talks in Submission No 1 of 27 January 1966 'Papua New Guinea – Constitutional Development'. Barnes advised the Cabinet that he intended to bring forward a submission on the possible long-term relationship between Australia and the Territory. Text of Submission No 1 and background information contained in Stuart Doran (ed.), *Documents on Australian Foreign Policy: Australia and Papua New Guinea 1966–1969*, Department of Foreign Affairs and Trade, Canberra, 2006, pp. 20-34. A copy of Cabinet Decision No 23 of 15 February 1966 in response to the submission is on p. 59.
60 ibid. Text of submission No 71 of 10 March 1966 'Papua and New Guinea: Ultimate Status' in pp. 86-103.
61 ibid. p. 91.
62 ibid. p. 91.
63 ibid. p. 92. The text of the Defence Committee's report was attached to the Submission and is reproduced as pp. 99-103.
64 Cabinet Notebook 1/78, meeting on 29 March 1966. NAA A11099, 1/78.
65 Cabinet Minute 24 and 29 March 1966, Decision No 138. NAA A5839, Vol 1.
65a Report by Sir Henry Bland, 31 March 1969, 'Some Observations on my Visit to PNG', 16–22 March 1969, NAA A1838 TS689/2, part 4.
66 Submission 577, 9 May, 1969, 'Papua and New Guinea: National Unity and Public Order', in Doran (ed.), *Documents on Australian Foreign Policy, Australia and Papua New Guinea 1966-1969*, pp. 760-763.
67 Gorton referred to Biafra again in a TV interview broadcast on 19 July 1970. Cable 43 from Canberra to Lagos of 5 August 1970 contains transcript of TV interview on Channel 7 on 17 July 1970 and broadcast on 19 July 1970. NAA A1838, 936/3/21 part 4. In the interview Gorton said 'I think it is not putting it too high to say that if one were not careful something even like a Biafran situation could develop if we just moved out and said "Right, you are on your own. We wash our hands of you". I believe it possible'.
68 Cabinet Notebook 1/274 meeting on 20 May 1969. NAA A11099 1/274.
69 Cabinet Decision No 1044 of 20 May 1969 in Doran (ed.), *Australia and Papua New Guinea*, ibid, pp. 771-772.
70 Defence Committee Minute of 2 September 1969, 'Violence in Rabaul', NAA A452, 68/5748 part 1.

NOTES (CHAPTER 9)

71 See note by G. L. V. Hooton, Attorney-General's Department, 'Military Aid to the Civil Power in Papua/New Guinea', 26 March 1971 for a detailed chronology of the role played by the issue of the calling out of the PIR in the political confrontation between Gorton and Fraser. See also a note prepared by Governor-General Hasluck dated July 1970 in NAA M1768 Item 2. See also I. Hancock, *John Gorton: He Did It His Way*, pp. 291-294 for a further account of the political crisis. In March 1971 when Malcolm Fraser resigned as Minister for Defence he cited Gorton's handling of the decision-making behind the call out of the PIR as one of the reasons he could no longer serve in his government.

72 Study in relation to Internal Security, Report by Interdepartmental Committee. 11 September 1972, NAA A452 T29, 1975/26.

73 National Intelligence Committee Report 'International Developments up to 1980', NAA A452, 1970/4122.

74 Speech by Prime Minister Gorton, ABC Radio, Port Moresby, 6 July 1970. ibid.

75 Handwritten comment by Waller to Deputy Secretaries Shann and Border, 8 December 1971, NAA A1838 3080/10/1 part 1.

76 See A1838, TS689 parts 3 to 6 for details of the review of the Defence Forces in Papua New Guinea.

77 Defence Committee Minute of 17 September 1970. Agendum 14/1970 Minute No 19/1970, Review of Defence Forces in Papua/New Guinea. NAA A1838, 679/2/2/4 part 7.

78 See Australian Defence Review, Department of Defence, 28 March 1972, Australia, House of Representatives, *Debates* Vol 77, 28 March 1972.

79 ibid.

80 ibid.

81 For details on the crisis, see note prepared by Governor-General Hasluck dated July 1970, 'Events Associated with Proposal to Use Defence Forces to Maintain Civil Order in Papua New Guinea, July 1970', NAA M1768 Item 2. In Malcolm Fraser's 'Political Memoirs' he and Margaret Simons refer only to Fraser telephoning the Governor-General while the Note prepared by Hasluck records Fraser as calling on him. Malcolm Fraser and Margaret Simons, *Malcolm Fraser: The Political Memoirs*, pp. 205-207. Cabinet Notebook 1/111 meeting on 19 July 1970. NAA A11099, 1/111. See also Cabinet Decision No 486 of 21 July 1970, 'Military Aid to the Civil Power in Papua and New Guinea', NAA A452, 1961/3329, part 5 and the Explanatory Note attached to the Minute for the Executive Council, 19 July 1970, NAA A432, 1961/3329.

82 Cabinet Notebook 1/87 of 6 September 1967. NAA A11099. 1/87.

83 Cabinet Notebook 1/34 of 4 September 1956. NAA A11099, 1/34.

84 Cabinet Notebook 1/56 of 1 May 1962. NAA A11099. 1/56.

85 Garry Woodard, *Asian Alternatives*, p. 346.

86 Submission No 107 of 19 May 1971, 'The Strategic Basis of Australian Defence Policy – 1971' and Decision No 197 of 8 June 1971. NAA A5908, 107. See 'Strategic Basis of Australian Defence Policy March 1971', pp. 411ff. in S. Frühling (ed.) *A History of Australian Strategic Policy Since 1945*, Defence Publishing Service, Canberra, 2009. See P. Dibb and R. Brabin-Smith, 'Indonesia in Australian Defence Planning', *Security Challenges*, Vol 3, No 4, November 2007, pp. 78-79.

87 S. Frühling (ed.), ibid., p. 413.

88 ibid., p. 414.
89 ibid.
90 ibid.
91 ibid.
92 ibid., p. 415.
93 Cabinet Minute, Decision No 452, 23 June 1970, NAA A5869, Vol 19.
94 Press Release No 907, 20 May 1971, 'National Unity', NAA A1209, 1971/9229.
95 Letter, Waller to Hay, 14 December 1971 NAA A1838, 3080/10/1 part 1.
96 Department of Defence, *Australian Defence Review*, Australian Parliament, 1972.
97 Australia, House of Representative, 1972, *Debates* Vol 77, 28 March 1972, p. 1252.
98 Statement by Minister for Defence to the Administrator's Executive Council, 15 June 1972, NAA A1838, 3080/4/1 part 1.
99 Comments made by W. Conroy in Record of Conversation W. L. Conroy, Director, PNG Department of Foreign Relations and Trade and L. H. Border, A/g Deputy Secretary, Department of Foreign Affairs, 6 August 1973. NAA A1838, 3080/1/2/3A, part 1A.
100 Cable PR11590 from Commander PNG Force to Defence, 15 June 1972, NAA A1838, 3080/4/1 part 1.
101 Interview with Minister for Defence, David Fairbairn, Australian Broadcasting Commission, 15 June 1972, Port Moresby.

Chapter 10

1 Whitlam was sworn in as Prime Minister on 5 December following the general election held on 2 December. He also held the portfolio of Minister for Foreign Affairs until 6 November 1973. Don Willesee served as Minister for Foreign Affairs from 6 November 1973 to 11 November 1975. Lance Barnard served as Deputy Prime Minister and Minister for Defence from 5 December 1972 to 6 June 1974. Bill Morrison served as Minister for External Territories from 19 December 1972 to 30 November 1973, Minister Assisting the Minister for Foreign Affairs in matters relating to Papua New Guinea from 30 November 1974 to 6 June 1975 and Minister for Defence from 6 June 1975 to 11 November 1975.

2 For an overview of Labor's policy approach to Papua New Guinea, see P. Westerway, 'The ALP and New Guinea', *New Guinea*, June/July 1965, pp. 37-39; Downs, *The Australian Trusteeship*, Chs 13–14; E. G. Whitlam, *The Whitlam Government 1972–1975*, Viking Press, Ringwood, 1985, pp. 71-101; E. G. Whitlam, Text of Address given by the Prime Minister and Minister for Foreign Affairs when opening the Australian Institute of Political Science Summer School, Canberra, 22 January 1973, in D. Pettit (ed.), *Selected Readings in Australian Foreign Policy*, Sorrett Publishing, Toorak, 1973; K. Beazley Snr, 'The Future of Papua New Guinea', *World Review*, Vol 11, No 2, July 1972, pp. 3-18; J. Griffin (ed.), *A Foreign Policy for an Independent Papua New Guinea*, Angus and Robertson in association with the Australian Institute of International Affairs, Sydney 1974, contains 'Labor's Plans for Papua New Guinea', Statement by the Leader of the Opposition Mr E. G. Whitlam, Port Moresby, 12 January 1970, pp. 145-49; E. G. Whitlam, *Beyond Vietnam: Australia's Regional Responsibility*, Victorian Fabian Society, Pamphlet 17, Melbourne, 1968; E.G. Whitlam, 'Australia and Her Region', in J. McLaren (ed.), *Towards a New Australia*,

Victorian Fabian Society, Melbourne, 1972, pp. 17-19; and G. Pemberton, 'Whitlam and the Labor Tradition' in D. Lee and C. Waters (eds), *Evatt to Evans: The Labor Tradition in Australian Foreign Policy*, Allen & Unwin, Canberra, 1997, pp. 131-62. An analysis of the transfer of power can be found in H. Nelson, 'Liberation: The End of Australian Rule in Papua New Guinea', *The Journal of Pacific History*, Vol 35, No 3, 2000, pp. 269-80.

3   The details of Whitlam's visits to Papua New Guinea are available in E.G. Whitlam, 'The Decolonisation of Papua New Guinea', paper delivered at 'Hindsight' seminar, *A Retrospective Workshop: Decolonisation and Independence in Papua New Guinea*, ANU Canberra, 3–4 November 2002. In 1971 the House of Assembly adopted Papua New Guinea as the official name of the country. Henceforth in this book the term Papua New Guinea or PNG will be used.

4   Text quoted in E.G. Whitlam, *The Whitlam Government 1972–1975*, p. 79.

5   Quoted by R. Waddell, 'January–April 1970' in C. Moore with M. Kooyman (eds), *A Papua New Guinea Political Chronicle 1967–1991*, Crawford House Publishing, Bathurst, 1998, p. 100. Chief Minister Somare later told Australian Ambassador to Indonesia, Bob Furlonger, that 'he had been impressed with Mr Whitlam in the past and that many of the things he had said during his visit in 1970 had had the agreement of the Pangu Party'. See Record of Conversation Furlonger and Somare, 5 December 1972, Port Moresby. NAA A452, 1972/3190.

6   Text of Labor's Plan for New Guinea in *Canberra Times*, 13 January 1970, p. 7.

7   Downs, *The Australian Trusteeship*, p. 464.

8   ibid., p. 465.

9   *The Australian*, p. 8, 3 July 1970.

10 Comments made by Tange to J. F. Robertson, Secretary, New Zealand Department of Defence and Lt General R. J. Webb, 21 January 1973. NAA A1838, 689/2/9 part 5.

11 In an interview on arrival in Port Moresby, 3 January 1971, Whitlam said, in relation to the future of Papua New Guinea, 'Australia has to decide whether or not she is willing to continue as a colonial power. This is a decision by Australians about Australia's place in the world ... The Australian Labor Party will not accept a colonial rule on Australia's behalf'. Text reprinted in *The Canberra Times*, 4 January 1971, NAA A 5882, CO66 part 1.

12 Policy statement delivered by Whitlam on 13 November 1972. NAA A1838, 3080/11/6/2 part 1.

13 ibid.

14 Barnard had visited Papua New Guinea with Whitlam in July 1960.

15 For a description of Morrison and his approach to Papua New Guinea, see Donald Denoon, *A Trial Separation: Australia and the Decolonisation of Papua New Guinea*, Pandanas Books, Canberra, 2005. p. 105. See also W. Morrison, 'Papua New Guinea: The Quiet Achievement' in T. Bramston, *The Whitlam Legacy*, The Federation Press, Annandale, 2013.

16 Comments by Morrison to author, 4 November 2002 and comments at 'Hindsight' seminar, Australian National University, Canberra, 3–4 November 2002. See Donald Denoon, *A Trial Separation*, pp. 145-150 for details and a critique of Australia's approach to the defence relationship with PNG.

17 Hank Nelson, *Papua New Guinea: Black Unity or Black Chaos*, Penguin Books, Ringwood, 1972, pp. 236-237.

18 Donald Denoon, *Trial Separation*, p. 4.
19 *Sydney Morning Herald*, 2 January 1975, Editorial 'As the Sun Sets'.
20 Papua New Guinea Press Release No 3437 of 3 December 1972, 'Chief Minister Congratulates A.L.P'. NAA A1838, 3080/11/6/2 part 1.
21 Address by Lance Barnard, Deputy Leader of the Australian Labor Party, to the Army Staff College, Queenscliff, 1 May 1972, NAA A1838, 3080/4/1 part 1.
22 ibid.
23 ibid.
24 Walsh and Munster, *Documents on Australian Defence and Foreign Policy 1968–1975*, Paper by Joint Intelligence Organisation, 11 January 1973, pp. 293-98.
25 ibid.
26 Record of Meeting between Minister for Defence, Minister Assisting the Minister for Defence and Minister for External Territories, Canberra, 18 January 1973, NAA A452 1972/4109.
27 See letter, Morrison to Barnard, 16 January 1973, NAA A 452, 1972/3889. Morrison argued 'whilst it had to date been able to maintain law and order, there is as least some doubt as to whether, without being strengthened, it will be able to do so in the future … I think that early consideration should be given to the formation of a police field force which could engage in the control of law and order in rural areas, controlling riots and border supervision. … The possibility of PIR personnel being used in the proposed field force could be explored'.
28 ibid. See also W. Morrison, 'Draft Notes on the Transfer of Defence Powers', Paper presented at 'Hindsight' seminar, Australian National University, Canberra, 3–4 November 2002. Morrison had served in Kuala Lumpur as Deputy High Commissioner before being elected to Parliament in 1969.
29 ibid.
30 ibid.
31 ibid.
32 Record of Meeting between Barnard and Morrison, 11 April 1973. Others present: David Hay, Secretary, Department of External Territories and G. Blakers, Deputy Secretary, Department of Defence. NAA A452, 1972/3889.
33 ibid.
34 Donald Denoon, *A Trial Separation*, pp. 147-148.
35 Record of Conversation Furlonger and Somare, 5 December 1972, Port Moresby. NAA A452, 1972/3190. Furlonger had visited Papua New Guinea in July 1970 as Director, Joint Intelligence Organisation.
36 ibid.
37 Cable 5290 of 11 December 1972 from Jakarta to Canberra, ibid.
38 ibid.
39 Cable 675 of 12 February 1973 from Jakarta to Canberra. ibid.
40 ibid.
41 Record of Meeting, Chief Minister of Papua New Guinea and Minister for Defence, Minister Assisting the Minister for Defence (Senator Bishop), and Minister for External Territories, Canberra, 18 January 1973, NAA A452, 1972/4109.
42 ibid.
43 ibid.

44 Ron May, *The Changing Role of the Military in Papua New Guinea*, Strategic and Defence Studies Centre, Canberra, 1993, pp. 14-56.
45 Text of Address, Minister for Defence, Lance Barnard, to the Administrator's Executive Council, Port Moresby, 25 January 1973, NAA A1838, 3080/4/5, part 1.
46 ibid.
47 ibid.
48 ibid.
49 Minute, Jackson to Blakeney DFA, 13 April 1973. NAA A9737, 1991/70805. Minute reported conversation with G. R. Marshall, Chief Planning Officer, Defence Planning, Department of Defence.
50 ibid.
51 Telex 519 of 1 February 1973 from the Department of External Territories, Canberra, to Administrator, Port Moresby. Press conference held on aircraft descending into Canberra on 29 January 1973. According to the telex message, Barnard initially used the word 'essential' to describe Manus and the refuelling base and this was later amended to 'desirable'. NAA A452, 1972/4109.
52 Minute, Hay (Secretary Department of External Territories) to FAS (GL), John Greenwell, 30 January 1973 reporting debriefing by Gordon Blakers (Deputy Secretary, Defence) on Barnard's visit. Ibid.
53 ibid.
54 Letter, Somare to Morrison, 18 May 1973. NAA A4087, D923/1/1. Morrison wrote to Barnard on receipt of Somare's letter seeking a transfer of part of the budget for the PNGDF to the Police Force.
55 Record of conversation, Whitlam and Somare, Port Moresby, 20 February 1973, NAA A1838, 3080/16/15 part 1.
56 Speech, Prime Minister Whitlam at a Papua New Guinea Government Dinner, Port Moresby, 18 February 1973, NAA A1838, 3080/16/15 part 1.
57 Address by Prime Minister Whitlam at a state banquet given by the Government of Indonesia, Jakarta, 20 February 1973. NAA A1838, 3080/16/15 part 1.
58 Speech by Minister for Defence, National Press Club, Canberra, 15 March 1973, NAA A1838, 677/1, part 11.
59 Australia, House of Representatives, 1973, *Debates*, Vol 84, 24 May 1973, pp. 2646.
60 ibid. Peacock had used similar language in June 1972 when he said 'while Australia will remain important to Papua New Guinea, we should not seek to build an exclusive relationship based on a mistaken belief that past assistance places Papua New Guinea under an obligation to us. Looked at from Papua New Guinea's point of view, Indonesia, Singapore, Malaysia, the Philippines and Japan, as well as the island nations of the Pacific, will have important places in the eyes of Papua New Guinea Governments'. Speech reprinted in W. J. Hudson, *New Guinea Empire: Australia's Colonial Experience*, Cassell, Melbourne, 1974, p. 115.
61 Letter, Somare to Whitlam, 6 August 1973. NAA A1838, 3080/4/4 part 2. Various annotations on the letter by departmental officers indicate a sense of confusion as to what had motivated Somare to write three months after the speech had been delivered. Whitlam had made no reference to a defence treaty.

62 News Release No 1229 of 17 May 1973 'Policy Guidelines Agreed'. NAA A1838, 3080/4/1 part 3.
63 Defence Committee Agendum, 'Strategic Basis Paper 1973', 29 and 31 May 1973, NAA A1838, 677/3, part 22. A copy of the Strategic Basis Paper is also contained in S. Frühling (ed.), *A History of Australian Strategic Policy Since 1945*, Defence Publishing Service, Canberra, 2009. The extracts following are taken from the edition released in Frühling's book.
64 ibid., para. 50.
65 Report by the Joint Planning Committee, 'Australian Access to Base Facilities in Papua New Guinea after Independence, 28 June 1973', NAA A1838, 3080/4/5 part 1. The Joint Planning Committee was established in 1940 to advise the Defence Committee and the Chiefs of Staff Committee on operational aspects of defence planning, plans for combined operations, co-ordination of inter-service training and strategic appreciation. The Department of Foreign Affairs was represented on the Committee.
66 ibid.
67 ibid.
68 Defence Committee Minute No 8/1973, 'Australia's Defence Relations with Papua New Guinea', 1 November 1973, NAA A4087, D923/13/3 part 1.
69 Minute, Pritchett to Tange, October 1973, 'Australia's Defence Interests with Papua New Guinea'. Pritchett told Tange that 'because of practical exigencies I have not called together a writing group but have written the paper myself'. He did, however, consult 'as to the concept' with Defence and Foreign Affairs officials. NAA A4087, D923/13/3 part 1.
70 Minute, Border to Waller, 7 February 1973, NAA A1838, 689/2/9 part 1.
71 Defence Committee Agendum No 5/1973, Minute No 8/1973, Minute of meeting on 1 November 1973, Australia's Defence Relations with Papua New Guinea. NAA A4087, D923/13/3 part 1. The subsequent extracts have been taken from the paper 'Australia's Defence Relations with Papua New Guinea'.
72 R. O'Neill, 'Australia's Future Defence Relations with Papua New Guinea', *Australian Outlook*, Vol 26, No 2, August 1972, p. 201.
73 H. Bull (ed.), *Foreign Policy for Australia: Choices for the Seventies*, Australian Institute of Political Science, Proceedings of the 39th Summer School, Angus and Robertson, Sydney, 1973, p. 149.
74 H. Bull, quoted in 'Summary of Discussion', in E. Wolfers (ed.), *Australia's Northern Neighbours: Independent or Dependent?*, Nelson, Melbourne, 1976, p. 180.
75 J. A. C. Mackie, *Konfrontasi: The Indonesia–Malaysia Dispute 1963–1966*, Oxford University Press, London, 1974.
76 J. A. C. Mackie, 'The External Dimension: Regional Problems and Policy Decisions Confronting Australia', in Wolfers (ed.), *Australia's Northern Neighbours*, p. 180.
77 F. A Mediansky, 'Defence', in W. J. Hudson (ed.), *Australia's New Guinea Question*, Nelson, in association with the Australian Institute of International Affairs, Melbourne, 1975, p. 140.
78 Comments by Professor O. Harries, in Bull (ed.), *Foreign Policy for Australia*, p. 172.

Chapter 11

1. P. Mench, *The Role of the Papua New Guinea Defence Force*, Development Studies Centre, Monograph No 2, Australian National University Press, Canberra, 1975, p. 78.
2. Morrison's account was conveyed to the author at the 'Hindsight' seminar, Australian National University, 4 November 2002.
3. According to an article in *Tribune*, the union leader Bill Hartley spoke on the issue and argued that 'such a treaty could involve Australia in military activity in PNG to defend the unity of the country against the tendency to communal disintegration which is evident today'. *Tribune*, July 17–23, 1973.
4. Mench, *The Role of the Papua New Guinea Defence Force*, p. 74.
5. See comment by Prime Minister and Foreign Minister Whitlam on departmental minute, 20 July 1973, NAA A1838, 689/1 part 1.
6. See text of the 1962 ANZUS Communiqué, Canberra, 8–9 May 1962, *CNIA*, Vol 33, No 5, 1962.
7. J. Starke, *The ANZUS Treaty Alliance*, Melbourne University Press, Carlton, 1965, p. 145.
8. See handwritten comment by Tange on a draft Defence Committee report, 7 February 1963, NAA A1838, 696/3/3 part 3.
9. Attachment, 'Australia's Defence Relations with Papua New Guinea: Note on PNG and ANZUS', Defence Committee Minute No 8/1973, 'Australia's Defence Relations with Papua New Guinea', 1 November 1973, NAA A1838, 3080/4/5 part 1. The US Embassy advice was contained in a letter, 7 May 1973, ibid.
10. ibid.
11. ibid.
12. James Curran, *Unholy Fury: Whitlam and Nixon at War*, Melbourne University Press, Carlton, 2015.
13. Record of the Joint Australian/Papua New Guinea Steering Committee on the Transfer of Defence Power, Canberra, 5–6 February 1974, para. 5, NAA A1838, 3080/4/1 part 1.
14. Record of the Australia/Papua New Guinea Ministerial Defence Meeting, Canberra, 4 April 1974, NAA A1838, 3080/4/1 part 5.
15. ibid.
16. ibid.
17. ibid.
18. Mench, *The Role of the Defence Force in Papua New Guinea*, pp. 92–93.
19. Papua New Guinea House of Assembly 1974, *Debates*, Vol III, no 28, p. 3681. Speech by Albert Maori Kiki, Minister for Defence, Foreign Relations and Trade, 25 April 1974.
20. ibid., p. 3685.
21. Submission Pritchett to Barnard, 9 July 1974, NAA A9737, 1991/70805.
22. ibid.
23. ibid.
24. Records of Conversation, Sir Victor Smith with Somare and Kiki, Port Moresby, 15 and 16 July 1974, NAA A1838, 689/2/12/1 part 1.

25 Speech by Minister for Defence at the CGSE Opening Royal Military College, Duntroon, 12 August 1974. NAA A1838, 3081/2/6/3/1 part 2.
26 Australia, House of Representatives, 1974, *Debates*, Vol 91, 24 October 1974, p. 2819.
27 See Australia, House of Representatives, 1975, *Debates*, Vol 10, 4 March 1975, p. 984 and Statement 'Transfer of Defence Power to Papua New Guinea' dated 4 March 1975, tabled by Barnard. The statement repeated the description of the future defence relationship set out in Barnard's speech in Parliament on 24 October 1974.
28 ibid.
29 ibid.
30 Papua New Guinea House of Assembly 1974, *Debates*, Vol III, no 38, pp. 4965-4966, 24 October 1974.
31 Department of Foreign Affairs submission, 3 September 1975, NAA A1838, 689/2/18 part 1.
32 Annotation by Whitlam on submission from B. C. Hill, First Assistant Secretary, Pacific and Western Division, Department of Foreign Affairs, 25 June 1974. NAA A1838, 1490/17/5, part 4.
33 Letter, Whitlam to Somare 19 June 1975 in cable CH232318 from Canberra to Port Moresby, 19 June 1975. NAA A1838, 3081/2/6/3 part 4.
34 See W. Way (ed.) with D. Browne and V. Johnson, *Australia and the Indonesian Incorporation of Portuguese Timor, 1974–1976*, Melbourne University Press, Carlton South, 2000, for a number of examples of Australian officials drawing attention to the impact on Papua New Guinea of Indonesia's actions against East Timor. See, in particular, Document No 24, 'Brief for Whitlam', Canberra 2 September 1974, pp. 90-93; Document No 81, Letter from Barnard to Willesee, Canberra 11 February 1975, pp. 176-80; and Document No 393, Cable to Canberra from Jakarta, 5 January 1976, pp. 652-60. In Barnard's letter to Willesee (Document No 81), Barnard notes 'A further aspect concerns Papua New Guinea. At present there seems little awareness of Portuguese Timor; but we cannot be confident that this would continue were Indonesia to take immoderate action in Timor. I would expect people in Papua New Guinea to think about the implications for their relations with Indonesia and in this respect to look again at their defence relationship with Australia. This could well be at the very time that we are finalising a defence relationship with PNG that, at the wish of both parties, will now contain no Australian commitment to the security of PNG after independence. Such a commitment would, of course, have direct implications for the structure of the Defence Force and for the size of our defence expenditure'.
35 May, *The Changing Role of the Military in Papua New Guinea*, p. 15.
36 The critical section of this document noted that 'the Papua New Guinea authorities will in good time provide to the Australian High Commissioner information, reports and assessments about politically sensitive situations in which Australian loan personnel might be involved'. The document noted that the arrangements allowed for direct consultation between the High Commissioner and the Papua New Guinea authorities. Department of Defence, *Documents Relating to Interim Defence Arrangements between Australia and Papua New Guinea*, tabled in the House of Representatives, 9 October 1975.
37 ibid. See text of Joint Statement 'PNG – Interim Arrangements for Post-Independence Defence Relations', 9 October 1975.

38 ibid. See text of letter from Morrison to Kiki, dated 10 September 1975.
39 Submission, Blakeney (FAS, Defence Division, Foreign Affairs) to Minister, 'PNG: Future Defence Relations with Australia', undated. NAA A9737, 1991/70805.

Chapter 12

1 Press Statement of 5 May 1967 by Malcolm Fraser. The University of Melbourne Digitised Collection, Malcolm Fraser Visit to PNG, 5 May 1967. Fraser had also visited Port Moresby in February 1968.
2 Editorial in *The Age*, 11 April 1972 'Changing Pace'.
3 Letter, Peacock to Somare, 11 May 1972. NAA A1838, 3080/10/1 part 2.
4 Speech by Andrew Peacock, Minister for External Territories, 'Independence – Papua New Guinea Style', to the Australian Institute of International Affairs, Melbourne, 4 July 1972. NAA A1838, 3080/11/1/2 part 1.
5 Speech by Peacock to the New South Wales Branch of the Australian Institute of International Affairs, Sydney, 8 June 1972, 'Future Relations Between Australia and Papua New Guinea', NAA A1838, 3080/10/1 part 2.
6 J. Killen, *Inside Australian Politics*, Methuen Haynes, 1985, p. 170.
7 Letter, Somare to Fraser, 30 January 1976. NAA A10756, LC211.
8 Cabinet Decision No 280 (FAD), 26 February 1976. NAA A13075, 280 FAD.
9 ibid.
10 Cabinet Notebook 3/13 meeting on 26 February 1976, NAA A11099, 3/13.
11 Minute, Renouf to G. Feakes, First Assistant Secretary, South East Asia and PNG Division, DFA, 2 March 1976. NAA A1838. 3081/2/6/3 part 17.
12 Letter of 15 September 1976, G. R. Marshall, Senior Assistant Secretary, Strategic Analysis and International Policy Division, Department of Defence, to M. Lyon, Assistant Secretary, PNG Branch, DFA. Marshall had earlier conveyed a similar message to the Director of Joint Intelligence Office. In that message Marshall had said the paper requested by the Cabinet should 'examine all possibilities for Australian involvement in ensuring a united PNG – including the use of force from Australia, particularly if other powers or interest groups become involved on the side of the secessionists'. Defence Department minute, 23 June 1976 Marshall to DJIO and DGJOP. NAA A1838, 3081/2/6/3/1 part 5.
13 P. Hastings, 'Interview with Prime Minister Fraser', *Sydney Morning Herald*, 7 May 1976.
14 Peacock wrote to Fraser on 12 April 1977 seeking his formal agreement that officials not proceed with the paper. Fraser replied on 26 April 1976 agreeing to Peacock's recommendation but asking that the situation be kept under review. NAA A1838, 3081/2/6/3/1.
15 Foreign Affairs and Defence Submission No 7, February 1976, 'Australia's Defence Relations with Papua New Guinea'. NAA A10756, LC264 part 1.
16 ibid.
17 ibid.
18 ibid.
19 ibid.
20 Cabinet Decision No 289 (FAD) of 2 March 1976. NAA A13075, 289/FAD.

21 Minute, I. D. Emerton, FAS Cabinet and Parliamentary Division, Prime Minister and Cabinet to Prime Minister, 4 March 1976 and letter, J. L. Menadue, Secretary to Cabinet to E. W. Dwyer, Acting Secretary, Department of Defence, 23 March 1976. NAA A10756, LC264 part 1.
22 See letter, Menadue to Dwyer. ibid
23 Joint Communiqué issued on 4 March 1976. *Australian Foreign Affairs Record*, Department of Foreign Affairs, Canberra, March 1976, pp. 153-156.
24 Submission No 487 of July 1976, 'Australia's Defence Relations with Papua New Guinea', NAA A10756, LC264 part 1.
25 Briefing note to the Prime Minister from Allan Griffith, First Assistant Secretary, External Relations and Defence Division, Department of Prime Minister and Cabinet, 10 July 1976. ibid.
26 Cabinet Notebook 3/19, meeting on 14 July 1976. NAA A11099, 3/19.
27 ibid.
28 Papua New Guinea Parliament 1976, *Debates*, Vol 1, No 17, p. 2260, 2 December 1976, *Defence Report 1975–1976*.
29 'Australian Strategic Analysis and Defence Policy Objectives (September 1976)', in S. Frühling (ed.), *A History of Australian Strategic Policy Since 1945*, pp. 543-623.
30 ibid. See Chapter 6.
31 ibid, p. 589.
32 ibid.
33 ibid., p. 590.
34 ibid., p. 591.
35 ibid., p. 592.
36 ibid., p. 594.
37 ibid.
38 Australian Parliament 1976, 'Australian Defence', Presented to Parliament by the Minister for Defence, the Hon D. J. Killen, November 1976.
39 Cabinet Submission No 946 'Australia's Defence relations with Papua New Guinea' and Decision No 2021 (FAD) of 16 December 1976. NAA A10756, LC264 part 1.
40 ibid.
41 ibid.
42 Cabinet Notebook 3/60, meeting on 16 December 1976, NAA A11099, 3/60.
43 Text of Press Conference by Prime Minister Somare, 13 January 1977, Jakarta. NAA A1838, 689/2/28 part 5.
44 Agreed Summary Record of Meeting, Prime Minister of Papua New Guinea and Prime Minister of Australia, 8 February 1977. NAA A1838, 3081/10/11/4 part 5.
45 ibid.
46 Joint Statement by the Prime Minister and the Prime Minister of Papua New Guinea on the Defence Relationship Between Papua New Guinea and Australia, 11 February 1977. ibid.
47 Transcript of Prime Minister Fraser's Press Conference, 11 February 1977, Port Moresby. NAA A1838, 3080/18/1 part 1.
48 Papers of Malcolm Fraser. NAA M1269, 9 part 2.
49 Australia, House of Representatives, 1977, *Debates*, Vol 103, 23 February 1977, pp. 345-346.

Chapter 13

1. Port Moresby Ministerial Directive from Senator Don Willesee, Minister for Foreign Affairs, to T. K. Critchley, 5 April 1974. NAA A1838, 3036/10/6/1 part 6.
2. See speech by E. G. Whitlam, 'Papua New Guinea – The Dangers of Separatism', Monash University, 29 July 1971. NAA M170, 71/61, Personal Papers of Prime Minister E. G. Whitlam. Kim Beazley served in the Australian Paarliament from 1945 to 1977 and was Minister for Education in the Whitlam Government.
3. Cabinet Submission No 4956 and Decision No 9702 of 11 August 1987. NAA A14039, 4956.
4. ibid.
5. ibid., Attachment C, para 21.
6. ibid., Submission, para 9.
7. ibid., Attachment C, para 5.
8. For an interpretation of Dibb's work, see Peter J. Rimmer amd R. Gerard Ward, 'The Power of Geography' in Desmond Ball and Sheryn Lee (eds.), *Geography, Power, Strategy and Defence Policy: Essays in Honour of Paul Dibb*, ANU Press, Australian National University, Canberra, 2016, pp. 45-69.
9. Cabinet Submission No 4956, Attachment C, para 8. NAA A14039, 4956.
10. ibid.
11. ibid., para 23.
11a. ibid., Attachment D, paras 10 and 11.
12. Decision No 9702, 11 August 1987. NAA A14039, 4956.
13. ibid.
14. Text available on website of the Department of Foreign Affairs and Trade, www.dfat.gov.au/geo/png/jdpgr_aust_png.
15. Text available on website of the Department of Foreign Affairs and Trade, www.dfat.gov.au/geo/png/joint-declaration.
16. ibid.
17. Cabinet Submission 209 of 6 June 1983 'Australian Defence Relations with Papua New Guinea', NAA A11116, CA3159 part 1.
18. P. Dibb, *Review of Australia's Defence Capabilities*, AGPS, Canberra, 1986, p. 37.
19. Australia, Senate 1989, *Debates*, Vol 138, 6 December 1989, p. 4023.
20. 2016 Australian Defence White Paper, Department of Defence, Canberra, 2016, para 3.7.
21. Stewart Firth, 'Security in Papua New Guinea: The Military and Diplomatic Dimensions', *Security Challenges*, Vol 10, No 2 (2014), p.109.
22. *PNG Defence White Paper 2013*, Independent State of Papua New Guinea, Port Moresby, 2013, p. 31.
23. Stewart Firth, 'Security in Papua New Guinea: The Military and Diplomatic Dimensions'. ibid.
24. *The Age*, 31 July 1972, p. 31.

BIBLIOGRAPHY

Primary sources

Research for this book has drawn primarily and extensively on the records of the National Archives of Australia in both Canberra and Melbourne, the National Library collection of Private Papers and the Australian War Memorial. In addition, use has been made of the United States National Archives, particularly the libraries of Presidents Truman, Kennedy and Johnson, the UK National Archives at Kew, the private papers of David Lloyd George held at Parliament House, London, and the National Archives of the Netherlands. Details of primary sources are cited in the endnotes.

Australian published government records
Australian Defence, Commonwealth Parliament of Australia, November, 1976.
Australian Defence Review, Commonwealth Parliament of Australia, March 1972.
Australian Foreign Affairs Record 1965–1977, Department of Foreign Affairs, Canberra.
Australia and the Indonesian Incorporation of Portuguese Timor 1974–1976, Documents on Australian Foreign Policy, Melbourne University Press, Carlton South, 2000.
Commonwealth Parliamentary Debates, 1901–1977, Commonwealth Government Printer, Canberra.
Current Notes on International Affairs (CNIA), Australian Government Publishing Service, Canberra, 1940–1977.
Defending Australia, Defence White Paper, Department of Defence, Australian Government Publishing Service, Canberra, 1994.
Dibb, P. *Review of Australia's Defence Capabilities*, Australian Government Publishing Service, Canberra, 1986.
Documents on Australian Foreign Policy, 1937–1949, Vols I–XVI, Department of Foreign Affairs and Trade, Canberra.
Documents Relating to Interim Defence Arrangements between Australia and Papua New Guinea, Commonwealth Parliament of Australia, October, 1975.
New South Wales Defences – Preliminary report by Sir William Jervois, Parliament of New South Wales, Sydney, 1877.
Statements on Foreign Policy, December 1975–March 1977, Department of Foreign Affairs, Canberra, 1977.
The Territory of Papua and New Guinea, Policy Statements 1960–1963, issued under the authority of the Minister for Territories, the Hon. Paul Hasluck, Canberra, 1963.
The Defence of Australia 1987, Australian Government Publishing Service, Canberra, 1987.

Bibliography

Papua New Guinea published government records
Defence Report 1975-1976, Papua New Guinea Parliament, Port Moresby, December 1976.
Papua New Guinea House of Assembly Debates 1965-1975, Port Moresby.
Papua New Guinea National Parliament Debates, 1975-1977, Port Moresby.
Universalism: Guidelines to the Foreign Policy of Papua New Guinea, Department of Foreign Affairs and Trade, Port Moresby, November 1976.
Papua New Guinea Defence White Paper 2013, The Independent State of Papua New Guinea, Port Moresby, 2013.

United States Government records
Foreign Relations of the United States (FRUS), Volumes XXIII and XXVII.

Interviews and correspondence
Bailey, Peter. Department of Prime Minister and Cabinet, interview, 11 February 2014.
Critchley, T. K. Australian High Commissioner, Papua New Guinea, interview, 8 February 1998.
Furlonger, R. Ambassador, Jakarta 1972–1974, 13 February 1998 and 12 February 2003, interviews.
Greenwell, J. Department of External Territories, interview, 13 February 2003.
Hay, Sir David. Secretary, Department of External Territories, interview, 4 November 2002.
Ingram, J. Department of External Affairs, Counsellor, Australian Embassy Jakarta, July 1962 to July 1964, interviews, 23 and 30 May 2016.
Jockel, G. Director, Joint Intelligence Organisation, telephone interview, 29 January 2003.
Lawler, Sir Peter. Department of Prime Minister and Cabinet, interview, 1 October 2014.
Lyon, M. Department of Foreign Affairs, interview, 2 February 1998.
Morrison, W. Minister for External Territories and Minister Assisting the Minister for Foreign Affairs in matters relating to Papua New Guinea, 4 November 2002, interview.
Tange, Sir Arthur. Secretary, Department of Defence, 3 November 1999, letter.
Woodard, G. Department of External Affairs, interview, 27 May 2016.

Secondary sources

Books
Aitkin, D. (ed.). *The Howson Diaries: The Life of Politics*, The Viking Press, Ringwood, 1984.
Andrews, E. M. *Isolationism and Appeasement in Australia: Reactions to the European Crisis, 1935–39*, Australian National University Press, Canberra, 1970.
Andrews, E. M. *The ANZAC Illusion: Anglo-Australian Relations During World War I*, Cambridge University Press, Cambridge, 1993.
Australian Institute of Political Science. *Foreign Policy for Australia: Choices for the Seventies*, Proceedings of the 39th Summer School, Australian Institute of Political Science, Angus and Robertson, Sydney, 1973.
Ball, D. (ed.). *The Anzac Connection*, Allen & Unwin, North Sydney 1985.

Ball, D. and Lee, S. (eds.). *Geography, Power, Strategy and Defence Policy: Essays in Honour of Paul Dibb*, ANU Press, Australian National University, Canberra, 2016.

Barwick, Sir Garfield. *A Radical Tory: Garfield Barwick's Reflections and Recollections*, Federation Press, Leichhardt, 1995.

Beale, H. *This Inch of Time: Memoirs of Politics and Diplomacy*, Melbourne University Press, Carlton, 1977.

Beddie, B. D. *Advance Australia–Where?* Oxford University Press in association with the Australian Institute for International Affairs, Canberra, 1975.

Bell, C. (ed.). *Agenda for the Eighties: Contexts of Australian Choices in Foreign and Defence Policy*, Australian National University Press, Canberra, 1980.

Bell, R. J. *Unequal Allies: Australian–American Relations and the Pacific War*, Melbourne University Press, Carlton, 1977.

Beaumont, J. (ed.). *Australia's War 1939–1945*, Allen & Unwin, St Leonards, 1996.

Beaumont, J. et al. *Ministers, Mandarins and Diplomats: Australian Foreign Policy Making 1941–1969*, Melbourne University Press, Carlton, 2003.

Beaumont, J. *Broken Nation Australians in the Great War*, Allen & Unwin, Crows Nest, 2014.

Bird, D. J. A. *Lyons – The 'Tame Tasmanian': Appeasement and Rearmament in Australia 1932–39*, Australian Scholarly Publications, North Melbourne, 2008.

Birman, J. (ed.). *Australia's Defence*, University of Western Australia Extension Service, East Fremantle, 1976.

Bolton, G. *Paul Hasluck: A Life*, UWA Publishing, Crawley, 2014.

Bramston, T. *The Whitlam Legacy*, The Federation Press, Sydney, 2013.

Bridge, C. (ed.). *Munich to Vietnam: Australia's Relations with Britain and the United States since the 1930s*, Melbourne University Press, Carlton, 1991.

Bridge, C. *William Hughes Australia*, Haus Publishing Company, London, 2011.

Brown, B. (ed.). *Australia and the Pacific in the 1970s: The Roles of the United States, Australia and New Zealand*, Australian National University Press, Canberra, 1971.

Buckle, K., Dale, B. and Reynolds, W. *Doc Evatt, Patriot, Internationalist, Fighter and Scholar*, Longman, Cheshire, Melbourne, 1994.

Bull, H., Cairns, K., Whitlam, G., and Teichmann, M. *Australian Foreign Policy in the Seventies*, Australian Institute of International Affairs, North Queensland branch, Townsville, 1968.

Bull, H. (ed.). *Asia and the Western Pacific: Towards a New International Order*, Nelson, Melbourne, 1975.

Bullock, K. *Australia and Papua New Guinea: Foreign and Defence Relations Since 1975*, Strategic and Defence Studies Centre, Australian National University, Working Paper No 227, March 1991.

Bunting, J. *R. G. Menzies: A Portrait*, Allen & Unwin, North Sydney, 1988.

Cain, F. (ed.). *Menzies in War and Peace*, Allen & Unwin in association with the Australian Defence Studies Centre, Australian Defence Force Academy, St Leonards, 1997.

Camilleri, J. and Teichmann, M. *Security and Survival: The New Era in International Relations*, Heinemann, Melbourne, 1973.

Camilleri, J. *An Introduction to Australian Foreign Policy*, Jacaranda Press, Milton, 1973.

Casey, R. G. *Australian Foreign Minister: The Diaries of R. G. Casey 1951–1960*, Collins, London, 1972.

Casey, R. G. *Friends and Neighbours: Australia, the United States and the World*, Michigan State College Press, East Lansing, 1955.

Cheeseman, G. *The Search for Self Reliance: Australian Defence Since Vietnam*, Longman Cheshire, Melbourne, 1993.

Bibliography

Cheeseman, G. and Bruce, R. (eds). *Discourses of Danger and Dread Frontiers: Australian Defence and Security Thinking After the Cold War*, Allen & Unwin, Canberra, 1996.

Chiddick, J. P. and Teichmann, M. *Australia and the World: A Political Handbook*, Macmillan, Melbourne 1977.

Clark, C (ed.). *Australian Foreign Policy: Towards a Reassessment*, Cassell, Melbourne, 1973.

Clark, C. M. H. *A History of Australia: The People Make Laws 1888–1915*, Vol V, Melbourne University Press, Carlton, 1981.

Conley Tyler, M. (ed.). *R. G. Casey: Minister for External Affairs 1951–60*, Australian Institute of International Affairs, Deakin, 2012.

Conley Tyler, M. (ed.). *Ministers for Foreign Affairs 1960–72*, Australian Institute of International Affairs, Deakin, 2014.

Connor, J. *ANZAC and Empire: George Foster Pearce and the Foundations of Australian Defence*, Cambridge University Press, Cambridge, 2011.

Cumpston, I. M. *Australia's Defence Policy 1901–2000*, Volumes I and II, Privately published, Canberra, 2001.

Curran, J. *Unholy Fury: Whitlam and Nixon at War*, Melbourne University Press, Carlton, 2015.

Day, D. (ed.). *Brave New World: Dr H. V. Evatt and Australian Foreign Policy*, University of Queensland Press, St Lucia, 1996.

Day, D. *Reluctant Nation: Australia and the Allied defeat of Japan 1942–45*, Oxford University Press, Melbourne, 1992.

Day, D. *The Great Betrayal: Britain, Australia and the Onset of the Pacific War 1939–1942*, Oxford University Press, Melbourne, 1988.

Day, D. *John Curtin: A Life*, Harper Collins, Sydney, 1999.

Dean, P. (ed.). *Australia 1942: In the Shadow of War*, Cambridge University Press, Cambridge, 2013.

Dean, P. (ed.). *Australia 1943: The Liberation of New Guinea*, Cambridge University Press, Cambridge, 2014.

Dennis, P. and Grey, J. (eds). *Serving Vital Interests: Australia's Strategic Planning in Peace and War, Proceedings of the 1996 Australian Army History Conference*, Australian Defence Force Academy, Canberra, 1996.

Dennis, P. and. Grey, J. *Emergency and Confrontation: Australian Military Operations in Malaya and Borneo 1950–1966*, Allen & Unwin in association with the Australian War Memorial, St Leonards, 1996.

Denoon, D. *A Trial Separation Australia and the Decolonisation of Papua New Guinea*, Pandanus Books, Canberra, 2005.

Dorney, S. *Papua New Guinea: People, Politics and History since 1975*, Random House, Sydney, 1990.

Dorney, S. *The Embarrassed Colonialist*, Lowy Institute, Penguin Books, Sydney, 2016.

Downs, I. *The Australian Trusteeship: Papua New Guinea 1945–1975*, Australian Government Publishing Service, Canberra, 1980.

Easter, D. *Britain and the Confrontation with Indonesia 1960–66*, I. B. Tauris, London, 2012.

Edgar, B. *Warrior of Kokoda: A Biography of Brigadier Arnold Potts*, Army Military History Series, Allen & Unwin, St Leonards, 1999.

Edwards, P. *A Nation at War: Australian Politics, Society and Diplomacy during the Vietnam War 1965–1975*, Allen & Unwin in association with the Australian War Memorial, St Leonards, 1997.

Edwards, P. *Australia and the Vietnam War*, New South Publishing, Sydney, 2014.

Edwards, P. *Arthur Tange: Last of the Mandarins*, Allen & Unwin, Crows Nest, 2006.
Edwards, P. with Pemberton, G. *Crises and Commitments: The Politics and Diplomacy of Australia's Involvement in Southeast Asian Conflicts 1948–1965*, Allen & Unwin in association with the Australian War Memorial, North Sydney, 1992.
Eggleston, F. (ed.). *The Australian Mandate for New Guinea: Record of Round Table Discussion*, Macmillan and Melbourne University Press, Melbourne, 1928.
Evans, R., Moore, C., Saunders, K., and Jamison, B. *1901 Our Future's Past: Documenting Australia's Federation*, Macmillan, Sydney, 1997.
Evatt, H. V. *Foreign Policy for Australia – Speeches*, Angus and Robertson, Sydney, 1945.
Firth, S. *New Guinea Under the Germans*, Web Books, Port Moresby, 1986.
Fitzhardinge, L. F. *The Little Digger 1914–1952: William Morris Hughes A Political Biography*, Vol II, Angus and Robertson, Sydney, 1979.
Frühling. S. (ed). *A History of Australian Strategic Policy Since 1945*, Defence Publishing Service, Canberra, 2009.
Gallaway, J. *The Odd Couple: Blamey and MacArthur at War*, University of Queensland Press, St Lucia, 2000.
Gelber, H. (ed.). *Problems of Australian Defence*, Oxford University Press, Melbourne, 1970.
George, M. *Australia and the Indonesian Revolution*, Melbourne University Press in association with the Australian Institute of International Affairs, Melbourne, 1980.
Golding, P. *Black Jack McEwen: Political Gladiator*, Melbourne University Press, Carlton South, 1996.
Goldsworthy, D. (ed.). *Facing North: A Century of Australian Engagement with Asia*, Vo 1, 1901 to the 1970s, Department of Foreign Affairs and Trade, Melbourne University Press, Carlton South, 2001.
Goldsworthy, D. *Losing the Blanket: Australia and the End of Britain's Empire*, Melbourne University Press, Carlton South, 2002.
Gordon, K. (ed.). *Agenda for the Nation*, The Brookings Institution, Washington, 1968.
Greenwood, G. and Grimshaw, C. (eds). *Documents on Australian International Affairs 1901–1918*, Nelson, in association with the Australian Institute of International Affairs and the Royal Institute of International Affairs, Melbourne, 1977.
Greenwood, G. and Harper, N. (eds). *Australia in World Affairs 1950–1955*, Cheshire, for the Australian Institute for International Affairs, Melbourne, 1957.
Greenwood, G. and Harper, N. (eds). *Australia in World Affairs 1956–1960*, Cheshire, for the Australian Institute for International Affairs, Melbourne, 1963.
Greenwood, G. and Harper, N. (eds). *Australia in World Affairs 1961–1965*, Cheshire, for the Australian Institute for International Affairs, Melbourne, 1968.
Greenwood, G. and Harper, N. (eds). *Australia in World Affairs 1966–1970*, Cheshire for the Australian Institute for International Affairs, Melbourne, 1974.
Grey, J. *A Military History of Australia*, Cambridge University Press, Cambridge, 1990.
Griffin, J. (ed.). *A Foreign Policy for an Independent Papua New Guinea*, Angus and Robertson and the Australian Institute for International Affairs, Sydney, 1974.
Guha, R. (ed.). *Makers of Modern Asia,*, The Belknap Press, Cambridge, USA, 2014.
Hall, T. *New Guinea 1942–1944*, Methuen Australia, Sydney, 1981.
Hegarty, D. and O'Hare, M. *Defending the Torres Strait: The Likely Reactions of Papua New Guinea and Australia to Australia's Initiatives*, Strategic and Defence Studies Centre, Australian National University, Working Paper No 191, September 1989.
Hasluck, P. *Australia in the War of 1939–1945: The Government and the People*, Vol 1, Australian War Memorial, Canberra, 1952.
Hasluck, P. *A Time for Building: Australian Administration in Papua and New Guinea 1951–1963*, Melbourne University Press, Carlton, 1976.

Bibliography

Hasluck, P. *The Chance of Politics*, Text Publishing, Melbourne, 1997.
Hastings, P. *New Guinea: Problems and Prospects*, Cheshire, Melbourne, 1969.
Henderson, A. *Menzies at War*, New South Publishing, Sydney 2014.
Henderson, W. *West New Guinea: The Dispute and Its Settlement*, Seton Hall University Press, 1973.
Hetherington, J. *Blamey: The Biography of Field Marshal Sir Thomas Blamey*, Cheshire, Melbourne, 1954.
Heydon, P. *Quiet Decision: A Study of George Foster Pearce*, Melbourne University Press, Carlton, 1965.
Hilsman, R. *To Move A Nation: The Politics of Foreign Policy in the Administration of John F. Kennedy*, Doubleday and Company, New York, 1967.
Horner, D. *Inside the War Cabinet: Directing Australia's War Effort 1939–1945*, Allen & Unwin, St Leonards, 1997.
Horner, D. *Blamey: The Commander-in-Chief*, Allen & Unwin, St Leonards, 1998.
Horner, D. *Defence Supremo: Sir Frederick Shedden and the Making of Australian Defence Policy*, Allen & Unwin, St Leonards, 2000.
Horner, D. *Making the Australian Defence Force, The Australian Centenary History of Defence*, Vol IV, Oxford University Press, South Melbourne, 2001.
Howard, J. *The Menzies Era*, Harper Collins Publishers, Sydney, 2014.
Hudson, W. J. (ed.). *Australia in World Affairs 1971–1975*, Cheshire for the Australian Institute for International Affairs, Melbourne, 1980.
Hudson, W. J. and North, J.(eds) *My Dear P. M.: R. G. Casey's Letters to S. M. Bruce, 1924–1929*, Australian Government Publishing Service, Canberra, 1980.
Hudson, W. J. *New Guinea Empire: Australia's Colonial Experience*, Cassell, Melbourne, 1974.
Hudson, W. J. *Australia and the Colonial Question at the United Nations*, Sydney University Press, Sydney, 1970.
Hudson, W. J. (ed.). *Australia and Papua New Guinea*, Sydney University Press, Sydney, 1971.
Hudson, W. J. (ed.). *Australia's New Guinea Question*, Nelson, in association with the Australian Institute of International Affairs, Melbourne, 1975.
Hudson, W. J. *Australia and the League of Nations*, Sydney University Press, in association with the Australian Institute of International Affairs, Sydney, 1980.
Hudson, W. J. *Australia and the New World Order: Evatt at San Francisco – 1945*, Australian National University, Canberra, 1993.
Jinks, B., Biskup, P. and Nelson, H. (eds). *Readings in New Guinea History*, Angus and Robertson, Sydney, 1973.
Jones, M. *Conflict and Confrontation in South East Asia 1961–1965: Britain, the United States and the Creation of Malaysia*, Cambridge University Press, Cambridge, 2002.
Kerr, A. *A Federation in These Seas*, Attorney General's Department, Canberra, 2009.
Kiki, A. M. *Ten Thousand Years in a Lifetime: A New Guinea Autobiography*, Cheshire, Melbourne, 1968.
Lane, P. *An Introduction to the Australian Constitution*, The Law Book Company Limited, Sydney, 1974.
Lee, D. *The Search for Security: The Political Economy of Australia's Postwar Foreign and Defence Policy*, Allen & Unwin in association with the Department of International Relations, Research School of Pacific and Asian Studies, Australian National University, Canberra, 1995.
Lee, D. and Waters, C. *Evatt to Evans: The Labor Tradition in Australian Foreign Policy*, Allen & Unwin in association with the Department of International Relations, Research School of Pacific and Asian Studies, Australian National University, Canberra, 1997.

Legge, J. *Sukarno: A Political Biography*, Penguin Press, 1972.
Lijphart, A. *The Trauma of Decolonization: The Dutch and West New Guinea*, Yale University Press, New Haven, 1966.
Lloyd, C. and Hall, R. *Background Briefings: John Curtin's War*, National Library of Australia, Canberra, 1997.
Louis, W. R. *Great Britain and Germany's Lost Colonies 1914–1919*, Clarendon Press, Oxford, 1967.
Lowe, D. (ed.). *Australia and the End of Empires*, Deakin University Press, Geelong, 1996.
Lowe, D. *Menzies and the 'Great World Struggle'*, University of New South Wales Press, Sydney, 1999.
Mackenzie, S. A. *The Australian at Rabaul: The Capture of the German Possessions in the Southern Pacific*, Vol X, Official History of Australia in the War of 1914–1918, University of Queensland Press in association with the Australian War Memorial, St Lucia, 1987.
Mackie, J. A. C. (ed.). *Australia in the New World Order: Foreign Policy in the 1970s*, Nelson, in association with the Australian Institute of International Affairs, West Melbourne, 1976.
Mackie, J. A. C. *Konfrontasi: The Indonesia–Malaysia Dispute 1963–1966*, Oxford University Press, London, 1974.
Maga, T. *John F. Kennedy and the New Pacific Community 1961–63*, Macmillan, Press Ltd, Houndsmills, 1990.
Marr, D. *Barwick*, Allen & Unwin, Sydney, 1980.
Martin, A. W. *Robert Menzies: A Life* Vol 2 1944–1978, Melbourne University Press, Carlton South, 1999.
Martin, A, and P. Hardy (eds.). *Dark and Hurrying Days: Menzies' 1941 Diary*, National Library of Australia, Canberra, 1993.
May, R. J. *The Changing Role of the Military in Papua New Guinea*, Strategic and Defence Studies Centre, Research School of Pacific Studies, Australian National University, Canberra, 1993.
May, R. J. and Selochan, V. (eds). *The Military and Democracy in Asia and the Pacific*, Crawford House Publishing, Bathurst, 1998.
McLaren, J. (ed.). *Towards a New Australia*, Cheshire, Victorian Fabian Society, Melbourne, 1972.
McGarr, P. *The Cold War in South Asia: Britain, the United States and the Indian Subcontinent, 1945–1965*, Cambridge University Press, Cambridge, 2013.
McMahon, R. *Colonialism and Cold War: The United States and the Struggle for Indonesian Independence, 1945–49*, Cornell University Press, Ithaca, 1981.
Meaney, N. *The Search for Security in the Pacific 1901–1914*, Vol I, Sydney University Press, Sydney, 1976.
Meaney, N. *Australia and World Crisis, 1914–1923*, Sydney University Press, Sydney, 2009.
Meaney, N. *Fears and Phobias: E. L. Piesse and the Problem of Japan 1909–39*, National Library of Australia, Canberra, 1966.
Mench, P. *The Role of the Papua New Guinea Defence Force*, Development Studies Centre, Monograph No 2, Australian National University Press, Canberra, 1975.
Millar, T. B. *Australia's Defence*, Melbourne University Press, Carlton, 1965.
Millar, T. B. *Australia's Defence Policies 1945–1965*, Working Paper No 7, Department of International Relations, Australian National University, Canberra, 1967.
Millar, T. B. (ed.). *Australian–New Zealand Defence Cooperation*, Australian National University Press, Canberra, 1968.

Millar, T. B. *Australia in Peace and War: External Relations 1788–1977*, Australian National University Press, Canberra, 1978.
Millar, T. B. (ed.). *International Security in the Southeast Asian and Southwest Pacific Region*, University of Queensland Press, St Lucia, 1983.
Miller, J. D. B. *Australia and Foreign Policy*, The 1963 Boyer Lectures, ABC Publications, Sydney, 1963.
Moses, J. and Pugsley, C. (eds). *The German Empire and Britain's Pacific Dominions 1871–1919: Essays on the role of Australia and New Zealand in World Politics in the Age of Imperialism*, Regina Books, Claremont California, 2000.
Moore, C. with Kooyman, M. *A Papua New Guinea Political Chronicle 1967–1991*, Crawford House Publishing, Bathurst, 1998.
Murphy, J. *Evatt A Life*, New South, Sydney 2016.
Nelson, H. *Papua New Guinea: Black Unity or White Chaos*, Penguin Ringwood, 1974.
Nelson, H. *Taim Bilong Masta: The Australian Involvement with Papua New Guinea*, ABC Books, Sydney, 1982.
Newton, D. *Hell-Bent: Australia's Leap into the Great War*, Scribe Publications, Brunswick, 2014.
O'Neill, R. (ed.). *The Official History of Australia in the War of 1914–1918*, Vols I–XII, University of Queensland Press in association with the Australian War Memorial, St Lucia, 1987.
Osmond, W. *Frederic Eggleston: An Intellectual in Australian Politics*, Allen & Unwin, Sydney, 1985.
Pemberton, G. *All the Way: Australia's Road to Vietnam*, Allen & Unwin, North Sydney, 1987.
Pettit, D. (ed.). *Selected Readings in Australian Foreign Policy*, Sorrett Publishing, Toorak, 1973.
Porter, R. *Paul Hasluck: A Political Biography*, University of Western Australia Press, Nedlands, 1993.
Pybus, C. *The Devil and James McAuley*, University of Queensland Press, St Lucia, 1999.
Reese, T. R. *Australia, New Zealand and the United States: A Survey of International Relations 1941–1968*, Oxford University Press, London, 1969.
Renouf, A. *The Frightened Country*, Macmillan, Melbourne, 1979.
Robertson, J. and McCarthy, J. *Australian War Strategy 1939–1945: A Documentary History*, University of Queensland Press, St Lucia, 1985.
Robson, L. L. *Australian Commentaries: Select Articles from the Round Table 1911–1942*, Melbourne University Press, Carlton, 1975.
Rowley, C. D. *The Australians in German New Guinea 1914–1921*, Melbourne University Press, Carlton, 1958.
Schreuder, D. and Ward, S. *Australia's Empire*, Oxford University Press, Oxford, 2008.
Sinclair, J. *To Find a Path: The Papua New Guinea Defence Force and the Australians to Independence, Vol II, Keeping the Peace 1950–1975*, Crawford House Press, Bathurst, 1992.
Sligo, G. *The Backroom Boys: Alfred Conlon and the Army's Directorate of Research and Civil Affairs, 1942–46*, Big Sky Publishing, Newport, 2013.
Souter, G. *New Guinea: The Last Unknown*, Angus and Robertson, Sydney, 1963.
Spartalis, P. *The Diplomatic Battles of Billy Hughes*, Hale and Ironmonger, Sydney, 1983.
Spender, P. *Politics and a Man*, Collins, Sydney, 1972.
Stanley, P. *Invading Australia: Japan and the Battle for Australia, 1942*, Viking Press, Camberwell, 2008.
Starke, J. G. *The ANZUS Treaty Alliance*, Melbourne University Press, Carlton, 1965.

Stevens, D. (ed.). *In Search of Maritime Strategy: The Maritime Element in Australian Defence Planning since 1901*, Strategic and Defence Studies centre, Australian National University, Canberra, 1997.

Stevens, D. and Reeve, J. (eds.). *Southern Trident: Strategy, History and the Rise of Australian Naval Power*, Allen & Unwin, Crows Nest, 2001.

Stockings, C. and Connor, J. *Before the ANZAC Dawn: A Military History of Australia to 1915*, NewSouth Publishing, Sydney, 2013.

Stone, P. *Hostage to Freedom: The Fall of Rabaul*, Oceans Enterprises, Yarram, Victoria, 1995.

Subritzky, J. *Confronting Sukarno: British, American, Australian and New Zealand Diplomacy in the Malaysian–Indonesian Confrontation, 1961–1965*, Macmillan Press, London, 2000.

Tarling, N. *Britain and the West New Guinea Dispute, 1949–62*, The Edwin Mellen Press, Lewiston, New York, 2008.

Thompson, A. (ed.). *Papua New Guinea: Issues for Australia Security Planners*, Australian Defence Studies Centre, Australian Defence Force Academy, Canberra, 1994.

Thompson, R. C. *Australian Imperialism in the Pacific: The Expansionist Era 1820–1920*, Melbourne University Publishing, Carlton, 1980.

Turner, M. *Papua New Guinea: The Challenge of Independence: A Nation in Turmoil*, Penguin Books Australia, Ringwood, 1990.

Walsh, R. and Munster, G. J. (eds.). *Documents on Australian Defence and Foreign Policy 1968–1975*, Angus and Robertson, Sydney, 1980.

Warner, G. *In the Midst of Events The Foreign Office Diaries and Papers of Kenneth Younger, February 1950–October 1951*, Routledge, Abingdon, 2005.

Waters, C. *Australia and Appeasement: Imperial Foreign Policy and the Origins of World War II*, I. B. Tauris, London, 2012.

Watt, Sir Alan. *The Evolution of Australian Foreign Policy 1938–1965*, Cambridge University Press, London, 1967.

Watt, Sir Alan. *Australian Diplomat: Memoirs of Sir Alan Watt*, Angus and Robertson, in association with the Australian Institute of International Affairs, Sydney, 1972.

Whitlam, E. G. *Beyond Vietnam: Australia's Regional Responsibility*, Victorian Fabian Society Pamphlet No 17, Melbourne, 1968.

Whitlam, E. G. *The Whitlam Government 1972–1975*, Viking Press, Ringwood, 1985.

Whittaker, J. L., Gash, N. G., Hookey, J. F. and Lacey, R. J., *Documents and Readings in New Guinea History: Prehistory to 1889*, The Jacaranda Press, Milton, 1975.

Wigmore, L. *They Dared Mightily*, Australian War Memorial, Canberra, 1963.

Wilkes, J. (ed.). *New Guinea and Australia*, Papers from the 24th Summer School of the Australian Institute of Political Science, Canberra, January 1958, Angus and Robertson, Sydney, 1958.

Wilkes, J. (ed.). *New Guinea … Future Indefinite?* Papers of the 34th Summer School of the Australian Institute of Political Science, Canberra, January, 1968, Angus and Robertson, Sydney, 1968.

Willmott, H. P. *The Second World War in the Far East*, Cassell and Co, London, 1999.

Wolfers, E. (ed.). *Australia's Northern Neighbours: Independent or Dependent?*, Nelson, in association with the Australian Institute of International Affairs, Melbourne, 1976.

Woodard, G. *Asian Alternatives: Australia's Vietnam Decision and Lessons in Going to War*, Melbourne University Publishing, Carlton, 2004.

Young, M. *Australian Labor Party Platform, Constitution and Rules*, ALP Federal Secretariat, Adelaide, 1971.

Journals and speeches

Atkin, D. and Wolfers, E. P. 'Australian Attitudes towards the Papua New Guinea Area Since World War II', *Australian Outlook*, Vol 27, No 2, August 1973, pp. 202-214.

Babbage, R. 'Australia and the Defence of Papua New Guinea', *Australian Outlook*, Vol 41, No 2, August 1987, pp. 87-93.

Beaumont, J. 'The Evolution of Australian Foreign Policy, 1901–1945', Occasional Paper No 1, Australian Institute of International Affairs (Victoria branch), 1989.

Ball, D. 'The Politics of Defence Decision Making in Australia: The Strategic Background', Reference Paper No 93, Centre for Strategic and Defence Studies, Australian National University, March–April 1979.

Barwick, Sir Garfield,. 'Australian Foreign Policy 1962', Thirteenth Roy Milne Memorial Lecture, 31 July 1962, Australian Institute of International Affairs, Perth, 1962.

Beazley, K. E. 'Papua New Guinea and Independence – Some Fatal Motives', *World Review*, Vol 9, No 2, July 1970, pp. 14-20.

Beazley, K. E. 'The Future of Papua New Guinea', *World Review*, Vol 11, No 2, July 1972, pp. 3-18.

Beazley, K. 'Thinking Defence: Key Concepts in Australian Defence Planning', *Australian Outlook*, Vol 42, No 2, August 1988, pp. 71-76.

Beddie, B. 'Indonesian Attitudes Towards East New Guinea – Restraint?, *New Guinea*, September/October 1965, pp. 17-26.

Benvenuti, A. Anglo–Australian Relations and the 'Turn to Europe', *The Royal Historical Society*, The Boydell Press, 2008, pp. 153-162.

Black, H. D. 'Review of Seminar, April 1972', *United Service*, October 1972, pp. 65-71.

Bull, H. 'Australia's Foreign Policy in the Seventies', Papers for a Seminar at Townsville, 20 July 1968, arranged by the Australian Institute of International Affairs and the Townsville University College.

Bull, H. 'The Defence of Australia to the 1980s: The Problem', *United Service*, Vol 26, No 2, October 1972, pp. 2-10.

Bull, H. 'Australia and the Great Powers in Asia', in *Australia in World Affairs 1966–1970*, eds G. Greenwood and N. Harper, Cheshire, Australian Institute of International Affairs, Melbourne, 1974.

Bull, H. 'Australia's Involvement in Independent Papua New Guinea', Fourth Heindorff Memorial Lecture, *World Review*, March 1974, pp. 3-18.

Calwell, A. 'Australian Foreign Policy', Inaugural H. V. Evatt Memorial Lecture, Melbourne University, 16 May 1966.

Camilleri, J. 'Australia's Involvement in Nuigini', *Ccaesarian (publication of the Canberra College of Advanced Education Student Association)*, Vol 4, No 6, April 3, 1974.

Camilleri, J. '"Internal Conflict in an Independent Papua New Guinea": A Rejoinder', *Australian Outlook*, Vol 28, No 3, December 1974, pp. 308-312.

Casey, R. G. 'Australia: The Foreign Policy of a Small Power', Reprinted from the *Centennial Review*, Vol 3, No I, Winter, 1959, pp. 1-18.

Cheeseman, G. 'From Forward Defence to Self Reliance: Changes and Continuities in Australian Defence Policy, 1965–1990', *Australian Journal of Political Science*, Vol 26, No 3, November 1991, pp. 429-445.

Cranston, R. 'International Law and Australia's Defence Obligations in South-East Asia', *World Review*, October 1973, pp. 28-39.

Crouch, H. 'Indonesia and the Security of Australia and Papua New Guinea', *Australian Outlook*, Vol 40, No 3, December 1986, pp. 167-174.

Dibb, P. 'Issues in Australian Defence', *Australian Outlook*, Vol 37, No 3, December 1983, pp. 160-166.

Dibb, P. 'Australia's Security Environment and Defence Policy', *Journal of the Royal United Services Institute of Australia*, June 1985, Vol 7, No 2, pp. 16-22.

Dibb, P. and Brabin-Smith, R. 'Indonesia in Australian Defence Planning', *Security Challenges*, Vol 3, No 4 (November 2007), pp. 67-93.

Dibb, P. 'The Importance of the Inner Arc to Australian Defence Policy and Planning', *Security Challenges*, Vol 8, No 4, (Summer 2012), pp. 13-31.

Doran, S. 'Toeing the Line: Australia's Abandonment of Traditional West New Guinea Policy', *The Journal of Pacific History*, Vol 36, No 1, 2001, pp. 5-18.

Edwards, P. 'Learning from History: Some Strategic Lessons from the "Forward Defence" Era', *Strategy*, May 2015, pp. 1-25.

Farran, A. '"The Freeth Experiment"', *Australian Outlook*, Vol 26, No 1, April 1972, pp. 46-58.

Firth, S. 'Security in Papua New Guinea: The Military and Diplomatic Dimensions', *Security Challenges*, Vol 10, No 2 (2014), pp. 97-113.

Fitzhardinge, L. F. 'W. M. Hughes and the Treaty of Versailles, 1919', *Journal of Commonwealth Political Studies*, Vol V, No 2, July 1967, pp.130-142.

Gelber, H. G. 'The Importance of Papua New Guinea to Australian Foreign Policies and Strategy', *United Service Institution of South Australia*, Proceedings of a Seminar on Papua New Guinea, Adelaide 1971, pp. 27-31.

Gelder, H. G. 'Australia and the Great Powers', *Asian Survey*, March 1975, Vol XV, No 3, pp. 187-201.

George, M. 'The Annexation of New Guinea', *Australian National University Historical Journal*, Vol 1, No 3–No 8, 1966, pp. 17-23.

Gibbney, H. J. 'The Interregnum in the Government of Papua', *Australian Journal of Politics and History*, Vol XII, No 3, December 1966, pp. 341-359.

Gow, N. 'Australian Army Strategic Planning 1919–1939', *Australian Journal of Politics and History*, Vol XXIII, No 2, August 1977 pp. 169-172.

Gray, G. G. '"The next focus of power to fall under the spell of this little gang": Anthropology and Australia's Post-war Policy in Papua New Guinea,' *War and Society*, Vol 14, No 2, October 1996, pp. 101-117.

Griffin, J. 'Cautious Deeds and Wicked Fairies: A Decade of Independence in Papua New Guinea', *The Journal of Pacific History*, Vol XXI, No 4, October 1986, pp. 183-201.

Gunther, J. 'What Do New Guineans Want? They Don't Know…', *New Guinea*, June/July 1966, pp. 22-29.

Hastings, P. 'The Future: A Weak, Client State…', *New Guinea*, March/April 1970, pp. 8-27.

Hastings, P. 'Comment', *New Guinea*, May/June 1975, pp. 2-3.

Hastings, P. 'The Papua New Guinea–Irian Jaya Border Problem', *Australian Outlook*, Vol 31, No 1, April 1977, pp. 52-60.

Heatu, B. 'New Guinea's Coming Army: To prevent a Coup or Lead One', *New Guinea*, September/October 1967, pp. 32-33.

Hegarty, D. 'Issues and Conflict in Post Colonial Papua New Guinea', *World Review*, Vol 18, No 3, August 1979, pp. 37-40.

Herr, R. 'The American Impact on Australian Defence Relations with the South Pacific Islands', *Australian Outlook*, Vol 38, No 3, December 1984, pp. 184-190.

Horner, D. 'Defending Australia in 1942', *War and Society*, Vol 11, No 1, May 1933, pp. 1-20.

Jackman, H. 'PNG Super Tribe?', *Pacific Defence Reporter*, September 1974, pp. 29-30.

Jackman, H. 'Jim and the Kiaps', *Quadrant*, March, 1977, pp. 71-74.

Bibliography

Jackman, H. 'Papua New Guinea in the Defence of Australia', *Journal of the Royal United Services Institute of Australia*, Vol 6, No 1, April 1983, pp. 32-36.

Jinks, B. 'Australia's Post-War Policy for New Guinea and Papua', *The Journal of Pacific History*, Vol 17, No 2, April 1982, pp. 86-100.

Jinks, B. 'Alfred Conlon, The Directorate of Research and New Guinea', *Journal of Australian Studies*, No 12, June 1983, pp. 21-33.

Johns, E. 'Labor and Papua New Guinea: 1941-1949', *New Guinea*, October 1974, pp. 23-64.

Kerr, J. 'An Australian View', *New Guinea*, A series of lectures to the NSW Branch of the Australian Institute of International Affairs, The Anglican Press, Sydney, September 1961.

Kerr, J. 'A Debate – Now! New Guinea's Constitutional Future', *New Guinea*, March/April 1966, pp. 17-22.

Kerr, J. 'Some Australian Problems: From Every Point of View – Independence', *New Guinea*, June/July 1966, pp. 37-45.

Kerr, J. 'From the Defence Angle – No Great Prize', *New Guinea*, December 1966/January 1967, pp. 25-32.

King, P. 'The Papua New Guinea/Australia Defence Relationship', *The Australian Quarterly*, Spring, 1984, pp. 277-285.

Lake, M. 'The Australian Dream of an Island Empire: Race, Reputation and Resistance', *Australian Historical Studies*, 46:3, pp. 410-424.

Lee, D. 'Britain and Australia's Defence Policy, 1945-1949', *War and Society*, Vol 13, No 1, May 1995, pp. 61-80.

Lee, D. 'The National Security Planning and Defence Preparations of the Menzies Government, 1950-1953', *War and Society*, Vol 10, No 2, October 1992, pp. 119-138.

Lee, D. 'Australia and Allied Strategy in the Far East 1952-1957', *The Journal of Strategic Studies*, Vol 16, December 1993, No 4, pp. 511-538.

Lynch, P. R. 'The Coming Army: Loyalty, Stability, Discipline', *New Guinea*, March/April 1969, pp. 21-25.

Mackie, J. A. C. 'Indonesia's New Look: An End to Confrontations?', *New Guinea*, September/October 1966, pp. 55-62.

Mackie, J. A. C. and Clark, C. 'Reconsidering Australian Foreign Policy', *Australia's Neighbours*, November-December 1967, pp. 4-5.

Mackie, J. A. C. 'Australia's Relations with Indonesia: Principles and Policies, Part I', *Australian Outlook*, Vol 28, No 1, April 1974, pp. 3-14.

Mackie, J. A. C. 'Australia's Relations with Indonesia: Principles and Policies, Part II', *Australian Outlook*, Vol 28, No 2, August 1974, pp. 118-178.

Mackie, J. A. C. 'Australian Foreign Policy – From Whitlam to Fraser', *Dyason House Papers*, Vol 3, No 1, August 1976, pp. 1-5.

Mackie, J. A. C. 'Australian-Indonesian Relations', *Current Affairs Bulletin*, Vol 53, No 5, October 1976, pp. 12-21.

McAuley, J. 'Defence and Development in Australian New Guinea', *Public Affairs*, Vol XXIII, No 4, December 1950, pp. 371-380.

McAuley, J. 'Australia's Future in New Guinea', *Public Affairs* Vol XXVI, No 1, March 1953, pp. 59-69.

McCarthy, J. 'The Imperial Commitment 1939-1941', *Australian Journal of Politics and History*, Vol XXIII, No 2, August 1977, pp. 178-181.

McDougall, D. 'Australian and British Military Withdrawal from East of Suez', *Australian Journal of International Affairs*, Vol 51, No 2, 1997, pp. 183-194.

MacQueen, N. 'Papua New Guinea's Relations with Indonesia and Australia', *Asian Survey*, Vol XXIX, No 5, May 1989, pp. 530-541.
Mattes, J. R. 'Constitutional Development: A Short History', *New Guinea*, June/July 1972, pp. 4-29.
Meaney, N. '"A proposition of the highest international importance": Alfred Deakin's Pacific Agreement Proposal and Its Significance for Australian–Imperial Relations', *Journal of Commonwealth Political Studies*, Vol V, No 3, November 1967, pp. 200-213.
Meaney, N. 'Look Back in Fear: Percy Spender, the Japanese Peace Treaty and the ANZUS Pact'. Discussion Paper No IS/01/426, The Suntory Centre, London School of Economics and Political Science, London, 2001.
Meaney, N. 'The Making of the Commonwealth and The Defence of Australia,' Chauvel Seminar Series, University of New England, Armidale, 2000.
Mediansky, F. A. 'New Guinea's Coming Army: Acquiring Politically Useful Skills', *New Guinea*, June/July 1970, pp. 37-42.
Mediansky, F. A. 'Now Here Is Our Foreign Policy', *Current Affairs Bulletin*, Vol 49, No 4, September 1972, pp. 98-112.
Mediansky, F. A. 'The Defence White Paper', *Pacific Defence Reporter*, December 1976/January 1977, pp. 9-13.
Mench, P. 'The Future II – After Independence … Australia's Military Involvement', *New Guinea*, January 1975, pp. 44 54.
Millar, T. B. 'The Defence of New Guinea: Still Only Three New Guinean Officers', *New Guinea*, March/April 1965, pp. 68-75.
Millar, T. B. 'Australian Defence: Two Views: Effective Forces and Powerful Friends', *Australia's Neighbours*, Fourth Series, No 26–27, July–August 1965, pp. 1-4.
Millar, T. B. 'Melanesia's Strategic Significance: An Uncertain Future', *New Guinea*, June/July 1970, pp. 30-35.
Millar, T. B. 'Defence Under Labor', *Current Affairs Bulletin*, Vol 52, No 7, December 1975, pp. 4-15.
Millar, T. B. 'The Defence of Australia during the Next Ten Years', *World Review*, Vol 16, No 1, March 1977, pp. 14-26.
Miller, J. D. B. 'Papua New Guinea in World Politics', *Australian Outlook*, Vol 27, No 2, August 1973, pp. 191-201.
Mullins, S. 'Queensland's Quest for Torres Strait: The Delusion of Inevitability', *The Journal of Pacific History*, Vol XXVII, December 1992, pp. 165-180.
Murfett, M. H. 'Living in the Past, A Critical Re-examination of the Singapore Naval Strategy, 1918–1941, *War and Society*, Vol 11, No 1, May 1993, pp. 73-103.
Nelson, H. 'Papua New Guinea's Foreign Policy: Universalism, Trade, Aid and Borders', *India Quarterly: A Journal of International Affairs*, Vol XXXIV, No 2, April–June 1978, pp. 176-187.
Nelson, H. 'Liberation: the End of Australian Rule in Papua New Guinea', *The Journal of Pacific History*, Vol 35, No 3, 2000, pp. 269-280.
O'Neill, R. 'New Attitudes for a New Decade: Some Conclusions for Australian Policy Towards Asia in the 1970's', *Australian Outlook*, Vol 24, No 2, August 1970, pp. 111-123.
O'Neill, R. 'Future Tendencies with Emphasis on Political Development, the Economy and Defence', *United Services Institution of South Australia*, Proceedings of Seminar on Papua New Guinea, Adelaide, 1971, pp. 52-60.
O'Neill, R. 'The Future – I: The Army in Papua New Guinea: Current Role and Implications for Independence', *New Guinea*, March/April, 1971, pp. 6-27.

O'Neill, R. 'Australia's Future Defence Relations with Papua New Guinea', *Australian Outlook*, Vol 26, No 2, August 1972, pp. 193-203.
O'Neill, R. 'New Objectives in Australian Foreign Policy in the 1970s', *United Service*, October 1972, pp. 19-31.
O'Neill, R. 'Australian Defence Policy Under Labour', *Royal United Services Institute*, September 1973, pp. 30-36.
O'Neill, R. 'The Defence Relationship', *New Guinea*, December 1976, pp. 61-70.
O'Neill, R. 'Present and Future patterns of Conflict: Some Thoughts on the 1980s', *Australian Journal of Defence Studies*, Vol 1, No 1, March 1977, pp. 16-27.
Overlack, P. 'Australian Defence Awareness and German Naval Planning in the Pacific, 1900–1914, *War and Society*, Vol 10, No 1, May 1992, pp. 37-51.
Overlack, P. '"Bless the Queen and Curse the Colonial Office": Australasian Reaction to German Consolidation in the Pacific 1871–1899', *The Journal of Pacific History*, Vol XXXII, September 1998, pp. 133-152.
Perkins, J. '"Sharing the White Man's Burden": Nazi Colonial Revisionism and Australia's New Guinea Mandate', *The Journal of Pacific History*, Vol XXIV, April 1989, pp. 54-69.
Premdas, R. R. 'A Non-Political Army: An Answer to Sundhaussen', *New Guinea*, March/April 1974, pp. 29-37.
Premdas, R. R. 'Toward a Papua New Guinea Foreign Policy: Constraints and Choice', *Australian Outlook*, Vol 30, No 2, August 1976, pp. 263-279.
Primrose, B. N. 'Equipment and Naval Policy 1919–1942', *Australian Journal of Politics and History*, Vol XXIII, No 2, August 1977, pp. 165-168.
Pritchett, W. B. 'Defending Australia and its Interests', *Pacific Defence Reporter*, July 1982, pp. 58-62.
Purdey, J, 'Scholarships and Connections: Australia, Indonesia and Papua New Guinea', *Working Paper Series Two*, Alfred Deakin Research Institute, August 2004, pp. 7-25
Richardson, J. L. 'Australian Strategic and Defence Policies' in *Australia in World Affairs 1966–1970*, eds G. Greenwood and N. Harper, Cheshire, Australian Institute of International Affairs, Melbourne, 1974.
Robertson, J. 'Australian War Policy 1939–1945', *Historical Studies*, Vol 17, No 69, October 1977, pp. 489-504.
Shann, K. C. O. 'Indonesia and Australia', *New Guinea*, June/July 1968, pp. 21-32.
Simington, M. 'The Southwest Pacific Islands in Australian Interwar Defence Planning', *Australian Journal of Politics and History*, Vol XXIII, No 2, August 1977, pp. 173-177.
Smith, S. 'British New Guinea: System of Administration', *The Review of Reviews for Australasia*, Vol XXVI, No 6, June 1905, pp. 552-558.
Standish, W. 'New Guinea Review, July–December 1972', *Australian Quarterly*, Vol 45, No 1, March 1973, pp. 107-121.
Sundhaussen, U. 'Australia's Future Defence Relations with Papua New Guinea: A Second Look', *Australia's Neighbours*, February–March 1973, pp. 6-7.
Sundhaussen, U. 'New Guinea's Army: A Political Role? *New Guinea*, July 1973, pp. 29-40.
Talbone, O. L. 'Papua New Guinea – The Realities', *Pacific Defence Reporter*, September 1975, pp. 13-14.
Tange, Sir Arthur. 'Defence Policy Making in Australia', *Pacific Defence Reporter*, February 1976, pp. 6-10.
Teichmann, M. 'Australian Defence: Two Views: Armed Neutrality', *Australia's Neighbours*, Fourth Series, No 26–27, July–August 1965, pp. 4-8.
Thompson, R.C. 'Making a Mandate: The Formation of Australia's New Guinea Policies 1919–1925', *The Journal of Pacific History*, Vol XXV, June 1990, pp. 68-84.

Twomey, P. 'Small Power Security through Great Power Arms Control? Australian Perceptions of Disarmament, 1919–1930', *War and Society*, Vol 8, No 1, May 1990, pp. 71-99.
Verrier, J. 'Priorities in Papua New Guinea's Evolving Foreign Policy: Some Legacies and Lessons of History', *Australian Outlook*, Vol 28, No 3, December 1974, pp. 290-307.
Viviani, N. 'Australia–Indonesia relations – Bilateral Puzzles and Regional Perspectives', *Australian Outlook*, Vol 36, No 3, December 1982, pp. 26-31.
Warubu, K. 'That Army Again! Fences, Boots and All That', *New Guinea*, June/July 1968, pp. 8-10.
Waters, C. The Last of Australian Imperial Dreams for the Southwest Pacific: Paul Hasluck, the Department of Territories and a Greater Melanesia in 1960, *The Journal of Pacific History*, Vol 51, No 2, pp. 165-185.
Watt, A. 'The ANZUS Treaty: Past, Present and Future', *Australian Outlook*, April 1970, Vol 24, No 1, pp. 17-36.
Wolfers, E. P. 'Papua New Guinea and Coming Self Government', *Current Affairs Bulletin*, Vol 48, No 5, October 1971, pp. 132-153.
Wolfers, E. P. 'Australia's Relations with Papua New Guinea', *United Service*, Vol 31, No 2, October 1977, pp. 15-17.
Woodard, G. 'Ministers and Mandarins: The Relationships between Ministers and Secretaries of External Affairs 1935–1970', *Australian Journal of International Affairs*, Vol 54, No 1, 2000, pp. 79-95.
Woodard, G. 'The Diplomacy of Appeasement', *Quadrant*, February, 1999.

Addresses and seminar papers

Joyce, R. 'The Future of Papua New Guinea in South East Asia', Seminar at the Australian National University, 'The Future of Free Institutions in Papua New Guinea', May 1965, Australian National University, Canberra, 1965.
Latham, J. 'The Significance of the Peace Conference from the Australian Point of View', An address delivered before the Melbourne University Association on 23 October 1919, reprinted by Melville and Mullen Pty Ltd, Melbourne, 1920.
Miller, J. D. B. 'Future Links between Australia and New Guinea', Paper delivered at Seminar on New Guinea Problems, Canberra, 30 May 1965.
Miller, J. D. B. 'Papua New Guinea and Australia in World Politics', Public Lecture at the Australian National University, Canberra, 11 April 1973.
Millar, T. B. 'Strategic Significance of the Melanesian Area', in M. W. Ward (ed) *The Politics of Melanesia*, Fourth Waigani Seminar, University of Waigani, Port Moresby, 9–15 May 1970, Australian National University, 1970, pp. 273-281.
Morrison, W. 'Draft Notes on the Transfer of Defence Powers', 'Hindsight': A Retrospective Workshop: Decolonisation and Independence in Papua New Guinea, Australian National University, 3–4 November 2002.
Nelson, H. 'The Enemy at the Door: Australia and New Guinea in World War II', Seminar Paper delivered at Tsukuba University, Japan, 21 July 1998.
O'Neill, R. 'Problems in Defence Relations between Australia and Papua New Guinea', Lecture delivered at Australian National University, Canberra, May 1976 to a Conference on 'Australia, Papua New Guinea and Indonesia' held under the auspices of the Strategic and Defence Studies Centre and the Council on New Guinea Affairs.
Whitlam, E.G. 'The Decolonisation of Papua New Guinea', 'Hindsight': A Retrospective Workshop: Decolonisation and Independence in Papua New Guinea, 3–4 November 2002.

Online (electronic) material
http://www.users.bigpond.com.battleforaustralia/intro.html.

Theses
Dee, M. Australian Policy: The Ministers for External Affairs and the West New Guinea Dispute 1949–1962, M. Litt dissertation, University of New England, 1996.

Dee, M. In Australia's Own Interest: Australian Foreign Policy During Confrontation 1963–1966, PhD dissertation, University of New England, 2001.

Doran, S. R. Western Friends and Eastern Neighbours: West New Guinea and Australian Self Perception in Relation to the United States, Britain, and Southeast Asia, 1950–1962, PhD dissertation, Australian National University, 1999.

George, M. L. Australian Attitudes and Policies towards the Netherlands East Indies and Indonesian Independence, 1942–1949, PhD dissertation, Australian National University, 1973.

Jinks, B. E. Policy, Planning and Administration in Papua New Guinea, 1942–1952, with Special Reference to the Role of Colonel J.K. Murray, PhD dissertation, University of Sydney, 1975.

Melhuish, K. J. Australia and British Imperial Policy: Colonial Autonomy and the Imperial Idea, 1885–1902, PhD dissertation, University of Sydney, 1965.

Primrose, B. N. Australian Political Involvement in New Guinea 1883–1908, MA Thesis, University of New South Wales, 1968.

Standish, W. Attitudes of New Guinea Student Leaders to Asia, BA (Hons) Thesis, Monash University, 1966.

INDEX

Abaijah, Josephine 215
Acheson, Dean 69–70, 76, 79
'active offence' policy 8
aid
   to Indonesia 204, 309n17
   to Papua New Guinea 271–2, 275
air defence 35
Amery, Leo 20
Anderson, H.D. (David) 157
Anglo–French Condominium of the New Hebrides 13, 29, 55, 72
Anglo–Japanese Alliance 8, 12–14, 21, 27, 296n40
Anglo–Malaysia Defence Agreement (AMDA) 174, 212
ANZAC Pact 43
ANZAM (Australian, New Zealand and Malaya) 75, 82, 92, 156
ANZUS Treaty
   application to independent Papua New Guinea 214, 247, 255–7, 268
   application to Territory of Papua New Guinea 105, 107, 131, 148–9, 163, 170–1, 172, 174, 181, 255–6
   Australian contributions to 125
   Australian obligations 196
   and defence of Malaysia 164, 170–1, 173, 177, 327n103, 328n122
   defence of the Pacific 75, 95, 194–5
   membership 79
   signing of 75
   Spender's advocacy for 71, 73
   US expectations of allies 164, 165
Asia
   Australia's relationship with 104–5, 109, 115, 120, 122, 127, 135, 198, 198–9
   decolonisation 48, 53
   nationalism 52
Asian–African Conference, Bandung, 1955 87
Atlee, Clement 65
Australasian Convention, Sydney, 1883 4
Australia, HMAS 11, 25
Australian Army

return of land to Administration in Port Moresby 71
   strength 80, 95, 115, 192
Australian Defence Force
   access to facilities in PNG 235
   defence preparedness 80, 95, 103, 115, 180, 324n68
Australian imperialism 5–6
Australian Labor Party
   during early 1960s 153
   'faceless men' 180
   on Indonesian sovereignty over West New Guinea 54
   interest in developments in PNG 227
   policy on defence treaty with PNG 255, 268
   policy for PNG independence 227
Australian nationalism, place of PNG 42
Australian Naval and Military Expeditionary Force 10, 25, 26
Australian New Guinea *see* Territory of Papua and New Guinea

Balfour, Arthur 21
Ball, George 175
Barnard, Lance
   on access to military facilities in PNG 259
   on Australia's defence relationship with PNG 239–40, 252, 258, 260, 262–4
   on establishment and development of PNGDF 231, 242
   as Minister for Defence 228, 232
   on need for PNG military capability 235, 238–9
   on ongoing support for PNGDF 241
   on PNG's internal security challenges 235
   on PNG's responsibility for its own defence 258
   retirement from Parliament 264
   visit to PNG 233
Barnes, Charles 181, 213, 216–17, 221, 224, 271

Barton, Edmund 5, 6, 7
Barwick, Sir Garfield
   on application of ANZUS Treaty 148–9, 173, 175, 177, 255, 329n4
   appointed Minister for External Affairs 124, 143
   as Chief Justice of High Court 181, 329n4
   on defence of Malaysia 184–5
   on Indonesian agreement to terms of settlement 150
   on Indonesian expansionist ambitions 172, 176–7, 183
   on Indonesian–Australian relationship 158, 161, 173, 175, 183, 184
   on lack of international response to Indonesian threat 147
   on lack of rapport with US on West New Guinea 129
   meeting with Kennedy 175, 176
   meeting with Lord Home 177
   meetings with Rusk 157, 175
   meetings with Sukarno 149, 174–5
   on military support for Dutch 109
   political career 143, 153
   on regional security policy in 1950s 72–3
   on strategic importance of New Guinea 127
   on support for Malaysia 161, 162, 163
   on US policy towards Indonesia 170
   visit to United States 175–7
   visits to Indonesia 149, 174
   on West New Guinea policy 143–6
Battle of the Coral Sea 41, 42
Battle of Kokoda xvii, 42
Battle, Lucius 255
Battle of Midway 41
Battle of Milne Bay 42
Battle of Tsushima 7
Beale, Howard
   on application of ANZUS to Papua New Guinea 163
   at quadripartite talks in Washington 161, 163
   meeting with Kennedy 131, 134

INDEX

misjudgment of US policy 129–30, 134
political career 129
representations to US re Indonesian aggression 147–8, 317n37
on US expectations of allies 164
Beaumont, Joan 19, 42
Beazley, Kim 227, 284
Bevin, Ernest 65–6, 68–9, 76, 111, 203
Bird, David 36
Bishop, Reg 233, 237
Blamey, General Sir Thomas 41, 43–4
Bland, Sir Henry 215
Bonar Law, Andrew 14
Boram, airfield at 169, 190
Border, L. H. 246
Borneo 162, 189–90
Bougainville
  Australian involvement 275, 278
  political crisis over Panguna mine 215, 216, 217, 218
  secessionist movement 254, 265, 272–3, 275
Bougainville Agreement 273
Bougainville Provincial Government 273
Britain
  alliance with Japan 8, 12–14, 21, 27, 296n40
  Australian relationship with 122
  Cold War strategy 140–1
  concern over Indonesian ambitions 160–1, 163
  defence facilities in Singapore 155
  defence of Malaysia 163, 187–8, 195, 196, 212, 327n106
  negotiations resolve West New Guinea dispute 140
  policy on West New Guinea dispute 63, 66–7, 68–9, 70
  proposed Federation of Melanesia 130, 132
  requests for defence assistance from Australia 187, 195, 196, 205–6
  review of policy on West New Guinea 130, 137
  role in establishment of Malaysia 155
  support for negotiated settlement over West New Guinea dispute 144
  withdrawal of military forces from Southeast Asia 200,
205, 210–12
British New Guinea
  annexation xxvi, 5
  Australia's acquisition of 6–7
  protectorate established 5
Brunei, rebellion 155, 160
Bull, Hedley 250, 251
Bunker, Ellsworth 148
Bunting, Sir John 143, 167, 197

Cabinet Notebooks xxiii–xxiv, 72, 294n21
Calwell, Arthur 54, 63, 150, 153, 180
Carnarvon, Earl of 3
Carola, SMS 3
Caroline Islands 11, 20, 32
Carrington, Peter 122–3, 152–3
Casey, Richard G.
  Cabinet submission on West New Guinea dispute 100–2
  character and personal style 75
  diplomatic campaign over West New Guinea 76–8, 84, 106–7
  diplomatic career 74–5
  on Dutch view of Australian policy 102
  on German demands for return of colonial possessions 37
  on Indonesia forcefully acquiring West New Guinea 106–7
  on Indonesian expansionist ambitions 83
  meeting with Dulles 106–7
  meeting with Subandrio 110
  meeting with Sukarno 77–8
  on military support for Dutch 100
  as Minister for External Affairs 71, 75
  on policy on West New Guinea 58
  political career 74
  on purchase of Dutch New Guinea 83
  retirement from Parliament 124
  visit to The Hague 76
  visits to Indonesia 76, 77–8, 86
  visits to Washington 106–7
  war service 74
Chamberlain, Neville 40
Chan, Julius 230
Chauvel, Lt General Sir Harry G. 29, 34
Chauvel, Richard 60, 70, 72

Chester, Henry 3
Chifley, J. B. (Ben) 44
Chifley Labor Government 49, 53
China, Japanese invasion 26
Churchill, Winston 28, 74, 196
Clemenceau, Georges 21
Cochran, Merle 69
Cold War 63, 70
Colombo Plan 71, 73, 78, 116
colonialism 61, 69, 109, 117, 118, 132, 134
Commonwealth Brigade 189
Commonwealth Strategic Reserve 156, 184, 197
communism
  fears of spread throughout New Guinea 67, 125
  threat in Indonesia 67, 73, 84, 85, 89, 90, 94, 98, 101, 112, 118, 129, 135, 136
  threat of spread in Asia 67, 73, 78, 80, 82, 94, 95, 118
compulsory military service 193
Conlon, Colonel Alf 43
conscription
  for home service 70
  for overseas service 196
  selective military service 194, 195, 196
Constitution, Commonwealth powers in relation to Pacific islands 5–6
Conzinc Rio Tinto (CRA) 215, 216
Cook Islands 6
Cook, Joseph 6
Council of Defence 32–3, 34, 38, 45
Council of Ten Meeting, Paris, 1919 21
Creswell, Rear Admiral William 9
Critchley, Tom 49, 284, 303n4
Crocker, Walter 50
Curtin, John 41, 42, 43, 44

Day, David 40
de Quay, Jan 141
Deakin, Alfred 4, 6, 7, 14, 69
decolonisation in Asia 48, 53
Dee, Moreen 156, 183
Defence Act 1903 (Cth) 7
defence budget 37
  under Lyons Government 40
  under Menzies Government 70, 95, 115, 165, 169–70, 171–2, 194, 196
Defence Committee
  on communist expansion in Asia 165

– 365 –

on Indonesian ambitions 165
on military importance of
  Netherlands New Guinea
  125
on place of Indonesia in
  strategic outlook 113–14
on strategic importance of
  New Guinea 86–9, 101,
  114, 165–7
on strategic significance of
  Papua New Guinea 219–20
on strategic value of the New
  Hebrides 56
Defence Review (1964) 194
defence strategy
  reliance on allies 114
  reliance on Royal Navy 27,
    29, 32, 40
  self-reliance 114
  shift in focus from Middle
    East to Southeast Asia 82
Defence White Papers
  1987 xiv
  2016 xiv, 290
Democratic Labor Party 195
Denoon, Donald 230, 235
Derby, Earl of 3
Dibb, Paul xxi, 287
Dibb Report xiv, 287–8, 290
Dihm, Bill 284–5
Directorate of Research and Civil
  Affairs 43
Disraeli Government (UK) 2–3
Djuanda Kartawidjaja 107, 116,
  117
Doran, Stuart 60, 72, 143
Douglas-Home, Alec, Earl of
  Home 133, 177, 182, 186
Downer, Alexander 315n106
Drees, Willem (Jr) 64, 65, 76,
  102
Dulles, Allen 96, 157
Dulles, John Foster 97, 99,
  106–7
Dutch East Indies *see*
  Netherlands East Indies
Dutch New Guinea
  Australian support for Dutch
    sovereignty 57–61, 62,
    69–70, 76–82
  opposition to Indonesian
    claim over 53–4, 58–9,
    64–6, 71
  possible purchase by Australia
    83
  sovereignty over 51–2
  strategic importance for
    Australia 68, 87–90
Dutch–Australian relations
  possible military assistance
    for Dutch 89, 100, 102,

103–4, 106–7, 108, 115, 136,
  139, 145
regarding sovereignty over
  West New Guinea 81–2, 85,
  86, 103, 127
Dutch–Indonesia Union 93
Dutch–Indonesian relations
  51–2
Dutch–Indonesian Round Table
  Conference Agreements 52–3,
  93

Eden, Anthony 76–7, 78–9
Edwards, Peter 48, 80, 95–6,
  143, 150, 178, 179, 202
Eisenhower Administration 84,
  133
Erskine, Commodore J. E. 5
Evans, Gareth 290
Evatt, H. V. 28, 42–3, 45, 50, 51,
  60, 113, 204

Fadden, Arthur 41, 303n2
Fairbairn, David 224–6, 232,
  240, 241–2
Fairhall, Allen 216, 221
federal elections
  1958 122
  1961 152
  1963 152, 153, 173, 180–1
  1972 228
Federation of Melanesia,
  proposal for 130, 132
Fiji 2
First World War
  Australian occupation of
    German New Guinea 10–14
  peace settlement 19–23
Fisher, Andrew 6, 13, 14, 20
Fisher Government 15
Five Power Defence
  Arrangement 212, 239, 246,
  281, 288
Foreign Affairs and Defence
  Committee of Cabinet
  (FADC) 185, 272
forward defence strategy 27, 75,
  80, 94, 180, 213, 221, 244
Four Power Talks 176
Fraser Government
  concern for PNG national
    unity and stability 272,
    275
  Joint Statement on defence
    279–82
  policy towards PNG 271, 282
  strategic defence outlook
    277–9
Fraser, Malcolm
  on acts of secession in Papua
    New Guinea 216

on Joint Statement on defence
  281
on long-term defence
  relationship with PNG 276
meetings with Somare and
  Kiki 280
as Minister for the Army 270
as Minister for Defence 220,
  270
objection to use of PIR to
  assist police 270, 337n71
as Prime Minister 270
resignation from Gorton
  Cabinet 220, 337n71
view of Gorton 210, 220
visits to PNG 270, 280
Furlonger, Robert (Bob) 199,
  236–7, 333n94

Galvin, Pat 231
General Scheme of Defence
  (1913) 8
George, Margaret 3, 52
German New Guinea
  Australia occupation 10–14,
    26
  Australian administration of
    League of Nations mandate
    23, 26, 29
  German control xxvi
  Japanese occupation of islands
    north of Equator 12–14
  protectorate established by
    Germany 4–5
German Samoa 11
Germany, demands for return of
  colonial possessions 36–7
Gilbert and Ellice Islands 29
Gillard, Julia 289
Gladstone Government (UK)
  3, 5
Goa, Indian takeover 140, 141
Goldsworthy, David 205, 206,
  211
Gorton Government 212–13
Gorton, John
  approach to security matters
    210
  on British withdrawal from
    Southeast Asia 210–11
  character and personal style
    153, 209–10
  on Indonesian–Australian
    relationship 204
  loss of leadership 220
  on Manus Island naval base
    45, 213
  on military assistance to
    Malaysia 211
  as Minister for Defence 220,
    222

INDEX

as Minister for the Navy 45, 148, 181, 210
as Prime Minister 204, 209, 210
on successions movements in PNG 336n67
visit to Indonesia 218
visit to Papua New Guinea 218
Great Depression 35
Greenwall, John 231
Grey, Sir George 2
Griffith, Alan 166–7
Guise, John 213

Harcourt, Lewis 10, 11–14
Harries, Owen 252
Harriman, Averell 163, 170, 175–6, 255
Hartley, Bill 343n3
Hasluck, Paul
  on alliance with United States 95, 98
  approach to foreign policy and security issues 197
  at ANZUS Council meeting 189
  on Australia's relations with Asia 144
  on Casey's effectiveness in Cabinet 75
  on communist tactics 109
  on Confrontation policy 203, 207
  conservatism 221
  on defence of Australian New Guinea 105, 330n19
  as Defence Minister 181
  on defence obligations and security priorities 196–7
  as External Affairs Minister 181, 188
  on future of Dutch New Guinea 125–6, 145–6
  on Gorton 210
  as Governor-General 221
  on Indonesian–Australian relations 146, 172–3, 189
  on involvement in Vietnam 209
  on linking Solomon Islands to Papua New Guinea 123, 126
  meeting with General Nasution 188
  meeting with Johnson 189
  meeting with Subandrio 188
  on need for stability in Indonesia 204
  on need to reassure Australian public 168

on policy on West New Guinea dispute 139
reputation 153
on support for Malaysia 187, 189
on unifying Australian and Dutch New Guinea 85
on UN's handling of West New Guinea dispute 95, 146
visit to United States 189
visits to Indonesia 188, 203–4
Hawke Labor Government
  aid to PNG 284–5
  Joint Declaration of Principles 247, 285–9
Hay, David 224, 231, 245
Hayden, Bill 285–6
Healey, Dennis 206–7
Heath, Edward 211
Henderson, Anne 52
Herbert, Henry Howard Molyneux (4th Earl of Carnarvon) 2
Heydon, Peter 117, 124
Hicks, Sir Edwin 168
Highlands Liberation Front 215–16
Hitler, Adolf 36, 37
Holt Government 203, 213
Holt, Harold
  on avoiding war with Indonesia 108
  death 202, 209
  on defence budgets 193
  on end of Confrontation policy 207
  on Indonesian–Australian relations 207
  on Indonesia's Confrontation policy 173
  on Manus Island base 148
  meeting with Hubert Humphrey 208
  as Minister for Labour and National Service 97
  on political instability in Indonesia 97
  as Prime Minister 202
  reputation 153
  on support for Malaysia 174
  on support for PNG's development 208
  as Treasurer 153, 165, 193, 207
  on US alliance 108
Holyoake, Keith 137, 189, 196
Hood, John 50
Hoover, Herbert 84
Howson, Peter 190
Hudson, W. J. 7

Hughes, William Morris
  annexation of former German possessions in Pacific xxi
  antipathy towards Japan 299n112
  at Council of Ten Meeting 21–3
  on Australia's strategic interests in the Pacific 18–23, 29
  character and personal style 14–15, 20, 21, 36
  on control of mandated territory 37
  on control over British New Guinea 6
  Imperial War Cabinet meetings 19–20
  on importance of New Guinea in Australia's defence 15, 18, 21–2, 28, 37
  misreading of Wilson 133
  on post-war defence policy and expenditure 26–8
Hughes-Onslow, Captain C. 9
Humphrey, Hubert 207–8
Hunt, Atlee 7
Hyde, Sir George 38

Ichirō, Motono 21
Imperial Conferences
  London, 1921 27
  London, 1937 26, 36–7
Imperial War Cabinet 19, 20
India, takeover of Goa 140, 141
Indonesia
  actions against Dutch interests 93–4, 97
  aid from Australia 204, 309n17
  attempted coup 197, 199
  claim over Dutch New Guinea 48, 51–2, 54–5, 57–8, 111–12, 117, 135, 136
  communist threat 67, 73, 89, 90, 94, 96, 98, 101–2, 112, 118, 129, 135, 136
  Confrontation policy towards Malaysia 93, 154, 155–6, 174–5, 197, 203, 206
  constitutional reform 93, 97
  as direct threat to Australia 191–2, 277
  Dutch 'police action' 51
  economic decline 119, 123, 153
  expansionist ambitions 60–1, 78, 83, 103, 104, 111–12, 136, 149, 157, 158–9, 162, 175, 182, 183–4

– 367 –

Foreign Minister's visit to
    Australia 107–13
Guided Democracy 93, 97,
    119, 123
independence 47, 49, 51–2, 53
invasion of East Timor 265
nationalism 48, 51, 175, 182,
    204
political instability 93, 97,
    99–100, 123, 182
repression of communism
    199, 203
strategic importance to
    Australia 113–14, 125,
    243, 277
terms of settlement regarding
    West New Guinea 149–50
trade with Australia 204
weapons purchases 94, 107
withdrawal from United
    Nations 156
Indonesian Army 123
    capability 102–3
Indonesian independence
    movement 53
Indonesian–Australian relations
    Australian support for
        independence 49, 51, 52
    Australia's approach to 72, 73
    British concerns over 66, 68
    Casey–Subandrio Joint
        Announcement 112–13, 117
    Colombo Plan and 116
    conflict over UN debate on
        West New Guinea 140
    development of bilateral
        relationship 50, 58, 78,
        84–5, 86–7, 96, 151
    during Suharto's presidency
        203–5
    during Sukarno's presidency
        49–50, 51, 57, 200
    fears of Indonesia forcefully
        acquiring West New Guinea
        107, 111–12, 117, 118–19,
        120–1
    friction over West New
        Guinea dispute 94, 117,
        118, 135
    Joint Statements on bilateral
        relationship 86, 112–13, 117
    Menzies visit to Jakarta
        116–19
    strain over Confrontation
        policy 159–60, 162, 175,
        182–3, 203
    threat of military force to seize
        West New Guinea 140, 148
    trade agreement 116
    visit by Subandrio to Australia
        107, 109–14

Indonesian–British relations
    66, 141
Indonesian–Dutch relations 94
Indonesian–Papua New Guinea
    border
    demarcation 175, 188
    incursions by Indonesian
        troops 277–8
    management of 200, 205,
        237, 243
    patrolling of 169
Indonesian–PNG relations
    236–7, 277
    Treaty of Mutual Respect,
        Friendship and Cooperation
        286
Indonesian–US relations 98,
    141, 148
Ingram, James 153–4, 318–
    19n64
Integrated Development Package
    285
inter-war diplomacy 25–6
International Court of Justice
    85, 117
Irian Barat (West New Guinea)
    107
Irian Jaya separatist movement
    265, 276
Irian Jaya–Papua New Guinea
    border
    demarcation 175, 188
    incursions by Indonesian
        troops 277–8
    management of 200, 205,
        237, 243, 276
    patrolling of 169

Japan
    advance into Southeast Asia
        and South Pacific 40
    alliance with Britain 8,
        12–14, 21, 27, 296n40
    declaration of war against
        Germany 11–12
    defeat of Russian navy 7
    invasion of China 26
    military strategy regarding
        Australia 41–2
    objection to White Australia
        policy 32
    occupation of German islands
        north of Equator 12, 15,
        17–18, 20, 22
    as perceived military threat
        to Australia 7–8, 9, 17–18,
        27–8, 29, 32, 41–2, 46
Japanese collaborators 53
Jockel, Gordon 203, 245–6
Johnson, Charles 209
Johnson, Les 224, 233

Johnson, Lyndon 189
Joint Declaration of Principles
    (1987) 247, 285–9
Joint Declaration of Principles
    (2013) 289
Joyce, Roger 4

Keating, Paul, on Kokoda war
    memorial xvii
Kellogg–Briand Pact 25
Kennedy Administration 129,
    130, 133, 139, 164, 172, 175
Kennedy, John F.
    on application of ANZUS
        Treaty 327n103
    approach to West New Guinea
        dispute 133, 140
    assassination 181
    communications with Sukarno
        140
    concerns about events in Asia
        133
    intervention to achieve
        negotiated settlement on
        West New Guinea 149
    meeting with Barwick 175
    meeting with Beale 131, 134
    meeting with Luns 134
    meeting with Menzies 131–3
    meeting with Sukarno 131,
        133, 135
    meetings with Macmillan
        131, 133, 140–2
    on US policy towards
        Indonesia 176, 182
Kennedy, Sir Arther 3
Kent-Hughes, William 57
Kerr, Alan 231
Kerr, John 317n38
Kiki, Albert Maori
    background 230
    on defence relationship with
        Australia 264, 269, 280
    as Defence spokesman 225
    first Defence Report to PGN
        Parliament 276–7
    meeting with Fraser 280
    as Minister for Foreign
        Relations and Defence
        230
    as Minister for Lands and
        Environment 230
    in negotiations over
        establishment of PNGDF
        254, 258–9, 260
    on PNG's defence and security
        policy 260–2, 269
    pro-Australian stance 230
Killen, James
    on Defence Cooperation
        Program with PNG 274

INDEX

on defence relationship with PNG 273–5, 275–6, 279–80, 281–2
on Joint Statement on defence 279–80, 281–2
as Minister for the Navy 271
as Minster for Defence 271
visits to PNG 271
Kitchener, Field Marshal Horatio Herbert (1st Earl Kitchener) 7
Kokoda Track xvii
Korean War 50, 63, 67, 70, 75, 76, 185

Ladrone Islands 20
Lake, Marilyn 5
Laos 97, 133, 139, 154, 169, 222
Latham, Sir John 17–18, 39
League of Nations mandates 21, 22–3, 44
Legge, Colonel Gordon 13, 14
Legge, John 123
Lepani, Charles 230
Levi, Noel 230, 254, 258
Lloyd George, David 20, 21
London Agreement 155
Lowe, David 71
Luns, Joseph 81, 86, 131, 134, 141
Lyons Government 35, 36, 40, 74
Lyons, Joseph 26, 35, 36, 37

Macandie, George 17
MacArthur, General Douglas 41
McBride, Philip 67, 68, 85, 94–5, 100, 102–4, 107
McEachern, Sir Malcolm 6
McEwen, John
 approach to international diplomacy 98, 138
 on approach to West New Guinea dispute 107–8, 138
 on Australia's relationship with Asia 104–5, 109, 115, 120, 198–9, 222
 on British withdrawal from region 206, 209, 211
 on defence of East New Guinea 105
 on defence obligations and security priorities 195
 on defence support for Malaysia 187, 188, 189–90, 195, 222
 on future defence relationship with Papua New Guinea 214
 on Indonesian control of West New Guinea 83, 137

on Indonesian–Australian relations 98, 104, 108, 127, 146, 163, 190, 204
influence on security policies 98, 221–2
on influencing public opionion 146
on involvement in Vietnam War 197–8, 209
on law and order problems in Papua New Guinea 216–17
as Minister for External Affairs 221
as Minister for Trade 221
on political/defence committments 185–6
on possibility of war with Indonesia 115
on possible guerrilla action in New Guinea 193
as Prime Minister 202, 209
on prioritising security commitments 191
on reliance upon military alliances 114–15
reputation 153
retirement from Parliament 221
role in foreign policy towards Southeast Asia xxiii–xxiv
on Singapore's departure from Malaysian federation 198–9
status in Cabinet 221
on Sukarno 187
on takeover of Solomon Islands 57, 305n36
on United States alliance 105, 107, 109, 209, 222
McIlwraith, T.J. 3–4
McIntyre, Lawrence (Jim) 50, 96, 100, 107, 117, 123, 313n68
Mackie, Jamie 113, 250, 251
McMahon, William
 approach to Papua New Guinea 220
 on Cabinet Notebooks xxiii
 character and personal style 153, 220
 political career 220
 as Prime Minister 205, 220
 visit to Indonesia 205
Macmillan Government 130
Macmillan, Harold 99, 131, 133, 140–2, 171, 182, 184
McNamara, Robert 189
Makino Nobuaki (Baron) 21, 22
Malaya 45
Malayan Emergency 75
Malaysia
 Australian support for 50, 156, 173, 184–8

defence by Britain 156, 163, 212, 327n106
establishment of federation 154–5
Five Power Defence Arrangement 212
inauguration 155, 174, 322n8
Indonesian military attacks 155–6
Michelmore Enquiry and Report 175, 322n8, 328n110
military assistance from Australia 50, 156, 186, 196, 197, 211, 327n106, 330n30, 335n46
succession by Singapore 156, 198–9
Malaysia Day 155, 174
Malik, Adam 203, 204, 230
Malphilindo/Malphindo 173, 326n98
Manila Summit 155
Manus Island naval base 45, 64, 68, 70, 94, 148, 219, 240, 243, 244, 245
Marianne Islands 11
Marshall Islands 11, 12, 20
Martin, Alan 181
Massey, William 22
Mataungan Association 215, 218, 271
May, Ron 238
Meaney, Neville viii, 5, 7, 8, 26, 32, 40
Mediansky, F. A. 251–2
Menadue, John 275
Mench, Paul 254, 255, 260
Menzies Liberal government
 Cabinet debates over defence obligations and security priorities 190–3
 Cabinet debates over response to Confrontation 161–3, 172–3, 186–8
 Cabinet debates over West New Guinea dispute 50–1, 72–3, 82–3, 100–7, 107–9, 113–15, 123–8, 130–1, 137–9, 143–6
 conscription 70
 defence arrangements for Malaysia 174
 defence budget 70, 95, 115, 165, 169–70, 171–2, 194, 196
 economic policies 152
 electoral success 122, 152, 180–1
 foreign policy 62, 73, 116
 national development 95, 163
 support for Malaysia 173, 174

– 369 –

West New Guinea policy
  58–60, 62–7, 68–70, 73,
  76–82, 87, 96, 100, 103,
  106, 110–11, 113, 117, 120,
  124–5, 126, 146–50
Menzies, Robert
  on Australia's influence on
    PNG's development xx
  character and personal style
    48, 50, 152
  on defence of Malaysia 162
  on defence obligations and
    security priorities 196
  on defence of Papua New
    Guinea 168, 169–70
  distrust of Sukarno and
    Indonesia 63, 100, 119, 121,
    128, 132, 158, 172, 194,
    200, 331–2n67
  on Dutch rule of West New
    Guinea 52–3, 66
  involvement in Suez Crisis 93
  meeting with Kennedy 131–3
  meeting with Wilson 196
  meetings with Churchill
    78–9, 80
  meetings with General
    Nasution 136–7, 318n64
  meetings with Macmillan 171
  meetings with Rusk 171–2
  meetings with Subandrio
    110–11
  meetings with Sukarno
    116–19
  mindset 132
  as Minister for External
    Affairs 124, 130
  on PNG 28
  political career 47, 48, 116,
    122, 123, 152
  on possibility of war with
    Indonesia 108
  retirement from Parliament
    200, 202
  on Tunku Abdul Rahman 119
  on United Nations 53, 63
  visit to Indonesia 92, 93,
    116–19, 200, 311n1
  visit to Netherlands East
    Indies 311n1
  visits to London 62–3, 68–9,
    78–80, 92, 93, 171
  visits to Papua New Guinea
    93, 174
  visits to United States 92,
    131–3, 171–2
  on war with Indonesia 196
Menzies UAP Government's
  approach to defence of PNG
    39
  bolstering of defences in New
    Guinea 39
  on Manus Island base 45
  reliance on Royal Navy for
    defence 40
Michelmore Enquiry and Report
  175, 322n8, 328n110
Middle East, deployment of
  Australian troops 79–80
middle power diplomacy 72
military conscription *see*
  conscription
Millar, T. B. 250
Millen, E.D. 10
Miller, J. D. B. 250
Momis, John 230
Monash, Lt General Sir John 29
Monroe Doctrine 4, 19, 69
Morauta, Mekere 230
Moresby, Captain John 2
Morrison, Bill
  on development of PNG
    police force 234
  as Minister for External
    Affairs 228
  on police field force 340n27
  portfolios in Whitlam
    Government 264, 338n1
  quashing of notion of defence
    treaty with PNG 255
  visit to PNG 228, 232
Mountbatten, Louis, Earl
  Mountbatten of Burma 205
Munro Ferguson, Sir Ronald 10,
  12–14
Murray, Sir Hubert 34–5

Nadzab airfield 45, 169, 190, 243
Nasser, Gamal Abdel 92, 93
Nasution, General 116, 136–7,
  188, 318n64
National Front for the Liberation
  of West Irian 136
National Intelligence Committee
  217
National Service training
  program 95, 115
nationalism, in Asia 52
Nauru 23, 36, 37
Naval Board 9, 10, 32
naval defence plans, Thring
  Plan 9
naval disarmament 25
'naval frontier' 9
Nelson, Hank 34, 42, 229
Netherlands
  policy towards West New
    Guinea 127, 134, 137, 141
  proposal to UN General
    Assembly 140
  self-determination for West
    New Guinea 127
  sovereignty over Dutch New
    Guinea 51–2, 64–5, 80–2,
    87–8, 134
  on UN trusteeship for West
    New Guinea 137
Netherlands East Indies
  decolonisation and
    independence 48
  police action against
    Indonesian nationalists 52
New Caledonia 8, 29
New Guinea (island)
  possible unification 124
  as single strategic entity 52,
    60, 62, 73, 77
New Guinea (League of Nations
  mandated territory) (1921)
    xxvi
New Guinea Volunteer Rifles 70
New Hebrides 6, 13, 14, 16, 29,
  55–7, 72, 308n94
New South Wales Colonial
  Government, calls for British
    possession of New Guinea 2–3
New Zealand
  ANZAC Pact 43
  calls for annexation of Tonga
    and Fiji 2
Nixon Administration 257
Noel-Baker, Philip 55
Non-Aligned Movement 116
North Borneo 45, 61, 154, 175,
  322n8, 328n110
North West Cape Naval
  Communications Station 180
nuclear weapons 115, 315n106

Okuma Shigenobu (Marquis) 20
O'Neill, Robert 250, 251
Organisasi Papua Merdeka
  (OPM) 265
Orlando, Vittorio 21
Overlack, Peter 6

Pacific Islands Regiment (PIR)
  capabilities 171
  conversion to PNGDF 238
  deployment to support police
    in PNG 216, 217, 220, 224,
    337n71
  disbanding of 70
  halt to build-up 212–13
  increase in size 168, 171, 212
  re-establishment as battalion
    of Australian Army 70
  third battalion 232
Pacific policy, during First World
  War 11
Page, Earle 39
Palar, L. N. 61
Paltridge, Shane 181, 190, 193

Index

PANGU Party 229, 230
Papua Act 1906 7
Papua Besena Movement 215–16, 218, 254
Papua New Guinea Act 1949 (Cth) xxvi
Papua New Guinea Defence Force (PNGDF)
  Australian servicemen subject to Village Court jurisdiction 265–6
  budget for 229, 238
  establishment and development 231, 232, 235–6
  financial assistance from Australia 266
  interim Status of Forces Arrangement 266
  involvement in internal security issues 277
  'loan' personnel 266
  major function 277
  need for 238–9
  negotiations over establishment and development 253–4, 257–60
  redesignation ceremony 233, 238
  Status of Forces Agreement 280–1
  Supply Support Arrangements 281
  transfer of personnel and defence assets 266
Papua New Guinea (PNG) (formerly Territory of Papua and New Guinea)
  access to Australian-built military bases 244–5, 250
  aid from Australia 271–2, 275, 284–5
  assessment of prospects 233
  border control and management 200, 205, 237, 243, 276, 277–8
  Bougainville Agreement 273
  Bougainville crisis 215, 216, 217, 218
  civil unrest in Gazelle Peninsula 215, 217, 218
  defence relationship with Australia 212, 222–3, 229, 231–2, 238–43, 245–52, 262–4, 273–5, 278–82, 290
  defence and security policy 260–2, 269, 276–7
  future defence arrangements 219–20, 224–5
  interim defence understandings 266–7
  interim Status of Forces Arrangements 266
  internal instability 249–50, 278
  internal security problems 215–17, 224, 228, 234, 240, 241, 243–4, 254
  Joint Declaration of Principles (1987) 285–9
  Joint Statement on defence (1977) 274, 279–82
  law and order problems 215–17, 218, 223, 224
  maritime resources 276
  naming of country xxvi, 339n3
  national unity 254, 265, 268, 272, 278
  path to self-government and independence 218–19, 224, 227–8, 231, 237, 264–7, 271
  place in Australia's defence outlook xiii–xvii
  place in Australia's security environment 290–1
  police force 228–9, 234, 238, 240, 241
  relationship with Australia xvii–xxi
  secession threats 241, 254, 278
  as South East Asian country 215
  strategic importance to Australia 243–5, 267–8, 277–8, 282–3, 286–8
  secessionist threats 215–16, 218, 223, 224, 254, 265, 272–3, 275
  tribal fighting in the Highlands 217
  Village Court system 265–6
  visit by Gorton 218
  visits by Fraser 270, 280
  visits by Peacock 270, 280
  visits by Whitlam 227
Papua New Guinea Provisional Administration Act 1945–46 (Cth) xxvi
Papua and New Guinea Select Committee on Constitutional Development 213–14
Papua New Guinea–Australian relations 228, 230–1, 242, 272
  annual security dialogue 290
  Integrated Development Package 285
  Joint Declaration of Principles (1987) 247, 285–9
  Joint Declaration of Principles (2013) 289
Joint Statement on defence (1977) 279–82, 286, 288
Ministerial Forum 285
Status of Forces Agreement 280–1
Papuan Black Power Group 215
Papuan campaign 41–2, 46
Papuan Infantry Regiment 167
Papuan separatism 215–16
Paris Peace Conference 21, 23, 45
Parkhill, Sir Archdale 37
Parsons, Graham 129
Peacock, Andrew
  as Minister for the Army 270
  as Minister for External Affairs 220, 221, 228
  as Minister for External Territories 270, 271
  as Minister for Foreign Affairs 270
  on PNG–Australia relationship 271, 341n60
  visits to PNG 270, 280
Pearce, Senator George 8, 13, 15–16, 27, 36–7
Pemberton, Gregory 150, 151, 189, 201
Petherbridge, Samuel 12
Petrov Royal Commission 50
Piesse, E. L. 28–9
PKI (Partai Komunis Indonesia) 49, 123
Plan Pygmalion 188
Port Moresby
  defence of 42
  as potential military base 37–8
Portuguese Timor, Indonesian claim to 61, 162, 171, 175, 326n89
Primrose, Brian 1, 3, 294n1
Pritchett, Bill 246, 247–9, 250, 261–2
Privy Council, appeals to 334n29

Queensland Colonial Government, attempted annexation of eastern New Guinea 3–4

Rabaul, US naval base 39
racial prejudice, against Indonesia 55
regional security policy
  during 1950s 73
  independence 60
Reid, Sir George 27
Renouf, Alan 151
Renville Agreement 51

Returned and Services League (RSL) 112
Robinson, Sir Hercules 2
role in foreign policy towards Southeast Asia 98
Rostow, Walt 131, 175
Roy Milne Lecture 184
Royal Australian Air Force, strength 80, 95
Royal Australian Navy
establishment 6, 7
strength 80, 148
Royal Navy, defence of Australia 27, 29, 32, 40, 45–6
Rusk, Dean
on coverage of ANZUS Treaty 256
on defence of Malaysia 164
on Indonesian interference in East New Guinea 175
on John Gorton 209
meeting with Barwick 175
meeting with Beale 147–8
meeting with Luns 134
meeting with Menzies 171–2
on UN trusteeship for West New Guinea 133, 317n37
on US policy regarding Indonesia 148
as US Secretary of State 131
Russo–Japanese War 1905 7

Sabah 154
Salisbury Government (UK) 5
Sandys, Duncan 184
Sarawak 154, 175, 322n8, 328n110
Scherber, Frederick 104, 313n53
Scholes, Gordon 290
Scullin Government 35
Second World War
Australian casualties 42
number of Australians who served in PNG xvi
in Pacific 40–5
Papuan campaign 41–2, 46
selective military service 194, 195
self-determination, Australian advocacy of principle 110, 112, 118, 127, 134, 136, 137, 140, 145
Service, James 4
Shann, K.C.O. (Mick) 50, 87, 153, 157, 182–4, 192, 303n4, 329n8
visits to PNG 246
Shaw, Patrick 50, 128, 140
Shedden, Sir Frederick 87
Sherger, Sir Frederick 168
Siaguru, Tony 230

Sinclair, Ian 276
Singapore
British Naval base 4, 9, 38, 40, 45–6, 205, 206–7
fall to Japanese 46
membership of Malaysia 154
succession from Malaysia 156, 198–9
Singapore Strategy 40, 45–6
Smith, Admiral Sir Victor 233, 262
Smuts, General Louis 22
Solomon Islands 6
acquisition by Australia 305n36
British protectorate 14, 29, 57
possible union with Papua New Guinea 123, 126
Somare, Michael
on aid from Australia 271–2
background 229
character and personal style 229–30
as Chief Minister in House of Assembly 229
on defence cooperation 262, 269, 280
as Defence spokesman in House of Assembly 225
development of Indonesian–PNG relationship 236–7
leadership of PANGU Party 229
meeting with Suharto 237
meetings with Fraser 280
in negotiations over establishment of PNGDF 254
on PNG–Australia relationship 230–1, 291
on PNG's defence force 238
on police field force 238
timeline for PNG independence 264–5
visits to Australia 233, 237–8, 271–2, 275
visits to Indonesia 237, 280
on Whitlam 3395
South East Asia Collective Defence Treaty (SEATO) 75, 83, 89, 125, 156, 185, 189, 196, 309n6
South Pacific, colonial calls for annexation of islands 1–5
South Pacific Commission 43
Spender, Percy
as Ambassador to Washington 71, 97
character and personal style 60, 66–7, 68, 71
delegate to United Nations

General Assembly 71
Hughes's influence 28, 56
on Indonesian sovereignty over West New Guinea 53–4, 58–9, 64–6, 71, 87, 91
meeting with Sukarno 57–8
meetings with British authorities 65–7
meetings with Dutch authorities 64–5
policy on West New Guinea 58–9, 65, 66, 73, 103, 110, 111
political career 53
retirement from Parliament 71
security screen initiative 55–61, 71
on United Nations 66
Spooner, William 83, 95, 98, 103, 109, 127, 138–9, 315n106
Squires, Lt General Ernest 38
Stanley, Edward Henry Stanley (15th Earl of Derby) 3
Stanley, Peter 40, 41–2
Status of Forces Agreement 280–1
Stevens, David 9
Stevens, Sir Roger 133
Stirling, Alfred 81
strategic arc north of the continent 38
Strategic Assessment Papers xx
strategic environment of Australia
during inter-war period 26–32
map presented to Hughes by American scholars 28, 30i
Piesse's map of Australian sphere of influence 28, 31i
place of Papua New Guinea 290–1
post-war zone of strategic responsiblity 45
prior to First World War 7–10
Street, Brigadier Geoffrey 37–8
Subandrio, Dr
assurances regarding Indonesian intentions 112, 117, 128, 135, 149, 314n88
Australian visit 86, 107, 109–14
on Australia's attitude towards Asia 135
on colonialism 118
on East New Guinea 128
on Indonesian–Australian relations 96, 112–13, 117, 135
joint announcement with Casey 112–13, 117

Index

on Malaysia 155
meeting with Menzies in
    Jakarta 116, 118
personality and character 96,
    154
on racial difference 118
on West New Guinea dispute
    96, 112
Subardjo 76
Subritzky, John 154, 155, 194,
    201, 211–12
Suez Crisis 50, 92–3, 105, 221
Suharto, General
    on Indonesian–PNG
        relationship 236–7
    meeting with Somare 237
    as president 197, 199, 201,
        203
    on stability of PNG 237
    visit to Australia 205
Sukarno, Achmad
    character and personal style
        48–9, 50, 119, 153–4
    on claim to West New Guinea
        107, 117, 118, 119, 135, 140
    Guided Democracy policy 93,
        97, 119, 123
    independence declaration 47
    invitation to visit to Australia
        118, 119, 160
    loss of leadership 197, 200,
        203
    on Malaysia 155
    meeting with Casey 77–8
    meeting with Kennedy 131,
        135
    meeting with Spender 57–8
    meeting with Tunku Abdul
        Rahman 155
    meetings with Barwick 149,
        174–5
    meetings with Menzies
        116–19
    overseas visits 93
    political career and power 48,
        116, 123, 154
    as President 48–9, 119
    support for dissident
        movement in East New
        Guinea 176
    view of Australia 49–50
    'Year of Living Dangerously'
        speech 192

Tamzil 117
Tange, Sir Arthur 123, 136, 142,
    149, 159, 161–2
    on application of ANZUS
        Treaty to PNG 256
    at meeting with General
        Nasution 136

Cabinet submission on West
    New Guinea 123
on defence preparedness 164
on deployment of PIR in
    Papua New Guinea 217
distrust of Indonesia 149
on friction in Indonesian–
    Australian relations 142–3
on Indonesian threats to
    Australian interests 161,
    161–2
meeting with Rusk 164
on military assistance to
    Malaysia 327n106
on PNG Defence Force 229
as Secretary of the
    Department of External
    Affairs 87
on self-determination for
    Papua New Guinea 162
on strategic importance of
    West New Guinea 87–8
Tarling, Nicholas 73
Territory Intelligence Committee
    325n71
Territory of New Guinea,
    Australian UN trusteeship
    over 44
Territory of Papua, Australian
    control over xxvi, 7
Territory of Papua and New
    Guinea
    adoption of name Papua New
        Guinea 339n3
    Australian administration
        xxvi, 45
    Australian responsibility for
        defence 89, 101–2, 125, 127,
        145, 151, 194, 197
    development to serve security
        interests 62
    Indonesian claims to 61
    strategic importance to
        Australia 44
    strengthening of defences
        167–70, 171–2, 180–1, 190,
        192
    visit by Menzies 93
Thomas, Peter 170
Thomson, George 210–11, 212
Thorneycroft, Peter 171
Thring, Commander W. H. C. S.
    (Hugh) 8–9, 26, 44
Timbs, Maurice 117
Tonga 2, 6
Townley, Athol 148, 153, 167,
    181
    correspondence with General
        Nasution 137
    on Indonesian–Australian
        relations 146

on inevitability of Indonesian
    takeover 138
on Manus Island naval base
    148
meetings with General
    Nasution 136, 137
reputation 153
submission on military
    importance of West New
    Guinea 123
trade, with Indonesia 204
Treaty of Versailles 23, 36
Truman Administration 84
Tunku Abdul Rahman
    meeting with Sukarno 155
    personality and character 119
    on UN trusteeship for West
        New Guinea 129, 132
Turner, Mark 34, 42

United Nations
    Evatt's role at 44–5
    and Indonesian independence
        51–2, 53
    negotiations over Dutch New
        Guinea 83–4, 85
United Nations General Assembly,
    Indonesian resolution 97
United Nations Good Offices
    Committee (GOC) 51, 304n8
United States
    Cold War strategy 70, 99,
        140–1
    concern over political
        instability in Indonesia 96,
        99, 129
    defence of Pacific 95
    expectations of allies 164
    non-engagement policy on
        West New Guinea dispute
        69–70, 79, 84, 97, 99, 106–7,
        128
    policy towards Indonesia 170,
        176, 182
    policy towards Malaysian
        crisis 170
    proposed UN trusteeship for
        West New Guinea 129,
        130–1, 133
    relations with Indonesia 98,
        170
    requests for military assistance
        in Vietnam 195
    review of policy on West New
        Guinea 129–30
    support for negotiated
        settlement on West New
        Guinea 142, 148, 149
    sympathy for Australia's stance
        on West New Guinea 84,
        95, 106–7

– 373 –

United States Air Force 45
United States–Australian
  relations, conflict of interest
  over West New Guinea 98,
  140–1, 142, 147–8, 150
US alliance
  concerns over 95, 98
  sole reliance upon 212
  support for 109
  see also ANZUS Treaty

Vanimo, patrol base at 70
Vietnam War
  Cabinet debates over 50, 102,
  197–8, 208–9
  increase in Australia's
  commitment by Holt 208–9
  initial deployment of
  Australian troops 197–8
  opposition to Australian
  involvement 153, 185
  possibility of Australian
  involvement 185, 190
  US request for assistance
  195–6

Walker, Patrick Gordon 60
Waller, Sir Keith 218, 224, 246
Walstab, Lieutenant Colonel 35
War Book 33–4
War Cabinet 39
Washington Naval Treaty 25, 34
Waters, Christopher 126
Watt, Alan 68–9, 81
Wells, Lt General Sir Henry 105
White Australia policy 8, 26, 29, 32, 36, 53, 77, 119, 151
Whitlam, E. Gough
  at ALP Special National
  Conference in 1963 180
  as Deputy Leader of ALP
  153, 180
  on Indonesian–Australian
  relations 241
  as leader of ALP 227
  meetings with Somare 241
  on PNG–Australian
  relationship 228, 242,
  339*n*11
  visit to Indonesia 241
  visits to PNG 227, 233, 241,
  271
Whitlam Government
  constitutional crisis 265
  defence cooperation
  arrangements with Indonesia
  242
  defence policy towards PNG
  233, 235, 240

desire for national unity in
  PNG 265, 268
  dismissal 270
  long-term defence
  relationship with PNG
  252, 255–7
  policy on PNG independence
  231, 254, 268–9
  study of defence bases and
  facilities within Australia
  242–3
  timeline for PNG self-
  government and
  independence 231, 237,
  264–5
  transfer of defence
  responsibilities to PNG
  263
Willesee, Don 258, 259, 284
Wilson Government 205, 210
Wilson, Harold 195, 203, 205
Wilson, Woodrow 18–19, 21, 22, 133
Wilton, General John 151
Wilton, Sir John 193
Wingti Government 285, 289
Wingti, Paias 284–5, 289
Wisdom, Evan 35
Woodard, Garry
  on Australia's objective in
  West New Guinea dispute
  52
  on Barwick's approach to
  foreign policy 178, 179
  on Barwick's approach to
  West New Guinea dispute
  143
  on Beale's misunderstanding
  of US policy 130
  on British concerns over
  Indonesian amibitions 160
  diplomatic career 304*n*13
  on fears associated with
  West New Guinea dispute
  55, 150
  on Menzies' misreading of
  Kennedy 133
  on racial prejudice against
  Indonesia 55

Yamin, Mohammed 60–1
Yap 11, 12, 20
Young, Sir John 2
Younger, Kenneth 62–3, 132

Zijlstra, Jelle 141